AF844509

Taking American Citizenship Seriously

Taking American Citizenship Seriously

The Recovery of the Fourteenth Amendment

David R. Upham

BLOOMSBURY ACADEMIC
NEW YORK • LONDON • OXFORD • NEW DELHI • SYDNEY

BLOOMSBURY ACADEMIC
Bloomsbury Publishing Inc, 1359 Broadway, New York, NY 10018, USA
Bloomsbury Publishing Plc, 50 Bedford Square, London, WC1B 3DP, UK
Bloomsbury Publishing Ireland, 29 Earlsfort Terrace, Dublin 2, D02 AY28, Ireland

BLOOMSBURY, BLOOMSBURY ACADEMIC and the Diana logo are
trademarks of Bloomsbury Publishing Plc

First published in the United States of America 2026

Copyright © Bloomsbury Publishing, Inc., 2026

For legal purposes the Acknowledgments on p. viii constitute
an extension of this copyright page.

Cover image © iStock.com/eurobanks

All rights reserved. No part of this publication may be: i) reproduced or transmitted in any form, electronic or mechanical, including photocopying, recording or by means of any information storage or retrieval system without prior permission in writing from the publishers; or ii) used or reproduced in any way for the training, development or operation of artificial intelligence (AI) technologies, including generative AI technologies. The rights holders expressly reserve this publication from the text and data mining exception as per Article 4(3) of the Digital Single Market Directive (EU) 2019/790.

Bloomsbury Publishing Inc does not have any control over, or responsibility for, any third-party websites referred to or in this book. All internet addresses given in this book were correct at the time of going to press. The author and publisher regret any inconvenience caused if addresses have changed or sites have ceased to exist, but can accept no responsibility for any such changes.

A catalog record for this book is available from the Library of Congress.

ISBN: HB: 978-1-6669-4385-6
ePDF: 979-8-216-26225-1
eBook: 978-1-9787-6143-8

Typeset by Deanta Global Publishing Services, Chennai, India

For product safety related questions contact productsafety@bloomsbury.com.

To find out more about our authors and books visit www.bloomsbury.com and
sign up for our newsletters.

Taking American Citizenship Seriously

The Recovery of the Fourteenth Amendment

David R. Upham

BLOOMSBURY ACADEMIC
NEW YORK • LONDON • OXFORD • NEW DELHI • SYDNEY

BLOOMSBURY ACADEMIC
Bloomsbury Publishing Inc, 1359 Broadway, New York, NY 10018, USA
Bloomsbury Publishing Plc, 50 Bedford Square, London, WC1B 3DP, UK
Bloomsbury Publishing Ireland, 29 Earlsfort Terrace, Dublin 2, D02 AY28, Ireland

BLOOMSBURY, BLOOMSBURY ACADEMIC and the Diana logo are trademarks of Bloomsbury Publishing Plc

First published in the United States of America 2026

Copyright © Bloomsbury Publishing, Inc., 2026

For legal purposes the Acknowledgments on p. viii constitute an extension of this copyright page.

Cover image © iStock.com/eurobanks

All rights reserved. No part of this publication may be: i) reproduced or transmitted in any form, electronic or mechanical, including photocopying, recording or by means of any information storage or retrieval system without prior permission in writing from the publishers; or ii) used or reproduced in any way for the training, development or operation of artificial intelligence (AI) technologies, including generative AI technologies. The rights holders expressly reserve this publication from the text and data mining exception as per Article 4(3) of the Digital Single Market Directive (EU) 2019/790.

Bloomsbury Publishing Inc does not have any control over, or responsibility for, any third-party websites referred to or in this book. All internet addresses given in this book were correct at the time of going to press. The author and publisher regret any inconvenience caused if addresses have changed or sites have ceased to exist, but can accept no responsibility for any such changes.

A catalog record for this book is available from the Library of Congress.

ISBN: HB: 978-1-6669-4385-6
ePDF: 979-8-216-26225-1
eBook: 978-1-9787-6143-8

Typeset by Deanta Global Publishing Services, Chennai, India

For product safety related questions contact productsafety@bloomsbury.com.

To find out more about our authors and books visit www.bloomsbury.com and sign up for our newsletters.

To my sons and daughters: May you cherish the freedom and citizenship with which God and your country have endowed you.[1]

[1] This dedication is adapted from the dedication that John Mercer Langston composed for his collected works, *Freedom and Citizenship: Selected Lectures and Addresses* (1883).

Contents

Acknowledgments

This work would have been utterly impossible without the contribution of so many people, to whom I am greatly indebted.

My teachers, classmates, colleagues, and students at the University of Dallas, for countless conversations that have inspired and shaped this work.

The dozens of scholars who, for over a century, have labored to recover the Fourteenth Amendment.

Richard Aynes, David Fowler, Christopher Green, Kurt Lash, and Earl Maltz, for their helpful commentary on previous drafts of this work.

The scholars with whom I've conversed at many academic conferences, especially those sponsored by the Center for the Study of Constitutional Originalism at the University of San Diego Law School, and the Pontifical John Paul II Institute for Studies on Marriage and Family at the Catholic University of America.

Many librarians, especially Ron Scrogham and the late Alice Puro of the University of Dallas, for their assistance.

My research assistants at St. Thomas University, Alfredo de Zayas and John Mendez.

St. Thomas University, the University of Dallas, the Civitas Institute at the University of Texas, and the Tennessee Family Action Council, for substantial financial support.

My students and new colleagues at St. Thomas University, for so much encouragement.

My teachers, especially Richard Dougherty, Thomas West, Murray Dry, and the late David Lowenthal.

My father and mother, for first teaching me to love our Republic.

My wife and our children, for countless blessings.

The first chapter of this work is an adaptation of my previously published article, *A Coherent Measure*, 48 Perspectives on Political Science 234 (August 2019).

Portions of the fourth chapter are derived from my article, *An Essay on Substantive Due Process and the Original Meaning of the Fourteenth Amendment's Due Process Clause*, 11 Faulkner L. Rev. 35 (2019).

Introduction

Our Constitution's Central Amendment

I am but God's humble instrument; but you may rest assured that as long as I live no one shall put a shackle on your limbs, and you shall have all the rights which God has given to every other free citizen of this republic.
—Abraham Lincoln, Remarks to Freedmen in Richmond (Apr. 4, 1865)[1]

The right of American citizenship means something.
—Senator Lyman Trumbull, Speech on the Civil Rights Bill (Apr. 4, 1866)[2]

Born in 1776, on the Fourth of July, our Republic is two and a half centuries old. Our federal Constitution is nearly as old.

Since its ratification, this Constitution has been amended twenty-seven times. Of those amendments, perhaps none is more important than the middle amendment—the fourteenth of the twenty-seven—ratified in 1868.

The Fourteenth Amendment may properly be called the Central Amendment, for it is central not only in number but also to our political life. This Amendment addresses truly foundational questions: Who are the members of our Republic, and what are our fundamental rights?

The most consequential portions of our Central Amendment are as follows:

> Section 1. All persons born or naturalized in the United States, and subject to the jurisdiction thereof, are citizens of the United States and of the State wherein they reside. No State shall make or enforce any law which shall abridge the privileges or immunities of citizens of the United States; nor shall any State deprive any person of life, liberty, or property, without due process of law, nor deny to any person within its jurisdiction the equal protection of the laws.
>
> Section 5. The Congress shall have power to enforce, by appropriate legislation, the provisions of this article.[3]

The Amendment thus (1) defines certain persons as bona fide citizens of our Republic; (2) guarantees to all citizens certain privileges and immunities; (3) secures to all persons, whether citizens or not, a certain legal process and legal protection; and (4) authorizes Congress to enforce the foregoing guarantees by national law.

This Central Amendment was designed to foster a more perfect Union. According to John Bingham, the chief drafter of the first section, the Amendment was supposed to establish "one country, one Constitution, and one people."[4]

Nonetheless, for a century and a half now, this one Amendment seems to have sown more discord than unity. By generating numerous, intensive, and protracted controversies, Bingham's amendment has yielded not "one Constitution," but many—*ex uno plures* rather than *e pluribus unum*.

The Amendment has sharply divided American jurists no less than the people in general. Some have read the Amendment quite narrowly—for example, that its Due Process Clause guarantees only the procedural rights of notice and a hearing,[5] and its Equal Protection Clause only an immunity from racial and national-origin discrimination.[6] Others have read it quite broadly—to protect an indeterminate and protean set of equality and liberty rights, substantive as well as procedural.[7]

"Originalism," despite its promise, has done little to resolve these divisions. Self-described originalists have endorsed the full panoply of readings, from the most indefinite to the most circumscribed.[8] Originalism has been, one might say, part of the problem, not the solution. As Kurt Lash recently noted, the originalist literature on the Fourteenth Amendment still features a "cacophony" of competing theories.[9]

The failure of Fourteenth-Amendment originalism was manifest at the momentous close of the Supreme Court's 2021–2022 term. In three high-profile cases—concerning religion, arms, and abortion—the nine justices all professed fidelity to the Amendment's original understanding, but divided sharply in their accounts of that understanding.

The three progressives, avowedly "true to the Framers' principles," contended that the Amendment's "guarantees of 'liberty' and 'equality' for all" were, by design, "majestic but open-ended" so as to "permit future evolution in their scope and meaning." By this account, fidelity to the original understanding requires the Court to discern and implement this evolution in light of "new societal understandings and conditions."[10]

The six conservatives likewise professed to "faithfully" follow the Framers' original "understanding";[11] hence, "constitutional rights" have "the scope they were understood to have *when the people adopted them*."[12] But according to the conservatives, Fourteenth-Amendment rights were originally deemed not *evolutionary* but *determinate*. These rights included only those "deeply rooted in our Nation's history and traditions," as evinced either by enumeration in the national Constitution or otherwise;[13] with each right's definition fixed no later than 1868 (when the Amendment was ratified).[14] By this account, it seems, the rights cannot be subject to any post-ratification expansion or contraction.[15]

At the same time, neither the progressives nor the conservatives provided any substantial evidence for their competing historical claims. Indeed, the Faithful Nine, despite their proclamations, seemed coldly indifferent even to the most important original evidence: the Framers' actual text.[16] In all three cases, the words of the Amendment barely made an appearance.[17] The three progressives seemingly could not be bothered even to read the text; they misquoted it to secure "equality"[18]—a word that appears nowhere in the Amendment nor anywhere else in the Constitution. Meanwhile, all the conservatives, save Justice Thomas, clung to the oxymoronic, antitextual doctrine of "substantive due process," and treated the Privileges or Immunities Clause as largely irrelevant.[19]

A year later, however, there was something of an originalist rapprochement. In *Students for Fair Admissions*, the majority and dissent, over several pages, both quoted the actual text of the Equal Protection Clause and cited extensive evidence as to its original meaning and purpose.[20] Moreover, the two sides, to a certain extent, adopted one another's approach from the prior year. The progressive dissent followed the conservative majority in *Dobbs* by treating as dispositive the enactment of certain laws at the time of the Amendment's adoption: *viz.*, certain "race-conscious policies" that left "no doubt that the Equal Protection Clause permits" comparable policies today.[21] That is to say, the Amendment cannot be interpreted to prohibit the sort of laws passed by the same officials who adopted the Amendment. Conversely, the conservative majority emulated the progressives in *Dobbs* by setting aside such laws in favor of the purportedly "broad sweep" and "transcendent aims" of the Amendment.[22]

At the same time, however, the conservatives stopped short of ascribing any evolutionary meaning to the Amendment. Indeed, both sides seemed to celebrate *Brown v. Board of Education* not as evolution but as restoration of the better, original understanding.[23] Both sides, then, seemingly agreed that one goal of constitutional interpretation should be originalist restoration.

Despite this rapprochement, the two sides remained estranged not only from one another, but also from the Amendment's actual text. Neither the conservative nor the progressive side sought to explain how its respective claims represented an interpretation of the actual Equal Protection Clause; that is, how a guarantee of "equal protection of the laws" could either (1) encompass any non*protective* benefit like education, or (2) invalidate the very *laws* defining this benefit. Further, with the exception (again) of Justice Thomas, no one contended that the Court should look instead to the Privileges or Immunities Clauses.[24]

This estrangement is not new. For generations, the judiciary has long interpreted the Amendment with scant regard to the text or other original evidence. This neglect has been most acute with respect to Section 1's primary purpose: to establish more firmly the basic rights of American *citizenship*. According to the Joint Committee on Reconstruction, which Congress authorized to draft the Amendment, its first section would "determine the civil rights and privileges of all citizens."[25] Moreover, just two days after Congress formally approved the Amendment, the Senate and House of Representatives passed a concurrent resolution condensing all of Section 1 in one word: "citizenship."[26]

Yet for the courts, citizenship has little to do with the rights secured by the Amendment. In particular, as to equality rights, the Supreme Court has long identified "suspect" or "quasi-suspect" classifications via formulas unrelated to citizenship; for example, where the members of a class have some "immutable" characteristic, or have been subject to stereotyping, or remain vulnerable as a "discrete and insular minority."[27] The Court has gone so far afield from the text as to declare that non-citizenship itself is a suspect classification.[28]

As to liberty rights, the Court has likewise used categories unrelated to citizenship; for example rights "essential to the orderly pursuit of happiness by freemen,"[29] or to "a scheme of ordered liberty,"[30] or to "the autonomy of the person," including "the right to define one's own concept of existence, of meaning, of the universe, and of the mystery of human life."[31] These rubrics concern the person who is *in* or *under* or even *over* the Republic, but not necessarily *of* the Republic—that is, a member or a citizen of our political community.

Why has the American judiciary thus neglected American citizenship? Constitutional historians have a ready answer: *The Slaughter-House Cases* (1873).[32] In that case, the Court nullified the very provision expressly securing the rights of citizenship. The Court held that the Privileges or Immunities Clause protected not the fundamental rights of American citizenship, but only rights that "owe their existence to the Federal government, its National character, its Constitution, or its laws."[33] But given the Supremacy Clause of Article VI,[34] such federally created rights had been amply secure from the beginning against state abridgment; hence, as the dissenting judges then aptly remarked, the majority's opinion rendered the Privileges or Immunities Clause a "vain and idle enactment."[35]

Since this dormition of the Privileges or Immunities Clause, the judiciary has instead relied on the Due Process Clause to secure certain "liberty" rights, and on the Equal Protection Clauses to safeguard certain "equality" rights.[36] And because these two provisions guarantee rights to "persons," and not just "citizens," the reigning liberty and equality jurisprudence has long been, both textually and conceptually, untethered to citizenship.[37]

Virtually all scholars agree that the Supreme Court misconstrued and therefore nullified the Privileges or Immunities Clause. And constitutional historians largely agree that the Court's substitute reliance on the Due Process and Equal Protection Clauses has distorted these in turn.[38] Hence, for decades, dozens of scholars have proffered a multitude of studies to support alternative interpretations of the Amendment—above all to recover the dormant Privileges or Immunities Clause, what Mary Hinman first aptly called "The Lost Clause."[39] The attention and affection paid to this sleepy clause have been so ardent that the late Justice Scalia called it the "darling of the professoriate."[40]

Despite all the professorial devotion, their "darling" remains a sleeping beauty. Fifteen years ago, the Supreme Court flatly rejected a petition to awaken her. In *McDonald v. City of Chicago* (2010), eight of the nine justices, over different opinions, expressly declined to revisit *Slaughter-House* and instead agreed that all claims of individual liberties under the Amendment would remain the domain of the Due Process Clause.[41] Only Justice Thomas was inclined to overturn *Slaughter-House* and revive the Privileges or Immunities Clause.[42]

In justifying their decision, the Court's conservatives and progressives both acknowledged the scholarly *consensus* repudiating the *Slaughter-House* opinion, but pointed to the scholarly *dissensus* as to the best substitute.[43] In other words, the Justices decided to let this sleeping beauty lie—largely because the legal academics weren't sure what she'd say if awakened.

In the last decade and a half, little has changed. Despite many new scholarly contributions, and the intervening appointment of three self-described "originalist" members, Justice Thomas remains alone.[44]

This dormition of the Privileges or Immunities Clause would seem a scandal. By adopting the Fourteenth Amendment, the American people sought to safeguard their essential rights as Americans. If so, the job of the American judiciary might seem straightforward: to understand and obediently apply this most vital constitutional mandate. And if there should be any obscurity as to what our political ancestors meant—especially an obscurity so severe as to cripple the courts—the job of the American legal academy would seem equally straightforward: to recover that meaning from obscurity.

Because this constitutional issue is so central, all this gloom might constitute not only a failure in jurisprudence but also a crisis in American identity. What does it mean to be a citizen of the United States? Does American membership have any privileges at all? Is the "citizen of the United States" entitled to anything else except the nametag?

To these vital questions of American identity, American jurists, of the bench and the academy, have proffered this dismal answer: "We don't know."

This book's principal ambition is to tackle this truly fundamental problem and to recover the meaning of American citizenship, as originally guaranteed in our Constitution's Central Amendment—and more broadly, to recover the original meaning of the Amendment's guarantees for the rights of *persons* as well as American *citizens*.

A New Approach

It may well be asked whether the world needs yet another book on the Fourteenth Amendment. This work, I believe, will be a genuine contribution, distinguishable from other studies in the following ways.

First, I will respect the Amendment's authors by affording them a strong *presumption of coherence*. I will assume, absent evidence to the contrary, that there was no substantial gap between the original "meaning" and original "understanding" or "purpose" of the Amendment. Such discord has been presumed or asserted in recent originalist efforts to conclude that the Amendment's original meaning imposes restraints wholly foreign to the authors' understanding.[45] Further, I will presume that this original understanding was itself coherent, and thus I will hesitate to impute any substantial misunderstanding among the legislators who made the Amendment. I will not, therefore, join those scholars who have assumed or asserted, based on some apparent discord, that these lawmakers were mired in mutual contradiction, if not outright confusion.

This presumption of coherence, in my view, seems necessary, in turn, to the presumptive legal validity of the Fourteenth Amendment. True law, according to most jurists, must be "known" at the time of promulgation.[46] If the lawmakers uttered words without any common understanding among themselves, let alone those who were to be bound, these utterances were not laws.

As I will elaborate in Chapter 1 ("An Original Consensus"), there is substantial *prima facie* evidence of this coherence. During the Amendment's adoption, proponents repeatedly emphasized the measure's clarity and coherence, and otherwise indicated a common understanding as to its meaning.

Second, I will respect the authors' authority by seeking, first and foremost, the original *official* understanding. Under this approach, evidentiary priority belongs to the words and deeds, actions and omissions, of those officials to whom the people of the United States delegated authority to propose and adopt constitutional amendments: namely, (1) the national Congress vested with proposal authority, (2) the state governors vested with transmittal and recommendatory authority, and (3) the state legislatures vested with ratification authority.

In Chapter 2 ("The Official Consensus"), I will defend this approach and argue that the most authoritative official exposition was provided by the Joint Committee on Reconstruction, which Congress had authorized to propose and explain the Amendment. And in the third chapter ("The Fundamentalist Consensus"), I will show that the Committee's formal report, as amply confirmed and explicated by other official evidence, shows an original fundamentalist consensus. The Amendment's first section, as the Committee certified, was designed to "determine" certain fundamental "civil rights and privileges" for the benefit of all Americans, while its fifth section was to provide Congress with power solely to enforce this determination.

Third, I will respect the authors' own words by clearly distinguishing the rights of *citizenship* from those of *personhood*. The Amendment's text makes a very clear differentiation in this regard. As Lincoln said in another context, "*This they said, and this meant*."[47]

But with one exception, seemingly no extended study has given substantial attention to this distinction.[48] Many have contended that the privileges of citizens refer to the natural rights of human beings, without reference to membership in a civil society.[49] Others have identified these rights as the creations of positive law, whether federal positive law (e.g., the rights enumerated in the first eight amendments),[50] or state law,[51] but again without any reference to the *citizenship* of the rights-bearers.

As the prominent jurist Richard Epstein has noted, this distinction between personhood and citizenship "receives only scant attention. But it should provoke a structural reexamination of the entire Fourteenth Amendment."[52] Or, as Justice Thomas has recently suggested, any recovery of the Amendment requires us to discern "the longstanding right[s] of citizenship."[53]

In this work, I will undertake this long-overdue "structural reexamination." Most notably, I will seek to distinguish the equal protection and due process owed to human persons under American jurisdiction from the "longstanding rights of citizenship." Chapter 4 will be devoted to the former; Chapters 5 and 6 to the latter.

Along the way, I will present a number of conclusions, some of them new, but many old and familiar. Perhaps my most noteworthy contribution will be my identification of the rights of American citizenship. I will argue that these "privileges" include, *inter alia*, the rights of travel, residence, commerce, and *some* of the procedural and nonprocedural rights recognized in the Bill of Rights, precisely because these were deemed rights of *citizenship*—rights to participate in the Republic's territory, markets, tribunals, deliberations, and so on. The "immunities" of citizenship, I will contend, include the freedom from unequal taxes and regulations that burden a citizen on three (and *only* three) bases: (1) a citizen's race and other heredity, (2) his place of birth or residence, or (3) his creed, whether political or religious. Citizenship implied exemption from such unequal burdens because they were badges of alienage.

Fourth, I will offer significant new evidence, some of which is only now readily available thanks to large, searchable databases, especially the Library of Congress's "Chronicling America" records and "Google Books." This new evidence includes some initial eyewitness reports of key congressional speeches, prominent speeches in the state legislatures, prominent newspaper editorials, and contemporaneous unreported judicial opinions.[54]

Fifth, I hope to foster scholarly conversation by presenting my findings through a series of discrete and severable conclusions as to the Amendment's key words and phrases ("State," "person," "due process," etc.). Such partition, I hope, will not only rightly prioritize the Amendment's text, but also promote scholarly consensus. By this method, other scholars might be able to accept or reject my findings *à la carte*, so to speak—to separate the wheat from the chaff. At least some parts of this study then might prove generally acceptable and thus provide solid building blocks of a future scholarly consensus, while other parts will prove less persuasive and rightly discarded.

Finally, in deference to the scholars' consensus, this study will proceed from a *presumption of rupture*. That is to say, there is a radical disconnect between the Amendment's original meaning and its subsequent exposition by the judiciary, beginning with the *Slaughter-House* decision (1873) (or very soon thereafter).[55]

These judicial opinions, then, will be set aside as a hindrance. To adopt Socrates' image for recovering the true nature of philosophy, those surveying later judicial reports to discern the Amendment's original meaning are like seafarers who may "catch sight of the sea Glaucus,"[56]

> [but] can no longer easily see his original nature, [because over time] some parts of his body have been broken off and others have been ground down and thoroughly maimed by the waves at the same time as other things have grown on him—shells seaweed, and rocks—so that he resembles any beast rather than what he was by nature.[57]

The Fourteenth Amendment, it seems, has likewise been misshapen into a beast by generations of judicial subtraction and addition. We will not, therefore, discover the Amendment's "original nature" by a voyage among the judicial reports.

In the conclusion of the book, "A Multiracial Republic—If We Can Keep It," I will suggest some explanation for this rupture. I will hypothesize that the Amendment's first section, though originally quite intelligible, was peculiarly vulnerable to judicial misconstruction and consequent obscurity due to the influence of powerful, subrational, and disintegrative influences in our Republic. These included the American passions for commerce and equality, and, more corrosively, American racism. The Fourteenth Amendment, I will propose, was nullified and obscured probably because the American people proved too *commercial*, too *egalitarian*, and too *racist* for their own Constitution.

* * *

This work is thus admittedly ambitious and avowedly patriotic. I hope to show my fellow citizens that our Constitution's Central Amendment had an original intelligible meaning; that in adopting this Amendment, our political ancestors acted with reason and purpose; and that we can recover that original understanding—so central to our common identity, and thus so vital to our Union.

This work is not partisan. I do not here offer any prescription for what Americans should do with this recovered understanding. The readers can accept any or even all of my conclusions, and still decide to reject the old American law in favor of something else. But in making that decision, my fellow citizens will have, I hope, the advantage of knowing what they are rejecting.

Sixty-five years ago, a leading Fourteenth-Amendment historian, Howard Jay Graham, praised another such historian in these words: "Dr. James has helped us to realize what our fourteenth amendment means, and so what it means to be an American."[58] My ambition here is to be worthy of similar praise.

Notes

1 David Dixon Porter, Incidents and Anecdotes of the Civil War 295 (1885) (quoted in Allen C. Guelzo, Reconstruction: A Concise History 8 (2018)).

2 Cong. Globe, 39th Cong. 1st Sess., 1757 (1866).

3 U.S. Const. amend XIV. The text of the Amendment is the version promulgated by Secretary of State William Seward in his proclamation of the Amendment's ratification. 15 Stat. 708, 709 (July 28, 1868).

4 One Country, One Constitution, and One People: Speech of Hon. John A. Bingham, of Ohio, in the House of Representatives, February 28, 1866, In Support of the Proposed Amendment to Enforce the Bill of Rights (1866).

5 *Chaloner v. Sherman*, 242 U.S. 455, 461 (1917) (holding that "notice and opportunity to be heard" satisfied all "the essential elements of due process of law").

6 *Trimble v. Gordon*, 430 U.S. 762, 780–1 (1977) (Rehnquist, J., dissenting) (arguing that "suspect classifications" should be limited to race and national origin). *Cf. Strauder v. West Virginia*, 100 U.S. 303, 307 (1880) (quoting the whole second sentence of the first section and asking rhetorically, "What is this but declaring that the law in the States shall be the same for the black as for the white; that all persons, whether colored or white, shall stand equal before the laws of the States?").

7 *See, e.g.*, *Harper v. Virginia Bd. of Elections*, 383 U.S. 663, 669 (1966) (affirming that, under the Amendment, neither "the catalogue . . . of fundamental rights" nor "equality" are "confined to historic notions" but rather "*do* change" with the times)

(emphasis in original); *McDonald v. City of Chicago*, 561 U.S. 742, 876–7 (Stevens, J., dissenting) (affirming that the "liberty" guaranteed by the Amendment is a "dynamic concept," the changing meaning of which was to be defined by "future generations,"—a "task the Constitution assigned to [the judiciary]").

8 *Compare* Randy E. Barnett & Evan D. Bernick, The Original Meaning of the Fourteenth Amendment: Its Letter and Spirit 152, 191 (2021) (contending that the Privileges or Immunities Clause prohibits the states from "unreasonably discriminating" by treating "similarly situated" citizens differently, and that the Due Process Clause bans all "arbitrary" laws), *with* Raoul Berger, Government by Judiciary: The Transformation of the Fourteenth Amendment 17–18 (2d ed. 1997) ("The three clauses of §1 were three facets of one and the same concern: to insure that there would be no discrimination against the freedmen in respect of 'fundamental rights,' which had a clearly understood and narrow compass").

9 Kurt T. Lash, *An Incomplete Introduction to the Fourteenth Amendment*, Law and Liberty, Jan. 20, 2021, https://lawliberty.org/book-review/an-incomplete-introduction-to-the-fourteenth-amendment/ (reviewing Ilan Wurman, The Second Founding: An Introduction to the Fourteenth Amendment (2020)).

10 *Dobbs v. Jackson Women's Health Org.*, 597 U.S. 215, 374 (2022) (Breyer, Sotomayor, Kagan, JJ., dissenting).

11 *Kennedy v. Bremerton Sch. Dist.*, 597 U.S. 507, 536 (2022) (quoting *Town of Greece v. Galloway*, 572 U.S. 565, 577 (2014)).

12 *N.Y. State Rifle & Pistol Ass'n v. Bruen*, 597 U.S. 1, 34 (2022) (quoting *District of Columbia v. Heller*, 554 U.S. 570, 634–5 (2008)) (emphasis added by Court).

13 *Dobbs*, 597 U.S. at 237–40.

14 *Bruen*, 597 U.S. at 83 (noting but not resolving an "ongoing scholarly debate" as to whether 1791 or 1868 is the date to identify the proper scope of the right to bear arms incorporated under the Fourteenth Amendment).

15 *Id.* at 17 (holding that the right to bear arms cannot be regulated in any manner inconsistent with "this Nation's historical tradition of firearm regulation"); *Kennedy*, 597 U.S. at 535 (noting that the incorporated freedom from religious establishment must be circumscribed with "reference to historical practices and understanding" and "focused on original meaning and history") (quotations omitted).

16 "Constitutional analysis must begin with 'the language of the instrument.'" *Dobbs*, 597 U.S. at 235 (quoting *Gibbons v. Ogden*, 22 U.S. 1, 186–9 (1824)).

17 In *Kennedy*, across 75 pages and multiple opinions, the Justices mentioned the Amendment by name only once. 597 U.S. at 524.

18 *Dobbs*, 597 U.S. at 374 (Breyer, Sotomayor, Kagan, JJ., dissenting).

19 *Id.* at 240, n. 22; *id.* at 331–6 (Thomas, J., concurring).

20 *Students for Fair Admissions, Inc. v. President & Fellows of Harv. Coll.*, 600 U.S. 181, 201–2 (2023); *id.* at 321–6 (Sotomayor, J., dissenting).

21 *Id.* at 322 (pointing to "a number of race-conscious" federal laws passed around the time of the Fourteenth Amendment's enactment).

22 *Id.* at 202 (maj. op.).

23 *Id.* at 203 (stating that by 1950, "the truth of the Fourteenth Amendment had thus begun to reemerge"); *id.* at 327 (Sotomayor, J., dissenting) (chastising the Court for curtailing the Reconstruction Amendments and noting that it was not until *Brown* that the Court "honored the guarantee of equality in the Equal Protection Clause").

24 *Id.* at 240–2 (Thomas, J., concurring).
25 Report of the Joint Committee on Reconstruction, 39th Cong., 1st sess. (1866), at i, xxi.
26 John Bingham proposed the resolution in the House. Jacob Howard moved for a concurring vote in the Senate. *See* Cong. Globe, 39th Cong., 1st Sess. 3241 (June 18, 1866); H. Journal, 39th Cong., 1st Sess. 859 (June 18, 1866); S. Journal, 39th Cong., 1st Sess. 541–2 (June 18, 1866).
27 *See, e.g.*, Susannah W. Pollvogt, *Beyond Suspect Classifications*, 16 U. PA. J. Const. L. 739, 742 (2014) (discussing the various judicial tests for identifying improper classifications).
28 *Graham v. Richardson*, 403 U.S. 365, 372 (1971).
29 *Meyer v. Nebraska*, 262 U.S. 390, 399 (1923).
30 *Palko v. Connecticut*, 302 U.S. 319, 325 (1937).
31 *Lawrence v. Texas*, 539 U.S. 558, 574 (2003) (quoting *Planned Parenthood of Southeastern Pa. v. Casey*, 505 U.S. 833, 851 (1992)).
32 83 U.S. 36 (1873). Some scholars date the rupture a bit later. *See, e.g.*, Bryan H. Wildenthal, *The Lost Compromise: Reassessing the Early Understanding in Court and Congress on Incorporation of the Bill of Rights in the Fourteenth Amendment*, 61 Ohio State L.J. 1051, 1151–2 (2000) (arguing that the Court's opinion in *United States v. Cruikshank*, 92 U.S. 542 (1876), served as "the origin of the narrow conventional reading" that largely nullified the Privileges or Immunities Clause).
33 *Slaughter-House Cases*, 83 U.S. at 79.
34 "This Constitution, and the Laws of the United States which shall be made in Pursuance thereof . . . shall be the supreme Law of the Land; and the Judges in every State shall be bound thereby, any Thing in the Constitution or Laws of any State to the Contrary notwithstanding." U.S. Const. art. VI.
35 *Slaughter-House Cases*, 83 U.S. at 96 (Field, J., dissenting).
36 *See, e.g.*, John Harrison, *Reconstructing the Privileges or Immunities Clause*, 101 Yale L.J. 1385, 1387 (1992).
37 *See, Students for Fair Admissions, Inc. v. President & Fellows of Harv. Coll.*, 600 U.S. 181, 242 (Thomas, J. concurring) (indicating that the immunity against racial discrimination seemed more connected with citizenship).
38 *See, e.g.*, Harrison, *supra* note 36, at 1387 (noting that the subsequent interpretation of these clauses has seemed "upside down" and involves various stubborn problems).
39 Mary Karlynn Hinman, The Lost Clause: An Analysis of the Privileges and Immunities of Citizens of the United States (1967) (Ph.D. dissertation, Harvard Univ.).
40 Transcript of Oral Argument at 7, *McDonald v. City of Chicago*, 561 U.S. 742 (2010) (No. 08-1521) (comment of Justice Scalia).
41 *McDonald v. City of Chicago*, 561 U.S. 742, 758 (plurality opinion) (2010); *id.* at 859–60 (Stevens, J. dissenting); *id.* at 934 (Breyer, J., dissenting).
42 *Id.* at 803–58 (Thomas, J., concurring).
43 *Id.* at 758 (plurality op. of Alito, J.); *id.* at 859, n. 2 (Stevens, J., dissenting).
44 *Dobbs v. Jackson Women's Health Org.*, 597 U.S. 215, 331–6 (2022) (Thomas, J., concurring).
45 *See, e.g.*, Jack M. Balkin, Living Originalism 104 (2014) (critiquing some originalists for treating "originally expected applications" as dispositive of "original meaning").

46 *See, e.g.*, 1 St. George Tucker, Blackstone's Commentaries 45 (1803) ("It is likewise 'a rule prescribed.' Because a bare resolution, confined in the breast of the legislator, without manifesting itself by some external sign, can never be properly a law. It is requisite that this resolution be notified to the people who are to obey it.").

47 Speech at Springfield, Illinois (June 26, 1857), *in* 2 Abraham Lincoln, Collected Works 398, 406 (1953).

48 A century ago, a political scientist based his doctoral dissertation on this distinction, but the study spanned only seventy pages and included very little legal history. Chin-Yung Yen, Rights of Citizens and Persons Under the Fourteenth Amendment (1905) (Ph.D. Dissertation, Columbia Univ.).

49 *See, e.g.*, Barnett & Bernick, *supra* note 8, at 144.

50 *See, e.g.*, Kurt T. Lash, The Fourteenth Amendment and the Privileges and Immunities of American Citizenship 278 (2014) (concluding that the Clause secures the "textually enumerated personal rights" of the federal Constitution).

51 *See, e.g.*, Harrison, *supra* note 36, at 1424 (1992) (concluding that the privileges and immunities include "rights as defined by the positive law of their states;" as well as "rights created or protected by national law"); Wurman, *supra* note 9, at 102 (stating that these privileges and immunities are "state defined privileges and immunities").

52 Richard A. Epstein, *Of Citizens and Persons: Reconstructing the Privileges or Immunities Clause of the Fourteenth Amendment*, 1 N.Y.U. J.L. & Liberty 334, 340 (2005).

53 *Am. Legion v. Am. Humanist Ass'n*, 588 U.S. 19, 33 (2019) (Thomas, J., concurring) (emphasis added).

54 For instance, *see Barnes v. Browning*, (Ind. Cir. Ct., Lafayette, IN) (Apr. 13, 1866), *reprinted fully in*, *Judge Test's Decision on the Case Under the Civil Rights Bill*, The Richmond Palladium (Richmond, IN), Apr. 26, 1866, at 1, http://chroniclingamerica.loc.gov/lccn/sn86058250/1866-04-26/ed-1/seq-1.

55 *See* Wildenthal, *supra* note 32, at 1134.

56 According to the story, Glaucus was a fisherman who became a sea god upon eating magic herbs.

57 Plato, The Republic 295 (Allan Bloom trans. 1968).

58 Howard Jay Graham, *The Framing of the Fourteenth Amendment, by Joseph B. James*, 32 Ind. L.J. 285, 293 (1957) (book review).

1

An Original Consensus

There is no ambiguity in the language of the proposed amendment.

—Message of Governor Francis H. Pierpont to the Virginia Legislature (Dec. 3, 1866)[1]

[We] demanded as a bond of security for the future that every person born on American soil or naturalized thereon is an American citizen, entitled to the rights and immunities of citizenship . . . this provision [is] so plain that no judicial blindness henceforth shall fail to read and understand it. (Great applause).

—Speech of Galusha A. Grow, Former Speaker of the House of Representatives, at Poughkeepsie, NY (November 1867)[2]

For seventy-five years now, jurists have offered sharply different accounts of the original meaning of the Fourteenth Amendment, and in particular, the Amendment's first section. And there has been little progress toward any consensus.

The discord has been so intractable that many have concluded that the blame lies not with the modern inquirers, but with the object of their inquiry. The Amendment's terms, Justice Robert Jackson lamented, remain "enigmatic and abstruse."[3] Nor has history clarified these terms. As various jurists have remarked, the evidence from the original debates seems "confusing and conflicting."[4]

Many have alleged that the confusion lay in the minds of the authors. In his landmark study, Charles Fairman said that the congressional drafters were beset with mental "confusion" and unresolved "ambiguity."[5] Subsequent scholars, including Hermine Herta Meyer and Paul Moreno, have leveled a similar charge.[6] More moderately, Christopher Wolfe has found "vagueness and some confusion in the minds of the framers about the actual language of the amendment."[7]

By some accounts, the problem was simply disagreement among the authors. Writing a half-century ago, Mary Karlynn Hinman concluded that these "potentially vital concepts" bore no common definition, but only a common vague purpose: "to accomplish something good," and for the most part, "the something good was for the Negro."[8] Cass Sunstein has similarly alleged that "no single or simple view can be found in history" because among the "many framers and ratifiers" there were "many different understandings."[9]

In contrast, many jurists have concluded that vagueness *was* the original consensus. Justice William Brennan, for instance, asserted that contemporaries generally knew Section 1 to be "vague and imprecise"[10] Accordingly, Father Francis Canavan charged that the prohibitions of Section 1 "were not in the proper sense of the term laws," but simply broad "political ideals."[11] More recently, Thomas Colby has contended that the Amendment's "language was, even then, recognized to be highly ambiguous and indeterminate," consisting of "soaring and ambiguous platitudes."[12]

For some scholars, the intentional ambiguity served one of two purposes: either to build a coalition or to deceive the citizenry. According to William Nelson, the drafters needed language "sufficiently ambiguous and broad" to forge a winning coalition in Congress and the states.[13] Alfred Kelly, in turn, claimed that congressional proponents used vagueness to deceive; "the technique of lofty, expansive, and highly generalized language" served to obscure the potentially broad sweep of the Amendment.[14] More recently, Susan Carle has likewise concluded that "the choice of language reveals obvious and likely intentional ambiguity."[15]

But as we will see in this chapter, a review of the commentary from the drafting and ratification of the Amendment provides substantial *prima facie* evidence of an original coherence—and original consensus. This evidence indicates that the major interpretive disagreements arose not among supporters but between supporters and some opponents. Moreover, even those disagreements were generally limited to three discrete and intelligible issues: (1) whether the "privileges and immunities of citizens of the United States" extended to intermarriage and political rights, (2) whether these "privileges and immunities" could be subject to congressional redefinition under Section 5, and (3) whether federal enforcement of the Due Process and Equal Protection clauses would not merely supplement, but even supplant the states' primary authority to secure life, liberty, and property against unlawful violence.

Supporters' Coherent Compromise

The recorded comments of the drafters and ratifiers of the Fourteenth Amendment provide direct and substantial evidence for an original coherent understanding of Section 1. The Amendment was first formulated by the Joint Committee on Reconstruction, which completed its draft on April 28, 1866. Its first section was drafted chiefly by Ohio Representative John Bingham. Bingham composed what would become the Amendment's momentous second sentence:

> No State shall make or enforce any law which shall abridge the privileges or immunities of citizens of the United States; nor shall any State deprive any person of life, liberty, or property, without due process of law, nor deny to any person within its jurisdiction the equal protection of the laws.[16]

Publicly, Bingham avowed this sentence a "simple, strong, plain declaration."[17]

To be sure, as the Republicans on the Committee publicly acknowledged, they had begun their deliberations with "conflicting opinions."[18] Two major points of dispute are relevant here. First, some Republicans favored an immediate guarantee of racial equality as to voting rights, while at the other extreme, some preferred silence,[19] mainly because they feared that northern white voters would reject such a reform.[20] Second, Republicans also disagreed as to civil rights (e.g., travel, contract, property, etc.), with some favoring an express provision for racial equality, which would constitutionalize the recently passed Civil Rights Act,[21] and others opposing any civil rights provision whatsoever, probably because they believed that any constitutional restatement was unnecessary and would even represent a tacit admission that the Act had been unconstitutional.[22]

When the Committee moved to finalize a proposal in late April 1866,[23] there were two major rival plans that reflected these disagreements: (1) the Owen Plan (drafted by noted reformer Robert Dale Owen), which the Committee had initially approved but then moved to reconsider on Wednesday April 25;[24] and (2) the New York Plan, drafted by a caucus of New York Republican congressmen later that evening.[25] The Owen Plan would have secured racial equality, first as to civil rights immediately, and then as to voting rights by 1876:

> Section 1. No discrimination shall be made by any state, nor by the United States, as to the civil rights of persons because of race, color, or previous condition of servitude.
>
> Sec. 2. From and after the fourth day of July, in the year one thousand eight hundred and seventy-six, no discrimination shall be made by any state, nor by the United States, as to the enjoyment by classes of persons of the right of suffrage, because of race, color, or previous condition of servitude.[26]

In sharp contrast, the New York Plan, as published in the *New York Tribune*, contained no guarantee for racial equality, either civil or political. Instead, the plan merely encouraged equality by reducing a state's congressional representation in proportion to the state's racial disenfranchisement of its population.[27]

At their next meeting, on Saturday, April 28, the Committee resolved these controversies, not by confusion, nor by a mere agreement to disagree, but by intelligible compromise. Their eventual proposal, as they later avowed in their formal report, resulted from "mutual concession" after lengthy discussion of their disagreements.[28] This claim is corroborated by other evidence. Just after the meeting on April 28, a newspaper reporter heard that after an "animated session of nearly five hours," the twelve Republican members had attained unanimity only after "mutual concession," with each member yielding at least "one point."[29] And Iowa Senator James Grimes, in a letter to his wife, reported that his colleagues had become "unexpectedly harmonious."[30]

As to the suffrage, the Committee accepted the approach of the New York Plan. The Committee voted to reject the racial equality guarantee and approved New York's representation-reduction formula, which would become Section 2 of the

Amendment.[31] The Committee thus settled on what Gabriel Chin has aptly called a "No-Fifths Compromise."[32]

But as to civil rights, Bingham's prohibitory sentence represented an apparent compromise between the two plans. On the one hand, Bingham's formula retained a guarantee for equal civil rights (as under the Owen plan). On the other hand, Bingham's formula, by its breadth and constitutional depth, addressed the concerns of the drafters of the New York Plan. The prohibitions were not redundancies as they were much broader than the Civil Rights Act.[33] And Bingham's formula, by reflecting guarantees already found in the Constitution ("due process," and "privileges and immunities") mitigated any tacit admission of the Act's unconstitutionality.

Nor, *pace* Justice Brennan, did the Bingham Compromise indicate a rejection of "Owen's rather specific language" in favor of "Bingham's far more elastic language."[34] To the contrary, Bingham's version, though broader in scope, was, by Owen's recollection, decidedly less elastic. It served, he said, to "*specify*, in *detail*, the civil rights which we propose to assure," which "specification" Owen rejected as "out of place . . . in a constitutional amendment" even if appropriate to a civil rights statute. That is to say, Owen favored the undefined "civil rights," while Bingham's formulas—the "equal protection of the laws," "due process of law," and the "privileges and immunities of citizens"—specified these "civil rights."[35] Accordingly, in their formal report on the Amendment, the Committee's Republican majority certified that Section 1's prohibitory sentence would "*determine* the civil rights and privileges of all citizens in all parts of the Republic."[36]

During the congressional debates, supporters likewise emphasized the clarity of Section 1. Rather than something nebulous, it was, for James Garfield, something solid and terrestrial—the "firm earth" as compact as "solid granite," and thus it would be an "enduring and indubitable principle." And when he turned to the sky for celestial metaphors, he saw a star—and not of the wandering sort: the section would "fix" the Civil Rights Act "in the serene sky, in the eternal firmament of the Constitution, where no storm of passion can shake it and no cloud can obscure it."[37]

Moreover, during the subsequent political campaign of 1866, when "from Maine to California" the proposed Amendment "was virtually the platform which was submitted to the people,"[38] supporters reemphasized the clarity of Section 1. It was "simple, just, and moderate";[39] the text itself provided its own "irresistible argument";[40] and "[n]o man can vote misunderstandingly who carefully reads and ponders" the proposal.[41] In Indiana, Governor Oliver Morton said Section 1 had a "clear meaning" with a "manifest spirit and purport,"[42] and the state's lieutenant governor likewise called it a "plain, unambiguous proposition."[43] And in North Carolina, the pseudonymous "Union Citizen" said the Amendment was "so plain and so easy of comprehension as to require no exposition, except with a view to answering object[ions] which have been made to it."[44]

Following the Republican triumph in those elections, official proponents expressed even more confidence in the Amendment's clarity. New York's governor recommended ratification to his legislature, but declined to discuss the Amendment because its provisions were already so widely "understood, appreciated and approved."[45]

Indiana's Governor Morton told his state legislature that "[n]o public measure was ever more fully discussed before the people, better understood by them, or received a more distinct and intelligent approval" and that he would "enter into no argument in its behalf" because "[e]very member of it understands it, and is prepared, I doubt not, to give his vote for or against, on the question of ratification."[46] In the subsequent debates in that legislature, supporters left the floor to the opposition, because, as one senator remarked, "every Republican in the State of Indiana fully understands the question—it has been discussed from every stump and school house—the people have voted for it, and we know where they stand."[47]

Illinois's governor likewise noted that the people had "after full and deliberate discussion" given a "most emphatic approval and indorsement."[48] Most emphatically, Virginia's governor declared there was "*no ambiguity* in the language of the proposed amendment."[49]

To my knowledge, the *only* possible exception to the supporters' professed clarity is Senator Jacob Howard's remark, as reported in the *Congressional Globe*, that the "privileges and immunities of citizens" could not "be fully defined in their entire extent and precise nature[.]"[50] The statement has been, in our times, sometimes quoted to support the conclusion that the Clause is elastic, including an indefinite variety of rights.[51]

In sharp contrast with modern scholars, neither Howard nor his contemporaries seemed to take his comment very seriously. He did not deem the remark important enough to include in his lengthy preparatory notes, nor did news reporters include it in their accounts of his speech.[52] The indifference was understandable, for on its face, the statement was a mere truism; of course no legal category can be defined perfectly, with entire precision. What James Madison had once said of "executive," "legislative," and "judicial" power probably applies to "privileges," "immunities," and "citizens":

> [As] to the institutions of man, in which the obscurity arises as well from the object itself as from the organ by which it is contemplated, we must perceive the necessity of moderating still further our expectations and hopes from the efforts of human sagacity. Experience has instructed us that no skill in the science of government has yet been able to discriminate and define, with sufficient certainty, its three great provinces the legislative, executive, and judiciary; or even the *privileges* and powers of the different legislative branches.[53]

In regard to Howard's remark, Christopher Green has reminded us of Aristotle's maxim that "it belongs to an educated person to seek out precision in each genus to the extent that the nature of the matter allows."[54] Indeed, a week later, Howard himself would exhibit such intellectual moderation in defending his proposed Citizenship Clause: "I think the language as it stands is *sufficiently* certain and exact."[55]

If, however, Howard meant something much more than this truism—if he meant that Section 1's language was, relative to other constitutional terms, peculiarly vague or obscure—then not only was he contradicted by every supporter who spoke of the measure's clarity, but he was contradicting himself. Howard's remark occurred just after he quoted with approval Justice Bushrod Washington's indication that the "privileges and immunities" could be known insofar as they were enjoyed in *all* the states since Independence, and that their complete enumeration would be "more tedious than difficult."[56] Further, a few weeks later, Howard would sign the Committee's formal report certifying that Section 1 would "determine" certain civil rights and privileges.

Further proof of the supporters' clear consensus can be found in the conspicuous absence of any acknowledgment, concession, or even accusation, whether in public or private remarks, that the proponents of the Amendment disagreed among themselves as to its meaning. My research has revealed no evidence of any adversary highlighting, or any proponent conceding, some major discord among proponents. Nor have I found evidence of anyone contesting those issues that have generated so much contention among today's scholars. Hence, for instance, no opponent or supporter pointed to any dispute as to whether the provision was a guarantee of absolute rights or equality in rights, or whether or how the Amendment "incorporated" the federal Bill of Rights. Participants in the debates, supporters and opponents alike, did not seem to notice any such discord at all.

Opponents' Allegations of Incoherence

Unlike supporters, many prominent opponents did indeed allege that Section 1 was vague—with particular reference to the Privileges or Immunities Clause. During the House debates, Representative Benjamin Boyer objected to Section 1 in part because "its phraseology [was] open to ambiguity and admitting of conflicting constructions."[57] In the Senate, on the last day of debate, Indiana's Thomas Hendricks objected that the "rights and immunities of citizenship" secured by the Privileges or Immunities Clause had not been "accurately defined," either by his colleagues or other statesmen, so the phrase was "not very certain but to some extent vague." An hour or so later, Maryland's Reverdy Johnson, a member of the Joint Committee, likewise objected to the Clause "simply because I do not understand what will be the effect of that."[58]

In a similar vein, during the first wave of ratification debates (1866–1867), members of several legislative committees objected to Section 1 as too vague. In North Carolina, the Joint Select Committee on Federal Relations opposed the Clause because "those privileges and immunities are . . . not defined[,]"[59] and Texas's House Committee on Federal Relations complained that the clause was a "generality."[60] The minority on Tennessee's senate committee protested that the Amendment was "couched in language ambiguous, uncertain and liable to various constructions, concealing a purpose to strike down and overthrow the legitimate rights of the States, and consolidate all power in the hands of a great centralized Government."[61] And the minority on New Hampshire's house committee likewise alleged that "the proposed Amendment is ambiguous or contradictory in its provisions[.]"[62]

Furthermore, when New Jersey's legislature, having flipped to Democratic control in 1868, voted to rescind its earlier ratification vote, the vagueness of the Amendment's language was a leading objection. Speaking with apparent reference to Section 1, the legislature claimed that its language was deliberately "vague for the purpose of facilitating encroachments upon the lives, liberties and property of the people," such that the "national judiciary" might exploit this ambiguity to invalidate even parts of the "common law."[63]

Despite the apparent vigor and sweep of these objections, for the most part they proved either transient or narrow in scope. As to Reverdy Johnson, his reticence seems more fleeting than well-considered. Johnson had voted for Bingham's substitute in the Joint Committee and made no objection to Section 1 in the lengthy and detailed report he subsequently prepared for the Committee's minority.[64] And within a year, while the Amendment's ratification was still pending, Johnson published a pamphlet indicating that whatever doubts he had had as to the Clause's meaning had been resolved. He explained that apart from the Citizenship Clause, all of Section 1 was merely declaratory of principles already contained in the Constitution:

> Under the Constitution, independent of this supposed amendment, the provisions as to the rights of citizens are the same as those of the amendment. . . . Will [any man] of sense, maintain that under the Constitution, without the amendment, a State could, by law, "abridge the privileges and immunities of citizens," or deprive any person "of life, liberty or property without due process of law." And these are all that the amendment prohibits. The fact is, that the provisions just referred to are wholly unnecessary.[65]

Thus Johnson adopted the view of some supporters and opponents that the clauses of the second sentence were merely declaratory if not wholly redundant.[66]

As to the vagueness objections, these seemed limited to two discrete issues. First, there was significant debate in the states as to whether the "privileges and immunities of citizens" would include the political and intermarriage rights of citizenship. Hence, during the election campaign, Hendricks seemingly abandoned his prior doubt and boldly charged that the privileges and immunities of citizenship would definitely include "voting and holding office" so that "negroes and Indians" would be endowed with "the high right and privilege of participating in the control of the affairs of the Government."[67] In Tennessee, the author of the minority report, Beriah Frazier, similarly suggested that the harmful ambiguity extended no further than to the possible inclusion of intermarriage and political rights; he proposed, as an adequate cure, the following amendment:

> That the foregoing proposed amendment to the Constitution of the United States shall not be so construed as to confer the right of suffrage upon a negro or person of color, or to confer upon any negro or person of color the right to hold office, sit upon juries or to intermarry with white persons; nor shall said proposed amendment be construed as to prohibit any State from enacting and enforcing such laws as will secure these ends, not inconsistent with the present Constitution of the United States; nor shall said proposed amendment be so construed as to

abridge the reserved rights of the States in the election and qualification of their own officers and the management of their domestic concerns, as provided and secured by the present Constitution of the United States."[68]

In New Hampshire, the minority similarly specified the harmful "ambiguity": whether the "right of suffrage" would be claimed as one of the "privileges."[69]

Second, there was substantial allegation, chiefly in the states, as to whether Congress's enforcement power under Section 5 would include the power to redefine these "privileges" and "immunities," whether by addition or subtraction. Texas's House Committee thus explained the danger:

> [I]n these privileges would be embraced the exercise of suffrage at the polls, participation in jury duty in all cases, bearing arms in the militia, and other matters which need not be here enumerated. It is unnecessary to appeal to the fact that in most of the original free States, negroes have been by law, and in all of them by immemorial usage, excluded from these "privileges and immunities," now sought to be forced on the Southern States, to show that the amendment proposed in this section contemplates and intends a violation not only of justice, but of the common instincts of our nature. . . .
>
> There is scarcely any limit to the power sought to be transferred by this section from the States to the United States. Congress might declare almost any right or franchise whatever, to be the privilege or immunity of a citizen of the United States and it would immediately attach to every citizen of every State, whether white man or descendant of African. To estimate the comprehensive scope of the power herein sought for Congress—that body might declare miscegenation a "privilege or immunity."[70]

North Carolina's joint committee presented the risk in similar (though more moderate) terms:

> Whether reference is had only to such privileges and immunities as may be supposed now to exist, or to all others which the Federal Government may hereafter declare to belong to it, or may choose to grant to citizens, is left in doubt, though the latter construction seems the more natural, and is one which that Government could at any time insist upon as correct and entirely consistent with the language used. With this construction placed upon it, what limit would remain to the power of that Government to interfere in the internal affairs of the States? And what becomes of the right of a State to regulate its domestic concerns in its own way? Whatever restrictions any State might think proper, for the general good, to impose upon any or all its citizens, upon a declaration by the Federal Government that such restrictions were an abridgement of the privileges or immunities of the citizens of the Union, such State laws would at once be annulled. For instance: the laws of North Carolina forbid the inter-marriage of white persons and negroes. But if this Amendment be ratified, the Government of the United States could

> declare that this law abridged the privileges of citizens, and must not be enforced; and miscegenation would thereupon be legalized in this Commonwealth.[71]

Both these interpretive objections were widespread, understandable, and plausible. And proponents' responses to both these objections were equally understandable and, in my opinion, more persuasive.

As to the first objection, of course political rights were undoubtedly privileges of citizenship. As Bingham himself had acknowledged, since Aristotle, political thinkers have treated decisional authority as the central element of citizenship;[72] and in *Corfield v. Coryell*, the leading antebellum case on "privileges and immunities," Justice Bushrod Washington had said that political rights "may" be included.[73] The Joint Committee likewise spoke emphatically of the "civil and political" rights of "citizenship."[74]

But supporters could rightly point to the qualifier "of the United States" as precluding any incorporation of political rights. As Indiana's Governor Morton explained, the right of suffrage is "conferred, bestowed, regulated, [and] withheld, by the several States," and therefore cannot be a privilege of "citizens of the United States."[75] As Morton (and also Senator Howard) explained, these fundamental rights belonged to citizens of the United States "as such" and thus could never be "abridged or interfered with by the laws of any State."[76] These privileges are not "conferred, bestowed, [or] regulated" by the states, and could never be "withheld."

Moreover, to interpret the Clause to encompass political rights would be absurd. In effect, the text seems to protect rights belonging to *all* citizens of the United States, but decisional rights were (and still are) routinely reserved to only a portion of the citizenry, not only on such controversial bases as sex, property, and religion, but also on such relatively uncontroversial bases as age and residence. As Reverdy Johnson explained, if the "privileges [and] immunities of citizens" included the suffrage, it would be "the duty of Congress to secure the franchise to every citizen, irrespective of age, residence, sex or color."[77]

During the campaign of 1866, Indiana's lieutenant governor, Conrad Baker, responded to opponents' political-rights reading with less moderation: "Never in the history of political discussion in this country has a plain, unambiguous proposition been so shamefully and willfully perverted as this."[78]

In contrast, as to intermarriage, proponents did not issue such a denial. Supporters treated this particular objection with deafening silence—and at times, tacit or express concession.[79] Indeed, as I have contended elsewhere, a strong preponderance of the evidence indicates that those who adopted the Amendment generally (though not unanimously) understood, but rarely proclaimed, that it would prohibit the states from adopting laws prohibiting or invalidating interracial marriage between citizens.[80]

As to the second objection—congressional power—some opponents had good reason to fear that, in conjunction with Section 5, the "privileges and immunities of citizens of the United States" would be subject to congressional redefinition. Some in Congress had already presumed to exercise that definitional authority by passing the Civil Rights Act, with reliance on the similar enforcement clause of the Thirteenth Amendment.[81]

But supporters had good reason to say otherwise. As the Constitution's sheer text indicates, American citizenship is anterior to the Constitution and the Congress established by it.[82] Because the rights of citizenship are thus fundamental, Congress could not have the power to redefine them. Rather, the Amendment would, according to the Joint Committee, "*determine* the civil rights and privileges of all citizens in all parts of the Republic," with Congress's power limited to enforcement of this determination.[83] I will elaborate this interpretation in Chapter 3.

Moreover, among antebellum authorities, the phrase, "privileges and immunities of citizens of the United States" did not refer to any federal power to create or destroy rights, but served as a gloss on the "privileges and immunities" guaranteed to citizens under Article IV. Perhaps most notably, two decades earlier, Justice Nathaniel Reed, of Ohio's Supreme Court, had interpreted the Clause to read as follows: "That 'the citizens (of the United States) of each State,' or belonging to each State, 'shall be entitled to all the privileges and immunities of citizens (of the United States) in the several States.'"[84] According to Reed, the Clause protected certain nationwide privileges: "the spirit and intention" of the Clause is "not to secure to the nonresident the same rights and indulgence with the resident in every State, but simply to secure to the citizen of the United States, whether a State resident or not, the full enjoyment of all the rights of citizenship, in every State throughout the Union."[85] These nationwide "rights of citizenship," which "[t]he legislation of the States cannot violate . . . in any way or degree," were not creatures of federal law. But they could "be *determined* by a reference to the spirit and letter of our national constitution, and also to the general custom of other nations."[86]

Still, these two interpretive disagreements did not reflect confusion. Rather, these intelligible and definable disputes represented a coherent set of disagreements. Such coherent disagreements were themselves evidence of an underlying coherence of opinion among both proponents and opponents of the Fourteenth Amendment.

There is, however, one exception: New Jersey's rescission resolution of 1868. As far as I know, it was the first and only instance where any participant in the adoption of the Amendment alleged either that it might be construed to invalidate the common law, or that such legal novelty might be imposed not by Congress but by the federal judiciary. Indeed, as I will discuss in Chapter 3, it was *supporters* who most feared judicial innovation; they endorsed Section 1 precisely to correct and retrain judicial activism.

Consensus Interpretation of the Citizenship, Due Process, and Equal Protection Clauses

In contrast, there was comparatively little disagreement as to the *meaning* of the Citizenship, Due Process, and Equal Protection Clauses—and almost no allegation of ambiguity. Of these three, only the Citizenship Clause gave rise to any noticeable interpretive debate. The provision was introduced in the Senate, and there, opponents charged that persons born under (Indian) tribal relations were indeed "subject to the jurisdiction thereof" and thus would qualify for *ius soli* citizenship. Supporters, however, rejected this interpretation, explaining that "jurisdiction" in this Clause implies "a full and complete jurisdiction," and those born under tribal governments were subject to only a partial jurisdiction.[87]

Further, of these three provisions, only the Citizenship Clause prompted opposition to its *justice* or *policy*. Some opposed it because they flatly opposed the multiracial citizenry that the Amendment established. Indiana's Senator Hendricks decried the Clause for degrading the status of American citizenship: when the "rank and title" of American citizen was reserved to whites, it "conferred honor at home and secured kindness, respect, and safety everywhere abroad; but if this amendment be adopted we will then carry the title and enjoy its advantages in common with the negroes, the coolies, and the Indians . . . races that ought not to mingle."[88]

Yet supporters favored the measure as declaratory of the existing law of the land: America *already was* a multiracial republic. As I will elaborate in Chapter 5, the provision was merely declaratory of the "great fact" that all persons born in and under the jurisdiction of the United States are citizens;[89] or as Senator Howard (the Clause's chief sponsor) affirmed, the provision was "simply declaratory of what I regard as the law of the land already. . . . It settles the great question of citizenship and removes all doubt as to what persons are or are not citizens of the United States."[90]

But as to the Due Process and Equal Protection Clauses, neither their meaning nor their policy was a matter of any significant dispute. Opponents, like supporters, routinely endorsed these principles. Most notably, in August 1866, at the Johnsonite "National Union Convention" in Philadelphia, prominent southern and northern Democrats, united in opposition to congressional Reconstruction, resolved that [the] "enfranchised slaves in all the States of the Union should receive, in common with all their inhabitants, *equal protection* in every right of person and property."[91] President Johnson had said much the same thing in his December 1865 message to Congress: "good faith requires the security of the freedmen in their liberty and their property."[92] Leading southern opponents of the Amendment repeatedly endorsed this principle in similar terms, including the governors of Mississippi, North Carolina, and Texas.[93] Accordingly, in his July veto of the Second Freedmen's Bureau Bill, Johnson protested that the law was unnecessary, in part because the former insurgent states had already "conferred by law upon the freedman" the same "protection granted to the white citizen . . . and it is believed that ample protection will be afforded him by due process of law."[94]

Instead, it was the *federalization* of due process and equal protection that provoked intense opposition. One controversial effect was the way in which the Due Process Clause might substantially increase the supervisory authority of the federal courts. In a widely published letter, Secretary of the Interior Orville Browning protested that the proposed Due Process Clause would "subordinate the State judiciaries in all things to federal supervision and control," for the federal courts would have authority to review every decision, in every criminal or civil case, by which any party was deprived of property, liberty, or life:

> [I]f adopted, every matter of judicial investigation, civil or criminal, however insignificant, may be drawn into the vortex of the Federal judiciary. In a controversy between two neighbors about the ownership of a pig, the unsuccessful party may allege that the State tribunals have deprived him of his property without due process of law, and take the case before the Federal tribunals for revision. So if a man may be indicted for larceny or other crime, convicted and sentenced upon allegation of deprivation of liberty with due process of law, he may bring the case before the federal tribunals for revision and reversal. So, too, if a murderer be arrested, tried, convicted and sentenced to be hung, he may claim the protection of the new constitutional provision, allege that a State is about to deprive him of his life without due process of law, and arrest all further proceedings until the Federal Government shall have inquired whether a State has a right to punish its own citizens for an infraction of its own laws.[95]

A joint committee of North Carolina's legislature likewise feared that any due-process claimant, however "groundless" his claim, would be entitled to an automatic "rehearing" before the federal courts.[96] In the Pennsylvania legislature, one opponent complained that "[t]he merest vagrant," upon his detention, would have "the right to appeal to the courts of the United States, for them to decide whether he has been deprived of his liberty justly and in due process of law."[97] Alabama's governor went a step further, contending that the Amendment would give the federal courts "complete and unlimited jurisdiction over every conceivable case" originating in state courts.[98] With more moderation, the author of the minority report from the Wisconsin Senate's Committee on Federal Relations feared the same, but suggested that the federal courts would first need congressional authorization before exercising such power.[99]

Still, neither Browning nor virtually anyone else objected to "due process of law" as an ambiguous, nebulous, or otherwise improper restraint on government.[100] To the contrary, as Browning noted, the principle was well established in American law, found not only in the federal Constitution as a restraint on Congress but also, as a restraint on the states, in "most of the State Constitutions," if not "all of them." Accordingly, the proposed provision was "simply a repetition of a limitation upon the powers of State Governments which is already present in the State Constitution[s]."[101] In the Ohio legislature, Samuel Bloom elaborated Browning's objection:

> It is already a provision of the Federal as well as every State constitution in the Union. Why this repetition? Hitherto each citizen looked to the courts of his own State for protection in this regard. This is to create in the federal government a guardian of the States, to see that they do not violate their own Constitutions. Does not this provision also vastly change our judicial system? Suppose a citizen of Ohio should feel aggrieved by the decision of a State Court, and should appeal to the Supreme or District Courts of the United States, upon the ground that he had been deprived unlawfully of liberty or property, or was about to be unlawfully deprived of life? Would not the United States Courts be compelled to assume jurisdiction?[102]

Bloom added that this subordination of the state judiciary would make litigation more expensive, and thus cause injustice to the poor:

> Would not this remove the administration of justice still further from the people? Would a poor man stand an equal chance with the rich? Would not the result be an almost total destruction of the poor man's hopes for justice[?] It would inaugurate a system of expensive justice, giving to wealth an undue advantage of poverty.[103]

In response, supporters did not deny that the Amendment's Due Process Clause would, at least potentially, expand the appellate jurisdiction of the federal courts over state deprivations of life, liberty, or property. In direct response to Browning's objection, the *Chicago Tribune* happily conceded that the Amendment would provide every freedman with "the right to appeal from the action of his State taking his life, liberty or property without due process of law."[104]

Unlike the Due Process Clause, the Equal Protection Clause did not, by its own force, provoke fears of such automatic and massive expansion of federal authority. This contrast probably resulted from the difference between judicial and executive authority, for the judiciary has the primary responsibility for conducting any *process* that might be due, but the executive is the principal initiator and provider of that *protection* that must be provided (or not denied), as I will discuss at length in the fourth chapter. If a state executive denied that protection by a failure of initiative (e.g., by arrest and arraignment), there would be no "case" of "controversy" to which the federal courts could have any jurisdiction.

Dissensus as to Congressional Power to Protect Life, Liberty, and Property

Still, in conjunction with Congress's enforcement powers under Section 5, both "equal protection" and "due process" provoked strong federalism objections. For many opponents, Congress would have the power to largely destroy the states' protective role. Congress, by law, could establish the required *protection* and *process*, entrust its enforcement to the federal executive, and grant the federal courts original as well as appellate jurisdiction over such cases. Federal authority would thus not merely supplement and supervise, but *supplant* state government. Accordingly, Maryland's legislators feared that Congress would thus have the "power of supervision, interference and control over State legislation affecting the lives, liberty, and property of its citizens and persons subject to its jurisdiction," which power was so broad as "to enable Congress to abolish the State governments."[105]

North Carolina's governor elaborated how congressional enforcement of equal protection might involve radical federal interference in the administration of intrastate justice:

> If the design of this fifth section is simply to reaffirm the long established principle of power necessarily implied under the provision just recited, it is needless

> surplusage; but if, as its special insertion indicates, it is intended to amplify the various powers which would be reasonably implied from the sections which precede it, and to give to Congress a peculiar authority over the subjects embraced in the proposed fourteenth article, it is mischievous and dangerous. If there be any feature in the American system of freedom which gives to it practical value, it is the fact that a municipal code is provided under the jurisdiction of each State, by which all controversies as to life, liberty or property, except in the now limited field of Federal jurisdiction, are determined by a jury of the county or neighborhood where the parties reside and the contest arises; but if Congress is hereafter to become the protector of life, liberty and property in the States, and the guarantor of equal protection of the laws, and, by appropriate legislation, to declare a system of rights and remedies, which can be administered only in the Federal Courts, then the most common and familiar offices of justice must be transferred to the few points in the State where these courts are held, and to judges and other offices, deriving and holding their commissions, not from the authority and people of the State as heretofore, but from the President and Senate of the United States. The States, as by so much, are to cease to be self-governing communities as heretofore, and trespasses against the person, assaults and batteries, false imprisonments and the like, where only our own citizens are parties, must be regulated by the Congress of the nation and adjudged only in its courts.[106]

Supporters of the Amendment did not agree. They indicated that congressional enforcement would be merely corrective and otherwise supplemental to state authority. As I will discuss in a subsequent chapter, supporters indicated that the Equal Protection Clause would not infringe the states' primary authority to make "the laws" defining protection, but only bar the states from refusing to equally provide the protection defined by those laws.[107]

Further, as to Congress's power to redress such denial, official supporters treated it as merely secondary and auxiliary. Congressional power would remain "in abeyance" unless the states demonstrated "bad faith" or an absence of "good faith."[108] The power was not preemptive, but exclusively remedial of culpable state misconduct.

On this point, an exchange between the two Wisconsin Senators, James Doolittle and Timothy Howe, clearly highlighted the sharp interpretive disagreement between supporters and some opponents. During the summer of 1866, Doolittle (a Johnsonite opponent) charged that "the first section . . . annihilates state sovereignty," for "Congress shall have the power by law to enforce the administration of equal justice in all the States, among all the people of the States." Doolittle concluded that the Amendment thus forced the naked question: "the problem of the hour is, whether the state shall live, or whether the state shall die."[109] In response, Howe insisted that the states would retain the primary authority over interpersonal justice: if "the several States administer and enforce equal justice between their citizens . . . there will be nothing for Congress to do, and the amendment will be inoperative." Congress's power to redress state denial of equal protection was thus limited: "The *only* effect of the amendment if it is adopted is to enable the National Legislature, representing the people of the United States, to enforce equal justice when the several States *refuse* to enforce it."[110]

Just after Republicans' success in the fall elections, the editors of *The Independent* reaffirmed that the states would retain primary protective responsibility: "If the States protect life and property, good and well; if not, the people intend that the Federal Government shall, and that is one of the reasons why they voted for the amendment." [111]

Supporters did not, of course, deny that the Amendment would represent a significant redistribution of political powers, by extending to the federal government what the Founders had left almost entirely to the states: substantial corrective authority as to justice between persons in the same state.[112] Supporters acknowledged the novelty, but argued that such redistribution had proven necessary by the *refusal* of the southern states to enforce their own laws securing life, liberty, and property against interpersonal violence. The Joint Committee, for instance, reported that a "deep-seated prejudice against color . . . leads to acts of cruelty, oppression, and murder, which the local authorities are at no pains to prevent or punish."[113] The *New York Tribune* explained the necessity of federal oversight: "the Rebel States have repeatedly and grossly outraged [the principle], and it is because life, liberty and property have been illegally taken away in spite of mere State laws that the Federal Government is bound to extend equal protection to all citizens."[114]

Some southern opponents acknowledged their states' abysmal failure. Before the Alabama legislature, in early 1867, former governor Lewis Parsons relayed reports that "in some portions of Alabama, men go at dead of night and steal from negroes, and burn their cabins, and leave by the light of the flames they kindle. The negro school houses, established to aid in their development and enlightenment, are burnt down." Such lawless violence, he warned, "must be put down" by Alabamians, "or the U.S. Government would put it down in such a manner as will be unpleasant to us."[115]

In public remarks, Republican congressmen acknowledged that their purpose was to provide this new power. Wisconsin Senator Howe asked, "If equal justice is the proper thing between man and man, does it make any possible difference who administers it? It is just as well, to be sure, to have it administered by the several States, *if they will administer it*, but if they will not administer it, somebody else should or else equal justice will not be done. [Cheers]."[116] Howe elaborated that his congressional colleagues had "thought this amendment not only proper, but absolutely necessary, because we thought we saw several of these States that were not only unwilling to enforce equal justice between their respective citizens but were absolutely determined that equal justice should not be administered."[117] John Bingham defended the Amendment on similar grounds. Quoting Kent, Bingham conceded that the Founders had left the enforcement of ordinary intrastate justice to the "*exclusive* cognizance of the State governments" and looked "essentially to the State courts for protection." Nonetheless, he explained, we now "have another state of affairs to deal with," for, in some parts of the South, "murder prevails by the consent of society," and officials use the "government and law . . . as a machine to give effect to a revengeful spirit and vent their will on whatever helpless ones they find within their reach. In such a case, the protection of property and personal right becomes a national object."[118]

The debate over federal enforcement of Section 1, then, reveals not confusion but intelligible disagreement as to both the propriety and the meaning of this change—with the disagreement arising not among supporters, but only between supporters and some opponents. Both sides understood that the Amendment would enhance federal power to secure life, liberty, and property against lawless violence. Supporters endorsed such centralization as necessary and proper, while opponents generally rejected it as unnecessary and dangerous. Further, there was an interpretive disagreement. Supporters thought that this new federal power would merely *supplement* the states' primary authority to protect persons and property, while some opponents argued that properly interpreted, the new powers would effectively *supplant* the states.

Conclusion

In sum, a review of the debates largely confirms the contemporaneous assessment of West Virginia's Governor, Arthur Boreman. In submitting the proposed amendment to his state's legislature, he remarked, only Sections 2 and 3 provoked "serious objection to the subject matter . . . of this amendment." As to Sections 1, 4, and 5, some were "not objected to at all; and the rest—except, perhaps, the clause regulating citizenship—are objected to only on the ground that they are proposed to be incorporated into the constitution of the United States—it being claimed that they appertain to matters that should be left to State regulation."[119]

As Boreman suggested, the prohibitions of the Equal Protection and Due Process Clauses gave rise to no controversies as to their meaning or policy, but substantial disagreement as to their federalization, especially as enhanced by Congress's enforcement power. And as he further indicated, the Citizenship Clause involved, in addition, some disagreement as to its meaning and also its policy, as many opponents rejected a multiracial republic.

But as Boreman failed to note, the Privileges or Immunities Clause likewise occasioned some dispute as to not only its federalization, but also its very meaning. Some opponents alleged that these "privileges" might include political rights and intermarriage rights, or would be subject to congressional redefinition. In response, supporters unanimously insisted that these rights were fundamental and civil; therefore, supporters not only denied any congressional power of redefinition, but also expressly and repeatedly denied that these privileges included political rights. Yet in sharp contrast, as to intermarriage rights, supporters observed a general silence if not tacit acknowledgment.

With these qualifications, we have reason to afford the Amendment a presumption of original coherence. The measure's proponents manifestly believed that they shared a common understanding. All this evidence, of course, does not tell us what the original understanding was. Nor does it prove that this understanding was unambiguous in ways that supporters or opponents could not then discern. Nor, for that matter, does this evidence indicate why any original consensus proved so fragile in the decades following ratification. Still, this evidence does show that the Amendment's authors believed the measure had some coherent meaning. We have good reason, then, to renew our efforts and seek to recover that meaning.

Notes

1 Journal of the Senate of the Commonwealth of Virginia, at 29, 34 (1866).

2 *Speech of Honorable Galusha A. Grow recently at Poughkeepsie*, Ashtabula Weekly Telegraph, Dec. 7, 1867, at 1–2, https://chroniclingamerica.loc.gov/lccn/sn83035216/1867-12-07/ed-1/seq-1/. The speech was delivered sometime in the week before Election Day, November 5, 1867. *Id.*

3 *Beauharnais v. Illinois*, 343 U.S. 250, 288 (1952) (Jackson, J., dissenting).

4 Lawrence Rosenthal & Joyce Lee Malcolm, *Colloquy Debate: McDonald v. Chicago: Which Standard of Scrutiny Should Apply to Gun Control Laws?* 105 Nw. L. Rev. 460 (2011) (noting "the confusing and conflicting evidence on the original meaning of the Fourteenth Amendment's Privileges or Immunities Clause").

5 Charles Fairman, *Does the Fourteenth Amendment Incorporate the Bill of Rights? The Original Understanding*, 2 Stan. L. Rev. 1, 12, 56 (1949).

6 Hermine Herta Meyer, The History and Meaning of the Fourteenth Amendment: Judicial Erosion of the Constitution Through the Misuse of the Fourteenth Amendment 91 (1977) ("Some of the speeches in the Congress displayed a great deal of confusion with respect to fundamental constitutional concepts"); Paul D. Moreno, How the Court Became Supreme: The Origins of American Juristocracy 122 (2022) (lamenting the "often incoherent debate in Congress").

7 Christopher Wolfe, The Rise of Modern Judicial Review 140 (1986).

8 Mary Karlynn Hinman, The Lost Clause: An Analysis of the Privileges and Immunities of Citizens of the United States 61 (1967) (Ph.D. dissertation, Harv. Univ.).

9 Cass R. Sunstein, *Originalism for Liberals: Book Review of The Bill of Rights by Akhil Reed Amar & For the People by Akhil Reed Amar and Alan Hirsch*, The New Republic, Sept. 28, 1998, at 31, https://home.uchicago.edu/~csunstei/originalism.html.

10 *Oregon v. Mitchell*, 400 U.S. 112, 274 (1970) (Brennan, J., dissenting).

11 Francis Canavan, *A New Fourteenth Amendment*, 12 Human Life Review 30, 40 (1986).

12 Thomas B. Colby, *The Federal Marriage Amendment and the False Promise of Originalism*, 108 Columb. L. Rev. 593, 596 (2008).

13 William E. Nelson, The Fourteenth Amendment: From Political Principle to Judicial Doctrine 143 (1988).

14 Alfred H. Kelly, *The Fourteenth Amendment Reconsidered, The Segregation Question,* 54 Mich. L. Rev.1049, 1077 (1956).

15 Susan D. Carle, *Liquidation and the Fourteenth Amendment*, 76 Fla. L. Rev. 103, 142 (2024).

16 U.S. Const. amend XIV. The text of the Amendment is the version promulgated by Secretary of State William Seward in his proclamation of the Amendment's ratification. 15 Stat. 708, 709 (July 28, 1868).

17 *The Constitutional Amendment: Exposition of Its Meaning, and Reasons for its Adoption*, The Weekly Perrysburg Journal, Sept. 7, 1866, at 1, https://www.loc.gov/resource/sn85026193/1866-09-07/ed-1/?sp=1&st=image&r=0.709,0.586,0.116,0.088,0.

18 Report of the Joint Committee on Reconstruction, H. R. Rep. No. 30, 39th Cong., 1st Sess., xxi (June 8, 1866) (hereinafter "Report").

19 In early April, Bingham circulated a proposal that said nothing about political rights. *Washington Topics and Gossip*, Cleveland Daily Leader, Apr. 18, 1866, at 1, https://chroniclingamerica.loc.gov/lccn/sn85042437/1866-04-18/ed-1/seq-1/. At the same time, Nevada's Senator William Stewart proposed a plan that required the enjoyment of the suffrage without regard to "race, color, or previous condition of servitude." See Cong. Globe 39th Cong. 1754, 1906 (Apr. 4, and Apr. 12). The Committee invited Stewart to present his proposal in person. Benjamin B. Kendrick, The Journal of the Joint Committee of Fifteen on Reconstruction 82 (1914) (hereinafter "Journal").

20 *See, e.g., Stand From Under!*, Evening Star, Apr. 26, 1866, at 2, https://chroniclingamerica.loc.gov/lccn/sn83045462/1866-04-26/ed-1/seq-2/ (reporting that in a meeting featuring "considerable heat" between Thaddeus Stevens's and Massachusetts's George Boutwell, the latter insisted that "two or three New England States were all that could be counted to sustain enforced Negro suffrage"); The Daily Mountaineer, Apr. 26, 1866, at 3, https://chroniclingamerica.loc.gov/lccn/sn89055266/1866-04-26/ed-1/seq-3/ (reporting opposition within the Indiana Republican caucus).

21 See Cong. Globe 39th Cong. 1754, 1906 (Apr. 4, and Apr. 12) (Senator Stewart's plan).

22 Chief Justice Salmon Chase, who contemporaneously was in conversation with Committee members, promoted a measure that would include antecedents to the eventual Sections 2 and 4, and said that a civil rights measure would be unnecessary "freight" on the Amendment and would "carry an admission that the Civil Rights Act lately passed by 2/3ds is unconstitutional." *See* Letter to Stephen Field, Apr. 30, 1866, and Letter to Wendell Phillips, May 1, 1866 *in* 5 Salmon P. Chase Papers 88, 89 & 90, 91 (John Niven ed. 1998). *See also The Question of Questions*, Daily Ohio Statesman, June 28, 1866, at 1, https://chroniclingamerica.loc.gov/lccn/sn84028645/1866-06-28/ed-1/seq-1/ (reprinting editorial from the *New York Evening Post* rejecting Section 1, for its proposal would represent a congressional admission that Congress had adopted an unconstitutional act, insisting that the Act was "in accord with the Constitution").

23 *The Reconstruction Committee's Final Session*, Chicago Tribune, May 1, 1866, at 1, https://chroniclingamerica.loc.gov/lccn/sn82014064/1866-05-01/ed-1/seq-1/.

24 Journal, *supra* note 19, at 83, 85–6 (Apr. 21); *id.* at 99–100 (Apr. 25) (narrowly approving the Owen plan for transmittal to Congress, then voting to reconsider the same).

25 New-York Tribune, Apr. 28, 1866, at 1, https://chroniclingamerica.loc.gov/lccn/sn83030214/1866-04-28/ed-1/seq-1.

26 Journal *supra* note 19, at 83–4 (Apr. 21) (noting Stevens's presentation of the plan); *id.* at 296 (noting Owen's authorship).

27 The New York Plan had four sections that corresponded roughly with the eventual sections 2–5. "Section I. Representatives shall be apportioned among

the several States which may be included within the Union, according to their respective numbers, which shall be determined by counting the whole number of persons, excluding Indiana net taxed; provided, that whenever male citizens of the United States not less than twenty-one years of age shall be excluded from the elective franchise in any State, except for participation in rebellion, the basis of representation therein shall be reduced in the proportion which the number thus included bears to the whole number of male citizens not less than twenty-one years of age, in such States." "Sec. 2. Until the ____ day of____ A.D. 187_ , all persons who voluntarily adhere to the late insurrection, giving it aid and comfort, shall be excluded from the right to vote for Representatives in Congress and for electors for President and Vice President of the United States." "Sec. 3. Debts or obligations already incurred or which may hereafter be incurred in aid of insurrection, or of war against the United States, and claims for compensation for loss of involuntary service or labor, shall not be paid by any State nor by the United States." "Sec. 4. Congress shall have power to enforce by appropriate legislation the provisions of this article." New-York Tribune, Apr. 28, 1866, at 1, https://chroniclingamerica.loc.gov/lccn/sn83030214/1866-04-28/ed-1/seq-1.

28 Report, *supra* note 18, at 15.

29 *Reconstruction Committee*, Chicago Tribune, Apr. 30, 1866, at 2, https://chroniclingamerica.loc.gov/lccn/sn82014064/1866-04-30/ed-1/seq-2/.

30 William Salter, The Life of James W. Grimes 292 (1876).

31 Journal, *supra* note 19, at 101–2.

32 Gabriel J. Chin, *Reconstruction, Felon Disenfranchisement, and the Right to Vote: Did the Fifteenth Amendment Repeal Section 2 of the Fourteenth Amendment?*, 92 Geo. L.J. 259, 266 (2004).

33 As Earl Maltz has noted, Bingham's broader language would also deflect the charge that Republicans were obsessed with the rights of freedmen to the neglect of other Americans. Earl M. Maltz, *Moving beyond Race: The Joint Committee on Reconstruction and the Drafting of the Fourteenth Amendment*, 42 Hastings Const. L.Q. 287, 315 (2015).

34 *Oregon v. Mitchell*, 400 U.S. 112, 263 (1970) (Brennan, J., dissenting).

35 Robert Dale Owen, *Political Results from the Varioloid*, 35 Atlantic Monthly 664, 666 (June 1875) (emphasis added). *See also Letter from Robert Dale Owen*, New-York Tribune, May 19, 1866, at 7, https://chroniclingamerica.loc.gov/lccn/sn83030214/1866-05-19/ed-1/seq-7/ (commenting on the draft approved by Congress, that he was "content to see civil rights asserted," so that the freedman is "not to exist among us as an outlaw, debarred from owning land, excluded from the witness-box, or from the courts of law, or from the rights of the testator, or subjected to punishments from which other races are exempt").

36 Report, *supra* note 18, at xxi.

37 Cong. globe, 39th Cong., 1st Sess. 2462 (1866).

38 H. 7th Sess., at 64, 68 (Kan. 1867) (Message of Kansas Governor, Samuel J. Crawford, to Kansas Legislature), https://babel.hathitrust.org/cgi/pt?id=nyp.33433004422956&seq=70.

39 *Congress vs. The President—The* Issue. The Daily Evening Telegraph, Sept. 24, 1866, at 6 (reprinting editorial from Frank Leslie's Illustrated Weekly), https://www.loc.gov/resource/sn83025925/1866-09-24/ed-1/?sp=6&st=image&r=0.327,0.607,0.291,0.21,0.

40 *The Congressional Plan of Reorganization.*, Belmont Chronicle, May 10, 1866, at 2 (reprinting editorial from Harper's Weekly), https://chroniclingamerica.loc.gov/lccn/sn85026241/1866-05-10/ed-1/seq-2/.

41 *Restoration: The Policy of the Union Party to Restore the National Union!*, Sunbury American, Sept. 29, 1866, at 2, https://chroniclingamerica.loc.gov/lccn/sn84026403/1866-09-29/ed-1/seq-2/.

42 *The Union in Indiana: Large Meeting at New Albany: Another Great Speech by Gov. Morton*, The Evansville Journal, July 21, 1866, at 2, https://newspapers.library.in.gov/?a=d&d=EJ18660721.1.2&e=-------en-20--1--txt-txIN-------.

43 *Grand Union Rally at Wheatland*, The Evansville Journal, Aug. 13, 1866, at 1, https://newspapers.library.in.gov/?a=d&d=EJ18660813.1.1&e=-------en-20--1--txt-txIN-------

44 *The Constitutional Amendment Calmly Reviewed in the Light of Free Discussion*, The Weekly North-Carolina Standard, Oct. 10, 1866, at 1, https://chroniclingamerica.loc.gov/lccn/sn85042148/1866-10-10/ed-1/seq-1/.

45 2 The Reconstruction Amendments: The Essential Documents 334 (Kurt T. Lash, ed. 2021) (hereinafter "Reconstruction Amendments").

46 *Id.* at 351.

47 9 Brevier's Legislative Reports of the General Assembly of the State of Indiana 44 (1867) (remarks of Mr. Bennett), https://indianamemory.contentdm.oclc.org/digital/collection/p15078coll21/id/78851.

48 1 Journal of the Senate of the Twenty-Fifth General Assembly of the State of Illinois 40 (1867).

49 Journal of the Senate of the Commonwealth of Virginia 29 (1866) (emphasis added).

50 Cong. globe, 39th Cong., 1st Sess. 2765 (1866).

51 *See, e.g.*, Nelson, *supra* note 13, at 123–4 (1998); Mark Kozlowski, The Myth of the Imperial Judiciary: Why the Right is Wrong about the Courts, at 38 (2003); *Littlejohn v. Sch. Bd. of Leon Cnty.*, 132 F.4th 1232, 1262 (11th Cir. 2025) (Rosenbaum, J., concurring).

52 On the absence of this remark in Howard's notes and the newspaper reports, *see* Andrew T. Hyman, *The Substantive Role of Congress Under the Equal Protection Clause*, 42 Southern Univ. L. Rev. 79, 105 n. 73 (2014).

53 The Federalist No. 37, at 224 (James Madison) (Clinton Rossiter ed., 2003) (emphasis added).

54 Aristotle, Nicomachean Ethics 41 (Robert C. Bartlett & Susan D. Collins, trans. 2011); Christopher R. Green, *Incorporation, Total Incorporation, and Nothing But Incorporation?*, 24 Wm. & Mary Bill Rts. J. 93, 125 (2015).

55 Cong. globe, 39th Cong., 1st Sess. 2895 (1866) (emphasis added).

56 *Id.* at 2765. Only in the 1870s does there appear substantial evidence of Republican uncertainty. *See* R. Christopher, Green, Equal Citizenship, Civil Rights, and the Constitution: The Original Sense of the Privileges or Immunities Clause 124 (2015).

57 Cong. globe, 39th Cong., 1st Sess. 2467 (1866).

58 *Id.* at 3039, 3041.

59 Journal of the Senate of the General Assembly of the State of North Carolina, 1866–1867 Sess., at 96 (Dec. 6, 1866).

60 Journal of the House of Representatives of the State of Texas, 11th Sess., at 578 (October 13, 1867), reprinted in Reconstruction Amendments, *supra* note 45, at

282; *see also* James E. Bond, No Easy Walk to Freedom: Reconstruction and the Ratification of the Fourteenth Amendment 216 (1997).

61 Senate Journal of the Called Session of the General Assembly of the State of Tennessee, 1866 Sess., at 41 (1866); *see also* Bond, *supra* note 60, at 22.

62 Journal of the House of Representatives of the State of New Hampshire, 1866 Sess., at 71 (1866).

63 *Joint Resolutions Withdrawing the Consent of New Jersey to the Proposed Amendment to the Constitution of the U.S., Entitled Article Fourteen, in* Documents of the Ninety-Second Legislature of the State of New Jersey 953 (1868).

64 Journal, *supra* note 19, at 22; Joint Committee on Reconstruction, Views of the Minority, 39th Cong., 1st sess., H. Rep. 30, pt. 2, at 1–12 (June 20, 1866).

65 Reverdy Johnson, A Further Consideration of the Dangerous Condition of the Country: The Causes Which Have Led to It, and the Duty of the People 14–15 (Baltimore: Sun Job Printing, 1867).

66 Cong. globe, 39th Cong., 1st Sess. 3031 (1866) (remark of Senator John Henderson that the Citizenship Clause will serve to make "plain only what has been rendered doubtful by the past action of the Government," but that the rest of Section 1 will "merely secure the rights that attach to citizenship in all free Governments").

67 Reconstruction Amendments, *supra* note 45, at 260.

68 *Id.* at 246; *see also* Horace Flack, The Adoption of the Fourteenth Amendment 163–4 (1908).

69 Journal of the House of Representatives of the State of New Hampshire, June 1866, at 71.

70 Reconstruction Amendments, *supra* note 45, at 282.

71 *Id.* at 311; *see also Speech of Geo. H. Pendleton, Esq., in Court Street Market Space, Wednesday Evening, September 19, in* Speeches of the Campaign of 1866 in the States of Ohio, Indiana and Kentucky 24 (1866) (hereinafter "Speeches of the Campaign") ("What are the rights of a citizen of the United States? They are those rights, and all of them, which Congress says shall belong to the citizens of the United States.").

72 Cong. globe, 39th Cong., 1st Sess. 1291 (1866) ("The term 'citizen' has had a definite meaning among publicists ever since the days of Aristotle. He interpreted and rendered that term to signify a person who was a partner in the government of the country."); Aristotle's Politics 64 (Carnes Lord trans., Univ. of Chicago Press 2d ed. 2013).

73 *See, e.g., Speech of Hon. Frank H. Hurd, in the Ohio Senate, on Thursday, January 3rd, 1867*, Daily Ohio Statesman, Jan. 5, 1867, at 1 (quoting *Corfield*'s dictum that to the list of privileges and immunities of citizens "may be added the elective franchise").

74 See chapter 2, *infra*.

75 *The Union in Indiana: Large Meeting at New Albany*, The Evansville Journal, July 21, 1866, at 2, https://www.loc.gov/resource/sn82014296/1866-07-21/ed-1/?sp=2&st=image&r=0.04,1.046,0.209,0.179,0.

76 *Id.*; Cong. globe, 39th Cong., 1st Sess. 2765 (1866).

77 Johnson, *supra* note 65, at 15.

78 *Governor Baker's Speech*, The Evansville Journal, Aug. 13, 1866, at 1, https://chroniclingamerica.loc.gov/lccn/sn82014296/1866-08-13/ed-1/seq-1/.

79 David R. Upham, *Interracial Marriage and the Original Understanding of the Privileges or Immunities Clause*, 42 Hastings Const. L. Q. 213 (2015).

80 *Id.* at 242–57.

81 Cong. globe, 39th Cong., 1st Sess. 2398 (1866) (remarks by Maryland Representative Charles Phelps ("I presume it will not be denied that under this amendment, if adopted, it would be for Congress to define and determine by law in what the 'privileges and immunities' of citizens of the United States consist, in like manner as Congress has already, under the constitutional amendment abolishing slavery and conferring the power to enforce its abolition by appropriate legislation, determined that the emancipated blacks are 'citizens of the United States,' and defined in what their civil rights as such citizens consist.").

82 So, for instance, it is the "people of the United States" who "ordain and establish" the Constitution for the same United States, and that Constitution reserves membership in the House and Senate to persons who had been citizens of the United States for several years before the Constitution's adoption—seven and nine years, respectively. U.S. Const. pmbl; *id.* art. I, § 2, cl. 1 & § 3, cl. 1. As Missouri Senator John Henderson explained, "[t]hese clauses show that such a thing as U.S. citizenship existed at and prior to the time when the Constitution was adopted." Cong. globe, 39th Cong., 1st Sess. 3032 (1866).

83 Report, *supra* note 18, at xxi (emphasis added).

84 Wm. H. Williams, *The Arrest of Non-Residents for Debt—Constitutionality of the Law*, 2 Western L.J. 265, at 266 (1844).

85 *Id.* at 267.

86 *Id.* at 266 (emphasis added). Reed, unfortunately for our study, did not enumerate those privileges. Still, he did explain that the "right of suffrage" was "not necessarily a right of citizenship, even though it is a right which none but the citizen can enjoy," for the "general custom of other nations" is to reserve the suffrage to only some citizens, and according to the letter of our national Constitution, "the individual States are expressly charged with the office of determining who shall be electors, even for officers of the general government." *Id.* Other antebellum authorities used some version of the phrase "privileges and immunities of citizens of the United States" to similarly interpret Article IV. *See Murray v. M'Carty*, 16 Va. (2 Munf.) 393, 398 (1811) ("But, although the constitution of the *United States* has wisely given to a citizen of each state the privileges of a citizen of any other state, yet it clearly recognises the distinction between the character of a citizen of the *United States*, and of a citizen of any *individual state*; and also of citizens of *different states*; and, although a citizen of one state may hold lands in another, yet he cannot interfere in those rights, which, from the very nature of society and of government, belong exclusively to citizens of that state. Such are the rights of election and of representation; for they cannot be imparted to any but citizens, without a subversion of the principles of the social compact." (emphasis in original)); *Douglass v. Stephens*, 1 Del. Ch. 465, 477 (1821) ("But, even supposing the design of this clause of the Constitution to have been to restrict the powers of legislation by the State Legislatures, it cannot be extended so far as that no peculiar advantage can be given by any State to its own citizens, but such as must be extended to all citizens in every State in the Union; because, the privileges secured are not such as are given to citizens in one or more States by the State laws, but must be such as the citizens in the several States, that is, in all the States, are entitled to. The great object to be attained was to prevent a citizen in one State from being considered an alien

in another State—to secure the right to acquire and hold real property. . . . The privileges and immunities, &c., are not enumerated or described; but they are all privileges common in the Union—which certainly excludes those privileges which belong only to citizens of one or more States, and not to those in every other State. It is more easy to ascertain whether the municipal law of this State giving a preference to State creditors is a law incompatible with the privileges secured by the second section of the fourth Article of the Constitution of the United States, than it is to define all the privileges and immunities which the section was intended to secure to the people of the United States; and this will be sufficient for the purpose of deciding the present case."); *Campbell v. Morris*, 3 H. & McH. 535, 565 (Md. 1797) (argument of Schaff for plaintiff in error) ("The object of the convention in introducing this clause into the constitution, was to invest the citizens of the different states with the general rights of citizenship . . . and not to put all the citizens of the *United States* upon a level; consequently, the injury, as to the effect of a law of any state, will not be whether it makes a discrimination between citizens of the several states; but whether it infringes upon any civil right, which a man as a member of civil society must enjoy." (emphasis added)); N.Y. Court of Appeals, *Report of the Lemmon Slave Case* 44 (1860) (argument of O'Conor) ("This means of course, the privileges of citizens of the United States. It does not mean the privileges of citizens of the particular State in which they are wayfarers, or of the State in which they are domiciled, but the general privileges of a citizen of the United States.").

87 Cong. globe, 39th Cong., 1st Sess. 2895 (1866).

88 *Id.* at 2939 (1866); *accord id.* at 2538 (1866) (remarks of Representative Andrew Rogers "that the American people believe that this Government was made for white men and white women").

89 *Message of Governor Oliver Morton to the Senate and House of Representatives of the State of Indiana*, Journal of the Senate of the State of Indiana, 45th Sess., Jan. 4, 1867, at 1.

90 Cong. Globe, 39th Cong., 1st Sess. 2890 (May 30, 1866); *id.* at 3032 (June 8, 1866) (reporting Senator Henderson's extensive argument that *ius soli* citizenship is already the law of the land).

91 *Declaration of Principles, reprinted in* Augustine Maverick, Henry J. Raymond and the New York Press, For Thirty Years: Progress of American Journalism From 1840 to 1870, at 459–60 (1870).

92 Andrew Johnson, *The Annual Message, December 4, 1865, in* Edward McPherson, The Political History of the United States During the Period of Reconstruction (From April 15, 1865 to July 15, 1870), at 66 (1871).

93 Edward Mayes, Lucius Q.C. Lamar: His Life, Times, and Speeches, 1825–1893, at 159 (1896) (quoting Governor Humphrey's message, to the special session of the Mississippi legislature, that justice demands "full *protection* in his person and property, real and personal" (emphasis added)); *Message of Governor to the General Assembly of North Carolina, in* Journal of the House of Commons at its Special Session of 1866, Jan. 19, 1866, 20 (claiming that already under North Carolina law, "the courts of justice were open to [free blacks'] complaints, with all the modes of relief to property or persons that were allowable to white men"); *Inaugural Address of Gov. J.W. Throckmorton, Delivered in the Representative Hall, Austin, August 9th, 1866*, Dallas Herald, Aug. 18, 1866 at 1, https://chroniclingamerica.loc.gov/lccn/

sn84022278/1866-08-18/ed-1/seq-1/ (advocating the adoption of further laws to "secure the freed people the full *protection* of all the rights of person and property guaranteed them by our Amended Constitution") (emphasis added)).

94 Andrew Johnson, *Veto of the Second Freedmen's Bureau Bill, July 16, 1866, in* McPherson, *supra* note 92, at 147.

95 *Letter from Secretary of the Interior O. H. Browning to W. H. Benneson and H.V. Sullivan, Oct. 13, 1866, in* Reconstruction Amendments, *supra* note 45, at 289–91. For a discussion of the publication and response to Browning's letter, see Kurt T. Lash, The Fourteenth Amendment and the Privileges and Immunities of American Citizenship 211–12 (2014).

96 Journal of the Senate of the General Assembly of the State of North Carolina, 1866–1867 sess., at 96 (Dec. 6, 1867). Mississippi's Joint Standing Committee on Federal Relations likewise decried the Amendment for transferring to the federal courts "a supervisory and appellate control" over the state courts in "questions arising on local law, on the predicate that the State courts will not deal between the parties with fairness or impartiality." Reconstruction Amendments, *supra* note 45, at 359.

97 *Id.* at 375. The Legislative Record: Containing the Debates and Proceedings of the Pennsylvania Legislature, for the Session of 1867, app. at xcvii (George Bergnor, ed. 1867). *Id.* at 375.

98 *Message from the Governor to the Senate and House of Representatives*, Journal of the Session of 1866–1867 of the House of Representatives of the State of Alabama, 33 (Nov. 12, 1866) ("A careful examination would show that the words, 'nor shall any State deprive any person,' which are contained in the first section, are of vast, if not dangerous import. It would enlarge the judicial powers of the General Government to such gigantic dimensions as would not only overshadow and weaken the authority and influence of the State courts, but might possibly reduce them to a complete nullity. It would give to the U.S. courts complete and unlimited jurisdiction over every conceivable case, however important, or however trivial, which could arise under the State laws. Every individual dissatisfied with the decision of a State court, might apply to a Federal tribunal for redress. It matters not what might be the character of his case. It might be civil. Or criminal. It might be a simple action of debt, or a suit in trover. It might be an indictment for assault and battery, for larceny, for burglary, for arson, or for murder. It would be all the same. Upon a simple complaint that his rights, either of person or property had been infringed, it would be the bounden duty of the tribunal to which he made his application, to hear and determine his case.").

99 State of Wisconsin: Journal of the Senate, Nineteenth Annual Session 99 (Jan. 22, 1867) (fearing that Congress will be able to "provide for a review of all matters and proceedings, in order to see if the state is depriving 'any person of life, liberty or property, without due process of law.'").

100 For one exception, see the unattributed allegation briefly mentioned and refuted by a supporter in Ohio. *Speech of General M.F. Force at Chillicothe, Sept. 22, in* Speeches of the Campaign, *supra* note 71, at 34, 34 (1866) ("An objection has been made that the phrase, 'due process of law,' is so vague that it might give the Federal Courts occasion to interfere too much in our affairs. As for this, in the first place, I don't know that the Federal Judges are any worse lawyers of any worse men than our State Judges; and, in the second place, this phrase is no new phrase. It is in the Constitution of the United States already.").

101 *Letter from Secretary of the Interior O. H. Browning to W. H. Benneson and H.V. Sullivan, Oct. 13, 1866, in* Reconstruction Amendments, *supra* note 45, at 289–91.
102 *Speech of Hon. S.S. Bloom*, Daily Ohio Statesman Jan. 24, 1867, at 1, https://chroniclingamerica.loc.gov/lccn/sn84028645/1867-01-24/ed-1/seq-1/.
103 *Id.*
104 *Browning's Letter*, Chicago Tribune, Oct. 27, 1866, at 2, https://chroniclingamerica.loc.gov/lccn/sn82014064/1866-10-27/ed-1/seq-2/.
105 Maryland General Assembly, Report of the Joint Committee on Federal Relations, Mar. 19, 1867, at 14 (1867). *See also* speech of Kentucky Representative Aaron Harding, in Cong. Globe, 39th Cong., 1st Sess. 3147 (June 13, 1866) ("[The Amendment] transfers all powers from the State governments over the citizens of a State to Congress").
106 *Message of the Governor to the Honorable, the General Assembly of North Carolina*," Journal of the Senate of the General Assembly of the State of North Carolina, 1866–1867 sess., at 28–9 (Nov. 20, 1866).
107 *See infra* chapter 3.
108 Cong. globe, 39th Cong., 1st Sess. 2768 (May 23) ("good faith"); *Governor's Message, in* Message and Annual Reports, for 1866, Made to the Fifty-Seventh General Assembly, of the State of Ohio, 2d sess., Jan. 2, 1867, part 1, at 282 (1867) (explaining that if the rights set forth in Section 1 "are in good faith protected by State laws and State authorities, there will be no need of federal legislation on the subject, and the power will remain in abeyance; but if they are systematically violated, those who violate them will be themselves responsible for all the necessary interference of the central government").
109 *The Campaign in Wisconsin: Speech of Senator T.O. Howe, at Madison, Wisconsin, Aug. 10,* Chicago Tribune, Aug. 14, 1866, at 2, https://chroniclingamerica.loc.gov/lccn/sn82014064/1866-08-14/ed-1/seq-2/.
110 *Id.* (emphasis added).
111 *Logic of the Secretary of the Interior*, The Evening Telegraph, Nov. 3, 1866, at 7, https://chroniclingamerica.loc.gov/lccn/sn83025925/1866-11-03/ed-1/seq-7/ (reprinting editorial from *The Independent*).
112 The Federalist No. 17, at 114 (Alexander Hamilton) (Clinton Rossiter ed., 2003) (noting that under the proposed Constitution, federal regulation of "private justice between the citizens of the same State" would be usurpation).
113 Report, *supra* note 18, at xvii.
114 *Secretary Browning and the Constitutional Amendment*, New-York Tribune, Oct. 25, 1866, at 4, https://chroniclingamerica.loc.gov/lccn/sn83030214/1866-10-25/ed-1/seq-4/. Similarly, Indiana's Governor Oliver Morton argued that Southern states had made the Due Process and Equal Protection Clauses necessary "by withholding the protection of the laws for life and liberty, and denying to [visiting citizens] the ordinary remedies in the courts for the vindication of their civil rights." *The Union in Indiana: Large Meeting at New Albany: Another Great Speech by Gov. Morton*," The Evansville Journal, July 21, 1866, at 1, https://chroniclingamerica.loc.gov/lccn/sn82014296/1866-07-21/ed-1/seq-1/.
115 *Speech of Ex-Governor Parsons, of Alabama*, The Charleston Daily News, Jan. 31, 1867, at 4, https://chroniclingamerica.loc.gov/lccn/sn84026994/1867-01-31/ed-2/seq-4/.

116 *The Campaign in Wisconsin: Speech of Senator T.O. Howe, at Madison, Wisconsin, Aug. 10,* Chicago Tribune, Aug. 14, 1866, at 2, https://chroniclingamerica.loc.gov/lccn/sn82014064/1866-08-14/ed-1/seq-2/ (emphasis in original).

117 *Id.*

118 *John A. Bingham*, Chicago Tribune, Dec. 12, 1868, at 2, https://chroniclingamerica.loc.gov/lccn/sn82014064/1868-12-12/ed-1/seq-2/ (emphasis added).

119 Journal of the Senate of the State of West Virginia, 5th Sess., at 19 (Jan. 15, 1867).

2

The Official Consensus

The conclusion of your committee therefore is, that . . . adequate security for future peace and safety . . . can only be found in such changes of the organic law as shall determine the civil rights and privileges of all citizens in all parts of the republic . . . together with an express grant of power in Congress to enforce those provisions.

—Report of the Joint Committee on Reconstruction (June 8, 1866)[1]

If the Fourteenth Amendment had some original coherent meaning, as supporters then asserted or assumed, where can this consensus be found? The text, by its own terms, has not yielded a generally accepted answer.

As to the contemporaneous discussion of the text, we have an abundant record, but it seems difficult to assess the relative value of the many different statements. It's hard to know even where to begin. As Christopher Wolfe has asked, "How can one tell whether a given speaker (in Congress or state legislatures or wherever) really spoke for a majority understanding of the amendment?"[2]

In this chapter, I will argue that, in recovering the Amendment's original coherent meaning, we have compelling reason to prioritize the original *official* understanding—that is, the understanding manifested by congressional and state officials pursuant to their authority to adopt the Amendment. And in seeking that understanding, we should give evidentiary priority to the explanation set forth by the Joint Committee on Reconstruction in its formal report: Section 1 would "determine the civil rights and privileges of all citizens in all parts of the republic," while Section 5 would provide an "express grant of power in Congress to enforce" this determination.[3] Though much neglected by American jurists of the bench and academy, this explanation represents the most authoritative and most exemplary evidence of the original official understanding.

The Original Official Understanding

In considering this question, we must never forget that it is a constitutional amendment we are expounding. A constitutional amendment is a peculiar sort of communication: it is a law, and more specifically, like a statute (and unlike a custom), a law made by a small and readily identifiable number of authorized persons. By their *authority*, we can readily identify a constitutional amendment's *authors*.

In our Republic, according to our founding principles, earthly political authority, under God, begins with the people of the United States, who have authority to institute, alter, or abolish their governments.[4] This people, in turn, expressly ordained and established not only the several state constitutions but also "this Constitution for the United States" as part of the supreme law of the land.[5] Through "this Constitution," this people reserved to themselves the power to elect (directly or indirectly) the members of the two houses of Congress.[6] And through this Constitution and these elections, the people have authorized and directed this bicameral Congress to propose any constitutional amendment whenever two-thirds of both houses might deem it "necessary."[7]

The people have delegated amendatory authority not only to Congress, but also to various state officials. State executives have transmittal authority pursuant to national custom and congressional directive[8] and recommendatory authority pursuant to their respective state constitutions.[9] State legislatures (or state conventions) have final, ratification authority under Article V of the Constitution.[10] All these congressional and state officials thus have, directly or indirectly from the people, the duty and authority to share in the making of constitutional amendments; thus, these officials' understanding can properly be termed the "original official understanding."

Moreover, as to the Fourteenth Amendment in particular, these congressional and state officials were not only the *authors* but also its primary *audience*. By its express terms, the Amendment placed restrictions on state officials (Section 1) and expressly empowered congressional officials (Section 5).

Therefore, because these officials were both the makers and chief recipients of this legal communication, their understanding must be the primary evidence of the communication's meaning. The communication was not made by, or for, any hypothetical member of the general public, but rather, the actual, official representatives of that public.

If so, we must agree with Lucile Lomen: "the best evidence of the meaning intended to be written into a measure" consists in "the contemporary utterances of the legislators," that is, "the explanations of it made by its framers."[11] It is this evidence, she noted eighty years ago, that the Court had disregarded in its misconstruction of the Privileges or Immunities Clause—such that the provision was "emasculated" and "almost forgotten."[12]

Among these framing officials, Congress had primary authority in the making of the Fourteenth Amendment. Congress initiated the process by drafting and proposing the measure. Moreover, of all these officials, Congress alone can be said to have represented the whole people of the Republic. Hence, if in making the Amendment, Congress provided an explanation, then Congress's explanation is the most authoritative among all other official explanations.

Congress's power to propose amendments seems to include the power to explain them. This authority seems unquestioned as to explanatory "preambles" incorporated into an amendment's ratified text. Where an "operative clause" has an attendant "prefatory clause" that "announces a purpose" (as in the Second Amendment), the judiciary must interpret the operative clause to be "consistent with the announced purpose."[13]

Congress's explanatory authority also seemingly extends to enacted but unratified preambles. In the resolution proposing the federal Bill of Rights, Congress explained that the amendments would provide "declaratory and restrictive clauses" in order to prevent "misconstruction" and "abuse" of the powers granted by the Constitution to the federal government.[14] From the beginning, American courts treated this enacted but unratified explanation as authoritative in interpreting the ratified text of the Bill of Rights.[15]

The Joint Committee's Report as Primary Authority

In proposing the Fourteenth Amendment, Congress did not enact any such explanatory preamble, whether ratified or unratified. But, as we'll see, Congress did delegate broad constitutional-design authority to a special committee: the Joint Committee on Reconstruction. And under this delegated authority, the Committee adopted a formal explanation of the Amendment.

Congress Delegates Authority to the Joint Committee.

The Committee received authority in this way.

When the Thirty-Ninth Congress met, on December 4, 1865, Republican majorities in the House and Senate refused to seat any putative representatives from the eleven insurrectionary states. Republicans believed that despite the defeat of secession and slavery, other evils in those states required redress before those states' representatives could be safely readmitted. These evils were chiefly the following:

> First, the states' failure to protect, against lawless violence, certain classes of persons—chiefly freedmen, northerners, and unionists;
>
> Second, the states' unjust "black codes," whereby American citizens were subject to racially discriminatory regulations as to such rights as travel, residence, commerce, property, speech, and arms-bearing; and
>
> Third, the grossly unjust and dangerous redistribution of political power, whereby the majority of the loyal citizenry in those states—African Americans—were wholly excluded from the suffrage, but the former rebels not only retained the vote but would enjoy augmented political power in the House of Representatives and the Electoral College because emancipation meant that millions of freedmen were now counted as whole persons rather than three-fifths thereof.

To redress these and other evils, Representative Thaddeus Stevens moved, on the first day of the Thirty-Ninth Congress, for the establishment of a "joint committee of fifteen members" on reconstruction to consider the conditions necessary for the admission of representatives from the insurrectionary states.[16] Within a fortnight, the House and Senate came to an agreement, and by concurrent resolution, (1) formed this Joint Committee, (2) directed it to "inquire into the condition of the States which formed the so-called Confederate States of America, and report whether they, or any of them, are entitled to be represented in either house of Congress" and (3) granted the Committee general "leave to report at any time, by bill or otherwise."[17]

From the beginning, constitutional remedies were primary to the Committee's mandate. On the first day of the session, just after the House endorsed the establishment of the Committee, several congressmen, including Stevens, John Bingham, and others, gave formal notice that each would propose a constitutional amendment.[18] On the next day, Stevens submitted a *restrictive* amendment to guarantee to every "citizen" the freedom from all racially discriminatory laws as to both civil and political rights; on the following day, Bingham proposed a *delegatory* amendment to empower Congress to secure to "all *persons* . . . equal protection in their rights of life, liberty, and property."[19] Each of these proposals, one for the *citizen*'s immunity against racial discrimination and one for the *person*'s right of equal protection, was captioned, by the editors of the Congressional Globe, "Equality Before the Law."[20] Soon thereafter, Congress named both of these egalitarian amendment designers to the fifteen-member joint committee, with Stevens named chairman on behalf of the House.[21]

Moreover, Congress subsequently sent to the Committee multiple other constitutional proposals; they were so numerous that by January 30, the House granted members blanket permission to submit proposals directly to the Committee without the need for any referral vote.[22] Of the proposals, two are of great interest here. First, on December 20, a week after the Committee's formation, the Senate sent the Committee a "petition of citizens of the United States" that the Constitution be "so amended that no State shall make any distinction in *civil rights or privileges* on account of race, color, or parentage among any of the *citizens of the United States*."[23] Like Stevens's proposal, this would have secured to American citizens, as such, an immunity against racial discrimination. The Committee later received several other versions of this popular petition.[24]

Second, on February 1, the whole Senate, by resolution, instructed the Committee to consider "amending the Constitution of the United States so as to declare with greater certainty the power of Congress to *enforce and determine*, by appropriate legislation, all the guarantees contained in that instrument," including "[t]hat which assures the citizens of each State all *privileges and immunities of citizens* in the several States."[25] Incidentally, on the very same day, Ohio Representative James Garfield told his colleagues in the House that such a clarificatory amendment should extend to enforcing the Due Process Clause as well as the Privileges and Immunities Clause.[26]

Scholars have not frequently highlighted the Senate's resolution. Yet as legal historian Herman Vandenburg Ames explained over a century ago, and Kurt Lash has noted more recently, this resolution, endorsed by the whole Senate, is critical evidence as to the method of the Amendment: To redress the evils of 1865, not by the invention of new constitutional norms, but by fuller enforcement of the existing Constitution.[27]

Meanwhile, consistent with its mandate, the Committee devoted its initial deliberations chiefly to various proposed constitutional amendments.[28] At the Committee's first substantive meeting (January 9), the chairman, Senator William Fessenden, announced that two matters required remedy, either by constitutional amendment "or otherwise": that "[1] the basis of representation shall have been modified, and [2] the rights of all persons amply secured."[29] As to constitutional remedies, he identified two possible approaches: by either "new provisions, or the necessary changes of existing provisions."[30]

To signal the importance of this twofold constitutional work, at the next meeting (January 12), the Committee entrusted it to a five-member subcommittee consisting of the two senior members from each house (Fessenden and Stevens), and three chosen by Fessenden. Fessenden then appointed Bingham, Representative Roscoe Conkling, and Senator Jacob Howard.[31]

Therefore, there was a general consensus that the Joint Committee had received congressional authority to discuss, frame, and explain constitutional amendments, chiefly, as Fessenden noted, (1) to modify representation (to redress the maldistribution of political power) and (2) to amply secure the equal rights of citizens and other persons, by additions to the Constitution that were either wholly new or enhancements to "existing provisions."

The Joint Committee's Initial Proposals

Accordingly, over the next few weeks, the Committee, after extensive deliberations, sent Congress two initial constitutional proposals, corresponding to these two goals.

The first of these, a modification of the rule of representation, was approved unanimously by the Republicans on the Committee on January 20,[32] and, submitted to Congress two days later. The proposal was a representation-reduction amendment—an antecedent to the eventual Section 2.[33] Under this early draft of the no-fifths rule, the emancipated, but disenfranchised freedmen would not be counted, and thus would not augment the political power of southern whites. The proposal passed the House but failed in the Senate.[34]

As to the rights of persons, after reviewing a proposal from the subcommittee of five, the Committee decided to recommit the question to a new "subcommittee on the powers of Congress," to be chaired by Bingham, who was joined by Massachusetts Republican George Boutwell and New Jersey Democrat Andrew Rogers.[35] The next day, Bingham alerted the full House that the Committee was considering measures to empower Congress to enforce the existing guarantees of the Constitution, including the Due Process Clause.[36]

Two days later, on January 27, Bingham returned to the Committee with the subcommittee's draft to empower Congress to secure (1) to "all persons" in the states "full protection in the enjoyment of life, liberty and property"; and (2) to all "citizens of the United States . . . the same immunities"; and also (3) to such citizens "equal political rights and privileges."[37] The three elements of this delegatory proposal seemed tailored to the three major inequalities of the unreconstructed South that we mentioned: (1) by "protection," to mitigate lawless violence against freedmen, unionists, and northerners; (2) by "same immunities," to relieve American citizens of racially discriminatory *munia*, or legal burdens; and (3) by "equal political rights and privileges," to further redress (beyond the representation-reduction measure the Committee had already approved) the unjust distribution of political power arising from racially discriminatory voting laws. Moreover, the first and second of these delegations could be correlated with two existing constitutional provisions: the Due Process Clause ("life, liberty, and property") and the Privileges and Immunities Clause ("same immunities" of "citizens," but modified by "of the United States").

The Committee stalemated on this second proposal.[38] A week later, on February 3 (two days after the Senate sent the Committee its Constitution-enforcing proposal), Bingham submitted a revision to the draft that made the connection between the proposal and these two existing constitutional provisions more emphatic and unambiguous. He (1) included express cross references, (2) reversed the order to conform with the sequence of their appearance in the Constitution (Article IV, then the Fifth Amendment), (3) mentioned the "privileges" as well as the "immunities" of "citizens," and (4) replaced the qualifier "of the United States" with "in the several states":

> The Congress shall have power to make all laws which shall be necessary and proper to secure to the citizens of each state all privileges and immunities of citizens in the several states (Art. 4, Sec. 2); and to all persons in the several States equal protection in the rights of life, liberty and property (5th Amendment).[39]

In making this proposal, then, Bingham proposed, as to the alternatives mentioned by Fessenden, plainly not to make wholly "new provisions," but to modify, by enlargement, certain "existing provisions." The decision was in accord with his own opinions and those of his fellow Buckeye, James Garfield,[40] and more importantly, in compliance with the Senate's recent resolution.[41]

This approach was neither novel nor peculiar to Bingham. Before the Civil War, the whole Republican Party had sought to redress southern evils by enforcement or enhancement of these same two constitutional provisions. Both the Due Process and Privileges and Immunities Clauses had figured prominently in the Republican Party's 1860 platform, which denounced territorial slavery as antithetical to the right to liberty secured by the Due Process Clause, and state repression of antislavery opinion as violative of the Privileges and Immunities Clause.[42] Further, in February 1861, delegates at the Washington Peace Conference had endorsed congressional enforcement of the latter clause. The Conference discussed and approved a Union-saving Thirteenth Amendment that would have, *inter alia*, required Congress to "secur[e] to the citizens of each State the privileges and immunities of citizens in the several States."[43] Four members of that Conference were among the fifteen later on the Joint Committee (Fessenden, Iowa's James Grimes, Massachusetts's George Boutwell, and Maryland's

Reverdy Johnson). A few weeks later, in his First Inaugural, Abraham Lincoln likewise called for congressional enforcement of the Privileges and Immunities Clause.[44]

In February 1866, Bingham's proposition, with its parenthetical references,[45] was approved narrowly, over the objections of three Republican members as well as the three Democratic members.[46] But when submitted to Congress on February 13, the references were gone,[47] probably because such overkill was unnecessary.

Like the Committee's first constitutional proposal, this second one also failed, but even more ignominiously. The Senate just laid it on the table and never took it up again.[48] The House debated the measure two weeks later, but decided on February 28 to postpone further consideration.[49]

This delegatory proposal failed mainly due to strong Republican opposition to the breadth of the "equal protection" power. Many contended it would authorize Congress to make all the "laws" protecting life, liberty, and property. Nevada's Senator William Stewart remarked that the proposed equal-protection delegation was so broad that it could "hardly have been intended by its framers."[50] In the House, New York's Robert Hale said that under the proposal, Congress might override "all State legislation, in its codes of civil and criminal jurisprudence and procedure, affecting the individual citizen"—a redistribution of power that would be "an utter departure from every principle ever dreamed of by the men who framed our Constitution."[51] Accordingly, *The Nation* reported that Bingham's proposal failed "chiefly because many members of the legal profession," though "[u]nimpeachable Republicans," believed the "equal protection" delegation would mean "a dangerous centralization of power."[52] In contrast, the "privileges and immunities" delegation seemed less controversial, probably because such proposals were already quite familiar.

The Joint Committee's Final Proposal

Two months later, on April 28, the Committee sent Congress a revised proposal: a unified, five-section amendment. This time, the twelve Republicans were unanimous.[53] To redress the unjust distribution of political power, the second section provided a new version of the representation-reduction proposal, and the third mandated some political disqualification for some former rebels. In addition, the fourth section invalidated any debt or claim arising from aid to the rebellion or from the loss of slave labor.

But what concerns us here are the first and fifth sections, concerning the ample security due to citizens and other persons, and congressional protection of the same. The first section, as redrafted by Bingham, adopted by the Committee, and then transmitted to Congress,[54] initially included only this prohibitory sentence:

> No State shall make or enforce any law which shall abridge the privileges or immunities of citizens of the United States; nor shall any State deprive any person of life, liberty, or property without due process of law; nor deny to any person within its jurisdiction the equal protection of the laws.[55]

The fifth section provided,

> The Congress shall have power to enforce, by appropriate legislation, the provisions of this article.[56]

This last sentence was copied from the Thirteenth Amendment and first proposed in Committee by Stevens.[57]

Bingham and the Committee thus significantly modified the February "Bingham Proposition," or "Bingham Amendment" as some reporters then called it.[58] On the one hand, the Committee strengthened the provision by replacing the delegatory language with direct restrictions on the states. On the other hand, the Committee softened the measure by subordinating Congress's power to the mere enforcement of these restrictions, and, most importantly, by adding the modifier "of the laws" to "equal protection." The new draft seemed to make clear that the states were to retain their primary authority to make, modify, and enforce "the laws" defining this protection, with Congress's power limited to redressing the states' refusal to enforce them.

Despite these important revisions, this new draft of the Bingham Proposition preserved the same method as the February version: to redress the evils of the unreconstructed South by enhancements to certain constitutional rights of citizens and of persons, already recognized and guaranteed in the Privileges and Immunities and Due Process Clauses, respectively.

Accordingly, in early June, Bingham would successfully move to permanently table his February proposal because the Committee's new draft, he said, concerned the same "whole subject matter."[59] Parenthetically, we note that the Supreme Court, along with many scholars, has not noticed that Bingham thus certified the continuity between his February and April drafts.[60]

Meanwhile, from May 8 to 10, the House of Representatives debated and approved, without amendment, the Committee's new draft.[61] The Senate, in turn, began formal discussions on May 23. In his remarks opening the debate, Senator Howard reminded his colleagues of the Committee's broad mandate: "to report by bill or otherwise *at their discretion*."[62] On Friday, June 8, after some major alterations—including the addition of the Citizenship Clause as the first sentence—the Senate finally approved the Amendment.[63] Five days later, on Wednesday, June 13, the House briefly discussed and approved the Amendment as revised by the Senate.[64] Hence, on that date, Congress, with two-thirds of both houses concurring, formally voted to propose the Fourteenth Amendment.

The Joint Committee's Belated Cover Letter

The Committee's Report, chiefly authored by Senator Fessenden, was not finalized until June 6 and was not presented to Congress until June 8, the last day of the Senate's deliberations and only a few days before the House's final vote.[65] Upon submitting the Report to the Senate, Fessenden declined to read or otherwise discuss it, in deference, he said, to his colleagues' desire to bring the Amendment to a speedy vote that day.[66] The Committee's minority drafted its own report, but it would not arrive in Congress until even later—a week after Congress gave its final approval to the Amendment.[67]

The majority Report could, then, be called the Joint Committee's "belated cover letter." The delay resulted from two facts: the chairman's acute illness and the general impatience of Republicans. As Fessenden explained to the Senate, the Committee had always hoped to present the proposed amendment along with an "extended report" setting forth the Committee's "reasons," but his present illness prevented him from drafting it.[68] So rather than wait for the explanatory report, the Committee thought it "advisable, as it was so late in the session, not to withhold the measures proposed for action."[69]

Despite this delay, the Committee retained its original mandate and began its belated cover letter by invoking its original authority "to report by bill or otherwise."[70] And as Fessenden's remarks indicate, that original authority would have allowed him, upon submission to the Senate, to make a discussion on this Report the order of the day.

Congress gave the Report not only prior authorization, but posterior approval. By separate resolutions in June, each chamber ordered special mass printing for distribution among the citizenry. The Senate ordered 50,000 copies,[71] and then the House, 100,000.[72]

To be sure, the reception and mass publication of the Report did not represent a formal adoption; Congress did not, for instance, enact the Report's explanation of the Amendment as a preamble to the enacted text. Further, congressional publication did not imply an endorsement of every word therein. After all, Congress had already signaled its disagreement with the Committee by amending the draft Amendment in various ways.[73] Moreover, the House of Representatives also directed (at Democratic insistence) the mass printing of the minority report; and such publication plainly did not signal endorsement.[74]

Despite these caveats, Congress's reception and mass distribution of the majority's Report did indicate a general approbation. Congress believed that the people at large should be acquainted with not only the proposed Amendment, but also the Committee's explanation of the same. Accordingly, at least one state legislature received the Report as Congress's official explanation of the proposal.[75]

Controlling or Merely Relevant?

But did the Committee's explanation—that Section 1 determined certain civil rights and privileges—establish not only an *official* but also a *controlling* principle of interpretation?

At first glance, the answer is "no," for Congress cannot delegate its bicameral authority to a mere committee. After all, as Justice Scalia once remarked, "[l]egislative history that does not represent the intent of the whole Congress is nonprobative; and legislative history that does represent the intent of the whole Congress is fanciful."[76]

Indeed, congressional committees would seem to be mere tools of their respective chambers, so their unenacted reports would not seem authoritative even on Congress itself. One might conclude, then, as Thurgood Marshall remarked at his 1967 confirmation hearing, that the Joint Committee's Report is "relevant but by no means controlling."[77]

On the other hand, as Justice Scalia conceded elsewhere, committee reports might be "controlling" insofar as they provide "an authoritative expression" of what the whole "Congress intended."[78] What sort of reports might qualify? A "conference report" would seem sufficient insofar as the conference receives bicameral and specific authorization to draft particular legislation.[79] Justice Frankfurter once explained, "[t]he most authoritative report is a Conference Report acted upon by both Houses and therefore unequivocally representing the will of both Houses as the joint legislative body."[80]

The Report of the Joint Committee on Reconstruction resembles an unenacted conference report. Congress established this bicameral committee, in part, for the specific purpose of drafting constitutional remedies to secure equal rights under law, and the Senate directed the Committee to consider the pursuit of that goal through enhancement of existing constitutional norms. Moreover, both houses of Congress not only adopted the Committee's proposed Sections 1 and 5 (with the addition of the introductory Citizenship Clause), but also approved the Committee's explanatory Report by ordering its mass publication and distribution.

So with good cause, John Codman Hurd (a then prominent jurist) would call the Joint Committee's Report, "the most *authoritative* declaration of principles supposed to have been afterwards carried out in political action."[81] Still, the Report was not the most authoritative of any such statement in American constitutional history. Of course, it had less authority (and was thus less controlling) than the congressionally *adopted* though *unratified* explanatory preamble to the first ten amendments, and even less authority than the *adopted* and *ratified* prefatory clause of the Second Amendment.

Conversely, however, the Report has greater authority than any statement made by the Constitutional Convention of 1787. That Convention acted *ultra vires*—in violation of its strictly limited mandate to propose revisions to the Articles. Hence, the proposed new Constitution represented, as Publius noted, a mere "informal and unauthorized" proposition.[82] In contrast, the Committee's proposition, and the explanations thereof, were *formal* and *authorized* by the people's representatives in Congress. The Report, then, should be received as more authoritative to the interpretation of the Fourteenth Amendment than all of Farrand's Records are to the interpretation of the original Constitution.

The Report as Exemplary Evidence

But even if the Committee's official explanation was not authoritative or "controlling," but only "relevant," their belated cover letter remains exceedingly relevant as the most exemplary evidence of the original understanding. After the sheer text of the Amendment, the Committee's explanation is the most important piece of originalist evidence.

The twelve signatories to the Report were manifestly exemplary men. By their election to Congress, they were eminent[83]—chosen by their fellow citizens to "refine and enlarge the public views,"[84] and received the high authority to alter the people's "supreme Law of the Land;" *viz.*, by making federal statutes and treaties, and by proposing constitutional amendments.[85] And by their subsequent election, the members of the Committee were preeminent among the eminent—elected by the elect for a task of vital importance to the whole Republic.

Because, as Akhil Amar has observed, the Committee was thus "all-important,"[86] the selection of these twelve was not casual. As Senator James Blaine recalled, the decision reflected a considered and universal respect among Republican congressmen:

> It is not often that such solicitude is felt in Congress touching the membership of a committee as was now developed in both branches. It was foreseen that in an especial degree the fortunes of the Republican party would be in the keeping of the [twelve] men who might be chosen. The contest, predestined and already manifest, between the President and Congress might, unless conducted with great wisdom, so seriously divide the party as to compass its ruin. Hence the imperious necessity that no rash or ill-considered step should be taken. Both in Congress and among the people the conviction was general that the party was entitled to the services of its best men. There was no struggle among members for positions on the committee and when the names were announced they gave universal satisfaction to the Republicans.[87]

The Committee's Republican members were, by this account, widely deemed "the best men."[88]

Among Committee members, the mutual respect was lavish. Elihu Washburne of Illinois called his colleagues "men of the most eminent ability, and the most unquestioned patriotism," whose Report was "one of the most complete, unanswerable and exhaustive papers ever presented to Congress."[89] A few years later, Jacob Howard hyperbolized, "[n]ever was a committee charged with a higher or more responsible duty than was that joint committee."[90] The encomia were not exclusively partisan. Reverdy Johnson, the leader of the Committee's Democratic minority, averred that despite his strong disagreements with the twelve Republicans, he "never saw the slightest reason to suspect that they designed anything that was not perfectly just and fair."[91]

In turn, each of the twelve "best men" lent his reputation to the explanation set forth in the Report. Ten of them attended the June 6 meeting devoted exclusively to the Report.[92] There, they heard Chairman Fessenden read the report, and all approved it "with one or two suggestions for alteration of phraseology."[93] Their ten signatures appeared on the Report as submitted to Congress.[94] The two absent Republicans were out of town on that day,[95] but each, upon his return, took pains to file a personal motion in the House for leave to add his signature.[96]

The primacy of the Report results not only from its authorship by men of eminent reputations, but also from the Report's enthusiastic reception. One of the signatories, Iowa Senator James Grimes, privately told his wife that the "final report of the committee . . . is regarded by everybody here, I think, as a very able paper; the ablest, in my opinion, submitted to Congress as a report, or in the form of a speech, since I have been in the Senate."[97] Publicly, Republicans' praise was extraordinary.[98] According to the *New York Tribune*, the Report provided "the complete, and, we may say, the official declaration of the principles which the Republican Party is bound to carry [into effect], and in the advocacy of which, we feel confident, the whole party will soon be a unit."[99] Fessenden's biographer aptly noted, "[t]he report has been called one of the greatest state papers in our political history" and proved "entirely satisfactory to the Republican party."[100]

The Report, for many, provided a *conclusive* explanation of the Amendment. The *Tribune*, like many newspapers, printed large excerpts, with special emphasis on the Report's concluding section:

> The conclusion of your committee therefore is, that the so-called Confederate States are not at present entitled to representation in the Congress of the United States; that, before allowing such representation, adequate security for future peace and safety should be required; that this can only be found in such changes of the organic law as [1] shall determine the civil rights and privileges of all citizens in all parts of the Republic, [2] shall place representation on an equitable basis, [3] shall fix a stigma upon treason, and [4] protect the loyal people against future claims for the expenses incurred in support of rebellion and for manumitted slaves, [5] together with an express grant of power in Congress to enforce those provisions. To this end they offer a joint resolution for amending the Constitution of the United States.[101]

After quoting this passage, the *Tribune* remarked,

> The report is very able, and will occupy a conspicuous place in the history of the Republican party. Whatever exceptions may be taken to one or another part, the whole will commend itself to the friends of the Union as a *conclusive* and admirable summary of the measures which the majority of the party regard as indispensable for securing the lasting restoration of the Union, and the triumph of the principles of Justice and Freedom.[102]

The *Cleveland Daily Leader* likewise celebrated the Report as "the *conclusive* document in explanation and defense" of the Amendment.[103]

Contemporary chroniclers agreed. In his history of Reconstruction, Edward McPherson (Clerk of the House during the Thirty-Ninth Congress) reserved a whole chapter to the Committee's majority and minority reports.[104] Likewise, in his 1868 *History of the Thirty-Ninth Congress*, William Barnes devoted a whole chapter to the

Report:[105] "It was drawn up with marked ability, and was destined to have a most important bearing upon public opinion."[106]

Two years after ratification, Senator Howard would venture to say, with specific reference to the Committee's explanation of the Amendment, that it had been "everywhere disseminated, read, [and] understood," and thus "received with approbation and even admiration throughout the northern states, and was accepted by every true loyal heart in the country."[107] He recalled that he had "never heard it criticized in Congress or out of Congress, verbally or in writing, by any person of any party."[108] Among Republicans, he added, the assent had been universal and "without dissent."[109] Further, he noted, the Report's explanation of the Amendment still reflected the "prevailing and next to unanimous sentiment of the Republican party of the United States, North and South."[110]

The Jurists' Neglect

Therefore, just a decade later, Hurd would explain that this document "for good or evil, will probably be regarded as one of the most important in the history of this country."[111] Accordingly, American historians, from Dunning to Du Bois, have featured it prominently in their studies of Reconstruction.[112]

But for well over a century, American jurists, of the bench, bar, and academy, have largely ignored it. As to scholars, my search across several databases,[113] over countless scholarly pages, yielded only a dozen or so references to the Committee's key explanatory phrase, "determine the civil rights and privileges"; and in most cases, the quotation was provided with little or no commentary.[114] Among living scholars, only a few have given the Committee's explanation more than a passing notice.[115]

Judges have been even more indifferent—and indeed, almost uniformly silent. To my knowledge, only three judicial opinions, from any tribunal, have included any mention of the Joint Committee's specific explanation of Section 1—and none of these in a majority opinion: Justice Black's dissent in *Adamson v. California*, Justice Thomas's concurrence in *McDonald v. City of Chicago*, and recently, a concurring opinion by Robert Wilkins, a federal appellate judge.[116] Moreover, for 150 years, across thousands of Fourteenth Amendment cases in various courts, judges have not deemed any part of the Report worthy of any mention at all—except in a dozen or so reported decisions.[117]

Recently, however, the Report has received new attention. In the Supreme Court's affirmative-action cases (*Students for Fair Admission*), the principal dissenters cited the Report prominently.[118] Still, in over two hundred pages, no member of the Court saw fit to mention the Committee's specific exposition of Section 1—that it would "determine the civil rights and privileges" of all Americans.

Jurists have seemed far more interested in other parts of the record. Nexis-Uni searches reveal that fifteen sources refer to Representative George Boutwell's quip, recorded thirty-five years after the fact, that Bingham chose the words "privileges and immunities" because their "euphony and indefiniteness of meaning were a charm to him."[119] Boutwell's stale quip, in turn, has been a "charm" to many, including both Robert Bork and Anthony Kennedy, though for antipodal purposes.[120] And dozens of scholars have quoted Jacob Howard's remark, set forth in his main speech in the congressional debates, that the Amendment "abolishes all class legislation."[121] This comment has further had pride of place in seven reported judicial decisions, including two majority opinions of the Supreme Court.[122] But Howard had hoped that "the world" would memorialize not his individual speech, but the written Report he co-signed with his esteemed colleagues.[123]

Among the most prominent jurists, there have been a few exceptions to this indifference. The first was William Guthrie, a leading member of the Supreme Court bar and arguably the founder of incorporationism. In his landmark *Lectures on the Fourteenth Amendment* (1898), he relied on the Report's determinative explanation and Senator Howard's opening Senate speech to conclude that the evidence was "entirely clear" that the original intention was to incorporate the rights set forth in the first eight amendments.[124] Justices Black and Thomas would likewise quote the Report and for a similar purpose, in their opinions in *Adamson v. California* (1947) and *McDonald v. City of Chicago* (2010), respectively.[125]

Why have the jurists, with so few exceptions, been so indifferent to the Report's explanation of the Amendment? There are, I think, at least three reasons.

First, the Report's brief explanation seems to say very little. Still, as Earl Maltz highlights, the Report remains a "key source" that "weigh[s] heavily in arguments over the intended meaning,"[126] and can indeed help resolve two important questions as to the Amendment's meaning: that it secures (1) only "civil" rights, and (2) to all Americans.[127] As I will elaborate in the next chapter, the Report provides strong, if not decisive, evidence to resolve not just these two matters, but two others—that it secures both a *determinate* set of goods, and a *plurality* of these rights and these privileges.[128]

Second, the Committee said nothing that one cannot find elsewhere in the record. The comment seems boring. It's normal. Many others said that Section 1 would secure various "civil rights."[129] But the Report's normalcy is precisely its value to the jurist. Our interest here is with discovering *norms*, and the original meaning thereof. And as I'll elaborate in the next chapter, the Committee's interpretation of Section 1 is indeed amply corroborated and explicated by other statements made by officials participating in the Amendment's adoption.

But there's a third explanation. The Report strongly indicates an original meaning and purpose that is wholly foreign to our governing jurisprudence. The Committee said that Section 1 would determine certain rights, but American judges have not interpreted the Amendment as determinate, and have had no reason to highlight their own infidelity to the official original purpose.

Still, the Committee's Report provides, by far, the most authoritative and exemplary original explanation of the Fourteenth Amendment. No other recorded comment, whether found in the *Congressional Globe*, state-legislative record, or elsewhere, provides such paramount evidence of the original understanding of Section 1. To recover that original consensus, so neglected by the courts, we scholars must prioritize this original official exposition.

Notes

1 Report of the Joint Committee on Reconstruction, H. R. Rep. No. 30, 39th Cong., 1st Sess., xxi (June 8, 1866) (hereinafter "Report").

2 Christopher Wolfe, The Rise of Modern Judicial Review: From Constitutional Interpretation to Judge-Made Law 124 (rev'd ed. 1994).

3 Report, *supra* note 1, at xxi.

4 *See generally*, The Declaration of Independence, paras. 1–2 (U.S. 1776).

5 U.S. Const. preamble & art. VI.

6 U.S. Const. art. I, §§ 2, 3; amend. XVII.

7 The language of Article V is in the form of obligation not mere permission: "The Congress, whenever two thirds of both houses shall deem it necessary, shall propose amendments to this Constitution." U.S. Const. art V.

8 The first ten amendments had been transmitted to the state legislatures indirectly, via the state executives, pursuant to Congress's resolution requesting President Washington to do the same. *Circular to the Governors of the States, Oct. 2, 1789*, National Archives, https://founders.archives.gov/documents/Washington/05-04-02-0087. After proposing the Fourteenth Amendment, Congress asked the President to do the same on June 18, 1866. S. Journal, 39th Cong., 1st Sess., 542 (1866). But two days earlier, and consistent with his practice in transmitting the Thirteenth Amendment, Secretary of State Seward had already assumed the duty. *See Report of Secretary of State William Seward to President Johnson, June 20, 1866, reprinted in* Cong. Globe, 39th Cong., 1st Sess., 3357 (1866) (reporting that on the same day (June 16) that the Secretary had received from the House an official copy of the proposed amendment, he then transmitted the proposal to the Governors of the several states via a circular letter, "in conformity with the proceeding which was adopted by him in 1865" as to the Thirteenth Amendment).

9 *See, e.g.*, Ohio Const. art. III, § 7 (1851) ("He shall communicate at every session, by message, to the General Assembly, the condition of the state, and recommend such measures as he shall deem expedient."); Pa. Const., art. II, § 11 (1838) ("He shall, from time to time, give to the general assembly information of the state of the commonwealth, and recommend to their consideration such measures as he shall judge expedient.").

10 U.S. Const. art. V.

11 Lucile Lomen, *Privileges and Immunities Under the Fourteenth Amendment*, 18 Wash. L. Rev. & St. B.J. 120, 128 (1943).

12 *Id.* at 128–9, 135. The late Ruth Bader Ginsburg noted the "remarkable staying power" of her article. Larry L. Jordan, *Historical Bar: Four Questions About the First Woman to Clerk at the United States Supreme Court*, 36 AK Bar Rag 4, 4 (2012).

13 *District of Columbia v. Heller*, 554 U.S. 570, 577–8 (2008).

14 *Legal Tender Cases*, 79 U.S. 457, 535 (1871) (quoting the "preamble to the resolution" submitting the amendments for ratification).

15 *Id.*; *Barker v. People*, 3 Cow. 686, 701 (N.Y. 1824) (relying exclusively on Congress's preamble to hold that the Amendments were "not to limit the power of the States, but to limit the power of the Union"); *Renthorp v. Bourg*, 4 Mart. (O.S.) 97, 131 (La. 1816) (relying chiefly on this preamble to hold that the Fifth Amendment's Takings Clause does not bind the states).

16 H. Journal, 39th Cong., 1st Sess., at 10 (Dec. 4, 1865) (approving Thaddeus Stevens's motion for a joint committee of fifteen).

17 S. Journal, 39th Cong., 1st Sess. 34 (Dec. 12, 1865) (approving an amended version of Stevens's resolution); H. Journal, 39th Cong., 1st Sess. 60 (Dec. 13, 1865) (concurring in the Senate version).

18 Bingham was the first to act, and then Stevens—just after the House approved the formation of a Joint Committee. *See* H. Journal, 39th Cong. 1st Sess., 13 (Dec. 4, 1865) (advance notice of constitutional proposals by Bingham, Stevens, and others).

19 *Id.* at 18 (Dec. 5, 1865) (Stevens's proposals submitted); *id.* at 34 (Dec. 6, 1865) (Bingham's proposal submitted); Cong. Globe, 39th Cong., 1st Sess. 10, 14 (Dec. 5 & 6, 1865) (noting Stevens's proposal that "All national and State laws shall be equally applicable to every citizen, and no distinction shall be made on account of race and color," and Bingham's proposal to "empower Congress to secure to all persons in every State equal protection in their rights of life, liberty, and property"). All emphases added.

20 *Id.* at 10, 14 (providing this caption to both these proposals).

21 H. Journal, 39th Cong., 1st Sess. 64 (Dec. 14, 1865).

22 *Id.* at 205 (Jan. 30, 1866).

23 S. Journal, 39th Cong., 1st Sess. 52 (Dec. 20, 1865) (emphasis added).

24 *See, e.g.*, *id.* at 183 (Feb. 23, 1866).

25 S. Journal, 39th Cong., 1st Sess. 126 (Feb. 1, 1866) (emphasis added); *see also* Cong. Globe, 39th Cong., 1st Sess. 566 (Feb. 1, 1865).

26 Cong. Globe, 39th Cong., 1st Sess. app. at 67 (Feb. 1, 1866); *see*, James A. Garfield, Restoration of the Southern States: Speech Delivered in the House of Representatives (Feb. 1, 1866), *in* 1 the Works of James A. Garfield 95, 110–11 (Burke A. Hinsdale ed., 1882) ("If our Constitution does not now afford all the powers necessary to that end, we must ask the people to add them. We must give full force and effect to the provision that 'no person shall be deprived of life, liberty, or property without due process of law.' We must make it as true in fact as it is in law, that 'The citizens of each State shall be entitled to all privileges and immunities of citizens in the several States.' We must make American citizenship the shield that protects every citizen, on every foot of our soil."). On January 25, Pennsylvania's Thomas Williams had already submitted to the House a measure that likewise would have amended the Necessary and Proper Clause, so it would now read, "To make all laws which shall be necessary for carrying into execution all powers vested by the Constitution in the Government of the United States, or in any department or officer thereof, and *enforcing all obligations, provisions, or disabilities imposed thereby on the several States* composing the same." Cong. Globe, 39th Cong., 1st Sess. 422 (Jan. 25, 1866) (emphasis added). This measure was referred on February 5, not to the Joint Committee but to the House Judiciary Committee. H. Journal, 39th Cong., 1st Sess. 230 (Feb. 5, 1866); Cong. Globe, 39th Cong., 1st Sess. 635 (Feb. 5, 1866).

27 Herman Vandenburg Ames, The Proposed Amendments to the Constitution of the United States During the First Century of Its History 220 (1897); Kurt T. Lash, The Fourteenth Amendment and the Privileges and Immunities of American Citizenship 184 (2014).

28 More particularly, the Committee considered antecedents of Sections 1, 2, and 5. *See* Benjamin Burns Kendrick, The Journal of the Joint Committee of Fifteen on Reconstruction 40–54 (New York, Negro Universities Press 1914).

29 *Id.* at 42.
30 *Id.*
31 Kendrick, *supra* note 28, at 46–7.
32 *Id.* at 53.
33 *See* H. Journal, 39th Cong., 1st Sess. 179 (Jan. 22, 1866), S. Journal, 39th Cong., 1st Sess. 96 (Jan. 22, 1866) (noting the submission).
34 H. Journal, 39th Cong., 1st Sess. 212–13 (Jan. 31, 1866); S. Journal, 39th Cong. 1st Sess. 221–2 (Mar. 9, 1866) (noting passage in the House but failure in the Senate).
35 Kendrick, *supra* note 28, at 55–6.
36 Cong. Globe, 39th Cong., 1st Sess. 429–32 (Jan. 25, 1866).
37 Kendrick, *supra* note 28, at 56.
38 *Id.* at 57–8.
39 Kendrick, *supra* note 28, at 61.
40 A week earlier, Bingham had announced to the House that he hoped for an amendment that would give Congress power to enforce certain guarantees of the Constitution, and indicated that these included the Due Process and Privileges and Immunities Clause. Cong. Globe, 39th Cong., 1st Sess. 429 (Jan. 25, 1866).
41 Ames, *supra* note 27, at 220.
42 Proceedings of the First Three Republican National Conventions 165 (1893).
43 David R. Upham, *The Meanings of the "Privileges and Immunities of Citizens" on the Eve of the Civil War*, 91 Notre Dame L. Rev. 1117, 1156 (2016).
44 *Id.* at 1158.
45 In his oral argument in *San Mateo County v. Southern Pacific R. Co.*, 116 U.S. 138 (1885), Roscoe Conkling recalled, "The committee took a week to consider this amendment, thus identified on its face with Article IV, Section 2, and with the fifth amendment, and on the tenth of February, by a vote of nine to five, ordered it reported to the two Houses." *Conkling's Argument, reprinted in* Howard Jay Graham, Everyman's Constitution: Historical Essays on the Fourteenth Amendment, the "Conspiracy Theory," and American Constitutionalism 595, 603 (1968).
46 Kendrick, *supra* note 28, at 61–2 (indicating opposition by Fessenden, as well as the New York Representative Conkling and Senator Harris).
47 Cong. Globe, 39th Cong., 1st Sess. 806, 813 (Feb. 13, 1866) (quoting text as submitted to the Senate by Fessenden and to the House by Bingham).
48 *Id.* at 806 (Feb. 13, 1866) (discussed in Op. O.L.C., Wrong Turns on the Road to Judicial Activism: The Ninth Amendment and the Privileges or Immunities Clause 60 (1987) stating that "[t]he measure was not debated in the Senate, but ordered to lie on the table, where it remained.")
49 H. Journal, 39th Cong., 1st Sess. 342 (Feb. 28, 1866) (noting vote in the House to postpone debate).
50 Cong. Globe, 39th Cong., 1st Sess. 1082 (Feb. 28, 1866).
51 *Id.* at 1063 (Feb. 27).
52 *Congress, in* 2 The Nation 291, 291 (Mar. 8, 1866) (quoted in *City of Boerne v. Flores*, 521 U.S. 507, 522 (1997)). *Accord* Earl M. Maltz, *Moving Beyond Race: The Joint Committee on Reconstruction and the Drafting of the Fourteenth Amendment*, 42 Hastings Const. L.Q. 287, 300 (2015).
53 Kendrick, *supra* note 28, at 101.
54 *Id. at* 106 (Apr. 28, 1866).

55 Cong. Globe, 39th Cong., 1st Sess. 2286–7 (Apr. 30, 1866).

56 *Id.*

57 Kendrick, *supra* note 28, at 84 (Apr. 21, 1866).

58 *Constitutional Amendment Proposed by the Reconstruction Committee*, Daily Union and American, Apr. 29, 1866, at 3, https://chroniclingamerica.loc.gov/lccn/sn85038519/1866-04-29/ed-1/seq-3/ (paraphrasing Section 1 as the "Bingham proposition, securing the rights of all citizens in every State, and forbidding state legislation to the contrary"); *Report of the Committee on Reconstruction*, The Portland Daily Press, May 1, 1866, at 2, https://chroniclingamerica.loc.gov/lccn/sn83016025/1866-05-01/ed-1/seq-2/ (mentioning reports of the "Bingham proposition" or "Bingham amendment" and connecting it to the February proposal).

59 H. Journal, 39th Cong., 1st Sess. 796 (June 5, 1866); Cong. Globe, 39th Cong., 1st Sess. 2980 (June 5, 1866).

60 *Compare* Robert J. Kaczorowski, *Revolutionary Constitutionalism in the Era of the Civil War and Reconstruction*, 61 N.Y.U. L. Rev. 863, 915 (1986) (noting the continuity), *with* City of *Boerne v. Flores*, 521 U.S. 507, 522 (1997) (stating erroneously that after February 28, "[t]he Amendment in its early form was not again considered").

61 Cong. Globe, 39th Cong., 1st Sess. 2545 (1866).

62 *Id.* at 2765 (emphasis added).

63 *Id.* at 3042.

64 *Id.* at 3149.

65 H. Journal, 39th Cong., 1st Sess. 811 (June 8, 1866); S. Journal, 39th Cong., 1st Sess. 505 (June 8, 1866). The Senate Journal indicates that Fessenden submitted the Report after the Senate's final vote. *Id.* But the Globe suggests that Fessenden submitted the Report beforehand—and even before the Senate's vote on various amendments (including Fessenden's last-minute motion to add "or naturalized" to the Citizenship Clause). *See* Cong. Globe, 39th Cong., 1st Sess. 3038–42.

66 Cong. Globe, 39th Cong., 1st Sess. 3038 (June 8, 1866).

67 The minority submitted their report to the House on June 19 and to the Senate on June 22. The House agreed to accept the Report without controversy, but there were some objections in the Senate, which delayed formal reception until July 7. *See* H. Journal, 39th Cong., 1st Sess. 866 (June 19, 1866); S. Journal, 39th Cong., 1st Sess. 563–4 (June 22, 1866) (noting submission and objection to reception of report); *id.* at 624–5 (July 7, 1866) (noting receipt despite objection). For the text, *see* Joint Committee on Reconstruction, Views of the Minority, 39th Cong., 1st sess., H. Rep. 30, pt. 2, at 1–12 (June 20, 1866).

68 Cong. Globe, 39th Cong., 1st Sess. 2265.

69 *Id.* On the illness, *see* Donald Dripps, *The Variola Variation*, 16 Const. Comment. 511 (1999).

70 Report, *supra* note 1, at vii; *see also id.* at iii (including the concurrent resolution as the first item in prefatory matter). There is evidence that some on the Committee feared its authority would be exhausted once it had submitted its constitutional proposals. On April 28, Stevens moved that the Committee report the constitutional and statutory proposals to the House and Senate, along with a request for "leave to submit at some future time reports to accompany the same." Kendrick, *supra* note 28, at 113–14. But the Committee never formally agreed; Stevens's motion

was superseded by Boutwell's motion to report the constitutional and statutory proposals separately, and his motion did not include any request for further permissions. *Id.* at 114–15. In submitting the proposals to the House, Stevens simply told the House that the Committee would later submit "a short report" in regard to the proposals. Cong. Globe, 39th Cong., 1st Sess. 2286 (Apr. 30); but Fessenden, for his part, entreated his colleagues that "perhaps we may ask leave to submit the report hereafter . . . if the Senate shall please to receive it." *Id.* at 2265 (Apr. 30, 1866); *see* H. Journal, 39th Cong., 1st Sess. 636–7 (Apr. 30, 1866); S. Journal, 39th Cong., 1st Sess. 384 (Apr. 30, 1866). And indeed, in submitting the already-authorized report, the Committee again "ask[ed] leave to report." Report, *supra* note 1, at ix. Still, despite all the courtesies, on June 6 the Committee decided simply to "submit the report." Kendrick, *supra* note 28, at 120 (June 6, 1866). Two days later, both houses received the Report without any further permission requested or granted. Cong. Globe, 39th Cong., 1st Sess. 3038, 3051 (June 8, 1866); H. Journal, 39th Cong., 1st Sess. 811 (June 8, 1866); S. Journal, 39th Cong., 1st Sess. 505 (June 8, 1866).

71 S. Journal, 39th Cong., 1st Sess. 511–12 (June 12, 1866). The resolution for 50,000 was "considered by unanimous consent and agreed to." Cong. Globe, 39th Cong., 1st Sess. 3098.

72 H. Journal, 39th Cong., 1st Sess. 878 (June 21, 1866); *see* Cong. Globe, 39th Cong., 1st Sess. 3326. *See also* Kendrick, *supra* note 28, at 264–5 (noting a total of 150,000 copies were ordered by the House and Senate).

73 *See, e.g.*, S. Journal, 39th Cong., 1st Sess. 471 (May 29, 1866) (reporting a unanimous vote to strike out the Committee's proposed third section that would have withheld the suffrage from formerly pro secession citizens).

74 H. Journal, 39th Cong., 1st Sess. 878 (June 21, 1866). Despite the House resolution, the minority report does not seem to have been thus printed. *See* H. Journal, 39th Cong., 1st Sess. 1005 (July 11, 1866) ("Mr. Le Blond, by unanimous consent, moved that it be referred to a select committee of five members to inquire why the minority views of the Committee on Reconstruction were not printed in the same volume with the majority report and testimony"). On the next day, however, the House rejected the motion. *Id.* at 1006 (July 12, 1866). Some Democrats accused the Republicans of dishonesty. *Another Trick Exposed*, The Daily Phoenix, at 2, July 19, 1866, https://chroniclingamerica.loc.gov/lccn/sn84027008/1866-07-19/ed-1/seq-2/.

75 Maryland General Assembly, Report of the Joint Committee on Federal Relations 4 (Jun. 16, 1866).

76 *Bank One Chicago, NA v. Midwest Bank & Trust Co.*, 516 U.S. 264, 280 (1996) (Scalia, J., concurring).

77 Nomination of Thurgood Marshall: Hearings Before the Comm. on the Judiciary, 90th Cong. 169 (1967).

78 *Pierce v. Underwood*, 487 U.S. 552, 566–7 (1988). *See* Mark Deforrest, *Taming a Dragon: Legislative History in Legal Analysis*, 39 Dayton L. Rev. 37, 70–1 (2013) (discussing *Pierce's* holdings on this point).

79 *Id.* at 71 & n. 267 (citing judicial authorities).

80 *Comm'r v. Acker*, 361 U.S. 87, 94 (1959) (Frankfurter, J., dissenting).

81 John C. Hurd, The Theory of Our National Existence: As Shown by the Action of the Government of the United States Since 1861, at 42 (1881) (emphasis added).

82 The Federalist No. 40, at 249 (James Madison) (2003).
83 Congressmen were "respectable"—because, by their election, they were likely, more or less, to have "the most attractive merit and the most diffusive and established [reputations]." The Federalist No. 10, at 77 (James Madison) (2003).
84 *Id.*
85 U.S. Const. art. VI.
86 Akhil Reed Amar, The Bill of Rights: Creation and Reconstruction 187 (1998).
87 2 James G. Blaine, Twenty Years of Congress: From Lincoln to Garfield 127 (Conn., The Henry Hill Publ'g Co. 1886).
88 For further evidence of this general respect, see the first remarks of Stevens in opening discussion of the Senate-amended version of the Amendment: "Mr. Speaker, that portion of the joint committee which is composed of the Union members of this House [seven Republicans] have examined the amendments which have been made by the Senate, and are unanimously of opinion that they ought to be adopted by the House [so Republican members] would be willing to take a vote upon it at once." Cong. Globe, 39th Cong., 1st sess. 3144 (June 13, 1866). The consensus of these seven House Republicans, then, was decisive evidence of the consensus of all Republicans in the House, and thus sufficient reason for their summary approval of the Senate's changes.
89 *Speech of Hon. E.B. Washburne Before the Jo Daviess County Republican Convention*, Chicago Tribune, Sept. 17, 1866, at 2, https://chroniclingamerica.loc.gov/lccn/sn82014064/1866-09-17/ed-1/seq-2/.
90 Cong. Globe, 41st Cong., 2d sess. 3614 (May 19, 1870).
91 Bernard C. Steiner, Life of Reverdy Johnson 133 (1914).
92 Kendrick, *supra* note 28, at 120 (June 6).
93 2 Francis Fessenden, Life and Public Services of William Pitt Fessenden 63 (1907) (citing Cong. Globe, 39th Cong., 1st sess. 3649 (July 7, 1866)).
94 *See* Report, *supra* note 1, at xxi.
95 Representatives Washburne and Henry Blow were absent from the Capitol at the time. *Reconstruction: Final Report of the Congressional Committee*, Cleveland Daily Leader, June 13, 1866, at 2, https://chroniclingamerica.loc.gov/lccn/sn85042437/1866-06-13/ed-1/seq-2/.
96 See H. Journal, 39th Cong., 1st Sess. 869 (June 20, 1866) (Washburne submitting a motion to sign the report of the Committee); *id.* at 915 (June 27, 1866). (Blow also submitting a motion to sign the report of the Committee). The Senate ordered the printing of copies (S. JOURNAL June 12) before either man returned, and the House ordered copies after Washburne signed but before Blow did. (H. JOURNAL June 21). All twelve signatures, however, appear on the report as reprinted in Edward McPherson's *Political Manual* for the year. Edward McPherson, A Political Manual for 1866–76, at 93 (Washington, DC, Philips & Solomons, 1867). Cong. Globe, 41st Cong., 2d sess. 3614 (May 19, 1870) (remarks of Senator Howard) (noting that the "Report is signed by all Republican members of the Committee," and naming each signatory).
97 William Salter, The Life of James W. Grimes 299 (1876).
98 *See Report of the Reconstruction Committee*, The Cecil Whig [Elkton, MD], June 23, 1866, at 1, https://chroniclingamerica.loc.gov/lccn/sn83016348/1866-06-23/ed-1/seq-1/ (celebrating the Report's "clear reasoning and formidable array of facts" and

the Report's vindication of the Republican majorities "in and out of Congress in their persistent efforts to restore the unity of the government on a just, permanent and enduring foundation"); *Final Report of the Reconstruction Committee*, Anderson Intelligencer [SC], June 21, 1866, at 1, https://chroniclingamerica.loc.gov/lccn/sn84026965/1866-06-21/ed-1/seq-1/ (calling the Report "the most important public paper issued in this country since President Johnson's first proclamation" of amnesty in May 1865); *Reconstruction*, The Evansville Journal, June 14, 1866, at 4, https://chroniclingamerica.loc.gov/lccn/sn82014296/1866-06-14/ed-1/seq-4/ (predicting that the people will "heartily indorse and approve the recommendations of the Committee, insisting upon Constitutional guarantees").

99 *Report of the Reconstruction Committee*, The Evening Telegraph, June 11, 1866, at 2, https://chroniclingamerica.loc.gov/lccn/sn83025925/1866-06-11/ed-1/seq-2/ (reprinting the Tribune's commentary); *see also The Reconstruction Report*, Chicago Tribune, June 11, 1866, at 2, https://www.loc.gov/resource/sn82014064/1866-06-11/ed-1/?sp=2 (contending that the Report "truly expresses the position of the majority of Congress and of the American people").

100 Fessenden, *supra* note 93, at 63.

101 See Report, *supra* note 1, at xxi (1866); *Report of the Reconstruction Committee*, The Evening Telegraph, June 11, 1866, at 2 (reprinting the Tribune's commentary), https://chroniclingamerica.loc.gov/lccn/sn83025925/1866-06-11/ed-1/seq-2/ The numbers in brackets are added.

102 Id.

103 *The Constitutional Amendment—the Union Platform*, Cleveland Daily Leader, June 15, 1866, at 2, https://chroniclingamerica.loc.gov/lccn/sn85042437/1866-06-15/ed-1/seq-2/ (emphasis added).

104 Edward McPherson, The Political History of the United States of America During the Period of Reconstruction 84–101 (Washington, DC, Philips & Solomons 1871).

105 William H. Barnes, History of the Thirty-Ninth Congress of the United States 466–72 (1868).

106 *Id.* at 466.

107 Cong. Globe, 41st Cong., 2d sess. 3614 (May 19, 1870). After quoting the Committee's exposition of the Amendment, he remarked, "I stand to that forever." *Id.*

108 *Id.*

109 *Id.*

110 *Id.* In sharp contrast, *see A Parliamentary Porcupine*, The Day Book [Norfolk, VA], June 11, 1866, at 2, https://chroniclingamerica.loc.gov/lccn/sn85025697/1866-06-11/ed-1/seq-2/ (denouncing the Report as "paltry in reasoning and malevolent in sentiment").

111 Hurd, *supra* note 81, at 42.

112 William Archibald Dunning, Essays on the Civil War and Reconstruction 115 (New York, The Macmillan Co. 1904) (1879); W. E. Burghardt Du Bois, Black Reconstruction 311–13 (1935). *See also* Readings in American Constitutional History, 1776–878, 518–27 (Allen Johnson, ed. 1912) (presenting, in a chapter on the "Origin of the Fourteenth Amendment," the Report first and then remarks by Bingham and other historical records). *But see* John G. Clark, *Historians and the Joint Committee on Reconstruction*, 23 The Historian 348, 358–9 (1961) (contending

that historians have assumed, without proper investigation, that the Report had a significant impact).

113 Google Books, JSTOR, Nexis Uni, and SSRN.

114 For significant discussions of the Report, *see* Earl A. Maltz, *The Concept of Equal Protection of the Laws—A Historical Inquiry*, 22 San Diego L. Rev. 499, 523 (1985) (providing perhaps the only extended discussion among living jurists); *see also* William D. Guthrie, Lectures on the Fourteenth Article of Amendment to the Constitution of the United States 60–1 (1898) (relying first on the Report, and then on Jacob Howard's Senate speech to support his incorporationist reading); Editorial, 6 Va. L. Rev. 50, 56 (1900) (noting critically Guthrie's reliance on the Report); Eugene Gressman, *The Unhappy History of Civil Rights Legislation*, 50 Mich. L. Rev. 1323, 1330 (1952) (contending that the Report shows the Amendment's prohibition was applicable to private as well as state action); James W. Fox, Jr., *Citizenship, Poverty, and Federalism: 1787–1882*, 60 U. Pitt. L. Rev. 421, 511–12 (1999) (quoting the Report to support the conclusion that Congress was to be "the national legislative body over the basic aspects of citizenship" with authority "in particularizing the rights and privileges of citizenship"); James W. Fox, *Publics, Meanings & the Privileges of Citizenship*, 2015 Const. Comm. 567, 582 (book review) (relying on the Report to insist that Section 1 was understood to protect "civil rights") (reviewing Lash, *supra* note 27); Gregory Maggs, *A Critical Guide to Using the Legislative History of the Fourteenth Amendment to Determine the Amendment's Original Meaning*, 49 Conn. L. Rev. 1069, 1080 (2017) (highlighting the Report's significance and providing some background). But many citations have been little better than perfunctory. *See* Nelson Lund, *Two Faces of Judicial Restraint (Or Are There More?) in McDonald v. City of Chicago*, 63 Fla. L. Rev. 487, 507 (2011) (briefly objecting to Justice Thomas's use of the explanation in his concurrence in *McDonald v. City of Chicago*); Vincent J. Samar, *The Analytic Aposteriori and a New Understanding of Substantive Due Process that Is Exhibited in the Lives of Those Seeking to Marry Someone of the Same Sex*, 30 St. Louis U. Pub. L. Rev. 377, 380 (2011) (merely noting Justice Thomas's quotation); Joshua A. Scott, Note, *The Right Thing for the Wrong Reasons? The Incorporation of the Second Amendment in McDonald v. Chicago*, 9 Ave Maria L. Rev. 335, 362 (2011) (same); Mark Graber, Constructing Constitutional Politics: Thaddeus Stevens, John Bingham, and the Forgotten Fourteenth Amendment (August 19, 2014), U of Maryland Legal Studies Research Paper No. 2014-37, https://ssrn.com/abstract=2483355 (quoting the Report only to support the conclusion that Section 1 did not have "a particular pride of place"); Brianne J. Gorod & Brian R. Frazelle, *Timbs v. Indiana: Mere Constitutional Housekeeping or the Timely Revival of a Critical Safeguard?*, 2018–2019 Cato Sup. Ct. Rev. 215, 221 (2019) (simply quoting the Report); David H. Gans, *The 14th Amendment Was Meant to Be a Protection Against State Violence*, The Atlantic, July 19, 2020 (providing the quote and noting only that the Report was "widely distributed across the country").

115 *See supra* note 114 (commentary of Maltz, Fox, and Maggs).

116 *Adamson v. California*, 332 U.S. 46, 109 (1947) (Black, J., dissenting); *McDonald v. City of Chicago*, 561 U.S. 742, 827 (2010) (Thomas, J., concurring); *Citizens for Const. Integrity v. Census Bureau*, 115 F.4th 618, 631 (D.C. Cir. 2024) (Wilkins, J., concurring).

117 *See McCleskey v. Kemp*, 481 U.S. 279, 346–7 (1987) (Blackmun, J., dissenting) (noting that the Report indicates "that discriminatory enforcement of States' criminal laws was a matter of great concern for the drafters"); *Patterson v. McLean Credit Union*, 491 U.S. 164, 194 n.4 (1989) (Brennan, J., dissenting) (involved Section 1981 claims and private performance of contracts); *Westberry v. Gilman Paper Co.*, 507 F.2d 206, 212 (5th Cir. 1975) (state action not sole purpose); *Poindexter v. Louisiana Financial Assistance Com.*, 275 F. Supp. 833, 839 n.23 (E.D. La. 1967) (detailing violence against freedmen's schools in Louisiana—desegregation case); *Butterworth v. Dempsey*, 229 F. Supp. 754, 778 n.6 (D. Conn. 1964) (Anderson, J., dissenting) (representative districting case). Significant quotations occurred in the dispute between Justices Harlan and Brennan over the Amendment's effect on political rights. *Oregon v. Mitchell*, 400 U.S. 112, 197–8 (1970) (Harlan, J. concurring in part); *id.* at 268 (Brennan, J., dissenting); *Reynolds v. Sims*, 377 U.S. 533, 594 (1964) (Harlan, J., dissenting) (redistricting—and discussing only the proposal not the explanatory report); Judge O'Scannlain of the Ninth Circuit has brought up the Report in connection with the right to bear arms in two panel opinions that were subsequently reversed upon *en banc* review. *See Young v. Hawaii*, 896 F.3d 1044, 1061 (9th Cir. 2018) (opinion of O'Scannlain) (guns case), *rev'd en banc*, 992 F.3d 765 (9th Cir. 2021) (O'Scannlain, dissenting on en banc review); *Nordyke v. King*, 563 F.3d 439, 455 (9th Cir. 2009) (opinion by O'Scannlain), *rev'd en banc* 681 F.3d 1041 (9th Cir. 2012).

118 *Students for Fair Admissions, Inc. v. President & Fellows of Harv. Coll.*, 600 U.S. 181, 321, 324 (2023) (Sotomayor, J., dissenting).

119 2 George S. Boutwell, Reminiscences of Sixty Years in Public Affairs 41–2 (1902).

120 Compare Robert H. Bork, The Tempting of America: The Political Seduction of the Law 39 (1989) (relying on the quip to speculate that it is "quite possible that the words meant very little to those who adopted them" and thus should not be a basis for judicial activism), *with* Anthony M. Kennedy, *William Rehnquist and Sandra Day O'Connor: An Expression of Appreciation*, 58 Stan. L. Rev. 1663, 1665 (2006) (relying on the quip to say that the Fourteenth Amendment was a "half-finished thought" and that had his late colleague (Chief Justice Rehnquist) been aware of this indeterminacy, he would have been "horrified").

121 Cong. Globe, 39th Cong., 1st Sess. 2766 (1866). For recent scholarship relying on this quotation, *see, e.g.*, Steven G. Calabresi & Hannah M. Begley, *Originalism and Same-Sex Marriage*, 70 U. Miami L. Rev. 648, 682 (2016).

122 *Plyler v. Doe*, 457 U.S. 202, 215 (1982); *Jones v. Helms*, 452 U.S. 412, 424 n.23 (1981). For other court opinions citing the remark, *see Barber v. Bryant*, 193 F. Supp. 3d 677, 706 n.27 (2016); *Catherine H. Barber Mem. Shelter, Inc. v. Town of N. Wilkesboro Bd. of Adjustment of N. Wilkesboro*, 576 F. Supp. 3d 318, 335 (W.D.N.C. 2021). For dissents, *see Reynolds v. Sims*, 377 U.S. 533, 600 (1964) (Harlan, J., dissenting); *Stern v. Tarrant County Hospital Dist.*, 778 F.2d 1052, 1062 (5th Cir. 1985) (Rubin, J., dissenting); *Harris v. Anderson*, 194 Kan. 302, 331 (1965) (Fatzer, J., dissenting).

123 Cong. Globe, 41st Cong., 2d sess. 3614 (May 19, 1870) ("[T]hese [twelve] names should be republished to the world, taking care always to place no particular stress upon one of the names on the list").

124 Guthrie, *supra* note 114, at 60–1. See also Frank Hendrick, The Power to Regulate Corporations and Commerce 222–3 (1906) (quoting Guthrie's lectures favorably).

125 332 U.S. 46, 109 (1947) (Black, J., dissenting); 561 U.S. 742, 827 (Thomas, J., concurring)
126 Maltz, *supra* note 114, at 523.
127 *Id.*
128 See *infra* ch. 3.
129 *Id.*

3

The Fundamentalist Consensus

We should endeavor to place [civil rights] above all courts, Supreme or otherwise, and embody them in the charter of our land—the Constitution itself.

—Senator Luke Poland's Speech to the Vermont General Assembly (Oct. 24, 1866)[1]

In recovering the Fourteenth Amendment's official meaning, we need not, and must not, rely exclusively on the Joint Committee's explanation. First and foremost, we must judge that explanation under the sheer text of Section 1, as proposed by the Committee and later incorporated into the Constitution: "Nothing but the text was adopted by the people."[2] Moreover, we must look to the rest of the Committee's lengthy formal Report, to see how the Committee's discussion sheds light on the text they proposed and the concluding explanation they offered.

Furthermore, we must look outside the Committee and assess the Report's consistency with other official explanations. These accounts are of two types. First, the pre-Amendment understanding of Section 1's terms is vital; this prior, received "legal meaning" is presumptively the original meaning of the new Amendment. Second, of course, we must consider the contemporaneous *official* understanding, as indicated by the words and deeds of other officials participating in the Amendment's adoption.

In this chapter, I will proceed analytically, by dividing the Committee's formal explanation into four parts: (1) that the prohibitions would "determine" certain rights, (2) that these rights were "civil," (3) that these consisted of a plurality of civil "rights" and civil "privileges," and (4) that these rights were guaranteed to "all citizens" and all "parts of the republic." I will consider each of these four aspects in relation to (a) the constitutional text, (b) the Committee's Report as a whole, (c) the official pre-Amendment understanding of the terms in that text, and (d) the prevailing understanding of that text among other officials who participated in the Amendment's adoption.

I will argue that the Committee's account, as amply corroborated and explicated by other official statements, shows that by its original official meaning, the Amendment's first section was not evolutionary but *determinate* and more specifically, a *fundamentalist* measure. Section 1 reaffirmed and further secured a set of civil rights and privileges that were fundamental to human personhood and American citizenship, and thus already foundational to our Republic. This securitarian Amendment gave neither the courts nor Congress, nor anyone else, any power to *define* (let alone *redefine*) these fundamental rights and privileges, but only enhanced power to secure them.

Determination

Determination and the Constitutional Text

By its very terms, Section 1's prohibitory sentence seems to refer to rights that are prior and fixed—for the language consists of a set of anti-negation rules. The states may not *abridge, deprive,* or *deny*. These bans, then, presuppose something already existing—something to be secured against partial or total negation. As anti-negation rules, they do not suggest a power to add or subtract.

Determination and the Whole Report

Elsewhere in its Report, the Committee repeatedly identified the securitarian goal: "security of future peace and safety," to "secure" the freedmen's "rights as free men and citizens," and more broadly, to "secure the civil rights of all citizens of the Republic."[3] Peace and safety were to be secured by the security of civil rights. These rights were not to be conferred, let alone to be reimagined or reinvented.

This determinate character was likewise indicated by an auxiliary statute drafted by the Committee. The Committee submitted, along with its constitutional proposal, two statutes that were "designed to carry the [Amendment] into effect."[4] One of these would have allowed congressional readmission to any of the former insurrectionary states, provided, in part, that the state "shall have modified its constitution and laws in *conformity*" with the proposed Amendment.[5] To require that a state "modify" its laws to be "in conformity" with the new Amendment[6] would seem to imply a definite *form* with which to con-*form*. Otherwise, the Committee's stipulation would make no sense: "Conform with this formless rule."

This *form*, the Committee indicated, arose from something fundamental, anterior to the laws and constitutions of the several and United States. The Committee's express aim was to secure to the former slaves their "rights as free men and citizens."[7] Freedom and citizenship, by their nature, implied the enjoyment of certain rights to be, not created by, but merely recognized and secured, by the constitutions and laws.

Some jurists, however, have ascribed indeterminacy to different terms of the Committee's proposal. *First*, some have found indeterminacy in the verb "abridge." They have said that "to abridge" meant "to regulate arbitrarily."[8] By this reading, Section 1 was to ban all state laws that arbitrarily abridge privileges and immunities, and thus to provide an undefined freedom from any and all unreasonable regulations.

But such a reading seems inconsistent with the meaning of "abridge" as used elsewhere in the Committee's proposal, where the verb refers to something that may sometimes be reasonable and proper. Their proposed section 2 reduced the representation of any state where citizens' right to vote was "abridged, except for participation in rebellion or other crime."[9] And the Committee's proposed third section would have temporarily withheld, and thus abridged, the voting rights of former rebels.[10] For the Committee, then, "to abridge" did not mean "to arbitrarily regulate," for the Committee did not deem the rebels' disenfranchisement as unreasonable or unjust. By the Privileges or Immunities Clause, the Committee sought to forbid all abridgment of a defined set of undoubted and prior goods. This forbidden abridgment was categorically bad because these rights were good. I will elaborate this point in the sixth chapter.

Second, some jurists have suggested indeterminacy in the words "privileges [and] immunities of citizens of the United States." This argument proceeds in two ways.

On the one hand, some scholars have read the "privileges" and "immunities" to mean whatever rights might be *conferred* by state or federal law. Such rights are indefinite; they may be subject to both addition and subtraction, for what the legislatures may give, the legislatures may take away. But nothing in the language of the proposal or elsewhere in the Report would seem to support this interpretation. This reading relies not on the text, but on a strained effort to read the text in light of (1) the so-called "orthodox" meaning of Article IV's Privileges and Immunities Clause, and (2) the contemporaneous discussion of Section 1. I'll discuss these matters later in this chapter.[11]

On the other hand, some jurists have contended that at least *one* of these rights of citizenship was an immunity against all "unreasonable" regulations.[12] This immunity would indeed have broad and indeterminate applications.[13]

But this reading would have a scandalous implication: that citizenship, not humanity, confers a freedom from unreasonable coercion. The Committee, however, seemed to presume, as we would today, that simple humanity gives such a right.[14] As indicated by their proposal, the Committee manifestly believed that all human persons have the rights of life, liberty, and property, and therefore, persons within American jurisdiction had a right to the security of those rights by a certain legal process and protection. Moreover, in their Report, the Committee indicated that some measure of justice and reasonability is owed even to the defeated rebels.[15] To be sure, the Committee charged that as "insurgents, rebels, traitors," they had "forfeited all civil and political rights and privileges"[16] and as conquered "enemies" they were entitled only "to such rights, privileges and conditions as might be vouchsafed by the conqueror"[17]—*viz.*, the "people of the United States."[18] Nonetheless, the Committee did not say that the conquered had forfeited any human rights that the conqueror was bound to respect. Instead, the Committee proposed to impose on the rebels a burden that was "not unreasonable" and "just and reasonable"—namely, to recover their full civil and political rights, the former rebels had to prove their renewed loyalty.[19] Even the defeated rebels had some right to reasonable treatment.

As a general rule, it would have been highly irregular for the Committee, in proposing an amendment to the law of our land, to suggest that reasonableness is not owed to the human being as such. In our first statement as an independent people, Americans had acknowledged that the human being, as such, has certain inalienable rights, and that "a decent respect to . . . mankind requires that [any people] declare the causes which impel them to [political] separation."[20]

The Constitution's Fourth Amendment, however, does seem to suggest that only citizens are entitled to reasonable treatment. The freedom from "unreasonable searches and seizures" is guaranteed only to "the people" and not all persons. We'll address this anomaly in the sixth chapter.[21]

Third, some jurists impute indeterminacy to the word "law," as used in the Due Process Clause. True law is reasonable or otherwise just, it is said, so to prohibit deprivations of liberty or property without "due process of *law*" is to prohibit any *unreasonable* deprivations, even if authorized by putative "laws."[22]

But such a reading is inconsistent with the word "law" or "laws," as used elsewhere by the Committee in both its proposal and its Report. As Christopher Green has pointed out, by banning "any law" that might abridge the rights of citizenship, the Committee presupposed that there was indeed such a thing as an unjust law.[23] Similarly, by requiring that the seceded states modify their existing "laws" to be in conformity with the Amendment,[24] the Committee understood that these nonconforming and otherwise unjust laws were still "laws," albeit in need of improvement.

Fourth, some jurists have found indeterminacy in Congress's power to "enforce" Section 1. By this account, Congress's power to *enforce* Section 1's prohibitions included a broader power to *determine* the rights to be thus secured.[25]

But Congress's power, under section 5, seems limited to an enforcement of Section 1's anti-negation rules, and thus merely to safeguard certain prior defined rights. Such enforcement cannot extend to *making* or *unmaking* any of these anti-negation rules, still less the making or unmaking of these anterior rights to be thus secured. Indeed, the text itself indicates a sharp distinction between making and enforcing: "No state shall *make or enforce* any law."

The Committee, in fact, seemingly decided against giving Congress power to "determine" as well as "enforce" any rules or rights. Recall that on February 1, the whole Senate had directed the Committee to consider establishing a congressional power to "enforce and determine" a number of constitutional terms, including the Privileges and Immunities Clause.[26] But instead, the Committee gave Congress the power to "enforce" only; the Committee decided that Section 1 itself would provide the *determination* of certain "rights and privileges," with Congress's Section 5 power limited to the *enforcement* of this determination.

The Committee's Democratic minority tacitly agreed. Had those members suspected that it would establish an indefinite, even protean, set of rights, subject to addition and subtraction by Congress, these members most certainly would have objected. Some opponents in the states would later prove quite vociferous in this regard.[27] But the Committee minority, in its lengthy report, was silent.[28]

Determination and the Prior Official Understanding

The Committee's determinate (and more specifically fundamentalist) understanding seems consistent with the prevailing pre-Amendment meaning of the text of Section 1. Before the Fourteenth Amendment, authorities generally concurred that these concepts—equal protection, due process, privileges of citizenship—were foundational to our Republic, dating to 1776 if not much earlier. These concepts corresponded to truly fundamental principles of human dignity and American citizenship.

Equal Protection of the Laws

As to "equal protection," this right does not seem to have been subject to significant antebellum judicial interpretation. Still, the term seems to have meant something definite, settled, and universally respected. Jurists had remarked, without apparent controversy, that equal protection was due to all human beings as such, the alien equally with the citizen,[29] the prostitute equally with the chaste,[30] and so on—with slavery identified by jurists (both pro-slavery and anti) as an anomaly that placed the slave outside or beneath ordinary equal protection.[31]

At the same time, the right included only one determinate right—"protection"—as defined by a plurality of variable "laws." The right to equal protection was determinate—but lawmakers could change the laws defining that protection.

As Christopher Green has conclusively shown, "equal protection of the laws," as understood before 1866, referred to "the equal fulfillment of . . . remedial and law-enforcement functions." It did not encompass "a generic guarantee against improper classifications."[32]

This principle was deemed not only determinate but fundamental. According to the Supreme Court in *Marbury v. Madison*, "the very *essence* of civil liberty certainly consists in the right of every individual to claim the protection of the laws."[33] Indeed, the right of equal protection seems a proximate conclusion of the "self-evident" truths of the Declaration of Independence. If all men are created equal with respect to the rights of "life, liberty, and the pursuit of happiness;" and if government is instituted "to secure these rights," then this security, it seems, must be "equal."[34]

Due Process of Law

"Due process of law" was likewise fundamental, in two senses. First, like equal protection, it expressly concerned the anterior, fundamental rights of human personhood—life, liberty, and property—rights that were, before state action, already "privy" to the person (hence the ban on *de-privation* absent a trial). Second, due process shielded these natural rights with conventional procedural norms that far predated 1776. The guarantee was medieval in origin—as old as the fourteenth century, if not older.[35] Three decades before the Fourteenth Amendment, Joseph Story had explained that "due process of law" affirmed "the right of trial according to the process and proceedings of the common law."[36] With more nuance, the Supreme Court confirmed, in *Murray's Lessee v. Hoboken Land & Improvement Co.* (1856), that the "process" must comport with "those settled usages and modes of proceeding existing in the common and statute law of England, before the emigration of our ancestors," and then preserved here insofar as proved suitable to our "civil and political condition."[37] "Due process of law," then, was a decidedly conservative, anti-innovation principle—to be truly process "of law" required conformity with the "old law of England" as Justice Thomas has recently noted.[38]

Nonetheless, as the Court in *Murray's Lessee* also indicated, due process of law did allow for one kind of change: contraction by desuetude. One or more of the old usages of England, the Court suggested, had been abandoned in the American colonies because of insuitability to local conditions. Perhaps such a precedent of lawful contraction might admit of repetition even after Independence—for example, new conditions prevailing in the nineteenth century, or even later, might make other old usages unsuitable, and thus require and permit further contraction.[39] In the years before and just after the Amendment's adoption, some authorities either expressly or impliedly approved of such development by contraction—most notably, in the deliberate, though controversial, abandonment of the grand jury indictment, even in capital cases.[40]

Such gradual contraction did not, strictly speaking, involve indeterminacy. Due process of law would remain determinate (establishing a *terminus* or end) and thus not expand, but still might contract via desuetude.

Privileges and Immunities of Citizens

The "privileges and immunities" of American citizenship were likewise fundamental and thus determinate—dating to 1776 if not earlier. In the decade before Independence, both the First Continental Congress and the British Parliament had recognized the existence of the "people of America."[41] On July 4, 1776, this "one people" called their fellow colonists "fellow citizens" and, via their representatives, declared that these "United Colonies" were "Free and Independent States"—and thereby renamed themselves the people of the United States of America.[42] Soon thereafter, in the Articles of Confederation, this one (but multistate) citizenry sought to "secure and perpetuate" their existing "mutual friendship and intercourse" by providing, in the Articles of Confederation, for their entitlement to "all privileges and immunities of free citizens in the several States."[43] The citizens secured this same unity in the Constitution of 1787.[44] This security for interstate citizenship was "so *fundamental* a provision" that Hamilton (as "Publius") called it the very "*basis* of the Union."[45]

As the American citizenry was thus fundamental to the Union, so too were their "privileges and immunities." According to the most respected antebellum definition, offered by Justice Bushrod Washington in *Corfield v. Coryell* (1823), these rights were "in their nature, fundamental; they belonged "of right, to the citizens of all free governments"; and they had, "at all times, been enjoyed by the citizens of the several states which compose this Union, from the time of their becoming free, independent, and sovereign."[46]

Some contemporary scholars have contended that despite this opinion, Justice Washington's determinate formula, "at all times" since Independence, was not definitional. They allege an absence of supporting evidence. Christopher Green has pointed to textual silence: that the "privileges and immunities" provisions of Article IV and the Amendment, unlike some other provisions, contain "no temporal qualifier" or "explicit time stamps."[47] Randy Barnett and Evan Bernick, in turn, point to official silence. No one "made a concerted effort to determine whether a purported privilege or immunity had always, universally been enjoyed by American citizens." Hence, "at all times . . . ought not to be taken literally."[48]

As to the absence of a "time stamp," I think the text of the Amendment does contain a temporal reference. The privileges and immunities are those of "citizens of the United States." That citizenry does indeed have a time stamp, a known baptismal date: July 4, 1776. On that day, the one people of the united American colonies were born again, so to speak, as the people of the United States. This birthday was, in turn, recognized in the text of the proposed Constitution of 1787: "Done in Convention . . . in the Year . . . of the Independence of the United States of America the Twelfth."[49]

As to the absence of any multistate and multiyear survey, the silence was entirely appropriate—and in fact was evidence of a general consensus across both the states and the generations. There was no need for a survey to show that, throughout the Union, American citizens could travel, acquire real as well as personal property, enjoy the writ of habeas corpus, and so forth, just as today there would be no need for such a study to show that in all states, Americans drive on the right side of the road, or use English to conduct public affairs. Today, as then, the enumeration of such universal American customs would be "more tedious than difficult," as Justice Washington avowed.[50] Such facts are so fundamental and so widely recognized, as to go without saying. Those matters that go without saying, regularly and appropriately, do go without saying.

According to many antebellum authorities, these fundamental American "privileges and immunities," recognized throughout the Union, were properly designated the rights of "U.S." citizenship, and *not* the rights of "state citizenship."[51] These authorities included, *inter alia*, Chief Justice Roger Taney, Stephen Douglas, Abraham Lincoln,[52] as well as the Supreme Courts of Delaware and Ohio.[53]

Concurrent with the Joint Committee's deliberations, various members of Congress likewise identified the "privileges and immunities" of American citizenship as thus foundational. In February, Bingham said that "privileges and immunities of citizens of the United States" were "essential to the unity of the people" and already recognized within the Constitution "as it stands . . . today."[54] Therefore, no state ever had "the right . . . to withhold from any citizen of the United States within its limits, under any pretext whatever, any of the privileges of a citizen of the United States."[55] A few months later, his fellow Buckeyes, Representatives Lawrence and Shellabarger, would say the same.[56] In early April, Senator Lyman Trumbull likewise identified the rights of contract, property, and so on, as enumerated in the Civil Rights Act, as some of the "inherent, fundamental rights, which belong to free citizens or free men in all countries [and] in all the States of the Union."[57]

Meanwhile, in a high-profile case, decided while the Joint Committee was preparing its final draft amendment, a circuit court in Indiana had said the same. In *Barnes v. Browning*, a free back man, born in the United States, challenged Indiana's constitutional provision that prohibited free blacks from entering the state and from enforcing labor contracts therein.[58] The case was widely reported, for it was the first case brought under the just-adopted and controversial Civil Rights Act—and in the swing state of Indiana, whose support would be essential to ratification. The decision was almost certainly known to the members of the Committee.[59] The court dodged the statutory question, but ruled in the plaintiff's favor on constitutional grounds instead. Even apart from the Act, the court noted, Article IV's Privileges and Immunities Clause secured the plaintiff's rights as "a citizen of the United States," including, *inter alia,* the right to reside, to make contracts, and "to sustain his action for his labor."[60] These general American rights, the court indicated, were, unlike the suffrage, not "depend[ent] on the legal laws of the State."[61] State laws, it seems, did not create (but could regulate) these anterior civil rights of American citizenship.

Nonetheless, some prominent scholars have contended that Section 1's terms, by their pre-Amendment meaning, did not involve fundamental or otherwise determinate rights. As indicated above, some jurists have contended that terms like "*abridge*" or "due process of *law*" implied an enormous and amorphous rule against arbitrary regulations. But with one exception, no scholar cites any pre-amendment authority in support of these interpretations.[62] As will be elaborated in a subsequent chapter, "abridge" was a neutral term; abridgment was good when the thing abridged was bad, and bad when the thing abridged was good. It bore no implied pejorative adverb like "unreasonably."[63] As I'll explain in the next chapter, although "due process of law" was widely thought to incorporate discrete requirements of reasonableness (e.g., need for a general trial, with a neutral judge, and conducted according to well-promulgated rules of general application), it did not encompass any general rule against all unreasonable regulations.[64]

In sharp contrast, with respect to the terms "privileges or immunities," there is substantial pre-Amendment evidence from which one might plausibly infer indeterminacy. Prominent antebellum jurists, like the New York Court of Appeals, Kent, and Story, had understood Article IV's Privileges and Immunities Clause to ban only interstate discrimination.[65] And on the basis of these authorities, the Supreme Court would, in the *Slaughter-House Cases*, later establish the now "orthodox" or "black-letter" reading by which the states "grant or establish" sundry rights.[66] From this observation, eminent scholars, such as Philip Hamburger, John Harrison, Ilan Wurman, and Kurt Lash, have plausibly concluded that the privileges and immunities themselves were understood to owe their existence to the positive law of the states, and are thus indeterminate, subject to addition and subtraction by state law. Each state "conferred" these rights, so each state was supposedly free to create or destroy any "privilege" or "immunity," subject only to a rule against interstate discrimination.[67]

But this inference is mistaken. By the most authoritative accounts, these privileges and immunities were indeed fundamental to American citizenship; the states could recognize, declare, or guarantee these rights, but did not *confer* them.[68] For instance, in *Dred Scott*, the Court's majority had already drawn a sharp distinction between the "rights of citizenship which a State may *confer* within its own limits"; for example, political rights, and those "rights of citizenship" that one enjoys simply "as a member of the Union."[69] These rights of U.S. citizenship, the Court indicated, included the rights of travel, speech, and arms throughout the Union, and a freedom from racially discriminatory criminal liability.[70]

To be sure, many pre-Amendment jurists had held that Article IV secured these fundamental rights only against interstate discrimination. But those favorable to the interstate-equality reading did not say the "privileges" and "immunities" were *created* by the respective states. It was the constitutional entitlement ("shall be entitled"), and not the "privileges and immunities of citizens," that was reducible to a freedom from discrimination. That seems to have been Kent's opinion.[71]

This approach was reflected in the bill, introduced by Ohio Representative Samuel Shellabarger in April 1866 and explained by him in July, that would "declare and protect" the "privileges and immunities of citizens of the United States." Hamburger rightly highlights this bill as illustrative of the original meaning of the Amendment.[72] The bill protected *only* citizens sojourning in another state, and *only* against interstate discrimination: "as fully as such rights and privileges are held and enjoyed by the other citizens of such State."[73] The limitation, Shellabarger explained in July, arose not because the rights were created by state law, but because of the very limited interpretation that the courts had applied to Article IV. The bill was aimed to protect the fundamental rights enumerated in *Corfield*,[74] but was limited to interstate discrimination only because, he specified, his bill was "confined to the enforcement of this single clause of the Constitution," as interpreted by the courts—who, he indicated, had limited the entitlement to out-of-state citizens in this way.[75] But the rights themselves were fundamental, and belonged to citizens as such. Hence, he said, these "fundamental" rights could not be *justly* "taken away from any citizen of the United States by the laws of any State"—even "from its own citizens."[76]

Further, he added, Congress might seek additional safeguards, *beyond interstate equality*, for these "rights of national citizenship," to benefit all Americans, "without regard to the fact of their passing from one State into another."[77] As to these additional safeguards, he almost certainly had in mind Congress's Civil Rights Act and the Fourteenth Amendment, which by their terms protected citizens of the United States against their own states.

Moreover, even if predominant, this interstate-equality reading was not unanimous. Most notably, in an unreported but high-profile case toward the end of the Civil War, Judge John Underwood, a Lincoln appointee, had held that the right to testify is one of the "fundamental" privileges to which sojourning citizens were entitled in every state, state laws to the contrary notwithstanding. The Clause secured an exemption not just against interstate discrimination, but also against local injustice; a state could not, on the basis of race, bar an incoming citizen from testifying, "[n]o matter with what wrongs" a state might "outrage humanity in the persons of colored men born and reared upon [the state's] own soil."[78]

Congress's Power to Enforce, by Appropriate Legislation

Further, Section 5's terms, "*enforce, by appropriate legislation*," as understood before the Amendment, might also imply indeterminacy. As used in the recently-adopted Thirteenth Amendment, this same language had received a very broad, if not implausible, construction by some congressmen. The Amendment's first section had mandated only the nonexistence of slavery and involuntary servitude (except as punishment for crime), and its second empowered Congress to "enforce" this mandate "by appropriate legislation."[79] Some had relied on this enforcement power to justify the passage of the Civil Rights Act, with its declaration of citizenship and its protection, against racial discrimination, of certain enumerated rights and immunities.[80] That is, some thought Congress's power to enforce mere emancipation encompassed a power to secure the rights of citizenship to the emancipated. Indeed, as the Report of the Joint Committee indicated, some Republican congressmen believed that under the Thirteenth Amendment, Congress already had the power to secure to freedmen the full *political* rights of citizenship as well.[81]

As we noted in the first chapter, *some* opponents of the Fourteenth Amendment, then, reasonably asked, if under the Thirteenth Amendment, Congress's power "to enforce" mere emancipation had included the power to enfranchise, then how much broader would be the power, under the Fourteenth, "to enforce" the civil rights guarantees of the first section.[82] As Robert Kaczorowski has plausibly inferred, this analogy indicates that Section 5 included a "plenary power" to "define" as well as "secure" an indefinite set of rights.[83]

But this "plenary power" reading has two weaknesses. On the one hand, because this broad interpretation of the Thirteenth Amendment was so implausible, it was by no means a consensus interpretation in 1866, even among Republicans. One critic pointed out the absurdity of contending that the power to emancipate implied the power to secure the rights of citizenship:

> The right of holding and conveying real estate . . . is withheld from foreigners in many of our States, and in most countries of the world, upon grounds of public policy. But the man would he laughed at who should assert that such persons, incapable of holding real estate, were for that reason not freemen, The power to enforce the abolition of slavery of negroes does not then extend to endowing them with all the privileges of citizenship in a State.[84]

Consequently, only some members of Congress had relied on the Thirteenth Amendment to justify the Act; others pointed to a variety of alternative bases.[85] Further (to my knowledge) no opponent of the Act (including, most notably, John Bingham)[86], ever conceded the constitutionality of the Civil Rights Act.

On the other hand, even those Republicans relying on the Amendment did not say that Congress could thereby *define* civil rights. Rather, as Senator Lyman Trumbull maintained, the Civil Rights Act merely enumerated and secured the "privileges which are essential to freemen," or the "great fundamental rights . . . appertaining to every freeman."[87] Freedom, mandated by Section 1 of the Thirteenth Amendment, implied citizenship. By this reading, it was *freedom* itself, and not Congress or the state legislatures, that *conferred* these fundamental rights. Congress was just protecting the rights of freedom.[88]

Missouri's John Henderson provided a fuller explanation of this position. Henderson had authored the Senate bill that would eventually become the Thirteenth

Amendment's first section. He later explained that the subsequent addition of Section 2 to his proposal "did not add to nor detract from the meaning or force of [Section 1]," but served only to make explicit what was already implicit in the first section.[89] In the Fourteenth Amendment debates, he elaborated that by adopting the Civil Rights Act, Congress had merely enforced the first section's mandate of freedom; the Act secured what he called the "muniments of freedom."[90] For Henderson, then, Congress's power under the Thirteenth Amendment did not encompass the conferral of new rights, but only the securing of the rights already conferred by freedom itself.

The Ninth Amendment and Other Prevailing Rules of Construction

Finally, some jurists have found indeterminacy not in the Fourteenth Amendment's text but in its constitutional context: specifically, the Ninth Amendment's rule that the enumeration of constitutional rights may not be "construed to deny or disparage" other rights. Most notably, in *Planned Parenthood v. Casey*, the Supreme Court said that by applying the Ninth Amendment's rule of construction, the "liberty" secured by the Amendment cannot be construed to have "outer limits" but must be, rather, a "rational continuum, which, broadly speaking, includes a freedom from all substantial arbitrary impositions and purposeless restraints."[91]

If indeed, the Ninth Amendment, as understood in 1866, did include such a prevailing rule, mandating an indeterminate reading of constitutional rights, then there would be good originalist reason to construe the Fourteenth Amendment in this way—perhaps so far as to embrace an expansive and indefinite immunity against unreasonable laws. As Michael Rappaport and John McGinnis have ably contended, the proper interpretation of a constitutional provision requires conformity with the interpretive rules prevailing at the time of its adoption.[92] That must include, of course, the interpretive rules already expressly incorporated into the Constitution.

But such an attempted use of the Ninth Amendment seems mistaken in four ways. First, it is inconsistent with the text of the Ninth Amendment. There is no mention of any expansive "freedom" from *all* "arbitrary" or "purposeless" burdens. Rather, it refers to a limited set of old rights: those "retained by the people." Moreover, as many jurists have pointed out, the Ninth Amendment, by its terms, was a mere rule of construction—it cannot add or take away anything substantive.[93] If the words of a constitutional prohibition are determinate, no construction can make them otherwise. The Ninth Amendment cannot transform the Second Amendment's limited right "to keep and bear" into "keep and bear *and discharge* arms," or the First Amendment's restrictions on laws made by "Congress" into "Neither Congress nor the state legislatures shall make." Similarly, the Ninth Amendment cannot transform any of the determinate prohibitions of the Fourteenth into a "freedom from all other unreasonable laws, deprivations, and denials." No rule of "construction" can impose the naked fallacy of *inclusio unius, inclusio alterius*.

Second, this reading is diametrically opposed to the express purpose of the Ninth Amendment. By an adopted preamble, Congress had explained that all the amendments proposed in 1789 were designed to guard against the "misconstruction" and "abuse" of the *federal* powers granted by the *federal* Constitution.[94] The legislative powers of the states are not thus granted and thus fall outside the scope of the Amendment. As applied to the states, this expansive reading would turn the Ninth Amendment, expressly designed to restrain federal power, into a tool for a massive expansion of the federal judicial power.

Third, this reading would arguably violate the Ninth Amendment itself. One of the rights retained "by the people" is their right, guaranteed by the Constitution, to republican state governments. An expansive reading of the Fourteenth Amendment, as enforced by judicial authority, would, to that extent, substitute government by a national oligarchic judiciary for popular state government.

Fourth, this application of the Ninth Amendment is antithetical to the interpretation of that Amendment (and its state-constitution analogues—the "Baby Ninth Amendments")[95] that prevailed at the time of the Fourteenth Amendment's adoption. By 1866, courts had held that this rule of construction, as applied to any constitution (federal or state), served to restrain the powers delegated in that same constitution, and not to enlarge the scope of any prohibitions therein.[96] Hence, as found in the state constitutions, the rule limited the powers granted to the state governments; as found in the federal constitution, the rule limited the powers granted to the federal government. Therefore, as found in the federal Constitution, it restricted federal powers only—including the federal judicial power.

Therefore, it was then agreed that the Ninth Amendment could not enlarge the construction of Article I, section 10—that "bill of rights for the people of each State"[97]—which prohibited the states from, *inter alia*, making ex post facto laws, bills of attainder, and laws impairing the obligations of contracts. At the time of the Fourteenth Amendment's adoption, jurists seemed unanimous on this point. Most notably, the Ninth Amendment made no appearance whatsoever in bolstering the expansive exposition of Article I, section 10 championed in *Cummings v. Missouri*[98] (the companion case to *Ex parte Garland*).[99] The case was argued in March 1866, with a decision published early in the December 1866 term.[100] The Court was sharply divided on a nakedly partisan basis, with all five Democrats in the majority, and the four Republicans in dissent. The majority concluded that by requiring clergymen to take an expurgative test oath against former disloyalty, Missouri had adopted a bill of attainder and an ex post facto law.[101] For present purposes, what's most stark is that throughout the protracted litigation, none of the critics of Missouri's law relied at all on the Ninth Amendment,[102] even to support their controversial and enlarged reading of Article I, section 10, and its enumerated rights. The silence was deafening and dispositive: the failure to even mention the Ninth Amendment as an auxiliary enlargement of Section 10 reflected not so much neglect as the consensus that no such argument was plausible.

Indeed, it was *defenders* of state test oaths, proponents of a strict interpretation of Section 10, that marshaled the Ninth Amendment on behalf of strict construction. As Kurt Lash has pointed out, in October 1865, the Maryland Supreme Court decided that the state's loyalty oath for voters did not violate Article I, section 10, in part because the "spirit and object" of the Ninth Amendment (along with the Tenth) imposed this rule: "*Prohibitions on the States are not to be enlarged by construction*."[103] The reasoning seemed to be as follows: to enlarge by construction the Constitution's limits on the states would enlarge the federal judicial powers granted by that same Constitution, to the disparagement of the people's retained right of republican self-government.[104]

The Ninth Amendment, as understood at the time of the adoption of the Fourteenth, *required* a strict construction of that amendment's prohibitions on the states, much as it required a strict construction of the prohibitions set forth in Article I, section 10. This was the prevailing rule of construction.

Moreover, any indeterminate reading of the Fourteenth Amendment's prohibitions would run afoul of another then-prevailing rule of construction. There was an "axiom in American constitutional law" whereby the long and conspicuous acquiescence of the bench and bar to a particular practice establishes a strong precedent against any constitutional challenge to such practice.[105] Hence, the Marshall Court had unanimously once declared that many years of judicial "practice and acquiescence," where a particular claim could have been made, such deafening silence provides an "irresistible answer" to that claim.[106] Stated otherwise, the "general acquiescence of legal men shows the prevalence of opinion in favor of the negative of [a] proposition."[107] Likewise, while the Amendment was pending, the Court unanimously endorsed the axiom that where there had been occasions to make a constitutional claim, the deafening silence of the bench and bar indicates "the general judgment of the profession that no such [claim] should be entertained."[108] And with specific reference to constitutional prohibitions on the states, the Taney Court had explained that "uniform [state] action, involving the right to the exercise of an important power by the state government for half a century; and this *almost without question*; is no unsatisfactory evidence that the [state] power is rightly exercised."[109] Protracted silence of the bar and bench meant consent. Long acquiescence established a binding permissive precedent.

As applied to the prohibitions of Section 1, this axiom would preclude all novel challenges to any state law or practice that had been long accepted by the bench and bar. As we've seen, these restrictions were founded on already well-established principles of "due process" and "privileges and immunities," recognized in the state and federal constitutions. Hence, where from the Founding to 1866, a particular sort of law or practice had never been challenged under these norms, the general and authoritative judgment of the bench and bar was, then, that no such challenge should be made.

Determination and the Contemporaneous Official Understanding

This determinate and, more specifically, fundamentalist understanding of Section 1 prevailed throughout the entire official discussion of the Fourteenth Amendment.

Supporters and many opponents generally said or implied that Section 1's terms were foundational to any just society and to our Republic in particular—and were already recognized in our Declaration of Independence, the federal Constitution, and the state constitutions. Upon introducing debate in the House, Thaddeus Stevens said the provisions of Section 1 were "all asserted, in some form or other, in our Declaration [of Independence] or organic law," and this foundation, in turn, was built on the "firm foundation of eternal justice."[110] John Farnsworth likewise noted that the Privileges or Immunities and Due Process Clauses were "already in the Constitution" while the Equal Protection Clause reflected a necessary implication of the Declaration's maxim that government is instituted to secure the universal human rights of life, liberty, and the pursuit of happiness.[111] In the Senate, Howard launched the debate by similarly explaining that the Privileges or Immunities Clause secured the fundamental privileges and immunities that were already guaranteed or recognized in the Constitution, whether in Article IV (as elaborated by Justice Washington in *Corfield v. Coryell*) or in the first eight amendments.[112] Section 1, as a whole, secured the "fundamental rights and privileges which pertain to citizens of the United States, and to all persons who may happen to be within their jurisdiction."[113] Such rights of American citizenship and human personhood were anterior to the state and federal governments; in contrast, the suffrage was "merely a creature of law." [114]

Other Congressmen similarly insisted that Section 1 was fundamental and already within the letter or spirit of the Declaration and/or the federal and state constitutions.[115] For instance, Vermont's Senator Luke Poland remarked that the Privileges or Immunities Clause was designed merely to enforce the original intent of Article IV's Privileges and Immunities Clause, while the Due Process and Equal Protection Clauses represented "the very spirit and inspiration of our system of government, the absolute foundation upon which it was established," and were already "declared in the Declaration of Independence and in all the provisions of the Constitution."[116]

Above all, Bingham, the principal author of the proposal, most emphasized its constitutional foundation. The goal was to safeguard "the privileges and immunities of all the citizens of the Republic and the inborn rights of every person within its jurisdiction whenever the same shall be abridged or denied by the *unconstitutional* acts of any State."[117] Where were these two sets of rights, of citizens and persons, already recognized? He and the Committee had answered the question in February: the Privileges and Immunities and Due Process Clauses.

This foundationalist feature was essential to the integrity of the whole Republican Party. By its 1860 national platform, the Party had promised to maintain "inviolate . . . the rights of the states, and especially the right of each state to order and control its own domestic institutions according to its own judgment exclusively."[118] Democratic partisans frequently cited the platform and charged that the Thirteenth Amendment, the Fourteenth Amendment, and other Republican policies violated "the rights of the states," and thus demonstrated Republicans' inconsistency if not dishonesty.[119] Hence, Republican supporters took pains to emphasize that the Amendment served merely to provide enhanced security for rights already recognized in the Constitution. In his main floor speech on May 10, Bingham insisted that Section 1 "takes from no State any right that ever pertained to it. No State ever had the right, under the forms of law or otherwise, to deny to any freeman the equal protection of the laws or to abridge the privileges or immunities of any citizen of the Republic."[120] Two days later, Maryland Senator John Creswell would likewise say of Section 1, "the Constitution [already] means that, if it does not say it," but "it has been interpreted differently," so as to render "due process" and "privileges and immunities" "mere guaranties." The Amendment would remedy the absence of federal enforcement power.[121]

Officials in the states said much the same—though without any consensus as to the precise place of these rights in our national foundation. Section 1 would merely "reaffirm"[122] or "reassert"[123] principles that were "vital,"[124] or "cardinal,"[125] that together were "manifestly an axiom of free government"[126] or the "very essence of free government,"[127] with foundations as deep as "the rights of man."[128] These principles, in turn, were also foundational to our Republic—the "cornerstone of American Independence"—and reflected the "immortal truths of the Declaration of Independence."[129] Section 1 provided "a declaration of the true intent and meaning of American citizenship."[130] Some supporters told their state legislatures that the principles were already "implied" or otherwise in "the principles of the Constitution itself."[131] Pennsylvania's outgoing governor said that the Amendment would incorporate "elements" already found in the "true spirit" of the Constitution, even if arguably absent from its original "express terms."[132] Such ideals were broad as well as deep: he explained that Section 1 embodied "principles which were never seriously doubted anywhere, until after the insane crusade in favor of slavery had been for some time in progress."[133] Indiana's governor said, in a campaign speech, that no "right-minded man" could object to Section 1, as it merely "establishes the fundamental principles upon which the Union is based."[134] One Indiana legislator put it bluntly: the Amendment secured "civil rights" that were "inherent" and "of God."[135]

So foundational were these prohibitions that many officials called Section 1's prohibitory sentence redundant—which became an argument both for and against the proposed Amendment. In the House, one supporter called the prohibitory sentence a harmless "surplusage."[136] In the Senate, among supporters of the Amendment, Nevada's William Stewart said the prohibitory sentence "adds nothing to the Constitution,"[137] and Missouri's John Henderson explained that that sentence's prohibitions were already fully implied by "citizenship," as declared by the newly added Citizenship Clause. His colleague, Kentucky's Garrett Davis, an opponent, likewise claimed that apart from the Citizenship Clause, Section 1 was wholly "unnecessary," for its restrictions were already effectively provided for in the federal and state constitutions.[138] In the states, the redundancy again became an argument for and against Section 1.[139] For instance, opponents in the Massachusetts legislature said it was "at best, mere surplusage," because various provisions of the Constitution, "upon any fair rule of interpretation," already covered "the whole ground."[140]

Foundation Repair

Parenthetically, *pace* Justice Thomas and many other learned commentators, the evidence is likewise overwhelming that the authors of the Amendment did not think they were engaged in any "second founding" or anything revolutionary at all.[141] Even for the most radical, the goal was not to lay a new foundation but to engage in what may be called *foundation repair*. Upon inaugurating debate in the House, Thaddeus Stevens said the Amendment would more securely establish the "principles" of the "great Declaration" and to this end, "to clear away the rotten and defective portions of the old foundations, and to sink deep and found the repaired edifice upon the firm foundation of eternal justice."[142] In the Pennsylvania legislature, the theme was renewed: The Amendment would "strengthen[] the weak points in our national fortifications;" it provided a "few plain and simple corollaries . . . by way of perfecting and rounding up the old charter of our liberties."[143]

The "rotten and defective" portions were, as Senator George Williams told voters, the Founders' concessions to slavery: "When the Constitution was formed, concession was made to wrong for the sake of union. Other concessions followed . . . and finally, the nation was required to recognize the right of secession, and when it refused war ensued."[144] The Amendment, however, was founded more squarely on the Founders' Declaration: "Lay down as the foundation that 'all men are created free and equal,' and your work will be like a 'house that is built upon a rock.'"[145]

Indeed, if truly revolutionary, the Fourteenth Amendment would not have qualified as an "amendment." Article V of the Constitution authorizes not constitutional "change" without qualification, but only the change that can be called an "amendment." And when proposed by Congress, such an amendment was lawful only by determination that such amendment is "necessary."

Nonapplication to Many Northern States

So well established were these principles that officials repeatedly affirmed that Section 1 would have no application to the many states where the rights were already well secured. Wisconsin Senator Howe said that the Privileges or Immunities Clause would have no application to "many" of the loyal states, for therein "no such abridgment of privileges or immunities is tolerated."[146] Bingham specified (as to the Committee's broader February proposal) that though the measure would "unquestionably" affect Oregon's laws and perhaps Indiana's laws,[147] still, "under *no possible interpretation*" could the measures "ever be made to operate in the State of New York" as long as it retained its current laws.[148] With reference to the closely related Civil Rights Act, Senator Lyman Trumbull reassured his colleagues that it would "have no operation in Massachusetts, New York, Illinois, or most of the States of the Union."[149] In Pennsylvania, future Governor John Geary told voters that in the "Northern States the people would not be affected" by Section 1 because "[l]ong ago our fathers made this provision for our people."[150] In his survey of the evidence, historian Joseph James found that the Amendment's "operation in the North was seldom alluded to and often denied."[151] Some opponents noted the Amendment's sectional nonapplication—and therefore complained that the measure was unjustly sectional.[152]

At the same time, the Amendment, on its face, plainly applied to all the states, even where no immediate effect was expected. Accordingly, in 1868, Georgia's new pro-Amendment governor answered opponents. The Amendment was "applicable to all the States," so "no one State can reasonably object to it on the ground of inequality."[153]

The suggestion, by these supporters and opponents, was that New York, Massachusetts, and many other loyal states had not adopted laws in violation of the

Amendment's principles. Unlike southern and some western states, these states had no need to "conform" their laws to these fundamental principles, for the states had so conformed from the beginning.[154] Such reassurances presupposed that Section 1 had a determinate form.

Moreover, while ratification was pending, Congress effectively certified seven states' constitutions as fully consistent with the Amendment. By the Reconstruction Acts of 1867, Congress mandated that the former rebel states ratify the Amendment and change its "constitution"—but not its "laws"—to be "in conformity with the Constitution of the United States in all respects."[155] These new constitutions had extensive provisions that could, like all laws, be challenged as unfair or unreasonable on countless grounds.[156] But Congress readmitted these states with these constitutions, and thereby indicated that none of these provisions violated the defined *forms* of the Amendment's prohibitions.

An Anti-Kritocratic Settlement

Finally, the Amendment's determinacy was essential to its central purpose: to provide a *settlement*. Missouri's legislature, in its formal ratification resolution, certified the Amendment as a "just and proper" basis for the "settlement of the issues growing out of the late rebellion."[157] The governors of New Jersey, New York, and Louisiana each formally recommended Section 1 as a "settlement."[158] Mississippi's unseated Senator-elect, James Alcorn, told his state's legislature that Section 1 would "finally . . . settle" the question of black citizenship that had been in dispute since the Missouri crisis.[159]

Republicans crafted this securitarian settlement because they were afraid. Theirs was the politics of fear, not hope. They meant not to empower but to restrain.

Their main fear was government by judiciary—*kritocracy*—which had proven so disastrous to the Union, and still threatened the Republic. To be sure, these securitarians were afraid of the unreconstructed southern white governments that were manifestly hostile to black citizenship. And they feared future congressional majorities. Representative Stevens, Broomall, and Garfield all said that the purpose of Section 1 was to place the Civil Rights Act beyond repeal by a mere congressional majority, and thus "above the reach of political strife."[160] Stevens identified the risk: "the first time that the South with their copperhead allies obtain the command of Congress [the Act] will be repealed."[161] Soon, he believed, Congress would be "flooded with rebels and rebel sympathizers" (that is, southern and northern Democrats, respectively).[162]

But even more so, these fundamentalists feared *present* as well as future judicial majorities. After all, Section 1 was necessary chiefly because the judiciary had distorted the Constitution. As to the Citizenship Clause, the Supreme Court's *Dred Scott* majority was the main villain. As Senator Yates declared in the debates, the Amendment would be "a guarantee which protects us from future judicial tyranny such as we have experienced under the decisions of the Supreme Court."[163]

But the courts were also partly responsible for the distortion of the Privileges or Immunities Clause. Senator Luke Poland, in recommending the provision, lamented the misconstruction of Article IV's Privileges and Immunities Clause:

> [The Clause] secures nothing beyond what was intended by the original provision in the Constitution, that "the citizens of each State shall be entitled to all privileges and immunities of citizens in the several States." But the radical difference in the social systems of the several States, and the great extent to which the doctrine of State rights or State sovereignty was carried, induced mainly, as I believe, by and for the protection of the peculiar system of the South, led to a practical repudiation of the existing provision on this subject.[164]

As James Wilson had remarked in the House (with reference to the closely related Civil Rights Act), federal enforcement of the privileges and immunities of citizenship would be wholly unnecessary if, "above all," state officials (including, presumably, state judges) would set aside the crabbed interpretation whereby Article IV protected only visitors and only against interstate discrimination, but instead accepted and enforced the better "doctrine" whereby certain rights belong to citizens as such, and "that a citizen does not surrender these rights because he may happen to be a citizen of the State which would deprive him of them."[165]

Even though many Republican judges were on the federal and state bench, the courts still menaced the rights of African Americans. By late May 1866, the Civil Rights Act had already been struck down by several southern judges, and many officials predicted, cheerfully or fretfully, that the present majority of the Supreme Court would do the same.[166] Of its ten seats, only three were occupied by reliable friends of the civil rights of African Americans: (Republicans Chase, Swayne, and Miller). Four hostile votes were certain from the four pre-Lincoln appointees: the three veterans of the infamous *Dred Scott* majority (Wayne, Nelson, and Grier) and their fellow traveler (Buchanan's appointee, Clifford).[167] A probable fifth or even sixth hostile vote could be reasonably expected from two more "moderate" Lincoln appointees: either the fifth Democrat on the Court, Stephen Field, or the fourth Republican, David Davis.[168] And another hostile vote was nearly certain from Henry Stanbery, Johnson's nominee to fill the vacant tenth seat. His nomination, one Republican alleged, was an "almost successful effort to pack the Supreme Court with judges who will declare the Civil Rights Bill unconstitutional."[169] The effort was only "almost successful," for at the close of the session in July, Congress reduced the number of permanent seats from ten to seven, so as to prevent Johnson from appointing any new justice, whether by Senate confirmation or by recess appointment.[170]

Even without Stanbery's tenth vote, the nine-member Court probably retained a majority hostile to Republicans' agenda. In October 1866, Senator Poland urged the Vermont legislature to ratify the Amendment, in part because the Civil Rights Act remained vulnerable to invalidation; there were still four members that had "concurred in that terrible Dred Scott decision."[171] The Amendment was thus necessary, he elaborated, to keep civil rights "*above all courts, Supreme or otherwise*."[172]

A few months later, Republican fears seemed confirmed when the Court invalidated two Republican policies in two sharply divided decisions where the majority consisted of the four pro-*Dred Scott* judges and one of Lincoln's appointees. In December, the

Court repudiated military tribunals, with Justice Davis providing the decisive vote and majority opinion;[173] and a month later, it was Justice Field who performed the same office in the Court's rejection of test oaths.[174]

As a result, animosity toward the Court's majority featured prominently in the subsequent ratification discussion.[175] Indiana's governor warned that the Civil Rights Act now "is liable to repeal or destruction at the hands of the Supreme Court."[176] Massachusetts's governor, likewise, said that civil rights needed constitutional reaffirmation, that is, "in the most solemn form, to the end that neither the Executive *nor the judicial power*, nor the local authorities, may render inoperative the deliberate verdict of the people."[177]

The general opinion confirmed the adversity between the Court and the Amendment. In Pennsylvania, the governor explained that Section 1 concerned "vital principles" that had "never seriously doubted anywhere," but that their reaffirmation was necessary because of the "insane crusade in favor of slavery," culminating in what was merely "*called* the decision . . . in the *Dred Scott* case."[178] In the legislature, one member reported the fear that the Supreme Court would declare the Amendment itself invalid.[179] One legislator met that concern with a threat: If these "five or six old gentlemen in black gown and powdered wigs" should attempt "to wrest from us the dearly earned fruits of this great war . . . they will all be impeached if necessary."[180] The "five or six" he had in mind were almost certainly the four pre-Lincoln appointees, the other Democrat Stephen Field, and the moderate Republican Davis.

In Congress, Bingham went further and threatened to neuter if not abolish the whole Supreme Court by constitutional amendment. If that tribunal "usurps power" so as to "defy a free people's will," Congress could strip the Court of its appellate jurisdiction and, if necessary, pass another constitutional amendment that would "defy judicial usurpation by annihilating the usurpers in the abolition of the tribunal itself."[181]

Opponents likewise treated the Court and the Amendment as adversaries. One Pennsylvania opponent defended the Court as the guardian of the Constitution, on whom we should rely "with perfect security."[182] Another remarked, with reference to the recent decisions, "[t]he Supreme Court has said that the Democratic party was right" and had justly "pronounced judgment" against the Republicans.[183] Likewise in the Wisconsin legislature, one opponent celebrated the Court as "the highest judicial tribunal of the government" and chief guardian "of the rights of states and of individuals."[184]

In any case, neither supporters nor opponents believed that the Amendment would generally *augment* the power of the Supreme Court. In Congress, there was, as Mary Karlynn Hinman found in her study, "no discussion of an extension of [such power] at any time in the debates."[185] My own review of the broader evidence, from the states and among the people at large, finds that no supporter *ever* said or suggested that the Amendment would empower the judiciary to discover new rights or discard old ones. The proponents of the Amendment had no such faith in the courts, still less the Supreme Court, and adopted the Amendment's first section precisely to correct and restrain that perverse tribunal.

Evidence of Indeterminacy

The chief evidence of indeterminacy comes from the claims of opponents. As we noted in the first chapter, some prominent officials did indeed say or suggest that Section 1 and Section 5 could involve a great deal of ambiguity. And ambiguity could imply indeterminacy.

At the same time, many opponents, while tacitly acknowledging the *coherence* of the Amendment, insisted that its proper interpretation would involve *indeterminate* applications. Some found such indeterminacy in the meaning of Section 1 itself. Representative Rogers, a member of the Joint Committee, contended "that the first section . . . is the most dangerous to liberty," for "all the rights we have under the laws of the country are embraced under the definition of privileges and immunities" and that if adopted, the Amendment would "prevent any State from refusing to allow anything to anybody embraced under this term of privileges and immunities."[186]

But this conclusion, he acknowledged, was "different to what some others have come,"[187] including, as we have noted, his own Democratic colleagues on the Committee. They said nothing against Section 1 in their joint report.[188] If anything, many opponents considered Section 1 to be innocuous. When President Johnson and various southern officials drafted an alternative "compromise" amendment in early 1867, they chose, by the most official account of their proposal, to retain Section 1 verbatim; it was the only section of the Amendment that the proffered substitute left untouched. In another version, there was some alteration to the Privileges or Immunities Clause.[189]

Section 5 was a different matter. The Johnsonite compromise omitted it.[190] As I noted in the first chapter, many opponents worried that Congress's power "to enforce, by appropriate legislation" would involve a broad power to define the rights of Section 1—including the power to give, and to take away. On the last day of debate in Congress, one opponent charged that Section 5 "transfers all powers from the State governments over the citizens of a State to Congress."[191] In some states, opponents charged that Congress may "declare" or "choose to grant,"[192] any right, and conversely, every right could be similarly "disposed of, destroyed, or abrogated," at Congress's discretion.[193] And as for what is "appropriate," Congress would claim and would provide this determination—a determination governed by the "prejudices and passions of the hour."[194]

Some opponents bolstered this objection by the analogy to Section 2 of the Thirteenth Amendment. Before formal debate had begun in the House, Maryland's Phelps initially alleged that a broad reading of Section 5 would result from the precedent set by Congress's outlandish reading of section 2 of the Thirteenth Amendment: that Congress's antislavery power was the basis for the Civil Rights Act.[195] In the Senate, Indiana's Thomas Hendricks said the same.[196] Upon transmitting the proposal, Maryland's governor renewed the charge.[197] Opponents in the Indiana and Pennsylvania legislatures, though repudiating this misconstruction, alleged that radicals would indulge in the same as to the Fourteenth Amendment.[198]

But even this objection could not be said to reflect a general consensus, even among opponents.[199] Some seemed unconcerned. Just as the Committee's minority took no pains to mention Section 5,[200] Representative Benjamin Boyer, in a lengthy speech, had only this to say: "Upon this [section], it will not be necessary to remark."[201] Early in the debates, Republican George Miller (R-Pa) said that, as far as he was aware, Section 5 was not "contested by any gentlemen in this House."[202] The objection was far more prominent during the ratification debates.

In any case, this interpretation of Section 5 certainly had no part in the consensus of *supporters*. No congressional supporter said or suggested, let alone hoped, that Section 5 would empower Congress to redefine the rights set forth in Section 1. The goal was to *determine* certain rights. Congressional supporters feared future Democratic congressional majorities almost as much as current Democratic judicial majorities.

In the states, only one pro-Amendment official indicated that Congress's enforcement power could include the redefinition of rights. Missouri's governor Thomas Fletcher told his legislature that Section 1 "prevents a State from depriving any citizen of the United States of any of the rights *conferred on him by the laws of Congress*, and secures to all persons equality of protection in life, liberty and property, under the laws of the State."[203] As Reagan's Justice Department opined, Fletcher's remark is evidence that a supporter understood Congress to have power to redefine the privileges and immunities of citizens of the United States.[204] It's also, I believe, the *only* such evidence. In a subsequent chapter, I will speculate as to why Fletcher offered such an idiosyncratic reading, so at odds with the prevailing understanding of supporters, both in Congress and the states.

But among jurists today, it is not Governor Fletcher's comment that has provided the chief evidence of indeterminacy. Rather, that distinction belongs to Jacob Howard's remark that the Amendment "abolishes all class legislation."[205] For decades now, that comment has long seemed promising as a sound basis for a federal power—congressional and even *judicial*—to invalidate any and all state laws that federal officials might deem unreasonable or otherwise unjust.[206]

The comment was indeed noteworthy. As reported in the *Congressional Globe*, it occurred during Howard's speech to inaugurate debate in the Senate. After a lengthy explanation of the Privileges or Immunities Clause, he then addressed the rest of Section 1:

> The last two clauses of the first section of the amendment disable a State from depriving not merely a citizen of the United States, but any person, whoever he may be, of life, liberty, or property without due process of law, or from denying to him the equal protection of the laws of the State. *This abolishes all class legislation in the States* and does away with the injustice of subjecting one caste of persons to a code not applicable to another. It prohibits the hanging of a black man for a crime for which the white man is not to be hanged. It protects the black man in his fundamental rights as a citizen with the same shield which it throws over the white man.[207]

From this remark, many jurists have inferred, as Robert Bork said in his confirmation hearings, that the Amendment prohibits any "distinction . . . between persons" that is not "a reasonable way to accomplish a valid legislative purpose."[208] That is to say, Bork and others have taken Howard to mean that the Amendment would bar all "arbitrary and irrational" legislative classifications of persons.[209]

Now, as Andrew Hyman has noted,[210] this remark may have never been uttered at all. This part of Howard's speech, though recorded in the *Globe*, was probably omitted from his actual address. Though several newspapers presented Howard's speech via an apparent transcription and other summaries or paraphrases, none included this remark.[211]

On the other hand, the remark was important enough to have appeared in Howard's prepared notes,[212] as well as the eventual record of the *Congressional Globe*.[213] Moreover, the remark was typical of what several other supporters had advocated: the Amendment was necessary to ensure equality for all "classes" of citizens.[214] The Joint Committee itself would express the hope that, someday, "all classes of citizens" might enjoy "equal rights and privileges."[215]

Nonetheless, Judge Bork and others have misunderstood the import of Howard's remark. Carefully examined, it provided not a *definition* of one or more of the discrete prohibitions of Section 1, but merely a *hyperbolic prediction* of the effect of all those prohibitions combined.

Let us review the parts of the statement. First, the subject, "This," seemed to refer to the entire prohibitory sentence, rather than to the Due Process and/or Equal Protection Clauses. To be sure, as printed in the *Globe*, it appears in the same paragraph that seems devoted to those latter provisions.[216] Howard's prepared notes, however, suggest a different division. "This" appears on a separate page and in its own separate paragraph; the sentence begins what appears to be a litany of comments referring to Section 1, as a whole, including his explanation that the right of voting is not one of the "privileges" guaranteed.[217]

Further, Howard proceeded to explain that the Amendment would secure not just the rights of persons (as secured by due process and equal protection) but the equal citizenship of black and white Americans: what he called the black man's "fundamental rights as a citizen," and protecting the citizens of the United States against caste legislation. As Christopher Green has perceived, the "re-entry of the rights of citizens into the discussion, immediately after Howard had distinguished the rights of persons from the rights of citizens, muddies the reference" such that the "antecedent" to "This" seems to be the entire sentence,, all three of the Section 1's prohibitions "as a whole."[218]

Second, the verb "abolishes" is not a legal term. By its terms, Section 1 does not abolish, but merely prohibits. Prohibitory laws do not, strictly speaking, abolish anything. Abolition may be a prohibition's aspiration—but rarely, perhaps never, fully achieved.

Third, the direct object, "class legislation," provided no legal definition but was only a nebulous pejorative. "Class legislation" was, in democratic America, a "harsh epithet," as one jurist said.[219] Nobody favored "class legislation"; everybody opposed it. The accusation thereof was common, applied indiscriminately, so to speak, to all sorts of discriminations.[220] Federal tax-exempt bonds, for instance, were denounced as "class legislation in its *most odious form*."[221] Many other examples of such rhetoric, as to many other legal distinctions, can be found in judicial reports.[222]

Opponents of Republican policies were not shy in using the same rhetoric. Justice Daniel, in *Dred Scott*, had denounced antislavery laws as "class" discrimination.[223] The Second Freedmen's Bureau Bill and the Civil Rights Act were likewise denounced as favoring a "class."[224] Some opponents of the Fourteenth Amendment said its Section 5 would lead to further class legislation: "We may find Congress conferring 'privileges and immunities' on one class to the exclusion of another class;"[225] laws will be passed "for the benefit of one class against the other."[226]

So all-encompassing was the term that Howard simply could not have meant the Amendment would prohibit "all class legislation." In the next paragraph, Howard made abundantly clear that Section 1 would not abolish one form of racially based class discrimination: "the first section of the proposed amendment does not give to either of these classes the right of voting."[227] But as this comment suggested—and as the Committee would indicate in its formal report—such racial discrimination was indeed unjust "class" legislation.[228]

The rest of Howard's sentence, the second part of the predicate, provides the discipline to his remark, by specification: "This abolishes all class legislation, *and* does away with the injustice of *subjecting one caste of persons to a code not applicable to another*." What is the import of "and"? The conjunction cannot mean "in addition," for caste legislation *was* a kind of class legislation: the primary meaning of "caste," according to Webster's dictionary, was "hereditary class."[229] Perhaps "and" meant only "for example." But the best reading is that "and" introduces a specification of the former, so the passage reads, "This abolishes all class legislation in the state *by* doing away with the injustice of subjecting one caste of persons to a code not applicable to another." Now the passage makes sense, for the Amendment would indeed prohibit arguably *the only* extant hereditary ("caste") codes in the United States: those state laws that imposed criminal liability on a racially discriminatory basis, and not the laws (though undeniably "class legislation") that *withheld* political privileges on such a basis.

Finally, by the modifier "in the States," rather than "by the states," Howard further indicated he was not *defining* the prohibitions of Section 1. Section 1 prohibits only laws made and enforced *by* the states. Laws made and enforced *in* the states by federal authorities plainly do not come with the legal meaning of Section 1. Howard could not have meant that, by its express terms, the Amendment would authorize judges to invalidate "all class legislation"—including any federal "class" law—such as, by some accounts, the Civil Rights Act itself.

Therefore, by saying "This abolishes class legislation in the States," Howard was not providing a definition, but instead a bold prediction that by prohibiting the imposition of hereditary criminal or civil liabilities on citizens, this Amendment would eradicate all extant unfair classifications in the states.[230] Such hyperbole, born of tunnel vision, was (and is) common in politics. For instance, in a campaign speech, one Committee member, Senator George Williams, likewise declared that by the Amendment, Congress aimed "to root out every ordinance of Government that works inequality or injustice among men."[231]

The Report of the Joint Committee, signed by Howard, likewise indulged in such hyperbole as to "class" injustice. The Committee's initial representation-reduction proposal specifically targeted only *racial* discrimination in state suffrage laws—requiring reduction "whenever the elective franchise shall be denied or abridged . . . on account of race or color."[232] The Committee said that this measure would, little by little, tend to extend the suffrage to "all classes of citizens."[233] The implication, then, was that once racial discrimination ended, so would *all* class legislation. In the passion of reform, it seems, racial discrimination seemed the sole "class discrimination" worth mentioning; to abolish race discrimination was to abolish all significant class injustice.

A similar tunnel vision probably moved Howard to similar hyperbole: by prohibiting states from including racial and other "caste" discrimination in their civil criminal codes, Section 1 meant the abolition of *all* the "class" legislation extant in the United States. It would be the Amendment to end all amendments!

But such dreams of injustice eradication were not *definitions* of the legal meaning of the Amendment or any part thereof. Howard's hyperbolic rhetoric, likewise, was not a legal definition.

Howard simply could not have meant that the Amendment's defined terms prohibited all unreasonable classifications—that the Amendment would thereby authorize Congress and even federal judges to roam among the states in an endless search of monsters of "animus" or "class legislation" to destroy. If that was his meaning, he thus read the Amendment to invite the Congress (with a future Democratic majority), or the Supreme Court (with its current Democratic majority) to repeal or invalidate any state or even federal law that Democratic officials might identify as "class legislation." If so, he was decidedly alone among supporters of the Amendment, and to my knowledge, never repeated it again. Such a reading would have been utterly inconsistent with (1) the original and fundamentalist meaning of Section 1, (2) the Ninth Amendment and other prevailing rules requiring strict construction of prohibitions on the states, (3) the official reassurances that the measure would have *no effect* on many states' laws, and (4) the decidedly securitarian and anti-kritocratic motives of the Amendment's authors.

In sum, the evidence is overwhelming. We must agree with Earl Maltz: the prohibitions of Section 1 were "perceived as guaranteeing a relatively small set of rights which, though somewhat unclear at the margins, was nonetheless fixed for all times in 1866."[234] Indeed, they were fixed even earlier; they were as old as the Republic.

Civil Rights

"Civil" Rights and the Constitutional Text

According to the Committee, the fundamental rights and privileges were *civil*. By its etymology and usual definition, *civil* rights would seem to refer to those that belong to individuals in the *city* or *society*.[235] Consequently, they are not, strictly speaking, rights of some state of nature—however they may correlate with natural rights as auxiliaries, substitutes, or otherwise.[236]

All the guarantees of Section 1 would seem to thus qualify as "civil" rights. The right to the protection and process of the "law" is a right to a civic benefit.[237] To be sure, these rights are auxiliaries to natural human rights of "life, liberty, [and] property" that belong to all persons, and not just citizens; consequently, the Amendment secures these rights for not just citizens but also persons, as I'll elaborate in the next chapter. Still, the beneficiaries are only that subset of humanity that happens to be under or within the jurisdiction of the states. That is to say, the Due Process and Equal Protection Clauses secure civil rights to persons as human beings *under* a particular civil society.

Equally "civil" is the Privileges or Immunities Clause: it protects the rights of *citizens*, who are not merely *subjects* but *members* of our civil society—the United States. Indeed, "civil" and "citizen" are close cognates; the very word "civil" is derivative of *civis*, the Latin noun for "citizen."[238] Of course the rights of citizenship are "civil" rights.

"Civil" Rights and the Whole Report

In one respect, the Report provides a very important qualification of the term "civil." By many accounts, the word was broad enough to include "political" rights, or more specifically, the right to participate directly in the decisional authority of the community—including authority to serve as voters, jurors, and other public officials.[239] But the Committee clearly distinguished "civil" from "political" rights, in discussing both the rights forfeited by the rebels[240] and those owed to the former slaves.[241]

In particular, the authors of the report hoped to protect the freedmen's "rights, *civil and political*." [242] Still, they declined to incorporate political rights into the Amendment except indirectly under Section 2, and for this express reason: The loyal states would not "consent to surrender a power they had always exercised"—the power to grant or withhold the suffrage.[243] Acquiescing to this state jealousy, the Committee modestly sought to extend political rights via Section 2's representation-reduction measure: "Such a provision would be in its nature gentle and persuasive, and would lead" the Committee hoped, "at no distant day, to an equal participation of all, without distinction, in *all* the rights and privileges of citizenship."[244] The Amendment's first section *determined* only some of these privileges of citizenship, the *civil* privileges, while the second section *promoted*, but did not *determine*, the *political* privileges of citizenship.

As the Committee indicated, the *civil* rights of citizenship were inherent in citizenship—they were to be merely *secured* by law. In sharp contrast, the *political* rights of citizenship were something that the states "granted" by law.[245]

This distinction, between civil rights to be secured and political rights to be granted, is vital to understanding the meaning of Section 1.

The Committee's minority members acknowledged this distinction as well, but attributed the decision to Republicans' fear of the voters. In their report, the minority observed that "the right is not directly asserted of granting suffrage to the negro"—and for "reasons so obvious that the dullest may discover them." *viz.*, such a measure "would be [so] obnoxious to most of the northern and western States . . . that their consent was not to be anticipated." [246] Instead, the minority taunted, the majority had shyly proposed Section 2 to impose black suffrage covertly and *indirectly*—by forcing the southern states to either "diminish their representation in Congress and of course in the electoral college or to admit to the right of suffrage their colored males."[247]

One question that the Report leaves unanswered is whether Section 1 embraced each and *every* civil right, or only determined *some* civil rights. The answer is probably the latter: that the Amendment secured only those civil rights that justly belonged to all persons and all citizens across the Republic. The Amendment concerned only those civil rights for which nationwide determination was proper because they were already recognized or guaranteed nationally, whether in our Declaration, the general common law, the state constitutions, the federal Constitution, or otherwise.

"Civil" Rights and the Prior Official Understanding

In this respect, the Committee's unanimous interpretation of Section 1 seems consistent with the pre-Amendment meaning of its terms. As to equal protection, it was never said to embrace political rights. In this sense, the equal protection of the laws was thus emphatically not a "pledge of protection by equal [political] laws."[248] Nor, it seems, is there any evidence that anyone deemed a denial of suffrage or other political rights a deprivation of life, liberty, or property so as to require "due process of law."

This distinction is fairly seen, for instance, in the opinions of the Supreme Court in two companion cases, *Cummings v. Missouri* and *Ex Parte Garland*, decided while the Amendment was pending. [249] There, the Court majority acknowledged that a disqualification from "political" and even some "civil rights" was not necessarily a "deprivation of life, liberty, or property" (and thus beyond the scope of the Due Process Clause). But a majority still held that such disqualification constituted a "punishment" and thus implicated Article I's bar to bills of attainder and ex post facto laws.[250]

As to the Privileges or Immunities Clause, the matter was more subtle. By general usage, the "privileges of citizenship" did, indeed, include political as well as civil rights.[251] The Committee itself had said the same; they hoped that Section 2 would, in time, lead to African Americans' enjoyment of "all the rights and privileges of citizenship," including access to the "ballot-box."[252] The "rights and privileges of citizenship," then, would seem to include the political rights of citizenship. The reading was consistent with the tradition: the First Continental Congress declared, that among their "the rights, liberties, and immunities" as "free and natural-born subjects" were not only such civil rights as the "privilege of being tried by their peers of the vicinage," but also the "right in the people to participate in their legislative council" via elected "representatives."[253]

Prior to the Amendment, the place of political rights among the "privileges and immunities of citizens," as set forth in Article IV, had occasioned significant disagreement. The sheer text of Article IV guaranteed "*all*" not *some* of these privileges, without qualification. Yet at the same time, all jurists seemingly agreed that Article IV could not, and thus did not, admit all sojourners immediately to the voting rights of citizens. The effect would destroy the republican character of the governments of the several states.

Jurists addressed this challenge in various ways. Some, like Delaware's Chancellor Nicholas Ridgely, sharply bifurcated the civil and political privileges of citizenship and declared that the Privileges and Immunities Clause immediately secured to citizens "all the civil rights of citizenship," but the "political rights" only after the citizens had satisfied the locally established "residence and other qualifications."[254] A few years later in *Corfield*, Justice Bushrod Washington drew the same distinction but suggested some doubt: citizens were simply entitled to the civil rights of travel, commerce, and so forth, and only *perhaps* to political rights, "as regulated and established by the laws and constitution" of the respective states.[255] Most critically, Washington's formulation acknowledged that unlike civil rights, the *political* rights of citizenship were "established" by state law.

But other jurists resolved the difficulty by categorically and entirely excluding political rights from these "privileges and immunities." In the first reported case on the clause, Maryland's Supreme Court had said "that a particular and limited operation is to be given to these words, and not a full and comprehensive one," such that the Clause in no way encompassed the "right of election, the right of holding offices, the right of being elected."[256] In *Dred Scott*, the Court majority likewise said that Article IV "gives [citizens] no political rights in the State, as to voting or holding office, or in any other respect."[257] "All" must be construed to mean "some."

Important for our purposes, some of these latter jurists preferred the formula: the privileges of "U.S." citizenship. The term provided an interpretive gloss that wholly excluded political rights. The phrase "of the United States" referred not to a federal source but nationwide enjoyment; that is, those rights to which all citizens were immediately entitled throughout the Union, and thus excluded the rights that a state could reserve to only local citizens.[258]

This formula had special prominence in the April debates of the Thirty-Ninth Congress, and in the Indiana case of *Browning v. Barnes*, decided at the same time.[259] Its chief proponents were John Bingham and other Ohioans—whose high court, twenty years earlier, had concluded that "certainly" these "rights of U.S. citizenship," as secured by Article IV, did not include "political rights," for the states reserve such rights only for some citizens, and have the exclusive authority to make such determinations.[260]

The circumstantial evidence is thus very strong: the Committee added the qualifier "of the United States," at least in part, to choose a formula that many jurists, including Bingham himself, had already used as a way of resolving the textual ambiguity as to interstate enjoyment of political as well as civil rights. The formula categorically excluded the political privileges of citizenship from the scope of Article IV—for these rights a state may reserve to its own residents.

The formula, however, now served a new purpose. Each state would retain the authority to reserve the suffrage not only to its own citizens, but *only to some* of these, even on the controversial basis of race.

Nonetheless, we must note some ambiguity in this formula. Before the Civil War, many had used this same language in a way that encompassed political rights. The Seneca Falls Convention demanded American women's "immediate admission to all the rights and privileges which belong to them as citizens of these United States"; the Convention understood these rights to include, above all, the "inalienable right to the elective franchise."[261] Similarly, the "rights, advantages and immunities of citizens of the United States," as extended by treaty to new citizens in the Louisiana Territory, were initially deemed to include the eventual *political* right of congressional representation (but subsequently the Supreme Court said otherwise).[262]

Nonetheless, as used to construe Article IV's Privileges and Immunities Clause, the formula "privileges and immunities of citizens *of the United States*" had usually served to exclude categorically the political rights of citizenship from all "privileges and immunities." And it was Article IV, not the citizenship provisions of the territorial treaties, nor the Seneca Falls Declaration, that was on the mind of those adopting the Privileges or Immunities Clause.[263]

"Civil" Rights and the Contemporaneous Official Understanding

Outside the Committee, the vast majority of officials likewise understood that Section 1 would secure civil but not political rights. Virtually all supporters said so; so did the best-informed opponents.[264]

Stevens, in introducing the Amendment, explained that Section 1 secured the same rights as those of the "civil rights bill," while Section 2, he lamented, "allows the States to discriminate" as to voting rights. Several other congressional supporters regretfully acquiesced to the failure to include political rights.[265] Bingham said emphatically that, as Section 2 indicates, the Amendment leaves the regulation of the suffrage with the state governments.[266] Howard, in his preliminary speech, likewise explained that Section 1 did not give "the right of voting."[267]

In the states, supporters again said that Section 1 would encompass civil, but not political rights. In the few New England states where the vote was available to non-whites, governors tended to report the result with lament. Vermont's governor said his state's citizens would have preferred an amendment that included "equal civil and political rights,"[268] and Maine's governor admitted that the Amendment was "imperfect" in failing to ensure political equality.[269] Elsewhere governors tended to report the matter without negative commentary: Section 1, they said, secured "civil rights," "equal civil rights," or "civil equality before the law,"[270] and "left with the states" the whole "power over the question of suffrage."[271]

To my knowledge, among official *supporters*, there was only one exception to this consensus—a lone supporter in the unreconstructed North Carolina legislature—who said that Section 1 granted the suffrage but reassured his colleagues that Section 2 took it away.[272] But otherwise, in 1866, at least, *all* official supporters, as the New York Times reported, "expressly admitted or tacitly assented to the admission that [the Amendment] did not touch the suffrage, or any other political right or franchise, in the slightest degree."[273]

For the most part, congressional opponents, along with the Committee minority, acknowledged that the Amendment would only indirectly promote black suffrage.[274] What some supporters lamented, these opponents ridiculed. Representative Eldridge mocked Republicans for their cowardice: the proposal "gives up universal suffrage."[275] Rogers taunted that the Committee majority had relinquished black suffrage out of "fear of not being able to deceive the people."[276]

But a few congressional opponents saw black suffrage lurking in Sections 5 and even still in Section 1. Some, as we've discussed, thought Section 5 would (or might) empower Congress to impose black suffrage.[277] As to Section 1, Maryland's Charles Phelps initially worried that "privileges" *might* be held to include political rights: "'[p]rivileges and immunities' [is] a much broader and more comprehensive term, [than civil rights] and may, by definition, include suffrage, jury duty, and eligibility to office."[278] Phelps's concern was perhaps temporary; he spoke before formal debate began, and before Republicans repeatedly explained that Section 1 secured only civil rights. For the most part, congressional opponents expressly or tacitly acknowledged that Section 1 would not, by its own force, impose black suffrage.

In sharp contrast, opponents in the states were divided. Some officials, such as the governors of Maryland and Delaware, like the Committee minority, charged that Republicans were trying, indirectly and surreptitiously, via Section 2, to impose black suffrage against the wishes of white citizens.[279] But many other opponents, as we saw, objected that Section 1 alone would compel the states to extend the suffrage to African Americans,[280] while others said Section 1 *might* be so construed.[281]

In this regard, Indiana's Republican lieutenant governor noted the sharp contrast between opponents on the Committee and those in his state:

> I beg leave to observe that it is not a little remarkable that Hon. Reverdy Johnson, the distinguished Senator from Maryland, who stands second to no man as a lawyer in the United States, did not make the discovery [that Indiana opponents] are so busily engaged in promulgating among the people. Senator Johnson made the Minority Report from the Joint Committee on Reconstruction, and . . . urging, as he does in that minority report, every possible objection that he could to the adoption of the amendment, it is quite wonderful that if so grave an objection as that it conferred negro suffrage really existed, he never once alluded to it.[282]

One may well speculate as to the reason for this sharp divide. The Committee's minority did not make the objection probably because, as participants in the initial drafting and debate, they well understood the terms of the compromise, and knew that supporters, including Stevens, had reluctantly abandoned blacks' political rights by assenting to secure only the civil privileges of citizenship. Some congressional opponents outside the Committee were somewhat less aware and could find black suffrage lurking in section 5. But in the states, opponents did not have the benefit of these discussions, and could plausibly argue that even Section 1, by itself, would mean the imposition of black suffrage on the states. Their misunderstanding, in turn, reflected the ambiguity in the antebellum uses of the phrase, "privileges and immunities of citizens of the United States."

In any case, the overwhelming preponderance of the evidence indicates that pro-Amendment officials in Congress and the states shared the formal conclusion of the Committee: Section 1 determined only civil, but not political rights. Virtually all supporters said so, as did most opponents, including the best-informed opponents.[283]

Plurality of "Rights" and "Privileges"

By explaining that Section 1 would "determine" various civil "rights" and civil "privileges," the Committee thereby affirmed that both these rights and these privileges were plural. Section 1 was not reducible to one fundamental "right," or one fundamental "privilege," whether equality or otherwise.[284]

Plurality and the Constitutional Text

At first glance, the Committee's reading seems thoroughly consistent with the plain terms of Section 1. The Privileges or Immunities Clause determines, against negation, at least four civil privileges (two or more "privileges" and two or more "immunities"). The Due Process and Equal Protection Clause secures against negation at least two other rights (legal "process" and "protection"). The determinate "rights and privileges," then, are at least six in number.

At the same time, the Committee's concise explanation was also politically prudent. The formula, no doubt, served as a gesture to the many American petitioners who had proposed to constitutionally outlaw any racial discrimination as to "civil rights and privileges."[285]

But there is an apparent incongruity between the Committee's text and the Committee's explanation thereof. The problem is threefold. First, as drafted, Section 1 is said to include not two clauses, but *three*: what we call the Privileges or Immunities, Due Process, and Equal Protection Clauses. Second, the Privileges or Immunities Clause mentions not only "privileges" but also "immunities." Third, Section 1 mentions "privileges" first, and then the other rights. Hence, to explicate the text, the Committee seemingly should have written, not "civil rights and privileges" but "civil privileges and immunities, process, and protection."

But as to the first problem, what we call three "clauses" actually consists of two independent clauses: the Privileges or Immunities Clause and then a second clause—which has a compound predicate, prohibiting certain deprivation and certain denial. We might call this the "Due Process-Equal Protection Clause." The first clause protects the rights of citizenship, the second the rights of personhood. Thus, it was appropriate for the Committee to characterize this two-clause sentence of Section 1 as securing two bundles: "rights" and "privileges."[286] I will elaborate on this point in the next chapter, devoted to the singular Due Process-Equal Protection Clause.

As to the second objection, the word "privileges" was actually broad enough to include "immunities," for an immunity is a species of privilege:[287] an immunity is that sort of privilege that exists only as an exemption from some burden.[288] As William Crosskey observed, "'privileges,' . . . could have been used alone, since, in its ordinary legal sense, it comprehends 'immunities' as one type of 'privilege.'"[289] In a subsequent chapter, I will defend the drafters' choice to mention, despite this redundancy, both privileges and immunities, instead of the more succinct "privileges."[290]

As to the third objection, the sequence (first "rights" and then "privileges") is appropriate if one considers the priority of human personhood to citizenship, both epistemologically and ontologically.[291] Accordingly, the Committee identified a primary duty to secure the freedmen's rights "as free men and citizens" (in that order). For a similar reason, in an initial draft considered by the Committee, the life, liberty, and property of "all persons" came before the "immunities" to be secured to "citizens of the United States."[292] I will discuss this priority further in the next chapter.

But as I mentioned in the previous chapter, Bingham and then the Committee decided to reverse this order. The Committee, after instruction from the Senate, ostentatiously collated the Amendment's remedial provisions with pre-existing constitutional norms, which happened to appear in that order: first the citizenship rights of Article IV, and then the personhood rights of the Fifth Amendment.[293] The April version of this proposal, as Bingham explained, covered the same "subject matter." [294] In his main floor speeches, in both February and May, Bingham told the House that his proposal would merely secure the rights of citizenship and personhood already recognized in the Constitution, first Article IV, then Amendment V.[295] Therefore, the final version properly retained this textual sequence.

Plurality and the Whole Report

There is, however, another problem with the Report's explanation. Even if appropriate to the constitutional text, the phrase "civil rights and privileges" seems grossly disproportionate to the Committee's (and Congress's) own stated motivations. Every evil mentioned by the Committee's Report could be classified as inequality—(1) protection denied on the basis of heredity (race), geography (northerners), and/or opinion (Unionist), and (2) the imposition of civil *munia* (either by formal burdens, duties, or by unlawful selective prosecutions) on the basis of race or Unionist allegiance.[296] One could say, then, that the original *motive* of Section 1 consisted exclusively in securing equality—a freedom from these discriminations; the goal, the Committee summarized, was to compel the states to provide "*equal* rights and privileges" to "all classes of citizens," regardless of blood, soil, or creed.[297] Free blacks, northerners, and unionists would enjoy civil equality before the law.

Indeed, an initial draft of the measure was more targeted to this egalitarian purpose. Recall that on January 27, Bingham, on behalf of his subcommittee, proposed to empower Congress to secure to "all persons" "equal protection" (without any mention of due process) and to all "citizens of the United States" the "same immunities" (with no mention of any civil "privileges").[298] In effect, this initial formula was more tailored to the actual problems in the South: the unlawful failure to provide equal legal protection (to freedmen, northerners, and unionists) and the legal imposition of unequal burdens (*munia*) on the basis of race.[299] To remedy these inequalities, Congress was to have express power to ensure this equal protection and these equal *in-munia*. There was, then, no need to speak about the "privileges" of citizenship or "due process of law."

But by collating its constitutional remedies with existing constitutional mandates, the Committee chose language that was necessarily more expansive. Article IV, by its terms, protected not just "immunities" but also "privileges," and the Fifth Amendment's Due Process Clause involved much more than the duty of equal protection of the laws.

The Committee thus chose to rely on a constitutional text with a meaning disproportionate to the Committee's immediate motive. The Committee's *method* established a *meaning* broader than the Committee's *motive*. Constitutional depth required greater breadth.

Plurality and the Prior Official Understanding

By their pre-Amendment meaning, Section 1's terms were plural and could not be reduced to an egalitarian principle. To be sure, "equal protection of the laws" was exclusively egalitarian—and protected only a single sort of equality (the "protection of the laws" that must be "equal"). But by no definition was "due process of law" reducible to interpersonal equality.[300] By seemingly all accounts, that norm incorporated a plurality of procedural rights, including a forensic trial, with notice to the defendant, hearing, evidence, and so on.[301] And by the prevailing account, "due process of law" also required conformity with a plurality of well-established "usages and modes of proceeding" of the Anglo-American tradition.[302] Further, many of these procedural rights involved formal *inequality*, favoring the defendant over the plaintiff in a civil case or over the complaining witness in a criminal prosecution.

But what of the "privileges" and "immunities"? According to some scholars, these rights were created by state law, with the *only* right to be "determined" being some immunity against racial, interstate, and similarly unfair discrimination. As Harold Hyman phrased it, the Privileges or Immunities Clause simply "forbade unequal deprivations of the *broad, uncodified, vague mass* of civil-rights practices which a state professed to afford equally to the generality of its citizens," the "catalogue" of which could change with any "given moment," depending on the customary, statutory, and constitutional law of each state.[303] Despite its manifest tension with the naked text, which mentions both "privileges" and "immunities," this one-immunity reading has seemed necessary to reconcile Section 1 with the purportedly "orthodox" meaning of Article IV's "Privileges and Immunities Clause," by which the rights are "created . . . by state law" and citizens enjoy only an immunity against interstate discrimination.[304]

Still, as we discussed above at length, the pre-Amendment meaning of these terms, as predominantly understood, included a plurality of fundamental rights. To be sure, by a widespread (but not unanimous) interpretation, Article IV secured these anterior, fundamental rights (1) only to out-of-state citizens, and (2) only against interstate discrimination.[305] But these rights were deemed to belong to all American citizens, as such, anterior to the federal and state governments created by that same American citizenry. These rights were thus not *created* by the state governments.

Accordingly, in the three most prominent antebellum judicial interpretations of the Privileges and Immunities Clause, courts did not reduce these rights to an immunity against discrimination. In the first reported state case, *Campbell v. Morris*,[306] the most respected federal decision, *Corfield v. Coryell*,[307] and in the Supreme Court's own opinion in *Dred Scott v. Sanford*,[308] the courts provided a list of rights that included several substantive privileges along with a distinct immunity against discrimination. Across these opinions, one finds such affirmative privileges as the right to travel, to enjoy the writ of habeas corpus, to file suits of all kinds, to acquire, hold, and convey real and personal property, to meet and speak publicly, and to bear arms. A *separate* immunity, usually listed last, protected against unequal taxation and regulations.[309] Therefore, the fundamental "privileges and immunities" of citizenship were indeed plural, only *one* of which was an immunity against discrimination.

Plurality and the Contemporaneous Official Understanding

Nonetheless, even if the Committee and pre-Amendment authorities understood Section 1 to determine a plurality of rights and privileges, there seems, at first glance, abundant evidence that the makers of the Amendment disagreed, with most officials suggesting that Section 1's prohibitory sentence guaranteed only equality, but with some officials identifying a plurality of rights. This apparently conflicting evidence has given rise to some of the most persistent and acute disagreements among scholars.

Most officials summarized *all* of Section 1's prohibitory sentence as a guarantee of equality only. In his introductory speech to the House, Stevens suggested that Section 1, as a whole, would prohibit "partial and oppressive laws" so that "the law which operates upon one man shall operate equally upon all."[310] Other congressmen said much the same.[311] In his speech, Howard recapped his introductory exposition of Section 1, including his lengthy enumeration of "privileges, immunities, and rights," as a two-part egalitarian guarantee: "equal justice to all men and equal protection under the shield of law."[312] Among state governors, the most common summary of Section 1 reduced the provision to equality: for example, "equal rights and impartial liberty," "equal civil rights," "equality before the law," or some variation thereof.[313] And many prominent citizens, like Senator Trumbull, suggested or plainly asserted that Section 1 was coextensive with the simple antidiscrimination norm of the Civil Rights Act.[314]

Conversely, some officials indicated that the Amendment would secure a plurality of rights. Howard began his speech with a very long list of privileges and immunities, some of them from Justice Washington's list in *Corfield*, some from the first eight amendments. These "privileges and immunities," he said later, included "a great number of particulars."[315] Senators Henderson and Howe, of Missouri and Wisconsin, respectively, also set forth lists, though shorter.[316] Bingham, in his speech to the House in May, likewise alluded to a plurality of rights, mentioning the freedom of loyal speech and opinion, and the immunity against "cruel and unusual punishments."[317]

Representative Thayer also said that Section 1 would secure the "fundamental rights of citizenship."[318] In three states (Ohio, Oregon, and Louisiana) the governors each suggested that Section 1 would protect a plurality of rights.[319]

In sum, as to the official discussion of Section 1, as Reagan's Justice Department concluded, there was a "major" theme of nondiscrimination, and only a "minor" theme of certain substantive "minimum civil rights standards."[320] At the same time, no supporter or opponent seemed to notice any disharmony between these two themes. No one alleged or acknowledged any such discord. Was there some great tone-deafness such that no participant in the debates could hear the dissonance? Could they not see that some thought Section 1 protected only the singular right of equality, while others thought it secured a plurality of rights? Were they blockheads incapable of seeing the fundamental difference between "the one" and "the many"?

But a simple answer is available—"rolling around our feet."[321] The apparent discord was harmony not understood.

This entire problem can be resolved by recalling the distinction between original *motive* and original *meaning*. The original motive of Section 1's prohibitory sentence was reducible to "equality before the law"—to address two forms of unjust discrimination: (1) the injustice whereby citizens of the United States, on the basis of race, were subject by law to unequal taxes and other liabilities, including criminal liabilities (*munia*), and thus certain *in-munia* of citizenship were abridged, and (2) the injustice whereby certain human beings were, on the basis of race, creed (Unionist or Republican), or state of origin (northern states), denied the equal protection of the laws. The practical effect of Section 1 was "equal citizenship," and so forth, and mainly equal citizenship regardless of race. This *motive* provided the "major" theme.

But surely the Amendment's prohibitions, by their original meaning, extended beyond addressing these immediate evils. The chosen method was to rely on deeper and broader principles already present in the Constitution. Section 1, via the Due Process Clause, incorporated multiple procedural safeguards, and not just some singular rule of equality. Similarly, Section 1 would safeguard all the "privileges" of citizens of the United States, and not only the immunity against racial or similarly improper discrimination. The *meaning*, compelled by the *method*, provided the "minor" theme.

Perhaps the clearest and most succinct official summary of Section 1, as to both its limited egalitarian motive and its broader meaning, was provided by Massachusetts's governor, Alexander Bullock:

> The first section guarantees to all persons born or naturalized in the United States, and subject to its jurisdiction, the right of citizenship and of civil equality before the law; *and* it protects them from any State legislation which might abridge their privileges, or deprive them of life, liberty or property, without due legal process.[322]

By this account, Section 1 (1) defines "citizenship" (by the Citizenship Clause) and (2) guarantees "civil equality before the law," but *in addition* (3) prohibits the states from abridging the "privileges" of citizenship and (4) from depriving citizens of life, liberty, or property without due process of law.

Bullock, who had studied law under Joseph Story, chose his sparse words carefully.[323] After mentioning "civil equality before the law," he mentioned "privileges" as well as rights of due process, but conspicuously omitted the "immunities" of citizenship or "equal protection of the laws"—and for good reason: "civil equality before the law" already encompassed both those elements. He understood, as had Bingham's subcommittee in January 1866, that "equal protection" to persons, and "the same immunities" to "citizens of the United States" would guarantee the "civil equality before the law" so lacking at the time. But though exhausting the immediate motive for Section 1, such "civil equality" did not exhaust the meaning of either the "privileges" of citizenship or the requirements of "due process of law" already recognized in the Privileges and Immunities and Due Process Clauses.

Yet many officials, however, took no pains to identify any meaning broader than "equality." Such discussion was simply unnecessary. The sole motive and practical effect of Section 1 was to ensure equality before the law—chiefly to African Americans, but also northerners and unionists—which was lacking in some states. The evil to be redressed was not any general indiscriminate abridgment, deprivation, or denial. Indeed, there appeared no likely danger that the free people of any state would thus turn on themselves, to consent to the general negation of their right to travel, trade, and converse, or their rights of protection and process. Such popular self-abnegation was not to be expected.

Indeed, in some northern states, any discriminatory abridgment or denial was highly unlikely. These states simply had not denied the equal protection of the laws, nor made and enforced any law that abridged the privileges or immunities of citizens of the United States—and were not likely to do so. Therefore, some proponents could reassure, and some opponents could complain, that the Amendment would have *no effect* on many loyal states, even though the Amendment's meaning plainly covered every state.[324]

Therefore, the Committee and the Congress could have written this section more succinctly:

> No state shall make or enforce any law which shall abridge the immunities of citizens of the United States, or deny to any person within its jurisdiction the equal protection of the law.

Initially, in January, Bingham's subcommittee on congressional powers had drafted a delegatory measure with similar precision: to secure "equal protection" and the "same immunities."[325] And on April 21, Bingham (with the support of Stevens) offered an amendment to the Owen plan by which Section 1 would have been similarly precise—addressing only racially discriminatory *munia* and the denial of equal protection (along with securing property against certain takings):

> No discrimination shall be made by any state, nor by the United States, as to the civil rights of persons because of race, color, or previous condition of servitude;

> nor shall any state deny to any person within its jurisdiction the equal protection of the laws, nor take private property for public use without just compensation.[326]

Such narrowly tailored language, however, would have obscured its grounding in the existing Constitution. Broader language, encompassing due process and the "privileges" of citizenship, was necessary to show that the Committee's constitutional remedies were simply enhancements to existing constitutional norms, to make abundantly clear that the Amendment in no way impaired any of the "rights" of the states, but enforced against the states standards already recognized in the federal Constitution.

In explaining the Amendment, most proponents emphasized the singular egalitarian motive and immediate effect; others emphasized the broader meaning, to include not only equality but also the plurality of due-process rights and fundamental privileges of citizenship. But this difference of emphasis was not a difference of opinion. The major and minor themes were harmonious.

For All Citizens in All Parts of the Republic

Finally, the Committee affirmed that this determination of these civil rights would benefit "all citizens in all parts of the republic." The Committee thus understood their proposal would extend to all Americans, including African Americans or southerners. Their conclusion seems consistent with the proposal's obvious text—all persons under or within the states' authority would enjoy certain rights of protection and process, and all citizens of the United States, as such, would enjoy, against any state's abridgment, certain privileges and immunities of citizenship. Indeed, the express motives for the Amendment were not limited to securing the rights of African Americans, but also to northerners or unionists, white and black.[327]

In this respect, little exposition is necessary. The Amendment's terms have not been a matter of serious disagreement. No one has, to my knowledge, denied that by their plain meaning, the Due Process and Equal Protection Clauses protect all persons who are under or within a state's jurisdiction, or that the Privileges or Immunities Clause protects all citizens of the United States.

But the Report's characterizations—all citizens in all parts of the republic—seem incongruous with Section 1 in two ways. On the one hand, the explanation seems underinclusive. The Due Process and Equal Protection Clauses encompass all "persons" and not just "citizens."

This discrepancy, as with others we have mentioned, can again be explained by the difference between motive and meaning. Injustice toward non-citizens, as such, was not a problem within the purview of the Committee. But to redress the injustice of lawless violence against Americans in the southern states, the Committee decided to ground the remedies in a deeper and broader constitutional principle that secured the rights of all human beings, *viz.*, the Due Process Clause of the Fifth Amendment.

On the other hand, the Report seems overinclusive. The Committee's draft of Section 1 (which consisted only in the prohibitory sentence) restricted only the states. But "all parts of the Republic" would seem to include places where the federal government has exclusive jurisdiction: the federal territories and the District of Columbia. Or was the Committee suggesting that "the Republic" did not include the very place where they were drafting the Amendment?

Perhaps in drafting its Report, the Committee simply forgot that "the Republic" is more than "the several states." Or perhaps the Committee's explanation reflects a certain understanding as to the meaning of the Constitution before the Amendment. As we've seen, Section 1's prohibitory sentence was understood to protect anterior fundamental rights of persons and citizens that no government whatsoever had a right to deny or abridge and were already recognized by the Constitution's Due Process and Privileges and Immunities Clauses. Perhaps the Committee, and Bingham especially, believed that the federal government, whether by these express provisions or otherwise, was already adequately barred from violating these rights of persons and citizens, so these rights, vis-à-vis the federal government, were already adequately "determined."[328] Therefore, the effect of the Amendment was, as a matter of organic law, to extend those prohibitions, already binding on the federal government, to the several states, especially those states where local governments had not respected these "civil rights and privileges."

* * *

In any case, this fundamentalist Amendment secured to all Americans, no more (but no less) than what Lincoln, just before his assassination, had promised the freedmen who had greeted him in Richmond: "you shall have all the rights which God has given to every other free citizen of this republic."[329] All Americans, as human beings and as citizens, had certain fundamental civil rights and civil privileges, the security of which was the purpose of the Amendment's first section.

Notes

1 *Speech of Honorable Luke P. Poland*, Green-Mountain Freeman (Montpelier, Vt.), Nov. 7, 1866, at 2, https://chroniclingamerica.loc.gov/lccn/sn84023209/1866-11-07/ed-1/seq-2/.

2 1 Joseph Story, Commentaries on the Constitution of the United States § 406 at 288 (William W. Story, ed., 2d ed. 1851).

3 Report of the Joint Committee on Reconstruction, 39th Cong., 1st Sess. xiii, xviii, xxi (1866) (hereinafter "Report").

4 *Id.* at xxi.

5 *Id.* at xxi, v (emphasis added).

6 *Id.* at v.

7 *Id.* at xiii.

8 Ilan Wurman, The Second Founding: An Introduction to the Fourteenth Amendment 137 (2020) (contending that to "abridge" civil rights means to "give civil rights based on arbitrary distinctions"); John Harrison, *Reconstructing the Privileges or Immunities Clause*, 101 Yale L.J. 1385, 1457 (1992) (concluding that the forbidden abridgment extended to restrict a right according to any "arbitrary or irrational" criterion); Christopher R. Green, Equal Citizenship, Civil Rights, and the Constitution: the Original Sense of the Privileges or Immunities Clause 43 (2015) (contending that "abridgement . . . was a standard way to express inequality"); William Baude et al., *General Law and the Fourteenth Amendment*, 76 Stan. L. Rev. 1185, 1238–9 (2024) (identifying as legal abridgment any "arbitrary or partial legislation" because it is not at the service of the "public good").

9 Report, *supra* note 3, at iv.

10 *Id.*

11 *Infra* text accompanying notes 63–74.

12 "[O]ne of the privileges of every American citizen [is] to adopt and follow such lawful industrial pursuit, not injurious to the community, as he may see fit, without unreasonable regulation." *Live-Stock Dealers' & Butchers' Ass'n v. Crescent City Live-Stock Landing & Slaughter-House Co.*, 15 F. Cas. 649, 652 (D.C.D. La. 1870) (No. 8,408).

13 As Harrison acknowledges, such a reading against "arbitrary or irrational" classifications does render a "confused concept" that cannot define improper classifications besides race, color, and previous condition of servitude. Harrison, *supra* note 8, at 1457–8.

14 *See, e.g.*, Universal Declaration of Human Rights, G.A. Res. 217 (III) A, U.N. Doc. A/RES/217(III) (Dec. 10, 1948), Arts. 9 & 12 (declaring that "No one shall be subjected to arbitrary arrest, detention or exile," and "No one shall be subjected to arbitrary interference with his privacy, family, home or correspondence").

15 See also Annual Message of Governor Marshall to the Legislature of Minnesota, Jan. 10. 1867, at 26, *compiled in* Annual Messages of Governors of Minnesota to the Legislature, 1864–1874 (compiled *circa* 1874) (contending that the Amendment established "reasonable, just and necessary conditions"). Further, to suggest that aliens, as such, may be treated arbitrarily seems inconsistent with the entire American legal tradition. *See,* among countless other sources, The Federalist No. 43 at 280 (James Madison) (Clinton Rossiter ed., 1961) (noting that "although no political relation can subsist between the assenting and dissenting States, yet the moral relations will remain uncancelled, [because the] claims of justice, both on one side and on the other, will be in force, and must be fulfilled [and] the rights of humanity must in all cases be duly and mutually respected").

16 Report, *supra* note 3, at xx (1866).

17 *Id.* at xix.

18 *Id.* at xx.

19 *Id.* at xvi.

20 The Declaration of Independence, para. 1 (U.S. 1776).

21 *See infra*, ch. 6.

22 Randy E. Barnett & Evan D. Bernick, *No Arbitrary Power: An Originalist Theory of the Due Process of Law*, 60 Wm. & Mary L. Rev. 1599, 1605 (2019).

23 Christopher R. Green, *Twelve Problems with Substantive Due Process*, 16 Geo. J. of Law & Pub. Pol. 398, 414 (2018).

24 Report, *supra* note 3, at v.

25 James Fox relies, in part, on the Report to conclude that, under Section 5, Congress was expected "to act as the national legislative body over the basic aspects of citizenship" with power to "particulariz[e] the rights and privileges of citizenship." James W. Fox, Jr., *Citizenship, Poverty, and Federalism: 1787–1882*, 60 U. Pitt. L. Rev. 421, 511–12 (1999); *see also, e.g.*, Jonathan P. Mitchell, *Textualism and the Fourteenth Amendment*, 69 Stan. L. Rev. 1237, 1244 (2017) (contending that Congress's power to "enforce" includes a power to enact (or retract?) "any equality norms," as to not only race, but also "sex, religion, disability or any other factor").

26 As Fox himself explained, the Senate thus proposed "to secure congressional power to not only enforce but also define citizenship, with citizenship understood broadly." Fox, *supra* note 25, at 496.

27 See *supra* ch. 1.

28 Joint Committee on Reconstruction, Views of the Minority, 39th Cong., 1st sess., H. Rep. 30, pt. 2, at 1–12 (June 20, 1866) (hereinafter, "Views of the Minority").

29 *Dias v. The Revenge*, 7 F. Cas. 637, 642 (C.C.D. Pa. 1814) (Case No. 3,877) (opinion of Washington, J.) (noting that "foreigners," as well as citizens, are "equally entitled to the protection of the law"); Letter from Alexander Hamilton to Thomas Jefferson (Jan. 7, 1802) *in* 25 The Papers of Alexander Hamilton, July 1800–April 1802, at 495 (Harold C. Syrett ed. 1977) ("Do we not protect [aliens] equally with our own citizens[?]").

30 *People v. Abbott*, 19 Wend. 192, 196 (N.Y. 1838) (insisting that the "common prostitute" and the "severely chaste" woman "are equally under the protection of the law" against rape).

31 *Neil v. Farmer*, 9 Ga. 555, 579 (1851) (acknowledging that "two races of men living together, one in the character of masters and the other in the character of slaves, cannot be governed by the same laws"); *United States ex rel. Wheeler v. Williamson*, 28 F. Cas. 686, 694 (E.D. Pa. 1855) (noting that in slaveholding states adjacent to Philadelphia, free and enslaved blacks were not "equally under the protection of the law"). *Cf.* Cong. Globe, 39th Cong., 1st sess. 2542 (May 10, 1866) (Bingham) ("No State ever had the right, under the forms of law or otherwise, to deny to any *freeman* the equal protection of the laws.") (emphasis added).

32 Christopher R. Green, *The Original Sense of the (Equal) Protection Clause: Pre-Enactment History*, 19 Geo. Mason U. C.R.L.J. 1, 44–5 (2008).

33 5 U.S. 137, 163 (1803) (emphasis added).

34 The Declaration of Independence, para. 2 (U.S. 1776).

35 25 Edw. III, stat. 5, c. 4 (1352) (providing that "no man ["nul homme"] of what estate or condition that he be, shall be put out of land, or tenement, nor taken, nor imprisoned, nor disinherited, nor put to death, without being brought in answer by due process of the law"). For a discussion of the statute, its original French text, and the relation of the statute to antecedent English law, especially the Magna Carta, *see* Charles Donahue Jr., *Magna Carta in the Fourteenth Century: From Law to Symbol?: Reflections on the "Six Statutes,"* 25 Wm. & Mary Bill Rts. J. 591, 601 n. 46 (2016).

36 Joseph Story, Commentaries on the Constitution § 1783 (Boston, Hilliard Gray, & Co. 1833)

37 59 U.S. 272, 277 (1856); *see also Huber v. Reily*, 53 Pa. 112, 117 (1866) (holding that "due process of law" required "a trial according to some settled course of judicial proceeding").

38 *Dobbs v. Women's Health Org.*, 597 U.S. 215, 331 (2022) (Thomas J., concurring).

39 *Cf.* Christopher Wolfe, The Rise of Modern Judicial Review: From Constitutional Interpretation to Judge-Made Law 124 (rev'd ed. 1994) ("Given the very nature of the common law . . . it seems unlikely" that the *Murray* Court meant that "the usages and proceedings as of 1789 were 'locked into' the Constitution").

40 *Hurtado v. California*, 110 U.S. 516, 530 (1884) (contending that "due process of law" is open to "a progressive growth and wise adaptation to new circumstances and situations of the forms and processes found fit to give, from time to time, new expression and greater effect to modern ideas of self-government"); *but see id.* at 545 (Harlan, J., dissenting) (concluding that due process of law required conformity with "settled usages and modes of proceeding," including indictment by grand jury); *see also* Donald A. Dripps, About Guilt and Innocence: The Origins, Development, and Future of Constitutional Criminal Procedure 153 (2003) (noting that contemporaneous with the Amendment, states were abandoning grand-jury indictment).

41 *See, e.g.*, The Declarations and Resolves of the First Continental Congress (Oct. 14, 1774), *reprinted in* 1 Sources and Documents of the U.S. Constitutions: National Documents 1492–1800, at 291 (William F. Swindler ed., 1982); The Declaratory Act (Mar. 18, 1766) *reprinted in* Danby Pickering, The Statutes at Large from 1225 to 1867 (London, Joseph Bentham 1869).

42 The Declaration of Independence, para. 1 (U.S. 1776).

43 Articles of Confederation of 1781, art. IV.

44 U.S. Const. art. IV, § 1.

45 The Federalist No. 80, at 478 (Alexander Hamilton) (Clinton Rossiter ed., 1961) (emphasis added).

46 6 F. Cas. 546, 551 (C.C.E.D. Pa. 1825) (No. 3,230).

47 Green, *supra* note 8, at 114.

48 Randy E. Barnett & Evan D. Bernick, The Original Meaning of the Fourteenth Amendment: Its Letter and Spirit 243 (2021).

49 U.S. Const. signatory clause.

50 *Corfield v. Coryell*, 6 Fed. Cas. 546, 551–2 (C.C.E.D. Pa. 1823).

51 *See* argument of counsel in *Campbell v. Morris*, 3 H. & McH. 535, 548 (Md. 1797).

52 [Dred] *Scott v. Sandford*, 60 U.S. 393, 425 (1857) (noting that under the Constitution any bona fide citizen would enjoy, "as a citizen of the United States[,]" the right to sojourn in any other state); Stephen Douglas, *Speech at Bloomington*, *in* Life of Stephen A. Douglas, To Which Are Added His Speeches and Reports 120 (H.M. Flint ed., 1863) (speech delivered on July 16, 1858) (speaking, with reference to Article IV, of the "rights and privileges awarded to citizens of the United States"); Abraham Lincoln, *Seventh and Last Debate with Stephen A. Douglas at Alton, Ill.* (Oct. 15, 1858), *in* 3 Collected Works of Abraham Lincoln 283, 299 (Roy P. Basler ed., 1953) (calling Article IV privileges the "rights of a citizen of the United States").

53 *Douglass' Admin. v. Stevens*, 2 Del. Cas. 489, 502 (1819) (holding that the "privileges and immunities to be secured to all citizens of the United States are such only as belong to the citizens of the several states, which includes the whole United States; and must be understood to mean such privileges as should be common, or the same in every state"); Wm. H. Williams, *The Arrest of Non-Residents for Debt—Constitutionality of the Law*, 2 Western L.J. 265, 266 (1844) (holding that the

"privileges and immunities" are those of "U.S. citizenship," and are "determined with reference to the letter and spirit of our national Constitution, and to the customs of other nations"). The published but unreported case is discussed in David R. Upham, *The Meanings of the "Privileges and Immunities of Citizens" on the Eve of the Civil War*, 91 Notre Dame L. Rev. 1117, 1122–3 (2016).

54 Cong. Globe, 39th Cong., 1st sess. 1088, 1090 (Feb. 28, 1866).

55 *Id.* at 1089.

56 *See infra* notes 71–6 & accompanying text.

57 Cong. Globe, 39th Cong., 1st sess. 1757 (Apr. 4, 1866).

58 *Barnes v. Browning*, Indiana Circuit Court (Lafayette, Ind.) (Apr. 13 1866), *reprinted in*, *Judge Test's Decision on the Case Under the Civil Rights Bill*, The Richmond Palladium (Richmond, Ind.), Apr. 26, 1866, at 1, http://chroniclingamerica.loc.gov/lccn/sn86058250/1866-04-26/ed-1/seq-1; (construing Ind. Const. art. 13 (1851)).

59 The opinion was elsewhere quoted and paraphrased in newspapers in Washington, D.C. and across the country, contemporaneously with the Committee's extended discussions and eventual decision as to the language of Section 1 (April 21–28). *See, e.g.*, The National Republican (Washington, DC), Apr. 23, 1866, at 2 https://chroniclingamerica.loc.gov/lccn/sn86053571/1866-04-23/ed-1/seq-2/ (summarizing this holding); *The First Case Under the Civil Rights Act*, The Daily Dispatch (Richmond, Va.), Apr. 20, 1866, at 1, https://chroniclingamerica.loc.gov/lccn/sn84024738/1866-04-20/ed-1/seq-1/ (quoting the final sentence of the opinion: "Without reference to the civil rights act, 1 shall sustain the demurrer to the defendant's answer, fully satisfied that the plaintiff is a citizen of the United States, independent of the act of Congress on that subject, with the right to sustain his action for his work and labor."); *see also Telegraphic Summaries*, The Placer Herald (Auburn, CA), Apr. 21, 1866, at 2, https://chroniclingamerica.loc.gov/lccn/sn82014998/1866-04-21/ed-1/seq-2/ (explaining that the decision rested on the plaintiff's status as "citizen of the United States"); *Judge Test Declares All Negroes Citizens*, Daily Ohio Statesman, Apr. 19, 1866, at 2, https://chroniclingamerica.loc.gov/lccn/sn84028645/1866-04-19/ed-1/seq-2/ (reprinting a summary published in the Indianapolis Herald on April 16, including the discussion of the Privileges and Immunities Clause); *The Negro Question in Indiana*, The Nashville Daily Union, Apr. 18, 1866, at 2, https://chroniclingamerica.loc.gov/lccn/sn83025718/1866-04-18/ed-1/seq-2/ (same). Many other newspapers commented on the case in April.

60 *Browning v. Barnes*, Indiana Circuit Court (Lafayette, Ind.) (Apr. 13 1866), *reprinted in*, *Judge Test's Decision on the Case Under the Civil Rights Bill*, The Richmond Palladium (Richmond, Ind.), Apr. 26, 1866, at 1, http://chroniclingamerica.loc.gov/lccn/sn86058250/1866-04-26/ed-1/seq-1.

61 *Id.*

62 *See* Barnett & Bernick, *supra* note 47, at 289 & 37 n. 3 (citing *Bank of Columbia v. Okely*, 17 U.S. 122 (1819) in support of the claim that "due process of law came to be understood as a guarantee against all arbitrary government action").

63 *See infra* chapter 6.

64 *See infra* chapter 4.

65 James Kent, 2 Commentaries on American Law 71 (2d ed. 1832) (noting that citizens in other states are entitled only to "the privileges the persons of the same description are entitled to in the state to which the removal is made"); Story, *supra*

note 36, at 1800 ("The intention of this clause was to confer . . . a general citizenship; and to communicate all the privileges and immunities, which the citizens of the same state would be entitled to under the like circumstances."); *Lemmon v. People*, 20 N.Y. 562, 599 (1860) (noting that the Privileges and Immunities Clause is only meant to "relieve [citizens] from any disabilities of alienage" and to prevent states from discriminating against out-of-state citizens).

66 *Slaughterhouse Cases*, 83 U.S. 36, 77 (1872).

67 *Id*. Philip A. Hamburger, *Privileges or Immunities*, 105 Nw. U. L. Rev. 61, 114 (2011) ("Bingham was fighting for the privileges and immunities secured by the Comity Clause, which in this instance were the privileges and immunities that [a state] *had given* its own citizens and now proposed to deny to visiting blacks") (emphasis added); Harrison, *supra* note 8, at 1469 (contending that Article IV secures "rights conferred upon citizens by state law"); Wurman, *supra* note 8, at 63 (identifying "privileges and immunities" as "state-conferred rights"); Kurt T. Lash, The Fourteenth Amendment and the Privileges and Immunities of American Citizenship 26 (2014) (stating that the prevailing antebellum interpretation was that Article IV secures "to sojourning state citizens equal access to a limited set of state-conferred rights"). From this common premise, each finds a different meaning in Section 1's Privileges or Immunities Clause. Hamburger contends that the Amendment secures to the citizen "[f]urther protection . . . against interstate discrimination." *Supra*, at 116. Harrison and Wurman say it secures these state-conferred rights against interstate and many other forms of discrimination. Harrison, *supra* note 8, at 1458 (concluding that the Amendment "requires caste-blindness with respect to privileges and immunities of citizens"); Wurman, *supra* note 8, at 133 (concluding that the Amendment requires that "one citizen be given the same rights as any other in similar conditions and that any condition must be rational and nonarbitrary"). Lash says, instead, that the Privileges or Immunities Clause secures a different, parallel set of rights—not those conferred by state law, but by federal constitutional law ("only those rights enumerated in the Constitution"), which rights could fluctuate with constitutional amendments. Lash, *supra* at xi.

68 *See, e.g.*, Pa. Const., Frame of Gov't, § 10 (1776) (requiring members of the state legislature to promise never to "propose or assent to any bill, vote, or resolution, which shall appear to me injurious to the people; nor do or consent to any act or thing whatever, that shall have a tendency to lessen or abridge their rights and privileges, as *declared* in the constitution of this state") (emphasis added): Tenn. Const., art IX, §2 (1796) (same).

69 *Scott v. Sandford*, 60 U.S. 393, 405 (1857) (emphasis added).

70 *Id*. at 416–17 ("For if [free blacks] were so received, and entitled to the privileges and immunities of citizens, . . . [they would have] the right to enter every other State whenever they pleased, singly or in companies, without pass or passport, and without obstruction, to sojourn there as long as they pleased, to go where they pleased at every hour of the day or night without molestation, unless they committed some violation of law for which a white man would be punished; and it would give them the full liberty of speech in public and in private upon all subjects upon which its own citizens might speak; to hold public meetings upon political affairs, and to keep and carry arms wherever they went"); *id* at 425 (remarking that if he were a citizen, a free black man "might have visited and sojourned in Maryland

when he pleased, and as long as he pleased, as a citizen of the United States; and the State officers and tribunals would be compelled, by the paramount authority of the Constitution, to receive him and treat him as one of its citizens . . . without respect to the laws of Maryland"); *but see id.* at 584 (Curtis, J., dissenting) (contending that neither the Constitution nor "naked citizenship" itself confers rights, but rather it is up to each state to determine whether to "confer" any privilege).

71 Kent *supra* note 65, at 71–2 (contending for an interstate-equality reading, but then quoting with approval *the* maxim that these rights are fundamental to all free governments and citing *Corfield v. Coryell* 6 Fed. Cas. 546 (no. 3,230 C.C.E.D.Pa. 1823)).

72 Hamburger, *supra* note 67, at 117–22.

73 *Id.* In April, another Buckeye, William Lawrence, would likewise call these Article IV rights the "privileges and immunities" that are "inherent in every citizen of the United States," and "fundamental" and thus not "dependent on local law." Cong. Globe, 39th Cong., 1st sess. 1836 (Apr. 7, 1866).

74 A Bill to Declare and Protect All the Privileges and Immunities of Citizens of the United States in the Several States, H.R. 437, 39th Cong. § 1 (as reported by H. Comm. on the Judiciary, Apr. 2, 1866, Printers No. 116) (discussed in Hamburger, *supra* note 67, at 118).

75 Cong. Globe, 39th Cong., 1st sess. app. at 293 (July 25, 1866).

76 *Id.*

77 *Id.*

78 *In re* Dorsey (E.D. Va. 1864), *decision reprinted in* Edward McPherson, The Political History of the United States of America, During the Great Rebellion app. 442, 442–3 (2d ed. 1865). The opinion was appended to a published address by a convention of African American men in Virginia. *See* Equal Suffrage: Address from the Colored Citizens of Norfolk, Va., to the People of the United States 23 (1865), https://omeka.coloredconventions.org/items/show/563.

79 U.S. Const. amend. XIII, §§ 1, 2.

80 Civil Rights Act of 1866, Ch. 31, 14 Stat. 27 § 1 (1866).

81 Report, *supra* note 3, at xiii ("Doubts were entertained whether Congress had power, even under the amended Constitution, to prescribe the qualifications of voters in a State, or could act directly on the subject"); *The Reconstruction Report*, Chicago Tribune, June 11, 1866, at 2, https://chroniclingamerica.loc.gov/lccn/sn82014064/1866-06-11/ed-1/seq-2/ (noting that the Committee had pronounced "no opinion upon the question whether Congress has power to admit the freedmen to the right of suffrage," but left the question "open").

82 *Supra* chapter. 1.

83 Robert J. Kaczorowski, *Congress's Power to Enforce Fourteenth Amendment Rights: Lessons from Federal Remedies the Framers Enacted*, 42 Harv. J. on Legis. 187, 200 (2005) (concluding that proponents of the Civil Rights Act, like Lyman Trumbull, understood the Thirteenth Amendment to confer a "plenary power . . . to define and secure the civil liberties of all Americans").

84 *The Civil Rights Bill*, The Columbian [Bloomsberg, PA], May 12, 1866, at 2, https://chroniclingamerica.loc.gov/lccn/sn83032011/1866-05-12/ed-1/seq-2/. Congress's power to enforce extended only to what was "appropriate" to the mandated nonexistence of "slavery [and] involuntary servitude"—a mandate with a long and

broad history in American law, which had never been held to require interracial equality as well as freedom. *See generally,* David R. Upham, *The Understanding of "Neither Slavery Nor Involuntary Servitude Shall Exist" Before the Thirteenth Amendment*, 15 Geo. J.L. & Pub. Pol'y 138, 170 (2017) (noting that "[f]or decades before the Civil War, many western states made and enforced laws that racially discriminated against free blacks, including restrictions on their right to travel, reside, make contracts, engage in trade, intermarry with whites, testify, and serve as voters and jurors, [but] there seems no record that anyone challenged them as violative of the prohibition of slavery and involuntary servitude").

85 *See, e.g.*, Cong. Globe, 39th Cong., 1st sess. 1293 (Mar. 9, 1866) (remarks by Representative Shellabarger relying on Congress's naturalization power); *id.* at 1294–5 (Mar. 9, 1866) (remarks by Representative Wilson relying on an interpretation of the Due Process Clause, in light of *Prigg v. Pennsylvania*, 41 U.S. 539 (1842), such that the Clause confers on Congress an affirmative power and duty to enforce the rights of "life, liberty, and property"); *id.* at 1757 (Apr. 4, 1866) (remarks by Trumbull relying on the implied or inherent power of Congress to protect its citizens, at home or abroad, in their fundamental civil rights).

86 Cong. Globe, 39th Cong., 1st sess. 1290–3 (Mar. 9, 1866).

87 *Id.* at 474–5 (Jan. 29, 1866).

88 Nor were these rights conferred by state law. The rights listed in the Act were among the "inherent fundamental rights which belong to free citizens or free men in all countries." *Id.* In sharp contrast, political rights "depend[ed] on the legislation of the various States." *Id.*

89 Wager Swayne, The Ordinance of 1787 and the War of 1861: An Address Delivered Before the New York Commandery of the Military Order of the Loyal Legion 72–3 (New York) (1892) (quoting letter from Henderson to Wager Swayne). The Senate Judiciary Committee, chaired by Trumbull, added the enforcement section to Henderson's original draft. *Id. see also* Cong. Globe 38th Cong., 1st sess. 1313 (Mar. 28, 1864) (speech of Trumbull presenting the revised version of Henderson's draft).

90 Cong. Globe, 39th Cong., 1st sess. 3035 (June 8, 1866). Unlike Trumbull, Henderson thought that one of these rights conferred by freedom was the "franchise," including the right to vote regardless of race. *Id.*

91 *Planned Parenthood v. Casey*, 505 U.S. 833, 848 (1992) (quoting *Poe v. Ullman*, 367 U.S. 497, 543 (1961) (Harlan, J., dissenting)).

92 *See, e.g.*, Mike Rappaport, *Original Methods Originalism Part I: The Basic Idea and the Different Versions*, Law & Liberty (May 26, 2017), https://lawliberty.org/original-methods-originalism-part-i-the-basic-idea-and-the-different-versions/.

93 "It is remarkable that, in the voluminous academic discussion of the Ninth Amendment, so little is made of the obvious textual fact that the Ninth Amendment is a rule of construction, not a substantive rule." Michael Stokes Paulsen, *Does the Constitution Prescribe Rules for Its Own Interpretation?* 103 Nw. U.L. Rev. 857, 884 (2009).

94 S.J. Res. of the First Congress Submitting Twelve Amendments to the Constitution, 1st Cong. (1789) *reprinted in* J. Comm. on Printing, Documents illustrative of the formation of the union of the American States, H. Doc. No. 398 at 1063 (1927). For a discussion of this preamble as providing an authoritative interpretation, *see supra* ch. 2.

95 A list of Little Ninth Amendments at the time of Reconstruction includes: Ala. Const. art. 1 § 30 (1819); Me. Const. art. 1 § 24 (1820); Ark. Const. art. 1 § 24 (1836); R.I. Const. art. 1 § 23 (1843); N.J. Const. art. 1 § 19 (1844); Cal. Const. art. 1 § 21 (1849); Ohio Const. art. 1 § 20 (1851); Md. Const. declaration of rights, art. 44 (1864); Minn. Const. art. 1 § 16; Or. Const. art. 1 Sec. 33 (1857); Kan. Const. art. 1 § 20 (1859); Nev. Const. art. 1 § 20 (1864); Fla. Const. art. 1 § 24 (1867). For a discussion of Baby Ninths in state constitutions, *see* Anthony B. Sanders, Baby Ninth Amendments: How Americans Embraced Unenumerated Rights and Why It Matters 41–64 (2023).

96 *See, e.g.*, *Coster v. Tide Water Co.*, 18 N.J. Eq. 54, 63–4 (1866) (citing the New Jersey analogue, in part, to hold that "the right of private property was made sacred by the constitution, to be invaded by no one, not even the [state] legislative power, except where such control was expressly given by that instrument"); *Lehman v. McBride*, 15 Ohio St. 573, 619 (1863) (relying on Ohio's analogue to "dismiss the idea that the general assembly is invested with the unlimited and undefined power to do anything and everything which is not found expressly prohibited"); *State ex rel. Burlington & M. R. R. Co. v. County of Wapello*, 13 Iowa 388, 412 (1862) (relying on the Iowa analogue "to determine the rightful exercise of a given power" including the power of the state legislature).

97 *Cummings v. Missouri*, 71 U.S. 277, 322, 325 (1867) (quoting *Fletcher v. Peck*, 10 U.S. 87, 138 (1810)).

98 71 U.S. 277 (argued in March 1866, decision published on January 14, 1867).

99 71 U.S. 333 (1867).

100 Peter Fish, *Secrecy and The Supreme Court: Judicial Indiscretion and Reconstruction Politics*, 8 Wm. & Mary L. Rev. 225, 233 (1967).

101 *Cummings*, 71 U.S. at 322–7.

102 *See id.* at 277–332; *State v. Cummings*, 36 Mo. 263, 263–79 (1865); *see also Garland*, 71 U.S. at 382–99 (Miller J., dissenting) (providing the dissent applicable to both *Garland* and *Cummings*).

103 *Anderson v. Baker*, 23 Md. 531, 624 (1865) (emphasis added) (discussed in Kurt T. Lash, *The Lost Jurisprudence of the Ninth Amendment*, 83 Tex. L. Rev. 597, 638–9 (2005)).

104 These powers include not only the "Judicial power of the United States" but also the greater judicial authority and responsibility transferred to the state courts by Article VI.

105 *Talcott v. Pine Grove*, 23 F. Cas. 652, 665 (C.C. Mich. 1872) (collecting many federal, state, and English authorities).

106 *Id.* (citing *Stuart v. Laird*, 5 U.S. 299, 309 (1803)).

107 *United States v. Hudson*, 11 U.S. 32, 32 (1812).

108 *Mississippi v. Johnson*, 71 U.S. 475, 500 (1867).

109 *Briscoe v. President & Dirs. of Bank of Ky.*, 36 U.S. 257, 318 (1837) (emphasis added).

110 Cong. Globe 39th Cong., 1st sess. 2459 (May 8, 1866).

111 *Id.* at 2539–40 (May 10, 1866).

112 *Id.* at 2765–6 (May 23, 1866).

113 *Id.* at 2766.

114 *Id.*

115 Cong. Globe 39th Cong., 1st sess. 2465 (May 8, 1866) (noting Representative Thayer's remark that Section 1 secured the "fundamental rights of citizenship" as

already "found in the bill of rights of every State of the Union"); *id.* at 2510 (May 9) (noting Representative Miller's claim that the Due Process and Equal Protection Clauses are "clearly within the spirit of the Declaration"); *id.* at 2539 (May 10) (Representative Farnsworth) (claiming that the Privileges or Immunities and Due Process Clauses are "already in the Constitution" and that the Equal Protection Clause reflected a principle that was plainly "self-evident and just"); *id.* at 2961 (June 5) (Senator Poland) (explaining that the Privileges or Immunities Clause encompassed nothing beyond the Privileges and Immunities Clause, as originally understood, and that Due Process and Equal Protection provisions were already "essentially declared" in the Declaration and Constitution, which principles were "at the very foundation of all republican government").

116 Cong. Globe 39th Cong., 1st sess. 2961 (June 5, 1866).

117 *Id.* at 2542 (May 10, 1866) (emphasis added).

118 Proceedings of the First Three Republican National Conventions 165 (1893).

119 *See, e.g.*, Wisconsin Senate Committee on Federal Relations, minority report, in 2 Kurt T. Lash, The Reconstruction Amendments: The Essential Documents 281 (2021) (claiming that the Amendment is "antagonistic to the principles of the republican party as asserted in the Chicago platform in 1860" and quoting this pledge).

120 Cong. Globe 39th Cong., 1st sess. 2542 (May 10, 1866). Bingham reemphasized this point during the 1866 campaign. In a speech that a newspaper entitled, "The Constitutional Amendment Discussed By Its Author," he declared that Section 1 "takes from no State any right which pertained to the several States of the Union, but it imposes a new limitation upon the State to correct their abuses of power." *See* Speeches of the Campaign of 1866, at 19 (1866); *see also* Weekly Perrysburg Journal, Sept. 7, 1866, at 1, https://chroniclingamerica.loc.gov/lccn/sn85026193/1866-09-07/ed-1/seq-1/ (reprinting the speech under the title, "Constitutional Amendment: Exposition of its Meaning, and Reasons for Its Adoption").

121 *Reconstruction*, The Cecil Whig, May 26, 1866, at 2, https://chroniclingamerica.loc.gov/lccn/sn83016348/1866-05-26/ed-1/seq-2/.

122 *Gov. David Butler, Message to the Legislature, Ratification of the Fourteenth Amendment* (July 6, 1866), Neb. S. Jour. 13 (1st Cong. 1866).

123 Governor A.G. Curtin, *Message to Legislature*, Pa. S. Jour. 16 (Jan. 2, 1867).

124 *Id.*

125 *Inaugural Address of His Excellency Andrew H. Bullock*, in Acts and Resolves Passed by the General Court of Massachusetts in the Year 1867, at 789, 821 (1867) (noting that these "cardinal" principles were "long recognized by the people of this Commonwealth, and endeared to them by the sanctions of their own history and usage").

126 *Id.*

127 *Governor's Message*, *in* Messages and Annual Reports For 1866 Made to the Fifty Seventh General Assembly of the State of Ohio 263, 282 (1867).

128 *Inaugural Address of Governor W.W. Holden*, Wilmington Journal, July 10, 1868, supplement, https://chroniclingamerica.loc.gov/lccn/sn84026536/1868-07-10/ed-1/seq-5/ (celebrating the Amendment, recently ratified by the North Carolina legislature).

129 *Debate on the Bill to Ratify the Constitutional Amendment—Speech of Mr. M.J. Scovel*, The Evening Telegraph, Sept. 11, 1866, at 1, https://chroniclingamerica.loc.gov/lccn/sn83025925/1866-09-11/ed-1/seq-1/.

130 H.R. Doc. No. 149, Mass. Gen. Ct. 1–4 (1867) *reprinted in* Reconstruction Amendments, *supra* note 119, at 285 (2021).

131 Urging ratification, Mississippi's Senator-elect (but unseated) James L. Alcorn reassured his state's unreconstructed legislature that "there was nothing in [Section 1] that has not been acknowledged by many of the best jurists in the land as the principles of the Constitution itself." *General Alcorn Before the Legislature*, The Weekly Clarion, (Jackson, MS), Jan. 31, 1867, at 8, http://chroniclingamerica.loc.gov/lccn/sn83016926/1867-01-31/ed-1/seq-8/.

132 *The Constitutional Amendment: Important Letter from Governor Curtin*, The Evening Telegraph (Philadelphia), July 13, 1866 at 8, https://chroniclingamerica.loc.gov/lccn/sn83025925/1866-07-13/ed-1/seq-8/.

133 *Gov. Andrew Curtin, Message to the Legislature*, Pa. S. Jour. 16 (Jan. 2, 1867).

134 *Speech of Gov. Morton*, Evansville Journal (Ind.), June 21, 1866, at 2, https://chroniclingamerica.loc.gov/lccn/sn82014296/1866-06-21/ed-1/seq-2/.

135 9 Brevier Legislative Reports 90 (1867) (quoted in Charles Fairman, *Does the Fourteenth Amendment Incorporate the Bill of Rights? The Original Understanding*, Stan. L. Rev. 5, 106 (1949)).

136 Cong. Globe 39th Cong., 1st sess. 2539 (May 10, 1866) (Rep. Farnsworth).

137 *Id.* at 2424 (May 7, 1866) (*quoted in* Earl M. Maltz, The Entire Fourteenth Amendment (Sept. 7, 2023) https://ssrn.com/abstract=4564980).

138 *Id.* at app. 240 (June 7) (Sen. Davis). *See also, e.g.*, the immediate response of a pro-administration newspaper: "The first section contains some generalisms about personal rights, all of which are sufficiently guaranteed not only by the Constitution and laws of the United States, but the constitutions and laws of the several States. It is therefore surplusage, and of no real value." *The Mountain and the Mouse*, National Republican, May 1, 1866, at 2, https://chroniclingamerica.loc.gov/lccn/sn86053571/1866-05-01/ed-1/seq-2/.

139 In North Carolina's unreconstructed legislature, one supporter (George Washington Logan) said that Section 1 was "already implied" in the Constitution. The Tri-Weekly Standard, Nov. 27, 1866, at 2, https://chroniclingamerica.loc.gov/lccn/sn85042146/1866-11-27/ed-1/seq-2/. *See also* H.R. Doc. No. 149, Mass. Gen. Ct. 1–4 (1867) *reprinted in* Reconstruction Amendments, *supra* note 119, at 385 (calling the first section "at best, mere surplusage"); The Legislative Record: Containing the Debates and Proceedings of the Pennsylvania Legislature, for the Session of 1867, app. at lxvii (George Bergnor, ed. 1867) (hereinafter Pennsylvania Legislative Debates) (contending that unless Section 1 was "mere surplusage" it was intended to mandate black suffrage surreptitiously); Journal of the House of Representatives of the State of Ohio For the Fifty-Eighth General Assembly 46 (1868) (purporting to rescind the state's ratification in part because "several" of the Amendment's provisions were "already fully provided for" in the federal Constitution).

140 H.R. Doc. No. 149, Mass. Gen. Ct. 3–4 (1867) *reprinted in* Reconstruction Amendments, *supra* note 119, at 385.

141 *See, e.g.*, *Students for Fair Admissions, Inc. v. President & Fellows of Harv. Coll.*, 600 U.S. 181, 231 (2023) (Thomas, J., concurring) (describing the Thirteenth and Fourteenth Amendments as a "second founding"); Ilan Wurman, The Second Founding: An Introduction to the Fourteenth Amendment (2020); Eric Foner, The Second Founding: How Civil War and Reconstruction Remade the Constitution (2019).

142 Cong. Globe 39th Cong., 1st sess. 2459 (May 8, 1866).
143 Pennsylvania Legislative Debates, *supra* note 139, app. at liv, lxv (remarks of Kinney and Jay, Jan. 31 & Feb. 6).
144 Speech of Hon. George H. Williams, of Oregon: At Wieting Hall, Syracuse, New York, October 24, 1866, at 7 (1866).
145 *Id.*
146 Cong. Globe 39th Cong., 1st sess., app. 219 (June 5, 1866).
147 Oregon's constitution excluded free lacks from the territory, courts, and real-estate markets of the state. Or. Const. amend. XVIII, § 4 (1859). *See also Oregon, Legislative Debate and Ratification, in* Reconstruction Amendments, *supra* note 119, at 279, 280 (indicating Senator Houston's argument that "[i]f ratified, the amendment nullifies the 35th section of the first article of the Constitution of Oregon").
148 Cong. Globe, 39th Cong., 1st sess., 1065–6 (Feb. 27, 1866) (emphasis added).
149 *Id.* at 1761 (Apr. 4, 1866).
150 *At Erie—Gen. Geary's Speech*, The Ebensburg Alleghanian, Sept. 20, 1866, at 1, https://chroniclingamerica.loc.gov/lccn/sn85054846/1866-09-20/ed-1/seq-1/.
151 Joseph B. James, The Framing of the Fourteenth Amendment 191 (1956).
152 *See* Cong. Globe, 39th Cong., 1st sess., 2506 (May 9, 1866) (Rep. Eldridge) (stating that the Due Process Clause has "reference only to the southern States, for there was never any necessity to apply it to the northern States"); *cf. Gov. Charles Jenkins Message to Ga. Legislature* (Nov. 1, 1866) *reprinted in* The Confederate Record of the State of Georgia 546 (1910) (contending, principally with reference to Section 2 but perhaps also the entire Amendment, that it would "fall upon citizens inhabiting one latitude like an avalanche from its mountain perch, crushing where it settles; whilst upon those of another latitude it will alight unfelt like a feather floating in still air").
153 Annual Message of the Governor, *in* Journal of the Senate of the State of Georgia 52, 67 (1868).
154 *Cf.* Cong. Globe, 39th Cong., 1st sess. 1761 (Apr. 4, 1866) (remarks by Lyman Trumbull reassuring his colleagues that the Civil Rights Act would have "no operation in Massachusetts, New York, Illinois, or most of the States of the Union" because these states' "municipal regulations" protect "all alike in their rights of person and property").
155 An Act to provide for the more efficient Government of the Rebel States, 14 Stat. 428–30 (March 2, 1867).
156 These included laws that restricted suffrage based on political opinion, reserved suffrage to males, and imposed sex-discriminatory taxes and regulations on males. *See generally*, David R. Upham, *The "Black and Tan Conventions," Diverse Originalism, and the Fourteenth Amendment*, 94 Miss. L.J. 1403 (2025).
157 Mo. S. Journal, 24th Gen. Assembly, 30 (Jan. 5, 1867).
158 *See* New York Governor Message to the Legislature, N.Y. S. Journal, 19th Sess. 7 (Jan. 2, 1867) (New York governor stating that the amendment provided "conditions of safety and justice indispensable to a permanent settlement,"); N.J. J. Assembly, 19th Gen. Assembly 8 (Sep. 10, 1866) (New Jersey Governor stating that the amendment was "the settlement of all the questions at issue."); *Louisiana, Gov. J. Madison Wells's Message to the Legislature, reprinted in* Reconstruction Amendments, *supra* note 119, at 362 (Louisiana Governor stating that the amendment was "adjusting and

settling, as it does, the rights of citizenship to all persons, without reference to race or color").

159 *Gen. Alcorn Before the Legislature*, The Weekly Clarion (Jackson, Miss.), Jan. 31, 1867, at 8 http://chroniclingamerica.loc.gov/lccn/sn83016926/1867-01-31/ed-1/seq-8/.

160 Cong. Globe, 39th Cong., 1st sess., 2462 (May 9, 1866).

161 *Id.* at 2459 (May 8, 1866); *accord id.* at 2498 (May 9, 1866) (Broomall saying the Amendment "will prevent a mere majority from repealing the law and thus thwarting the will of the loyal people").

162 *Id.* at 3148 (June 13, 1866).

163 *Id.* at 3038 (June 8, 1866).

164 *Id.* at 2961 (June 6, 1866).

165 *Id.* at 1118 (Mar. 1, 1866).

166 *See, e.g.*, *id.* at 3035 (remarks of Sen. Henderson) (June 8) (remaking that "[t]he State courts are already deciding the 'civil rights bill' to be unconstitutional" and worrying that the Supreme Court might agree); *id.* at 2397 (May 5) (Charles Phelps, cheerfully predicting that in several years, the Act would be "judicially negatived").

167 Benjamin Pomerance, *Justice Denied: The Peculiar History of Rejected United States Supreme Court Nominees*, 80 Alb. L. Rev. 627, 671 (2017).

168 *Id.* at 679.

169 *Debate on the Bill to Ratify the Constitutional Amendment—Speech of Mr. J.M. Scovel*, The Evening Telegraph (Philadelphia), Sept. 1, 1866, at 1, https://chroniclingamerica.loc.gov/lccn/sn83025925/1866-09-11/ed-1/seq-1/.

170 Stanbery had helped to draft Johnson's veto message of the Civil Rights Bill. The Senate took no action on the nomination, and Congress avoided the danger of his recess appointment by reducing the size of the Court from ten to seven by the Judicial Circuits Act, passed in July 1866. Joshua Braver, *Court-Packing: An American Tradition?*, 61 B.C. L. Rev. 2747, 2782 (2020).

171 *Speech of Honorable Luke P. Poland*, Green-Mountain Freeman, Nov. 7, 1866, at 2, https://chroniclingamerica.loc.gov/lccn/sn84023209/1866-11-07/ed-1/seq-2/.

172 *Id.* (emphasis added).

173 *Ex parte Milligan*, 71 U.S. 2, 118 (1866). Davis was reviled by Republicans for authoring what some called the new Dred Scott decision. Andrew L. Slap, The Doom of Reconstruction: The Liberal Republicans in the Civil War Era 147 (2006).

174 *Ex parte Garland*, 71 U.S. 333, 381 (1867); *Cummings v. Missouri*, 71 U.S. 277, 330 (1867).

175 On Republican outrage, *see* Walter Stahr, Salmon P. Chase: Lincoln's Vital Rival 557–8 (2021).

176 9 Brevier Legislative Reports 28 (1867).

177 *Inaugural Address of His Excellency Andrew H. Bullock*, *in* Acts and Resolves Passed by the General Court of Massachusetts in the Year 1867, at 789, 821 (1867).

178 *Gov. Andrew G. Curtin, Message to Legislature*, Pa. S. Jour. 15 (Jan. 2, 1867) (emphasis added).

179 Pennsylvania Legislative Debates, *supra* note 139, app. at xviii (remark of Bigham) ("I know some timid people are afraid that the Supreme Court of the United States will undertake at some future time to decide that it is not a part of the Constitution. I have no apprehension that such will occur during my lifetime").

180 *Id.* at xxviii (remark of Lowry).

181 Cong. Globe, 39th Cong., 2d sess. at 501–2 (Jan. 16, 1867) (mentioned in Guelzo, Concise history at 91).

182 Davis "I shall rely upon the Supreme Court . . . with perfect security"); Pennsylvania Legislative Debates, *supra* note 139, app. at xxi (Jan. 16).

183 *Id.* app at LX (Jan. 31).

184 *The Constitutional Amendment: Speech of Senator Geo. Reed of Manitowoc, delivered in the State Senate, January 23, 1867*, The Manitowoc Pilot, Feb. 8, 1867, at 2, https://chroniclingamerica.loc.gov/lccn/sn85033139/1867-02-08/ed-1/seq-2/.

185 *See* Mary Karlynn Hinman, The Lost Clause: An Analysis of the Privileges and Immunities of Citizens of the United States 62 (1967) (Ph.D. dissertation, Harvard Univ.) ("The Congressman did not anticipate that the new amendment would eventually enlarge substantially the judicial power of the United States").

186 Cong. Globe, 39th Cong., 1st sess. 2538 (May 10, 1866).

187 *Id.*

188 *See* Views of the Minority, *supra* note 28, at 1–12. Moreover, a few sentences later, Rogers said otherwise, by suggesting that the measure, via Section 2, provided only indirect imposition of black suffrage, and only on the South—an "attempt in this indirect way to inflict upon the people of the South negro suffrage." Cong. Globe, 39th Cong., 1st sess., 2538 (May 10, 1866). Rogers was not generally esteemed for the coherence of his floor speeches. The House clerk recalled that "he excelled any member of Congress at that time as a voluble speech-maker. . . . No matter what word came in his way when in the full onrush of speech-making, he crushed it into his sentence with a recklessness that was refreshing. Big or little, appropriate or inappropriate, fit or unfit, in it went, and on he rushed, a verbal torrent, scattering grammatical wrecks along his pathway." Edward W. Barber, *Men and Events in Washington During and After the Civil War*, 30 Collections and Researches Made by the Michigan Pioneer and Historical Society 212, 226 (1906).

189 Cong. Globe, 39th Cong., 2d sess. 1045 (Feb. 6, 1867) (proposal of Senator Dixon). The version thus published in the Congressional Globe seems to be the most official. The *Richmond Enquirer* perhaps had the initial scoop, publishing the draft on February 4. "*The Plan*," The Tri-Weekly *Standard*, Feb. 7, 1867, at 2, https://chroniclingamerica.loc.gov/lccn/sn85042146/1867-02-07/ed-1/seq-2/ (reprinting plan as published in the *Enquirer* on February 4). This version corresponds to a handwritten version provided by Lewis Hanes, a delegate to the conference. *The New Plan of Reconstruction*, The Daily Dispatch (Richmond), Feb. 8, 1867, at 3, https://chroniclingamerica.loc.gov/lccn/sn84024738/1867-02-08/ed-1/seq-3/. But by other reports, the proposal would have replaced the Privileges or Immunities Clause with a restatement of Article IV's Privileges and Immunities Clause, sometimes with the conspicuous replacement of "in the several States" with "*of* the several states." *See* Richard L. Aynes, *Constricting the Law of Freedom: Justice Miller, the Fourteenth Amendment, and the Slaughter-House Cases*, 70 Chi.-Kent L. Rev. 627, 660 n.228 (1994); and Lash, *supra* note 67 221–2 (both relying on the version discussed in Joseph P. James, The Ratification of the Fourteenth Amendment 137, 140 (1984)). The New York Times published this second version: *Andy's Proposed New Plan*, The Evening Telegraph (Philadelphia), Feb. 5, 1867, https://chroniclingamerica.loc.gov/lccn/sn83025925/1867-02-05/ed-1/seq-1/ (reprinting the version printed in

the New York Times). One manuscript, with notes added by President Johnson, reflected this second version. *A Southern Proposal for a Fourteenth Amendment*, in 1 Documentary History of Reconstruction: Political, Military, Social, Religious, Educational & Industrial 238, 240 (Walter L. Fleming ed., 1906). And, in contrast with the records of the *Congressional Globe*, some newspapers reported that Dixon had indeed submitted to the Senate a proposal with the Article-IV substitution. *See Congressional Proceedings*, The Evening Telegraph (Philadelphia), Feb. 7, 1867, at 6, https://chroniclingamerica.loc.gov/lccn/sn83025925/1867-02-07/ed-1/seq-6/ (reporting Dixon's submission in the Senate with this substitute). As submitted to the state legislatures, the versions differed. Compare the following: the version submitted to the North Carolina legislature, N.C. S. Journal, 388 (Mar. 1, 1867) (no change to Section 1); that presented to the Alabama legislature, Ala. H. Journal 457 (Feb. 14, 1867); and that presented to the Mississippi legislature (Feb. 11) (using the Article IV's language, including "*in* the several States"), *reprinted in* The Daily Clarion (Jackson, Miss.), Feb. 12, 1867, at 2, https://chroniclingamerica.loc.gov/lccn/sn83045232/1867-02-12/ed-1/seq-2. Still, even with this alteration, contemporary commentators treated the revised Section 1 as "substantially the same." *Johnsonion Reconstruction*, Delaware Gazette (OH), Feb. 15, 1867, at 2, https://chroniclingamerica.loc.gov/lccn/sn83035595/1867-02-15/ed-1/seq-2/; *Reconstruction*, Green-Mountain Freeman, Feb. 13, 1867, at 2 (specifying various differences but ignoring as insignificant the change to "privileges and immunities").

190 Cong. Globe, 39th Cong., 2d sess. 1045 (Feb. 6, 1867).

191 Cong. Globe, 39th Cong., 1st sess. 3147 (June 13. 1866).

192 *Journal of the Senate of the General Assembly of the State of North Carolina* 91 (1866–67) *reprinted in* Reconstruction Amendments, *supra* note 119, at 311.

193 Tex. H. Journal 580, 11th sess. (1866) *reprinted in* Reconstruction Amendments, *supra* note 119, at 282.

194 Tex. S. Journal 422, 11th sess. (1866) *reprinted in* Reconstruction Amendments, *supra* note 119, at 283; *see also Georgia Governor message to the Legislature*, Ga. S. Journal 8 (Nov. 1, 1866) ("It will be contended that [Congress] are the proper judges of what constitutes appropriate legislation").

195 *See* Cong. Globe, 39th Cong., 1st sess. 2398 (May 5, 1866) (Rep. Phelps of Md.) ("for Congress to define and determine by law in what the 'privileges and immunities' of citizens of the United States consist, in like manner as Congress has already, under the constitutional amendment abolishing slavery and conferring the power to enforce its abolition by appropriate legislation, determined that the emancipated blacks are 'citizens of the United States,' and defined in what their civil rights as such citizens consist."). *See also supra* text accompanying notes 79–80.

196 "When these words were used in the amendment abolishing slavery they were thought to be harmless, but during the session there has been claimed for them such force and scope of meaning as that Congress might invade the jurisdiction of the States, rob them of their reserved rights." Cong. Globe, 39th Cong., 1st sess. 2940 (June 4, 1866).

197 *Md. Governor Message to the Legislature*, Md. S. Journal, appx. 5 (1867) *reprinted in* Reconstruction Amendments, *supra* note 119, at 395 (cautioning that all of Section 1 "must be read in the light of the 5th section, and of the interpretation already given by Congress to the same language in the 13th Amendment already adopted,

namely, section 5: 'The Congress shall have power to enforce, by appropriate legislation, the provisions of this article'").

198 1 Indiana H. Journal, 101 (1867) *reprinted in* Reconstruction Amendments, *supra* note 119, at 355 (contending that because "in the last few years" there had been "many instances of stretching the powers of government . . . by resorting to new and startling constructions of what seemed to be plain provisions, plainly written," that Section 5 might be subject to similar (mis)construction and lead to further "centralizing" of the "power of the Federal Government"); Pennsylvania Legislative Debates, *supra* note 139, app. at lxviii ("A like provision was tacked upon the constitutional amendment abolishing slavery, and is made the pretext of unlimited bureau appropriations and civil rights bills").

199 *See, e.g.*, *supra* text accompanying notes 84–90 (discussing congressional Republicans' interpretation of the Thirteenth Amendment).

200 Views of the Minority, *supra* note 28, at 1–12.

201 Cong. Globe, 39th Cong., 1st sess. 2467 (May 8).

202 *Id.* at 2511 (May 9, 1866).

203 Thomas C. Fletcher, First Biennial Message, Jan. 4, 1867, *in* 4 The Messages and Proclamations of the Governors of the State of Missouri 80, 81 (1924).

204 Office of Legal Policy, Department of Justice, Wrong Turns on the Road to Judicial Activism: The Ninth Amendment and the Privileges or Immunities Clause 93 (1987).

205 Cong. Globe, 39th Cong., 1st sess. 2766 (May 23, 1866).

206 *See, e.g.*, *Plyler v. Doe*, 457 U.S. 202, 215 (1982).

207 Cong. Globe, 39th Cong., 1st sess. 2766 (May 23, 1866) (emphasis added).

208 *Confirmation Hearing on the Nomination of Robert H. Bork to the Supreme Court of the United States*, Senate Committee on the Judiciary, 100th Cong. 703 (1987).

209 Jack M. Balkin, Living Originalism 220–1 (2014); *see also* Michael Kent Curtis, *The Fourteenth Amendment: Recalling What the Court Forgot*, 56 Drake L. Rev. 911, 992 (2008); Steven G. Calabresi and Hannah M. Begley, *Originalism and Same-Sex Marriage*, 70 U. Miami L. Rev. 648, 671, 681, 687 (2016) (relying on Howard's quote and other sources to conclude that the Amendment barred all "arbitrary" classifications).

210 Andrew Hyman, *A Comment in Response to Dale Carpenter Regarding Equal Protection*, The Originalism Blog (Nov. 23, 2014), https://originalismblog.typepad.com/the-originalism-blog/2014/11/a-comment-in-response-to-dale-carpenter-regarding-equal-protectionandrew-hyman.html (discussing this evidence).

211 *Id.*

212 Howard's prepared notes were recently discovered by Andrew Hyman. *See id.* (linking to https://www.tifis.org/sources/Howard.pdf). A copy of the notes is also on file with the author.

213 Cong. Globe, 39th Cong., 1st sess. 2766 (May 23, 1866).

214 *See, e.g.*, remarks of Pennsylvania Governor Curtin, (claiming that the Amendment would give "to all classes the benefit of American civilization" and provide "that all persons, of whatever class, condition, or color should be equal in civil rights before the law"). For many other sources, *see* Steven G. Calabresi & Julia T. Rickert, *Originalism and Sex Discrimination* 90 Tex. L. Rev. 1, 34–7 (2011).

215 Report, *supra* note 3, at xvi.

216 *Accord* Green, *supra* note 8, at 50–1.
217 *See* Jacob Howard, Reconstruction Report of the Committee 4–5 (1866) (unpublished manuscript) (on file with author).
218 Green, *supra* note 8, at 50–1.
219 *See. e.g.*, *Crow v. State*, 14 Mo. 237, 324–35 (1851) (Napton, J., dissenting) (contending as to arguably preferential taxation law, "[i]t is in vain to denounce such legislation as class legislation, or to stigmatize it by any other harsh epithets" for "[i]f the Legislature pass unwise and unequal laws, their constituents will hold them responsible" and therefore it is not the judiciary's role "to review or amend constitutional enactments").
220 Andrew Johnson, Message of the President of the United States to the Two Houses of Congress, Dec. 4, 1865, at 8 (1865) ("Monopolies, perpetuities, and class legislation are contrary to the genius of free government, and ought not to be allowed").
221 Lamoille Newsdealer [Hyde Park, VT], May 16, 1866, at 2, https://chroniclingamerica.loc.gov/lccn/sn84023428/1866-05-16/ed-1/seq-2/ (reprinting editorial from the *Boston Post*).
222 *See, e.g.*, *Caruthers v. Andrews*, 42 Tenn. 378, 390 (1865) (discussing and rejecting the claim that an anti-usury law is "class legislation"); *Merrit v. Fisher*, 19 Iowa 354, 356 (1865) (denouncing a certain statutory remedy for landlords as "class" legislation). "The term 'class legislation' as used in nineteenth-century legal discourse could refer to any special-interest legislation." Bret Boyce, *The Magic Mirror of "Original Meaning": Recent Approaches to the Fourteenth Amendment*, 66 Me. L. Rev. 29, 67 (2013). *See also Goepp v. Bethlehem*, 28 Pa. 249, 255 (1857) (affirming that "class legislation is so manifestly wrong that its existence should not be presumed unless the legislative intent is free from doubt or difficulty" and indicating that only *some* class legislation can be said to be opposed to the "law of the land"). *But see Lehman v. McBride*, 15 Ohio St. 573, 606–7 (1863) (defining "class legislation" benignly as including any discrimination, including all laws "intended to operate exclusively, or mainly, upon certain classes of persons; as, for example, upon attorneys at law, auctioneers, brokers and bankers, etc." and noting that "criminal laws impose their penal sanctions only upon transgressors; and the elective franchise itself is, by the constitution, limited to a class of citizens composing less than one fourth of the whole").
223 *Dred Scott v. Sandford*, 60 U.S. 393, 489 (1857) (Daniel, J., concurring) (denouncing the antislavery law as an establishment of "inequalities amongst [American] citizens by creating privileges in one class of those citizens, and by the disfranchisement of other portions or classes [i.e., slaveholding citizens], by degrading them from the position they previously occupied").
224 *See, e.g.*, Johnson veto message, July 16, 1866, Cong. Globe, 39th Cong., 1st sess. 3839 (July 16, 1866) (identifying the Second Freedmen's Bureau Bill as "class legislation"); *Bowlin v. Commonwealth*, 65 Ky. 5, 7 (1867) (decrying the Civil Rights Act on similar grounds).
225 Letter of Governor W.L. Sharkey to Governor B.G. Humphreys, Sept. 17, 1866, *in* The Weekly Panola Star [Miss.], Oct. 6, 1866, at 1, https://chroniclingamerica.loc.gov/lccn/sn83016951/1866-10-06/ed-1/seq-1/.
226 *Miss. Legislative Committee Report, Rejection of the Fourteenth Amendment*, Jan. 30, 1867 *reprinted in* Reconstruction Amendments, *supra* note 119, at 359.

227 Cong. Globe, 39th Cong., 1st sess. 2766 (May 23, 1866).
228 Report, *supra* note 3, at xiii.
229 Noah Webster, An American Dictionary of the English Language 203 (rev'd ed. 1869). A secondary meaning referred to an "order or class in society." *Id.* In the second sense, the word could refer to any stable grouping. *Compare, e.g.*, *State v. Caesar*, 31 N.C. 391, 409 (1849) (Nash, J., concurring) (noting that in contrast with the statutory racial distinctions, "the common law . . . knows no difference of caste") *with Cost v. Genette*, 1 Port. 212, 214 (Ala. 1834) (referring to the "profession of the law" as a "caste").
230 Green, *supra* note 8, at 50–1 (attributing Howard's statement to an assumption that the Black Codes represented the only class legislation worth noticing).
231 Speech of Hon. George H. Williams, of Oregon: At Wieting Hall, Syracuse, New York, October 24, 1866, at 5 (1866).
232 Cong. Globe, 39th Cong., 1st sess. 433 (Jan. 25, 1866).
233 Report, *supra* note 3, at xiii.
234 Earl M. Maltz, Civil Rights, the Constitution, and Congress, 1863–1869, at 109 (1990).
235 *See, e.g.*, "Civil," Online Etymology Dictionary, https://www.etymonline.com/word/civil.
236 *See Corfield v. Coryell*, 6 Fed. Cas. 546, 551–2 (no. 3,230 C.C.E.D.Pa. 1823) (explaining that all the privileges and immunities of citizens might be categorized under certain "general heads," including these natural rights: "the enjoyment of life and liberty, with the right to acquire and possess property of every kind, and to pursue and obtain happiness and safety"). *See also Douglass Admin. v. Stephens*, 1 Del. Ch. 465, 470 (1821) (explaining that the rights life, liberty, and property "are the rights of a citizen; and all men by nature have them").
237 This civil right to equal protection was chiefly a guard against nonstate action. *See* Eugene Gressman, *The Unhappy History of Civil Rights Legislation*, 50 Mich. L. Rev. 1323, 1330 (1953) (noting that the Committee's Report indicates that the evils to be addressed by the Amendment were primarily the product of individual rather than state action and thus the Committee did not "limit the scope of the amendment to state action").
238 "Civil," Online Etymology Dictionary, https://www.etymonline.com/word/civil.
239 *See, e.g.*, Bingham's objection to the term "civil rights and immunities" in an early draft of the Civil Rights Act. Cong. Globe 39th Cong. 1st Sess. 1291 (1866).
240 Report, *supra* note 3, at xix–xx (stating that the "great mass" of the southern whites had become "insurgents, rebels, traitors," and thus "forfeited all civil and political rights and privileges").
241 *Id.* at xiii.
242 *Id.*
243 *Id.*
244 *Id.* (emphasis added).
245 *Id.* at xiii.
246 Views of the Minority, *supra* note 28, at 9.
247 *Id.*
248 *Yick Wo v. Hopkins*, 118 U.S. 356, 369 (1886); Alfred Avins, *Equal Protection against Unnecessary Police Violence and the Original Understanding of the Fourteenth Amendment: A Comment*, 19 Buff. L. Rev. 599, 600 (1970).

249 71 U.S. 277 (1867).

250 *Id.* at 320, 322. *Accord*, *Ex parte Garland*, 71 U.S. 333, 378 (1867) (conspicuously omitting any discussion of a possible violation of the Fifth Amendment, even though insisting that an attorney, who holds a position as officer of a court, "can only be deprived of it for misconduct ascertained and declared by the judgment of the court after opportunity to be heard has been afforded").

251 *Douglass v. Stephens*, 1 Del. Ch. 465, 469 (1821) (Ridgely, Ch.) ("the words 'privileges and immunities' comprehend all the rights, and all the methods of protecting those rights which belong to a person in a state of civil society").

252 Report, *supra* note 3, at xiii.

253 *Declaration and Resolves of the First Continental Congress*, Oct. 14, 1774, Online Library of Liberty, https://oll.libertyfund.org/pages/1774-declaration-and-resolves-of-the-1st-continental-congress.

254 *Douglass*, 1 Del. Cas., at 470 (Ridgely, Ch.).

255 *Corfield v. Coryell*, 6 Fed. Cas. 546, 552 (No. 3,230 C.C.E.D. Pa. 1823) (noting that the rights to the territory, tribunals, and markets of a state are "some of the particular privileges and immunities of citizens, which are clearly embraced by the general description of privileges deemed to be fundamental [and] to which *may* be added, the elective franchise, as regulated and established by the laws or constitution of the state in which it is to be exercised") (emphasis added).

256 *Campbell v. Morris*, 3 Harr. & McH. 535, 554 (Md. 1797),

257 *Scott v. Sandford*, 60 U.S. 393, 422 (1857).

258 *See, e.g.*, id. at 405, 422 (1857) (sharply distinguishing "the rights of citizenship as a member of the Union" from "the rights of citizenship which a State may confer within its own limits," and insisting that the former cannot include "political rights"); *Murray v. M'Carty*, 16 Va. 393, 398 (1811) (noting that, as a citizen of the United States, "a citizen of one state may hold lands in another, yet he cannot interfere in those rights, which, from the very nature of society and of government, belong exclusively to citizens of that state," such as "the rights of election and of representation").

259 *See* Upham, *supra* note 54; *Barnes v. Browning*, Indiana Circuit Court (Lafayette, Ind.) (Apr. 13 1866), *reprinted in*, *Judge Test's Decision on the Case Under the Civil Rights Bill*, The Richmond Palladium (Richmond, Ind.), Apr. 26, 1866, at 1, http://chroniclingamerica.loc.gov/lccn/sn86058250/1866-04-26/ed-1/seq-1; (construing Ind. Const. art. 13 (1851)).

260 Wm. H. Williams, *The Arrest of Non-Residents for Debt—Constitutionality of the Law*, 2 Western Law Journal 265, 266 (1844).

261 *Declaration of Sentiments*, *in* Woman's Rights Conventions: Seneca Falls & Rochester, 1848, at 5, 7 (1969).

262 Upham, *supra* note 54, 1124–7; Arnold T. Guminski, *The Rights, Privileges, and Immunities of the American People: A Disjunctive Theory of Selective Incorporation of the Bill of Rights*, 7 Whittier L. Rev. 783–5 (1985).

263 *See infra* ch. 6 (noting how seemingly all participants assumed or asserted that the Privileges or Immunities Clause was based on the Privileges and Immunities Clause).

264 Earl M. Maltz, Civil Rights, the Constitution, and Congress, 1863–1869, at 93–121 (1990).

265 Cong. Globe, 39th Cong., 1st sess. 2462 (May 8, 1866) (Garfield) (remarking he did "profoundly regret" the failure to protect black voting rights); *id.* at 2536 (May 10, 1866) (Kelley) (complaining that the Amendment "does not go far enough"); *id.* at 2539 (Farnsworth) (stating that in this respect the Amendment was "not all I could wish").

266 Bingham added, however, one "exception, that as the right in the people of each State to a republican government and to choose their Representatives in Congress is of the guarantees of the Constitution, by this amendment a remedy might be given [where] treason might change a State government from a republican to a despotic government"). *Id.* at 2542. In January he had specified that it was contrary to the "original intent and spirit" of the Constitution that, in any state, a majority of the free male citizens should be disenfranchised by the minority, which would render the government no longer Republican. *Id.* at 431 (Jan. 15, 1866). He thus indicated that racial exclusion from the suffrage could abridge the privilege of American citizens to a republican form of government, *provided* the excluded represented a majority of free male citizens, but not if the excluded were a decided minority, as in his own state at the time. The individual right of the citizen was not the right to vote, but the citizen's right to live under a government was not a racial or otherwise hereditary aristocracy.

267 *Id.* at 2766 (May 23).

268 *Gov. Paul Dillingham's Message to Vermont's Legislation*, Vt. S. Jour. 12, 24–9 (1866); *reprinted in* Reconstruction Amendments, *supra* note 119, at 288.

269 *Governor Chamberlain's Address, in* Acts and Resolves Passed by the Forty-Sixth Legislature of the State of Maine 135, 138 (1867).

270 George L. Woods, *Inaugural Address, in* Journal of the Proceedings of the Senate of the Legislative Assembly of Oregon For the Fourth Regular Session 26, 29 (1866) (endorsing the Amendment for "securing in the full exercise of all their civil rights, of all persons in the republic, whether native born or naturalized"); Annual Message of Governor Marshall to the Legislature of Minnesota, Jan. 10. 1867, at 25, *in* Annual Messages of Governors of Minnesota to the Legislature, 1864–1874 (1874) (explaining that the Amendment "secures to all citizens of the U.S. equal civil rights"); *Inaugural Address of His Excellency Andrew H. Bullock*, in Acts and Resolves Passed by the General Court of Massachusetts in the Year 1867, at 789, 821 (1867) (stating that the Amendment secures "civil equality before the law").

271 *Message of Governor F.G. Pierpont to the Virginia Legislature*, Va. S. Jour. 29 (Dec. 4, 1866).

272 In the legislature of North Carolina in the fall of 1866, a member of the small Republican minority, George Washington Logan, argued that the privileges of U.S. citizenship did indeed include political rights, but that what Section 1 secured, Section 2 took away: "while the first section denied any State to abridge privileges of its citizens, the 2nd section made certain exceptions and gave the States the right to abridge the privilege of voting." The Tri-Weekly Standard, Nov. 27, 1866, at 2, https://chroniclingamerica.loc.gov/lccn/sn85042146/1866-11-27/ed-1/seq-2/.

273 *The Suffrage Question Again—the Views of Thaddeus Stevens Upon It*, The Evening Telegraph [Philadelphia], Nov. 5, 1867, at 2, https://chroniclingamerica.loc.gov/lccn/sn83025925/1867-11-05/ed-1/seq-2/ (reprinting editorial from the New York Times).

274 "The first section embodies the principles of the civil rights bill, and is intended to secure ultimately, and to some extent indirectly, the political equality of the negro race." Cong. Globe, 39th Cong., 1st sess. 2467 (May 8, 1866) (Rep. Boyer).

275 *Id.* at 2506 (May 9) (Rep. Eldridge).

276 *Id.* app. at 230 (June 13).

277 *Gov. James Orr's Message to the Legislature*, SC H. Jour. 14, 32–5 (Nov. 27, 1866), *in* Reconstruction Amendments, *supra* note 119, at 365 (South Carolina Governor arguing that Section 5 would "confer upon Congress the absolute right" over suffrage); *Gov. Gove Saulsbury's Message to the Legislature*, Delaware S. Jour. 3 (Jan. 3, 1867) *in* Reconstruction Amendments, *supra* note 119, at 365 (Delaware governor alleging that the "ulterior motive" of the Amendment's proponents was the direct congressional imposition of the suffrage).

278 Cong. Globe, 39th Cong., 1st sess. 2398 (May 5, 1866) (emphasis added).

279 *See Gov. Gove Saulsbury's Message to the Legislature*, Delaware S. Jour. 3 (Jan. 3, 1867) *reprinted in* Reconstruction Amendments, *supra* note 119, at 365 (Delaware governor "decrying Section 2's "ulterior purpose, the bestowal of the elective franchise on the African race in this country"); *Md. Governor message to the legislature*, Md. S. Journal, app. at 22 (1867) (Maryland governor contending that the Amendment would mean the "enforcement of negro suffrage and negro equality, by indirect legislation"); *see also Miss. Joint Standing Committee on State and Federal Relations*, Miss. S. Jour. 196 (1867) *reprinted in* Reconstruction Amendments, *supra* note 119, at 359 (contending that Section 2's "object is to compel the Southern States" to allow blacks to vote).

280 *See, e.g.*, 9 Brevier Legislative Reports 80 (1867) (contending that Section 1 would "repeal all our State laws" that distinguished by race, and thus enacting black suffrage); Texas H. Jour. 577 (1866) *reprinted in* Reconstruction Amendments, *supra* note 119, at 282 (Texas Committee on Federal Relations stating that these privileges would include "suffrage at the polls").

281 *See, e.g.*, *Speech of Ex-Governor Parsons, of Alabama*, The Charleston Daily News, Jan. 31, 1867, at 4, https://chroniclingamerica.loc.gov/lccn/sn84026994/1867-01-31/ed-2/seq-4/ (warning that if "suffrage was not allowed" to free blacks, the "Radicals . . . would contend that it was an abridgment of the privileges and immunities of citizens of the United States").

282 *Governor Baker's Speech*, The Evansville Journal, Aug. 13, 1866, at 1, https://chroniclingamerica.loc.gov/lccn/sn82014296/1866-08-13/ed-1/seq-1/.

283 *See also Griswold v. Connecticut*, 381 U.S. 479, 501 (1965) (Harlan, J., concurring) (claiming that the redistricting cases had offered "an interpretation that was made in the face of irrefutable and still unanswered history").

284 *But see* Nelson Lund, *Two Faces of Judicial Restraint (Or Are There More?) in McDonald v. City of Chicago*, 63 Fla. L. Rev. 487, 507 (2011) (contending that "the nondiscrimination thesis" is reconcilable with the Report, which "does not necessarily imply that the law must 'determine' these rights by making them substantively uniform throughout the nation").

285 *See supra* ch. 2. Some scholars have contended that the Committee's consideration of a ban on all racial "distinctions," and the rejection of that language in favor of the Bingham Proposition, led the Committee to reject color-blindness. *See, e.g.*, Andrew Kull, The Color-Blind Constitution 62–9 (2009) (cited in *Students for*

Fair Admissions, Inc. v. President & Fellows of Harv. Coll., 600 U.S. 181, 322 (2023) (Sotomayor, J., dissenting)). But by incorporating the petitioners' formula in the explanation, the Committee suggested it had not rejected their aims. Indeed, if one of those privileges included an immunity against all state racial discrimination, then Section 1 did indeed incorporate such a ban.

286 For further discussion of the "Equal Protection-Due Process Clause," *see infra* chapter 3.

287 *Campbell v. Morris*, 3 H. & McH. 535, 553 (1797) (noting that "[p]rivilege and immunity are synonymous, or nearly so" for the former "signifies a peculiar advantage, exemption, [or] immunity," but immunity "signifies exemption, privilege").

288 It is an interesting question why the specification was made—why the need to add "immunities" in addition to "privileges." Privileges may be here used equivocally, with "privilege" representing not only the genus but also the chief species thereof. For a defense of this two-part language, *see infra* Chapter 4.

289 William W. Crosskey, 2 Politics and the Constitution in the History of the United States 1093 (1953).

290 *Infra*, ch. 6.

291 That is to say, we know what a human being is before we know what a citizen is (epistemology) and the civic order owes its existence more to the existence of men than the converse, so there is a reciprocal but asymmetrical dependence (ontology).

292 "Congress shall have power to make laws which shall be necessary and proper to secure to all persons in every State full protection in the enjoyment of life, liberty and property; and to citizens of the United States in every State the same immunities, and equal political rights and privileges." *See* Benjamin Kendrick, The Journal of the Joint Committee of Fifteen on Reconstruction 57–8, 60 (1914) (On Jan. 27 and Feb. 3 the Joint Committee considered the Amendment's initial draft).

293 Precisely because personhood is more knowable than citizenship, it was understandable that the original Constitution mentioned interstate citizenship but not personhood—for some Framers, the rights of persons to due process went without saying.

294 Cong. Globe, 39th Cong., 1st sess. 2980 (June 5).

295 *Id.* at 2542 (May 10).

296 Report, *supra* note 3, at xi (alleging that the insurgents "drove out from among them those who remained true to the Union, and heaped every imaginable insult and injury upon the United States and its citizens"); *id.* at xvi–xviii (discussing the persistent "abuse of the institutions and people of the loyal states," the widespread hatred of "southern men who adhered to the Union" and of "northern men who go south to engage in business," the intolerance of "Union men, whether of northern or southern origin . . . be they white or black," the refusal "to place the colored race . . . upon terms even of civil equality," and actual and threatened "prosecutions . . . in State courts against Union officers for acts done in the line of official duty").

297 *Id.* at xvi (emphasis added).

298 Kendrick, *supra* note 289, at 56.

299 As Bingham told the full House of Representatives, the measure the Committee was considering would thus "protect[] the rights of all persons, white or black, which had not heretofore been enforced owing to the want of power in Congress." *From*

Washington, Keowee Courier [S.C.] Jan. 25. https://chroniclingamerica.loc.gov/lccn/sn84026912/1866-02-10/ed-1/seq-1/. This racial specification does not, however, appear in the Globe. Bingham only mentions that "whenever the majority of a state inserted the word 'white' as a condition of the elective franchise, it deserved consideration whether such exclusion would not be opposed to the Constitution of the United States." Cong. Globe, 39th Cong., 1st sess. 430 (Ja. 25, 1866)

300 It included this principle in some respect. *See Cohen v. Wright*, 22 Cal. 293, 318 (Cal. 1863) ("The terms 'due process of law' have a distinct legal signification, clearly securing to every person whether a citizen or not, without distinction of sex or race, a judicial trial, according to the established rules of law, before he can be deprived of life, liberty, or property").

301 See *id.* at 304 ("no person can be held to answer for such crime, unless on presentment or indictment of a grand jury; and, in any trial, the party accused shall be allowed to appear and defend in person and with counsel; and, touching the truth of the charge, a jury trial is secured to him. Nor can the party accused be convicted of treason, unless on the evidence of two witnesses to the same overt act, or confession in open Court").

302 *Murray's Lessee v. Hoboken Land & Improvement Co.*, 59 U.S. 272, 277 (1856).

303 Harold M. Hyman, A More Perfect Union: The Impact of the Civil War and Reconstruction on the Constitution 467 (1973) (emphasis added) (quoted in Wrong Turns *supra* note 204, at 96).

304 Wrong Turns *supra* note 204, at 94 (1987); Harrison, *supra* note 8, at 1398–401; Wurman, *supra* note 8, at 54.

305 *See supra* text accompanying notes 65–78.

306 *Campbell v. Morris*, 3 H. & McH. 535 (Md. 1797).

307 6 Fed. Cas. 546 (C.C.D. Pa. 1823) (Case No. 3,230).

308 60 U.S. 393 (1857).

309 *Campbell*, 3 H. & McH. at 553–4 (declaring that these rights included the "privilege" or "peculiar advantage" of acquiring, holding, and conveying "real as well as personal property," in every other state, the right to protection thereof equally with citizens of that state, as well as the immunity from "any taxes or burdens which the property of the citizens is not subject to"); *Corfield v. Coryell*, 6 Fed. Cas. 546, 551–2 (no. 3,230 C.C.E.D. Pa. 1823) (declaring that these rights include not only the affirmative right "to pass through, or to reside in any other state, for purposes of trade, agriculture, professional pursuits, or otherwise; to claim the benefit of the writ of habeas corpus; to institute and maintain actions of any kind in the courts of the state; [and] to take, hold and dispose of property, either real or personal," but also "an exemption from higher taxes or impositions than are paid by the other citizens of the state"); *Dred Scott*, 60 U.S. at 417 (stating that the privileges of citizenship, to be enjoyed by the sojourning citizen, included "the right to enter [and] sojourn" in every other state, to go wherever, whenever, and "as long as they pleased," and also "the full liberty of speech in public and in private upon all subjects upon which its own citizens might speak; to hold public meetings upon political affairs, and to keep and carry arms wherever they went," but with an immunity against any racially discriminatory criminal liability that might restrict the general right of travel and sojourn).

310 Cong. Globe, 39th Cong., 1st sess. 2459 (May 8, 1866).

311 *Id.* at 2502 (Raymond) ("equality of rights to all citizens of the United States, and of all persons within their jurisdiction"); *id* at 2262 (Randall) ("equality . . . between the races").

312 *Id.* at 2766. With only one exception, all of these speakers attributed this egalitarian meaning to the whole of Section 1, and not some part thereof. For the exception, see Thomas Elliot's remark in House: "I support the first section because the doctrine it declares is right, and if, under the Constitution as it now stands, Congress has not the power to prohibit State legislation discriminating against classes of citizens, or depriving any persons of life, liberty, or property without due process of law, or denying to any persons within the State the equal protection of the laws, then, in my judgment, such power should be distinctly conferred." *Id.* at 2511 (May 9).

313 *Gov. Paul Dillingham's Message to Vermont's Legislation*, Vt. S. Jour. 12, 24–9 (1866), *in* Reconstruction Amendments, *supra* note 119, at 256–7 ("equal and impartial liberty"); *Annual Message of Governor Marshall to the Legislature of Minnesota*, Jan. 10. 1867, at 25, *compiled in* Annual Messages of Governors of Minnesota to the Legislature, 1864–1874 (1874) ("equal civil rights"); Second Biennial Message of Gov. Frederick F. Lowe, to the California Legislature, Seventeenth Session 23 (Dec. 2, 1867) ("equality before the law"); Message of the Governor, Journal of the Assembly of Wisconsin 14, 34 (1867) (claiming that the Amendment secures "to all men equality before the law"); *Tennessee, Governor William Brownlow's Proclamation*, June 19, 1866, *in* Reconstruction Amendments, *supra* note 119, at 243 (convening a special session of the legislature to adopt the Amendment, and summarizing all of Section 1 in these terms: "Equal protection of all citizens in the enjoyment of life, liberty and property"). Likewise, in a public statement calling for ratification in special summer sessions of the state legislatures, the governor of Pennsylvania remarked, "That all persons, of whatsoever class, condition, or color, should be equal in civil rights before the law, is demanded by the very form of our Government and it is a blistering stain on our nationality that slavery has been enabled . . . to deform our civil policy, and in many States to deny equal justice to a large class of people." *The Constitutional Amendment: Important Letter From Governor Curtin*, The Evening Telegraph, July 13, 1866, at 8, https://chroniclingamerica.loc.gov/lccn/sn83025925/1866-07-13/ed-1/seq-8/.

314 *Senator Trumbull in Chicago*, in Speeches of the Campaign of 1866, at 6 (1866) (affirming that Section 1 was a "reiteration of the rights as set forth in the Civil Rights Bill, an unnecessary declaration perhaps . . . that all good citizens were entitled alike to equal rights in this Republic"); Cong. Globe, 39th Cong., 1st sess. 2538 (May 10) (Rogers) (declaring that Section 1 is "no more nor less than an attempt to embody in the Constitution of the United States that outrageous and miserable civil rights bill").

315 *Id.* at 3039 (June 8).

316 *Id.*, app. at 217 (June 5) (Howe) (mentioning as among the plainest and most necessary "rights of citizenship" the rights "to hold land," "to collect their wages by the processes of the law," "to appear in the courts as suitors for any wrong done them or any right denied them," "to give testimony in any court, even when the facts might be within their knowledge," as well as equal enjoyment of common school taxation.) *Id.* at 3034 (June 8) (Henderson) (mentioning the rights "to hold real or personal property," to participate in the "courts as a witness," and receive "the means of education" as well as an immunity against "unequal burdens").

317 *Id.* at 2542 (May 10). Bingham would say much the same just after ratification. *The Great Importance of the Fourteenth Amendment*, New York Herald, Dec 3, 1868 *reprinted in* Reconstruction Amendments, *supra* note 119, at 430 (noting that "[s] ome of the immunities are freedom from cruel and unusual punishment and from unlawful seizures").

318 Cong. Globe, 39th Cong., 1st sess. 1152 (Mar. 3, 1866).

319 *Governor's Message*, *in* Messages and Annual Reports For 1866 Made to the Fifty Seventh General Assembly of the State of Ohio 263, 282 (1867) (mentioning a plurality of "immunities," including freedom of discussion); George L. Woods, *Inaugural Address*, *in* Journal of the Proceedings of the Senate of the Legislative Assembly of Oregon For the Fourth Regular Session 26, 29 (1866) (endorsing the Amendment for "securing in the full exercise of all their civil rights, of all persons in the republic, whether native born or naturalized"); *Governor's Message*, Documents of the Second Session of the Second Legislature of Louisiana 3, 4 (1867) (mentioning "rights of citizenship").

320 Wrong Turns, *supra* note 204, at 82–5.

321 Plato, The Republic 111 (Allan Bloom trans. 1968).

322 *Inaugural Address of His Excellency Andrew H. Bullock*, *in* Acts and Resolves Passed by the General Court of Massachusetts in the Year 1867, at 789, 821 (1867) (emphasis added).

323 *Alexander Hamilton Bullock*, 50 The New England Historical and Genealogical Register 153–4 (1896) (recalling Bullock as a "careful student" with speech marked by "graceful diction and elegant expression").

324 *See supra* text accompanying notes 146–56.

325 Kendrick, *supra* note 289, at 56.

326 *Id.* at 83, 85.

327 Report, *supra* note 3, at xvii.

328 This reflection has obvious implications for *Bolling v. Sharpe*.

329 David Dixon Porter, Incidents and Anecdotes of the Civil War 295 (New York, D. Appleton & Co. 1885) (quoted in Allen C. Guelzo, Reconstruction: A Concise History 8 (2018)).

4

The Human Person's Rights to Legal Process and Protection

The second part of the [second sentence] declares that no State shall deprive any person of life, liberty or property without due process of law, nor deny to any person within its jurisdiction the equal protection of the laws.

By this it is intended to throw the equal protection of the law around every person who may be within the jurisdiction of any State, whether citizen or alien, and without regard to condition or residence, not only as to life and liberty, but as to property. It has happened in times past that several of the Southern States discriminated against the citizens of other States by withholding the protection of the laws for life and liberty, and denying to them the ordinary remedies in the courts for the vindication of their civil rights, and hence the adoption of this provision.

—Speech of Governor Oliver Morton at New Albany, Indiana, July 18, 1866[1]

Our inquiry can now be refined. How did the text of Section 1 "determine" certain "civil rights and privileges"? These rights seem to encompass the *person's* rights to legal "process" and legal "protection," and the *citizen's* "privileges" and "immunities." I will discuss the rights of the person in this chapter, and the rights of the citizen in the following two chapters.

The Due Process-Equal Protection Clause

This method requires a defense, for it seems inappropriate in at least two ways.

First, my approach seemingly treats the provisions in the wrong order, as the constitutional text mentions citizenship first, and then personhood. This sequence, as I explained in the last chapter, seemingly resulted from the widespread opinion, embodied in a Senate resolution, that any constitutional remedies should refer back to existing constitutional provisions, which happen to appear in this order: Article IV Privileges and Immunities Clause, and then the Fifth Amendment's Due Process Clauses.[2]

Though contra-textual, my approach has a distinct advantage. By beginning with the rights of persons, the inquiry may begin with the relatively simple and uncontroversial before tackling the more complex. As I set forth in the first chapter, during the discussion of the Amendment, the due-process and equal-protection restrictions occasioned very little controversy as to their meaning or justice—but only as to their federalization.

Indeed, with the end of slavery in 1865, virtually all American officials, at least as a matter of public policy, endorsed the principle that every human person who might be under a state's jurisdiction ought to enjoy that state's legal process and protection. In contrast, the meaning of citizenship remained in dispute, with many opposed to the notion of black citizenship.

Georgia's constitution of 1865 is illustrative of the limited consensus. The first two provisions stipulated, respectively, (1) "Protection to person and property is the duty of government," and (2) "No person shall be deprived of life, liberty, or property, except by due process of law."[3] A subsequent provision required special legislation "for the governance of free persons of color, for the protection and security of their persons and property." All persons, including "free persons of color" then, were entitled to security to life, liberty, and property, via legal protection and process.

But this latter provision made clear that such persons were not citizens. Most strikingly, the legislature was directed to regulate "*their transactions with citizens*," including whether to admit black persons to enjoy the state's territory or testify in the state's tribunals (immigration and testimonial regulations, respectively).[4] Unreconstructed Georgia said, in effect, "Black personhood, yes. Black citizenship, no."[5]

This limitation was not surprising. The human person, or "man," is more knowable than "citizen"; and the rights of the human being to retain life, liberty, and property are easier to apprehend (and harder to forget) than citizenship and its privileges. Further, "due process of law," though peculiar to the Anglo-American legal tradition, was very old and well established. Conversely, America's multistate and multiracial citizenry, with its "privileges" and "immunities," was newer and more obscure. And this obscurity persists in our time.

Second, by bundling the person's rights of process and protection, my approach seems to improperly conflate two distinct provisions: what we lawyers call the Due Process Clause and the Equal Protection Clause.

But the text requires this bundling. The drafters deliberately divided the prohibitory sentence of Section 1, with its three restrictions, into two independent clauses—the first securing certain rights of citizens, the second certain rights of persons.

The rule of brevity, and the rhetorical rule of three, would ordinarily have required the reduction of the three prohibitions into one clause, with a compound predicate governed by one common subject ("No state"). This rule of brevity was exemplified in the seven prohibitions set forth in a single independent clause of Article I, section 10:

> No State shall enter into any Treaty, Alliance, or Confederation; grant Letters of Marque and Reprisal; coin Money; emit Bills of Credit; make any Thing but gold

> and silver Coin a Tender in Payment of Debts; pass any Bill of Attainder, ex post facto Law, or Law impairing the Obligation of Contracts, or grant any Title of Nobility.[6]

Section 1's prohibitions, then, should have been reduced to one independent clause with a nice tripartite predicate: "No State shall make or enforce any law . . . deprive any person . . . or deny to any person," and so on.

Now Bingham was well aware of this model. He recalled, five years later, that he had imitated the language of Article I, section 10 precisely to conform with the Court's holding in *Barron v. Baltimore*.[7] His recollection is confirmed by the text of a speech he delivered in March 1866—that except for the prohibitions of Article I, section 10, with their express language, "No state shall," the states are not restrained in the government of their respective populations.[8] President Johnson, in vetoing the Civil Rights Bill, would make a similar claim:

> [T]here is a Federal limitation that no State shall pass a law impairing the obligations of contracts; and as to crimes, that no State shall pass an ex post facto law; and as to money, that no State shall make any thing but gold and silver a legal tender. But where can we find a Federal prohibition against the power of any State to discriminate?[9]

In apparent response to these concerns, in early April, Bingham circulated to his colleagues this draft of his proposal:

> No State shall *pass* or enforce any law which shall *impair* or deny any of the privileges or immunities of citizens of the United States; nor shall any State deprive any person of life, liberty or property without due process of law, nor take private property for public use without just compensation, nor deny the equal protection of the laws to all persons therein.[10]

To begin the prohibition with the words "No state shall," and to bar the states from *passing* laws that might *impair* rights, surely harkened back to Article I's ban on the *passing* of contract-*impairing* laws.

Although thus imitating the vocabulary of that clause, Bingham did not imitate its concision. He drafted not an elegant three-in-one prohibition, but a clunky two-clause provision, where the second clause repeated the subject ("nor shall any state") and combined both due process and equal protection (and initially also a third prohibition on property-takings).[11] The twoness appears deliberate.

Accordingly, during the Amendment's adoption, most prominent commentators aptly distinguished the prohibitory sentence into its two parts: (1) the Privileges or Immunities Clause, and (2) what we might call the Due Process-Equal Protection Clause (or perhaps more precisely, the Legal Process and Protection Clause). These commentators included Senators Jacob Howard and Luke Poland in their principal floor speeches,[12] Senator Reverdy Johnson in a public pamphlet,[13] Indiana's Governor

Oliver Morton in a prominent campaign speech,[14] North Carolina's governor in his formal transmittal message,[15] Maryland's Joint Committee on Federal Relations in its formal report,[16] and the pseudonymous "Madison" in his commentary in the New York Times.[17]

In a similar vein, prominent officials followed the Joint Committee ("rights and privileges") in providing a two-part summary of Section 1's prohibitory sentence. In his main floor speech, Bingham identified two sets of rights: (1) "the privileges and immunities of all the citizens of the Republic" and (2) "the inborn rights of every person within its jurisdiction."[18] Likewise, Ohio's governor reduced the three prohibitions into two negatives, one against abridgment of citizens' privileges, and the other against attempts "to deprive [persons] of the equal protection of the laws."[19]

Conversely, some kept the two-part distinction, but summarized the second half of the prohibitory sentence, the one Due Process-Equal Protection Clause, as a single affirmative. Missouri's governor said the prohibitory sentence guaranteed both certain rights to citizens, and "to all persons equality of protection in life, liberty and property, under the laws of the State."[20] In a campaign speech, Indiana's governor also explained that the prohibitory sentence was intended both to secure certain "great privileges or immunities" of citizenship, and "to throw the equal protection of the law around every person who may be within the jurisdiction of any State, whether citizen or alien, and without regard to condition or residence, not only as to life and liberty, but also as to property."[21] During the campaign of 1866, Bingham likewise treated the Due Process-Equal Protection Clause as a single affirmative, distinct from the negative Privileges or Immunities Clause: "that every person hereafter, in every State, shall have equal protection of the laws, and no State shall make or enforce any law which shall abridge the privileges or immunities of citizens of the United States."[22]

Whether expressed affirmatively or negatively, such mergers of legal process and protection into one guarantee did not, as some have claimed, reflect any "confusion."[23] Rather, these officials all saw that the second clause was indeed one independent clause with a dual predicate serving a single set of "inborn" or human rights. As the political scientist Chin-Yung Yen observed a century ago, Section 1 has three clauses: the Citizenship Clause, the Privileges or Immunities Clause, and a third clause, with due process and equal protection constituting the two halves thereof.[24] And as political scientist Michael Zuckert has noted more recently, these last two restrictions have a unity; they "perfectly complement each other; each provides a constitutional right to one aspect of the security of natural rights."[25] Equal protection, the "positive" aspect (phrased as a double negative: no denial), "requires state provision of protection of rights," while due process, the "negative" aspect, "prohibits the states from depriving persons of rights."[26]

To be sure, not all officials thus merged these latter two prohibitions. Most notably, while launching debate in the House, Stevens reframed Section 1's prohibitory sentence as a nice three-in-one clause: "The first section prohibits the States from abridging the privileges and immunities of citizens of the United States, or unlawfully depriving them of life, liberty, or property, or of denying to any person within their jurisdiction the 'equal' protection of the laws."[27] His purpose here was either rhetorical elegance, or perhaps to anticipate a distinction he suggested: between the "privileges and immunities," and "due process of law" that were "already asserted [in] our organic law," and the "equal protection" found, perhaps not there, but "in our DECLARATION."[28] Illinois's John Farnsworth likewise identified "equal protection" as the sole part of the prohibitory sentence "not already in the Constitution." It was, however, implied by the "self-evident" truths of the Declaration: "How can [the individual] have and enjoy equal rights of 'life, liberty, and the pursuit of happiness' without 'equal protection of the laws?'"[29]

At the same time, Bingham (the main drafter) had always insisted on the merger of equal protection under due process, for he believed that the Fifth Amendment's Due Process Clause, rightly understood, already encompassed the duty of protection. He had based his February proposal on the grounds that if fully enforced, the negative anti-deprivation Clause implied an affirmative governmental duty of protection. He read the Clause to say that no person should be unlawfully deprived of life, liberty, or property, *by anyone*—so Congress had not only the express duty to refrain from unlawful deprivations, but also the implied duty to make that a reality wherever Congress had appropriate authority. Now Bingham conceded that the Supreme Court had conclusively held, in *Barron v. Baltimore*, that the Fifth Amendment constitutionally restricted only the federal government from making such deprivations.[30] But he championed his February proposal as a means to empower Congress with new nationwide authority to fully enforce the Due Process Clause, by protecting the rights of person and property against lawless deprivation by *anyone*—not only (1) federal actors, but also (2) state actors, and even (3) private actors. And in April, he transformed this guarantee into a twofold anti-deprivation and anti-denial restriction on each "State," coupled with a supplementary enforcement power in Congress.

This interpretation of the Fifth Amendment, though strange to us, was not unique to Bingham. It had been anticipated by the Republican Party in its first national platform (1856): Whereas "our Republican fathers . . . ordained that no person shall be deprived of life, liberty, or property, without due process of law, it becomes our duty to maintain this provision of the Constitution against all attempts to violate it," including by federal law "prohibiting [slavery's] existence or extension" in the federal territories.[31] That is to say, the Due Process Clause recognized a federal duty not only to refrain from any and all lawless deprivation of liberty, but also to protect persons against such unlawful deprivation by private actors—albeit only in the territories and other places where the federal government had general jurisdiction.

Accordingly, in support of the 1862 bill to abolish slavery in Washington, D.C., Bingham invoked the Due Process Clause as a "clear recognition of the rights of all . . . no matter whether citizens or strangers; no matter whether rich or poor; no matter whether wise or simple; no matter whether strong or weak," for this "Magna Charta to mankind declares that the rights of all to life and liberty and property are equal before the law."[32] Consequently, "the letter and spirit" of the Fifth Amendment required not only that Congress refrain from enslavement, but also congressional intolerance of slavery in the federal district and anywhere else Congress had general jurisdiction—to equally protect the right to liberty against unlawful deprivation—by anyone.[33]

As incorporated into the Fourteenth Amendment, now the states would be expressly bound by the same duties—the duties both to refrain (no unlawful deprivation) and to act (no refusal to protect). In this sense, the Amendment was not merely declaratory but restrictive. Therefore, Bingham appropriately phrased the new restriction in the future prescriptive: "nor *shall* any state deprive . . . nor deny."

In sum, we will treat the Due Process-Equal Protection Clause as one clause because it was one clause with a compound predicate. The Clause provided a new restriction, with enhanced security, against unlawful violence, for a single set of fundamental human rights of person and property: those already proclaimed in our Declaration, recognized in the Fifth Amendment, and partly secured by the same. And we will treat the Due Process-Equal Protection Clause first because its original meaning was less controversial and easier to grasp relative to the other two clauses of Section 1: the Citizenship and Privileges or Immunities Clauses, to be treated in Chapters 5 and 6, respectively.

No State

The subject of the Due Process-Equal Protection Clause, as well as the Privileges or Immunities Clause, is "State." The term appears well over 100 times in the original Constitution and is incorporated into the very name of our Republic: "United States of America." In the Amendment, the word appears two dozen times, and six times in Section 1 alone.

Such rich context largely precludes any substantial doubt as to the meaning of the word. The Amendment indicates that a "state" is one of the United States. Under Section 2 of the Amendment (as under the Republican Guarantee Clause), a state is a community of people—distinct from its government[34]—that has, roughly proportionate to its population, a right to representation in the House of Representatives. Under Section 1, by express terms or implication, each such popular community has (a) a territory in which persons might "reside" or otherwise be found, (b) the authority to make and enforce certain laws, (c) the duty within its territory to provide all persons with the equal protection of such laws, and (d) the authority under those laws to deprive those same persons of life, liberty, and property.

Not surprisingly, the definition of "state" occasioned almost no debate during the adoption of the Amendment. There was, of course, great concern over the status of the so-called seceded states—to what extent those entities were still "states" of the Union. But all seemed to concur that each of these, once fully readmitted to congressional representation and relieved of military governance, would be a "state" for all intents and purposes.

For much the same reason, there was almost no debate among jurists as to the meaning of "state" before the Civil War. All seemed to agree that "state" included only the states of the Union, including (1) the sovereign people thereof, and (2) every legislative, executive, and judicial agent that the people might authorize to make and enforce laws. But there was, however, some dispute as to the status of an entity on which the state might confer its wealth and prestige, but not its law-making or enforcement powers. The debate arose under the provision of Article I, section 10, by which "[n]o State shall . . . emit Bills of Credit."[35] In 1837, a divided Supreme Court held that under that provision, a state-chartered bank was not a "state," even where the state owned all the bank's shares, and the state's legislature appointed all the bank's officers.[36] Writing for the majority, Justice McLean acknowledged that a "state cannot do that which the federal Constitution declares it shall not do . . . either directly, or indirectly."[37] But a corporation, however much controlled by and subsidized by a state, is not a "state," unless the corporation was not just the sovereign's tool, but its authorized "agent," empowered to "bind the state" and endowed with the "attributes of sovereignty."[38] These attributes included the sovereign's immunity from suit without its consent.[39] In 1852, the Court reaffirmed the same.[40]

In sum, at the time of the adoption of the Fourteenth Amendment, a "state" included the sovereign people of a state, as well as the legislature thereof, and any other authorized agent of the people that shared in the sovereign's authority and the sovereign's immunity in making and enforcing laws—up to the violence of deprivation of life, liberty, or property. But a "state" did not include an entity merely subsidized and controlled by the state's government, which did not share in sovereign authority and consequent sovereign immunity.

Person

The "person," if within or under a state's jurisdiction, is the primary object of the Due Process-Equal Protection Clause. The word is common to both parts of the compound predicate, as direct and indirect object, respectively: the state may not deprive "any person" of life, liberty, or property, absent certain legal process, or deny "to any person" within its jurisdiction, certain legal protection.

The term "person" has long been a matter of extensive interpretive disagreement. The most prominent questions have been (1) whether the word encompasses *all* human beings, and (2) whether it encompasses *only* human beings. Clear and convincing evidence, I submit, provides an affirmative originalist answer to both these questions.

All Human Beings

"Person," as used in Section 1, was understood to encompass all human beings. The genealogy, purpose, and contemporaneous discussion of the Due Process-Equal Protection Clause all indicate that "any person" meant any "man" in the sense of "human being."

From its origin, "due process of law" was due to the human being. The rule is traceable to a 1354 statute that provided that "no man of what state or condition he may be" (whether free or not), shall be deprived of life, liberty, or property "without [being] brought to answer by due process of law."[41] The rule expanded the coverage of the Magna Carta, which protected each "*free* man" from certain deprivations except "by the judgment of his peers or the law of the land." In both cases, the protected individual was "man," in the sense of human being, as in Magna Carta's original Latin "*nullus homo liber*" or the 1354 statute's original Norman French ("*nul homme*").[42]

In antebellum America, due process of law (or law-of-the-land) was recognized not only in the federal charter but also "in some form of expression in the constitutions of nearly all the States."[43] The free states preserved the tradition and thus the protected individual was generally called "man."[44] In the slaveholding states, however, the violence necessary to slavery was flatly incompatible with the Anglo-American tradition. Therefore, such jurisdictions generally modified the traditional rule, sometimes by such innovations as rephrasing "due process of law" as "due course of law,"[45] or by the anachronism of reverting to the thirteenth-century "free man" (instead of "man").[46] But with emancipation, various southern white governments, though still regarding the freedmen as noncitizens, quickly restored the old rule by extending constitutional due process once again to any "person" or "man."[47]

The purpose of the Due Process-Equal Protection Clause likewise indicates that "person" included every human being. The goal, inspired by our Declaration, was to provide greater security to the inalienable rights with which the Creator endowed "all men."

This principle was not merely some relic of the eighteenth century or a glittering generality. The equal and inalienable rights of all men supplied a vital and absolutely primary rule of action. The preservation of these principles "promulgated in the Declaration of Independence, and embodied in the Federal Constitution," chiefly in the Due Process Clause, was the first plank in the Republican Party's first national platform (1856), and had inspired all emancipation efforts.[48] Moreover, these principles found pride of place as the first provision in most reconstruction-era state constitutions, including six of the eight accepted by Congress while the Amendment was pending.[49]

The primacy of this principle in Reconstruction is manifest in the record of the Thirty-Ninth Congress. In his *first* speech on the *first* day of the Thirty-Ninth Congress, the newly elected Speaker of the House (Schuyler Colfax) reminded his colleagues that Congress's "*primary*" duty was to establish, in states corrupted by rebellion, that government that would "afford what our Magna Charta, the Declaration of Independence, proclaims is the *chief* object of government—*protection to all men* in their inalienable rights."[50] By 1868, the national Republican Party celebrated all such efforts, whether in Congress or the several states, to establish the "great principles of the immortal Declaration of Independence" as "a living reality on every inch of American soil."[51]

Because of its primacy, the Declaration featured prominently in Republicans' explanation of the Due Process-Equal Protection Clause. In the House, Pennsylvania's George Miller found the Clause "clearly within the spirit of the Declaration of Independence" such that no one "can seriously object to it."[52] In the Senate, Vermont's Luke Poland said the Clause was "essentially declared in the Declaration" and throughout the Constitution.[53] The connection was obvious. By the Declaration, the government of each state had the duty "to secure these rights" that belong as inalienable endowment to every human being: life and liberty, as well as the property essential to the pursuit of happiness. The Clause enforced this duty by compelling the states to follow the laws defining the process and protection necessary to those human rights.[54]

For this reason, commentators said, without any controversy, that "person" thus encompassed every flesh-and-blood human being. Pennsylvania's Senator Cowan (an opponent) remarked that "every human being" in a state's "jurisdiction" was a "person entitled to protection";[55] Maine's governor said the amendment served "the rights of humanity."[56] In campaign speeches, prominent supporters announced that person included "any human being" or "every man, woman, and child."[57] And Bingham emphatically made this point. He repeatedly and publicly proclaimed that the Clause secured human or "inborn rights"[58] and appropriately encompassed "every human being," "no matter how friendless"[59] including the "fatherless," the "houseless," and the "humblest child in this land."[60]

But there are two sorts of human beings that arguably were not included by the word "person": (1) non-citizen humans and (2) prenatal humans.[61]

Non-citizens were outside the primary purpose of the foundational principles. Even though inalienable rights belong to "all men," a particular government is instituted for the security of only some men—those very men that institute it. This *people*, a small subset of humanity, has a primary claim to the government's protection. For this reason, Virginia's 1776 Declaration of Rights stipulated that although "*all men* are by nature equally free and independent, and have certain inherent rights," when such men "enter into a state of society," their government is "instituted for the common benefit, protection, and security of [that] people, nation or community."[62] Likewise, the first section of Kansas's 1861 bill of rights stipulated that "[a]ll men are possessed of equal and inalienable natural rights," but that "all free governments" are founded on "the people" and "are instituted for *their equal protection*."[63] Similarly, while the Amendment was pending, the Illinois Supreme Court declared that "[t]he great object of government is to afford protection to the life, liberty and property of the *citizen*."[64]

During the debates over the Civil Rights Act, many also suggested that citizenship, not personhood, conferred the right to protection: "No maxim is more generally acknowledged or more current in the mouths of men than that allegiance on the part of the citizens entitles [them] to protection on the part of the Government."[65] In Senator Lyman Trumbull's pithy phrase, "Allegiance and protection are reciprocal rights."[66]

Moreover, as we saw in the previous chapter, the Joint Committee had, contra-textually, identified "citizens" as the beneficiaries of all of Section 1 and made no mention of the rights of aliens. Others, such as the governors of Tennessee and Ohio, likewise identified "citizens" as those who would enjoy "equal protection" in the rights of life, liberty, and property under the Amendment.[67] Non-citizen persons were not worth mentioning and perhaps thereby excluded.

But there is another consideration. Whenever any people establish a government for themselves over a defined space, they establish a monopoly of coercive force over that space—a geographic "jurisdiction." Consequently, any human being found within that space is necessarily dependent on that government's protection. And because, as most

Americans then believed, God gives every such human being certain inalienable and equal rights, any governing people have an indefeasible duty, as a common carrier of sorts, to provide equal security to such equal human rights. Good government, under God, can never be a fee-for-service arrangement, a mere protection racket, let alone an extortion scheme. Accordingly, the maxim of Anglo-American law, from the Magna Carta to the state constitutions, was that *every* "person" or "man," whatsoever, for any "injury done him in his lands, goods, person or reputation, shall have remedy by the due course of law, and right and justice administered, without *sale*, *denial* or *delay*."[68] Even if the primary purpose of the civil order (including the primary purpose of the Due Process-Equal Protection Clause) is security for the citizen, the protection of the foreigner becomes an inalienable duty upon any people's establishment of a civil order.

Accordingly, both the centuries-old tradition and the Amendment's naked text guaranteed legal protection and legal process not only to the citizens, but to any human person who might be within or under a state's jurisdiction, "whatever estate or condition he may be." Thus, a few years before the Amendment, California's Supreme Court had remarked, without any apparent dissent, that constitutional due process embraced "every person whether a citizen or not, without distinction of sex or race."[69] In his opening speech, Howard likewise said Section 1 "relates to the privileges and immunities of citizens of the several States, and to the rights and privileges of *all persons, whether citizens or others*, under the laws of the United States."[70] Or, as Williams Lawrence said in an 1866 campaign speech, under the proposed Amendment, even the "foreigner who seeks any asylum on our shores . . . may rest under its protecting aegis, and no State can deprive him of the equal protection of the law."[71] And while the Amendment was pending, the Supreme Court declared simply, "By the protection of the law *human* rights are secured."[72]

As to prenatal humans, the question was not controversial until the last five decades. But the matter has divided scholars since, in *Roe v. Wade*, the Supreme Court said that if fetal "personhood is established . . . the fetus' right to life would then be guaranteed specifically by the Amendment."[73]

As many scholars have pointed out, the legal meaning of "person" in 1866 seemed to include prenatal humans.[74] Authorities frequently referred to such an individual as, in the old law French, a "person" who is "*en ventre sa mere*."[75] So, for instance, in one inheritance case, a girl "*en ventre sa mere* [was deemed] a person in *rerum natura*;" so "both by the rule of the common and civil law, she was, to all intents and purposes, a child, as much as if born in her father's lifetime. A child in the womb of the mother is under the protection of the law."[76]

This *protection*, of course, surrounded not only the girl's postnatal property but also her prenatal life (at least after that quickening that evinced the beginning of life). As James Wilson wrote in his *Commentaries,* "With consistency, beautiful and undeviating, human life, from its commencement to its close, is protected by the common law. In the contemplation of law, life begins when the infant is first able to stir in the womb."[77]

On the other hand, in at least two respects, prenatal humans seem not to qualify as "persons" under the Amendment. First, the Amendment requires that "all persons" be counted for purposes of congressional representation, but prenatal persons have seemingly never been included in this enumeration. Second, the Amendment guarantees "equal protection" to all persons within a state's jurisdiction, but the laws never treated prenatal humans, even after quickening, as deserving protection equal with postnatal humans. At common law, they were not, unless subsequently born alive, "persons" that could be victims of homicide. Moreover, the crime of prenatal feticide, even in the last weeks of pregnancy, was categorically a lesser offense than postnatal infanticide.[78] Moreover, although several states, at the time of the Amendment's adoption or soon thereafter, reformed their anti-abortion laws to provide some greater "protection" to prenatal life,[79] seemingly no one drew any connection between the "equal protection" due to persons under the Amendment and the enhanced "protection" to be afforded (or withheld) under the new anti-abortion statutes.[80] Such prenatal humans, it seems, were not Fourteenth-Amendment "persons."

To the first objection, however, the required enumeration can extend only to those persons readily countable. It was very difficult to count prenatal persons; even today, even when a woman appears to be "with child," only an intrusive exam can determine whether she is indeed carrying a living child, and if so, how many. For the same reason, transient persons are traditionally undercounted. But no one would argue that such uncounted persons are not "persons."

To the second objection, we should recall that, after strenuous objections by many Republicans, the equal-protection mandate was redrafted to ensure not equal protection simply, but equal protection as defined by "the laws." As I will elaborate below, the provision guaranteed not equal laws but equal enforcement of the laws. Hence, the Amendment, as adopted, was irrelevant to any critique or reform of "the laws" that distinguished feticide from infanticide, or post-quickening from pre-quickening feticide.

For much the same reason, the Amendment did not prohibit the states from withholding "equal protection" to certain persons under Indian-tribal immunity, even if fully "within" a state's jurisdiction. The "laws" defining equal protection included the federal laws that circumscribed a state's authority and responsibility vis-à-vis such persons.[81] The resulting inequality, then and now, reflects obedience to the very "laws" defining protection, and thus conformity with the Amendment. Such limited and unequal protection in no way suggests any human being's constitutional non-personhood.

Only Human Beings

The evidence is likewise clear and convincing that the word "person" included only human beings.

To be sure, the word was never simply synonymous with "human being"; one could speak of divine persons, angelic persons, and artificial persons (like corporations). In law, as Bouvier's dictionary then affirmed, "person" was "more extensive than man" and included not only "natural" persons but also "artificial beings, as corporations."[82] At the same time, the general rule was that "when the word 'persons' is spoken of in legislative acts, natural persons will be intended, unless something appears in the context to show that it applies to artificial persons."[83]

The context of the Amendment indicates, very strongly, that "person" here referred exclusively to "natural persons."[84] That context includes the preexisting Constitution. Most notably, in the Fifth Amendment, where "person" is the subject of the first few clauses, its reflexive pronoun is "himself." In the subsequent "Takings Clause," apparently designed to protect corporations as well as natural persons, the subject changes to "private property"—an unnecessary distinction if "person" included corporate as well as individual owners of private property. Otherwise, that Amendment could have read, more succinctly, "no person . . . shall be deprived of life, liberty, or property without due process of law, nor be obliged to relinquish his property, where it may be necessary for public use, without a just compensation." Incidentally, that was precisely the language of Madison's rough draft.[85]

The immediate context of the Fourteenth Amendment makes this limitation even clearer, as Judge William Woods pointed out soon after ratification:

> Are corporations persons within the meaning of the same amendments? The word "person" occurs three times in the first section, in the following connections: "All persons born or naturalized in the United States"—"nor shall any state deprive any person of life, liberty or property," etc.—"nor" shall any state "deny to any person within its jurisdiction the equal protection of the laws." . . . Only natural persons can be born or naturalized; only natural persons can be deprived of life or liberty; so that it is clear that artificial persons are excluded from the provisions.[86]

Three other textual considerations indicate that "persons" cannot include artificial persons. First, the Amendment guarantees equal protection only to stubbornly unilocational persons—those corporeal beings who might be "within" a state's jurisdiction. But incorporeal persons, whether divine, angelic, or corporate, can bilocate, trilocate, and even multilocate. Second, the possessive adjective "its" ("within its jurisdiction") has a clear antecedent in "state" only if the intervening noun "person" is only a male or female person. Third, Section 2 requires that "[r]epresentatives shall be apportioned among the several States according to their respective numbers, counting the *whole number of persons* in each State, excluding Indians not taxed," but corporations have never been so enumerated.[87] And unlike prenatal persons, the exclusion of corporate "persons" cannot be attributed to uncountability, as they are normally easier to count than human beings, especially if states require corporate registration. Moreover, the result would be absurd, as each state would infinitely increase the number of corporate "persons" to maximize its congressional apportionment.

Further, the pre-Amendment meaning of the Equal-Protection-Due Process provision further indicates that "person" is limited to human beings. In its medieval origins, as we saw, due process was due to *homines*. And for the most part, antebellum jurists assumed or asserted that the word "person" as used in due-process provisions of state constitutions, likewise encompassed only human persons.[88] Even when straining to extend rights to corporations, courts frankly acknowledged the *textual* non-personhood of artificial entities. In one case, the Supreme Court of Mississippi counted a corporation as an "accused" person under the state's due-process clause, but had to rely on the "spirit" and not the letter of the provision.[89] Similarly, a few years after the Amendment's adoption, the Supreme Court of Illinois declared that state's due-process provisions "are designed to apply only to natural persons, but artificial persons must be permitted to invoke the *spirit* of justice which prompted them."[90]

Likewise, "equal protection," as applied to "persons" before the Amendment, seemed reserved to human beings. Where used by antebellum authorities, "equal protection" seemingly always concerned the equality due to human persons—aliens as well as citizens. As Hamilton asked rhetorically, "Do we not protect [aliens] equally with our own citizens, in their persons and reputation; in the acquisition and enjoyment of property?"[91]

Furthermore, the *purpose* of the Due Process-Equal Protection Clause supports this limitation. Under the Declaration, "men" are *equally* endowed by God with certain rights. Corporations, in contrast, are made by men; in Chief Justice Marshall's phrase, a corporation is the "mere creature" of human law.[92] As creatures of men, corporations may be equal to one another, but cannot be equal to men, just as men, equal to one another, are not equal to their Creator.

To be sure, justice to the human makers of corporations may require some derivative and inferior measure of justice to the corporations they make,[93] just as justice to the divine Maker of humans might require some inferior and derivative measure of justice to such persons. Indeed, the justice due to human-made associations might be especially salient where the association was itself oriented directly to man's Maker: religious associations. Not surprisingly, when Massachusetts first constitutionally guaranteed "equal protection" to certain entities, the right was reserved to a peculiar sort of association: Christian "denominations."[94]

Furthermore, as we saw, Bingham repeatedly emphasized that Section 1 secured *human* rights granted by the Creator. He said much the same in private writings. Perhaps most notably, in a contemporaneous letter to a friend, he explained that in framing Section 1, his governing principle was a "conviction of the fundamental, eternal rights of humanity, rights that had been denied to the negroes. It surged from my understanding of the Divine Plan. . . . By persons I did not mean corporations."[95] And in a public speech, he paraphrased the restriction in these terms: "that no State shall hereafter deny to any *human being* within its limits the equal protection of the laws."[96]

In sum, therefore, the term "person" included any human being, and only human beings.

The Person's Right to Due Process of Law

As we saw in the first chapter, neither of the predicates of the Due Process-Equal Protection Clause occasioned much controversy as to their meaning or justice, but much as to their federalization. As to legal process, the human person's right to security in person and property against state violence, absent "due process of law" (and the related "law of the land"), seemed an old, familiar, even anodyne concept. When, early in the Thirty-Ninth Congress, the voluble Democrat Andrew Rogers[97] had asked for a definition of "due process of law," Bingham curtly responded, "the courts have settled that long ago, and the gentleman can go and read their decisions."[98] That seemed to settle the matter, as no one in Congress questioned further the meaning of "due process of law" as it would appear in the final version. Indeed, whether in Congress or the states, there was virtually no debate as to the provision except as to its federalization, for no one then seems to have noted any major substantive disagreement as to the meaning or value of "due process of law."

Therefore, it has been remarkable that this apparent original settlement has long given way to such discord among jurists of the bench, bar, and academy. One explanation has been that, despite Bingham's admonition, many officials adopting the Amendment simply never bothered to "read" the "decisions" and thus were ignorant of their complexity and even confusion. A century ago, in a now-obscure but important study, the legal historian Herbert Leyland read well over one hundred of these pre-Amendment judicial opinions, and saw not settlement, but "the spectacle of a confused mess of material with no clear, predominant and universally accepted reading of the phrase."[99] Leyland conceded that Bingham and his colleagues no doubt "had some idea of the meaning," but, Leyland charged, the framers cunningly exploited the widespread "ignorance of the very [complex] material which Bingham used in framing the Amendment,"[100] so as to conceal from "the people . . . the great power cloaked in comfortable words."[101] The Due Process Clause, then, was a successful conspiracy against the people to transfer power to the federal government, especially its courts.

In recent decades, however, several scholars have taken a fresh look at the pre-Amendment "decisions" and have discerned not so much original confusion, but coherence. Some, such as Frederick Gedicks and Ryan Williams, have found evidence supportive of what we now call "substantive due process."[102] In response, others, like Michael McConnell, Nathan Chapman, and Matthew Franck, have specified that the decisions stand for a more limited proposition: that "due process of law" required a genuine trial and must be "of law" such that the legislative act defining liability must not be a mere decree, tailored to identifiable persons, but a genuine rule with general and unpredictable applications.[103] Christopher Green has reviewed the congressional debates touching on "due process of law" in the five years before the Amendment and found further coherence: a "bipartisan consensus" that the phrase (1) mandated traditional judicial proceedings and (2) included a public safety exception.[104]

Building on the research and analysis of both Leyland and these recent scholars, I submit that an even richer consensus can be found if we read the judicial "decisions" in light of a close reading of the constitutional text. By collating the judicial conclusions with each of the terms, the verb "deprive," the nouns, "life, liberty, [and] property," the noun "process," and its modifiers, "due" and "of law," we can identify a fairly coherent and robust original understanding.

Deprive

While the subject of the prohibition is "state," the governing verb is "deprive." The question, then, is to ascertain what kind of state action might constitute state *deprivation*. The later contention that deprivation encompassed *regulation* was essential to the initial establishment of what was later called "substantive due process," beginning with economic substantive due process.[105] A century later, the suggestion that deprivation included *withholding* or *denial* was essential to the "due process revolution" that required due process in the denial of governmental benefits. [106]

Neither of these readings seems reconcilable with the original meaning of "deprive." The word strongly suggests both something that was privy or private to the person but is made no longer private by something extrinsic, something violent. Deprivation, then, would seem to require destruction or dispossession of a private good, and not its mere regulation.

Still less could deprivation mean the mere withholding or denial of a public good that is not yet privy to the individual. The immediate context of the prohibition on certain deprivation, paired with a prohibition on state *denial* of equal protection, would seem, by contrast, to preclude the sense that "to deprive" includes "to deny." Otherwise, the whole clause could have had one single governing subject (state) and verb (deprive): "No state shall deprive any person of the equal protection of the laws, or of life, liberty, or property without due process of law."

Moreover, the antecedents of the Due Process Clause used language that indicated only dispossession or destruction. Most notably, the original 1354 statute provided that absent due process of law, a man could not be "put out of his lands or tenements, nor taken, nor imprisoned, nor disinherited, nor put to death."[107] Each of these verbs, later replaced with the simple "deprive," suggests only violent interference with the person's body and property.

This original limitation is further confirmed by contemporaneous judicial opinions. In 1853, the Pennsylvania Supreme Court explained that "deprive" and "take" are synonyms, and that "take" is "one of the commonest and plainest in the language, and cannot easily be misunderstood either by a lawyer or layman"; the term, as to property, has "universally, in this state and elsewhere, been interpreted to mean a taking altogether, a seizure, a direct appropriation" and never when the object "is merely depreciated in value, or encumbered, or incidentally injured."[108] The same principle applied to liberty; just a few years before the Amendment, the California Supreme Court indicated that the deprivation of liberty required the confinement of the body of persons: "incarcerating in prison, selling or holding in slavery, or in any other way taking away their liberty."[109]

There were at least two antebellum exceptions to this judicial consensus: in opinions concerning (1) slaves and (2) intoxicating liquors. The first instance was in Justice Baldwin's concurring opinion in a case regarding the interstate slave trade; he briefly remarked that under the Fifth Amendment, property included slaves, and that the forbidden congressional deprivation included any interference "not merely in ownership," but also in "the right of disposing" of such property.[110] A regulation of the slave trade might represent a deprivation of property. More influential was the 1856 holding, by the New York Court of Appeals, that a law prohibiting the sale, or holding for sale, of intoxicating liquors was an unconstitutional *deprivation* of property.[111] According to the lead opinion in the case, a state deprivation occurs when any law or other state action "annihilates the value of property, and strips it of attributes, by which alone it is distinguished as property."[112] And a secondary opinion in the case clarified that deprivation of a person's chattel can occur by the subversion of his rights in the chattel, even "without its being seized or physically destroyed, or taken from his possession."[113]

Nonetheless, this holding was anomalous,[114] what William Crosskey aptly called the "*New York heresy.*"[115] It was, in fact, the subject of "widespread disapproval in New York itself" and "unfavorable comment" elsewhere.[116] Delaware's high court, in the same year, explained that "[t]he vendible quality of a thing is not of the substance of the thing in such sense that they may not be lawfully separated, and the right to have or own a thing does not oblige the State to furnish a market for its sale."[117] Three years later, Alabama's Supreme Court surveyed the decisions and noted that most courts "favor the proposition that a statute which entirely prohibits the sale of spirituous liquors does not, in the sense of this clause, deprive the owner of his property in them."[118] Instead, that court found more persuasive the interpretation that deprivation meant "dispossession."[119]

At the time of the adoption of the Amendment, even New York authorities seemed to disown the heresy.[120] As one court noted in 1866, the verb "deprive" under the constitution means "the taking away of a man's property" and not merely "regulating the manner of the use of it."[121] And soon after the Amendment's adoption, in the *Legal Tender Cases*,[122] the Supreme Court likewise noted that deprivation "has always been understood as referring only to a direct appropriation, and not to consequential injuries resulting from the exercise of lawful power"—even if such injuries resulted from a regulation that was "impolitic and unjust."[123]

Life, Liberty, or Property

The forbidden deprivation extends to these goods: "life, liberty, [and] property." As the text indicates, these are *privy* to the person, of which he or she cannot be *deprived* absent a certain condition: "due process of law." And as indicated by the whole discussion of the Amendment, these three things pertained to the person as "*rights*." The February proposal expressly referred to them as the "*rights* of life, liberty, and property,"[124] and though omitted from the April revision, Bingham and others still identified these goods as "rights" that were natural or "inborn."[125]

With a single major exception, these three rights were deemed straightforward and uncontroversial. In one well-respected decision,[126] Alabama's Supreme Court had noted, the "terms 'life, liberty or property' speak their own meaning, and clearly refer to the three great interests—human life—personal liberty—and private property, which it was the object of civil government to protect."[127]

Life, as "human life," seems clear. Liberty, or "personal liberty," was limited to locomotion or freedom from restraint.[128] Thus, North Carolina's high court explained that "liberty," when used in the state constitution's law-of-the-land provision, referred to an individual's bodily or "personal liberty" in contrast with the "liberties" that an individual or corporation might enjoy.[129] While the Amendment was pending, Missouri's supreme court (or at least a judge thereof) likewise said that under the Due Process Clause, "life, liberty, and property" meant "personal security, personal locomotion or freedom from arrest, and private property."[130] As Charles Warren found a century ago, in virtually every pre-Amendment case on due process, "liberty" was deemed to mean "freedom from physical restraint."[131]

Property, or "private property," also had a largely uncontroversial meaning: that "dominion which one man claims and exercises over the external things of the world."[132] Such "external things" included any real as well as personal property that might be privy to the individual person.[133] Incidentally, despite the efforts by John Locke and James Madison in their philosophical work, seemingly no American legal authority accepted that "property" was the paradigmatic right, including one's own life and natural liberty, or any other "internal" rights to one's body, conscience, or mind.[134] The Amendment, therefore, did not and could not simply read, "nor shall any state deprive any person of property without due process of law."

But slavery had occasioned a great definitional dispute. Pro-slavery Americans aimed to vindicate as "property" that "despotical dominion" over a peculiar sort of external thing: another human person. Speaking for the Court in the *Dred Scott* decision, Chief Justice Taney had concluded that under the Fifth Amendment, the right of the master to the slave represents "property" as much as any "other property owned by a citizen."[135]

Justice Curtis, a northern Whig (and future Democrat), provided a modest dissent. Slaves *could* represent constitutional "property," but only on a certain condition. Because slavery was "contrary to natural right," the enslaved person could be property only if so designated by local municipal laws, but would have no status as "property" outside the slave states recognizing such artificial property.[136]

But Republicans and other antislavery Americans claimed that true "property" could never include a human being. These Americans found the limitation in both the Declaration of Independence and the very meaning of "property" under the Constitution. Hence, the sole Republican on the Court, Justice McLean, denied that the Constitution recognized any kind of "property in man."[137] Many Republicans, like Lincoln, said the same.[138] Of course, by 1866, this entire question was resolved by the Thirteenth Amendment's declaration that such property was nonexistent, a declaration enhanced by the Fourteenth Amendment's invalidation of every claim, whatsoever, arising from the loss of such so-called property.[139]

However clear these terms were, this triad may seem inappropriate in two respects. The first problem is that the triad has too many elements, as the words "liberty" and "property" already imply "life": any destruction of life would necessarily destroy the person's locomotion or possession of property. Accordingly, as Andrew Bodoh has pointed out, several state constitutional antecedents had, in the interest of concision, omitted "life" but used "liberty" alone or both "liberty" and "property."[140]

Vermont's constitution, for instance, protected only "liberty," but the state's high court explained that the word implied "life":

> The closing paragraph of the tenth article in our bill of rights is, "nor can any person be justly deprived of his liberty, except by the laws of the land, or the judgment of his peers;" dropping the words, life and property, which are inserted in most of the state constitutions. The liberty, spoken of in our bill of rights, is the liberty of the person of every subject; and the right to the enjoyment of life is personal to all; and a proceeding affecting the life of a subject may well be termed a proceeding to deprive him of his natural personal liberty; all this is involved.[141]

Conversely, however, "liberty" could not imply "property"[142] The deprivation of life would always destroy liberty, but the deprivation of liberty would not destroy property. An incarcerated person could still own property, and conversely, a poor person could still have bodily liberty. The court elaborated: "The infliction of a fine does not act upon the personal liberty of the subject any more than it would to render judgment against him in a civil action."[143]

Because the human body and human property were not reducible to one another, proponents of the Amendment often spoke of the rights as only twofold—of person (body) and property. Most notably, the equal-protection element of the Civil Rights Act guaranteed "the security of person and property."[144] Senator John Henderson explained that these referred to the "fundamental rights of person and property which cannot be denied to any person without disgracing the Government itself."[145]

Therefore, the authors of the Fifth and Fourteenth Amendments, it seems, should have rejected the triad in favor of a more succinct, twofold formula, either "liberty or property" or "rights of person or property."

But the triad was appropriate in two respects. First, under the rule of three, it provided a certain rhetorical elegance, a sense of completion, wholeness. This wholeness, in turn, might suggest the inclusion of certain interstitial rights, as I'll note below. Second, the triad pointed to an essential threefold distinction. As we'll elaborate below, there were three standards of due process that varied relative to the three goods to be deprived: as one ascended, from alienable property, to inalienable liberty, to inalienable and almost-inviolable life, the state had a higher burden to justify the deprivation.

The *second* problem is the triad seems too short. Conspicuously omitted are two rights, privy to the human person, that had long been associated with due process: limb and (bodily) offspring.

The deprivation of limb (or any other destruction of the body short of death) had been encompassed by the Magna Carta: no freeman was to be "*in any manner destroyed*," without due process of law.[146] And in the Fifth Amendment, no person was, for the same offense, to be put in jeopardy of "life or limb." Yet the due process provisions of the Fifth and Fourteenth Amendments conspicuously omitted "limb."

Similarly, the deprivation of bodily offspring had likewise long been associated with due process. It was an established maxim that the parent could not be deprived of his or her offspring except by a judicial determination that the deprivation was justified. As future Justice Samuel Nelson said thirty years before the Amendment, the parent is "the natural guardian of his infant children [and] in the absence of good and sufficient reasons shown to the court, such as ill usage, grossly immoral principles or habits, want of ability, and so forth, is entitled to their custody, care and education. All the authorities concur on this point."[147] By 1866, the rule still prevailed: the Wisconsin Supreme Court explained that a child's mother, upon the death of the father, became the sole "natural guardian" of her child; therefore, there could be no "*depriving* the mother of the care and custody of the child" absent a showing of "good reason" or "just cause." And the burden of proof, the court said, was on those alleging such just cause—and not on the mother to disprove such cause: "An effort was made to show that she was destitute of affection for her offspring, or was of so quick and violent a temper as rendered her unfit or unsuitable to have charge of the child. The proof however fails to establish any such case."[148]

Moreover, just as the Fifth Amendment had expressly recognized the person's right to his or her limbs, the Fourteenth impliedly recognized the person's dominion over his or her offspring. Under the Citizenship Clause, a person's citizenship by birth required both birth in the United States and subjection to the jurisdiction thereof—which subjection was understood to be mediated through the newborn's subjection to his or her parents. As Senator Reverdy Johnson remarked, the measure would encompass children "born of parents who at the time of birth were subject to the authority of the United States."[149] And within two decades, the Supreme Court would agree that this subjection "relate[s] to the time of birth," and that such subjection to the United States depends entirely on whether the "parents" were subject to the same jurisdiction.[150]

At the very least, then, it would have been highly anomalous if the authors of the Bill of Rights decided to secure, against unlawful deprivation, a mother's right to a handkerchief, but not her right to her offspring. In this regard, consider the insistence of a Tennessee judge, future Justice John Catron, that a statute authorizing an unmarried man's right to legitimize and obtain custody of his offspring must be read to include, albeit impliedly, the mother's right to notice and a hearing:

> The woman cannot be deprived of any article of property of the least value, unless she has notice of the judgment by which it is decreed away; yet it is urged that her child, to whom she has the strongest right, possibly, to be found in the laws of nature, or the English common law, can be taken from her at discretion, without notice or the power of resistance, by an *exparte* [sic] judgment.[151]

Therefore, it might seem that the omission of the terms "limb" and "offspring" was conspicuous and thus arguably deliberate. Perhaps the authors of the Fifth and Fourteenth Amendments believed that the interests of limb and offspring, though traditionally associated with due process and recognized in the Fifth and Fourteenth Amendments, required no further constitutional guarantees.[152]

I think the better explanation for the omission of "limb" or "offspring" is that both these goods were adequately covered by the terms "life, liberty, or property"—and in two ways. First, these goods could be implied by the triad, taken not separately but as a unit. "Life, liberty, and property" together arguably include not just these three items but any interstitial right—the rights that lie in between. The right to limb is a sort of interstitial right between life and liberty, and bodily offspring between liberty and property.

Even if taken separately, one or more of these distinct terms probably covered limb and offspring. Insofar as "life" was understood as the union of the soul with the body,[153] the destruction of any part of a person's body was, to that extent, a destruction of the soul's unity with the body, and thus any destruction of a body part was a partial deprivation of "life." Accordingly, while the Amendment was pending, Missouri's supreme court defined "life," under the Due Process Clause, as synonymous with "personal security."[154]

If so, one might ask why the authors of the Fifth Amendment used the apparently redundant expression, "life or limb." One possible answer, as Akhil Amar has contended, is that the expression was simply a term of art, "a vivid and poetic metaphor for all criminal punishment."[155] Another explanation is that the addition of "limb" was simply clarificatory of the scope of the Double Jeopardy Clause—included in an abundance of caution to cover all destructions of the body, even those that did not involve the total loss of life—as would be, say, the amputation of the head from the body ("capital" punishment). Indeed, as I will note below, authorities read the first three clauses of the Fifth Amendment—Double Jeopardy, Self-Incrimination, and Grand Jury Clauses—as merely partly declaratory of what was implied by the subsequent, broader, and culminating Due Process Clause; so destruction of limb was incorporated into "life, liberty, or property."

As to parental custody of offspring, both "liberty" and "property" arguably sufficed. The child's right to liberty and property included the interest in his or her "natural guardian" or trustee. To deprive the child-beneficiary of this bodily trustee was a deprivation of the child's liberty, or perhaps more clearly, his or her property; the beneficiary of a trust has a sort of property interest in the trustee's care.

Conversely, one could speak of the parental-trustee as having a property interest in the custody of the child. The parent, it was said, had property in the child's services,[156] and this implied the child's custody as well. Further, the mother especially would seem to have something like a property interest in her infant. The child would seem close to an archetypical or paradigmatic form of property: the fruit of one's bodily labor. As one court explained a few years before the Amendment, property must include, first and foremost, "the fruits of toil and labor . . . and upon every principle of legal justice are entitled to the protection of the Courts."[157] If so, what is "proper" to the mother's body, and thus her property, must include not only the acorns she might collect with her bodily labor, but the child produced from both her body and her labor—a labor so laborious that we simply call it "labor."

To be sure, the slogan, "no property in man," seemed to preclude any claim that a parent has "property" in her offspring. And at least one antebellum court categorically rejected the notion of such parental "property."[158] But if instead, the child was understood not as chattel but as a trust, then to that extent the child was the trustee's property. As one court explained, the "right of guardianship is a trust for the benefit of the child, and the parent is not at liberty to abuse it."[159] As the mother's natural trust, not chattel, the child was truly a sort of property—indeed, more "proper" to her than her mule, her hat, or any other chattel.

Nonetheless, to my knowledge, before the Amendment, no judicial authority had, in connection with constitutional "due process," expressly identified "limb" as "life," or parental custody as the "property" or "liberty" of either child or parent. But no authority ever denied such notions.

Still, within a decade of the Amendment's adoption, at least one court would declare that the "right to life includes the right of the individual to his body in its completeness and without dismemberment."[160] And just a few months after the Amendment's ratification, Indiana's supreme court declared that "to *deprive* the father of his right to the *custody* of his infant child," without notice and a hearing, was to violate the father's more general right to retain his "*liberty* and *property*" unless deprived of them by a judicial determination that "he has forfeited them by the standing laws of the community, and has had opportunity to answer such charges."[161] And two years later, in an opinion authored by Judge Anthony Thornton—a Democratic member of the Thirty-Ninth Congress—the Illinois Supreme Court concluded that constitutional due process secured the child's liberty interest in his father's care. The Court found that, by compelling a poor child to live at a reform school, the state had engaged in deprivation without "due process of law" because there had been no judicial determination either that the child had forfeited his liberty by crime, or that his father had forfeited his custody by "gross misconduct" or was otherwise an unfit custodian.[162]

Without Due Process of Law

The person's rights to life, liberty, and property are secured against all state violence unless the state provides or follows something called "due process of law." The phrase has three elements: a substantive governed by two modifiers: (1) a process, (2) a process that is due, and (3) a process that is "of law."

Let's consider these three elements.

Process

"Process" is the object in this prepositional phrase, "without due process of law." The word, when first introduced into English in the fourteenth century, meant what we now call "judicial process."[163] That is to say, "process" meant a *trial*. This understanding still prevailed among antebellum jurists. In his commentaries, Kent remarked that the "better and larger definition of 'due process of law' is 'law in its regular course of administration through courts of justice.'"[164] Justice Benjamin Curtis, the preeminent antebellum judicial "authority on due process of law,"[165] read the phrase to prohibit the deprivation of "life, liberty or property without a trial."[166] The guarantee, then, was for due *trial* of law.

This understanding prevailed at the time of the Amendment's adoption. In 1863, the California Supreme Court declared that "[t]he terms 'due process of law' have a distinct legal signification, clearly securing . . . a judicial trial."[167] This trial, courts concurred, required "inquiry"[168] or "forensic trial and judgment" [169] or "judicial investigation."[170]

This forensic trial, in turn, required that there be a proper trier: a "*judex*" or "a regularly constituted court."[171] Various authorities quoted Kent's formula requiring "regular administration."[172] Further, as Christopher Green has discovered, during the Civil War, Democratic as well as Republican members of Congress agreed that due process meant a judicial trial.[173]

The trier, moreover, must have the requisite impartiality—and it was axiomatic that personal interest was disqualifying. Michigan's Supreme Court endorsed as "fundamental" to constitutional due process the "principle that no man shall be party and judge in his own case" and tried only "by impartial judicial authority."[174] The Delaware Supreme Court said much the same.[175]

Process, then, was not equivalent to mere method or manner. The significance of "*process*" instead of the more flexible "*course* of law," seems to have been noticed by some officials. As we noted, some antebellum slave states had substituted "due course of law" for "due process of law." Alabama's high court noted the flexibility of the substitute: "By 'due course of law,' we are to understand those forms of arrest, trial and punishment, guarantied by the constitution, or provided by the common law; *or else* such as the legislature . . . have enacted to ensure public peace, and elevate public morals."[176] Due *course* of law, it seems, need not involve the *process* defined by common or constitutional law. Perhaps aware of this legacy, the biracial reconstruction conventions in Alabama and Mississippi, each decided to discard the antebellum "due course of law" and restore the medieval "due process of law."[177]

We might pause here to note that the sheer necessity of a "process" would necessarily bar certain legislative enactments. Three extreme examples come to mind. First, if the state commanded the haphazard destruction of life, liberty, or property, it's hard to see what room would be left for any trial involving forensic investigation. The sole matter to be tried would be whether the defendant had a life to destroy, a body to detain, or property to be destroyed or seized. Second, the state could command the destruction of a specified person's life, liberty, or property. Here, there would be only one trivial matter to address and investigate—the identity of the defendant. Third, the state could command such destruction whenever it was some official's will or pleasure.[178] Here the investigation would be largely complete simply upon the official's communication of his feelings—for there would be little room for anyone to refute the official's account of his or her feelings. In all these cases, the state enactment would largely abrogate the necessity of any meaningful judicial investigation. Consequently, this deprivation under such enactments would occur without any real process—and hence be unconstitutional.

But there are at least two difficulties in reading "process" as a reference to an impartial trial. The *first* is contextual. As Christopher Green has noted, the word "process," as used elsewhere in the Constitution, refers to a largely summary mode of coercion that is merely ancillary to a trial—the Sixth Amendment's "compulsory process" for obtaining witnesses favorable to the accused.[179] Indeed, contemporaneous with the adoption of the Fifth Amendment, the word "process" often referred primarily to this usage and various other modes that did not, themselves, include a forensic trial but were only ancillary to such trial.[180]

This usage is indeed interesting, and it raises the question of how a word that originally came into English as *trial* had come to refer to a subordinate, ancillary part of the whole judicial proceeding. Perhaps the usage was (1) a certain noble synecdoche, where the most rational and respectable part, the evidentiary trial (the process, strictly speaking), becomes a word for the whole judicial proceeding, and then (2) a certain veil, where the more brutal parts of the proceeding are designated by the nobler end to which they are ordered. The whole proceeding is now called a "process," with the word "process" used *especially* to cover the least honorable subrational aspects, such as a judge's order to compel the testimony of a reluctant witness: "find him, grab him, drag him here, and make him talk." Better to call this ugly business "process."

A second problem with "process" as "trial" is there are so many exceptions that swallow the rule. The categorical language prohibits *all* deprivations of life, liberty, and property without due process. But summary coercion is quite normal, in the forms of pretrial arrest,[181] post-trial execution,[182] as well as war[183] and tax collection.[184] In all these instances, there is coercive state action brought to bear directly on the life, liberty, or property of persons, but without an individual forensic process to test the cause of such coercion.

But perhaps none of these instances of summary state coercion is truly an exception to the "process" requirement. They all seem to be not exceptions but necessary *auxiliaries* to the general rule. Pretrial arrest can be necessary to conduct the process—the defendant must "be brought in to answer."[185] Similarly "compulsory process" to obtain testimony favorable to the defendant may be essential to a just trial. Pretrial seizure and even sale may be necessary as to perishable goods—precisely to "protect the rights of all parties by a resort to the only mode to obtain any beneficial use from the property."[186] Post-trial execution of judgments, including seizure and forfeiture of property, is necessary to make the process effective.[187] To require a trial to determine whether there was a trial would result in an endless series of adjudications without effect.

War, like pretrial arrest, aims at satisfying a necessary condition for this process. Any just war, it seems, must aim at the peace absolutely necessary to judicial process.[188]

As to taxation, perhaps it is an exception. Before the Amendment, the Supreme Court said that the "general" rule requiring "a trial according to some settled course of judicial proceedings" admitted an exception: "process in its nature final, [that] issues upon the body, lands, and goods of certain public debtors without any such trial."[189] If so, then due process sometimes required a trial, sometimes not.

Nonetheless, the Court's statement may have been misleading. Such collection of public debt, chiefly tax collection, may also have been not an exception, but simply ancillary to "due trial of law." Taxation may provide the resources indispensable to the whole judicial process—and in the manner most conducive to justice and prudence. A judiciary dependent on voluntary and private funds would almost certainly fail to be (or at least appear to be) impartial between the rich and poor. Such a failure would probably be fatal to the legitimacy of the judicial process. Therefore, the Michigan Supreme Court rightly viewed the collection of revenue as necessary to the very existence of the tribunal and the rest of the government: "an act of the government in the exercise or pre-eminent sovereignty, to which all other rights are subordinate, a right necessary for the protection and preservation of the government."[190]

But perhaps taxation represents something even more anodyne—the mere enforcement of an anterior debt requiring no further judicial determination. Just as the Due Process Clause presupposes that human beings, as such, have a right to life, liberty, or property, the whole Constitution might also presuppose that members of civil society have a duty to financially contribute to its work.[191] Taxation, as defined by law, is not the imposition of a new burden but an ascertainment or "assessment" of an anterior debt. Tax collection, then, is merely enforcement of a debt that is already privy to the person. The tax collection process is like the post-trial execution of a judgment. There is no deprivation of property, for the creditor (in this case, the state) already has superior title.

Due

The process must have two discrete features: it must be both "due" and "of law." The two modifiers, "due" and "of law," are syntactically separate, and we may consider them both separately and in their proper order.

The word "due" came in as a past participle of the French *devoir* or "to owe," so it originally meant something "owed" to someone or something.[192] To whom is "process" thus due or owed? Is the process owed to the lawmaker—to give the legislature its due? Rather, the context strongly suggests that the obligee is someone far more important: the human person. The human person, created by God (as most Americans then believed), has certain anterior rights of life, liberty, and property far in excess of the legislature instituted by man. Such persons are prior to law: "Jurists as far back as Justinian in the sixth century saw clearly that law is *for* persons, not the other way around."[193]

One might, therefore, speak of "due process" alone, without any reference to "of law." Prior to any determinations of the positive law, something is due to the human being, as such. The text indicates this disjunction. A certain process is "due" apart from and prior to the "law."

A person whose body and property are threatened is owed not just a trial, but a *due* trial, a trial with certain features. According to pre-Amendment authorities, seemingly two features were thus due to the human being.

First, the person was entitled to conversation, and more specifically, *notice and a hearing*. From the beginning, this conversation was the core procedural right: to be brought to answer. This right is presupposed in the Fifth Amendment: to say that no "person shall be *held to answer* for a capital, or otherwise infamous crime." The implication is that no one can ever be prosecuted without this opportunity for "answer."

As to notice, the human being is, more specifically, entitled to know the *cause* for which he might be destroyed or dispossessed. After all, if "a decent respect [to] mankind requires a declaration of the *causes*" for the destruction of a people's political union, so much more does a decent respect to an individual require a declaration of the causes for the destruction of his own person or property. Both political violence to a people and bodily violence to an individual require a declaration of a cause.

As to a hearing, the person has a right to a voice in the proceeding concerning his or her own person and property. The value of the person's speech is not its reliability or veracity. Indeed, the presumption was always against the individual. No one can be a *judge* in his own case. Still, everyone has a right to a *voice* in his own case. Universal human corruption mandates the former, universal human dignity compels the latter.

Accordingly, at the time of the Amendment's adoption, authorities treated notice and a hearing as essential to due process.[194] To cite one example, the Pennsylvania Supreme Court, in 1866, said that due process involved not only *actor*, *reus*, and *judex*, that is "a complainant, a defendant and a judge," but also "regular allegations [and] opportunity to answer."[195]

Second, the threatened person was entitled to a *presumption against deprivation*, rebuttable only for good cause. This presumption was due by implication of the principle that life, liberty, and property are already *privy* to the person as rights. Any deprivation of what is otherwise rightful is violence, and for such violence, there is a trial of its justification or cause. Contrary to common usage, under our Constitution, what's "on trial" is not the defendant, but the *cause* justifying the proposed violence to his anterior rights of person or property.

Notice and a hearing, however, do not suffice. Due process must require, in addition, a presumption against deprivation. Otherwise the burden might belong to the person to show that deprivation was not proper. As Justice Harlan later charged in his dissent in *Hurtado v. California*, a person could be brought to answer "upon a rule to show cause why he should not be hanged."[196]

The necessity of this presumption to "due process" was, I believe, asserted or assumed by all pre-Amendment authorities. In the Petition of Right, after quoting the medieval "due process" provisions, Parliament denounced their violation by the detention of Englishmen where "no cause was certified, but that they were detained by your Majesty's special command," and, more generally, "without being charged with anything to which they might make answer according to the law."[197] The maxim seemed to be, "No cause, no deprivation."

A decade before the Fourteenth Amendment, the leading antebellum "authority on due process of law,"[198] Justice Curtis, explained that the human person is owed this presumption by "natural right":

> Natural right requires that no man should be punished for an offense until he has had a trial and been proved to be guilty; [otherwise] the legislative will could inflict a forfeiture of life, liberty or property without a trial. The exposition of these words, as they stand in Magna Charta, as well as in the American constitutions, has been that they require "due process of law;" and in this is necessarily implied

> and included the right to answer to and contest the charge, and the consequent right to be discharged from it unless it is proved.[199]

Furthermore, such proof could not be established by the defendant's silence.[200]

In criminal proceedings, this presumption against deprivation has long been known, more commonly, as the "presumption of innocence." As the Supreme Court later declared, "[t]he principle that there is a presumption of innocence in favor of the accused is the undoubted law, axiomatic and elementary, and its enforcement lies at the foundation of the administration of our criminal law."[201] Still, as I'll elaborate presently, the presumption was not only against criminal guilt, but against any other cause whereby an individual might lose his or her liberty or property. Therefore, the presumption of innocence is only the chief instance of the broader presumption against deprivation.

What "cause" would be sufficient to justify deprivation? A valid cause is certainly not the mere will and pleasure of those with sovereign authority. "The cause is in my will," said Caesar, "that will satisfy the Senate."[202] But such a "cause" would never satisfy Anglo-American due process.

Before the Fourteenth Amendment, authorities identified only a few discrete *causes* that, if proven, would rebut the presumption against deprivation. Two were usually mentioned: forfeiture by crime or another's superior title.[203] The New York courts provided perhaps the most commonly cited formula: "a prosecution or suit instituted and conducted according to the prescribed forms and solemnities *for ascertaining guilt, or determining the title to property*."[204] We can divide this second type of cause into two subtypes: superior title in another private party, and superior title in the political community (e.g., taxation). We can also discern another cause that authorities recognized; the adult person's nonculpable inability to manage his or her own person, offspring, or property.[205]

Hence, for our purposes, we can distinguish four causes that were thought to justify deprivation of the individual's rights of person and property: (1) forfeiture by crime, (2) the person's inability to manage his person, offspring, or property, (3) the political community's superior title, and (4) a private party's superior title.

Moreover, both the Amendment's context and all the discussion before its adoption strongly indicated three tiers of justification, corresponding to the parts of the triad of life, liberty, and property. Standards became stricter as one ascended from property to liberty to life. Let's consider these.

Property could be taken for any and all of these reasons, including forfeiture (fines), inability to manage one's property (guardianship or civil commitment), superior title in the state (taxation or eminent domain), and superior title in another individual (whether arising in property, contract, tort, or otherwise).

Personal liberty, in sharp contrast, could be subject to state violence for only three of these causes: forfeiture, inability to manage, or superior title in the community (e.g., compulsory public service)[206]—but *not* another private person's superior title. The right to liberty was nontransferable, or inalienable.[207] For this reason, California's Supreme Court, in enumerating the causes justifying deprivation, sharply distinguished the inalienable rights of life and liberty from property: "The great principle is, that a man's life, liberty, and property, is his own . . . until it is proved in due course of law that he has forfeited his life or liberty, or that the property is not his, but belongs to another."[208] The same implication could be drawn from the common formula that distinguished "superior title in property," but as to life and liberty, only "guilt."

This last point, of course, had remained unsettled until the Thirteenth Amendment. There had been some debate as to whether by sheer contract, a person could acquire superior title in another's body. For antislavery Americans, the matter was clear: the only lawful basis for depriving a human person of the *inalienable* goods of life *or* liberty was punishment for crime. The Free Soil Party, in the first plank of its 1852 platform, declared,

> That governments . . . are instituted among men to secure to all those inalienable rights of life, liberty, and the pursuit of happiness with which they are endowed by their Creator, and of which *none can be deprived by valid legislation, except, for crime.*[209]

Conversely, antebellum pro-slavery judges and legislators sometimes endorsed voluntary, contractual slavery. One Missouri judge defended slavery as entirely consistent with the natural, but *alienable* right to liberty. A person could thus effectively consent to enslavement and even hereditary slavery: "slavery may begin by a voluntary surrender of liberty; and that by the law of nature, children born of parents who are de facto slaves become ipso facto slaves themselves."[210] In the decade before the Civil War, several southern legislatures moved to make this theory a reality by legalizing voluntary self-enslavement by free blacks.[211]

As one Republican recalled in 1867, before the Thirteenth Amendment, a free black man had been deemed bereft of the inalienable "rights of manhood"; he was only property, either owned by another or "owned by himself," and thus "could have sold himself for so much money, and possessed the inestimable right to say how much he would take and from whom he would take it." But now such persons are "property no more" and no longer "the connecting link between beast and human, they stand forth in recognized manhood free American citizens."[212] That is to say, all human persons are *inalienably* free.

Finally, by virtually all accounts, only one cause could justify deprivation of life and limb: forfeiture by crime. The limitation was simply axiomatic in American law. No authority ever said or suggested that the state may impose *nonpunitive* death or dismemberment. The limitation was indicated by the Fifth Amendment. Under the Double Jeopardy Clause, no person could "be subject for the same offence to be twice put in jeopardy of life or limb." The implication was obvious; just as the Takings Clause, "by authorizing the appropriation of private property to public use, impliedly declares that, for any other use, private property shall not be taken,"[213] so the Double Jeopardy Clause, by authorizing jeopardy to a person's bodily integrity for an "offense," impliedly declares that for any other cause, life and limb shall not be jeopardized at all.

Moreover, under the Grand Jury Clause, we see that only *infamous* crimes may justify death. Any capital offense was, by definition, an "infamous" crime; that is, the sort of crime that, like treason, murder, mayhem, rape, and so on, is by its nature so grave a violation of the common good that the culprit would be of wicked repute (fame) in all civilized communities.[214]

Of Law

Lastly, this process must conform with one other requirement—it must be not only what is *due* to the human person, but also *of law*. The qualification was so important that we might, as Randy Barnett and Evan Bernick have recommended, speak of the "Due Process of Law Clause," instead of the "Due Process Clause."[215]

Law's definition is a matter of perennial dispute in jurisprudence, but the leading authorities tend to incorporate one or more of the following four elements: Law is (1) something made by those vested with legislative authority, (2) published so as to be known, (3) a rule of action with general and even unpredictable application and not a particularized precept or decree, and (4) for the public good and not merely the private good of the lawmaker.[216]

At the time of the adoption of the Fourteenth Amendment, the judicial decisions indicated that the process was not "of law" where it clearly violated one or more of these four elements.

First, as to legislative authority, courts were clear that the process required conformity with authoritative prescription. The oft-cited formula, mentioned above, required a finding of either guilt or superior title to property by the "*prescribed* forms and solemnities." According to another common formula, "due process of law" meant process "according to those rules and forms which have been established for the protection of private rights."[217]

Second, as to effective promulgation, the courts seemed to require a heightened standard for the laws prescribing any process that might jeopardize a person's life, liberty, or property. The rules had to be especially well known—with the necessary promulgation extending beyond a particular time and local lawmaker, with a preference for the traditional, if not ancient.

Kent said that the "better and larger definition of due process of law" is "*law* in its *regular* course of administration through courts of justice."[218] Story specified that the regularity had a certain antiquity: "trial according to the process and proceedings of the *common law*."[219] A decade before the Amendment, the Supreme Court, in a unanimous decision, provided more nuance. "Due process of law" required conformity with certain "settled usages and modes of proceeding" of England's common and statutory law, provided that such usages and modes had not been abandoned as incompatible with local conditions in America.[220] With some qualification, then, due process of law barred innovation.

At the time of the Amendment's adoption, courts similarly affirmed that the process must be well "settled,"[221] "regular,"[222] or "ordinary."[223] In 1863, the California Supreme Court declared that the trial must be "according to the established rules of law," that is, "according to the course of the common law regulating proceedings in like character."[224] And around the same time, as Christopher Green has found, Democratic as well as Republican members of Congress said much the same thing.[225]

By some accounts, the rule was inflexibly bound to the practices prevailing at the Founding. Twenty years before the Amendment, South Carolina's high court had said the rule required compliance with "common and statute law existing in this State at the adoption of our Constitution,[226] and Pennsylvania's high court said that due process of law required a traditional trial, "*more majorum*, according to the laws and customs of our fathers."[227] North Carolina's supreme court said the trial must be conducted "according to the course, mode and usages of the common law as derived from our forefathers."[228] And while the Amendment was pending, Virginia's supreme court, citing *Murray's Lessee*, said due process of law requires conformity with "the usages and modes of proceeding which prevailed in England or in this country before, or at the time of, the adoption of the constitution."[229] At the same time, this Founding-era prevalence did not require unanimity. Even if a rogue state, at Independence, had embraced a novel mode, a "single state adopting a new and exceptional mode of proceeding, could have no weight in the argument." [230]

But other courts allowed for more flexibility, some measure of post-Founding innovation. For instance, in 1859, Alabama's Supreme Court expressly declined to endorse North Carolina's formulation.[231] While the Fourteenth Amendment was pending, Nevada's high court declared that "the process" need not be the same as "pursued at common law, but that the mode and manner of their procedure may be regulated and prescribed by statute."[232] New Hampshire's highest court likewise said that the "law of the land" may be "shaped and altered by the legislature from time to time."[233] But we should note here the cautious language—*shape* or *alter*, but not abolish or reinvent.

Some authorities suggested a middle position—what was essential to heightened promulgation was not deep antiquity but wide acceptance. Michigan's supreme court said that, in contract disputes at least, the "process of law" must mean a "trial" either "by jury, *or* according to some *universally established* practice of courts."[234] A few years after ratification, Virginia's supreme court endorsed "any legal process, which was originally founded in necessity, has been consecrated by time, and approved and acquiesced in by universal consent, must be an exception to the right of trial by jury, and is embraced, by the alternative, 'the law of the land.'"[235] The suggestion was that the "law" of due process or "law of the land," then, might set aside old forms and accept new ones, but only slowly, and only upon confirmation by a broad consensus. And as we saw, the Supreme Court had suggested that the "law" of due process may involve an abandonment, by desuetude, of certain traditional usages or modes.

Why might the "law" defining the judicial process require so much antiquity and/or breadth of promulgation? Perhaps one reason was the peculiar vulnerability of poor litigants to unjust deprivation where procedural norms are protean. The poor (and their underpaid attorneys) are less likely to be familiar with the allegedly "new and improved" modes of procedure, and less likely to be attuned to the opinions and passions of the class of jurists occupying the bench. Stable, boring, and familiar judicial process, however inefficient and anachronistic, might provide substantial protection to the most vulnerable defendants.

The traditionalist standard, however, gives rise to an interpretive challenge. Many of these traditional usages were also enumerated in the state and federal constitutions. Indeed, such enumeration, especially in the national Constitution, was primary evidence that such modes and usages were, in fact, deeply and broadly established. But their enumeration, alongside a separate due-process provision, turns the enumeration into mere redundancies.

The problem was illustrated in a judicial opinion issued in May 1866, precisely while Congress was discussing the proposed Fourteenth Amendment. John Erskine declared that the Fifth Amendment's Due Process Clause "exhibits a summary of all the antecedent precautions contained in this [same] article."[236] Erskine's reading seemingly renders superfluous the other precautions of the Fifth Amendment itself. As the Supreme Court said twenty years later, such a reading ignores the "recognized canon of interpretation especially applicable to formal and solemn instruments of constitutional law" whereby judges "are forbidden to assume, without clear reason to the contrary, that any part of this most important amendment is superfluous."[237]

But a "clear reason" may be found by considering both the meaning of "due process *of law*" and the primary purpose for the first ten amendments. The meaning of "law" required that the procedures conform with *very* well-established norms. And the purpose of the first ten amendments, as set forth by Congress, was to preserve certain well-established norms via certain "declaratory" and "restrictive" clauses.[238] Constitutional enumeration, then, served to declare and thus make more enduring, at least some of the "usages and modes of proceeding" that were already well established—and thus essential to the "law" governing due process.

As to the Fifth Amendment in particular, a close reading of the five listed prohibitions shows how the fourth (due process) may justly be read—in part—as a culminating summary of the foregoing. That Amendment consists of three parts, each consisting of an independent clause: the first part, with person as subject, is the lengthy Grand Jury Clause; the second part repeats the subject "person" in a new clause (probably because the length of the grand jury provision required it to stand alone), and covers double jeopardy, self-incrimination, and due process of law. The third part, with a new subject "property," is the fifth prohibition, "Takings Clause," and it seemingly protects not only human persons but all other owners of property, as we discussed.

The first four restrictions, concerning human beings and ending with due process, have an integrity and order. The list begins with threats to human life (grand jury), then expands to threats to human life and limb (double jeopardy), then any threatened deprivations of human life, liberty, or property as punishment for crime (self-incrimination), and then culminates in a general rule covering all threatened deprivations of life, liberty, or property, whether in criminal or other proceedings. We now can see, with Akhil Amar, "the grand arc of ever-greater inclusion, the subtle spiraling outward of clausal scope, in the sequence of Fifth Amendment clauses," concluding with the Due Process Clause.[239] Therefore, we might read that Amendment to mean "nor shall any person be subject for the same offence to be twice put in jeopardy of life or limb; nor shall be compelled in any criminal case to be a witness against himself, nor *otherwise* be deprived of life, liberty, or property, without due process of law."

Even though constitutional enumeration (especially in the Fifth Amendment) was persuasive evidence that a usage was sufficiently settled as to be "of law," such enumeration was not always dispositive. On the one hand, enumeration was not necessary. Certain traditional modes were so very well established as to require no enumeration. In trials of serious crime, "beyond a reasonable doubt" was the sole governing rule. As Justice Henry Baldwin (while on circuit) informed the jury, "we know of no other rule."[240]

On the other hand, enumeration was not sufficient. Some usages, though specified in the federal Constitution, might never have reflected a genuine consensus. For example, trial by jury in civil cases, guaranteed by the Seventh Amendment, seems never to have been so universally established as to be "of law." As Hamilton had observed, "there is a material diversity, as well in the modification as in the extent of the institution of trial by jury in civil cases, in the several States," so there was "no general rule" reflecting an American consensus.[241] Similarly, though mandated by Article III, the trial by judges holding their office during good behavior was neither ancient nor universal. Even if, as Hamilton believed, such a mode was the very "best expedient which can be devised in any government, to secure a steady, upright, and impartial administration of the laws," this excellent mode was not a traditional or otherwise general mode, but merely a "modern improvement" that had been adopted only in some American states.[242]

Further, at least one constitutionally enumerated right had arguably been essential to "law" at the Founding but was no longer so in 1866: the grand jury. The broader question, left unanswered at the time of the Fourteenth Amendment's adoption, was whether due process of law was so inflexibly traditional that no procedure prevalent at a particular time (1776, 1789, or 1866) could ever be set aside. The matter was especially salient as to those rights that had once been so prevalent as to have an express place in the Bill of Rights.

The answer was probably no, as many states were moving away from the use of the grand jury, despite the standard of the Fifth Amendment. As Charles Fairman explained, before the Fourteenth Amendment's adoption, some states had modified or abolished the grand jury for infamous crimes. But there seems to be no evidence that anyone thought the pending Amendment would have any effect in repealing this progressive reform.[243]

This deafening silence, as George Thomas has observed, suggests a general consensus that the Amendment would leave the states a broad authority to modify traditional criminal procedures.[244] Perhaps that silence alone indicates that by 1866, the anti-innovation rule, as incorporated in "due process of law," had become sufficiently flexible so as to permit the states broad authority to set aside, after due reflection, the grand jury and some other traditional usages and modes of proceeding.

But at the same time, no authority before 1868 said what the Supreme Court would say a generation later: that "process of law" was so flexible as to allow "constant fluctuation" where each state legislature could freely change procedural laws, by addition or subtraction, to conform with the mere "wishes" of the public.[245] Rather, to be fully "of law," the procedural laws had to conform with some broadly or deeply settled usages or modes and not transient popular will or caprice.

Third, courts recognized that to be genuinely "of law," the proceeding must involve directives that were general in their application and not tailored to identifiable persons. As Matthew Franck has noted, unlike a decree, a law is "impersonal, general, or neutral in character."[216] By the "rule of law," the primary justice makers are the blindfolded lawmakers, who thus do not know whose ox will be gored.

Why should we prefer justice effectuated by partly blind lawmakers rather than fully sighted judges? Why should we favor the off-the-rack, one-size-generally-fits-most justice provided by the legislature, instead of the personally tailored justice provided by a wise magistrate?

Aristotle provided two reasons. First, tailored justice was impossible because of the absence of tailors; there were not enough magistrates to do justice on a truly case-by-case basis.[247] Law was thus more efficient, though inexact.

Second, and more importantly for our purposes, human tailors, if available, are too corrupt and need restraint:

> One who asks law to rule, therefore, seems to be asking God and intellect alone to rule, while one who asks man adds the beast. Desire is a thing of this sort; and spiritedness perverts rulers and the best men. Hence law is intellect without appetite.[248]

Human judges, then, require restraint by human laws.

But lawmakers have appetites no less than judges. Government by human laws most certainly does involve appetite as well as intellect. If passion corrupts the "best of men," it corrupts lawmakers no less than judges. Why should we prefer corruptible human legislatures to corruptible human judges?

The blindfold is the answer: the blindfold frustrates the corrupting effects of human passions. As Aristotle suggests, men are more inflamed by particulars than abstractions, especially as to human things; we love humanity but can't stand (some) people. The lawmaker, when partly blindfolded, and the judge when restrained by rules made by such blindfolded legislators, may be less unjust precisely insofar as these persons cannot consider the particularity of the person. On balance, then, the rule of law, made by partly blinded human lawmakers, is less arbitrary than rule by full-sighted human decree-makers.

Accordingly, Iowa's Supreme Court said that due process of law requires "a judicial determination, after due notice, in pursuant of a general law," not targeting an identifiable person; the so-called "law of the individual case" could not be made by the lawmaker.[249] The Pennsylvania Supreme Court likewise held that the "law of the land" means "laws that are general in their operation, and that affect the rights of all alike; and not a special act of the legislature, passed to affect the rights of an individual against his will, and in a way in which the same rights of other persons are not affected by existing laws."[250] Other courts agreed; the legislative enactment should not "operate[] upon a special case, person, or locality."[251] Rather, "law of the land," means "a general and public law, operating equally upon every member of the community."[252] It cannot be "a special act of the legislature, passed to affect the rights of an individual."[253]

For this reason, before the Fourteenth Amendment, courts held that an uncompensated property deprivation, targeting an identifiable person, deprived that person of property without due process of *law*.[254] Contrary to the Supreme Court's subsequent *dictum*, this limitation on targeted deprivations was not "substantive" due process.[255] Rather, it was essential to legal process: to be "of law," any procedure must be governed by rules of unpredictable application.[256]

Fourth, in a significant but limited way, the original meaning of due process prohibited deprivations under general directives that were not for the general good but the private good of identifiable individuals. Just as the generality element precluded directives that targeted identifiable persons for deprivation, the public-purpose element prohibited directives that targeted identifiable persons for private benefit.[257] These considerations might explain why jurists at the time presented, as paradigmatically violative of due process of law, a legislative directive transferring the property of "A" to "B."[258] In effect, the targeting of "A" meant the directive lacked the necessary generality, while the exclusive benefit to "B" meant the directive lacked a public purpose. Failing in both these respects, such a legislative decree, however formally promulgated and however authorized by the legislative body, was not "of law."

In the words of a New York court, the "taking of property without due process of law, refers to a transfer of property from one person to another; and not to the taking of private property for *public use*."[259] The Iowa Supreme Court elaborated the principle a few months after the Fourteenth Amendment's ratification. The state constitution's due process clause, in conjunction with its takings clause, "prohibits by implication the taking of private property for any private use whatever, without the consent of the owner," even if compensated.[260] But in assessing whether a use was "private" or "public," the court urged a very strong presumption that the legislature had a public purpose, "*unless* it *manifestly* appears by the provisions of the act, that they can have no tendency to advance and promote the public use."[261]

But could this "public good" principle be extended to disqualify as "law" any legislative act that might be otherwise unjust? After all, is not justice the chief part of the public good? Doesn't the Declaration of Independence indicate that the securing of natural rights is the chief reason for which governments are instituted? If so, then any unjust law is "no law at all," and any process based on this directive cannot be "due process *of law*," and so the judiciary must invalidate any such directive.

The objection is intelligible, but I think unpersuasive. Indeed, the preceding considerations in this section provide strong reasons against any interpretation that would authorize the judiciary to nullify, as non-law, any otherwise valid law simply because the judges might deem it unjust or otherwise without a proper purpose.

Recall that if "law" is to rule, then it must be genuine law: that is, (1) made by the legitimate representative of the community, (2) promulgated fully, (3) formed as a rule of general (and unpredictable) applications, and (4) designed for justice and otherwise for the public good. But in a judicial proceeding, the first three of these features are all woefully lacking. First, the community has no representative there. The judge cannot seriously claim to represent the whole community. Even a relatively large bench, like the Supreme Court, could not be called the Judicial House of Representatives, or "The People's Court." The judge is a subordinate officer of, not a representative of, the sovereign people. To be sure, in some cases there may be a lawyer claiming to represent "the state" or "the people" or "the United States," but neither in fact nor in function is that lawyer entrusted with the common good. The very nature of our adversarial judicial process reduces "the United States" or a state to a mere party or a faction in the courtroom.

Second, there is the problem of promulgation—whether the relevant standard is *known*. The justice-seeking judge—who demands that the parties prove or disprove to his personal satisfaction the justice of the community's *promulgated public acts*—would place the litigants in the difficult position of having to know the judge's *unpromulgated private thoughts*; and that burden would generally fall more heavily on the poorer litigants whose representatives are less likely to be in the same socioeconomic circles as the judge.

Third, because the judicial process involves specific, identified parties, it lacks the discipline of the veil that tempers the legislature when it makes general rules. In a particular case or controversy, the judge would know *precisely* whose ox will get gored precisely when he or she decides that a law is just or unjust. Passions corrupt the "best of men"—even the best judge.

In sum, "of law" arguably involves four prerequisites, including a rule that laws be for the public good. But the judge has little to no authority to enforce this last requirement. Such judicial oversight would make the administration of justice lawless precisely in relation to the first three aspects of law. Such a reading, further, would have been diametrically opposed to the anti-kritocratic purpose of the Amendment's proponents. Accordingly, during the adoption and initial interpretation of the Fourteenth Amendment, there was no record of *anyone* suggesting that the required "due process of law" would give such sweeping power to the judiciary.

Professors Barnett and Bernick, however, have written that such was the original meaning, even if not recognized in 1866–1868. Before the Amendment, they write, "due process of law came to be understood as a guarantee against all arbitrary governmental action . . . by denying that an arbitrary act of a legislature qualified as 'a law.'" To support the claim, they provide one citation: the remark of the Marshall Court, that the analogous state "law of the land" provisions secured "the individual from the arbitrary exercise of the powers of government, unrestrained by the established principles of private rights and distributive justice."[262] Indeed, during the adoption of the Amendment, one official made a similar observation. In his letter opposing the Amendment, Interior Secretary Orville Browning celebrated the rule, as incorporated in the federal and state constitutions, as a "guarantee against arbitrary and oppressive invasions of the rights of the citizen."[263]

But neither Browning nor the Marshall Court identified non-arbitrariness as the *definition* of "due process of law." None of these officials said that the Due Process Clause (or its analogues), by its express terms, bans all arbitrary deprivations. The definition was far more precise. Anti-arbitrariness was the purpose or *genus*, and "process of law" was merely a determination or one *species* thereof. Due process of law functioned as one of the many constitutional restraints on *arbitrio* (will), in one very peculiar and important way: by binding the government, including the courts, to the *ratio* of a trial (process), conducted in obedience to the *ratio* embodied in well-established procedural laws. The principle was not designed to liberate the judge so he or she might second-guess the lawmakers. Such a liberation of the judge's *ratio* would also liberate his *arbitrio*, and to the authors of the Amendment, the greater risk was arbitrary kritocracy rather than arbitrary laws.

Accordingly, neither Browning nor any other opponent, let alone any supporter, said or suggested that the restriction would empower a judge to invalidate laws simply because he or she deemed them arbitrary. On this point, the silence was deafening. Opponents vociferously denounced the due process provision for its subordination of the state courts to the federal. Samuel Bloom, in the Ohio legislature, remarked, "This is to create in the Federal government a guardian of the States to see that they do not violate their own Constitutions."[264] The charge then was that federal authorities would humiliate state officials by overseeing their compliance with state law, not that the federal judges would rewrite state laws.

Opponents had no reason to fear that anyone would interpret "due process of law" to allow federal or state judges to review state laws for reasonableness, because no one had ever said so. State courts had emphatically denied that any provision of the federal or state constitutions would give such power. In New York, one judge both celebrated "due process of law" as a restraint against "mere arbitrary legislation, under whatever pretext of private or of public good" and disavowed any judicial power "to annul any law solemnly passed, either on an assumed ground of its being contrary to natural equity, or from a broad, loose and vague interpretation of a constitutional provision, beyond its natural and obvious sense."[265] Georgia's Supreme Court likewise said with reference to the state and federal constitutions, "Is there anything contained in either, that says, that no unjust law shall be passed? There is not."[266]

Michigan's high court, in a due-process case, likewise chastised any judicial activism that would seek to use constitutional adjudication to enforce the judges' supra-legal sense of justice:

> If it be said, the law is unnecessarily severe, and may sometimes do injustice, without fault in the sufferer under it, our reply is: these are considerations that may very properly be addressed to the legislature, but not to the judiciary—they go to the expediency of the law, and not to its constitutionality. When courts of justice, by reason of such objections, however well founded, seek for some hidden or abstruse meaning in one or more clauses of the constitution, to annul a law, they encroach on the power of the legislature, and make the constitution instead of construing it. They declare what the Constitution should be,—not what it is.[267]

* * *

In sum, by following Bingham's advice, we can read the "decisions" of the court before 1866 and see, with him, that the courts had indeed, "settled" the meaning of "due process of law." The phrase did not imply an indefinite power to nullify purportedly unreasonable state laws. It did, however, set forth substantial safeguards for human dignity against arbitrary power. In sum:

Any state deprivation of a human person's life, liberty, or property required,

(1) a judicial "process" (trial) that tested the justification for the deprivation;
(2) a trial giving what was "due" to the threatened human person, *viz.*,
    (a) notice.
    (b) a hearing, and
    (c) a presumption against deprivation, to be rebutted only upon cause shown, that is, proof that
        (i) the person had forfeited his life, liberty, or property by crime,
        (ii) the person was unable to manage his liberty or property,
        (iii) the political community had superior title in the person's personal services (liberty) or property, or
        (iv) another private entity had superior title to the person's property.
(3) which trial must be conducted in accord with "law"—that is,
    (a) authorized prescriptions,
    (b) that conformed with traditional or otherwise well-established procedural norms,
    (c) did not target identifiable persons for deprivation, and
    (d) did not target an identifiable private individual or group for the benefit of such deprivation.

I believe that this schema provides a fairly comprehensive account of the prevailing understanding of the "due process of law" in 1866. If my conclusions are correct, then the courts, indeed, had already thus "settled" the meaning of "due process of law." Bingham was right.

The Person's Right to Legal Protection

Any person who happens to be within a state's jurisdiction is guaranteed a certain legal protection. To him or her, no state may "deny . . . the equal protection of the laws."

Deny

"Deny" here seems to mean to deliberately refuse or withhold. Denial was not mere absence of action, nor mere forgetfulness or even culpable "neglect."[268] Deny is a transitive verb that thus takes a direct object. By its Latin etymology, the word had the sense of actively pushing something away—to negate away (*negare* + *de*).[269] In procedural law, for instance, the thing pushed away was an allegation: a "denial" was defined as a "traverse of the statement of the opposite party."[270] A denial, then, was not mere silence or even a *nolo contendere*. In the Ninth Amendment, denial likewise refers to something deliberate and active—the enumeration of rights shall not be construed so as to negate away ("deny") other rights retained by the people. Therefore, to ban state denial is not to ban mere state silence or other inaction, but some sort of state rejection.

Therefore, it is not quite true, as Christopher Green has claimed, that "prohibiting states from denying the protection of the laws is, as a matter of grammar, a requirement that states supply protection of the laws."[271] Rather, the prohibition extends only to a *deliberate refusal* to supply such protection, not the mere failure to do so.

In ordinary speech, the thing "pushed away" is not a claim but a request or demand; for example, to refuse a petition, to refuse admission, and so forth. Section 2 of the Amendment seems to use the word in this sense: a state will lose representation to the extent the right to vote is "denied" to law-abiding adult male citizens; their right to vote was, it seems, something requested or demanded either by the citizen or by our democratic standards. Hence for Thaddeus Stevens, to "deny" under Section 2 was synonymous with affirmative *exclusion*.[272]

In Section 1, however, the protection not to be denied was commanded as a matter of fundamental right. It was axiomatic, said the Texas Supreme Court, that no state may withhold "that protection, which it is the duty of government and the intention of the law to afford."[273] The states had no right whatsoever to refuse to protect a human person within its jurisdiction. Slavery had obscured the principle, to be sure—hence, as Bingham explained, no state "*ever* had the right, under the forms of law *or otherwise*, to deny to any *freeman* the equal protection of the laws," but now that slavery was legally nonexistent, even the pretext as to unfree persons was gone.[274]

Accordingly, during the adoption of the Amendment, supporters indicated that the forbidden state denial involved not merely inaction, but something akin to a deliberate policy of *dereliction*. According to Ohio's Samuel Shellabarger, the prohibition targeted the "*systematic* and universal murder of the Union men of the South."[275] Indiana's governor, Oliver Morton, told citizens that the measure concerned not merely state neglect, but a conscious discriminatory failure to provide: southern states had "discriminated against citizens of other States, by withholding the protection of the laws for life and liberty."[276] The *New York Tribune* found evidence of such a policy of discrimination in "serious" and "pervasive" lawless violence (as employment lawyers today might say). The rebel states "have repeatedly and grossly outraged" the right of legal protection, as "life, liberty and property have been illegally taken away."[277]

This forbidden dereliction required something more than mere negligence. Senator Howe told voters that the Amendment prohibited only state *refusal*: "The only effect of the amendment if it is adopted is to enable the National Legislature, representing the people of the United States, to enforce equal justice when the several States *refuse* to enforce it."[278]

For Bingham, the forbidden denial seems to have required some overt state action—an "enactment." In two public speeches, Bingham identified such denial as an "abuse" of state power.[279] And in his main speech in Congress, Bingham emphatically specified that Section 1's prohibitions, including equal protection, concerned *only* "state enactments"—with "that extent . . . no more."[280]

What constituted a state *enactment* or other policy of denial of legal protection? These enactments or other policies could not, of course, be laws, for the bar extended only to the refusal to enforce laws. One oft-cited example of such denial, by sublegal enactment, was the bill of expulsion that South Carolina's legislature had passed two decades earlier against Samuel Hoar, an attorney who had come to the state to bring a challenge to the state's black-exclusionary laws.[281] We might also consider, as a more notorious example of sublegal enactments, Joseph Goebbels's declaration, within his office as Propaganda Minister, that encouraged the lawless violence of Kristallnacht.

But generally, the Amendment's supporters suggested that even without such official enactments, a state could still adopt a policy of denial. Such a policy was inferred where there was (1) pervasive popular hatred toward an individual or group, (2) pervasive violence against such persons, and (3) official inaction. In explaining the need for the Amendment, the Joint Committee (including Bingham) cited evidence of a pervasive or "general feeling and disposition" of intolerance toward "any class of people friendly to the Union, be they white or black," resulting in "acts of cruelty, oppression, and murder, which the local authorities are at no pains to prevent or punish."[282]

Vermont's Senator Luke Poland, before his state's legislature, recounted the fear of a Union veteran in Virginia. If white Virginians could elect whomever they wished to office, the veteran said, "every man like himself throughout Virginia in one week would be hanged upon a tree." Poland added, "And precisely so with the freedmen." The Amendment, therefore, was necessary "to save the Union men in the South, white or black."[283]

The *New York Herald* was more blunt: the *people* of the rebel states—and thus the states—were "preaching and practicing" the "right to shoot n-----s and Yankees."[284] General George Thomas likewise reported that at least in some parts of the South, "murder prevails with the consent of society."[285]

In all these cases, the state "enactment" or "policy" was effectively made by the ultimate sovereign—the people themselves (or large portions thereof). The people's adoption of such a policy could be proven by widespread public speech, resulting in widespread violence, and official compliance with the popular policy through deliberate inaction.

In sum, to "deny" meant "to refuse deliberately," which state refusal took the form of some state sublegal enactment or other policy. The authors of the policy could be the state legislature, other state officials, or even the people themselves.

Equal Protection of the Laws

The states may not deny to any person within their respective jurisdictions a certain good: the "equal protection of the laws." The term, by its own terms, seems to refer to equal enforcement of those laws that shield the person's body and property against external harm.

Protection

"Protection" is the direct object. By its etymology, the term has the sense of shield, from *pro* (in front of, before) and *tegere* (to cover).[286] And accordingly, before and during the Amendment's adoption, authorities generally spoke of the protection as a shield against external harms. As Christopher Green has demonstrated with abundant evidence, protection referred to "fulfillment of the government's remedial and enforcement functions," and could not include all other governmental "advantages" or "benefits."[287] To be sure, as of 1866, such protection was the principal work of the government; Senator Stewart remarked, the "great body of the laws of the several States[,] as in fact of any government[,] relate to the protection of life, liberty, and property."[288] Nonetheless, protection did not exhaust *all* of the benefits of government, like education and healthcare.

The main external evil was interpersonal violence—"cruelty, oppression, murders," as the Joint Committee stated. In addition, perhaps the "protection" also covered nonhuman external threats, such as floods, wild animals, communicable diseases, and so on. But government could not, strictly speaking, "protect" (shield) persons against nonexternal dangers or other evils, such as degenerative diseases, ignorance, and so forth. To that extent, healthcare and education were not "protection."

As the text of the Due Process-Equal Protection Clause indicates, the shield extended to the person's *rights* of life, liberty, and property. Such protection was already owed or "due" to the person, for these rights were already "privy" to the person. The February draft had made this connection explicit: Congress would be empowered to secure "equal protection in the *rights* of life, liberty, and property."[289] And in reading the final draft, Indiana and Missouri's governors still thought that Section 1 secured equal protection of "rights."[290]

Here again, limb and offspring were almost certainly included. The "protection" of the law surely shielded the person against not only homicide, personal kidnapping, and theft, but also mayhem and kidnapping of offspring.

Curiously, seemingly no one mentioned protection to "reputation"—even though the interest had often ranked alongside body and property as a good to be secured by government.[291] Perhaps reputation was too intangible, too amorphous for any "shield," so the laws securing such goods could not represent "protection," strictly speaking. Moreover, the limitation to life, liberty, and property seemed implied by the due-process rule with which equal protection was tightly paired. And recall that for Bingham, at least, the duty of equal protection was derived from the general principles of the Due Process Clause. Hence, his February draft, as adopted by the Joint Committee, mentioned protection only as to these rights. Accordingly, it is probable that equal protection secured these three rights, including interstitially or otherwise, the rights of limb and bodily offspring.

Equal

The protection must be "equal." This modifier, as to its purpose or meaning, does not appear to be difficult to grasp. "Equal," as attached to protection, served to affirm and secure the equality of the natural rights with which every human being is endowed, and the security of which is the purpose of government. And its meaning seems to prohibit any unequal protection, whatsoever.

Of The Laws

"Protection," however, has a second modifier besides "equal": "of the laws." This latter modifier indicated that the Amendment secured not equal protection simply, but rather as required by "the laws." These protective laws were found chiefly in the common law, as codified or modified by state statutes or local ordinances, but also in some federal laws. The states had the primary, but not exclusive, authority over these protective "laws," as Representative Farnsworth and Senator Howard both indicated by paraphrasing "of the laws" as "of its laws."[292]

This modifier no doubt served to allay the fears, provoked by the February draft, that the Amendment might be construed to empower Congress to secure not merely equal law enforcement but even equal laws, and thereby supplant the primary legislative authority of the states. Recall that his February proposal made no such limitation: Congress would have power to secure "equal protection in the rights of life, liberty, and property."[293] But "after the fiasco of his first version," as Hermine Herta Meyer aptly observed, Bingham "evidently took great pains to limit his second version."[294]

One of these "pains" was the addition of the qualifier "of the laws." The change seems to have settled the matter, in Congress at least. As Earl Maltz has explained, strong evidence can be inferred by the subsequent congressional silence:

> But the very lack of criticism from more mainstream Republicans in either the Senate or the House of Representatives was itself an important indicator of their view of the scope of section one. As we have already seen, conservative Republicans had vociferously attacked the Bingham amendment when it had come before the House of Representatives in February. Further, Republicans in general had shown no qualms in criticizing the language of the other provisions of the constitutional amendment reported by the Joint Committee, successfully arguing for not only the addition of the citizenship clause to section one, but also important changes in the language of sections two, three and four. Against this background, the failure to interpose any criticism . . . can only be viewed as an indication that Republicans in general believed that Bingham's change in the wording of the equal protection clause had obviated the potential ambiguity that some had found so objectionable in the original Bingham amendment.[295]

It was not just Republicans who were satisfied. As to the scope of "equal protection *of the laws*," Democrats on the Committee and Congress were equally silent: No one objected that congressional enforcement would now entail a power to supersede the states' principal power to modify or make the protective laws.

To be sure, as we saw, some opponents in the states would later renew the charge.[296] Still, to my knowledge, no official *supporter* ever, in or out of Congress, said or suggested that Congress would be empowered to supplant the states as the primary makers or modifiers of the laws defining equal protection.

After all, the motive or purpose of the "equal protection" restriction was not unequal laws but unequal enforcement. A member of the Pennsylvania legislature specified the evil to be redressed:

> that the grossest outrages, upon life, liberty and property, are constantly being perpetrated, in the broad glare of open day, by [the southern] people, and the victims to that state of society are utterly remediless. The courts of the South have neither the power nor the disposition to punish offenders unless they happen to be Union men or negroes. In either case they are remarkably prompt and . . . severe.[297]

The problem, as the *New York Tribune* likewise explained, was the violence "*in spite of* mere State laws," not *because of* such laws.[298] According to another commentator, the judiciary was "as cruel in its indifference as the mob in its crimes," as officials "complacently fold their hands while persons entitled to their protection are lawlessly doomed to death or to a living despair."[299]

Some opponents took umbrage at the suggestion that the southern states could not be trusted to enforce the laws. The new power would involve the "insulting" implication that a state's own judiciary "will not administer justice to all alike."[300] But Maryland's Senator Creswell, among others, responded that the former rebels had forfeited any such trust. By the widespread murder and banishment of "Union men," the rebel states had proved themselves "false to that responsibility imposed upon them by law, [so] it became necessary that another tribunal should assert the right."[301]

In the Reconstruction Acts, passed in spring 1867, Congress reached the same verdict: no "adequate protection for life or property now exists in the rebel States," so military authorities might now assume the obligation "to protect all persons in their rights of person and property," including, if necessary, by military tribunals.[302] The problem in the South was not the absence of protective laws, whether common law, statutory, or otherwise, but the absence of enforcement.

A few editorialists, however, did suggest that the guaranteed "equal protection" might extend to equal laws, and in particular, racially equal laws. Just after Congress proposed the Amendment, one Ohio newspaper alleged that radicals' "new trick" was "to force negro suffrage," and would use "equal protection of the laws" as the pretext.[303] And late in the ratification process, the *Cincinnati Commercial*, in supporting the Amendment, seemed to confirm the allegation: that the Amendment's equal-protection measure would bar "the creation of castes, aristocracies, monopolies of *political* and civil rights" adverse to African Americans.[304] "Equal protection" could even entail equal political rights.

With more moderation, a few commentators suggested that "equal protection of the laws" was a pledge of equal *procedural* laws. One Pennsylvania legislator, materially misquoting the Amendment to secure "equal protection of the law" rather than "laws," said that by this "talismanic charm," every person would enjoy "equality before the law," such that the court must "look solely at the merits of the claim which he presents, or the details of the crime with which he is charged," without regard to color or wealth.[305] Some also contended that the guarantee would invalidate procedural laws impairing equal protection by the courts, such as West Virginia's laws excluding former rebel-sympathizers from filing suits, and California's law excluding Chinese aliens from presenting testimony concerning a white defendant.[306] The implication was that the person's right to the equal protection of the *substantive* laws might invalidate certain unequal *procedural* laws.

These exceptions, however, were sporadic and never reflected in the official or otherwise general understanding of supporters. Among public officials, supporters and most opponents seemed to concur: the guarantee of "equal protection of the laws" was *not* a guarantee of "equal laws," procedural or substantive.[307] Rather, it extended only to the equal enforcement of the laws defining that protection.

At the same time, "of the laws," probably did impose one important mandate on state legislators. The laws, perhaps, could not be altered by some mere sublegal enactment, such as a bill of outlawry (the analogue of a bill of attainder), excluding some identifiable person from ordinary protection. [308] The preexisting common and statutory laws remained valid for such a person unless altered by a *bona fide* law, with all the prerequisites, including unpredictable application.

In sum, the Due Process-Equal Protection Clause did indeed give to each human person, within or under a state's jurisdiction, both a certain negative freedom from lawless state violence against his or her rights of person or property, and a certain affirmative entitlement to equal legal protection in these same rights. But the affirmative right extended only against some deliberate state policy of refusal to enforce equally the laws defining that protection.

Notes

1 The Evansville Journal, July 21, 1866 at 1–2, https://www.loc.gov/item/sn82014296/1866-07-21/ed-1/.

2 *See supra* ch. 3.

3 Ga. Const. art. I, §§ 1–2 (1865).

4 *Id.* art. II, § 5.

5 *See also, e.g.*, Fla. Const. art. XVI, §§1–2 (1865) (stipulating that "all the inhabitants of the State, without distinction of color, are free, and shall enjoy the rights of person and property, without distinction of color," and that "in all cases affecting the rights and remedies of colored persons, no person shall be incompetent to testify as a witness on account of color" *but* that "in all other cases, the testimony of colored persons shall be excluded, unless made competent by future legislation").

6 U.S. Const. Art. I, § 10, cl. 1.

7 "I did imitate the framers of the original Constitution. As they had said no State shall emit bills of credit, pass any bill of attainder, ex post facto law, or law impairing the obligations of contracts; imitating their example and imitating it to the letter, I prepared the provision of the first section of the fourteenth amendment as it stands in the Constitution." Cong. Globe, 42d Cong., 1st Sess. app. at 84 (1871).

8 Cong. Globe, 39th Cong. 1st sess. 1291 (Mar. 9, 1866) ("The prohibitions of power by the Constitution to the States are express prohibitions, as that no State shall enter into any treaty, &c., or emit bills of credit, or pass any bill of attainder, &c. The Constitution does not prohibit States from the enactment of laws for the general government of the people within their respective limits").

9 *Id.* at 1679–1680 (President Johnson's veto message). *See* Thomas H. Burrell, *Dobbs v. Jackson Women's Health Organization: Revisiting the Fourteenth Amendment, Due Process of Law, and American Citizenship*, 49 Ohio Northern Univ. L. Rev. 259, 309 (2023) (discussing the significance of this objection to the Amendment's subsequent drafting history).

10 *Washington Topics and Gossip*, Cleveland Daily Leader, Apr. 18, 1866, at 1, https://chroniclingamerica.loc.gov/lccn/sn85042437/1866-04-18/ed-1/seq-1/ (emphasis added).

11 Bingham's proposal to the Committee used a semicolon between the two clauses and separated the due process and equal protection predicates by a comma. Benjamin B. Kendrick, The Journal of the Joint Committee of Fifteen on Reconstruction 106 (1914). But the version reported to Congress placed a semicolon between the due-process and equal-protection predicates. *Id.* at 116. It is possible that the substitution of the semicolon for Bingham's comma was the work of the Committee clerk, William Blair. Lord Kendrick, *supra* note at 39, 120 (identifying Lord as the clerk). In the version adopted by Congress, this semicolon remained, but in the version transmitted by Secretary of State William Seward, ratified by the state legislatures, and then proclaimed as ratified by Seward in July 1868, that comma was restored. *Compare* 2 Documentary History of the Constitution of the United States of America 638 (1894) (copying the congressional resolution) *with, id.* at 642, 646, 654, 658, 662 (showing ratification records from states of Connecticut, New Hampshire, Tennessee, New Jersey, and Oregon, respectively), *and* William H. Seward, Proclamation of July 28, 1868, at 15 Stat. 708, 709 (app. no. 13) (1868); *accord The Constitutional Amendment: Proclamation by Secretary Seward*, Chicago Tribune, July 23, 1868, at 1, http://chroniclingamerica.loc.gov/lccn/sn82014064/1868-07-23/ed-1/seq-1/.

12 Cong. Globe, 39th Cong. 1st sess. 2765, 2961; Bernard H. Siegan, The Supreme Court's Constitution: An Inquiry Into Judicial Review and Its Impact on Society 65 (1987) ("Instead of offering separate meanings," for the Due Process and Equal Protection Clauses, "Howard lumped them together in a short explanation").

13 Reverdy Johnson, A Further Consideration of the Dangerous Condition of the Country 14 (1867) (dividing Section 1 into three clauses).

14 *Governor Morton's Speech*, The Richmond Palladium [IN], Aug. 2, 1866, at 1, https://chroniclingamerica.loc.gov/lccn/sn86058250/1866-08-02/ed-1/seq-1/ (treating the whole prohibitory sentence as a single "clause" but referring to the Due Process-Equal Protection as the "second part of the clause").

15 *Journal of the House of Commons of the General Assembly of the State of North Carolina* 24–30 (1866–1867) *reprinted in* 2 The Reconstruction Amendments: The Essential Documents 309 (Kurt T. Lash, ed. 2021).

16 Md. S.J. app. 5 (1867) *reprinted in* Reconstruction Amendments, *supra* note 15, at 395.

17 "Madison," *Essays on the Fourteenth Amendment*, No. II (Nov. 15, 1866) in *id*, at 299–300.

18 Cong. Globe, 39th Cong. 1st sess. 2542 (May 10, 1866).
19 Ohio Executive Documents 281 (1867) *reprinted in* Reconstruction Amendments, *supra* note 15, at 336 (2021).
20 Thomas C. Fletcher, First Biennial Message, Jan. 4, 1867, *in* 4 The Messages and Proclamations of the Governors of the State of Missouri 80, 81 (1924).
21 *Governor Morton's Speech*, The Richmond Palladium [IN], Aug. 2, 1866, at 1, https://chroniclingamerica.loc.gov/lccn/sn86058250/1866-08-02/ed-1/seq-1/.
22 *The Constitutional Amendment: Exposition of Its Meaning, and Reasons for Its Adoption*, The Weekly Perrysburg Journal [OH], Sept. 7, 1866, at 1, https://chroniclingamerica.loc.gov/lccn/sn85026193/1866-09-07/ed-1/seq-1/.
23 Steven G. Calabresi & Julia T. Rickert, *Originalism and Sex Discrimination*, 90 Tex. L. Rev. 1, 40 (2011).
24 Chin-Yung Yen, Rights of Citizens and Persons Under the Fourteenth Amendment 36 (Ph.D. Dissertation, Columbia Univ. 1905).
25 Michael Zuckert, *On the Fourteenth Amendment: A Textual Analysis*, 48 Perspectives on Pol. Sci., 248, 250 (1992).
26 *Id.*
27 Cong. Globe, 39th Cong. 1st sess. 2459 (May 8, 1866).
28 *Id.*
29 *Id.* at 2539 (May 10).
30 *Id.* at 1065 (Feb. 27, 1866).
31 *Republican Party Platform of 1856*, The American Presidency Project, https://www.presidency.ucsb.edu/documents/republican-party-platform-1856.
32 John A. Bingham, *On the Bill to Emancipate Slaves, and to Prohibit Slavery and to Perpetuate Liberty in the National Capital*, Apr. 11, 1862, *reprinted in* Franklin College Register: Biographical and Historical 217–18 (1908).
33 *Id.* at 218.
34 The word "state," as used in the Constitution, can designate "the people of the several local communities as distinguished from their governments. The word used in this sense is found in the clause in which the United States guarantees to every State in the Union a republican form of government." Chin-Yung Yen, Rights of Citizens and Persons Under the Fourteenth Amendment 27 (1905) (Ph.D. Dissertation, Columbia Univ.).
35 U.S. Const. art. I, § 10, cl. 1.
36 *Briscoe v. President & Directors of Bank of Kentucky*, 36 U.S. 257, 319–20 (1837).
37 *Id.*
38 *Id.* at 320, 326.
39 *Id.* at 321.
40 *Darrington v. Bank of Alabama*, 54 U.S. 12, 16–17 (1852).
41 Edward S. Corwin, *The Doctrine of Due Process of Law before the Civil War*, 24 Harv. L. Rev. 366, 368 (1911) (quoting 28 Edw. III).
42 25 Edw. III, stat. 5, c. 4 (1352) (providing that "no man ["nul homme"] of what estate or condition that he be, shall be put out of land, or tenement, nor taken, nor imprisoned, nor disinherited, nor put to death, without being brought in answer by due process of the law"). For a discussion of the statute, its original French text, and the relation of the statute to antecedent English law, especially the Magna Carta, *see* Charles Donahue Jr., *Magna Carta in the Fourteenth Century: From Law to Symbol?: Reflections on the "Six Statutes,"* 25 Wm. & Mary Bill Rts. J. 591, 601 n.46 (2016).

43 *The Slaughter-House Cases*, 83 U.S. 36, 80 (1873).
44 *See, e.g.*, Penn. Const., Dec. of Rights, § IX (1776) ("nor can any man be justly deprived of his liberty except by the laws of the land, or the judgment of his peers"); Northwest Ordinance, Section 14, art. II (U.S. 1787) ("No man shall be deprived of his liberty or property, but by the judgment of his peers or the law of the land"); *see also* Mass. Const., art. I, § XII (1780) ("no subject shall be arrested, imprisoned, despoiled, or deprived of his property, immunities, or privileges, put out of the protection of the law, exiled, or deprived of his life, liberty, or estate, but by the judgment of his peers, or the law of the land").
45 *See, e.g.*, Miss. Const., art. I, § 10 (1817).
46 *See, e.g.*, Md. Const., Dec. of Rights, § XXI (1776); S.C. Const. art. XLI (1778); Ark Const. art. II, § 10 (1836).
47 *See, e.g.*, Md. Const., art. I, art. 23 (1864) ("no man"); S.C. Const. art. IX, § 2 (1865) ("No person"); Ark. Const., art. II, § 10 ("no man") (1864); Ga. Const. art I, § 2 (1865) ("No person").
48 Republican Platform of 1856, § 1.
49 Neb. Const, art. I, § 1 (1867); Fla. Const. art. I, § 1 (1868); N.C. Const. art. I, § 1 (1868); La. Const., art. I, § 1 (1868); S.C. Const. art. I, § 1 (1868); Ala. Const. art. I, § 1 (1868); *but see* Ark. Const. art. I, § 1 (1868) (beginning with popular sovereignty not universal human rights); Ga. Const. art. I, § 1 (1868) (beginning simply with the duty of protection to persons).
50 Cong. Globe, 39th Cong., 1st sess. 5 (Dec. 4, 1865) (emphasis added) (quoted and discussed in Alexander Tsesis, *The Thirteenth Amendment's Revolutionary Aims*, *in* The Promises of Liberty: The History and Contemporary Relevance of the Thirteenth Amendment 1, 9 (2010)).
51 *Republican National Platform of 1868*, § 14, The American Presidency Project, https://www.presidency.ucsb.edu/documents/republican-party-platform-1868.
52 Cong. Globe, 39th Cong. 1st sess. 2510 (May 9, 1866).
53 *Id.* at 2961 (June 5, 1866).
54 *Cf. Osborn v. Nicholson*, 18 F. Cas. 846, 855 (C.C.E.D. Ark.) (Jan. 1, 1870) ("By [the Thirteenth and Fourteenth Amendments], a living force and vitality were imparted to the words of the declaration of independence, 'that all men are created equal;' and to that clause of article 5 of the constitution of the United States, which declares that, 'No person shall be deprived of life, liberty, and property without due process of law'").
55 Cong. Globe, 39th Cong. 1st sess. 2890 (May 30, 1866).
56 *Governor Chamberlain's Address*, *in* Acts and Resolves Passed by the Forty-Sixth Legislature of the State of Maine 135, 138 (1867). *See also* https://thereconstructionera.com/joshua-lawrence-chamberlain-explains-why-the-14th-amendment-is-necessary-for-reconstruction-1867/.
57 *Speech of Gen. John A. Logan at Cairo*, Chicago Tribune, June 28, 1866, at 1, https://chroniclingamerica.loc.gov/lccn/sn82014064/1866-07-02/ed-1/seq-1/; Gen P.C. Shanks at Portland (Aug 25, 1866) *reprinted in* Speeches of the campaign of 1866, in the states of Ohio, Indiana, and Kentucky 22 (1866).
58 Cong. Globe, 39th Cong., 1st Sess. 2542 (May 10, 1866).
59 *Id.* at 1094 (Feb. 28); *see also Hon. John A. Bingham: His Speech at the Convention Last Wednesday*, The Wheeling Intelligencer (Wheeling W. Va.), Aug. 8, 1866, at 1,

https://chroniclingamerica.loc.gov/lccn/sn84026844/1866-08-13/ed-1/seq-1/; *Speech at Harrison County* (Aug. 24) *reprinted in* Speeches of the campaign of 1866, in the states of Ohio, Indiana, and Kentucky 19 (1866), and also https://chroniclingamerica.loc.gov/lccn/sn85026193/1866-09-07/ed-1/seq-1/.

60 *Mr. Bingham's Speech at Martinsville*, The Wheeling Intelligencer (Wheeling W. Va.), Sept. 4, 1866, at 2, https://chroniclingamerica.loc.gov/lccn/sn84026844/1866-09-05/ed-1/seq-2/. *See also* Cong. Globe, 39th Cong. 1st sess. 3979 (July 20, 1866) (declaring that Amendment "secures to every human being in every State the equal protection of the laws").

61 I have already treated this question at length. David R. Upham, *Prenatal Personhood, State Duties, and Congress's Abortion Power Under the Fourteenth Amendment*, 74 Cath. U. L. Rev. 427 (2025).

62 Va. Const. Dec. of Rights, §§ 1, 3 (1776) (emphasis added).

63 Kan. Const. Bill of Rights, §§ 1, 2 (1861) (emphasis added).

64 *Toledo, W. & W. R. Co. v. Harmon*, 47 Ill. 298, 304 (1868) (emphasis added).

65 *The Civil Rights Bill*, Marshall County Republican, April 5, 1866, at 2, https://chroniclingamerica.loc.gov/lccn/sn84038034/1866-04-05/ed-1/seq-2/ (reprinting editorial from the N.Y. Post).

66 Cong. Globe, 39th Cong., 1st sess. 1757 (Apr. 4, 1866).

67 *Gov. William Brownlow's Proclamation and Address*, Tenn. S. Journal 3 (1866) *reprinted in* Reconstruction Amendments, *supra* note 15, at 243 (2021); *Gov. Jacob Cox's Message to the Legislature*, Ohio Executive Documents 281 (1867), *in id.* at 335.

68 *See, e.g.*, Penn. Const. art. IX, § xi (1790) (emphasis added); N.C. Const. art. I, § 35 (1868) (same); Magna Carta, 25 Edw. 1 § 29 (1297) ("To no man (*nemini*) will we sell or delay or deny right").

69 *Cohen v. Wright*, 22 Cal. 293, 318 (1863).

70 Cong. Globe, 39th Cong., 1st sess. 2765 (May 23).

71 *Speech of Judge Lawrence at Piqua*, Bellafontaine Republican, Sept. 21, 1866, at 1. I found this speech thanks to the research of a student studying under Professor Richard Aynes. Jeremy D. Burkhart, *William Lawrence: Perspectives of a Reconstruction Republican on the 14th Amendment*, at 13, University of Akron Constitutional Law Center, 39th Congress Project (2010), https://ideaexchange.uakron.edu/conlawakron39th/9/.

72 *Ex parte Milligan*, 71 U.S. 2, 119 (1866).

73 *Roe v. Wade*, 410 U.S. 113, 156–7 (1973).

74 *See, e.g.*, Charles I. Lugosi, *Conforming to the Rule of Law: When Person and Human Being Finally Mean the Same Thing in Fourteenth Amendment Jurisprudence*, 4 Geo. J. L.& Pub. Pol'y 361, 395 (2006).

75 *See, e.g.*, *Hall v. Hancock*, 32 Mass. 255, 258 (1834) ("A child *en ventre sa mere* is taken to be a person in being, for many purposes. He may take by descent, by devise, or under the statute of distributions, and generally for all purposes where it is for his benefit." (citations omitted); *St. Amour v. Rivard*, 2 Mich. 294, 297 (1852) (referring to a "person" whether "born, or en ventre sa mere").

76 *Swift v. Duffield*, 5 Serg. & Rawle 38, 40 (Pa. 1819); *but see In re Succession of Packwood*, 12 Rob. 334, 359 (La. 1845) (suggesting a distinction between the person "en ventre sa mere" from the person "in esse").

77 2 James Wilson, Works 475 (1802).

78 C'Zar Bernstein, *Fetal Personhood and the Original Meanings of "Person" in the Constitution*, 26 Tex. Rev. Law & Pol. 485 (2022).

79 Lugosi, *supra* note 74, at 395.

80 The absence of evidence today is evidence of absence, given that for fifty years now, jurists and historians have been very, very eager to find some connection between abortion and the Amendment.

81 *See*, for instance, the majority and dissenting opinions in *Oklahoma v. Castro-Huerta*, 597 U.S. 629 (2022) (discussing at length the limits of states' territorial criminal jurisdiction but without ever mentioning the Fourteenth Amendment).

82 2 Bouvier Law Dictionary 326 (1868).

83 *Id.* (citing *Blair v Worley*, 2 Ill. 177, 179 (1835)).

84 *See, e.g.*, Lugosi, *supra* note 74, at 395–6 (2006); *but see* John Finnis, *Abortion is Unconstitutional*, First Things (Apr. 1, 2021), https://www.firstthings.com/article/2021/04/abortion-is-unconstitutional (contending that the protection of nonhuman "persons" like corporations was outside the purpose of the Amendment, but was within the meaning of the word "person").

85 *Rep. Madison Argues for a Bill of Rights* (June 8, 1789), Teaching American History, https://teachingamericanhistory.org/document/speech-on-amendments-to-the-constitution/.

86 *Insurance Co. v. New Orleans*, 13 F. Cas. 67, 68 (C.C.D. La. 1870) (No. 7052).

87 *See Connecticut Gen. Life Ins. Co. v. Johnson*, 303 U.S. 77, 89 (1938) (Black, J., dissenting) (making this argument).

88 A few apparently contrary cases involve state constitutional provisions that provided procedural safeguards for not only life, liberty, and property, but also various "privileges" or "franchises." See *State v. Heyward*, 37 S.C.L. (3 Rich.) 389, 412 (1832) (concluding that by the state constitution, "a corporation can only be deprived of its powers, rights, privileges, and immunities, by a judgment of forfeiture, obtained according to the law of the land. By this, I understand a trial had, and a judgment pronounced, in the court of law of this State"). The court acknowledged that a corporation is not a "freeman." *Id.* Still, the freemen composing the corporation were entitled to security in their corporate "privileges." *Id.* South Carolina's provision protected, against unlawful deprivation, the "freeman's . . . freehold, liberties, [and] privileges," in addition to his "life, liberty, [and] property," S.C. Const. art. IX, § 2 (1790). This case is discussed in Henry Thompson Leyland, The Concept of Due Process of Law in 1866 and Its Influence on the Fourteenth Amendment 69 (M.A. Thesis, Univ. of Wis. 1922). *Accord*, *Davidson v. N.Y.C.*, 27 How. Pr. 342, 345 (N.Y. Sup. Ct. 1864) (discussing and applying N.Y. Const. art I, § 1 (1846) to protect corporate franchises).

89 *Payne v. Baldwin*, 11 Miss. 661, 675 (1844) (interpreting Miss. Const. art. I, § 10 (1817), (and concluding that "the spirit" of the due-process provision, though covering only the "accused" in a "criminal" prosecution and identified as "he" nonetheless "extends undoubtedly to franchises granted to a body corporate" in a civil case), *rev'd on other grounds in Planters' Bank of Miss. v. Sharp*, 47 U.S. 301 (1848).

90 *Chi. & Alton R.R. Co. v. People*, 67 Ill. 11, 24 (1873) (emphasis added).

91 *But see Pennsylvania, D. & M. Steam Navigation Co. v. Dandridge*, 8 G. & J. 248 (Md. 1836) (holding that a corporate party's agent can be a competent witness, for corporations "are equally entitled to protection").

92 *Trs. of Dartmouth Coll. v. Woodward*, 17 U.S. (4 Wheat.) 518, 636–7 (1819) (discussed in Christopher J. Wolfe, *"An Artificial Being": John Marshall and Corporate Personhood*, 40 Harvard J. L. and Pub. Pol'y 201, 218–19 (2017)).
93 *Id.* at 218–23.
94 Mass. Const., Dec. of Rights, art. III (1780) ("And every denomination of Christians, demeaning themselves peaceably and as good subjects of the commonwealth, shall be equally under the protection of the law").
95 Erving E. Beauregard, *John A. Bingham and the Fourteenth Amendment*, 50 The Historian 67, 69 & n.11 (Nov. 1987) (quoting J. Bingham, conversation with John N. Haverfield, Cadiz, Ohio, 16 August 1866, in Haverfield, "Reminiscences," (unpublished, n.d.)), See also Hon. John A. Bingham: His Speech at the Convention Last Wednesday, The Wheeling Daily Intelligencer, Aug. 13, 1866, at 1 ("The first attribute of Deity is to be recognized in the Constitution of your country. I think this is one way to make a nation immortal, to do justice, to make the rights of all men as sacred as our own").
96 *Mr. Bingham's Speech* [at Martinsville], The Wheeling Daily Intelligencer. Sept. 5, 1866, at 2 (emphasis added).
97 See Edward R. Barber, *Men and Events in Washington During and After the Civil War*, 30 Collections and Publications of the Michigan Pioneer and Historical Society 212, 226 (1906).
98 Cong. Globe, 39th Cong. 1st sess. 1089 (Feb. 28, 1866).
99 Herbert Thompson Leyland, The Concept of Due Process of Law in 1866 and Its Influence on the Fourteenth Amendment, M.A. Thesis, University of Wisconsin 128 (1922).
100 *Id.* at 129.
101 *Id.* at 130.
102 Frederick Mark Gedicks, *An Originalist Defense of Substantive Due Process: Magna Carta, Higher-Law Constitutionalism, and the Fifth Amendment*, 58 Emory L.J. 585 (2009); Ryan C. Williams, *The One and Only Substantive Due Process Clause*, 120 Yale L.J. 408 (2010).
103 Nathan S. Chapman & Michael W. McConnell, *Due Process as Separation of Powers* 121 Yale L.J. 1672 (2012); Matthew J. Franck, *What Happened to the Due Process Clause in the Dred Scott Case? The Continuing Confusion over "Substance" versus "Process,"* 4 Am. Pol. Thought 120 (2015) ("every one of the pre–Dred Scott examples [Gedicks and Williams] adduce concerns an enactment that embodies an arbitrary decree in the mere form or guise of law (i.e., punitive, particularistic and/or retrospective deprivations of property or liberty) or an abject failure to provide notice and process").
104 Christopher R. Green, *Our Bipartisan Due Process Clause*. 26 Geo. M. L. Rev. 1147 (2019).
105 *Hepburn v. Griswold*, 75 U.S. 603, 624 (1870) (holding that a law that "compels all those who hold contracts for the payment of gold and silver money to accept in payment a currency of inferior value deprives such persons of property without due process of law"); *Munn v. Illinois*, 94 U.S. 113, 139–43 (1876) (Field, J., dissenting).
106 *Goldberg v. Kelly*, 397 U.S. 254, 261–2 (1971) (holding that the denial of welfare benefits was a deprivation governed by the clause, and discussing post-1945 cases involving the denial of governmental benefits).

107 Petition of Right (1628), Online Library of Law and Liberty, https://oll.libertyfund.org/pages/1628-petition-of-right (quoting a translated form of the 1354 statute).
108 *Sharpless v. Mayor & Citizens of Philadelphia*, 21 Pa. 147, 166–7 (1853).
109 *Cohen v. Wright*, 22 Cal. 293, 319 (1863).
110 *Groves v. Slaughter*, 40 U.S. 449, 515 (1841) (Baldwin, J., concurring) (cited in Howard Jay Graham, Everyman's Constitution: Historical Essays on the Fourteenth Amendment, the "Conspiracy Theory," and American Constitutionalism 49 (1968)).
111 *Wynehamer v. People*, 13 N.Y. 378, 486–7 (1856).
112 *Id.* at 398 (Op. of Comstock, J.).
113 *Id.* at 433 (Op. of Seldon, J.).
114 2 William Crosskey, Politics and the Constitution in the History of the United States 1115 (1953), *quoted in* Richard G. Stevens, Reason and History in Judicial Judgment: Felix Frankfurter and Due Process 70 (rev'd ed. 2017).
115 *Id.*
116 *Id.* See Andrew T. Hyman, *The Little Word "Due,"* 38 Akron L. Rev. 1, 24 n. 57 (2005) ("Wynehamer was not a typical case, and state courts usually reached the opposite conclusion.").
117 *State v. Allmond*, 7 Del. 612, 641 (1856).
118 *Dorman v. State*, 34 Ala. 216, 241–2 (1859).
119 *Id.* (quoting *Sharpless v. Mayor of Philadelphia*, 21 Pa. 147 (1853)).
120 *Roosevelt v. Godard*, 52 Barb. 533, 550 (N.Y. Gen. Term 1868) (noting that a harbor regulation "does not deprive the owners of the wharves to which it relates of any of their rights or privileges [but] merely regulates the manner in which they are to be used and enjoyed for the purpose of promoting the business, security and good order of the harbor"). The court did indicate that deprivation could occur where regulation rendered property unfit for the purpose it was designed for, but also suggested that such repurposing was not a deprivation: the regulation "does not deprive the owner of his property, nor subject it to new uses, neither does it prevent him from devoting it to the lawful uses and purposes for which it has been adapted and designed [but] merely prescribes the manner in which those uses and purposes are to be subserved by it").
121 *Cooper v. Schultz*, 32 How. Pr. 107 (N.Y. Comm. Pleas 1866) (holding that a regulation regulating the time when butchers can drive cattle through the street did not violate the state constitution, and noting that the "statute books abound with laws of this description, and without them the ordinary objects of civil government could not be effected").
122 79 U.S. 457 (1871).
123 *Id.* at 551–2.
124 Cong. Globe, 39th Cong. 1st sess., at 1034 (Feb. 26, 1866) (emphasis added).
125 *Id.* at 2542 (May 10).
126 *See Cummings v. Mo.*, 71 U.S. 277, 332 (1867) (contending that expositions of due process were "presented with great force in The matter of Dorsey").
127 *In re Dorsey*, 7 Port. 293, 404 (Ala. 1838); *see also Taylor v. Porter & Ford*, 4 Hill 140, 144 (N.Y. Sup. Ct. 1843) (indicating that the state's due-process restriction secured the "rights of personal liberty and private property); *Commonwealth ex rel. M'Lain v. Wright*, 3 Grant 437, 443 (Pa. 1863) (explaining that the "liberty" protected by the Due Process Clause and the writ of habeas corpus is that "personal liberty" that "is dearer to men than any other rights," that is, "a man's right to himself").

128 *Tuttle v. Wilson*, 24 Ill. 553, 554 (1861) (noting that the "right to personal liberty is one of the most valuable and most cherished rights appertaining to man in society, and one of which he cannot be deprived, except by the judgment of his peers, or by the law of the land" and decrying the barbarous law that once authorized the imprisonment of debtors).

129 Den ex dem. *Trustees of University v. Foy*, 5 N.C. 58, 87 (1805).

130 *Murphy & Glover Test Oath Cases*, 41 Mo. 339, 367 (1867) ("opinion of the court" by Holmes, J.); *but see* id. at 388 (Wagner, J., concurring) (stating that he and a third judge dissent from "much of the reasoning" in Judge Holmes's opinion).

131 Charles Warren, *The New Liberty Under the Fourteenth Amendment*, 39 Harv. L. Rev. 431, 443 (1926) (quoted in George W. Carey, In Defense of the Constitution 176–7 (rev'd ed. 1995)).

132 *Bruch v. Carter*, 32 N.J.L. 554, 562 (1867).

133 2 Bouvier Law Dictionary 387 (1868).

134 *Madison's Views on Property*, *in* American State Papers Bearing on Sunday Legislation 158, 158 (William Addison Blakely, ed. 1911) (rejecting Blackstone's definition, which limited property to "external things," but instead contending that property includes "every thing to which a man may attach a value and have a right," including the right to "conscience").

135 *Scott v. Sandford*, 60 U.S. 393, 451 (1857).

136 *Id.* at 625 (Curtis, J., dissenting).

137 *Id.* at 537 (McLean, J., dissenting).

138 Abraham Lincoln, Cooper Union Address, New York, New York (Feb. 27, 1860), https://www.abrahamlincolnonline.org/lincoln/speeches/cooper.htm (remarking that the Framers avoided using the word "slave" or "slavery" precisely "to exclude from the Constitution the idea that there could be property in man").

139 *Osborn v. Nicholson*, 18 F. Cas. 846, 856 (C.C.E.D. Ark. January 1, 1870) (concluding that Section 4 of the Amendment "is based on the broad principle that there shall be no further recognition by the national government or the states of the idea that there could lawfully be property in man").

140 Andrew T. Bodoh, *Liberty Is Not Loco-motion: Obergefell and the Originalists' Due Process Fallacy*, 40 Campbell L. Rev. 482, 491–2 (2018).

141 *Lincoln v. Smith*, 27 Vt. 328, 361 (1856).

142 *Id.* at 500 (contending that some state constitutions "seem to employ 'liberty' standing alone almost interchangeably with 'life, liberty, and property' or similar language").

143 *Id.*

144 14 Stat. 27 (Apr. 9 1866).

145 Cong. Globe, 39th Cong. 1st sess., at 3035 (June 8).

146 1 St. George Tucker, Blackstone's Commentaries app. (1803) ("Which words, '*aliquo modo destruatur,*' according to Sir Edward Coke, include a prohibition not only of killing, and maiming, but also of torturing (to which our laws are strangers) and of every oppression by colour of an illegal authority").

147 *People ex rel. Nickerson v.* ______, 19 Wend. 16, 16 (N.Y. Sup. Ct. 1837). *Accord Dalton v. State*, 6 Blackf. 357, 358 (Ind. 1843) (holding that the "mother, being the natural guardian of the child, could not be deprived of that guardianship by the appointment of another guardian, of the application for which appointment

she had no notice"); *Reidell v. Morse*, 36 Mass. 358, 359–60 (1837) (affirming that "[t]he power of taking children from their parents and families and homes, and binding them to strangers, as servants . . . should only be exercised in cases of clear necessity [which] must be shown affirmatively [by] adjudication"). Story noted that the right might arise not from the siring but from the subsequent care of offspring. "By the common law, the father has a right to the custody of his children during their infancy. In whatever principle this right is founded, whether it result from the very nature of parental duties, or from that authority, which devolves upon him, by reason of the guardianship by nature, or nurture, technically speaking, its existence cannot now be brought into controversy." *United States v. Bainbridge*, 24 F. Cas. 946, 949 (C.C.D. Mass. 1816). At least one court anticipated a contemporary approach that treated parental authority as arising from a prudential legislative presumption. *See, e.g., Striplin v. Ware*, 36 Ala. 87, 89–90 (1860) (remarking that "[t]he law devolves the custody of infant children upon their parents, not so much upon the ground of natural right in the latter, as because the interests of the children, and the good of the public, will, as a general rule, be thereby promoted" given the "fair presumption, that so long as children are under the control of their parents, they will be treated with affection, and their education and morals will be duly cared for").

148 *Ramsay v. Ramsay*, 20 Wis. 507, 508 (1866)

149 Cong. Globe, 39th Cong. 1st sess., 2893 (May 30, 1866).

150 *Elk v. Wilkins*, 112 U.S. 94, 102 (1884).

151 *Lawson v. Scott*, 9 Tenn. 92, 94–5 (1825).

152 *Cf. People v. Goodwin*, 18 Johns. 187, 201 (N.Y. 1820) ("The expression, jeopardy of limb, was used in reference to the nature of the offense, and not to designate the punishment for an offense; for no such punishment as loss of limb was inflicted by the laws of any of the states at the adoption of the Constitution. Punishment by deprivation of the limbs of the offender would be abhorrent to the feelings and opinions of the enlightened age in which the Constitution was adopted, and it had grown into disuse in England for a long period antecedently. We must understand the term, 'jeopardy of limb,' as referring to offenses which, in former ages, were punishable by dismemberment, and as intending to comprise the crimes denominated in the law felonies").

153 John Wharton, The Law Lexicon, Or Dictionary of Jurisprudence 274 (1867) (defining "death" as the "departure of the soul from the body").

154 *Murphy & Glover Test Oath Cases*, 41 Mo. 339, 367 (1867).

155 Akhil Reed Amar, *Double Jeopardy Law Made Simple*, 106 Yale L.J. 1807, 1810 (1997).

156 *Musgrove v. Kornegay*, 52 N.C. 71, 74 (1859); *Johnson v. Terry*, 34 Conn. 259, 263 (1867).

157 *Rogers v. Soggs*, 22 Cal. 444, 453–4 (1863) (holding that despite a statute giving miners certain priority rights in adjacent lands, the farmers using those same lands had superior rights to "permanent improvements, such as houses, orchards, vineyards," as well as "such products of the soil as are the fruits of toil and labor").

158 *Bennet v. Bennet*, 13 N.J. Eq. 114, 118 (1860) (rejecting "the assumption that the parent has the same right of property in the child that he has in his horse, or that the master has in his slave, and that the transfer of the custody of the child from the

father to the mother is an invasion of the father's right of property," for the "father has no such right . . . no property whatever in his children").

159 *People ex rel. Brooks*, 35 Barb. 85, 88 (N.Y. Sup. Ct. 1861).

160 *Bertholf v. O'Reilly*, 74 N.Y. 509, 515 (1878); *accord* House Report No. 373, Criminal Procedures in Cases of Crimes Punishable by Loss of Life or Liberty, at 4–5, 48th Cong., 1st sess. (Feb. 20, 1884) (noting that "when . . . it is said, 'nor be deprived of life, liberty, or property without due process of law,' no one would hold because the word 'limb' is omitted that he might be deprived of limb without such due process").

161 *Lee v. Back*, 30 Ind. 148, 152–3 (1868) (emphasis added) (quoting *Chase v. Hathaway*, 14 Mass. 222, 224 (1817)).

162 *People ex rel. O'Connell v. Turner*, 55 Ill. 280, 287–8 (Ill. 1870) (Court opinion by Judge Anthony Thornton). Thornton did not specify whether he was referring to the Fourteenth Amendment's due-process provision, or the virtually identical stipulation of the state constitution, Ill. Const., art. II, § 2 (1870) ("No person shall be deprived of life, liberty or property without due process of law"). For Thornton's biography, *see* 1 The Bench and Bar of Illinois: Historical and Reminiscent 458 (John M. Palmer ed. 1899).

163 *Process*, Online Etymological Dictionary, https://www.etymonline.com/word/process.

164 *Jones v. Robbins*, 74 Mass. 329, 361 (1857) (quoting with approval James Kent's formula).

165 Curtis was "the authority on due process of law," for no other antebellum jurists had "so many due process decisions to his credit." Leyland, *supra* note 99, at 19–20.

166 *Greene v. Briggs*, 10 F. Cas. 1135, 1140 (C.C.D.R.I. 1852) (emphasis added).

167 *Cohen v. Wright*, 22 Cal. 293, 318 (1863).

168 *Baker v. Kelley*, 11 Minn. 480, 498 (1866) (quotations omitted); *East Kingston v. Towle*, 48 N.H. 57, 61 (1868).

169 *Starr v. Hamilton*, 22 F. Cas. 1107, 1110 (C.C. D. Ore., 1867) (No. 13,314); *Rockwell v. Nearing*, 35 N.Y. 302, 306 (1866) (quotations omitted).

170 *State ex rel. Pittman v. Adams*, 44 Mo. 570, 587 (1869); *Beaupre v. Hoerr*, 13 Minn. 366, 369 (1868).

171 *Bullock v. Geomble*, 45 Ill. 218, 222 (1867); *cf.* Veto of the Second Freedmen's Bureau Bill, July 16, 1866, *in* Edward McPherson, A Political Manual for 1866 and 1867, at 147, 148 (1867) (objecting to the measure because it would "confer upon the commissioners judicial powers, by which citizens of the United States are to be deprived of their property in a mode contrary to [the Due Process Clause]").

172 *Beaupre v. Hoerr*, 13 Minn. 366, 367 (1868); *Rison v. Farr*, 24 Ark. 161, 175 (1865); *Jones v. Robbins*, 74 Mass. 329, 361 (1857).

173 Green, *supra* note 104, at 1186–9.

174 *Parsons v. Russell*, 11 Mich. 113, 121 (1863).

175 *State v. Allmond*, 7 Del. 612, 639 (1856) (affirming that any "law that should make a man a Judge in his own cause would violate" the right to "an impartial trial").

176 *In re Dorsey*, 7 Port. 293, 404–5 (Ala. 1838) (emphasis added); *accord Wammack v. Holloway*, 2 Ala. 31, 34 (1841) (indicating that "due course of law," on its own, would not require conformity with the common law's requirement of trial by jury).

177 *Compare* Ala. Const. art. I § 10 (1819); Miss. Const. art. I, § 10 (1817); *with* Ala. Const. art. I, § 8 (1867); Miss. Const. art. I, § 2 (1868).

178 *See* Petition of Right (1628), Online Library of Law and Liberty, https://oll.libertyfund.org/pages/1628-petition-of-right (denouncing, as a deprivation of liberty without due process, the seizure of persons without any cause shown wave the King's "special command").
179 Christopher R. Green, *Twelve Problems with Substantive Due Process*, 16 GEO. J. L. & PUB. POL'Y 397, 407 (2018).
180 Max Crema & Lawrence B. Solum, *The Original Meaning of "Due Process of Law" in the Fifth Amendment*, 108 Va. L. Rev. 447 (2022).
181 *Cooper v. Schultz*, 32 How. Pr. 107, 123–4 (N.Y. Comm. Pleas 1866).
182 *Pitt v. Davison*, 37 N.Y. 235, 373–4 (1867) (noting that post-trial execution does not necessarily require notice and hearing).
183 *Compare* Military Commissions, 11 Op. Att'y Gen. 297, 313 (1865) (concluding that to encompass warfare within the Due Process Clause would have the "absurd consequences" by treating soldiers as murderers for killing an enemy combatant) *with In re Bergen*, 3 F. Cas. 261, 263 (C.C.N.C. 1870) (No. 1,338) (affirming, provocatively, "that when the civil power appeals to force to support its authority, the sword is due process of law").
184 *Compare Howell v. Buffalo*, 37 N.Y. 267, 270 (1867) (concluding that the state's due-process clause "could not have been intended as a restriction upon the taxing power of the legislature"), *with Mason v. Rollins*, 16 F. Cas. 1061, 1063 (C.C.N.D. Ill. 1869) (No. 9,252) (conceding that such seizure is not "judicial process" but still "is an executive process [that] has been expressly decided to be due process of law within the meaning of the constitution").
185 *Westervelt v. Gregg*, 12 N.Y. 202, 212 (N.Y. 1854) (opinion of Denio, J.).
186 *Parsons v. Russell*, 11 Mich. 113, 122 (1863).
187 Such methods are lawful, of course, "only on conviction or after a trial may be had by the accused, as in the case of the seizure of gunpowder." *Ex Parte Grace*, 12 Iowa 208 (1861); *see also* Leyland, *supra* note 99, at 30.
188 *See, among countless sources*, Abraham Lincoln, Second Inaugural Address, Mar. 4, 1865, *in* Abraham Lincoln: His Speeches and Writings 792 (Roy P. Basler ed. 1946) (referring to the "progress of our arms, on which all else chiefly depends").
189 *Murray's Lessee v. Hoboken Land & Improvement Co.*, 59 U.S. 272, 279 (1856).
190 *Parsons*, 11 Mich. at 122–3.
191 *Mason v. Rollins*, 16 F. Cas. 1061, 1063 (C.C.N.D. Ill. 1869) (No. 9,252) (noting that "[a]ll property of the citizen is subject to the imposition of taxes for the support of the government and the payment of its debts").
192 *Due*, Online Etymology Dictionary, https://www.etymonline.com/word/due.
193 Gerard V. Bradley, *Moral Truth and Constitutional Conservatism*, 81 La. L. Rev. 1317, 1328 (2021) (emphasis in original) (citing John Finnis, *The Priority of Persons Revisited*, 58 Am. J. Juris. 45, 46 (2013)).
194 *See, e.g., Winner v. Fitzgerald*, 19 Wis. 393 (1865) (noting that "due process of law . . . means that every person shall have the privilege of being heard"); *State ex rel. Pittman v. Adams*, 44 Mo. 570, 587 (1869) (noting that the process must include a "full and fair hearing"); *Bullock v. Geomble*, 45 Ill. 218, 223 (1867) (due process requires "notice to the [person] that he may be heard").
195 *Murray v. Hoboken Land & Improv. Co.*, 59 U.S. 272, 280 (1856); *Huber v. Reily*, 53 Pa. 112, 117 (1866).

196 110 U.S. 516, 548 (1884) (Harlan, J., dissenting) (quoted in Robert A. Fairfax, Jr., *Interrogating the Nonincorporation of the Grand Jury Clause*, 43 Cardozo L. Rev. 855, 886 (2022)). Or, as Harlan wrote for the whole Court a decade later, "[n]otice to the owner to appear in some judicial tribunal and show cause why his property shall not be taken for public use without compensation would be a mockery of justice." *Chicago, Burlington & Quincy Railroad Co. v. Chicago*, 166 U.S. 226, 236 (1897).

197 Petition of Right (1628), Online Library of Law and Liberty, https://oll.libertyfund.org/pages/1628-petition-of-right.

198 Leyland, *supra* note 99, at 19–20.

199 *Greene v. Briggs*, 10 F. Cas. 1135, 1140 (C.C.D.R.I. 1852).

200 *In re Dorsey*, 7 Port. 293, 404 (Ala. 1838).

201 *Coffin v. United States*, 156 U.S. 432, 453 (1895).

202 Julius Caesar, Act II, Scene 2.

203 *Baker v. Kelly*, 11 Minn. 480, 497 (1866) (holding that absent a judicial determination that a person's life, liberty, and property "are held contrary to the existing law, or are forfeited by its violation" these rights may not be "taken from him"); *Green v. Shumway*, 39 N.Y. 418, 426 (1868); *Rockwell v. Nearing*, 35 N.Y. 302, 306 (1866) (noting that the judicial process is for "ascertaining guilt or determining the title to property").

204 *Taylor v. Porter & Ford*, 4 Hill 140, 147 (N.Y. Sup. Ct. 1843); *quoted with approval in Rockwell v. Nearing*, 35 N.Y. 302, 306 (1866); *Ames v. Port Huron Log Driving & Booming Co.*, 11 Mich. 139, 143 (1863); *Ex parte Grace*, 12 Iowa 208, 214 (1861).

205 *Chase v. Hathaway*, 14 Mass. 222, 224–5 (1817) (holding in an adult-guardianship case that "whenever the legislature has provided that, on account of *crime or misfortune*, the public safety or convenience demands a suspension of these essential rights of the individual, and has provided a judicial process, by which the fact shall be ascertained, it is to be understood as required that the tribunal, to which is committed the duty of inquiring and determining, shall give opportunity to the subject to be heard in support of his innocence or his capacity"). *In re Janes*, 30 How. Pr. 446, 449 (N.Y. Sup. Ct. 1866) (holding that due process requires a judicial determination as to whether a person was "lost to self control, unable . . . to attend to business, and dangerous to remain at large"); *In re Petition of Goodenough*, 19 Wis. 274, 278–9 (1865) ("where it appears that the father is an improper person to have the care and management of the child . . . [the fact] be sustained by clear and satisfactory proofs"); *People ex rel. O'Connell v. Turner*, 55 Ill. 280, 284 (1870) (holding that Due Process Clause prohibits transferring a child's custody from a parent to a reform school absent a showing of "gross misconduct or almost total unfitness on the part of the parent"). *See also Van Deusen v. Newcomer*, 40 Mich. 90, 105 (1879) (argument of counsel for defendant in error) ("One cannot be restrained of his personal liberty on an ex parte proceeding and without notice" and citing multiple sources).

206 *Kneedler v. Lane*, 3 Grant 523, 545 (Pa.1864) (Agnew, J., concurring) (contending that compulsory military service is not incompatible with "due process of law").

207 As to offspring, the matter was complicated because two parents, mother and father, could make the claim of superior title. *See, e.g.*, *Lawson v. Scott*, 9 Tenn. 92, 94–5 (1825).

208 *Cohen v. Wright*, 22 Cal. 293, 318–19 (1863).

209 *See* Jacobus tenBroek, The Antislavery Origins of the Fourteenth Amendment 120 (1951) (quoting the platform).
210 *Marguerite v. Chouteau*, 3 Mo. 540, 573–4 (1834) (Wash, J., dissenting).
211 David R. Upham, *The Understanding of "Neither slavery nor involuntary servitude shall exist" Before the Thirteenth Amendment, 15 Geo.* J.L. & Pub. Pol'y 137, 150–1 (2017).
212 *Two Pictures* (reprinted from the *Chicago Republican*), The Evening Telegraph, Dec. 31, 1867, at 2, https://chroniclingamerica.loc.gov/lccn/sn83025925/1867-12-31/ed-1/seq-2/.
213 *Taylor v. Porter & Ford*, 4 Hill 140, 146–7 (N.Y. Sup. Ct. 1843) (citing *In re Albany St.*, 11 Wend. 149, 151 (N.Y. Sup. Ct. 1834)); *accord Coster v. Tide Water Co.*, 18 N.J. Eq. 54, 65 (1866).
214 *Clellans v. Commonwealth*, 8 Pa. 223, 228 (1848) (mentioning murder and rape as "offences in their nature infamous"). *Cf. Bartholomew v. People*, 104 Ill. 601, 607 (1882) (citing statutory and other authority to contend that what made a person incompetent as a witness for "infamous crime" depended on the nature of the offense and not the punishment). After the Fourteenth Amendment, the Supreme Court decided, instead, that what makes a crime infamous is the infamy of the punishment prescribed rather than the nature of the crime. *Ex parte Wilson*, 114 U.S. 417, 423–4 (1885) (affirming that "by an elementary rule of construction" the term must include "crimes subject to any infamous punishment, even if they should be held to include also crimes infamous in their nature, independently of the punishment affixed to them"). This seems mistaken; what makes a punishment "infamous" as to the punished man is that the punishment seems to be evidence that he had committed an infamous crime, for decent communities do not gravely punish persons except for grave offenses. If a person were subject to death for jaywalking, the punishment would be infamous not to the person killed, but to the state actors responsible for such infamously unjust punishment.
215 Randy E. Barnett & Evan D. Bernick, The Original Meaning of the Fourteenth Amendment: Its Letter and Spirit 19 (2021).
216 *See, e.g.*, Francis Peter LeBuffe, S.J., Outlines of Pure Jurisprudence 18–21 (1924).
217 *Westervelt v. Gregg*, 12 N.Y. 202, 209 (1854).
218 *Jones v. Robbins*, 74 Mass. 329, 361 (1857) (quoting with approval James Kent's formula) (emphasis added).
219 3 Joseph Story, Commentaries on the Constitution of the United States § 1783 (1833) (emphasis added) (quoted in, *inter alia*, *Ex parte Grace*, 12 Iowa 208, 214 (1861).
220 *Murray's Lessee v. Hoboken Land & Improvement Co.*, 59 U.S. 272 (1856).
221 *Huber v. Reily*, 53 Pa. 112, 117 (1866)
222 *Cooper v. Schultz*, 32 How. Pr. 107, 124 (N.Y. Sup. Ct. 1866); *Weaver v. Lapsley*, 43 Ala. 224, 232 (1869).
223 *Green v. Shumway*, 39 N.Y. 418, 428 (1868).
224 *Cohen v. Wright*, 22 Cal. 293, 318 (1863).
225 Green, *supra* note 104, at 1185–6.
226 *State v. Simmon 2 Spears,* 761 (S.C. 1844).
227 *Brown v. Hummel*, 6 Pa. 86, 91 (1847)
228 *Hoke v. Henderson*, 15 N.C. 1, 16 (1833).

229 *Martin v. Snowden*, 59 Va. 100, 141 (1868).
230 *Id.*
231 *Dorman v. State*, 34 Ala. 216, 237 (1859).
232 *State v. Millain*, 3 Nev. 409, 466 (1867); *but see Gibson v. Mason*, 5 Nev. 283, 302 (1869) (referring to the modes "as were known either to the common law or as were generally recognized in this country at the time of the adoption of the constitution").
233 *East Kingston v. Towle*, 48 N.H. 57, 60 (1868) (quotations and citations omitted).
234 *Parsons v. Russell*, 11 Mich. 113, 121 (1863) (emphasis added).
235 *Commonwealth v. Byrne*, 61 Va. 165, 193 (1871) (citation omitted).
236 *In re the Oath to be taken by Attys. & Counsellors*, 35 Ga. 286, 293–4 (May 31, 1866) (quoted in Leyland, *supra* note 99, at 25). Here he was probably relying on the antebellum jurist William Rawle. William Rawle, A View of the Constitution of the United States of America 127–32 (H.C. Carey & I. Lea eds., Philadelphia 1825) (contending that the Due Process Clause "exhibits a summary" of the procedural rights listed in the Fourth, Fifth, Sixth, and Eighth Amendments), quoted and discussed in Williams, *supra* note 102, at 453 & n. 197.
237 *Hurtado v. California*, 110 U.S. 516, 534 (1884).
238 *Bill of Rights*, National Archives, https://www.archives.gov/founding-docs/bill-of-rights.
239 Akhil Reed Amar, *Double Jeopardy Law Made Simple*, 106 Yale L.J. 1807, 1812 (1997).
240 *See, e.g.*, *United States v. Wilson*, 28 F. Cas. 699, 709 (C.C.E.D. Pa. 1830) (jury charge) ("If a jury have a reasonable, well founded doubt of guilt, they must acquit of even the lowest offences—we *know of no other rule* for the highest.") (emphasis added).
241 The Federalist No. 83, at 503 (Hamilton) (Clinton Rossiter ed., 1961).
242 *Id.*, No. 78, at 463 (Hamilton).
243 Charles Fairman, *Does the Fourteenth Amendment Incorporate the Bill of Rights? The Original Understanding*, Stan. L. Rev. 5, 106, 115 (1949).
244 George C. Thomas, III, *When Constitutional Worlds Collide: Resurrecting the Framers' Bill of Rights and Criminal Procedure*, 100 Mich. L. Rev. 145, 203–4 (2001).
245 *Holden v. Hardy*, 169 U.S. 366, 387 (1898).
246 Franck, *supra* note 103, at 125.
247 Aristotle's Politics 93 (second ed., Carnes Lord, ed. 2003).
248 *Id.*
249 *Reed v. Wright,* 2 G. Greene 15 (Iowa 1849) (discussed in Leyland, *supra* note 99, at 62).
250 *Kneedler v. Lane*, 3 Grant 523 (Pa. 1864).
251 *Standeford v. Wingate*, 63 Ky. 440, 459 (1866) (Williams, J., dissenting).
252 *Jones' Heirs v. Perry*, 18 Tenn. 59, 72 (1836).
253 *Sears v. Cottrell*, 5 Mich. 251, 254 (1858).
254 *See, e.g.*, *Alexander v. Baltimore*, 5 Gill 383, 392–3 (Md. 1847); *Lindsay v. Commissioners*, 2 S.C.L. (2 Bay) 38 (Ct. App. 1796) (discussed in Chapman & McConnell, *supra* note 103, at 1760–1).
255 *Twining v. New Jersey*, 211 U.S. 78, 110 (1908) (mentioning "the effect of due process in restraining substantive laws, as, for example, that which forbids the taking of private property for public use without compensation").

256 *But see Corbin v. Marsh*, 63 Ky. 193, 225–6 (1865) (Williams, J., dissenting) (contending that uncompensated targeted taking would be compatible with "due process of law," under the Fifth Amendment, but for the addition of the Takings Clause, for otherwise "the government would have had the most absolute power, by due process of law, to take the citizen's property, without compensation").

257 *See, e.g.*, *Nesbitt v. Trumbo*, 39 Ill. 110, 113–16 (1866) (citing various cases and holding that a legislative act, whereby a person was deprived of his property for the creation of a private right of way, was not the "law of the land").

258 *See, e.g.*, *People ex rel. Matthews v. Toynbee*, 12 How. Pr. 238, 249–51 (N.Y. March 1, 1856) (op. of Comstock, J.)

259 *Jordan v. Hyatt*, 3 Barb. 275, 281 (N.Y. Sup. Ct. 1848) (emphasis in original).

260 *Bankhead v. Brown*, 25 Iowa 540, 545 (1868).

261 *Id.* at 545–6 (emphasis added). *See also Gibson v. Mason*, 5 Nev. 283, 304, (1869) (conceding that if the tax law at issue "is simply for a private purpose, that it is levied for the benefit of private individuals, or that it is taking the property of one citizen and giving it to another . . . we should unhesitatingly declare the law unconstitutional").

262 Barnett & Bernick, *supra* note 215, at 289 (citing *Bank of Columbia v. Okely*, 17 U.S. 235, 244 (1819)).

263 *Letter from Secretary of the Interior O. H. Browning to W. H. Benneson and H.V. Sullivan, Oct. 13, 1866*, *in* Reconstruction Amendments, *supra* note 15, at 289–91.

264 *Speech of Hon. S.S. Bloom, in the Ohio House of Representatives* (Jan. 4, 1867), Daily Ohio Statesman, Jan. 24, 1867, at 1, https://chroniclingamerica.loc.gov/lccn/sn84028645/1867-01-24/ed-1/seq-1/.

265 *Cochran v. Van Surlay*, 20 Wend. 365, 383 (N.Y. County Ct. 1838) (Verplanck, Sen., dissenting); *quoted in* Theodore Sedgwick, A Treatise on the Rules which Govern the Interpretation and Application of Statutory and Constitutional Law 185 (1857), and *Gibson v. Mason*, 5 Nev. 283, 297 (1869).

266 *Powers v. Inferior Court of Dougherty County*, 23 Ga. 65, 77 (1857)

267 *Soars v. Cottrell*, 5 Mich. 251, 254–5 (1858); *accord People ex rel. Detroit & H. R. Co. v. Township Bd. of Salem*, 20 Mich. 452, 504 (1870).

268 On "state neglect" as a significant injustice at the time, *see generally*, Pamela Brandwein, Rethinking the Judicial Settlement of Reconstruction 29–31 (2011).

269 *Deny*, Online Etymology Dictionary, https://www.etymonline.com/word/deny.

270 1 Bouvier Law Dictionary 459 (1868).

271 Christopher R. Green, *The Original Sense of the (Equal) Protection Clause: Pre-Enactment History*, 19 Geo. Mason U. C.R.L.J. 1, 42 (2008).

272 "If any State shall exclude any of her adult male citizens from the elective franchise, or abridge that right, she shall forfeit her right to representation in the same proportion." Cong. Globe, 39th Cong. 1st sess., at 2459 (May 8).

273 *Lander v. State*, 12 Tex. 462, 485 (1854).

274 Cong. Globe, 39th Cong. 1st sess. 2542 (emphasis added).

275 Samuel Shellabarger, Speech at Springfield, OH, Aug. 16, 1866, *in* Speeches of the Campaign of 1866, at 11 (1866) (quoted in James H. Bond, *The Original Understanding of the Fourteenth Amendment in Illinois, Ohio, and Pennsylvania*, 18 Akron L. Rev. 435, 446 (1985).

276 *Governor Morton's Speech*, The Richmond Palladium [IN], Aug. 2, 1866, at 1, https://chroniclingamerica.loc.gov/lccn/sn86058250/1866-08-02/ed-1/seq-1/.

277 *Secretary Browning and the Constitutional Amendment*, New-York Tribune, Oct. 25, 1866, https://chroniclingamerica.loc.gov/lccn/sn83030214/1866-10-25/ed-1/seq-4/.

278 *The Campaign in Wisconsin: Speech of Senator T.O. Howe, at Madison, Wisconsin, Aug. 10,* Chicago Tribune, Aug. 14, 1866, at 2, https://chroniclingamerica.loc.gov/lccn/sn82014064/1866-08-14/ed-1/seq-2/ (emphasis added).

279 *Speech at Harrison County* (Aug. 24) *reprinted in* Speeches of the campaign of 1866, in the states of Ohio, Indiana, and Kentucky 19 (1866), and also https://chroniclingamerica.loc.gov/lccn/sn85026193/1866-09-07/ed-1/seq-1/ (stating that the prohibitory sentence of Section 1 limits the States' "abuses of power"); *Mr. Bingham's Speech at Martinsville*, The Wheeling Intelligencer (Wheeling W. Va.), Sept. 4, 1866, at 2, https://chroniclingamerica.loc.gov/lccn/sn84026844/1866-09-05/ed-1/seq-2/ (explaining that the equal-protection guarantee "declares against the abuse of powers hitherto exercised by States, in which they denied the equal protection of the laws, or any protection of the laws whatever, to some of the noblest men in the Republic").

280 Cong. Globe, 39th Cong. 1st sess., at 2543 May 10.

281 Joint Resolution Endorsing Report of Committee on Federal Relations, Dec. 5, 1844, *in* Acts and Joint Resolutions of the General Assembly of the State of South Carolina, Passed in December 1844 159, 160 (1845) ("Resolved, That the emissary sent by the State of Massachusetts to the State of South-Carolina, with the avowed purpose of interfering with her institutions, and disturbing her peace, is to be regarded in the character he has assumed, and to be treated accordingly. Resolved, That his Excellency the Governor be requested to expel from our territory the said Agent, after due notice to depart, and that the Legislature will sustain the Executive authority in any measures it may adopt for the purpose aforesaid"). Horace Greeley, 1 The American Conflict: A History of the Great Rebellion in the United States of America 181 (1865); *John A. Bingham*, Chicago Tribune, Dec. 12, 1868, at 2, ihttps://chroniclingamerica.loc.gov/lccn/sn82014064/1868-12-12/ed-1/seq-2/ (emphasis added) (explaining that the Amendment "gives us full power to protect our citizens, and it was needed," because when a great "outrage was committed in South Carolina" against Hoar, "there was no remedy under any authority").

282 Report of the Joint Committee on Reconstruction, H. R. Rep. No. 30, 39th Cong., 1st Sess., xvii–xviii, (June 8, 1866). Jack M. Balkin, *The Reconstruction Power*, 85 N.Y.U.L. Rev. 1801, 1807 (2010) (noting that the failure of state and local governments to guarantee equal protection of the laws was a central focus of the Report).

283 *Speech of Honorable Luke P. Poland*, Green-Mountain Freeman, Nov. 7, 1866, at 2, https://chroniclingamerica.loc.gov/lccn/sn84023209/1866-11-07/ed-1/seq-2/.

284 New York Herald, Jan. 31, 1867, at 6, https://chroniclingamerica.loc.gov/lccn/sn83030313/1867-01-31/ed-1/seq-6/.

285 *John A. Bingham*, Chicago Tribune, Dec. 12, 1868, at 2, ihttps://chroniclingamerica.loc.gov/lccn/sn82014064/1868-12-12/ed-1/seq-2/.

286 *Protect*, Online Etymology Dictionary, https://www.etymonline.com/word/protect.

287 Green, *supra* note 271, at 44–72.

288 Cong. Globe, 39th Cong. 1st sess., at 1082 (Stewart, Feb. 28).

289 *Id.* at 813 (Feb. 13).

290 *See supra* text accompanying notes 20–1.

291 *See, e.g.*, Penn. Const. art. IX, § xi (1790) (providing that "every man, for an injury done him in his lands, goods, person or reputation, shall have remedy by the due course of law, and right and justice administered, without sale, denial or delay"); N.C. Const. art. I, § 35 (1868) (same).

292 Cong. Globe, 39th Cong. 1st sess., at 2539 (May 10) (Farnsworth) (loosely quoting the proposal to require a state to provide equal protection "of its laws"); *id.* at 2765 (May 23) (Howard) (likewise paraphrasing the proposal). Still, as Andrew Hyman has pointed out, the Amendment does not read "of its laws," so the laws are not limited to laws made by the states. Andrew Hyman, *The Substantive Role of Congress Under the Equal Protection Clause*, 42 S.U.L. Rev. 79, 81 (2014).

293 Cong. Globe, 39th Cong. 1st sess., at 813 (Feb. 13).

294 Hermine Herta Meyer, The History and Meaning of the Fourteenth Amendment: Judicial Erosion of the Constitution Through the Misuse of the Fourteenth Amendment 294 (1977).

295 Earl M. Maltz, *Moving beyond Race: The Joint Committee on Reconstruction and the Drafting of the Fourteenth Amendment*, 42 Hastings Const. L.Q. 287, 317 (2015).

296 *See supra* chapter 1.

297 The Legislative Record: Containing the Debates and Proceedings of the Pennsylvania Legislature, for the Session of 1867, app. at civ. (George Bergnor, ed. 1867) [hereinafter "Pennsylvania Legislative Record"].

298 *Secretary Browning and the Constitutional Amendment*, New-York Tribune, Oct. 25, 1866, at 4 https://chroniclingamerica.loc.gov/lccn/sn83030214/1866-10-25/ed-1/seq-4/.

299 *Mr. Browning's Letter*, Worcester Daily Spy, Oct. 26, 1866, at 2, https://chroniclingamerica.loc.gov/lccn/sn83021205/1866-10-26/ed-1/seq-2/.

300 *The Howard Amendment*, The Western Sentinel [N.C.], Oct. 4, 1866, at 2, https://chroniclingamerica.loc.gov/lccn/sn84026526/1866-10-04/ed-1/seq-2/.

301 *Speech of Senator Creswell of Maryland*, The Evening Telegraph. Sept. 22, 1866, at 3, https://chroniclingamerica.loc.gov/lccn/sn83025925/1866-09-22/ed-1/seq-3/.

302 Reconstruction Act, ch. 153, 14 Stat. 428 (1867).

303 *The New Trick to Force Negro Suffrage Upon the People of the United States*, Bedford Gazette [Penn.], June 22, 1866, at 2, https://chroniclingamerica.loc.gov/lccn/sn82005159/1866-06-22/ed-1/seq-2/.

304 *Rescinding the Fourteenth Amendment*, Delaware Gazette [OH], Jan. 24, 1868, at 1, https://chroniclingamerica.loc.gov/lccn/sn83035595/1868-01-24/ed-1/seq-1/.

305 Bond, *supra* note 275, at 463 (quoting Pennsylvania Legislative Record, *supra* note 297, app. at xcix).

306 *A Pair of Amendments*, Wheeling Daily Register, June 19, 1866, at 2, https://chroniclingamerica.loc.gov/lccn/sn84026847/1866-06-19/ed-1/seq-2/ (stating that the proposed Fourteenth Amendment "though not so intended" was a "decided rebuke to [West Virginia's] radical extremists," who they cannot "prevent *any person* from bringing suit to enforce his legal rights, for they must then no longer deny to any one the equal protection of the laws" (emphasis in original)); *The Fourteenth Amendment*, The Pacific Commercial Advertiser, Aug. 22, 1868, at 3 (reprinting California editorial on effects of the newly adopted Amendment).

307 *Yick Wo v. Hopkins*, 118 U.S. 356, 369 (1886).

308 Akhil Reed Amar, *Attainder and Amendment 2*, 95 Mich. L. Rev. 203, 212 (1996).

5

American Citizenship

A Partial Declaration

There is room also for a more critical examination of the Constitutional meaning of the term "Citizens" than has yet taken place; and of the effect of the various civil disqualifications applied by the laws of the States to free people of colour.

—Letter of James Madison to James Monroe (Nov. 19, 1820)[1]

It would be just as legitimate to inquire whether the African race intended to admit the whites to the privileges of citizenship. They all resided together, participants of that freedom which was the fruit of their common struggles and sacrifices. Whatever their disparity in numbers, or condition, neither had the right to eject the other from the common purchase, or make them aliens from the commonwealth.

—Justice Woodbury Davis, Maine Supreme Court (Aug. 20, 1857)[2]

Our inquiry now turns from personhood to citizenship. Over the next two chapters, I'll address first the status of citizenship, and then the privileges thereof. This order conforms with the sequence of the text—the Citizenship Clause comes first, then the Privileges or Immunities Clause. Furthermore, this order follows the order of apprehension; from its drafting and until our time, the former clause has occasioned far less disagreement and confusion than the latter.

American citizenship is older than our Republic. Upon Independence Day, the American people avowed that they already formed "one people," that is, the "good people" of certain "United Colonies."[3] Indeed, within the previous few years, this one colonial people, through their congressional representatives, had already officially called themselves the "American people," the "people of America," or simply, "Americans."[4]

As the Declaration of Independence indicates, the individual members of this American people were, as colonists, already "fellow Citizens," and thus "friends and Brethren."[5] And one of the rights of American colonial citizenship was the freedom from compulsory military service against one another. The violation of this immunity was one of the "abuses" that rendered the British king a "tyrant," and thus "unfit to be the ruler of a free people."[6]

With independence of the "United Colonies," as declared by the renamed "United States,"[7] this colonial "free people" was now the "people of the United States," and the members thereof "citizens of the United States."[8] As indicated by the Constitution the citizenry subsequently adopted, at least some citizens were "natural-born citizens" (without the qualifier "of the United States"), and some others were "citizen[s] of the United States, at the time of the adoption of this Constitution," and some others might become citizens through "naturalization." Further, these Americans, if also citizens of a "state," could, under Articles III and IV of that charter, sue or be sued in federal courts under diversity jurisdiction, and were "entitled to all Privileges and Immunities of Citizens in the several States."[9]

The Declaration and Constitution did not otherwise define the status or rights of American citizenship.[10] Still, these concepts were not new; they had clear antecedents in classical Greece and Rome, as well as English law, which provided a generally accepted framework for American citizenship.

American Citizenship (1776–1865)

I'll here provide a rough but serviceable sketch of this framework, as received and preserved by the American people.

The Classical Citizen and the English Subject

The word "citizen" is a Latinate word, derived from *civis* (citizen), that is, a member of the *civitas* (commonwealth). *Civis* and *civitas* were the Latin translations of the Greek *polites* and *polis*, respectively.

Aristotle had provided the most thorough and respected discussion of the citizen and the commonwealth. He observed that the commonwealth, by its nature, is an association of members, called "citizens," for their comprehensive earthly good. This commonwealth superintends the whole, but is not totalitarian—it does not destroy the individual or the anterior relations of the household (between parent and offspring, wife and husband, etc.). Rather, the commonwealth presupposes the existence of individuals, households, and even villages or tribes (what we might call the "extended family"). At the same time, neither the individual nor the household, nor even the tribe, is a self-sufficient community. The commonwealth, however, is the self-sufficient community, providing its constituents, both individuals and families, with what they need for earthly flourishing.[11]

Aristotle identified seven goods of the commonwealth in which the members thus share: (1) a common territory, (2) markets for inter-household exchange, (3) a community for inter-household marriage (exogamy), (4) tribunals to resolve conflicts, (5) public discussion as to the common good, (6) arms (coercion) both to enforce the community's decisions and to protect the community's territory against external enemies, and (7) superintending the whole *polis*, a common *politeia*, a regime or constitution—governing the distribution of authoritative offices.[12] This seventh good, unlike the others, necessarily involves stark inequality because decisional authority is necessarily hierarchical. Still, some constitutions are more democratic, less hierarchical, than others.[13]

This last good concerns what American officials, in 1866, would call "political" rights, and which the states might reserve to only *some* citizens. Still, the politically unequal citizenry shares the *politeia* in common—via a common agreement or at least acquiescence as to the distribution of decisional authority ("political power," in today's parlance).[14] Or as Cicero remarked, the commonwealth necessarily involves a "consilium primum"—a first counsel or decision—as to that "constitution."[15] Political authority is distributed unequally, but pursuant to a general agreement or acquiescence among the citizenry.

Consistent with this definition of the commonwealth, Aristotle offered three definitions of its membership. First, *the citizen by common usage* is any free person born to a mother and father who are both bona fide citizens. This universal convention arises from the very nature of the commonwealth as an association of households; any issue of two citizens' marriage is thus, by necessity, a member of the parents' commonwealth. Second, the *inchoate citizen* is any free person who shares in the territory and other parts of the commonwealth, chiefly the markets and tribunals; this person is *in*, but only partly *of*, the commonwealth. Third, *the citizen-in-full* is the citizen who participates not only in the commonwealth's territory, markets, deliberations, and so forth, but also in decisional authority as distributed by the constitution. To use the terminology of 1866, the citizen-in-full enjoyed the full rights of citizenship, both "civil" and "political."[16]

Roman law likewise identified citizens as persons with some share in these elements of the commonwealth. As a nineteenth-century textbook explained, the rights of Roman citizens included certain *iura privata*, such as the right to acquire, transfer, and hold real property, and to intermarry with citizens of other classes, as well as certain *iura publica*, such as the right to make certain judicial appeals, to vote, and to hold office.[17]

In medieval and early modern England, the civic member was demoted to a "subject." And in apparent opposition to Aristotle, English law defined native citizenship with reference to place of birth (*ius soli*) rather than parentage (*ius sanguinis*). For the most part, all persons born on English soil, and only such persons, were natural-born subjects.

But here we should note the two ways in which English law still acknowledged Aristotle's purportedly universal norm of heredity (blood). Persons born on the soil still needed some measure of qualifying blood—and could thus be subject to hereditary disqualification. Persons were not English subjects if born to parents who were themselves immune from ordinary local jurisdiction, whether *de jure* (as foreign ambassadors) or *de facto* (as members of invading armies).[18] Conversely, qualifying blood could be sufficient to transmit citizenship even to persons born abroad, if born to (1) the sovereign monarch, (2) his or her ambassadors, or (3) other English subjects.

By 1776, these persons were deemed natural-born subjects by force of common law or well-established statutory law.[19]

I venture to add another consideration: the Anglo-American *ius soli* rule may not have been so much an alternative as an auxiliary to the more fundamental *ius sanguinis* rule. In a large, mobile, and commercial nation like England or America, paternity was especially uncertain. The obscurity was all the more acute in 1866, when a large portion of our people was emerging from chattel slavery—which rendered paternity haphazard and difficult to adjudicate. To address this uncertainty, the overinclusive *ius soli* rule provided a noble and useful veil. Like the old marital presumption of paternity, it served as a prophylactic rule. Anyone born to a woman on English or American soil presumptively was the child of an English or American father, much as anyone born to a married woman was presumptively the child of her husband.[20]

Moreover, the English "subjects," despite their designation, increasingly resembled classical citizens. The English subject, unlike the alien, had certain rights to the territory, markets, and tribunals of the commonwealth; for instance, he had a right to remain in the territory (e.g., to not be "transported beyond seas"), to acquire permanent interests in real as well as personal property, to be tried by a jury of the vicinage, and an exemption from certain regulations and higher taxes imposed on foreigners.[21]

Further, by at least the seventeenth century, the English subject had the right to participate not only in the kingdom's territory, markets, and tribunals, but in the higher goods of the community, such as public *deliberations* and *arms*, and with some share, albeit partial and remote, in *decisional* authority. According to the English Bill of Rights of 1689, among their "ancient rights and liberties," the "subjects" had the right to speak publicly on public matters, via the "right to petition the king." Moreover, the subjects had two complementary rights as to arms: the right (if Protestant) to "have arms for their defense," and the freedom from a peacetime standing army, with both martial privileges subject to definition by law. More generally, the whole "people" had the right to share in government through representation in Parliament, which was said to "fully and freely represent . . . this nation," that is, "all the estates of the *people* of this realm," and without whose consent the people could not be taxed.[22]

The American Subject and Citizen

In America, the same principles obtained. Any person born within and under the King's dominion, including the American colonies, was a fellow British subject. Moreover, an alien-born person might become a member by naturalization in the colonies. By statute, naturalization required both a durational residence (seven years) and the appropriate political and religious creeds (allegiance to the Crown, and a Protestant or Jewish religion).[23]

As to rights, American subjects claimed all these rights of Englishmen. These included not only their rights as human persons, such as the right to "life, liberty, and property," but also their rights as English subjects, such as trial "by their peers of the vicinage," the right to petition, the freedom from standing armies, and, most saliently (at the center of the controversy), the political right of representation in the legislature.[24]

With the Revolution, these principles required some modification. First and foremost, the "one people" of America dissolved all their "political connections" with the British people. The American people were now "separate and equal." At the same time, the civil war compelled a provisional rule of membership that was more inclusive and easier to adjudicate. Ten days before declaring independence, Congress sweepingly declared that "all persons abiding within any of the United Colonies, and deriving protection from the laws of the same, owe allegiance to the said laws, and are members of such colony."[25] Consistent with this inclusive rule, Congress soon thereafter approved an Articles of Confederation that secured the "privileges and immunities" of citizenship to virtually all the "free inhabitants" of states.[26] This revolutionary *ius soli* rule, unlike the ordinary common-law rule, depended on (1) American soil of *residence* (not birth), along with (2) enjoyment of American jurisdiction.

As Aristotle might say, during the Revolution, America prudently decided to turn all the inchoate citizens (those already sharing in the soil and tribunals), regardless of parentage or place of birth, into ordinary citizens, and require of them the full duties of allegiance. Indeed, we might say that such a rule arose not merely from prudence but also justice. These Americans were not so much *naturalized* as *proto-natural*, for they shared, by their blood, sweat, and tears, in the very founding of the Republic. As Aristotle observed, those participating in the constitution at the time of commonwealth's founding are the primordial parental citizens from whom membership by parentage subsequently derives.[27]

Nonetheless, the old birthright rule was not forgotten. Even if absent during the whole conflict, the *antenati* (born on American colonial soil) were still presumptive citizens of the Republic. Virginia's legislature, for instance, claimed as citizens all (white) persons who had been *either* resident thereon for two years after Independence *or* native to the state's soil.[28] Further, well after the war, the general rule was that though absent during the Revolution, the *antenati* could return as loyal citizens, without naturalization, provided they had made their election within a reasonable amount of time.[29]

With the close of the war, in 1783, the old peacetime order returned. Going forward, citizenship once again would require birth or naturalization—mere residence was insufficient. Accordingly, under the post-war Constitution of 1787, the privileges and immunities of citizens were secured no longer to "free inhabitants" but only to "citizens."

As to citizenship by birth, the old laws persisted. As before Independence, there was little doubt that the common-law rule still encompassed all persons born in the United States and subject to the jurisdiction thereof—with one naked exception to be discussed below.[30] Further, as to persons born abroad, Americans retained and reaffirmed the old statutory right of *ius sanguinis* membership. The First Congress declared that foreign-born offspring of American citizens "shall be considered as natural born Citizens," provided their fathers had not lost or abandoned heritable citizenship by absence from American soil.[31]

As to citizenship by naturalization, the power was first assumed by the several states upon Independence, and then transferred through the Constitution to the national Congress. Congress proceeded to establish a "uniform rule of naturalization" that, like the colonial antecedent, extended citizenship to the alien born on two fundamental criteria: durational *residence* and political *creed* (to "support the Constitution of the United States"). But unlike the colonial antecedent, this rule did not require any religious creed.[32] Conversely, the statute imposed a new hereditary exclusion: only "white" persons were eligible.[33] Nonetheless, under treaty law, the naturalization of non-whites remained lawful. Under the Louisiana Purchase and other territorial treaties, as well as various treaties with discrete Indian tribes, both the non-white members of those tribes and the non-white residents in the ceded territories became citizens of the United States without significant controversy.[34]

We pause here to recapitulate what has been suggested. Americans deemed *three* factors as decisive in distinguishing aliens from citizens, whether by birth or by naturalization. These three included (1) heredity, (2) birth or residence on the soil, and (3) political creed; or stated tersely, American *blood,* American *soil,* and American *creed.* These three elements all corresponded to the three foundational elements of the commonwealth, as identified by Aristotle: community of households (blood), occupying a common territory (soil), and sharing a common constitution (creed)—and each of these factors had a rough correlative in Aristotle's three definitions of citizenship: the citizen by heredity, the inchoate citizen by residence on the soil; and the citizen in full, who, under the constitution, shares in authoritative office.

As a general rule, citizenship required participation in two of these three elements. So citizenship by birth on the soil also required hereditary jurisdiction—that is, birth to parents who were under American jurisdiction (soil and blood). Citizenship by birth to American parents abroad also required some participation on the soil—paternal residence (blood and soil). Naturalization required both residence and the oath to support the Constitution (soil and creed). And as we'll discuss, ex-citizenship by expatriation required departure from two of the three (soil and creed).[35]

These considerations will prove very helpful in the next chapter, when we seek to identify the *immunities* of American citizenship.

The Revolution involved not only some temporary modification of the criteria for citizenship, but also permanent enlargement of the privileges thereof. First, as citizens and thus co-sovereigns (and no longer mere subjects), Americans did not so much petition the sovereign as deliberate with one another. Accordingly, the state and federal constitutions generally recognized and secured to "the people" or "the citizens" the full freedoms of discussion: not only petition, but also assembly, press, and speech.[36] Second, as a multireligious citizenry, every member of the American "people," regardless of religious faith, enjoyed all civil rights, including the right to keep and bear arms.[37] Non-Protestants were no longer, as to any *civil* right, second-class citizens. Finally, as citizens under a republican government, the people were entitled not only to representation in the legislature, but to a wholly popular government where all officials received their authority "directly or indirectly from the great body of the people" and were accountable to the same.[38]

In large measure, all these principles of citizenship, as modified and Americanized, occasioned very little controversy. Americans generally endorsed a common view of citizenship—a view plainly developed from the Western tradition and more specifically, Anglo-American law.

The African American?

But here as elsewhere, American slavery did much violence to the broader and deeper tradition. By some antebellum accounts, even if free and native to the soil, and even if they had shed blood, sweat, and tears for American Independence, African freedmen and their descendants did not enjoy *ius soli* membership, and could thus be subject to hereditary burdens and outright exclusions from the commonwealth.

At the Founding, this matter was quite ambiguous. Despite the inclusiveness of both the common-law birthright rule and the revolutionary residence rule, some states subjected free blacks to legal restrictions concerning two significant features of citizenship: intermarriage and voting. About half the states (mostly southern) prohibited free blacks from intermarriage with whites, and a minority (all southern) reserved the suffrage to "whites." These anomalies became more widespread, if not normative, during the next century. By the Civil War, a clear majority of the states invalidated and/or prohibited blacks' intermarriage with whites, and all the states outside New England denied or abridged blacks' right to vote.[39] In these two respects, free blacks were treated as resident aliens, or mere inchoate citizens, who still participated in the territory, markets, and tribunals, even if barred from intermarriage and political rights.

These restrictions occasioned some local controversy, but little national debate. But when some states went much further, and undertook an even more radical alienation of native-born black persons—even from the soil itself—an intense national controversy ensued.

This issue first rose to national prominence during the debates over the admission of Missouri. The people of the territory proposed to be admitted as a state with a constitution that both protected slavery and impeded the immigration of free blacks, even those born on American soil. These two matters required not one, but two Missouri Compromises—the first as to slavery, the second as to black citizenship. The first of these is well known, the second is not.

Most northern congressmen insisted that the limitation violated the black citizen's constitutional entitlement to the "privileges and immunities of citizens in the several states." In response, southerners flatly denied that free blacks were "citizens."[40] The acrimonious debate ended with the Second Missouri Compromise. Unlike the first, the second was little more than a mere agreement to disagree.[41] Congress required that Missouri agree that its state constitution "shall never be construed" such that "any citizen of either of the States of this Union shall be excluded from the enjoyment of any of the privileges and immunities to which such citizen is entitled under the Constitution of the United States."[42] But Congress refused to resolve the very issue in dispute: whether native-born free blacks were, in fact, constitutional "citizens," and thus entitled them to a right to travel throughout the Union free from racial obstructions.

The constitutional issue was obscure even to James Madison, the so-called "father of the Constitution." In the midst of the second crisis, in a letter to President Monroe, he lamented the absence of "a more critical examination" as to both the "meaning of the term 'Citizens'" and "the effect of the various civil disqualifications applied by the laws of the States to free people of colour."[43] Madison, it seems, was not sure whether, under his and our Constitution, free blacks, though native to the soil, could ever be American citizens, and to what extent they could be subject to various "civil disqualifications."

These controversies persisted until the Civil War. By 1860, officials had adopted roughly three different positions. First, pro-slavery jurists generally denied categorically that the free descendants of black slaves could ever be American citizens—in part because, if citizens under Article IV, they would be entitled (racial disqualifications notwithstanding) to the privileges of travel, residence, speech, and arms-bearing while sojourning in other states, including slaveholding states: a veritable parade of horribles. Such was the opinion of the Court majority in *Dred Scott*.[44] Mississippi's high court went further, declaring that free blacks were not just aliens, but presumptively "alien enemies"; it was state policy "to interdict all intercourse, commerce, and comity with this race."[45]

Second, more moderate officials, northerners like Justice Curtis, relied on a states-rights approach, whereby each state determined the citizenship status of persons born on the state's soil. Further, when going to another state, such citizens were entitled only to a freedom from interstate discrimination; they enjoyed only whatever rights that state might afford to persons "under the same circumstances."[46] Accordingly, free blacks could be citizens only if recognized as such in their state of birth; and while traveling to another state, they were entitled only to whatever rights (if any) in-state free blacks might enjoy. These officials helped establish what would become, *after* the Fourteenth Amendment's adoption, our "orthodox" reading by which Article IV only protects out-of-state citizens against interstate discrimination.[47]

Third, however, was the view increasingly held by Republicans: all free persons, native to American soil and American jurisdiction, were American citizens. As such, they were entitled, throughout the Union, to certain fundamental privileges of American citizenship, state laws to the contrary notwithstanding.[48] This law was not only our national law, but natural law. Indeed, insofar as it was the natural law, it must be our constitutional rule. After all, the Constitution is made by "we the people," and by necessity "the people" cannot lawfully unmake themselves; the majority, as such, cannot exclude the minority, any more than the minority can lawfully exclude the majority.

Consider, in this regard, the response of Judge Woodbury Davis, of the Maine Supreme Court, to the originalist claim that white Americans, at the Founding, did not consider free blacks as fellow members of "the people":

> If it be said that history shows that at the time when the federal constitution was adopted, the white population of the country did not intend to admit colored persons of African descent to the privileges of citizenship, while the assertion is denied, it is *also* replied that we have *no right to inquire* what one class of persons

> intended, in derogation of the rights of any other class. *It would be just as legitimate to inquire whether the African race intended to admit the whites to the privileges of citizenship.* They all resided together, participants of that freedom which was the fruit of their common struggles and sacrifices. Whatever their disparity in numbers, or condition, neither had the right to eject the other from the common purchase, or make them aliens from the commonwealth.[49]

We are a multiracial republic by not only original opinion but original natural right. The very nature of our people, then, forbids any such inquiry into whether any majority or minority intended to exclude any portion of our citizenry. From the beginning, Americans were a multiracial people, and as such, they could not alienate any portion of themselves on the basis of race.

By 1866, the first position (pro-slavery) was no longer viable. The second position was still endorsed by many northern Democratic officials and was adopted by southern Democrats as well. But among the Republicans that adopted the Fourteenth Amendment, the third position prevailed. In fact, the Joint Committee on Reconstruction aimed to secure to African Americans not only civil rights but *all* their rights as full "citizens"—both "civil and political." But the white loyal electorate was not with them. When the Amendment was adopted, all but five states (all in New England) still limited the suffrage to whites. And in 1865, even in strongly Republican states like Connecticut, Wisconsin, and Minnesota, the electorate rejected proposals to extend equal voting rights to blacks.[50] The white voters' message was fairly clear: Civil rights, yes. Political rights, no (or not yet). The Committee's majority had to acquiesce to public opinion.

In this chapter and the next, I will address how the Fourteenth Amendment's Citizenship and Privileges or Immunities Clauses were designed to settle some of these controversies in favor of African Americans' status and "civil privileges" as citizens—albeit by means of language with a *meaning* that plainly exceeded this *motive*.

The Citizenship Clause

As first proposed to Congress by the Joint Committee, the Amendment included no definition of citizenship. Republicans on the Committee initially thought such a constitutional definition unnecessary. The holding of the Supreme Court in *Dred Scott* was so erroneous that it should simply be ignored.

In his speech of May 23, inaugurating the discussion of the Committee's proposal, Senator Howard remarked that there already was an existing, well-established norm of "*national* law, or rather of *natural* law which recognizes persons born within the jurisdiction of every country as being subjects or citizens of that country. Such persons were, therefore, citizens of the United States, as were born in the country or were made such by naturalization."[51]

Nonetheless, a few days into the Senate's deliberations, Republicans came to agree that, among other changes, some declaratory provision as to citizenship was needed.

After deliberations in a Republican caucus, Howard presented various proposals to the full Senate on May 30—a series of changes so significant that the whole Amendment became known (at least in North Carolina) as the "Howard Amendment."[52] One of these changes was a new first sentence: "All persons born in the United States and subject to the jurisdiction thereof are citizens of the United States and of the States wherein they reside."[53] The proposed addition, he reiterated, was "simply declaratory of what I regard as the law of the land already . . . by virtue of natural law and national law."[54] The measure was the subject of an extended debate between Senators Howard, James Doolittle, and others, chiefly as to whether its terms improperly extended citizenship to persons born under (Indian) tribal immunity.[55]

As first submitted to the Senate, this declaration included only citizens by birth on American soil, without any mention of others; for example, citizens by naturalization or by birth abroad to American parents. But in the last hour of the Senate's debate, just before the final vote on the whole Fourteenth Amendment, Fessenden moved to insert "or naturalized" in between "born" and "in the United States." There was, Howard tersely announced, "no objection" to the proposal, and the insertion was summarily approved without discussion.[56] This eleventh-hour change made little news.[57]

Persons Born or Naturalized in the United States

"All persons, born or naturalized"

The first few words of the Amendment have never involved substantial controversy. As we saw, "person" was clear in meaning: any "human being."

"Born," by universal experience, was, of course, familiar. Birth was the culmination of maternal gestation: the universal mode for the prenatal care and reception of new human persons. We may here note that when extracorporeal, motherless gestation is achieved (whether via "artificial wombs" or otherwise), there will be persons who will not have been born. The citizenship of such motherless persons will involve interesting questions.[58]

"Naturalized," by constitutional and historical context, was likewise a straightforward term. The Constitution expressly vests statutory "naturalization" power in Congress, and the United States had also naturalized by treaty.[59]

Parenthetically, we can see that as of 1866, there were still three qualifications that Congress deemed decisive as to whether a foreigner satisfied our "uniform rule of naturalization." These are the same three that were essential to citizenship at the Founding: soil, creed, and blood. The first prerequisite was a share in American *soil*; durational residence (typically five years) was required. The second was the adoption of the American *creed*: foreigners had to renounce all foreign allegiance and instead credibly promise to "support" the Constitution—with special emphasis on our constitutional intolerance of hereditary titles, as foreigners had to specially renounce any personal title of nobility. The third was *blood* or heredity, as all aliens had to satisfy the hereditary qualification of "white" (or, alternatively, from 1870, "African"). Conversely, for some alien minors, American *blood* could substitute for American creed; if resident, such minors could enjoy naturalization simultaneous with their Americanized parents.[60]

The statute also mandated two other requisites—freedom and "good moral character"—but these differed in kind from the foregoing. These qualities concerned not whether a person might be a member of *our* civil society, but a good member of *any* civil society. Freedom was essential to citizenship everywhere.[61] And to be of "good moral character" (as first interpreted after the Civil War) was a euphemism for a non-felon. The term referred not to a peculiarly virtuous person, but rather the person who had *not* engaged in conduct generally recognized as evil and harmful to any human community: either grave *mala in se* as "murder, robbery, theft, bribery, or perjury," or, by habitual or other repeated violations of local law, mere *mala prohibita*, like gambling.[62] Good moral character, like judicial "good behavior," established a very low bar.

In the United States

The requisite birth or naturalization must occur "in the United States." This phrase was then not difficult to understand. Without significant controversy, the "United States" included, of course, the several states.[63] Further, as Michael Ramsey has pointed out, it was well established that the "United States" encompassed the federal district and the federal territories. The Supreme Court had held that "[t]he district of Columbia, or the territory west of the Missouri, is not less within the United States, than Maryland or Pennsylvania."[64] Indeed, beginning with the 1795 revision of the naturalization rule, Congress expressly identified an alien residing in the territories as someone "within the limits . . . of the United States" and thus eligible for naturalization as "a citizen of the United States" even though never a state resident.[65] Moreover, in various territorial treaties, the United States incorporated most of the territorial inhabitants as naturalized "citizens of the United States," without any state residence or citizenship.[66] Accordingly, as Ramsey notes, during the Senate debate over the proposed Citizenship Clause, all participants "seemed to assume that the Howard proposal encompassed the territories (including unorganized frontier territories)."[67]

Yet as the Thirteenth Amendment indicated, there may be "places" outside the "United States" but still subject to the jurisdiction thereof. Ramsey has explained that such places included areas subject to temporary military jurisdiction—such as the port of Tampico occupied during the Mexican-American War.[68] The Supreme Court had noted in *Fleming v. Page* that the military may "invade the hostile country, and subject it to the sovereignty and authority of the United States" but absent formal legislative acquisition by treaty or otherwise, such conquest did "not enlarge the boundaries of this Union," so the place "was out of the limits of the United States" even though subject to the martial jurisdiction thereof.[69]

Subject to the Jurisdiction Thereof

Besides birth or naturalization *in* the United States, the Citizenship Clause requires subjection to American jurisdiction. At first glance, we may ask whether this second requirement is redundant. Jurisdiction, from the Latin *dicere* (to say) and *ius* (law or right), meant the power to say what the law is, and usually, with respect to particular parties in a lawsuit. Jurisdiction, then, was the "authority by which judicial officers take cognizance of and decide causes."[70] From the Thirteenth Amendment and the *Fleming* decision, we learn that jurisdiction refers to *place*. Therefore, it would seem that anyone "in" the United States, by his very presence, is *ipso facto* subject to the jurisdiction thereof.

But as we will see below, this requirement, though superfluous as to domestic naturalization, was not redundant as to citizenship by domestic birth.

At Birth

Both the constitutional context and the official discussion of the Citizenship Clause indicate that, as originally understood, "subject to the jurisdiction" meant birth to parents who were "subject to the full ordinary authority of the United States."

At birth, this jurisdiction was mediated through the parents. As we noted in the previous chapter, a person was born subject to the jurisdiction of the United States precisely because he or she was born subject to parents "who at the time of birth were subject to the authority of the United States."[71] This understanding was uncontroversial; by the opinion prevailing in 1866, the parents had, by natural right, the primary authority over their bodily offspring.

Ordinary "jurisdiction" under Section 1 seems to involve that space in which a state has the authority and duty to provide the "equal protection of the laws," and wherein a person might be subject to governmental deprivation of property, liberty, and even life. Hence, jurisdiction seems to suggest involving the authority to make and enforce civil and criminal laws in furtherance of these duties.

It turns out, however, some persons *in* the United States are not subject to its full ordinary jurisdiction. Over some persons, the United States lacked "legal" or "actual" authority, as Gerard Magliocca has observed.[72] Diplomats and members of Indian tribes enjoyed a substantial *de jure* immunity from the ordinary civil and criminal jurisdiction—such persons and their children are not subject "fully and completely" to the American jurisdiction, as one Senator explained.[73] Likewise, members of invading armies had a certain *de facto* immunity, which placed them outside that ordinary jurisdiction of any and all the United States.

One matter that remains very controversial among scholars is whether for a child to qualify for this *ius soli* citizenship, his parents' subjection to the United States must be *exclusive* as well as complete. The question, sometimes very loosely referred to as the debate over "birthright citizenship," divided the Supreme Court in *United States v. Wong Kim Ark*,[74] and still occasions sharp discord. Some contend that the Clause should be read, "and subject to the exclusive jurisdiction thereof," such that the Clause does not recognize as citizens those persons born to parents subject concurrently to a foreign power, for they remain, even while in the United States, the subjects or citizens of that sovereign. Such concurrent subjection was common. By international law, even while residing abroad and thus subject to local jurisdiction, subjects or citizens were still substantially and concurrently under the jurisdiction of their sovereigns. As Robert Mensel notes, "it was well-settled . . . in 1866, that a foreigner could be domiciled in the United States but remain subject to a foreign power."[75]

The Clause's text alone does not solve the question as to whether the jurisdiction need be exclusive or could be merely concurrent. To be sure, the word "exclusive" is absent. But as Chief Justice Marshall observed in another context, "affirmative words are often, in their operation, negative of other objects than those affirmed" such that "a negative or exclusive sense must be given to them."[76]

Many scholars have listed good reasons to give an "exclusive sense" to the phrase "subject to the jurisdiction thereof."[77] First, this reading renders Section 1 consistent with the Civil Rights Act, the constitutionalization of which was a motive for Section 1. That Act "declared" all persons "born in the United States and *not subject to any foreign power*, excluding Indians not taxed . . . to be citizens of the United States."[78]

Second, this reading seems consistent with a plausible reading of Senator Howard's explanation that the Clause would "not include persons born in the United States who are foreigners, aliens, who belong to the families of ambassadors or foreign ministers."[79] By this account, one should here read "ambassadors or foreign ministers" as mere exemplars of alien parents, so his remark best reads "who are foreigners, aliens [such as, but not limited to] persons who belong to the families of ambassadors."

Third, such a reading seems necessary to Howard's express purpose of vindicating an anterior "natural law" of citizenship.[80] Now, we might agree with Bingham that citizenship, as a matter of right, includes "every human being born within the jurisdiction of the United States of parents not owing allegiance to any foreign sovereignty," so "neither the Congress nor the States can justly or lawfully take it from him."[81] But no natural law compels a country to receive as citizens every person, regardless of parentage, born on the country's soil. Indeed, in apparent contravention of any such law, our Republic, from the Founding until today, has claimed as American citizens those persons born on foreign soil to American parents.[82]

On the other hand, critics of the exclusive-jurisdiction reading have plausible responses to these points. As to the first, Chin-Yung Yen and others have answered that the definitions provided by the Civil Rights Act and the Amendment do not seem coextensive. The Act sets forth three requirements, but the Amendment only two.[83]

As to the second point, Howard's mention of ambassadorial families could be read as definitional, and not merely exemplary. That is to say, Howard's remarks should be read this way: "persons born in the United States who are [complete] foreigners, aliens [because they] belong to families of ambassadors."

As to the third point, Howard also mentioned a "national" law, but our national law had never excluded the children born here to aliens; indeed prevailing antebellum authority held that our national law recognized as native citizens persons born to alien sojourners. In *Lynch v. Clarke*, New York's high court had identified this old common-law rule as our "national unwritten law" that was "coeval with the existence of the Union."[84] That is, this rule was logically prior to the state and federal constitutions, and was foundational to the Union itself. The law, the court said, is constitutive of the very "people" by and for whom our Constitution was made.

To be sure, not all proponents of black citizenship fully endorsed the rule. During the framing of the Amendment, Wendell Philips and Horace Greeley proposed a constitutional definition to exclude persons born to merely sojourning aliens.[85] Joseph Story had proposed a similar rule, whereby alien-parental residence was necessary. But as he noted, such a definition had never been our national law.[86]

Finally, as Michael Ramsey and others have noted, the exclusive reading is inconsistent with the rest of the extended debate in the Senate. The interlocutors on both sides all seemed to assert or assume that the Clause would encompass children born to alien Chinese and Gypsies.[87]

The debate has been extensive and perhaps will not be resolved. The evidence is sufficiently mixed that reasonable jurists will differ, and a consensus may be difficult.

Still, I add here a few remarks that may contribute to some resolution in favor of reading the term "jurisdiction" in a nonexclusive way—and thus support the broader, common-law *ius soli* citizenship.

First, during the 1866 election campaign, various supporters and opponents of the Amendment again said or assumed that children born to aliens were citizens under the Citizenship Clause. In late summer 1866, two congressmen from Ohio—a state with large Irish and German populations—celebrated the Amendment for securing citizenship to the children of immigrants. William Lawrence told voters at Piqua that though the Citizenship Clause was "unnecessary," for its terms were "never doubted by any jurist," still it was well "to make it an unalterable law, so that the children born here of parents coming from Germany and Ireland, and other nations, should never be denied the rights or character of citizens by any law of the land."[88] A month later, down the road in Madisonville, Representative Benjamin Eggleston used near-identical language; the Clause would declare the citizenship of "children born here of parents coming to our shores from Germany, Ireland, and other countries."[89] Conversely, in Pennsylvania, Senator Cowan again complained, as he had in the Senate, that the Amendment would confer citizenship on "all" Chinese persons "born in the United States,"[90] and thus prevent any state from expelling all such persons if necessary to the public safety.[91] Maryland's Senator Creswell ridiculed such concerns; opponents were afraid that American citizenship might make "civilized people out [of] Chinese and gipsies [sic]."[92] On this point, I am aware of no evidence where anyone said or assumed otherwise—that the children of unnaturalized immigrants, of whatever ethnicity, were excluded from the Clause's definition of birthright citizenship.

Second, many officials spoke as if the measure would encompass all persons born in the United States, and thus strongly suggested that any exceptions were negligible in number. Supporters frequently omitted entirely the phrase "subject to the jurisdiction thereof." Upon introducing the Senate's amendments to the House, Stevens said the Clause declares citizenship "to belong to every person born or naturalized in the United States."[93] Missouri's governor said the Amendment secured to "every person, born or naturalized in the United States, the rights of a citizen thereof."[94] Before the Vermont legislatures, Senator Poland said the Amendment reaffirmed that "a person born upon our soil—who should first see the light upon our soil—and should live here from that time forward, was a citizen."[95] And to voters, Illinois's John Logan said, "Ever since we have had a Government, I tell you, all free persons born in the United States, negroes and all have been recognized as citizens. Everybody has."[96] These speakers all thus strongly suggested that any exceptions were *de minimis*. This suggestion makes sense if the exceptions were limited to those born to parents with diplomatic or tribal immunity, but would have been absurd if the Clause excluded the many persons born in the country to unnaturalized immigrants.[97]

Third, opponents were deafeningly silent as to the citizenship of children born to European immigrants. No opponent said or suggested that the Citizenship Clause neglected the children of unnaturalized immigrants in favor of blacks. Opponents would surely have loudly raised the objection, as I'll discuss below.[98]

On balance, then, I believe the strong preponderance of the evidence indicates that, as understood by those that adopted the Amendment, the term "subject to the jurisdiction thereof" did not mean "subject to the exclusive jurisdiction thereof." Under the Fourteenth Amendment, citizenship by birth on American soil extends to any person born to parents subject to the ordinary jurisdiction of the United States, even if those parents are concurrently subject to a foreign sovereign.

At Naturalization

As paired with naturalization, the qualifier "subject to the jurisdiction thereof" is entirely redundant. Anyone naturalized inside the United States, by United States officials, is *ipso facto*, at the moment of naturalization, subject to the jurisdiction of the United States. Indeed, from the beginning of the process, by establishing the necessary residence, the foreigner becomes subject to a concurrent American jurisdiction.

Indeed, the whole mention of "naturalization" was entirely unnecessary—and to that extent, the Citizenship Clause fails the requirements of Article V of the Constitution, which directs Congress to propose amendments they deem "necessary." To write in the Constitution that naturalized citizens of the United States are citizens of the United States was "an absurd declaration," as the New Jersey rescinding legislature charged.[99]

We might, then, well wonder why Fessenden proposed, and why the Senate so readily accepted, the unnecessary and absurd insertion of "or naturalized." The hasty and eleventh-hour decision seems ill-conceived.

I believe the necessity was not so much constitutional as political. The omission had become a political liability. Earlier in the day, Missouri Republican John Henderson had, at length, waxed eloquently but loosely. He said, among other things, the following:

> But now upon the moment of *naturalization* the foreigner becomes a citizen of the United States, and may become a citizen of any one of the States by the same residence and under the same circumstances as native-born citizens of other States.
>
> Now, if there be any force in the reasoning to which I have referred, or any weight in the authorities cited, U.S. citizenship is *just what it is defined to be* in the first section of this amendment. I mean that those persons who are to be made citizens by this amendment are the persons, and none others, who have ever been citizens of the United States, under a fair and rational interpretation of the Constitution since its adoption in 1789.[100]

But at this point the definition was utterly silent as to the naturalized Americans celebrated by Henderson. Had the Senate proceeded to adopt the Amendment without some mention of the naturalized, opponents would surely have lambasted the so-called "Black Republicans" for their neglect of the European immigrant in favor of their alleged favorite constituency—the blacks.

President Johnson had already rehearsed this argument in his message vetoing the Civil Rights Bill.[101] And in the press, opponents of the Joint Committee's initial proposal had been quick to level this charge of anti-immigrant bias:

> [Section 1] certainly places the negro above every non-naturalized person in the county, and confers upon these late slaves privileges and immunities which are denied to every freeborn Irishman, yeoman, or other foreigner that resides in our midst.[102]

Republicans were always vulnerable to this indictment. Their party had been formed, in part, from former Know-Nothings. Among leading Republicans were delegates at the 1855 Know-Nothing Convention, including Senator Henry Wilson of Massachusetts and the Speaker of the House, Schuyler Colfax.[103]

The Senate's haste resulted chiefly from Republicans' impatience with any further delay. Meanwhile, Senate Democrats had their own reasons for silent acquiescence. It would not have profited them to quibble about the inclusion of their preferred constituency (European immigrants), or to save Republicans from embarrassment at their mistake in phraseology.

As a political matter, the insertion largely worked. Although some critics would still charge Republicans with comparative disdain for immigrants, by Fessenden's amendment, the charge was largely blunted and limited to *unnaturalized* immigrants. For instance, in the Pennsylvania legislature, one opponent denounced Republicans for making the "person who comes into this country at five years of age" worse off than "the most illiterate negro."[104] But no opponent spoke of the children born here to immigrants.

In sum, the inclusion of "or naturalized" was politically necessary but legally unnecessary. It was, to that extent, a constitutional error. This error would prove harmful, for it has fostered, in turn, the persistent error that the Citizenship Clause offered an exhaustive, comprehensive definition rather than a merely *partial* declaration (as I will explain below).

Are

The principal verb of the Citizenship Clause is "are"; that is, the verb "to be," in the third-person plural, indicative mood, and present tense. The Clause, then, seems to be a declaration of a present fact rather than a prescription for the future.

The constitutional context confirms this inference. Unlike nearly all provisions of the Constitution, including the subsequent provisions of Section 1, the Citizenship

Clause's main verb does not adopt the prescriptive future; it does not read "all persons born or naturalized in the United States . . . *shall be* citizens of the United States." It is the only provision of the Fourteenth Amendment, and one of the few in the whole Constitution, where the principal verb is in the present indicative.

In this respect, the Citizenship Clause resembles the Tenth Amendment, which likewise uses the present indicative: "The powers not delegated to the United States by the Constitution, nor prohibited by it to the States, *are reserved* to the States respectively, or to the people." To adopt the terminology of the First Congress, the Tenth Amendment was thus "declaratory" and not "restrictive."[105] So too is the Citizenship Clause.

The statutory context likewise supports this reading. The closely related (though not identical) Civil Rights Act was quite explicit in this regard: "That all persons born in the United States, and not subject to any foreign Power, are *hereby declared to be* citizens of the United States."[106] The Act and the Amendment did not confer, but merely declared, citizenship of a certain subset of humanity.

A Mere Declaration

Indeed, the whole discussion of the Amendment confirms that the Clause was understood as only a declaration of legal fact. Richard Aynes has pointed out, virtually all supporters concurred that the Citizenship Clause simply recognized the existing citizenship of persons born within and under American jurisdiction.[107] To cite but one of many prominent examples, Howard said so,[108] Steven said so,[109] and Indiana's governor (Oliver Morton) informed the state legislature that the Clause "establishes *the great fact* that all persons born in the United States [and] subject to the jurisdiction thereof, are citizens of the United States."[110]

To be sure, many opponents disagreed. Reverdy Johnson, who had successfully argued against black citizenship in the *Dred Scott* case, supported a new constitutional definition, but deemed it a necessary *clarification* and not just a declaration.[111] And less moderate opponents denounced the Clause as a radical and harmful innovation, as we saw in Chapter 1.[112]

But for supporters, the Amendment emphatically did not "confer citizenship" on the freedmen, or "overturn" the *Dred Scott* decision.[113] All official supporters seemingly agreed that *Dred Scott* was manifestly erroneous. It was never the true law of our land; it did not need to be "overturned" but simply set aside, or even ignored.

The Citizenship Clause was declaratory as to both aspects of the defined citizenship—not just "of the United States" but also "of the State" of residence. In this latter respect, unlike *ius soli* citizenship, the question had never been controversial, so the declaration was largely unnecessary. In *Gassies v. Ballon* (1832), the Supreme Court had already unanimously held that "a citizen of the United States, residing in any state of the Union, is a citizen of that state."[114] Other authorities, including pro-slavery jurists, later cited this holding without controversy, as did members of the Thirty-Ninth Congress.[115]

Still, at least some opponents in the states seemed unaware of this basic law.[116] And to that extent, the specification was helpful.

Some scholars, nonetheless, have characterized this latter part of the Clause as more than declaratory—as an inversion of the former relation between national and state citizenship. Richard Aynes, for instance, has contended that "the citizenship clause indicates a change: that instead of national citizenship being derivative from state citizenship, and state citizenship being primary, the framers made national citizenship primary."[117] But the framers seemed unaware that they were making any such fundamental change. With reliance on authority like *Gassies*, they reasonably believed that such was already the true relation between national and state citizenship.

A Merely Partial Declaration

Like the affirmative words "subject to the jurisdiction thereof," the verb "are" may or may not have an "exclusive sense." Should the Citizenship Clause be read, "All persons . . . *and only such persons*"?

The answer is almost certainly no. As Chin-Yung Yen observed a century ago, the Fourteenth Amendment provided only a "partial definition of citizenship."[118]

If the definition was comprehensive, the result would have been unjust, if not absurd. Though purportedly a mere constitutional declaration, the Clause would have then abrogated a prevailing statutory declaration,[119] recently reaffirmed in 1855, that persons born abroad to American parents, "are declared to be citizens of the United States."[120] This provision was retained in the Revised Statutes, as adopted by Congress a few years after the Amendment.[121] No one, during the adoption and initial interpretation of the Amendment, seems to have said or suggested that the Amendment's declaration contradicted any existing statutory declaration.

Indeed, any such alienation would have been revolutionary and not constitutional. The very people that have ordained and established the Constitution could not, by mere constitutional amendment, declare as aliens any portion of themselves. And without good cause, this expulsion of a minority of the citizenry from the commonwealth would have been flatly unjust.

Moreover, if comprehensive, the Citizenship Clause's definition would have excluded from American citizenship not only those born abroad to Americans, but also the first citizens of the Republic—including the patriots who, by offering their blood, sweat, and tears, risked their "lives, fortunes, and their sacred honor," and had founded the Republic. None of these first citizens was "born or naturalized in the United States." The "United States" did not exist until July 4, 1776. Accordingly, the Constitution's Article II distinguished between persons who were (1) "natural-born citizens" but not "of the United States," as well as (2) "citizens *of the United States* at the time of the adoption of this Constitution."[122] The former group encompassed persons who were natural-born American "citizens" (but not yet "of the United States") by birth in the colonies, but whose designation became "citizens of the United States" at Independence. This latter group included persons, like Alexander Hamilton and James Wilson, who were born abroad but became citizens, not by naturalization, but simply by their residence in America around the time of Independence.

By 1866, of course, most of our first citizens were dead. Nonetheless, there were still many undoubted "citizens of the United States," though they had never been born or naturalized in the United States, but were born on colonial soil and/or resident in the United States in 1776. These included, incidentally, John Gray, the last surviving veteran, "the last soldier of the Revolution."[123] John Bingham "almost adored the glorious old hero," and while the Amendment was pending, introduced a bill to give him a special pension.[124]

Indeed, the drafters of the Citizenship Clause had originally intended to address only *ius soli* citizenship.[125] They tacitly rejected any comprehensive proposal. A few weeks before the Republican Senate caucus drafted the Clause, Nevada's William Stewart had proposed this nearly exhaustive declaration: "All persons, Indians not taxed excepted, born within the limits or within the jurisdiction of the United States, and all persons naturalized under its laws, are and shall be both citizens of the United States and citizens of the several States within which they reside."[126]

Still, such a comprehensive definition was unnecessary; the only Americans whose citizenship had been widely denied were the American-born descendants of African slaves. Accordingly, Republican senators initially settled on a more targeted, merely partial declaration, limited to reaffirming citizenship to persons native to our soil.

But as we saw, at the eleventh hour, the Republicans hastily abandoned this approach, with the legally unnecessary but politically strategic insertion of "or naturalized" just before "in the United States." Still, neither the text nor the context suggests that this patch was understood to make the definition exhaustive.

A Merely Defeasible Declaration

Finally, this declaration was not only merely partial, but defeasible. Persons who "are" citizens today could lawfully become ex-citizens tomorrow. Membership was not inalienable or otherwise perpetual.

This question of "perpetual allegiance" had not been entirely settled at the Founding. To be sure, Americans agreed that a whole people, for compelling cause, could renounce their allegiance. After all, our Republic began with the American people's renunciation of allegiance to the British crown. A people, as a community, could indeed rightfully alienate their birthright subjecthood or citizenship wherever necessary to secure their more fundamental inalienable rights as human persons.

The same principle no doubt applied to any subset of a people or even an individual citizen. Here the right could take the form of peaceful expatriation. Whenever any form of government becomes "destructive of these ends," it is, of course, the right of the individual simply to leave its jurisdiction.

Nonetheless, such a right, whether popular or individual, was not constitutional, strictly speaking. Thus framed, the right to sever allegiance, whether by the people's right to violent revolution or by the individual's right to departure, presupposed the government's forfeiture of allegiance by grave wrong. Thereby the citizens were forced to become either revolutionaries (collectively) or refugees (separately).

Conversely, a citizen could lose citizenship by his or her own crime. An individual who commits a crime punishable by deprivation of life or liberty thereby forfeits citizenship, the enjoyment of which depends upon such fundamental goods.

But could a citizen—without committing a crime, or imputing some crime to his or her (former) government—constitutionally and otherwise lawfully, set aside this allegiance? An affirmative answer seemed implied by our law of naturalization. The rule never required the applicant to prove or even suggest that he or she was a refugee. There was no requirement or implication that the alien's former sovereign had *forfeited* any right to allegiance. Our naturalization law, though fairly generous to foreign immigrants, was not thereby insulting to foreign sovereigns.

Still, as to the alienability of *American* citizenship, some antebellum authorities resisted the conclusion. Most notably, Justice Bushrod Washington, on circuit, could not "admit that a citizen of the United States can throw off his allegiance and his country without some law authorizing him to do so," for by his "original character," he is a "subject or citizen of the country where he was born, and to which his perpetual allegiance is due."[127]

But by the time of the adoption of the Fourteenth Amendment, the matter was settled. Jacob Howard, the chief sponsor of the Citizenship Clause, took it "for granted" that the citizen can lose his or her status by "expatriation" as well as by "the commission of some crime by which his citizenship shall be forfeited."[128] Accordingly, on the day before Seward's formal declaration of the Amendment's ratification, Congress declared "the right of expatriation" to be "a natural and inherent right of all people, indispensable to the enjoyment of the rights of life, liberty, and the pursuit of happiness."[129] As subsequently expounded by the Grant Administration, the declaration meant the American citizen could exercise this right by a twofold departure—from both the Republic's soil and our creed. The American could lawfully become an ex-citizen by taking two steps: (1) his establishment of a residence in another country and (2) by some word or deed demonstrating allegiance to that country.[130] Note that the combination of two familiar elements—soil and creed—again served to mark the ex-citizen from the citizen.

Citizens of the United States and of the State of Residence

In the declaratory Citizenship Clause, the predicate nominative has a single substantive: "citizens." This one noun has two modifying genitive phrases, "of the United States" and "of the State wherein they reside." The phraseology suggests the declaration of a single status, "citizen," with two aspects, first of the Union, second of the state of residence, if any.

Both the legal context and the contemporaneous discussion confirm this textual inference. American citizenship has a primary relation to the Union, with a merely secondary, derivative, and contingent relation to a state. Indeed, our naturalization law, as promulgated by statutes and treaties, had already naturalized aliens as "citizens of the United States" even if such new citizens had never stepped foot in a state, let alone established residence therein. As Indiana's governor said to a mass meeting in July 1866, the Amendment will protect "Citizens of the United States, as such, though they may not be citizens of any State."[131] And, he explained, in this respect the measure was merely declaratory: "It is as well settled as any other proposition connected with constitutional law, that a person may be a citizen of the United States, and yet no citizen of any State."[132] In Congress, Democrat Andrew Rogers had said the same.[133]

Therefore, contrary to the Supreme Court, it does violence to the text and original understanding of the Citizenship Clause to interpret these two genitive phrases—mere modifiers—as establishing two substantives, "a citizenship of the United States, and a citizenship of a State, distinct from each other, and which depend upon different characteristics or circumstances in the individual."[134] Rather, the Amendment declared only one citizenship, with a primary and essential relation to the Union, and a derivative and contingent relation to whatever state, if any, wherein an American may happen to reside. The Citizenship Clause is *not* the Citizenships Clause.

Moreover, this Citizenship Clause declares only an existing status and does not, by its own force, confer rights. Contrary to the readings recently offered by scholars such as Gregory Dolin, Ryan Williams, and Kurt Lash, the Clause cannot be read, by its own force, to impose new restrictions on the federal or state governments.[135] Instead, as Governor Morton explained, because the Clause merely declared an existing status, it "gives no right, power, or privilege to citizens of the United States which they have not always possessed."[136] To be sure, some opponents, especially in the states, did contend that state citizenship, as enforced by Congress under Section 5, would compel the states to admit African Americans to the suffrage.[137] Still, no supporter agreed.[138]

Moreover, to read the Citizenship Clause as rights-conferring would, in fact, defeat the original purpose of Section 1. Recall that the Committee aimed to determine the civil rights of "all citizens." Yet the Citizenship Clause was only partly declaratory of the class "citizens of the United States," so if that Clause conferred privileges, it would do so not universally, but for only some Americans.

In sum, the Citizenship Clause provided a merely defeasible and partial declaration of status, encompassing only *some* of the persons who qualify as "citizens of the United States." These persons include all persons naturalized in the United States, or born in the United States to parents subject to the ordinary jurisdiction of the United States. This partial declaration of citizenship status, by its own force, confers no new rights or privileges on any portion of the citizenry.

Notes

1 9 Writings 30, 32 (Gaillard Hunt, ed. 1910).

2 Opinion of the Supreme Judicial Court, 44 Me 507, 586, 594–5 (1857) (Op. of Davis, J.). The opinion is undated, but the approximate date may be inferred from the date of the first newspaper reports. *See, e.g.*, *Negro Citizenship in Maine*, Burlington Free Press, Aug. 21, 1857, at 2, https://chroniclingamerica.loc.gov/lccn/sn84023127/1857-08-21/ed-1/seq-2/.

3 Declaration of Independence, para. 1 (U.S. 1776).

4 Declaration and Resolves on Colonial rights of the First Continental Congress, Oct. 14, 1774, *in* 1 Journals of the Continental Congress, 1774–1789, at 63–4 (1904)

[hereinafter "Journals of the Continental Congress"]; Olive Branch Petition, July 8, 1775, *in* 2 Journals of the Continental Congress 160, 161 (1905) (referring to "your American people"); *see also* The Declaratory Act (Mar. 18, 1766) *reprinted in* Danby Pickering, The Statutes at Large from 1225 to 1867 (London, Joseph Bentham 1869).

5 Declaration of Independence (U.S. 1776).

6 *Id.*

7 *Id. See also* 5 Journals of the Continental Congress 747 (1906) (resolution of September 9, 1776, "That in all continental commissions, and other instruments, where, heretofore, the words 'United Colonies' have been used, the stile be altered, for the future, to the 'United States'") (cited in 1 George Ticknor Curtis, Constitutional History of the United States from Their Declaration of Independence to the Close of Their Civil War 36, n. 1 (1897)).

8 See U.S. Const. art. I, §§ 2–3.

9 *Id.* arts. III, IV.

10 "It cannot escape notice that no definition of the nature and rights of citizens appears in the Constitution. The descriptive term is used, with a plain indication that its meaning is understood by all." William Rawle, A View of the Constitution of the United States of America 79 (1825).

11 Aristotle's Politics, Book I, chs. 1–3; Book II, chs. 2–3, at 2–6 (Carles Lord ed., 2d ed. 2013) (rejecting the destruction of the household, via the sharing of wives and children, as contrary to the nature of the commonwealth); *id.* Book III, ch. 9, at 75–7 (calling the commonwealth "a community of families and villages in a complete and self-sufficient life").

12 *Id.* (stating that a city includes a common location, trade, and common justice for "not committing injustice against each other," and also "intermarriage"); *id.* at Book I, ch. 2, at 2–5 (affirming that the city exists for "adjudication" and defining both the household and the commonwealth as discussion about the "good and bad, just and unjust, and other things of this sort"); *id.* at Book II, chs. 5 & 8, at 33, 43 (remarking that the disarmed portion of a community is a way for keeping them as slaves, not citizens); *id.* at Book III, ch. 6, at 71 (defining a *politeia* as "an arrangement" of a commonwealth "with respect to its offices").

13 *Id.*

14 *Id.* Book 4, ch. 1, at 97–8.

15 De Republica, Book I, § 41, https://www.perseus.tufts.edu/hopper/text?doc=Perseus:abo:phi,0474,043:1:41.

16 *See supra*ch. 2.

17 William Ramsay, An Elementary Manual of Roman Antiquities 39, 122 (1859).

18 Gerard N. Magliocca, *Indians and Invaders: The Citizenship Clause and Illegal Aliens*, 10 Univ. Penn. J. Con. L. 499, 503, 526 (2008).

19 James H. Kettner, The Development of American Citizenship, 1608–1870, at 15 (1978).

20 Cf. Aristotle, *supra* note 11, at Book III, ch. 5, at 71 (noting that some communities accept as members persons born to a citizen-mother alone, "and it is the same way with bastards in many regimes"). *Cf.* Scott Titshaw, *Inheriting Citizenship*, 58 Stan. J. Int'l L. 1, 17–18 (2022) ("Every country in the world provides for inherited citizenship. . . . The real contrast is not between birthplace citizenship regimes and inherited citizenship regimes, but between regimes recognizing both rules and those

rejecting birthplace citizenship in favor of an exclusive, or nearly exclusive, focus on inherited citizenship.").

21 Habeas Corpus Act of 1679, Online Library of Liberty, https://oll.libertyfund.org/pages/1679-habeas-corpus-act (providing that "no subject of this realm" shall be removed "beyond the seas" or otherwise outside the kingdom). 1 William Blackstone, Commentaries on the Laws of England 360 (1766) (noting that aliens are subject to some higher taxes, may not acquire permanent interest in real estate and may participate in trade only as a matter of "indulgence to strangers"—a generous and prudential policy that fostered the "advancement of trade").

22 The English Bill of Rights (1689), Online Library of Liberty, https://oll.libertyfund.org/pages/1689-english-bill-of-rights.

23 See generally Kettner, *supra* note 19, at 65–105.

24 Declaration and Resolves on Colonial rights of the First Continental Congress, Oct. 14, 1774, *in* 1 Journals of the Continental Congress, at 63–4.

25 5 Journals of the Continental Congress 475 (1906). *See also Inglis v. Trustees of Sailor's Snug Harbor*, 28 U.S. 99, 165 (1830) (quoting the definition adopted by New York's Council of Safety in July 1776 "that all persons abiding within the state of New York, and deriving protection from the laws of the same, owe allegiance to the said laws, and are members of the state"); *Jackson v. White*, 20 Johns. 313, 326 (N.Y. 1822) (concluding that as "members" these were "citizens").

26 A week after Independence, a committee chaired by John Dickinson proposed a rule guaranteeing interstate rights of interstate travel, commerce, and so on, to all "inhabitants." *Id.* at 547. After significant debate and revision, in November 1777 Congress approved and distributed to the state legislatures the Articles of Confederation, which secured "all privileges and immunities of free citizens" to "the free inhabitants of each of these states, paupers, vagabonds and fugitives from Justice excepted." Articles of Confederation, art. IV, National Archives, https://www.archives.gov/milestone-documents/articles-of-confederation.

27 Aristotle, *supra* note 11, at Book II, ch. 2, at 64.

28 An act declaring who shall be deemed citizens of this commonwealth, Act of May 3, 1779, ch. 55 (declaring as citizens "all white persons born within the territory of this commonwealth and all who have resided therein two years next before the passing of this act"), reprinted in 10 William Waller Hening, The Statutes at Large; Being a Collection of All the Laws of Virginia, from the First Session of the Legislature, in the Year 1619, at 129 (1822) (cited in Michael D, Ramsey, *The Original Meaning of "Natural Born,"* 20 U. Pa. J. Const. L. 199, 233, n.117 (2017))

29 *Ainslie v. Martin,* 9 Mass. 454, 459 (1813) (holding that "all persons born within the territories of the government and people, although before the declaration of independence, were born within the allegiance of the same government"). See Kettner *supra* note 19, at 191–208 (discussing cases).

30 *Lynch v. Clarke*, 1 Sand. Ch. 583 (N.Y. 1844) (discussed in Kettner, *supra* note 19, at 318).

31 An Act to Establish An Uniform Rule of Naturalization, 1 Stat 103, 103–4 (Mar. 26, 1790).

32 *Id.*

33 *Id.*

34 *See, e.g.*, *Dred Scott v. Sandford*, 60 U.S. 393, 533 (1857) (McLean, J., dissenting) (noting that under the territorial treaties, "we have made citizens of all grades,

combinations, and colors"); Kettner, *supra* note 19, at 292–3 (discussing tribal treaties); Christopher R. Green, Equal Citizenship, Civil Rights, and the Constitution: the Original Sense of the Privileges or Immunities Clause 24–5 (2015) (noting that the Florida cession incorporated as American citizens a significant population of African ancestry, especially near Mobile, Alabama).

35 *See infra*text accompanying notes 126–9.

36 *See, e.g.*, U.S. Const. amend. I; Mass. Const. Declaration of Rights, art. XIX (1780).

37 *See, e.g.*, U.S. Const. amend. II; Penn. Const. art. IX, § xxi (guaranteeing to "the citizens," without further qualification, the right to bear arms). During the French and Indian War, several colonies, including Pennsylvania, had enacted statutes disarming Roman Catholic subjects. Graham Ambrose, Note, *Gunmaking at the Founding*, 77 Stan. L. Rev. 235, 270 (2025).

38 Federalist No. 39, at 36 (Clinton Rossiter ed. 1961).

39 On intermarriage, see David R. Upham, *Interracial Marriage and the Original Understanding of the Privileges or Immunities Clause*, 42 Hastings Const. L.Q. 213, 235 n.107 (2015). On voting restrictions from the Founding to the 1860s, *see* Hanes Walton, Jr. et al., The African American Electorate: A Statistical History 118–20 (2012); *The History of the Negro Vote*, 40 The Crisis 128, 128 (W.E.B. Du Bois ed. 1933).

40 Lewis H. LaRue, Liberty, Equality, Privileges, Immunities: Lost Knowledge 12–26 (Wash. & Lee Pub. Law & Legal Theory Research Paper Series, Working Paper No. 00-4, 2000), http://papers.ssrn.com/paper.taf?abstract_id=247655.

41 Merrill D. Peterson, The Great Triumvirate: Webster, Clay, and Calhoun65 (1987).

42 Proclamation Respecting the Admission of the State of Missouri into the Union, Aug. 10, 1821, 3 Stat. 797, app. II. The resolution, in context, is found in Revised Statutes of Missouri 29 (1845); *but see Dred Scott v. Sandford*, 60 U.S. 393, 588 (1857) (Curtis, J., dissenting) (interpreting this resolution as favorable to black citizenship).

43 9 Writings 30, 32 (Gaillard Hunt, ed. 1910).

44 *Dred Scott*, 60 U.S. at 417.

45 *Heirn v. Bridault*, 37 Miss. 209, 233 (1859).

46 *Lemmon v. People*, 20 N.Y. 562, 610 (1860) (opinion of Denio, J.); *Dred Scott*, 60 U.S. at 583–4 (Curtis, J., dissenting)

47 *Paul v. Virginia*, 75 U.S. 168, 180 & n.7 (1869) (holding that the Privileges and Immunities Clause places "the citizens of each State upon the same footing with citizens of other States" and citing in support only *Lemmon v. People*, 20 N.Y. 562 (1860)).

48 See generally, David R. Upham, *The Meanings of the "Privileges and Immunities of Citizens" on the Eve of the Civil War*, 91 Notre Dame L. Rev. 1117, 1148–54 (2016).

49 Opinion of the Supreme Judicial Court, 44 Me 507, 586, 594–5 (1857) (Op. of Davis, J.) (emphasis added).

50 1 Ellis Paxson Oberholtzer, History of the United States Since the Civil War 140 (1917).

51 Cong. Globe, 39th Cong. 1st sess. 2765 (May 23) (emphasis added).

52 These May proposals "ultimately identified him so closely with the Fourteenth as to give it his name"—the "Howard Amendment." 3 Francis Newton Thorpe, The Constitutional History of the United States 264–5 (1901). For perhaps the first use of the term, *see Restoration—Mr. Howard's Amendment*, The Weekly North-

Carolina Standard, June 6, 1866, at 3, https://chroniclingamerica.loc.gov/lccn/sn85042148/1866-06-06/ed-1/seq-3/ (discussing the many Howard amendments under the title "Howard Amendment"). It was not Howard's May 23 speech that seemed responsible for this designation. It seemed a regional expression. *See, e.g.*, S. Rep. No. 5, 42d Cong., special sess., Report of the Select Committee to Investigate Alleged Outrages in the Southern States 37 (Mar. 10, 1871) (including testimony by a North Carolinian that the Amendment was "known with us there as the Howard Amendment").

53 Cong. Globe, 39th Cong. 1st sess. 2869 (May 29). The final 's' in States was deleted as a printing error. *Id.* at 2892 (explained in Robert E. Mensel, *Jurisdiction in Nineteenth Century International Law and Its Meaning in the Citizenship Clause of the Fourteenth Amendment*, Saint Louis Univ. Pub. L. Rev. 330, 364 n. 235 (2012)).

54 Cong. Globe, 39th Cong. 1st sess. 2890 (May 30).

55 *Id.* at 2890–7.

56 *Id.* at 3040 (June 8).

57 *See, e.g.*, from Fessenden's home state, The Portland Daily Press, June 12, 1866, at 1, https://chroniclingamerica.loc.gov/lccn/sn83016025/1866-06-12/ed-1/seq-1/ (briefly mentioning the addition as one of "several changes, most of them verbal" made by the Senate in the last days of its deliberations); Worcester Daily Spy, June 9, 1866, at 2, https://chroniclingamerica.loc.gov/lccn/sn83021205/1866-06-09/ed-1/seq-2/ (mentioning several amendments but omitting as unimportant the insertion of "or naturalized").

58 David R. Upham, *The New Motherless Child and Our Old Constitution*, Humanum Review, Mar. 6, 2025, https://humanumreview.com/articles/the-new-motherless-child-and-our-old-constitution.

59 Kettner, *supra* note 19, at 52–3.

60 For the laws in force in 1866 (or soon thereafter) see Revised Statutes §§ 2165–74, pt. 1 at 380–3 (1875).

61 *Dred Scott v. Sandford*, 60 U.S. 393, 427 (1857) (noting that "no one supposes that a slave is a citizen of the State or of the United States").

62 *In re Spenser*, 22 F. Cas. 921, 922 (C.C.D. Or. July 8, 1878).

63 U.S. Const. art. I § 9.

64 Michael D. Ramsey, *Originalism and Birthright Citizenship*, 109 Geo. L.J. 405, 426 (2020) (quoting *Loughborough v. Blake*, 18 U.S. 317, 319 (1820)).

65 Naturalization Act of 1795, §§ 1–2; *accord* Revised Statutes of the United States § 2165 (1875) pt 1, p. 380. *See* Frank George Franklin, The Legislative History of Naturalization in the United States (1906) (discussing Congress's 1795 decision to allow territorial naturalization).

66 *See, e.g.*, *American Insurance Company v. Canter*, 26 U.S. 511, 542 (1828) (affirming that the Adams-Onis Treaty "admits the inhabitants of Florida to the enjoyment of the privileges, rights, and immunities of the citizens of the United States").

67 Ramsey, *supra* note 64, at 429.

68 *Id.* at 430 (citing *Fleming v. Page*, 50 U.S. 603 (1850)).

69 *Fleming*, 50 U.S. at 615–16.

70 1 Bouvier Law Dictionary 769 (1868)

71 Cong. Globe, 39th Cong. 1st sess. 2893 (May 30) (comments of Reverdy Johnson); *see also id.* at 2897 (May 30) (remarks of George Williams indicating that parental diplomatic or tribal immunity is imputed to the offspring).

72 Gerard N. Magliocca, *supra* note 18, at 503, 526.
73 Cong. Globe, 39th Cong. 1st sess. 2897 (May 30).
74 169 U.S. 649 (1898).
75 Mensel, *supra* note 53, at 342–3.
76 *Marbury v. Madison*, 5 U.S. 137, 174 (1803).
77 Mensel, *supra* note 53, at 371 (concluding that the "greater weight of the historical record supports the conclusion that the intention . . . of the Fourteenth Amendment was to exclude from citizenship children born here of citizens or subjects of foreign powers, including [any] nations with which the United States entered into treaties"); John C. Eastman, *Born in the U.S.A.? Rethinking Birthright Citizenship in the Wake of 9/11*, 42 U. Rich. L. Rev. 955, 960 (2008) (arguing that "any child born on U.S. soil to parents who were temporary visitors to this country and who, as a result of the foreign citizenship of the child's parents, remained a citizen or subject of the parents' home country" were not deemed "subject to" U.S. jurisdiction).
78 Ch. 31, 14 Stat. 27.
79 Cong. Globe, 39th Cong. 1st sess. 2890 (May 30).
80 *Id.*
81 *Id.* at 1291 (Mar. 9).
82 Revised Statutes §§ 2165–74, pt. 1 at 380–3 (1875).
83 *See* Chin-Yung Yen, Rights of Citizens and Persons Under the Fourteenth Amendment 16 (Ph.D. Dissertation, Columbia Univ. 1905) ("The Civil Rights Act requires three elements to constitute the status of citizenship of the United States; namely, the element of birth, the element of subjection to the jurisdiction of the United States and the element of freedom from any foreign jurisdiction. The Fourteenth Amendment, however, requires only two; the element of birth and the element of subjection to the United States' jurisdiction. From this it will be seen that the main difference between the two lies in the element of relation to foreign jurisdiction, though they both agree in exempting from their operations all diplomats, their families and servants, Indians, and children born to a member of a foreign force during hostile occupation.").
84 *Lynch v. Clarke*, 1 Sand. Ch. 583, 655 (N.Y. Ch. 1844). *See also Lyndon v. Danville*, 28 Vt. 809, 816 (1856) (citing this holding with approval); *United States v. Rhodes*, 27 F. Cas. 785, 789 (C.C.D. Ky. 1867) (same); *But see Dred Scott v. Sandford*, 60 U.S. 393, 476 (1857) (Daniel, J., concurring) (quoting Vattel's remarks that "[t]he natives or natural-born citizens are those born in the country of parents who are citizens.").
85 Phillips's proposal appeared as the banner in many issues of his *National Anti-Slavery Standard*: "No State shall make any distinction in civil rights and privileges among the naturalized citizens of the United States residing within its limits, or among persons born on its soil of parents permanently resident there, on account of race, color, or descent." *Quoted in* Andrew Kull, The Color-Blind Constitution 62 (1992). Greeley, in the *New York Tribune*, offered an amendment that excluded "Indians not taxed and the children of foreigners who choose to remain subject to some foreign power." *See The Cabinet and Congress*, The Plymouth Weekly Democrat, May 10, 1866, at 1 (quoting from the Tribune's editorial).
86 Joseph Story, Commentary on the Conflict of Laws 48 (1834) (quoted in Mensel, *supra* note 53, at 341).
87 Ramsey *supra* note 64, at 447–8.

88 *Speech of Judge Lawrence at Piqua* (Aug. 15), Bellefontaine Republican, Sept. 21, 1866, at 1. *See* Jeremy D. Burkhart, *William Lawrence: Perspectives of a Reconstruction Republican on the 14th Amendment*, The 39th Congress Project, at Center for Constitutional Law, University of Akron, https://ideaexchange.uakron.edu/cgi/viewcontent.cgi?article=1008&context=conlawakron39th (citing the speech). The speech was separately published as *National Politics. The Real issue. Speech at Piqua, Ohio*, Aug. 15, 1866 (mentioned in Robert J. Kaczorowski, The Nationalization of Civil Rights: Constitutional Theory and Practice in a Racist Society, 1866–1883, at 69 (1987).

89 *Speech of the Hon. Benjamin Eggleston* (Sept. 25), in Speeches of the Campaign of 1866, in the states of Ohio, Indiana, and Kentucky 37 (1866) [hereinafter "Campaign Speeches"] (cited in Matthew Ing, *Birthright Citizenship, Illegal Aliens, and the Original Meaning of the Citizenship Clause*, 45 Akron L. Rev. 719, 745 (2012)). A year later, during the 1867 campaign, Ohio Democrat Hugh Jewett objected that the Citizenship Clause would cover not only children of European immigrants, but "all persons born in the United States, be they Chinese, Indians, negroes, or people of any other race or color." *Speech on Hon. H.W. Jewett*, July 5, 1867, Daily Ohio Statesman, July 16, 1867, at 1, https://chroniclingamerica.loc.gov/lccn/sn84028645/1867-07-16/ed-1/seq-1/.

90 Cong. Globe, 39th Cong. 1st sess. 2890–1 (May 30).

91 *Speech of Senator Cowan, at Latrobe, PA, Sept. 11, 1866*, Clearfield Republican. Sept. 26, 1866, at 1, https://chroniclingamerica.loc.gov/lccn/sn83032199/1866-09-26/ed-1/seq-1/.

92 *Speech of Senator Creswell of Maryland*, The Evening Telegraph. Sept. 22, 1866, at 3, https://chroniclingamerica.loc.gov/lccn/sn83025925/1866-09-22/ed-1/seq-3/.

93 Cong. Globe, 39th Cong. 1st sess. 3148 (June 13).

94 Thomas C. Fletcher, First Biennial Message, Jan. 4, 1867, *in* 4 The Messages and Proclamations of the Governors of the State of Missouri 80, 81 (1924).

95 *Speech of Honorable Luke P. Poland*, Green-Mountain Freeman (Montpelier, Vt.), Nov. 7, 1866, at 2, https://chroniclingamerica.loc.gov/lccn/sn84023209/1866-11-07/ed-1/seq-2/.

96 *Speech of Gen. John A. Logan, at Cairo, June 28, 1866*, Chicago Tribune, July 2, 1866, at 1, https://chroniclingamerica.loc.gov/lccn/sn82014064/1866-07-02/ed-1/seq-1/.

97 By 1870, nearly 15% of the population (over 5 million) was foreign born. United States Census Office, A Compendium of the Ninth Census 376 (1872). No doubt a large portion of such persons, while yet unnaturalized, gave birth to children in the United States.

98 Cong. Globe, 39th Cong. 1st sess. 1756 (Apr. 4) ("But the President tells us that the bill in effect proposes a discrimination against large numbers of intelligent, worthy, and patriotic foreigners and in favor of the negro").

99 *New Jersey, Legislature Rescinds Prior Ratification* (1868) in 2 Reconstruction Amendments: The Essential Documents 409 (Kurt T. Lash ed. 2021).

100 Cong. Globe, 39th Cong. 1st sess. 3033 (June 8).

101 "The bill in effect proposes a discrimination against large numbers of intelligent, worthy, and patriotic foreigners, and in favor of the Negro." *Id.* at 1858 (Apr. 9).

102 *The Radical Plan*, The Evening Telegraph, May 1, 1866, at 2, https://chroniclingamerica.loc.gov/lccn/sn83025925/1866-05-01/ed-1/seq-2/ (reprinting an editorial from the "Daily News").

103 Willard H. Smith, *Schuyler Colfax and Reconstruction Policy*, 39 Indiana Mag. of His. 383, 391–4 (Dec. 1943). By one report, Colfax had, in his Know-Nothing days, publicly delivered this fiercely anti-Irish and anti-German tirade: "Look at a German, how he smokes his pipe, and if you observe one feature of intelligence in his smeary, imbecile countenance, show him to me. See the drunken, degenerate Irishman, with his whisky bottle in his pocket, how he swears, drinks and raves; and show me on his filthy countenance one feature of morality, sense or education; the thought is foolish and insane. . . . They are beneath the American in sense and comprehension, and must be put down; and, if needs be kept down with the bayonet, and with ball and powder. There is no ground for talking allegorically or caring the consequences. A great cry has been raised that foreigners are driven from the ballot box, and hindered from voting. This is, as I believe, in some cases true. Shall the American citizen stand back and let a degenerate, red nosed, drunken Irish creature vote instead? And just look at a long-eared, long-mouthed, uncombed German, that has just arrived from some cavern in his cabbage land, the beer foam sticking to his bristly beard, and smelling like garlic and onion." *The Man the Republicans Want the Adopted Citizens to Vote For—Schuyler Colfax on Foreigners in [1855]*, The Wheeling Daily Register, Oct. 30, 1868, at 1, https://chroniclingamerica.loc.gov/lccn/sn84026847/1868-10-30/ed-1/seq-1/.

104 The Legislative Record: Containing the Debates and Proceedings of the Pennsylvania Legislature, for the Session of 1867, app. at xiii (George Bergnor, ed. 1867) [hereinafter "Pennsylvania Legislative Debates"]; Reconstruction Amendments, *supra* note 99, at 368. *See also, e.g.*, *The Radical Plan*, The Evening Telegraph, May 1, 1866, at 2, https://chroniclingamerica.loc.gov/lccn/sn83025925/1866-05-01/ed-1/seq-2/ (objecting that the proposed Amendment "places the negro above every non-naturalized person in the country, and confers upon these late slaves privileges and immunities which are denied to every freeborn Irishman, yeoman, or other foreigner that resides in our midst"); *Speech of Col. R.P.L. Baber*, Daily Ohio Statesman, Sept. 11, 1866, at 2, (denouncing the Citizenship Clause as "simply a confession that the negro is entitled to greater protection than our unnaturalized population"); *The Radical Plot to Keep the Union Divided*, The Evening Argus [Rock Island, IL], Sept. 24, 1866, at 2, https://chroniclingamerica.loc.gov/lccn/sn84038628/1866-09-24/ed-1/seq-2/ (charging that the Amendment is a "confession that the negro is entitled to *greater* protection than our unnaturalized population").

105 Bill of Rights, National Archives, https://www.archives.gov/founding-docs/bill-of-rights.

106 Ch. 31, 14 Stat. 27.

107 Richard L. Aynes, *Unintended Consequences of the Fourteenth Amendment and What They Tell Us About its Interpretation*, 39 Akron L. Rev. 289, 290–300 (2006).

108 Cong. Globe, 39th Cong. 1st sess. 2890 (May 30) ("simply declaratory of . . . the law of the land") (May 29).

109 *Id.* at 3148 (June 13). ("It declares [citizenship] to belong to every person born or naturalized in the United States").

110 *Message of Governor Oliver Morton to the Senate and House of Representatives of the State of Indiana*, Journal of the Senate of the State of Indiana, 45th Sess., Jan. 4, 1867, at 41. *But see Speech of Senator Creswell of Maryland*, The Evening Telegraph. Sept.

22, 1866, at 3, https://chroniclingamerica.loc.gov/lccn/sn83025925/1866-09-22/ed-1/seq-3/ (suggesting that the Amendment will "make" native blacks into "citizens" or at least "relieve that question from all doubt and uncertainty").

111 Because the *Dred Scott* decision might still be a binding precedent, "the object [black citizenship] can only be safely and surely attained by an amendment to the Constitution." Cong. Globe, 39th Cong. 1st sess. 504 (Jan. 30).

112 *See supra* chapter. 1. *See also, e.g.*, Cong. Globe, 39th Cong. 1st sess. 2939 (June 4) (reporting remarks of Senator Hendricks that the Clause would "add many millions to the class of persons who are citizens").

113 *Slaughterhouse Cases*, 83 U.S. 36, 37 (1873) ("The first clause of the fourteenth article was primarily intended to confer citizenship on the negro race").

114 *Gassies v. Ballon*, 31 U.S. 761, 762 (1832).

115 *Marshall v. Baltimore & Ohio R.R.*, 57 U.S. 314, 329 (1854); *Baker v. Wise*, 57 Va. 139, 212 (1861); Cong. Globe, 39th Cong. 1st sess. 1756 (Apr. 4) (citing *Gassies* for the proposition that a citizen of the United States "is also a citizen of every State where he may happen to be"); *id.* at 3032 (remarks of Henderson on June 8).

116 "Further, we are not aware that there has been any decision, or that there is any agreement among legal authorities as to what constitutes citizenship of a State, apart from citizenship of the United States." —H.R. Doc. No. 149, Mass. Gen. Ct. 3–4 (1867) *reprinted in* Reconstruction Amendments, *supra* note 99, at 385.

117 Richard L. Aynes, *Enforcing the Bill of Rights Against the States: The History and the Future*, 18 J. Contemp. Legal Issues 77, 113 (2009).

118 Yen, *supra* note 83, at 11.

119 *See also* William T. Han, *Beyond Presidential Eligibility: The Natural Born Citizen Clause As A Source of Birthright Citizenship*, 58 Drake L. Rev. 457, 476–8 (2010).

120 10 Stat. 604.

121 Revised Statutes, § 1993, pt. 1, at 351 (1875).

122 U.S. Const. art. II.

123 James M. Dalzell, John Gray, of Mount Vernon: The Last Soldier of the Revolution (1868).

124 *Id.* at 32.

125 But see *Speech of Hon. Geo. F. Edmunds Delivered Before the General Assembly, Oct. 24, 1866*, Green-Mountain Freeman, Nov. 21, 1866, at 1, https://chroniclingamerica.loc.gov/lccn/sn84023209/1866-11-21/ed-1/seq-1/ (noting that because of the "infamous Dred Scott decision," it is "necessary that the supreme law of the land should declare who are and who are not citizens of the United States").

126 Herman Vandenburg Ames, The Proposed Amendments to the Constitution of the United States During the First Century of Its History 221 (1897). *See Senator Stewart's Restoration Amendment*, Chicago Tribune, May 18, 1866, at 2, https://chroniclingamerica.loc.gov/lccn/sn82014064/1866-05-18/ed-1/seq-2/.

127 *United States v. Gillies,* 25 F. Cas. 1321, 1322 (C.C.D.Pa. 1815) (No. 15, 206).

128 Cong. Globe, 39th Cong. 1st sess. 2895 (May 30, 1866).

129 An Act Concerning the Rights of American Citizens in Foreign States, July 27, 1868, 15 Stat. 223, ch. CCLXIX; first codified as Title XXV, Revised Statutes § 2004 (1875).

130 Opinion of Secretary of State Hamilton Fish, Aug. 25, 1873, *in* Opinions of the Principal Officers of the Executive Departments, and Other Papers Relating to Expatriation, Naturalization, and Change of Allegiance 10, 11 (1873) ("The quitting

of the country must be real, that is to say, actual emigration for a lawful purpose, and should be accompanied by some open avowal or other attendant acts showing good faith, and a determination and intention to transfer one's allegiance").

131 *The Union in Indiana: Large Meeting at New Albany: Another Great Speech by Gov. Morton*, The Evansville Journal, July 21, 1866, at 2, https://newspapers.library.in.gov/?a=d&d=EJ18660721.1.2&e=-------en-20--1--txt-txIN-------.

132 *Id.* See also Reconstruction Amendments, *supra* note 99, at 251.

133 Cong. Globe, 39th Cong. 1st sess. app. at 231 (June 13) ("Everybody here knows that under the old [Constitution] now proposed to be amended a man may be a citizen of the United States and yet have no citizenship in any State."). *But see Speech of Hon. S.S. Bloom in the Ohio House of Representatives* (Jan. 4), Daily Ohio Statesman, Jan. 24, 1867, at 1, https://chroniclingamerica.loc.gov/lccn/sn84028645/1867-01-24/ed-1/seq-1/ (calling the Citizenship Clause revolutionary, for "under the present Constitution, an individual becomes a citizen of the United States, by virtue of being the citizen of a State," but under the Amendment "persons become the citizens of a State by virtue of being a citizen of the United States").

134 *Slaughterhouse Cases*, 83 U.S. 36, 74 (1873).

135 According to Williams and Dolan, it is this Clause that arguably bars the federal government from imposing racially discriminatory burdens—and thus provides a basis for *Bolling v. Sharpe*. Ryan C. Williams, *Originalism and the Other Desegregation Decision*, 99 Va. L. Rev. 493, 499 (2013); Gregory Dolin, *Resolving the Original Sin of Bolling v. Sharpe*, 44 Seton Hall L. Rev. 749 (2014) For Lash, this Clause, in reference to state citizenship, bars the states from doing the same—and thus it is this Clause that constitutionalized the Civil Rights Act. Kurt T. Lash, *The State Citizenship Clause*, 25 U. Pa. J. Const. L. 1097, 1098, 1140–50 (2023).

136 *The Union in Indiana: Large Meeting at New Albany: Another Great Speech by Gov. Morton*, The Evansville Journal, July 21, 1866, at 2, https://newspapers.library.in.gov/?a=d&d=EJ18660721.1.2&e=-------en-20--1--txt-txIN-------. Morton's New Albany speech can also be found in Campaign Speeches, *supra* note 89, at 3. *See also The Fourteenth Constitutional Amendment*, The Portland Daily Press, July 21, 1868, at 2, https://chroniclingamerica.loc.gov/lccn/sn83016025/1868-07-21/ed-1/seq-2/ (contending that the Clause "does not, in fact, establish any new principle, being merely declaratory of what has been the law ever since slavery was abolished").

137 Journal of the Wisconsin Senate, 19th Ann. Sess. 96 (1867) (contending that by the Citizenship Clause, as enforced by Section 5, Congress would have "the power to make them citizens of the several states wherein they reside, and thereby to extend to them the right of suffrage") Reconstruction Amendments, *supra* note 99, at 379; General George W. Morgan at Coshocton, OH, Aug 21, 1866, *in* Campaign Speeches, *supra* note 89, at 15–16 (quoting the Citizenship Clause and that of "the Federal Government had the power to determine who should be citizens of a State, it would be at once claimed she also had the power to define the rights of such citizens, and we should soon have negro jurors, voters, judges and legislators in Ohio by virtue of laws of Congress").

138 One possible exception may be found in the remarks of the New Jersey governor, in 1868, vetoing the legislature's rescission of ratification: "Its first section defines and settles the hitherto disputed question of citizenship, by declaring all persons born or naturalized in the United States, and subject to the jurisdiction thereof, to

be citizens of the United States and of the State wherein they reside, *and as such*, entitled to the equal benefit of the laws." Message of Governor Marcus L. Ward, Feb. 25, 1868, 92 Journal of the Senate of the State of New Jersey 252 (1868) (emphasis added). Ward thus suggested that it was the Citizenship Clause that gave rise to equality under the laws.

6

American Citizenship

Its Privileges—Its Immunities

Have the words, civil rights, immunities, privileges[,] such precise & definite meaning as to be practicable[;] or must we specify, rights of citizenship, residence in the state—to hold property, be a party and witness?

—Lot Morrill to Charles Sumner (November 1865)[1]

We now, at last, turn to the long-dormant Privileges or Immunities Clause. The topic remains the "darling of the professoriate"—a matter of great academic interest and decided judicial disinterest.

No State Shall Make or Enforce Any Law

Much of the text of the Privileges or Immunities Clause is not obscured by controversy. The subject, verbs, and direct object of the primary clause ("state," "make or enforce," and "law") have occasioned very little dispute. These terms are familiar and seem straightforward. For our purposes, we may rely on the definitions of "state" and "law" provided in the fourth chapter.

The verbs "make" and "enforce" seem to refer, respectively, to the legislative and executive powers of the state. Those terms already had a certain degree of precision. We saw that the Amendment itself authorizes Congress to legislate so as to "enforce" the prohibitions of Section 1—but not to "make" (or unmake) these restrictions. But otherwise, nothing in the Amendment serves to clarify those terms.

The verbs are modified by the auxiliary "shall." Therefore, unlike the Amendment's first sentence—the Citizenship Clause—and like its companion in the second sentence, the Due Process-Equal Protection Clause, the Privileges or Immunities Clause is in the prescriptive future. Both these clauses, then, appear *restrictive* and not merely *declaratory*. They add a new limitation to the Constitution.

At the same time, these new restrictions were not wholly new. As we've seen, by these new provisions, Bingham and his colleagues sought to determine old civil rights and privileges already fully recognized in the Constitution's Privileges and Immunities and Due Process Clauses.[2]

What has been obscure, instead, is the subordinate clause that modifies "law": "which shall abridge the privileges or immunities of citizens of the United States." What are these privileges, these immunities, and what constitutes the forbidden legislative abridgment? These are the questions that have proven so difficult to answer.

Abridge

Let's begin with the verb. Each state is forbidden to legislatively *abridge* certain privileges or immunities. As mentioned in a previous chapter, several contemporary scholars have imputed an inherently pejorative sense, such that "to abridge" means "to unreasonably regulate" especially in the sense of unfairly or "unequally regulate."[3]

There is, however, almost no evidence to believe that the verb had such a meaning. As today, the verb simply meant "to shorten"; in Bouvier's Law Dictionary, the principal meaning was "to shorten a [litigant's] declaration or count by taking away or severing some of the substance of it."

Whether such shortening or abridgement was reasonable or unreasonable, good or bad, depended on the thing abridged. To abridge a bad thing was good. Hence, several states constitutionally commanded the state's legislature to "abridge" the needlessly complex rules of judicial procedure.[4]

Conversely, to abridge a good thing was bad. Therefore, many state constitutions had prohibited the abridgment of certain rights. Pennsylvania's Constitution of 1776 declared that no one "who acknowledges the being of a God, [can] be justly deprived or abridged of any civil right as a citizen, on account of his religious sentiments or peculiar mode of religious worship,"[5] and required state legislators to swear to never "consent to any act or thing whatever, that shall have a tendency to lessen or abridge [the people's] rights and privileges, as declared in the constitution of this state."[6]

But in American constitutional law, the most prominent and common use of "abridge," as a prohibition, was in connection with legislative abridgment, and abridgment of one particular good thing—the people's freedoms of discussion. In the First Amendment, "we the people" barred Congress from making any law "abridging the freedom of speech, or of the press; or the right of the people peaceably to assemble, and to petition the Government for a redress of grievances." In subsequent state constitutions, in apparent imitation, the verb "abridge" served again to safeguard these same freedoms of discussion against adverse legislation.[7]

Abridgment v. Lawful Regulation

It would seem, then, that to "abridge" meant simply to shorten. To abridge rights was simply bad, so the anti-abridgment rule of the Fourteenth Amendment prohibits any and all state legislative reductions of the rights of citizenship.

But at least some of these rights of citizenship, especially commerce, are always subject to regulations. How might one distinguish legislative abridgment, which is categorically banned, from lawful regulation? Given the repeated reassurances that the Amendment would have no effect on many loyal states' laws, there must have been a very broad field of regulations left to the states.

It seems that whether any regulation was an abridgment of the citizen's privileges or immunities depended on two discrete factors: (1) the scope of the particular privilege or immunity and (2) the scope of the particular citizen's capacity to participate in that right.

Scope of the Privilege or Immunity

First, as to the scope of the right, we must recall that these privileges and immunities of citizens were diverse. As Howard explained, these rights "necessarily include within themselves a great number of particulars." They were not some "indivisible unit."[8] If so, the meaning of abridgment must vary with the scope of each right.

Among the "privileges" the scope varied significantly, and the precise boundaries were somewhat vague. At one extreme was the citizen's right to the territory of the commonwealth. This right to travel and reside included a right to move about the country, for any reason or no reason at all. This freedom of movement meant the freedom to do what one pleases—to move arbitrarily, capriciously, or otherwise without any *reason* whatsoever. In *Dred Scott*, the Supreme Court said that the citizens of the United States, as such, were entitled to enter other states and go "wherever they *pleased*, singly or in company" and sojourn there "as long as they *pleased*."[9] Louisiana's supreme court had said much the same twenty years earlier: "every citizen [may] select his domicil accordingly, as his interest, inclination, or *even caprice*, may direct." Accordingly, "any restraint upon his choice would be an *abridgment* of his rights."[10]

At the other extreme, we might identify the right to testify. The individual's right was highly ordered to a rational and public purpose. It concerned the citizen's right and enforceable duty, pursuant to oath (testimony), to present evidence in a highly regulated manner: as a response to particular questions. The witness box was certainly not the citizen's soapbox, to say whatever he pleased.

Other rights seemed to lie somewhere between the very broad "go wherever in the country you please," and the very narrow "answer the question." Most notably, the freedom of discussion was not, on the one hand, a "freedom of expression," as we call it today. It was not a freedom to utter as one's will or caprice may direct. Rather, as Jud Campbell has noted, the freedom of speech itself was ordered to the "public good."[11] According to Kent's widely quoted definition, this freedom meant the right to speak or publish "the truth, with good motives, and for justifiable ends, whether it respects government, magistracy, or individuals."[12] As the Ohio Supreme Court explained in 1860, as "thus defined," this freedom of discussion categorically excluded defamation, obscenity, and the like, so any restraints on such utterances did not "abridge" the freedom at all.[13]

On the other hand, surrounding this general freedom of discussion was a prophylactic freedom to publish anything, without any submission to a censor; that is, without prior restraint ("freedom of the press"). To that extent, this right, more procedural than substantive, suggested a broad license: the publisher could, without any prior restraint, express or emote, even arbitrarily or capriciously. Still, liability for abusing this unrestrained freedom, by utterances without good cause and harmful to the public good (and thus properly called tortious or even criminal) could be assessed by post-publication correctives, imposed via due process of law.

Perhaps somewhat more ordered and thus limited was the privilege to engage in commerce. It seems that at the time, the citizen was not at liberty to buy and sell, arbitrarily or capriciously, but rather to participate in markets, as established and regulated by the community. One might even say that the citizen's claim of *right* depended on some *rational basis*, good motive or purpose. The precise scope of this ordered freedom was, of course, always controversial. But for present purposes, we might note that contemporaneous with the ratification of the Amendment, several state legislatures debated, at length, maximum-hours laws (the eight-hour day demanded of some labor groups),[14] but no one seems to have claimed that such controversial regulations of labor markets would "abridge" some right to make contracts as the citizen's will or caprice might direct.[15] Indeed, I know of no evidence that anyone thought such laws, however unreasonable, might run afoul of the pending Amendment. The liberty of contract, then, was more circumscribed than the liberty of movement.

In sharp contrast, however, the scope of an *immunity*, strictly speaking, was easiest to see. An exemption (*in-*) from a burden (*munia*) prohibits any such burden, even if otherwise negligible. So if, as I will argue, one of the immunities of citizenship was a freedom from any racial or other hereditary tax, then any such tax, even a one-penny "black tax" or "Russian-American tax," would represent an abridgment of that immunity. The meaning of abridgment here is quite clear.

Scope of the Particular Citizen's Capacity to Participate

Second, as to the scope of the citizen's capacity, persons are often, by facts anterior to citizenship, unable to participate in one or more privileges of the commonwealth. We can distinguish these anterior incapacities in three ways. *First*, the most common, is personal, unchosen, nonculpable incapacity. All persons, at one or more points in their lives, lack the requisite reason to participate in certain matters, such as the making of enforceable contracts. Such incapacity includes the universal human experiences of immaturity, disease, and old age. This incapacity also includes the common (but not universal) inability to do certain work, such as the study and practice of medicine. The laws defining and recognizing such nonculpable personal inability, whether particular or general, do not violate the Privileges or Immunities Clause. They are, of course, perennially controversial.

Consider, most notably, the age-of-consent rules governing participation in commerce. These do not proceed from the assumption that children are not citizens. As Roscoe Conkling explained during the ratification debates, "[c]hildren, for example, *have every right* here referred to." The Amendment was merely "merely declaratory," designed to "settle the law and quiet controversy," so "the law of this country and of every civilized nation, is now exactly as it will be after this clause is ratified."[16] Under the Amendment, children were citizens, but the long-established laws that defined their inabilities would be unaffected, for such laws did not abridge their privileges as citizens; these laws did not create but merely recognized (albeit imperfectly) the child's disabilities.

Second, one might speak of personal and culpable incapacity, resulting from culpable misconduct and resulting forfeiture. Crime, as defined and punished by the state, can strip the citizen of liberty or even life and thus impair, suspend, or even destroy his ability to travel, trade, and otherwise participate in the goods of the community. Such disabilities, enforced by law, are not legislative abridgments of citizenship, for such persons have forfeited their citizenship, in whole or part, by gravely harming the very community of which they are a member.

Third, some other particular incapacities may arise not from culpable *wrongs* but from *rights*. These incapacities are even praiseworthy. By exercising the natural right of conscience, the citizen may be under creedal incapacities (testamentary incapacities of those who are conscientiously unable to take an oath). By exercising the natural right of contract, the citizen may be under contractual incapacities (e.g., a non-compete provision of an employment contract).[17] This latter category can include even terms implied by law (e.g., various incapacities imputed to the attorney-client relation, or the employer-employee contract).

Here again, laws defining these incapacities did not abridge the citizen's privileges. The human person, by creed or contract, had shaped his or her own incapacity. And like the laws defining unchosen and culpable incapacities, the laws defining these disabilities are fallible. They identify but never simply create the disability.

These considerations as to incapacity seem relevant only to the regulations of affirmative privileges. But as to purely negative rights, those that consist purely in an exemption, the citizen's incapacity is irrelevant. If there are certain burdens that may not be imposed on any citizen (e.g., a racial tax), then no citizen, regardless of any personal, contractual, or creedal capacity, may be subject to such burdens.

Controversial Regulations v. Abridgments

To be sure, such laws defining personal, creedal, or contractual incapacity were (are) *always* subject to dispute as to their justice or prudence. The proper age (or ages) of consent is a perennial topic of dispute. Criminal laws and their execution may often be grossly unjust; lawmakers, executives, judges, and juries all fail.

Perennially controversial is the imputation of a term to a contract—without the express consent of the parties. Such terms, given the asymmetry of the employer-employee relation, might include a minimum-wage or maximum-hours law. Such regulations may be unjust or imprudent, but insofar as they serve to acknowledge and/or redress certain anterior inequalities, do not abridge the rights of citizenship.

To us, one asymmetrical, disability-defining law, still recognized in 1866, may seem peculiarly unjust: marital coverture. The common law had imputed to wife and husband a radical unity as to property rights, with the husband designated as the sole authorized agent to make enforceable contracts concerning the spouses' separate and joint property. As a practical matter, the rule (though encompassing many equitable exceptions) substantially impaired a married woman's ability to make enforceable contracts and otherwise participate in commerce.[18]

Nonetheless, this disability, however unjust or foolish, was not understood to be in conflict with the Fourteenth Amendment. To my knowledge, at the time of the Amendment's adoption, no one said that by making or enforcing a law that imputed coverture to the marital contract, a state thereby "abridged" any individual's rights of *citizenship*.

The silence cannot, as some have assumed, be attributed to some general opinion that married or unmarried women were not citizens. Officials were unanimous in stating the obvious: that the "persons" born or naturalized in the United States included all such human beings whatsoever, regardless of "age, residence, sex," and so on.[19] The question was not in doubt or in any way controversial. Consider these remarks by congressional candidate John Logan of Illinois in response to opponents' allegation that Section 1 would secure not only civil rights but also political rights. He explained that *all* citizens, "male or female, white, black or red" have the "rights of citizenship," including the right "to sue and to be sued, to own property, to have process of court, to have protection of life, liberty, and property"[20] But to say that citizenship also includes the suffrage would have an absurd implication:

> What says the law? You can't prosecute an action in the U.S. Court [under diversity jurisdiction] unless you are a citizen of another State. Suppose some lady in Missouri wanted to bring some suit in the State of Illinois, [and] the defendant by his attorney . . . says and asserts that Mrs. Mulligan or Stephens is not a citizen of the United States because she is a female woman [laughter and applause]. What do you think Judge [Samuel] Treat will say to [that] lawyer? He would say, young man, where did you study law? He would say that you are the first man I ever knew to say that a woman was not a citizen of the United States.[21]

Nor did the silence reflect some general, thoughtless acceptance of traditional coverture. While the Amendment was pending, several states debated and adopted reforms that significantly modified coverture in favor of married women's rights to "sue and be sued" and to acquire and convey property.[22] Indeed, as one jurist noted at the time, reforms were "still in progress," the result of which "will probably be an entire revolution in the law affecting the rights and liabilities of married women."[23] But seemingly no one drew any connection between these reforms and the pending Amendment.

The silence, instead, reflected the general consensus that marital contracts were anterior to citizenship, so laws ascertaining and defining the terms thereof could not abridge any right of citizenship. The best evidence for this consensus was the Supreme Court's unanimous decision, ten years before the Amendment, in *Conner v. Elliott* (1855).[24] There, a widow residing in Mississippi had challenged a Louisiana law that reserved certain rights of community property to in-state persons, more specifically, those who had married or resided in the state. She claimed that by discriminating against her on the basis of state residence, Louisiana marital-property law violated her entitlement to the "privileges and immunities of citizens" under Article IV. The Court denied her claim. Of course, neither the Court nor anyone else made the absurd argument that because a female, she was not a citizen, nor did the Court ignore the law's obvious interstate discrimination. Rather, in a terse opinion, the Court held that by "the express words and clear meaning of this clause, no privileges are secured by it, except those which belong to citizenship." Therefore, those rights "attached by the law to contracts . . . wholly irrespective of the citizenship of the parties to those contracts, cannot be deemed 'privileges of a citizen,' within the meaning of the constitution."[25]

In sum, neither coverture nor any other widespread regulation of citizens' rights fell under the prohibited legislative abridgment. As originally understood, the Privileges or Immunities Clause would not impair the broad authority of the states to regulate commerce, speech, and so forth, by laws identifying (though not creating) certain anterior incapacities of citizens to participate in those privileges, including various personal, contractual, or creedal incapacities. These laws were necessarily imperfect, often very unjust or imprudent, but not unconstitutional.

Exemplars of Prohibited Abridgment

The tacit consensus on this point prevailed throughout the entire discussion of the Amendment. To my knowledge, there were only two kinds of laws then in force that anyone, supporter or opponent, *ever* identified as potentially violative of the pending Privileges or Immunities Clause.

First and foremost, of course, were the "black codes" and other racially discriminatory laws that burdened African Americans' participation in not only political but also civil rights. These laws were not adopted pursuant to any effort by lawmakers to identify any anterior personal, creedal, or contractual incapacity of African Americans. Rather, the laws proceeded from the more fundamental assumption that "African Americans" simply were not Americans to begin with.[26]

This point has often been overlooked. The real point of controversy concerned who was a citizen, and not what were the rights of citizenship.

A second challenged regulation was the "ironclad oath" that some states made a condition for participating in not only *political* but also *civil* rights. During and after the War, various states (especially border states like Missouri and West Virginia) had required persons to swear that they had never supported secession or other rebellion and had otherwise been loyal. Most controversially, Missouri's 1865 constitution had imposed such an expurgative oath as a prerequisite, even "to teach or preach, or solemnize marriages" as a clergyman of "any religious persuasion, sect, or denomination."[27] According to critics (such as Chief Justice David Walker of the Arkansas Supreme Court), Missouri had thus "by a constitutional provision, attempted to *abridge the rights of a certain class of her citizens*, among which were clergymen, whose right to preach the gospel of Christ was attempted to be lettered by an oath."[28]

The Supreme Court heard the case in March 1866 and struck down this oath requirement nine months later while the Fourteenth Amendment was pending. In January 1867, in *Cummings v. Missouri*, a divided Court found this barrier to be a bill of attainder and thus a violation of Article I, section 10.[29]

Though sharply divided on a strictly partisan basis, the Justices largely agreed about the nature of the oath: the prerequisite served not to identify a citizen's personal incapacity (or "unfitness"), but to identify a citizen's forfeiture. According to the majority, the oath

> was exacted not from any notion that the several acts designated indicated *unfitness* for the callings, but because it was thought that the several acts deserved punishment, and that, for many of them, there was no way to inflict *punishment* except by depriving the parties who had committed them of *some of the rights and privileges of the citizen*.[30]

The Court held that such a deprivation of a citizen's privilege was a punishment—and thus constituted a bill of attainder—even if not a deprivation of life, liberty, and property.[31] A few years later, the Court, citing *Cummings*, summarily overturned West Virginia's law that imposed a similar oath on litigants.[32]

The dissenting judges in *Cummings*, though denying that the restriction was a "punishment," likewise treated it as a means of identifying those who had forfeited their privileges by disloyalty. Speaking with reference to the right to practice law (at issue in a companion case (*Ex parte Garland*)), the dissenters said that a person who had "voluntarily borne arms against the government of the United States while a *citizen* thereof," or assisted the rebellion, "has, by doing those things, *forfeited his right* to appear in her courts."[33] The real disagreement, between majority and dissent, was whether a citizen's forfeiture of civil rights could be proven simply by his or her refusal to take an oath.

Because the Amendment was not yet ratified, the Court did not consider whether the Privileges or Immunities Clause might invalidate such laws as abridgments of the privileges of citizenship. Still, opponents in some border states made precisely this charge. The Amendment, it was said, put the local "radicals" in an "awkward dilemma," for they "must condemn their own favorite State measures."[34] The *Wheeling Daily Register* called the Amendment a "Candid Confession": local "radicals" deny to a "certain class of persons . . . the right to earn a livelihood by the practice of the law. But Congress[,] after declaring them citizens, say that no State shall pass or enforce any laws abridging their privileges or immunities."[35] Missouri's *Weekly Caucasian* saw a naked contradiction between Republicans' proposed amendment and their local policy:

> it is a nice question for Missouri and Tennessee radicals to decide, how, under this amendment, they could make their test oath work with it, for, it is said. "No State shall make or enforce any law which shall abridge the privileges or immunities of citizens of the United States." So much for the test oath.[36]

I do not know whether or how the Amendment's supporters answered this charge. The issue was, perhaps, already moot even before Congress proposed the Amendment. Even after oral argument in March 1866, there was confidence that the Court would invalidate the oath.[37] And with the *Cummings* decision nine months later, the question was settled. Soon thereafter, courts in Missouri and West Virginia would acquiesce to the Supreme Court's holdings as to the civil rights to teach and to file suit.[38] And afterwards, West Virginia and other states repealed the oath, even as to the legal profession.[39]

Still, we may reasonably infer how many Republicans would have responded. As to the legal profession, one answer had already been provided. In 1866, the West Virginia Supreme Court sharply distinguished the "right of every citizen to appear in court by attorney," a fundamental civil right, from the "right to appear in court as an attorney-at-law for another," for the latter, like political rights, was among the "privileges and immunities *conferred* by law."[40] Because conferred by law, these rights could be subject to a test oath. The Republican dissenters in *Garland* would say the same: even if still full citizens, those refusing to take the oath could be excluded from such political rights.[41]

But what of undoubted fundamental *civil* privileges, such as the right to file suit, to teach—even the freedom of public and sacred speech—anterior rights that the lawmakers did not confer, but merely recognized and secured? Some, perhaps, would have joined the suggestion of the Republican dissenters in *Cummings*: that test-oath laws—even as to the right to teach—did not abridge any citizen's privilege, but merely served to identify those citizens who had forfeited their citizenship. But here, I suspect that, on cooler reflection, even the most radical Republicans would have hesitated to pronounce the sentence of forfeiture based solely on the person's silence.

A few may have taken a more disingenuous approach. This was probably the tactic adopted by Missouri's governor, Thomas Fletcher, in his message to his state's legislature on January 2, 1867, when he recommended adoption of the Amendment and offered a brief description of the Privileges or Immunities Clause.

Fletcher was in a tough political spot. He favored (1) the ratification of the Republicans' Fourteenth Amendment, and (2) extension of the suffrage to African Americans, but also (3) the repeal of the local test oath.[42] But the oath was fiercely defended by many radicals whose votes he needed for the first two reforms. And the radicals, as spirited men, were in no mood to retreat on any point so fiercely contested.

When the legislature met on January 2, the nation still waited for the Supreme Court's opinion in *Cummings* (it would be announced two weeks later, on January 14). The whole matter had excited great passions: including local and nationwide Democratic denunciation, and stubborn local defensiveness. The radicals were understandably suspicious of the state's population, as a large percentage had been rebels or rebel-sympathizers. In the 1865 Drake Constitution, the radicals had decided to impute to all Missourians a presumption of disloyalty (and thus forfeiture of civil rights), to be rebutted by taking an expurgative oath.

Fletcher thus had compelling reasons not to suggest that the oath was unjust or even unconstitutional; he could not safely suggest that anyone voting for the Amendment would effectively concede the injustice or unconstitutionality of the oath. He would thereby have insulted his own base, and thus alienated many legislators upon whom he would rely to ratify the Amendment, extend the suffrage, and otherwise do justice to African Americans.

Instead, Fletcher made two understandable moves. First, he decided to challenge the oath solely on grounds of prudence: it should be repealed, he said, simply because it was unenforceable. But he did not hint at its injustice or unconstitutionality.[43]

But as to the pending Privileges or Immunities Clause, he offered a novel reading whereby he could both preserve the proposal's chief purpose (the constitutionalization of the Civil Rights Act to protect African Americans) but not even suggest that the Clause would touch the rights abridged by the oath. Fletcher declared that the privileges and immunities of a citizen of the United States are not fundamental rights, but those "*conferred* on him by the laws of Congress."[44] That plainly implicated the whole Civil Rights Act. At the same time, his definition would leave the states free to abridge such basic civil rights as the right to teach, unless such rights were first *conferred* by Congress.

We may now venture an explanation as to the anomaly we noted in a prior chapter: Fletcher provided the only recorded remark, by *any official supporter*, indicating that the "privileges and immunities of citizens of the United States" were not the fundamental civil rights of the citizen, but "the rights conferred" on the citizen by the government. Fletcher offered this inverted and anomalous reading, I believe, precisely to address an anomalous and extreme political situation in his state.

But most Republicans, on cooler reflection, I believe, would have conceded that the pending Privileges or Immunities Clause would abrogate, as to civil rights, all expurgative test oaths, especially Missouri's. These could not properly serve as a test or trial of a citizen's forfeiture and did not otherwise identify any other anterior incapacity, whether personal, creedal, or contractual. Therefore, the oath requirement did, indeed, abridge the citizen's privileges as a citizen of the United States and would be abrogated by the Fourteenth Amendment. By ratifying the measure, the radicals in border states would indeed condemn some of their own policies.

During the Civil War, the Supreme Court of Minnesota had already exemplified such cool reflection. The state's legislature had passed its own anti-disloyalist laws that barred pro-secession citizens from suing in the state's courts. When citizens from Mississippi (then in rebellion) filed suit against local citizens, their suit was dismissed. But on appeal, the high court struck down the law, precisely because it abridged the privileges of citizens of the United States.

The court began by emphasizing the judicial duty to give heightened scrutiny to laws adopted during times of heightened passion, like wartime:

> [T]he very fact that the act was passed under such a state of excitement, admonishes us of the necessity of carefully examining its several provisions, lest in our anxiety to punish the guilty authors and abettors of our national troubles, we do far greater injury to ourselves, by forgetting justice, and disregarding the wholesome restraints of our fundamental law.[45]

The court set aside the legislature's hot-headed measure as violative of "privilege of suing and defending in our courts," secured to the "citizens of this state," by the state constitution, and to citizens of other states, by the federal Constitution's Privileges and Immunities Clause (citing *Corfield v Coryell*). As long as the government of the Union, "still regards the people of [Mississippi] as citizens," Minnesota could not constitutionally "treat them as alien enemies, for the purpose of depriving them of rights which they enjoy as citizens of the United States."[46]

In sum, we can discern an original understanding of the verb "abridge": to shorten. The states may not make or enforce any law that in any way shortens any privilege or immunity of a citizen of the United States. Whether a law does so "abridge" any such right depends on (1) the scope of the particular privilege or immunity affected and (2) the scope of the particular citizen's anterior capacity to participate in a particular right. The Amendment thus leaves with the states a very broad authority to pass regulations that defined—but did not create—the citizen's anterior incapacities (whether personal, creedal, or contractual) to participate in the rights of citizenship. The black codes and the expurgative test oaths, however, did not define any such incapacity, but abridged the fundamental rights of citizenship.

The Privileges and Immunities of Citizens of the United States

We now turn, at last, to the great unanswered question: What are these "privileges [and] immunities of citizens of the United States" to be secured against legislative abridgment?

There is no consensus, even among those who have concluded that there was an original consensus. As to their "darling," the scholarly amorists, at times, seem quarrelsome rivals; they all admire her, but debate endlessly as to her true excellence.

Three Main Originalist Approaches

But the discord is not all cacophony. There is a certain order to the rival accounts. As the late Professor Calvin Massey pointed out, while "there is no agreement concerning a single original meaning of the Privileges or Immunities Clause, it is possible to identify three distinct, plausible, and credible original understandings."[47] These three are (1) the equal rights, (2) the incorporationist, and (3) the fundamental rights readings.

To identify these three approaches, I will instead categorize them relative to the source text that is foundational to each: (1) the Civil Rights Act ("CRA") (equal rights) (2) the Bill of Rights ("BOR") (incorporationist), and (3) the Declaration of Independence ("DOI") (fundamental rights). Each of these readings finds, in its respective source text, a set of rights that are paradigmatic, if not exhaustive, of the "privileges and immunities of citizens of the United States."

According to the CRA reading, these "privileges and immunities" include certain equal civil rights and immunities: the rights to "[1] make and enforce contracts,

[2] to sue, be parties, and give evidence, [3] to inherit, purchase, lease, sell, hold, and convey real and personal property, and [4] to full and equal benefit of all laws and proceedings for the security of person and property," and a freedom from [5] any racially discriminatory "punishment, pains, and penalties," along with perhaps some other rights. By this equal-rights reading, a state "abridges" these rights by any regulation of them that discriminates against citizens on the basis of race or any similarly unreasonable classification.[48] The Clause secures only an equality with respect to these rights.

According to the BOR reading, these privileges and immunities are chiefly, if not exclusively, the personal rights found in the original Constitution (such as the privilege of the writ of habeas corpus), or enumerated in the first eight amendments.[49] By this "substantive" account, the Privileges or Immunities Clause protects these rights absolutely, even if all citizens are equally affected. The Clause provided enhanced security for these rights, already valid against federal abridgment (as held in *Barron v. Baltimore*), but now also against state abridgment.

According to the DOI reading, the privileges of U.S. citizenship are chiefly found in the fundamental natural rights of life, liberty, and pursuit of happiness, as set forth in the Declaration and in some of the first state constitutions. By this account, the privileges of citizenship are certain "retained natural rights," as defined or modified (but never destroyed) by law, especially state law or "general law."[50] This reading can be quite expansive, and thus more inclusive; it can encompass both the equality mandated by the Civil Rights Act and various liberties, including, but not limited to, the rights enumerated in the Bill of Rights.

There is substantial evidence supporting each of these originalist readings. I provide here just a short summary.

The *CRA Reading* finds much support in the pre-Amendment understanding of the "privileges and immunities of citizens." Several of the Act's enumerated rights had long been authoritatively identified as privileges or immunities of citizens, including the right to sue and be sued, the right to acquire real as well as personal property, the immunity against interstate discrimination in taxation and regulation, and, by some accounts, the immunity against racial discrimination as to criminal liability.[51]

Even more abundant evidence is found in the debates over the adoption of the Civil Rights Act. Several speakers, including the chief proponents, the chairmen of the Judiciary Committees of the House and Senate (James Wilson and Lyman Trumbull, respectively) identified the rights enumerated in the Act as privileges and immunities of American citizenship. Wilson said that "this bill refers to those rights which belong to men as citizens of the United States and none other" and was necessary because some states had failed to "practice" and "enforce" the "privileges and immunities citizens" as defined by Justice Washington's exposition in *Corfield v. Coryell*.[52] Likewise, Trumbull said,

> To be a citizen of the United States carries with it some rights; and what are they? They are those inherent, fundamental rights which belong to free citizens or free men in all countries, such as the rights enumerated in this bill, and they belong

> to them in all the States of the Union. The right of American citizenship means something.[53]

Trumbull then proceeded to cite Kent's paraphrase of Washington's explanation of "privileges and immunities of citizens" in *Corfield*.[54] Several others, including a leading opponent, Reverdy Johnson, said the Act would secure the "rights of citizenship."[55]

Members of the Joint Committee and their close associates acknowledged a close connection between the prohibitions of the Act and those of Section 1. According to one newspaper report, behind closed doors, Bingham had persuaded his colleagues to adopt his proposal precisely to redress the unconstitutionality of the Civil Rights Act:

> Mr. Bingham, of Ohio, then insisted that the present Civil Rights Bill was unconstitutional, and that an amendment to the Constitution guaranteeing civil rights to persons in all of the states should be agreed to. The committee adopted that proposition.[56]

Although the Committee thus replaced Robert Dale Owen's more precise racial-egalitarian "civil rights" formula, the consensus was that Bingham's formula had the same effect. Owen himself seemed satisfied with the change. A few weeks later, he publicly recommended a number of changes to Sections 2 and 3 that would have restored aspects of his initial proposal, but he approved the new Section 1. An advocate of "equal civil rights," he was "content to see civil rights asserted," for the freedman must not "exist among us as an outlaw, debarred from owning land, excluded from the witness-box, or from the courts of law, or from the rights of the testator, or subjected to punishments from which other races are exempt."[57]

Bingham's proposition, of course, did more than constitutionalize the Act. It also would extend its egalitarian guarantees to all Americans. Accordingly, insiders were quick to highlight its effects beyond the Act. The day after the Committee's decision, Roscoe Conkling's close advisor—the Senate Secretary John Forney[58]—publicly wrote that Section 1 "embodies the guarantees of the Civil Rights Law into the national compact." More specifically, he explained, the Section would have two effects: (1) put to "rest all [constitutional] doubts on that point," and (2) secure "that protection to the American citizen, until now omitted in our fundamental law, and even in the laws themselves."[59]

A week later, the close relationship between the Act and Section 1 was axiomatic to the public debates in the House. In his speech initiating debate, Stevens noted that Section 1 barred certain racially discriminatory "unjust legislation of the States," and acknowledged that it was "partly true" that the Civil Rights Act "secures the same things."[60] Many others said or suggested the same.[61] And no one in the House seemed to disagree.

In the ratification discussion in the states, the same connection was made—the Amendment would readopt the Act but make its benefits available to all Americans. For instance, Trumbull told voters that Section 1

> declares the rights of the American citizen. It is a reiteration of those rights as set forth in the "Civil Rights Bill"—an unnecessary declaration, perhaps because all those rights belong to the citizen, but to avoid cavil it was thought proper to put in the fundamental law the declaration that all the citizens were entitled alike to equal rights in the Republic.[62]

Oregon's Senator George Williams told voters that Section 1 would "protect every citizen in the enjoyment of his civil rights against the partial and prejudicial legislation of any State."[63] Many, many other speakers indicated that Section 1, as a whole, corresponded to the Civil Rights Act.[64]

Most speakers, in this regard, spoke of Section 1 indiscriminately. But a few did identify the Privileges or Immunities Clause as the primary correlative to the Civil Rights Act. In the House, Massachusetts's Thomas Eliot indicated that the Clause specifically barred "state legislation discriminating against classes of citizens."[65] In the New Jersey Senate, James Scovel remarked that the Amendment "reaffirms the provisions of the Civil Rights bill, that no State shall abridge the privileges and immunities of citizens of the United States."[66]

Perhaps the most nuanced account of the relation between the Civil Rights Act and the discrete prohibitions of Section 1 was offered on the campaign trail by Schuyler Colfax. He announced that the Act "specifically and directly declares what the rights of a citizen of the United States are—that they may make and enforce contracts, sue and be parties, give evidence, purchase, lease, and sell property, and be subject to like punishments." Colfax here conspicuously omitted the rights to "hold" property and to "the full and equal benefit of all laws and proceedings for the security of persons and property."[67] The omission was probably deliberate, for those rights belonged to personhood, not citizenship, and represented those parts of the Civil Rights Act that seem covered by the Due Process-Equal Protection Clause—*viz.*, the right to hold property (against unlawful deprivation) and the right to receive equal security (or a certain "equal protection").[68]

The *BOR Reading* likewise has much supporting originalist evidence. The language of the Privileges or Immunities Clause strongly indicates an intentional and close connection with the deliberative rights of the First Amendment. Recall that in April, Bingham had initially imitated Article I, section 10 in using the terms "No state," "pass," and "impair or deny."[69] But upon revision, he adopted language from the First Amendment; he replaced "pass" with "make," and "impair or deny" with "abridge." This choice alone, as Akhil Amar notes, provides very strong evidence of an intent to subject the states, equally with Congress, to the norm against making laws *abridging* the freedoms of discussion.[70]

Another textual argument proceeds from the relation between the Constitution "of the United States" and the rights of citizens "of the United States." Michael Zuckert has articulated the inference: "Because privileges and immunities belong to citizens of the United States, and because the fundamental document governing the United States is the Constitution, it is reasonable to conclude that the privileges and immunities are special rights enjoyed by the citizens of the United States by virtue of the Constitution."[71]

Or in Amar's apt phrase, the "privileges and immunities of citizens of the United States" are "most obviously those declared in the Bill of Rights."[72] According to these scholars, by a certain logic, the Constitution *of the United States* is what defines the rights of citizens *of the United States.*

Both these textual inferences have limited support in the official pre-Amendment meaning. The Ohio Supreme Court, two decades earlier, had insisted that one should look to the U.S. Constitution (as well as the law of nations) to identify the fundamental "privileges and immunities of citizens of the United States," as secured by Article IV.[73] Further, many authorities had identified the freedoms of discussion as among the chief privileges or immunities of citizens—including the Supreme Court in *Dred Scott*, treatise writers, and Republican officials on the eve of the Civil War.[74] Accordingly, in the Thirty-Ninth Congress, Pennsylvania's John Broomall, in recalling the "the rights and immunities of citizens" that had been "habitually and systematically denied in certain States to the citizens of other States," mentioned certain freedoms of discussion, as both first and last on his list: "the right of speech, the right of transit, the right of domicil, the right to sue, the writ of habeas corpus, and the right of petition."[75]

More direct evidence can be found in the emphatic statements made during the Amendment's adoption, especially by Section 1's chief drafter, Bingham, and its chief advocate in the Senate, Jacob Howard. In May, Bingham mentioned, among the secured privileges and immunities, both the freedom of loyal speech and the freedom from "cruel and unusual punishments."[76] For his part, Howard said the "privileges and immunities" included, *inter alia*, "the personal rights guaranteed and secured by the first eight amendments of the Constitution," and then proceeded to list some of them, largely in the order they appear, including the freedoms of deliberation, the right to bear arms, and others (though with some interesting interpolations and omissions, to be discussed below).[77]

Further, during the ratification debates, various officials and other commentators indicated that the Amendment would secure, against state abridgment, the rights of deliberation and the right to bear arms.[78] And Ohio's governor, in his formal transmittal message, likewise said that the Amendment would secure the "freedom of discussion" because "immunities of this kind . . . are of the very essence of free government."[79]

Of particular note was Bingham's turn, during the 1866 campaign, from the freedom of loyal speech to the freedom of *sacred* speech. Defending the Amendment, he said, "Freedom of conscience is one of the privileges of citizens of the United States, and men are not to be put to torture, sent to the dungeon, walk the narrow steps of the scaffold, for teaching their children the holy principles of our Lord and Master."[80] Bingham was far from alone; violence to this freedom of sacred speech, especially the freedom to proclaim universal human dignity under God, had long been a complaint by many antislavery northerners.[81]

The *DOI Reading* likewise has substantial support in the pre-Amendment meaning. In *Corfield*, Justice Washington had relied on the rights of life, liberty, and pursuit of happiness as the principles or headings for categorizing the fundamental privileges and immunities of citizenship:

> They may . . . be all comprehended *under the following general heads*: Protection by the government; the enjoyment of life and liberty, with the right to acquire and possess property of every kind, and to pursue and obtain happiness and safety; subject nevertheless to such restraints as the government may justly prescribe for the general good of the whole.[82]

Washington probably had in mind Lockean natural rights as set forth in the first provision of his home state's constitution:

> That all men are by nature equally free and independent, and have certain inherent rights, of which, when they enter into a state of society, they cannot, by any compact, deprive or divest their posterity; namely, the enjoyment of life and liberty, with the means of acquiring and possessing property, and pursuing and obtaining happiness and safety.[83]

But note that, contrary to some scholars,[84] Washington did not here say that the rights of life, liberty, and so on, were themselves privileges of citizenship, but rather that these natural rights provided the "general heads" by which to classify these privileges.[85] The distinction is subtle but vital to the integrity of Washington's exposition. To call the right to "life" a privilege of citizenship is to deny the principle that it is the Creator who directly endows every human being with life—and thus far above the power of civil society to add or subtract.

Consistent with this rule of categorization, Washington proceeded to identify five of the fundamental rights of citizenship, and he seemed to order them in relation to two of these "general heads": "liberty" and "property." He first mentioned two liberty rights: (1) the "right of a citizen of one state to pass through, or to reside in any other state, for purposes of trade, agriculture, professional pursuits, or otherwise," and (2) "to claim the benefit of the writ of habeas corpus." Then he added one right pertaining to both liberty and property, (3) "to institute and maintain actions of any kind in the courts of the state." Last, he mentioned two rights of property: "(4) to take, hold and dispose of property, either real or personal" and (5) "an exemption from higher taxes or impositions than are paid by the other citizens of the state."[86] This enumeration, ordered to the headings of liberty and property, though expressly incomplete, was no mere "laundry list."[87]

During the adoption of the Amendment, several officials expressly quoted this natural-rights passage from *Corfield* as expository of the proposed Privileges or Immunities Clause. Among these were Jacob Howard in the Senate,[88] and Ohio's William Lawrence in a campaign speech.[89] Other officials likewise treated the Declaration's rights as foundational to the Privileges or Immunities as well as the Due Process-Equal Protection Clause. Tennessee's governor said *all* of Section 1 was a guarantee "to all citizens" of "equal protection in the enjoyment of life, liberty and property."[90] Nebraska's governor likewise indicated that Section 1, as a whole, "accepts fully, and forever vindicates by the solemn pledge of a nation the idea that was the corner-stone of American Independence, but has been for a time rejected by the builders of the national superstructure"[91]

The Deficiencies of These Accounts

But each of the readings, while supported by substantial evidence, fails to account for other substantial evidence. In particular, the readings fail to integrate coherently (1) some major portion of the official discussion, (2) the Joint Committee's official explanation, and, above all (3) the constitutional text, with its manifest distinction between the rights of persons and of citizens.

First, as to the official discussion, supporters of the rival CRA and BOR readings have had great trouble in making a persuasive account of the evidence supporting the other reading. The CRA proponents have dealt with the BOR evidence in two ways. First, some have tended to dismiss Bingham and Howard as idiosyncratic or incoherent.[92] But as Richard Aynes, *inter alia*, has emphasized, members of Congress and the Joint Committee afforded these men great respect, by assigning them leading roles in the drafting and explanation of Section 1.[93] Second, some have attempted to impute to Bingham and Howard some implied restraining principle, by which the rights of discussion, arms-bearing, and so forth, are fully subordinate to the sole right to equality.[94] But this claim cannot be squared with the naked text of Section 1, which protects a plurality of rights against *all* abridgment, and not just a single immunity against interracial, interstate, or similarly improper discrimination.[95]

BOR proponents have, in turn, treated the CRA evidence in two unpersuasive ways. First, some have ventured to say that the Civil Rights Act itself incorporates the Bill of Rights.[96] The effort, as Ilan Wurman observes, does violence to the text of both the Act and the Bill.[97] Second, by sharply distinguishing the Act from the Privileges or Immunities Clause, proponents have tried to reassign the Civil Rights Act wholly to other parts of Section 1, whether the Citizenship Clause or the Due Process-Equal Protection Clause.[98] Now some *parts* of the Act plainly correlated with these two clauses: the Act's declaration of *ius soli* citizenship correlates with the Citizenship Clause; the Act's enumerated rights, to hold property and to equal security of person and property, seemed encompassed by the Due Process-Equal Protection Clause, as Colfax arguably noticed. But other rights, especially the right to *acquire* real and personal property, found a home in the Privileges or Immunities Clause.[99] And accordingly, the vast bulk of the originalist evidence indicates that *each* clause of Section 1, including the Privileges or Immunities Clause, had some correlative in the Civil Rights Act.[100]

In contrast, by its great breadth and imprecision, the DOI reading can account for both sides' evidence: equal civil rights, enumerated rights, and an indefinite list of other rights.[101] Still, no proponent of any of these readings has ever ventured to explain one salient point of evidence: Jacob Howard's peculiar enumeration of only some of the rights in the first eight amendments. His list includes curious interpolations and conspicuous omissions (e.g., of the Religion Clauses and the entire Fifth and Seventh Amendments). Yet only a few scholars have even mentioned these additions and subtractions, and none have offered a persuasive explanation. Howard Jay Graham, and more recently, George Thomas, have noted that Howard seems to endorse "selective incorporation,[102] but neither identified any rationale for his selection. Jay Bybee has dismissed Howard's enumeration as an incoherent "laundry list,"[103] and other scholars have simply declared the omissions insignificant.[104] But we now know, thanks to the research of Andrew Hyman, that Howard, a respected jurist, prepared written notes that indicate deliberate omissions and inclusions, which we'll address below.[105]

Second, contrary to the Joint Committee's official explanation—that Section 1 would "determine" a plurality of "rights" and "privileges"—none of the readings provide a *determinate* account of both "privileges" and "immunities." The CRA reading reduces all these privileges to a single immunity against discriminatory regulation, but with an expansive, indeterminate application to countless forms of unreasonable regulations. The DOI reading, rooted in broad natural rights language, likewise opens to an indeterminate extension to both natural and derivative civil rights.

The BOR approach, in contrast, does propose a determinate set of privileges. The basis for determination is very clear: constitutional enumeration. Not surprisingly, then, only incorporationists or semi-incorporationists (like Justice Thomas) have bothered to cite the Committee's formal explanation.

But neither the BOR nor the other readings provide a "determinate" account of the "equality" rights that are also secured by Section 1. Whether finding this equality in the Privileges or Immunities Clause, or elsewhere in Section 1, none of these readings can offer any clear limit to the antidiscrimination norm. What besides race represents a forbidden basis for imposing regulatory or fiscal burdens? Scholars have usually settled on the conclusion that the Amendment bars racial and similarly *unreasonable* classifications. But such an open-ended rule is unsupported by the Amendment's text and utterly adverse to its original, determinate, and anti-kritocratic purpose.

Finally, and above all, none of the accounts indicates how these liberty and equality rights are those of "citizens." Despite the Amendment's sheer text, none addresses the clear distinction between the rights of human personhood and the privileges and immunities of citizenship.

A New Approach

Let's take a fresh look.

The Fourteenth Amendment's rule against legislative abridgment safeguards certain defined goods: the "privileges [and] immunities of citizens of the United States." This compound direct object has two nouns, "privileges" and "immunities," which are modified by "of citizens," which, in turn, is modified by "of the United States."

In reading this text anew, at least four questions present themselves.

First, what is the relation between the "privileges and immunities of citizens" of this Amendment and those already mentioned in the Constitution? The original fourth article had already entitled the citizens of "each state" to certain "privileges and immunities of citizens," but without the qualifier "of the United States." The context indicates some strong connection between the Amendment and the Fourth Article. Are these parallel rights, or the same rights, and if the latter, was the second Privileges or Immunities Clause a mere redundancy?

Second, we see another redundancy problem. Why does the Amendment speak of "immunities" as distinct from the "privileges"? The word "privilege," derived from *privus* and *lex*, points to a private or special law, and the word "immunity," from *in* and *munia* (burdens), indicates an exemption from some burdens.[106] Accordingly, Lincoln's attorney general had provided these definitions: "*Privileges* are special rights belonging to the individual or class, and not to the mass. *Immunities* are rights of exemption only—freedom from what otherwise would be a duty, obligation, or burden."[107] But every special exemption (immunity) is a kind of special right (privilege), so in drafting the Clause, the Joint Committee should have omitted "immunities" and used the word "privileges" alone (as the Committee did in their formal Report). Conversely, some of the affirmative privileges seem to consist chiefly (if not exclusively) of an immunity—for example, the freedom of speech and freedom of commerce consist in a freedom from certain state interference. Hence Ohio's governor classified the freedom of discussion as an "immunity."[108] So perhaps either "immunities" or "privileges" alone would have sufficed, as William Crosskey argued.[109]

Third, in what way are these rights "*of*" citizens of the United States? The suggestion is that there are special rights and peculiar exemptions that belong to "citizens" and more specifically, those "of the United States." But the text does not indicate whether "of" serves to identify (a) the class of persons secured, (b) the class of rights secured, or (c) both.

Fourth, what, in particular, are these "privileges" and "immunities" of citizens of the United States? If the classification is determinate, some enumeration must be possible—but no enumeration has proven satisfactory except to pure incorporationists.

A Necessary Enhancement to Article IV

As to the first question, the evidence is overwhelming: that as originally understood, the "privileges and immunities of citizens of the United States" were substantially the same as the "privileges and immunities of citizens" secured by Article IV.

Most notably, in his prepared written remarks,[110] Senator Luke Poland (a former Chief Justice of the Vermont Supreme Court) certified that the Privileges or Immunities Clause "secures nothing beyond what was intended by the original provision in the Constitution, that 'the citizens of each State shall be entitled to all privileges and immunities of citizens in the several States.'"[111]

Other officials likewise equated these privileges and immunities. My own research confirms what Chester Antieau, David Bogen, and James Bond found in their extensive surveys of the congressional and state discussions: *everyone* who spoke on the topic directly and expressly confirmed that the privileges and immunities were the same; no one said otherwise.[112]

As we saw, the enforcement of the Privileges and Immunities Clause had been a prevailing method throughout the drafting process: to redress the evils of the unreconstructed states by constitutional enhancements to existing constitutional provisions.[113] This was a well-worn approach. From before the Civil War, Republicans aimed to protect Americans in the South by enhanced federal enforcement of that same Clause—understood as securing something more than just an immunity against interstate discrimination.[114]

Now a remark in Senator Howard's main speech may seem to provide some contrary evidence. After quoting from both *Corfield* and the amendments, he said "here is a mass of privileges, immunities, and rights, *some* of them secured by the second section of the fourth article of the Constitution, which I have recited, *some* by the first eight amendments of the Constitution," and all of them "guaranteed by the Constitution or recognized by it."[115] From this comment, Chin-Yung Yen and later scholars have concluded that Howard deemed "privileges and immunities" to consist in "*two things*; namely, those rights secured by the second section of the fourth article of the Constitution and those conferred by the first eight amendments."[116]

Still, one might instead read Howard so that he treats the "privileges and immunities" of the Amendment as the equivalent to those of Article IV, with *some* of the exemplars *evinced* by Justice Washington's partial enumeration, and *some* others *evinced* by express enumeration in the Constitution. That is to say, we should read his comment to say, "some of them secured by *the leading judicial exposition of* the second section of the fourth article of the Constitution, which *exposition* I have recited, some of them by the first eight amendments." Justice Washington enumerated some of these "privileges and immunities," the Constitution enumerated some others, but they all could be found under Article IV.

There are several good reasons to read Howard in the latter way. First, this reading explains Howard's use of the verb "recite," which seems to refer to his lengthy quotation from Washington's enumeration, and not the nineteen words of the Privileges and Immunities Clause, for recitation usually refers to something longer than a short sentence. Second, this reading is probably what Howard intended to say. In his prepared notes (on pages 2–3), Howard initially planned first to quote from *Corfield*'s list of rights, and then to affirm that the Amendment's Privileges or Immunities Clause would protect these same "fundamental civil rights of the citizen" secured by Article IV.[117] But later, Howard decided to add, as pages 2a–2b, a list of rights from the amendments, along with an allusion to *Barron*.[118] This insert thus appeared as an *internal amendment* to his original discussion of *Corfield* and Article IV; the enumeration from the Bill of Rights served to flesh out further Justice Washington's partial list.[119] Third, this reading is consistent with two different newspaper paraphrases of the speech—that altogether omitted Howard's insertion as to the Bill of Rights, and thus indicated that the Privileges or Immunities Clause would secure the same "fundamental rights" or "fundamental guarantees" encompassed by Article IV's Privileges and Immunities Clause.[120] Fourth, this reading makes Howard's remark consistent with his purpose of representing the general opinion of his colleagues (none of whom distinguished the rights of Article IV from those of the Amendment), and not Howard's idiosyncratic view. Fifth, the reading coheres with Howard's subsequent explanation, offered in Congress in early 1869, that the Privileges or Immunities Clause served to enforce the same rights: it "grew out of the fact that there was nothing in the whole Constitution to secure absolutely the citizens of the United States in the various States against an infringement of their rights and privileges under the second section of the fourth article of the old Constitution."[121]

Finally, as I will explain below, this reading best explains Howard's omissions and interpolations in listing the rights recognized in the first eight amendments. Howard, I will show, surveyed these amendments precisely to distinguish those rights, among others found in the amendments, that might satisfy Washington's general definition of "privileges and immunities of citizens."

But if the new Privileges or Immunities Clause did indeed "secure nothing beyond" what was originally intended by Article IV (as Senator Poland claimed), why was it proposed and adopted? Was it not a mere redundancy, and thus wholly unnecessary, as many opponents alleged—and thus violative of Article V's standard that Congress's proposal authority extended only to changes they deem "necessary"?

By the naked text, there must have been some general opinion that the entire prohibitory sentence, including the Privileges or Immunities Clause, like the Due Process Clause, was in some sense a new restriction and not a mere restatement. The verbs are all in the prescriptive future: "No State *shall* make or enforce . . . deprive . . . or deny." These provisions cannot be merely declaratory, but restrictive.

Howard's remark from 1869 provides some clue as to why the Privileges or Immunities Clause was necessary: there was nothing "to absolutely secure the citizens of the United States" in their fundamental "rights and privileges" under Article IV, section 2. And in his prepared remarks, Poland indicated that some amendment was necessary to remedy the slavery-induced nullification of the original Privileges and Immunities Clause:

> But the radical difference in the social systems of the several States, and the great extent to which the doctrine of State rights or State sovereignty was carried, induced mainly, as I believe, by and for the protection of the peculiar system of the South, led to a practical repudiation of the existing provision on this subject, and it was disregarded in many of the States.[122]

Still, neither Howard nor Poland here specified how the Old Clause had been frustrated, and precisely how the new Clause would remedy the defect.

This question has proven difficult to me. I have not identified any consensus view as to the precise necessity of any of the restrictive clauses of Section 1. The Joint Committee, in its formal report, offered no explanation for the necessity of Section 1, other than the certification that the restrictions would "determine" certain "civil rights and privileges." The Committee was deafeningly silent as to the Committee's initial abortive proposal to empower Congress to enforce the Privileges and Immunities and Due Process Clauses, the predecessor to Sections 1 and 5; in contrast, the Committee candidly mentioned and discussed the initial proposal that would become Section 2.[123] Nor can I glean a general consensus from the remarks of various supporters.

This dissensus and resulting silence, I think, was a function of Republicans' dissensus, not as to the meaning of Sections 1 and 5, but as to the meaning of the Constitution of 1865. Republicans did not agree as to what extent the Constitution might already both "determine [these] civil rights and privileges" and empower Congress to enforce this determination.

In this regard, we must not forget that the Republican Party of 1866 was a fragile coalition, composed of formerly bitter rivals, divided along two main fault lines. These lines did not, as some have supposed, correspond to some division between "radicals" and "moderates." Rather, the most important divisions concerned (1) federalism (old Whigs v. Jacksonian Democrats) and (2) the Compromise of 1850 (with many who supported the measure and some bitterly opposed, especially Free Soilers). In 1854, these old Democrats, Whigs, and Free Soilers had been united only by their common devotion to the Declaration of Independence and their hostility to slavery's expansion in the federal territories.[124] By 1865 that unity had extended further—to national intolerance of secession and slavery, and then to the conviction that free blacks, native to the soil, were not only entitled to freedom, but also American citizenship and the full civil rights thereof. But as to this last goal, Republicans had never settled their old disagreements as to the scope of federal and state power under the old Constitution.

One especially divisive matter had been whether Congress ever had the power to enforce Article IV's Fugitive Slave Clause (the companion to the Privileges and Immunities Clause). Congress's Fugitive Slave Act had been affirmed in *Prigg v. Pennsylvania* (1842) and then strengthened by the Compromise of 1850. Those Republicans who had entered the GOP as old Whigs and Compromisers (like Lincoln) usually agreed with *Prigg*: that Article IV conferred on Congress the power and duty to return fugitives to slavery. For Republicans like Lincoln, it was therefore natural to propose a congressional Privileges and Immunities Act. But at the other extreme, those who had been both Jacksonian Democrats and anti-Compromise Free Soilers (like Bingham and Chase) had rejected *Prigg* and denounced the law as unconstitutional, on both antislavery and states' rights grounds. In their view, Article IV's mandate, "shall be delivered up," was exclusively a state power and duty. So divisive was this issue that when Chase proposed to raise it at the 1860 national convention, Lincoln privately warned him that it would "explode the convention and the party."[125]

For this and other reasons, no consensus, even in 1866, was possible as to the precise necessity of an enhancement to the old Privileges and Immunities Clause. The topic was better left undiscussed lest it blow up the Republican congressional coalition.

Instead, one finds, among supporters, at least four disparate diagnoses of the problem to be remedied—but not one of which seemed to reflect a consensus.

First, by some accounts, Article IV's Privileges and Immunities, like the Fifth Amendment's Due Process Clause, did not clearly bind the states at all. A new, unambiguous formula—"No State shall . . ."—was necessary to bind the states to respect both "privileges and immunities," and "due process of law."

The problem was what I will call the *Barron-Prigg* rule. As strange as it may seem today, as of 1866, it was not yet settled that Article IV's Privileges and Immunities Clause bound the states. To be sure, most authorities had come to endorse this reading,[126] and indeed, the language "shall be entitled" would seem to require both the federal and state governments to respect the citizens' entitlements. But earlier in the century, two state supreme courts had concluded that the Clause, with its passive voice "shall be entitled," bound impliedly only the federal government.[127] This holding anticipated the Supreme Court's subsequent holdings as to other passive-voice clauses of the Constitution, in the famous cases of *Barron v. Baltimore* (1835) and *Prigg v. Pennsylvania* (1842). In both cases, the Court held that where a constitutional command takes the passive voice without an express agent, expressed in "general terms," the implied agent is "the federal government." In *Barron*, as we know, the rule was applied to the Fifth Amendment's Takings Clause ("shall not be taken," and by implication to all the passive-voice constructions of Amendments II–VIII); and in *Prigg*, to Article IV, section 2's Fugitive Slave Clause ("shall be delivered up"). In contrast, the Court said that restrictions on the states must expressly identify "state," and typically took the active voice (as in Article I, section 10 "No State shall").[128]

This *Barron-Prigg* rule, it was feared, could plausibly apply to that other provision of Article IV, section 2: the Privileges and Immunities Clause. Much as the Supreme Court had effectively held that the Due Process Clause reads, "No person shall be deprived *by the federal government* of life, liberty, or property without due process of law" (as Bingham expressly pointed out),[129] the Court might hold that the Privileges and Immunities Clause should be read, "The citizens of each state shall be entitled *by the federal government* to all privileges," and so forth.

In their speeches inaugurating debate in their respective chambers, both Thaddeus Stevens and Jacob Howard suggested that the *Barron-Prigg* rule was the main rationale for the Amendment's new and enhanced Due Process and Privileges or Immunities Clauses. In the House, Stevens noted that all three prohibitions of Section 1 were "asserted, in some form or other, in our Declaration or organic law. But the Constitution [in these respects] limits only the action of Congress, and is not a limitation on the States." The existing Due Process and Privileges and Immunities Clauses, he suggested, bound only federal authorities. In the Senate, with specific reference to the Privileges or Immunities Clause, Howard likewise noted that although all its "privileges, immunities, and rights" were already asserted—or in his words, "guaranteed" or "recognized"—by Article IV and Amendments I–VIII, these guarantees were not a limitation on the states:

> [T]he course of decision of our courts and the present settled doctrine is, that all these immunities, privileges, rights, thus guaranteed by the Constitution or recognized by it, are secured to the citizen solely as a citizen of the United States and as a party in their courts. They do not operate in the slightest degree as a restraint or prohibition upon State legislation. States are not affected by them, and it has been repeatedly held that the restriction contained in the Constitution against the taking of private property for public use without just compensation is not a restriction upon State legislation, but applies only to the legislation of Congress.[130]

The last allusion there was, of course, to the *Barron* decision.

The purpose of the new phrasing of Section 1, it seems, was not to *overturn* either *Barron* or *Prigg*, but rather to *accept* the rule of construction and specify unambiguously that the states were now fully bound by both Article IV's Privileges and Immunities Clause and the Fifth Amendment's Due Process Clause.

Now a year after the Amendment's adoption, in late 1869, the Supreme Court, in the unanimous decision in *Paul v. Virginia*, would settle the issue: the old Privileges and Immunities Clause does indeed bar certain "legislation by [the] states."[131] Accordingly, in January 1871, Bingham (as chair of the House Judiciary Committee) offered a milder explanation of the original motive: "It had been judicially determined that the first eight articles of amendment of the Constitution were not limitations on the power of the States, and it was apprehended that the same *might be held* of the provision of the second section, fourth article."[132]

As to the "*Barron-Prigg* rule," the reader will note that neither Stevens nor Howard, in 1866, nor Bingham in 1871, made any reference to *Prigg* in connection with Section 1. Howard and Bingham alluded only to *Barron*, while Stevens mentioned neither case. This silence was almost entirely political. While the "*Barron* contrarians" (in Akhil Amar's nice term) were few in number and mild of spirit, in the Republican coalition, the *Prigg* contrarians (or perhaps, the "anti-*Prigg* prigs") had been numerous and indignant—including Bingham.[133] Any focus on *Prigg* would have divided the Republican caucus. Hence, Howard and Bingham had good reason to explain the Amendment as a corrective to *Barron*, which had never occasioned bitter divisions.

Second, by the most authoritative accounts, the old formula excluded from its protection not only territorial citizens but also citizens in their home states.[134] The entitlement "in the *several* States," was read, contra-textually, to mean "in the *other* States." Ohio's Shellabarger accepted that interpretation as authoritative, without apparent complaint.[135] But Iowa's James Wilson said so with lament: if only, he said, "the States should admit, and practice the admission, a citizen does not surrender these rights because he may happen to be a citizen of the State which would deprive him of them," then the Civil Rights Act would have been unnecessary.[136]

The Amendment would now unambiguously protect every citizen in every state, including his or her home state, and not merely sojourners from other states. And it would encompass even those territorial "citizens of the United States" who were citizens of no state. As Indiana's governor explained, the Clause concerned all "citizens of the United States," including any that "may not be citizens of any State."[137]

Third, the old Clause, according to many prominent authorities, secured fundamental rights only against interstate discrimination.[138] Consequently, American citizens, in many states, had been subject to discrimination and outright exclusion on other bases—chiefly race and opinion (antislavery or loyalist). The strictly interstate-equality reading had served to defeat their constitutional claims under Article IV.[139]

It was probably this crabbed reading (though now "orthodox") that Senator Poland had in mind when he mentioned slavery's practical nullification of the old Clause. The *Worcester Daily Spy* likewise endorsed the Privileges or Immunities Clause as redressing the "years of false interpretation," that had been "fatal" to the "vital spirit of the constitution."[140]

For many, creedal discrimination was chief among the evils to be remedied by the new Clause. Similarly, Maryland's Senator John Creswell told voters that it would restore the old Clause that already protected these "privileges and immunities" but had "been interpreted differently." In particular, "in some of the Rebel States the people say now, that loyal men shall not settle among them."[141] Ohio's William Dennison explained the Amendment as a vindication of Article IV. Republicans had not been free to enjoy their privileges and immunities, but the Amendment would now secure "to every citizen a right to go where he pleases within the limits of the United States, and then and there to assert his high and noble rights and dignity as an American citizen."[142]

During the fall campaign, the *Chicago Tribune* would elaborate on this point in an extended, learned editorial, entitled "American Citizenship." Here the emphasis was not on creedal, but racial and other hereditary discrimination. Despite Article IV, section 2, Americans still lacked a "uniform citizenship," because each state had authority to exclude citizens from various civil rights. The problem was that the old Privileges and Immunities Clause had been "expounded as only meaning that a citizen of Maine moving into another State is entitled only to the privileges and immunities which the laws of that other State accords to the citizens of Maine of his class." The Amendment would correct this "anomalous condition of civil rights," by declaring that the citizen of the Union "shall no longer be deprived of his civil rights by the local regulations of any of its parts."

> [T]he naturalized Irishman, the naturalized German, the Yankee, and last, but not less horrible, the colored man [will have] the right to enter any court of justice, and there on terms of equality, to be plaintiff in any action against any of the first families. [The Amendment] gives to either of these classes, in defiance of State laws to the contrary, the right to purchase and hold real estate, to sell and lease the same, and, when dying, to devise it; it even permits them to inherit as heirs, or receive as devisees, real and personal property on an equality with the old first-class people.[143]

That is to say, the Amendment now secured the citizen against not only interstate discrimination but also all hereditary and national-origin discrimination.

Note that the motive (and hence expected application) of this correction was to expand the interstate-equality rule to encompass interracial and creedal equality. Still, this egalitarian motive would not exhaust the meaning. This equality would result from the establishment of a uniform standard of nationwide privileges. Senator Creswell, for instance, noted that by Section 1, a "citizen of the United States" would no longer, in some states, be denied the "privileges and immunities" that he enjoyed in "other states."[144] The *Burlington Free Press* (in Poland's home state) likewise explained that "the privileges and immunities of citizens of the United Stiles shall [no longer] be subject to the varying caprices and prejudices which may prevail in different States."[145]

Celebrating ratification, the *Chicago Tribune* noted that Section 1 would secure the "legal equality of all citizens of the United States," but by a "common citizenship" to belong to a citizen "wherever he may be" and no longer a hodge-podge of "citizenships, each varying and to be varied according to the whims and passions of a majority in each State."[146]

Fourth, the new Amendment supplemented the old constitutional guarantee with a new express congressional power. By many accounts, especially among *Prigg* opponents, the old Privileges and Immunities Clause lacked any federal enforcement mechanism. Hence, in his opening speech, Representative Stevens announced, "This amendment supplies that defect, and allows Congress to correct the unjust legislation of the States, so far that the law which operates upon one man shall operate equally upon all."[147] And in his leadoff speech, Senator Howard likewise noted that if these fundamental guarantees "are to be effectuated and enforced, as they assuredly ought to be, that additional power should be given to Congress to that end. This is done by the fifth section of this amendment . . . a power not found in the [current] Constitution."[148]

But here again, note the lack of Republican unity. Some believed that *Prigg* had already established an adequate foundation for such congressional power. Congress could and must enforce *all* the mandates of the Constitution, equally with the Fugitive Slave Clause. Iowa's James Wilson, an old Whig but Free Soiler, had relied on *Prigg* to claim that the Civil Rights Act was an exercise of Congress's power to enforce, against the states, both the Privileges and Immunities and the Due Process Clauses.[149] But many demurred. To men like Bingham, such reasoning was identical to the argument *ad absurdum* they had leveled against *Prigg* before the War.[150] Bingham, thus, sought an amendment to *grant* decidedly new powers to Congress. For him, the measure was *delegatory*.

Maryland Senator Creswell seemed to take a middle approach. Section 1 was already in the Constitution, but "it has been interpreted differently" so a corrective amendment was necessary.

> We intend by these provisions to empower Congress to legislate upon the subject, and design to remove [Due Process and Privileges and Immunities] from the [class] of mere guaranties, as they used to be called, and to place them among the express powers, so that wherever in this broad land, any man, a citizen of the United States, shall he assailed in any of his rights of life, liberty or property, he shall be able to throw around his shoulders the protecting aegis of the Stars and Stripes, and say, "I am an American citizen, and no man dare assail me, because the Constitution and the laws protect me the world over."[151]

Section 1, as enhanced by Section 5, would be corrective and clarificatory; it was somewhere between purely declaratory and purely delegatory.

So when speaking collectively, Republicans had to hedge their language.[152] As to Section 1, the Joint Committee was largely noncommittal: the Amendment would "determine" certain civil rights and privileges, without specifying further how the Amendment would change the Constitution by imposing truly new restrictions on the states. And Section 5 would provide Congress with an "express grant" of enforcement power. The Committee thus left open the question of whether the Constitution already included an "implied grant" of such authority to enforce the Privileges and Immunities or Due Process Clauses.

In sum, a constitutional enhancement to the old Privileges and Immunities Clause was indeed necessary for one or more of at least four disparate reasons: (1) to clearly bind the states to respect these privileges and immunities (as a corrective to the *Baron-Prigg* rule), (2) to secure these rights to all citizens in all the states (not just citizens of other states), (3) to protect these rights against all infringement (not merely interstate discrimination), and (4) to arm Congress with an express and therefore undeniable power to enforce this restriction against the states. Republicans did not seem united on any one of these reasons.

Parenthetically, we may notice how Republican disunity as to the meaning of the existing Constitution has impaired our ability to ascertain the original meaning of their amendment to it. The disagreement concerned the precise effect of these changes. In what sense were the prohibitions of Section 1 restrictive and not merely declaratory? To what extent, if any, was the "express" power of Section 5 delegatory and not merely declaratory? Where such disagreement threatened the Republican coalition, Republican leaders tended to remain silent.

At the same time, for our purposes, I must emphasize that in no respect did this veiled disunity as to the effect of Sections 1 and 5 indicate any dispute as to their meaning. The real dissensus concerned the meaning of the Constitution of 1865.

Why Distinguish "Privileges" from "Immunities"?

If, as the Maryland Supreme Court had said in 1797, the words "privileges" and "immunities" are "synonymous, or nearly so,"[153] why this repetition? If an immunity was just a type of privilege, and if every privilege implied an immunity, for what good reason did the authors of the Fourteenth Amendment distinguish "immunities" from "privileges"?

An immediate answer can be found in the drafters' purpose. The goal was to redress certain present injustices by enhancements to undoubted provisions of the old Constitution. The authors of the original Constitution had referred to the "privileges and immunities of citizens," so the Amendment's authors followed suit—even if the original repetition was an error.

Moreover, not only the constitutional text, but a certain interpretive tradition had already distinguished "privileges" from "immunities." Various authoritative enumerations of the rights of citizenship had included, first, various *privileges to* certain goods (travel, residence, property acquisition), and second, certain *immunities from* unequal taxes or other burdens. This order appeared in the Articles of Confederation,[154] in *Campbell v. Morris* (Md. 1797) (the first reported state interpretation of the Privileges and Immunities Clause),[155] and in *Corfield* (the leading federal exposition of the same).[156] In a similar vein, as Hermine Herta Meyer observed, congressional drafters of the Second Freedmen's Bureau and Civil Rights Bills deliberately listed certain affirmative "civil rights" followed by separate "immunities" against racially defined liabilities.[157] The demarcation was especially clear in the Bureau Bill; the category, certain "rights and immunities," was expressly divided into the "civil right[s] secured to white persons" (e.g., to make and enforce contracts, acquire property, etc.) and the immunities against "any other or different punishment than white persons are subject to for the commission of like acts or offences."[158]

The tradition, in turn, provided a significant conceptual clarification. Some of the rights of citizenship implied an affirmative entitlement. The rights to petition, to sue, to testify, for instance, all implied not merely an immunity against obstacles but also a right to be received. They were not reducible to "leave me alone." These involved the right to *participate*, to be welcome in the deliberations of the community. But "immunities," strictly speaking, consisted *only* in an exemption from certain coercion. Hence, in his famous letter to the Hebrew congregation in Rhode Island, President Washington had used the term with a certain precision. He remarked that in all the states, Jews, equally with Christians, enjoyed "liberty of conscience and immunities of citizenship." He omitted "privileges," for in some states non-Protestants did not enjoy equal *political* rights of citizenship.[159]

Moreover, when discussed in reference to citizenship, the distinction between privileges and immunities also corresponded roughly to the distinction between substantive and equality rights. The affirmative privileges of citizenship lent themselves to a universal baseline of substantive rights, while the immunities *of citizenship* took an exclusively egalitarian form. Commenting on a draft of the Civil Rights Act, Representative James Wilson said the word "immunities" guarantees "citizens of the United States *equality in the exemptions* of the law. A colored citizen, because he is colored, shall not be subject to obligations, duties, pains, and penalties from which other citizens are *exempted*."[160]

As early as January, Bingham and his colleagues on the Committee seemed to have understood this distinction between "privileges" and "immunities." On January 9, Bingham told the full House that he was seeking a delegatory amendment to empower Congress to enforce the Privileges and Immunities Clause, in order to secure "equal and exact justice to all men."[161] On January 24, the Committee chairman, Senator Fessenden, appointed him as chairman of the three-man "subcommittee on the powers of congress."[162] The next day, Bingham alerted the full House that the Joint Committee was considering a measure to grant an "express power to the Congress of the United States to enforce in behalf of every citizen of every State and of every Territory in the Union the rights which were guarantied to him from the beginning" in the Constitution, and here mentioned the Due Process Clause.[163] Two days later, Bingham presented to the Committee the subcommittee's proposal to empower Congress to secure, to persons, the rights of life, liberty, and property, and to "citizens of the United States" the "same immunities." Bingham and his colleagues almost certainly understood these two powers to concern, respectively, the Due Process Clause and the Privileges and Immunities Clause.

But the latter power initially encompassed only certain "immunities." The omission of "privileges" here was surely deliberate. Bingham and the subcommittee, it seems, initially tailored the proposal to the particular evils of the time: the injustice of laws imposing racially discriminatory *munia*. There was no need for Congress to enforce the "privileges" because all the evils of the black codes, even those affecting rights of speech and arms, arose entirely from the imposition of unequal burdens on the basis of race—and thus were violations of the immunities of citizenship.

But this tailored approach tended to obscure the proposal's grounding in the existing Constitution. Hence, as we noted, on February 3, Bingham would redraft the proposal to relate the measure more clearly to the broader language of the existing Constitution. Bingham was so eager to emphasize the relation that he (1) quoted virtually the whole "privileges" and "immunities" provision, (2) thus changed "citizens of the United States" back to "citizens in each State," (3) reordered the two clauses so they appeared not in the logical sequence but in the original textual sequence—Article IV and then the Fifth Amendment—and (4) in an excess of caution, temporarily included express parenthetical references.[164]

In vindicating this revised version, Bingham expressly noted the distinction between the affirmative, substantive "privileges" to be provided (or not withheld), and the negative, egalitarian "immunities" not to be burdened:

> Who ever before heard that any State had reserved to itself the right, under the Constitution of the United States, to *withhold* from any citizen of the United States within its limits, under any pretext whatever, any of the *privileges* of a citizen of the United States, or to *impose* upon him, no matter from what State he may have come, any *burden* contrary to that provision of the Constitution which declares that the citizen shall be entitled in the several States to all the *immunities* of a citizen of the United States?
>
> What does the word immunity in [Article IV] mean? *Exemption from unequal burdens.*[165]

So the privileges of citizens were something affirmative, something that the states may not "withhold," but the immunities of citizens were negative rights, exemptions from certain "unequal burdens" that a state may not "impose."[166]

Even with the new draft, Bingham still understood the principal motive to be security of "immunities" from unequal burdens, and chiefly racially unequal burdens. In the House debate, New York's Giles Hotchkiss noted that Bingham's manifest object was "to provide that no State shall discriminate between its citizens and give one class of citizens greater rights than it confers upon another." Bingham replied, with apparent agreement, that the restriction was implied by Article IV—if only the states would not "interfere, those *immunities* follow."[167]

This distinction between egalitarian motive and broader meaning was, as we noted, evident in Massachusetts Governor Bullock's brief exposition of Section 1. By his careful phrasing, he indicated that the guarantees for the "immunities of citizens" and "equal protection" both concerned "civil equality," while the "privileges of citizens" and "due process" involved something else.[168]

In sum, both a certain tradition and the drafting history provide substantial evidence that the Amendment's authors viewed "immunities" as materially distinct from "privileges." Immunity meant *only* exemption, and the "immunities of citizens" meant exemptions from certain unequal burdens (racial *munia*, for instance). In contrast, privileges seemed to refer to some affirmative substantive rights that did not seem reducible to either equality or an exemption from coercion. To be sure, the principal if not sole motive was the protection of these "immunities," but the Privileges or Immunities Clause would encompass certain affirmative "privileges" as well.

Of Citizens of the United States, As Such

Both these "privileges" and "immunities" are "of" citizens of the United States. Does "of" serve to identify the class of persons, the class of rights, or both?

With Richard Aynes and Akhil Amar, I think the evidence overwhelmingly supports the third answer.[169] These rights pertain to citizens of the United States, *as such*—that is, they were the rights of *citizenship*, and more specifically of citizenship *of the United States*. As Amar writes, the phrase is best read as "defining the rights of Americans as Americans."[170]

The Supreme Court had already unanimously indicated this understanding. A decade before, in *Conner v. Elliott*, the Court held that these "privileges and immunities" were solely those that pertained to "citizenship."[171] In *Corfield*, Justice Washington likewise explained that the "privileges and immunities of citizens" under Article IV were "fundamental"; they belonged, "of right, to the citizens of all free governments." [172]

Moreover, Washington further indicated that at least some of these rights were subject to local specification or determination, but in all the states of the Union—the rights of citizens *of the United States*. They "have, at all times, been enjoyed by the citizens of the several states which compose this Union, from the time of their becoming free, independent, and sovereign." Accordingly, as his enumeration indicates, these rights included both the universal citizenship rights to the territory, markets, and tribunals, but also certain specifications of these rights by our Anglo-American law, chiefly procedural rights like "the benefit of the writ of habeas corpus."[173]

Therefore, we see that the specification "of the United States," by referring to rights to be enjoyed by all Americans, throughout the Union, served two purposes. On the one hand, it provided some determinations or specifications, peculiar to all the United States. These specifications might include, in addition to habeas corpus, the freedom from prior restraint as an American specification of the general freedom of discussion. On the other hand, as we saw in previous chapters, the term also made abundantly clear that the term could not include political rights, for states properly served these rights to only some citizens.

This understanding prevailed throughout the official discussion of the Amendment. In the House, various speakers said that the Amendment would secure to every "citizen of the United States the natural rights which necessarily pertain to *citizenship*" or the "fundamental rights of *citizenship*"[174] In the Senate, Wisconsin's Timothy Howe likewise referred to the "necessary rights of citizenship."[175]

In his main speech to his colleagues, Senator Howard unambiguously said the same. He told his Senate colleagues that the Privileges or Immunities Clause "relates to the privileges and immunities of citizens of the United States, *as such*, and as distinguished from all other persons not citizens of the United States."[176] Furthermore, his enumeration included a number of rights peculiar to American citizenship, such as habeas corpus and trial by jury of the vicinage.

In the states, various governors likewise called these privileges and immunities the rights of citizenship, *per se*. Tennessee's governor told his legislature that the Amendment guaranteed "the civil rights of the citizens" to which they were "entitled" by "the very laws of nature."[177] In their transmittal messages, the governors of Louisiana and Illinois mentioned, respectively, "the rights of citizenship," and the "civil rights" that "citizenship confers."[178] In a campaign address, Indiana's Governor Morton declared that "citizens of the United States, *as such*, though they may not be citizens of any State, have *certain great privileges or immunities* which are not to be abridged or interfered with by the laws of any State."[179]

Many other commentators said the Amendment secured the rights of citizenship. The leading Democrat on the Joint Committee, Reverdy Johnson, wrote that the Clause secured only those rights "incident to citizenship," belonging to *all* citizens of the United States, "irrespective of age, residence, sex or color."[180] Various prominent citizens, in newspapers and speeches, said the same.[181]

But there are two countervailing considerations. *First*, there seems to be substantial contradictory evidence. Various prominent officials seemed to conflate these privileges with general human rights. This commentary appeared chiefly in two contexts: (1) congressional speeches supporting the constitutionality of the Civil Rights Act, and (2) campaign speeches emphasizing the exclusion of political rights from Section 1. Lyman Trumbull, for instance, said that the Act included rights that were among "those inherent, fundamental rights which belong to *free citizens or free men* in all countries."[182] William Lawrence said that the Act vindicates the equality "before the law" of "all men in their civil rights," that is, such "rights of citizenship" as the "right to life, liberty, acquire property."[183] And, in the campaign, John Logan reassured Illinois's voters that the Amendment secured, not the suffrage, but "only protection of great natural rights, being equivalent of a declaration that every man is a human being."[184] Roscoe Conkling likewise explained that Section 1 "has no reference to the right to vote nor to any rights except those which belong to all human beings in this country."[185]

Still, I think we have reason to treat these remarks as relatively insignificant to the original understanding of Section 1. The speakers made no effort to square this equivalence with the sheer text, which made a naked distinction between persons and citizens. Moreover, there is reason to suspect, from the context of the remarks, that speakers were tempted to deliberate obfuscation. Proponents of the Civil Rights Act, relying on an implausible reading of the Thirteenth Amendment, had reason to argue that freedom, *ipso facto*, made the former slave not just a "freeman" but also a "citizen," for thereby the Act could be justified as an exercise of Congress's power under the Amendment. By this implausible reading, Congress's power to emancipate could thus be warped into a power to enfranchise with civil rights—freedom from slavery required admission to the privilege of holding real estate.[186] The reading required the absurd assertion that freedom necessarily implied citizenship—and thus an obfuscation of the rights of "free men" and those of "citizens."

A temptation to obfuscate also affected speakers during the Campaign of 1866. Many voters in the Midwest fiercely opposed black political equality but did favor universal emancipation and blacks' enjoyment of other basic human rights. The speakers, then, had reason to allay racist fears, not by any subtle nuance as to the "civil" v. "political" rights of citizenship (as one sees in the Joint Committee's Report), but rather to dig a wide and comforting chasm between universal human rights and black suffrage. It was easier to call free blacks fellow men than fellow Americans, and thus better to say that the Amendment secured human rights rather than the rights of citizenship. The result was to ignore the civil rights of citizenship lying in between the rights of personhood and the peculiar privileges of the elector, and thus to obscure the meaning of the Privileges or Immunities Clause.

Second, there is a conceptual obstacle: to define these rights as privileges of citizenship seems to leave us with an empty set. By custom, if not express constitutional right, aliens often enjoyed, equally with citizens, various rights of travel, commerce, speech, and so on. As Lawrence Solum has contended, to limit "privileges or immunities to those rights that are possessed by citizens of the United States qua their status as national citizens results in an extremely narrow set of privileges or immunities."[187] In fact, the set may be empty, as there were probably no rights for which citizenship was both a necessary and sufficient condition, except, perhaps, the enjoyment of the naked status "citizen."[188] American citizenship, it seems, has no exclusive privileges except the nametag.

But our inquiry does not seek those rights that only citizens enjoy, but those that citizens enjoy "of right." Aliens may indeed enjoy all of these rights—but not to the same extent as citizens. Very often the undoubted privileges of membership are extended to nonmembers. To use an analogy, the members of a tennis club have, by right of membership, the privilege to use the courts owned by the club; still, for various reasons, the club may permit nonmembers to use the courts (e.g., by permitting youth teams access). This extension may be such that nonmembers use the courts more frequently than members do. Such indulgence, such frequency, does not alter the fact that the use of the courts is still a privilege of membership; members, more than nonmembers, have a greater right to the courts, and will have different and greater reason to object if access is denied.

To pursue our inquiry, we might consider three ways in which noncitizens, despite their alienage, may still share in these rights of citizenship.

First, as to the territory and markets, the citizen, as a matter of justice, has the right to share in these goods. But for reasons of prudence and/or generosity, a community may extend one or more of the rights of trade or travel to foreigners. As Blackstone said, for the "advancement of trade," England has made an "indulgence to strangers" whereby aliens may enter and acquire and convey personal property.[189] These rights belong to members "of right," but to aliens only by "indulgence."

Second, as to many procedural rights of citizenship, aliens may also enjoy them "of right" precisely because they incidentally overlap with the requirements of due process of law owed to all human persons. For instance, the writ of habeas corpus, by requiring that detentions be publicized, and the right to trial by jury, by securing the decision to the person's "vicinage," were deemed privileges of citizenship insofar as these protected the criminal defendant as a member of the political community. At the same time, because these "usages and modes of proceeding" had become so well-established, they were also essential to that due process of law owed to all persons—even sojourners with little connection to either the community to be notified by habeas relief or empowered through the jury.

Third, some of the rights of citizenship, particularly arms and speech, had a dual aspect—one with reference to civic membership, and the other with reference to the person's anterior relation to self, household, or God. These rights thus sometimes appeared as privileges of citizenship, or fundamental human rights, or both. The right to bear arms, for instance, can be referred to the right of communal self-protection, "the best security of a free State," but also the right of the individual to defend himself and his household. Similarly, as Aristotle explained, discussion as to "the advantageous and the harmful, and hence also the just and the unjust" is essential to the political partnership as well as the household.[190] And, of course, speech is essential to the natural right of each human person to worship almighty God according to the dictates of his or her conscience. Hence, in the new state constitutions approved by Congress in 1867–1868, one finds the right to bear arms secured to "the people" or "every citizen" for both the defense of "himself and the state."[191] As to the freedom of speech, some states, like Georgia, emphasized its civic function: "Freedom of speech and freedom of the press are inherent elements of *political liberty*" and therefore, "every *citizen* may freely speak, or write, or print on any subject, but be responsible for the abuse of the liberty."[192] Conversely, Arkansas emphasized speech as a human right: "The free communication of thoughts and opinions is one of the invaluable *rights of man*, and all *persons* may freely speak, write and publish their sentiments on all subjects, being responsible for the abuse of such right."[193]

This difference of emphasis did not mean a difference of opinion. Insofar as one was bearing arms or speaking with reference to the public good, these rights were privileges of citizens, as such.

An Enumeration: More Tedious than Difficult?

What then are these determinate rights of American citizenship—these fundamental rights that (1) belong to the citizens under all free governments, and (2) in the manner that these rights have been enjoyed by the free citizens of the United States since Independence?

The authors of the Amendment did not provide us with an exhaustive list. At least one congressman anticipated the problem we still face. In the fall of 1865, before the start of the Thirty-Ninth Congress, Senator Lot Morrill of Maine privately sketched a constitutional amendment that would have redressed the evils of 1865 by saying that all "citizens of the United States," (1) are "equally entitled to protection in life liberty & property," (2) are "equal in their civil rights immunities & privileges," and (3) should enjoy the "elective franchise" free from any "distinction . . . on account of race, des[c]ent, or color." This proposal anticipated the same three evils in the South that confronted the Joint Committee: (1) unequal denial of protection, (2) inequality in various other civil rights, and (3) the unjust distribution of political power. Morrill seemingly thought the first and third proposals were adequately clear, but as to the second, he wondered whether "the words, civil rights, immunities, privileges," had "such precise & definite meaning as to be practicable" or "must we specify, rights of citizenship, residence in the state—to hold property, be a party and witness in [court]," and so forth.[194]

Morrill's comment is quite exasperating to us. He should have pressed this concern in Congress. More aggravating is the insouciance displayed by Justice Bushrod Washington in his *Corfield* opinion: "What these fundamental principles are, it would perhaps be more tedious than difficult to enumerate."[195] So he breezily mentioned only a handful of examples. Jacob Howard was, for some reason or other, anxious to withhold any full enumeration; in his notes, after he listed various privileges and immunities, he gave himself this reminder: "Don't *attempt* to define these."[196]

Scholars have sought to complete this list, but without success. Proponents of the three rival readings have relied on their respective source texts: (1) the Declaration of Independence, (2) the Bill of Rights, and (3) the Civil Rights Act.

Each of these starting points has failed to provide a full and persuasive exposition of these privileges and immunities. If "the beginning" is truly "more than one half of the whole," then any error here would be fatal.[197]

The error, I believe, that has crippled all these approaches is this: these documents are a bad place to begin. None of them is a list of the rights of citizenship; none was drafted to specify the rights of civic membership. In the Declaration, the Founders set forth a series of "self-evident truths" concerning natural rights of man and the revolutionary right of the people, with no attention paid to how "men" might become a "people," and rights of membership in a people. The fact that the American people existed, as "one people," and were fellow citizens, was simply assumed.

Neither was the national Bill of Rights a declaration of Americans' privileges. Rather, the Bill provides a list of various fundamental principles—including certain religious and procedural rights, belonging to all human beings, as well as rights of "the people." The distinction between personhood and citizenship, while suggested by the text, did little to determine the enumeration of rights. It was not the nature of the rights involved, but the nature of the powers restrained or defined, that determined the sequence. The express purpose of the amendments was to prevent "misconstruction" or "abuse" of the *powers* of the central government, so the Amendments proceed by addressing, first the legislative power (Amendment I), then, chiefly (but not exclusively), the executive power (Amendments II–IV), and then the judicial power (Amendments V–VIII).[198]

Nor did citizenship govern the enumeration in the Civil Rights Act. The list of rights bears no resemblance to any traditional conception of citizenship. Instead, the list seems to reflect the usual list of rights granted to a corporation: the power to make enforceable contracts, to sue and be sued, and to acquire property.[199]

We might well ask why Congress chose to model the freedmen's statutory rights on the customary rights of a corporation. I think it probable that the drafters were anticipating a judicial challenge to the law and seeking to establish a constitutional basis for a federal statute. Henry Wilson, an old Whig, was apparently the first to craft such a list, in his bill "to enforce" the just-ratified Thirteenth Amendment.[200] His list, we might speculate, reflected an effort to lay the groundwork for a peculiar and tenuous constitutional claim: Congress's enforcement power under the Thirteenth Amendment implied the power to "charter" new freedmen with the same rights that Congress had given the Bank of the United States, as upheld in *McCulloch v. Maryland*.[201] If Congress can *give* such rights to mere corporations, the argument might go, why cannot Congress *secure* those same rights to Americans?

Whatever may be the reason for these enumerations, neither the Declaration of Independence, nor the Bill of Rights, nor the Civil Rights Act has provided a reliable launchpad for identifying the rights of *citizenship*. But where can we find a point of departure for our inquiry?

As indicated in the prior chapter, I submit that Aristotle provides our best initial guide.

Why should we rely on some long-dead Athenian to understand modern American citizenship? There are three reasons. First, Aristotle was still, in 1866, the premier authority on "citizenship." Second, it turns out, even today the practices of nation states confirm Aristotle's insights. As Siegfried Wiessner found, in his meticulous comparative study of legal systems, the possession of *nationality* (membership) still normally entails certain enhanced rights to enter and remain in a nation's territory, and to participate in the nation's markets, tribunals, and public life.[202] Third, Aristotle's account provides us with a very serviceable set of categories in which to identify *all* the "privileges" and "immunities" of citizenship recognized in 1866.

The Privileges of American Citizenship

All of the rights that American officials generally recognized as privileges of citizenship, before and during the adoption of the Amendment, seem to fall into six categories—the same six parts of the commonwealth identified by Aristotle, those six shared goods of the community: territory, markets, intermarriage, tribunals, public deliberations, and arms. I am aware of no exception.

Territory

The citizen's right to participate in the territory of our commonwealth included the right to travel and reside throughout the Union. This right was mentioned near-ubiquitously, even though omitted from the Declaration, the Bill of Rights, or the

Civil Rights Act. The Supreme Court had mentioned this right in *Dred Scott*, Justice Washington mentioned it first in *Corfield*, and thus Howard mentioned it as well, as did many other participants during the adoption of the Amendment.[203] The matter seemed wholly uncontroversial.

Markets

The citizen's right to participate in the commonwealth's markets included the right to make enforceable contracts, and the right to acquire, hold, and convey property of all kinds, real as well as personal. Before and during the Amendment's adoption, judicial and congressional authorities regularly, and without controversy, included this right among the privileges of citizenship.[204] This right seemed to include the right to participate in all lawful modes of acquiring and conveying property, including earning a livelihood in the professions.[205]

Intermarriage

As I elaborated in a prior article, the citizen's right to intermarriage was what Roman law called the *ius connubii*—the right to intermarry with other citizens, including across class lines (plebeians and patricians), with the issue of such marriage recognized as full citizens. At the same time, in the Christian West, at least, marriage did not arise from citizenship. Marriage and parenthood were understood as fundamental human relations, anterior to the political community. But at the same time, citizenship provided a means to facilitate exogamy, intermarriage across lines of household, clan, and the like. This right of intermarriage consisted chiefly in both an immunity against barriers to exogamy, such as caste, creed, and so on, and the privilege of legitimizing offspring: the offspring of such marriages would be received as full citizens.[206] A multistate, multicreedal, and multiracial citizenry implied the right to marry across state, creedal, and racial lines.

For the most part, English and American authorities had had little occasion to even mention intermarriage as a right of citizenship. In modern times, aliens could generally intermarry citizens without impediment, so any conceptual relation between intermarriage and citizenship became obscure.[207] Moreover, in England and America, the broad *ius soli* rule avoided the delicacy of identifying paternity and thus legitimizing persons as the offspring of a citizen-father and citizen-mother. Sheer maternal presence, at the time of birth, was enough.

But American slavery, and the resulting American apartheid, gave rise to an American peculiarity: local statutes, in many states, invalidated or prohibited intermarriage between whites and blacks. As one jurist noted soon after the Civil War,

> Race, color and social rank, do not appear to constitute an impediment to marriage at common law, nor is any such impediment now recognized in England. But by local statutes in some of the United States, intermarriage has been discouraged between persons of [different] races. With the recent extinction of slavery, many of these laws have passed into oblivion.[208]

These statutes are so familiar to our history that we may lose sight of their sheer absurdity. The right of intermarriage was plainly essential to the very concept of a common citizenship. In our multiracial and multistate republic, laws prohibiting interracial marriage were as irreconcilable with our Union as laws against interstate marriage. However imprudent or prudent might be marriages across lines of clan, race, or state, the very notion of a common country precludes any legal barriers to such exogamy.

Before and during the adoption of the Amendment, advocates of black citizenship were sometimes reluctant to address the issue, for interracial marriage was widely disapproved. Nonetheless, one can glean a prevailing (but not unanimous) original consensus that the Amendment would prohibit the states from making or enforcing laws invalidating or prohibiting interracial marriage.

In my lengthy prior study, I drew the following conclusion:

> Opponents of black citizenship [often] insisted that free blacks' enjoyment of the status and privileges of citizenship would invalidate racial-endogamy laws. Some proponents of multiracial citizenship demurred (at least impliedly), but others plainly agreed with opponents. Still, many proponents treated the issue with deafening silence—but a silence that can best be interpreted as tacit agreement with opponents.[209]

Furthermore, during and immediately after ratification (1866–1873), nearly all Republican judges concluded that such laws had been invalidated by the Civil Rights Act and/or the Amendment.[210]

Tribunals

Our tribunals are critical to the protection of individual life, liberty, and property. And because these courts may not only protect but also threaten those same rights with unjust harm, the rights of judicial protection and process belong to the human person as such. In this sense, these rights are rights of personhood, not privileges of citizenship.

Still, even within the tribunals, the citizen, as such, has certain privileges. To identify these, we can distinguish the citizen in four capacities in which he may appear: as suitor, witness, defendant, and convict.

The citizen has special rights as a suitor. He or she has a right to file suits in defense of not only his or her own person, property, or reputation, but also the public good. Such suits may have included *qui tam* actions,[211] abatements of a common nuisance,[212] suits for punitive damages,[213] and challenges to sovereign immunity.[214]

Such suits also included the right to request a writ of habeas corpus on behalf of a detained third party. The most notable instance was the writ requested in 1852 by Louis Napoleon, "a colored citizen" of New York, to compel a traveling Virginian slaveholder, Jonathan Lemmon, to give cause for detaining eight persons as slaves in New York.[215] Napoleon's suit led first to these persons' immediate emancipation and then protracted litigation that generated nationwide debate on the rights of traveling slaveholders under the Privileges and Immunities Clause.[216]

Accordingly, before and during the making of the Amendment, officials concurred that the privileges of citizenship included the right, as Justice Washington phrased it, "to institute and maintain actions *of any kind* in the courts of the state."[217] Congress enumerated the right "to sue" in the Civil Rights Act; and many Republicans, in Congress and elsewhere, mentioned the right as a privilege of citizenship.[218]

Second, the citizen can appear as a witness. Here too the right may be a matter of human dignity: he may, as a complaining witness, civil defendant, or otherwise, testify on behalf of, or in defense of himself, his household, business partners, and so forth. In this respect, testimony is a right of personhood. But the citizen, as such, may also testify even where he has no such private interest, but only a public interest, as a member of the community.

In this latter respect, the exclusion of black persons' testimony was a badge not so much of slavery but of alienage. In 1854, California's Supreme Court explained the implication with approval. The purpose of the exclusion was "to throw around the [bona-fide] *citizen* a protection for life and property, which could only be secured by removing him above the corrupting influences of degraded castes." If non-whites had the equal right to testify, the "same rule would admit them to *all* the equal rights of *citizenship*."[219]

This distinction between personhood and citizenship is necessary to understand how the postbellum black codes defined the freedmen's right to testify. Acquiescing to black freedom, but still hostile to black citizenship, southern white lawmakers accepted black testimony—but only in cases in which black persons were interested. For example, Florida's 1865 constitution provided that in all proceedings "founded upon injury to a colored person," or otherwise "affecting the rights and remedies of colored persons, no person shall be incompetent to testify as a witness on account of color" but "in all other cases, the testimony of colored persons shall be excluded, unless made competent by future legislation."[220] The implication was that in disputes between citizens (all of them white), blacks' testimony was disfavored if not unwelcome.

In response, the Amendment's supporters declared emphatically that African Americans, as citizens, had an equal right, with other citizens, to "give evidence" in *all* cases[221] and "in any court," especially "when the facts might be within their knowledge."[222] As members of the community, they had a right (and duty) to participate, *especially* in criminal cases, where the community itself was harmed.[223]

Third, the citizen can appear as a defendant. For the most part, the rights of the defendant are mostly in furtherance of human dignity. Still, some of these rights secured either his or her interests as a citizen, or even the interests of the whole community. These included his general right of the citizen to "be sued" in local courts, as stated by the Civil Rights Act, and then reaffirmed by various supporters of the Amendment.[224] We might also add the right of the citizen, when charged with a crime, to return to his community during the pendency of the criminal proceeding—and hence Howard's express mention of security against "excessive bail."[225]

Of these procedural rights, two were especially prominent in Anglo-American law: the writ of *habeas corpus* and trial by jury of the vicinage. These were so important that "we the people" enumerated them in the original Constitution. Conversely, so *civic* were these rights that at times they were limited to only community members. Most notably, in the Northwest Ordinance, Congress guaranteed these rights *only* to "inhabitants," all while protecting every "person" or "man" in religious freedom and various other procedural rights.[226]

Accordingly, during the adoption of the Amendment, Jacob Howard and some other proponents declared that the privileges of citizenship included both the rights of habeas corpus and trial by jury.[227] The claim was elaborated by some African American leaders in the Midwest. Ohio's John Mercer Langston told the Missouri legislature that the citizen's privilege to trial by an "impartial jury of his peers" required the exclusion from the jury of all those "surcharged with prejudice" and the inclusion of "citizens . . . the legal and political equals of the person charged with crime before them, however black he may be."[228] The Illinois Convention of Colored Men asked rhetorically, "And where is the American citizen who does not deem this very sacred and time-honored right an essential part of his citizenship?" By the total exclusion of African Americans from juries, "no colored citizen . . . can have the reasonable privilege or right to be confronted by a jury composed either wholly or in part, of his equals," a right, they mentioned, was already "privileges and immunities of citizens" secured by Article IV.[229] By this account, the Amendment, properly enforced, would require modification of the whites-only laws whereby a black defendant might be tried by a jury from which members of his race were systematically excluded. This right was not the political right to serve on a jury, but the civil right to be tried by one's peers in the community.

Finally, the citizen can be convicted of a crime. As such, the citizen may thus forfeit the liberty and life necessary to enjoy the rights of membership. Still, even here, the citizen may retain some consideration as a member. He may not be subject to any cruel punishments that are contrary to the ordinary *usages* of his community. In this respect, though extended to all persons by force of due process of law, the immunity against cruel and *unusual* punishments belongs chiefly to the citizen.[230] Hence both Howard and Bingham mentioned this right in connection with the Privileges or Immunities Clause.[231]

Public Discussion

By the original understanding, the privileges of citizenship included the freedoms of discussion. The inclusion of this right is strongly suggested by the drafters' choice of the terms, "make any law" and "abridge." Further, in the decade before the Amendment, this right had been identified as a core privilege of citizenship by the Supreme Court in *Dred Scott* and by other authorities.[232] The right of discussion seems plainly to satisfy Justice Washington's definition of the rights of citizenship; his own law teacher, James Wilson, had written, "[t]he *citizen under a free government* has a right to think, to speak, to write, to print, and to publish freely, but with decency and truth, concerning publick men, publick bodies, and publick measures."[233] Accordingly, as we've noted above, during the discussion of the Amendment, Bingham, Howard, and various other prominent commentators agreed that the privileges included the various rights of public discussion: the freedom of speech (especially the highest forms of speech: loyal and sacred speech), the freedom of the press, and the right to assemble and petition.[234]

Arms

The right to keep and bear arms, like the freedom of discussion, was also endorsed as essential to free citizenship and among the "privileges" secured by the Amendment. Before the War, the federal and state constitutions generally reserved the right to keep and bear arms to "the people" or "the citizens." And as Robert Leider has recently emphasized, the common purpose of such provisions was to enable the citizen to protect, not so much his or her private interests, but the *public* good—the "common defense."[235]

Hence, according to pro-slavery jurists, the non-citizenship of free blacks was demonstrated by their exclusion from arms-bearing. Before the War, Georgia's Supreme Court, for instance, had concluded that a free black man "is not and cannot become a citizen," in part because "he is not allowed to keep or carry fire-arms, [nor] preach or exhort without a special license, on pain of imprisonment, fine and corporeal punishment."[236] Likewise in *Dred Scott*, Taney remarked that if citizens under Article IV, free blacks would be able to travel to other states, and there enjoy not only the rights of public speech, but also "to keep and carry arms wherever they went."[237]

Even after emancipation, some southern states retained such restrictions. Consequently, during the Amendment's adoption, Jacob Howard and other commentators also included arms-bearing among the rights of citizenship secured by the Amendment.[238] In newspapers, the pseudonymous "Madison" and "Moscow," in New York and North Carolina respectively, both listed this right.[239]

Although mentioned with less frequency than rights of commerce and discussion, the identification of arms-bearing as a privilege of citizenship seemed uncontroversial. Instead, the interesting controversies concerned whether certain regulations (e.g., disbanding militias, or banning the carrying of concealed weapons) represented an abridgment of that right.[240]

Constitutional Enumeration and Howard's End

Here, then, is a mass of privileges, some of them found in the most authoritative expositions of Article IV's "privileges and immunities of citizens," and some of them found, more prominently, in the declarations made by the American people in their national Constitution.

Constitutional enumeration, then, is not necessary to a right's inclusion among the fundamental privileges of American citizenship. Indeed, some rights are so foundational, so manifest, that no constitutional declaration was thought necessary. Even under an ordinary despotism, the mere subject, as a member of the community, would have a right to the primary goods of the community: the community's territory, markets, and intermarriage.

But as one ascends to free citizenship, to participation in the public tribunals, public discussion, and public defense, these privileges are less likely to be known, more easily forgotten. And for these, constitutional enumeration seemed necessary.

Such enumeration, in turn, provided powerful evidence that a right has indeed been enjoyed by the free citizens of our United States since Independence. And for good reason, then, Senator Howard relied on such enumerated rights in his exposition of the Privileges or Immunities Clause.

Let's turn, then, to Howard's discussion, as recorded in the *Congressional Globe*:

> To these privileges and immunities [as partly enumerated in *Corfield*] should be added the personal rights guaranteed and secured by the first eight amendments of the Constitution; such as the freedom of speech and of the press; the right of the people peaceably to assemble and petition the Government for a redress of grievances, a right appertaining to each and all the people; the right to keep and to bear arms; the right to be exempted from the quartering of soldiers in a house without the consent of the owner; the right to be exempt from unreasonable searches and seizures, and from any search or seizure except by virtue of a warrant issued upon a formal oath or affidavit: the right of an accused person to be informed of the nature of the accusation against him, and his right to be tried by an impartial jury of the vicinage; and also the right to be secure against excessive bail and against cruel and unusual punishments.[241]

The list appears to have been prepared by someone who had either memorized these Amendments or was reading them while preparing the list, all while making seemingly deliberate omissions and some interpolations. With one exception (the accused person's right to notice), the rights appear precisely in the order in which they appear in the Constitution. And with that same exception, the list, with its conspicuous omissions, corresponds with his prepared handwritten notes.

What was Howard's purpose in providing this partial enumeration, with his omissions and interpolations? No one, I believe, has proposed a satisfactory answer.

I submit that Howard's end was to discern and explain how our Bill of Rights recognized *some* of the rights of citizenship, and more particularly, the rights that belonged to the citizens throughout our Union since Independence. That is to say, his list was a further elaboration of the incomplete list of *Corfield*.

Howard begins by saying that these rights are "guaranteed and secured" by constitutional enumeration. Because these are fundamental rights, as old as the Republic (born 1776), the people's Constitution (drafted 1787–present) can only secure these rights, not create them.

Beginning with the First Amendment, Howard deliberately omits the religion clauses—and for good cause. From the Founding through Reconstruction, Americans agreed that the right to worship God according to the dictates of one's own conscience belonged to the human person as such. By the prevailing opinion, this duty and right was so vital that the human person could not be subject to any compulsory support for religion—however small and remote—in the form of taxation to support some established church.[242] This duty and right of man vis-à-vis God was prior and above citizenship—far beyond the poor power of any human authority to add or detract. For this reason and others (as I hope to elaborate in a subsequent publication) the evidence is clear and convincing that as originally understood, the Privileges or Immunities Clause did not incorporate either of the Religion Clauses against the states.

Howard, instead, begins with undoubted rights of citizenship. These are the rights that the First Amendment protects against *abridgment*: "the freedom of speech and of the press" and "the right of the people peaceably to assemble and petition the Government for a redress of grievances." As to assembly, Howard clarifies that this right pertains "to each and all the people"; that is to say, every citizen, as such, and not only some formal assembly of the citizenry, has the right to meet with others and petition their government.

Howard then turns to the Second Amendment. He mentions another well-established privilege of American citizenship: "the right to keep and to bear arms." Here he omits any mention of militia membership, probably for the same reason that he adds "each and all the people" in reference to the right of assembly: to emphasize that the right belongs to the whole citizenry, and not merely some gathering thereof.

Howard then mentions the Third Amendment's "right to be exempted from the quartering of soldiers in a house without the consent of the owner." Although the security of the home would seem to be a human right, the ownership of real estate may be reserved to citizens; furthermore, alien residents who own their homes (even if only by a leasehold) may be called inchoate citizens. To this extent, the right of the homeowner was a privilege of citizenship. Conversely, Howard omits the Amendment's exception, "in time of war, but in a manner to be prescribed by law." Howard probably thought the exception irrelevant to the Fourteenth Amendment, which restricted only the states. The war power belonged chiefly to the government of the Union.

Howard then mentions, from the Fourth Amendment, the general right "to be exempt from unreasonable searches and seizures," along with the specification thereof, the freedom "from any search or seizure except by virtue of a warrant issued upon a formal oath or affidavit." Howard's inclusion of this exemption, as a right of citizenship, seems compelled by the language of the Fourth Amendment. This right was expressly reserved to "the people" and not "persons." By the sheer text of our Constitution, then, it seems that citizenship, and not humanity, confers a freedom from certain unreasonable coercion. Howard complied.[243]

Nonetheless, we should note that in this respect, the Fourth Amendment was anomalous, probably reflecting one of our Founders' embarrassed concessions to slavery. The traditional view had treated the right to security of person and property as belonging to human persons. Hence, the Massachusetts Constitution (from which the phraseology of the Fourth Amendment seems derived) had guaranteed the freedom from unreasonable searches to every person "subject" to local jurisdiction.[244] But here and elsewhere, slavery distorted tradition. Slavery's enforcement required summary and arbitrary searches and seizures of enslaved persons. Hence, as proposed by three ratifying conventions, from states where slavery was not yet abolished (Virginia,

Pennsylvania, and New York), the freedom from such "unreasonable" coercion was to be limited to "every freeman." But Madison changed the term to "the people," probably to avoid defacing our national bill of rights with any further reference to unfree persons.[245] The result of this veil was (and is) persistent confusion among jurists as to the distinction between certain human rights and the rights of citizenship. Some American lawmakers seemed to have noted the anomaly; the authors of two subsequent state constitutions substituted "persons" for "the people," including the revised 1850 constitution in Michigan (Howard's home state) and the new Constitution drafted 1868 by the biracial loyalists in South Carolina, who restored the pre-1789 association of these rights with personhood.[246]

The foregoing rights all appeared in the transcription of Howard's speech, as provided to various New York newspapers.[247] We now turn to rights and omissions, the mention of which was not reported in any newspaper. Still, with one exception, each appeared in Howard's prepared notes as well as the *Congressional Globe*.[248]

Howard proceeds to completely omit the Fifth Amendment. The omission was plainly necessary not only to avoid the erroneous suggestion that the Fourteenth Amendment's Due Process Clause was superfluous, but also because neither that clause nor any other clause of the Fifth Amendment could qualify as a right belonging to citizens of the free governments of the several states since Independence. The rights protected by the Double Jeopardy, Self-Incrimination, Due Process, and Takings Clauses all secured the integrity of the human person, in his natural rights of bodily integrity, locomotion, conscience, and property. Like religious freedom, they concerned matters of fundamental human dignity, prior to and distinct from the person's relation to the commonwealth.

In contrast, the grand-jury indictment had some connection with civic membership. Howard omits it probably because it did not qualify as a right enjoyed in the several states since Independence. In Howard's home state—in 1859 (when he was its attorney general)—the state passed a statute that rejected the grand jury.[249]

Howard next turns to the Sixth Amendment and mentions "the right of an accused person to be informed of the nature of the accusation against him." As printed in the *Globe*, this comment was probably an error. It was anomalous in three respects. First, it is the only one that is mentioned out of the order in which it appears in the Bill of Rights. Second, it is the only term omitted from Howard's prepared notes. Third, it is difficult to see how this basic right to notice could be a privilege of citizenship. I cannot venture an explanation for the error, whether by the *Globe*'s editor or someone else. Still, the right's inclusion is the chief evidence against the argument I have advanced here: that Howard carefully distinguished the rights of citizenship from those of personhood.

Howard then mentions, from the Sixth Amendment, the citizen's "right to be tried by an impartial jury of the vicinage." As we saw, many deemed this right to be fundamental to American citizenship. Howard's addition of the term "vicinage" emphasizes this communal relation: the accused citizen's right to be tried by his or her neighbors.

As to the rest of the Sixth Amendment, Howard omits it entirely: the right to a "speedy" trial, to a district determined "by law," to compulsory process for favorable witnesses, and to assistance of counsel. Here again, each of these guarantees concerns the defendant as a human being, and not as a member of our political community.

Howard omits entirely the Seventh Amendment. Like the right of habeas corpus and trial by jury in criminal cases, the right arguably pertained to American citizenship. Indeed, the same Congress that proposed the Bill of Rights also, in the Judiciary Act of 1789, partly reserved this right to persons who were "citizens of the United States."[250] Still, unlike those two rights, the civil jury was never so universally established as to belong to the citizens of *all* our states.[251] And as Fairman pointed out, during the pendency of the Fourteenth Amendment, Congress accepted at least two state constitutions that withheld the jury from certain civil actions covered by the Seventh Amendment.[252] This right, then, was arguably a privilege of citizenship in some states, but not of the Union. The lack of universality was such that the right is neither a privilege of American citizenship nor an essential element of due process of law.[253]

Finally, turning to the Eighth Amendment, Howard mentions "the right to be secure against excessive bail and against cruel and unusual punishments." As we saw, both these rights concern the person, as defendant and convict, as a member of our political community.

Conversely, Howard conspicuously omits the freedom from "excessive fines." That immunity concerns the human person, as such. Consider the Magna Carta:

> A freeman shall not be amerced for a slight offense, except in accordance with the degree of the offense; and for a grave offense he shall be amerced in accordance with the gravity of the offense, yet saving always his "contentment"; and a merchant in the same way, saving his "merchandise"; and a villein shall be amerced in the same way, saving his "wainage."[254]

These concerns as to proportionality and the convict's livelihood both are referable to the human being as such. The limitation is an immunity of humanity, not of citizenship; it belongs, of right, to the alien equally with the citizen.[255]

The Immunities of American Citizenship

As we saw, the "immunities" of American citizenship, as distinct from other privileges, were understood to consist exclusively of exemptions from certain "unequal burdens." Any law that imposed on the citizen such unequal burdens (*munia*) would thereby abridge his or her *in-munia* as a citizen of the United States.

In defining these forbidden unequal burdens, at least two questions present themselves: (1) What represents a "burden" that the laws impose, whether justly or unjustly? And (2) what inequalities make a burden the sort of "unequal burden," the exemption from which is a fundamental immunity of citizenship?

Burdens: Fiscal and Regulatory

The notion of a burden, imposed by law, seems straightforward. A burden is something external, some weight imposed on someone or something. A law-imposed burden arises when a state makes and enforces a law, resulting in an imposition by legal coercion on someone. A burden, then, is not the state denial or withholding of a benefit; there is no *immunity* against a *denial*. Bingham, then, properly identified the abridgement of an immunity as the imposition of a burden.[256]

State-imposed burdens or *munia* seem to fall into two categories. First, the state may impose fiscal burdens, via taxes and other takings of property. Second, the state may impose criminal and other regulatory burdens by establishing rules and punishments.

Both fiscal and regulatory burdens featured prominently in discussions of the privileges and immunities of citizenship, both before and during the adoption of the Amendment. In *Corfield*, Justice Washington mentioned "an exemption from higher taxes or impositions than are paid by the other citizens of the state."[257] In *Dred Scott*, Chief Justice Taney referred to an immunity from racially defined criminal liability.[258] That latter immunity featured prominently in the Civil Rights Act: the citizen's right, equally with white citizens, to "like punishment, pains, and penalties, and to none other." Further, during the Amendment's adoption, proponents contended that Section 1 encompassed an immunity from discriminatory taxation and criminal liability. Senator Howe called racially discriminatory taxation a "crime" to be barred by the Amendment's Privileges or Immunities Clause—and its guarantee of "equal laws."[259] Senator Howard likewise said the Amendment would abolish, in the criminal laws, all "caste" legislation among citizens of the United States: "when one measure of justice is to be meted out to a member of one caste while another and a different measure is meted out to the member of another caste, both castes being alike citizens of the United States."[260]

Forbidden Inequalities: Blood, Soil, Creed

Of course, not all "burdens" are precluded by the "immunities of citizenship." Burdens are commonplace. Like death, taxes (and rules) will always be with us.

Nor do these immunities bar all "unequal burdens." The Amendment cannot nullify *all* unequal burdens. All laws imposing burdens discriminate, and on countless bases. Unequal classifications appear throughout the tax and criminal codes—and many of these classifications are (arguably) grossly unjust or imprudent.

What peculiar sorts of inequality, as to fiscal or criminal liabilities, offend the Fourteenth Amendment? This question has bedeviled American constitutional law for generations. The only point of consensus seems to be that the Amendment, by one provision or another, categorically (or nearly so) prohibits any state from making or enforcing any law which shall impose on an American citizen any racially unequal tax or criminal liability. But there is no consensus either as to what specific provision establishes this ban, or as to what other sorts of inequalities are likewise unlawful.

Still, as we have indicated here, both the naked text and the drafting history strongly suggest that the principal textual foundation for this "immunity" against racial burdens is the Privileges or *Immunities* Clause. Accordingly, after the Amendment's adoption (1868–1873), challenges to racially discriminatory laws generally were under the Privileges or Immunities Clause and not the Equal Protection Clause.[261]

If so, then, we can refine our inquiry further: we are seeking a certain type of immunity—the immunities of citizenship. We can therefore set aside the immunities of alienage (e.g., against liability for treason) or the immunities of humanity (e.g., against arbitrary coercion). Our goal is to identify those unequal burdens whereby a *citizen* is treated like an alien: what we might call the badges or burdens of alienage. What unequal burdens, besides racial burdens, represent such badges of alienage?

The contemporaneous discussion of the Amendment points to an answer. Across thousands of pages of discussion, officials seemed to identify three and only three illegitimate bases for imposing a burden on the citizen.

First and foremost, officials mentioned *hereditary* classifications. Of these, racial discrimination was the Amendment's principal target. More precisely, the immediate evil to redress was hereditary discrimination against the African freedmen and their descendants. The freedmen, markedly distinct by color, had been subject to hereditary servitude and alienage. Therefore, to secure these citizens' rights against the badges of alienage, the Amendment was designed to bar "discrimination . . . because of race, color, or previous condition of [hereditary] servitude," to use the formula initially adopted by the Joint Committee.[262]

According to some proponents, the revised (Bingham) version likewise barred any "regard" or "reference" to race. Louisiana's governor said it would secure "the rights of citizenship to all persons, without reference to race or color."[263] Ohio's Senator John Sherman told voters that the only effect of Section 1 was "that every body—man, woman and child—without regard to color, should have equal rights before the law; that is all there is in it." And John Geary, in his successful campaign for the Pennsylvania governorship, explained that the citizen, "without respect to color . . . shall be entitled to receive civil rights in all the States and Territories; the Amendment thus conformed with a provision already made in Pennsylvania by "our fathers": that everyone "without regard to color, so far as civil rights were concerned, should be equal before the law."[264] Several opponents in the Midwest likewise emphasized this race-neutral rule, but often to allege that it would extend to equal political rights.[265]

Parenthetically, this anti-"regard" formula would bind state legislators to be deliberately color-indifferent, and not exactly "color-blind" or "color-unconscious." To require the lawmakers' indifference seems more reasonable than to require their blindness or unconsciousness as to naked facts of color.

Various officials spoke more broadly, however, and indicated that the measure would prohibit all other hereditary burdens. Recall the popular petition that was repeatedly referred to the Joint Committee: "[N]o State shall make any distinction in civil rights or privileges on account of race, color, or *parentage* among any of the citizens of the United States."[266] As suggested by the Joint Committee's formal explanation and other sources, Section 1 seems to have likewise broadly barred hereditary discrimination. Several officials, such as Jacob Howard, and members of the Pennsylvania legislature, said the measure barred discrimination on the basis of "caste"[267] (the primary meaning of which, according to Webster's dictionary, was "hereditary class").[268] The *Chicago Tribune* elaborated the broad effect against all hereditary burdens. The Amendment would "knock down the barrier [of] aristocracy," and secure to "the naturalized Irishman, the naturalized German, the Yankee, and last, but not less horrible, the colored man," the right to go into all the states, and therein enjoy, in rights of property and commerce, "equality" with "any of the first families," that is, the "the old first-class people."[269]

Second, less frequently, the Amendment's supporters said it also barred *geographic* discrimination. As an enhancement of the old Privileges and Immunities Clause, of course the measure would ban interstate as well as interracial discrimination. Tennessee's governor explained that besides securing the freedmen's civil rights, Section 1 would "also prevent unjust and oppressive discrimination by one State against the citizens of other States."[270] Various commentators concurred.[271] The secondary evil to be redressed, then, was that southern states would, vis-à-vis northern citizens, not only withhold the equal protection of the laws, but also impose onerous legal burdens. Just after ratification was announced, Bingham explained the danger in a candid interview: Without the Amendment, he said, if a northerner went to the southern states, the former rebels "could tax his property to the extent of confiscation," and then use such confiscatory taxes "to pay for their lost n-----s."[272]

The freedom from discrimination on the basis of place, however, extended beyond state-origin discrimination but also national-origin discrimination. For instance, in 1867, Representative William Kelley of Pennsylvania celebrated the equality of all American citizens in every state, regardless of state or country of origin:

> No matter whether from the South or New England, or the Liffey or the Shannon, the Danube or the Rhine, the little words, "Our country," were dear to every man, and to none as much as to an American. . . . In this country, no matter where a man was born, he is entitled to all the privileges and immunities of every State as soon as he is naturalized; and if the citizen of Tennessee chose to go to Pennsylvania he can do so, and still be at home. . . . Into whatever State he may go he is still an American citizen; and if they chose to go to the late Russian possessions, to enter upon the ice trade or hunt walruses, they could do so, and [I] would recommend them to take a large American flag with them and hang it on the North pole.[273]

Third, even less frequently, supporters said that the Amendment prohibited *creedal* discrimination. Early in the Thirty-Ninth Congress, some Republicans urged Congress to proceed from the principle of equal rights, regardless of race, color, *or creed*.[274] In April 1866, Ohio's William Lawrence argued that the old Privileges and Immunities Clause already mandated such creedal and racial equality.[275]

Accordingly, after Congress proposed the Amendment, various commentators saw in it a ban on such discrimination. Senator Howe told voters that Section 1 prohibited creedal as well as racial discrimination. By this amendment . . . we propose to say that even if a majority "cherishes" some "animosity . . . it must not find expression in their legislation—that they must make equal laws for loyal and disloyal, for white and for black, let their feeling be what they may. [Cheers]."[276]

In a similar vein, during formal ratification debates, some state legislators in Wisconsin and Pennsylvania explained that Section 1 would guarantee equal rights "regardless of color, race, or creed," or "without distinction of race, color or religion."[277] On July 4, 1866, the *Chicago Tribune* likewise claimed that the Amendment (and other Republican policies) reflected the great principle of equal rights, "without distinction of color, race or religion."[278]

Many other Republicans implied the same, by appropriating the old Jeffersonian formula that had always treated creedal discrimination, along with interstate discrimination, as illicit. In his first inaugural address, Jefferson celebrated, as *first* among "the essential principles of our government. . . . Equal and exact justice to all men, of whatever state or persuasion, religious or political."[279] For antebellum Democrats, this principle became a favorite slogan. President Franklin Pierce likewise celebrated "the constitutional equality of each and all of the citizens of the United States as citizens, whatever their religion, wherever their birth or their residence."[280] On January 9, 1866, Bingham found the principle already embodied in Article IV's Privileges and Immunities Clause, and explained that he hoped for an amendment to give Congress the power to fully enforce that principle.[281] And during the Campaign of 1866, Bingham again appropriated this Jeffersonian slogan to explain the proposed Amendment.[282]

Of course, Jefferson, Pierce, and other Democrats had always omitted race from the list of required equalities. But Republicans were happy to correct the mistake.[283] A decade later, in their last great civil rights measure, Republicans began the Civil Rights Act of 1875 in these terms:

> we recognize the equality of all men before the law, and hold that it is the duty of government in its dealings with the people to mete out *equal and exact justice* to all, of whatever nativity, *race*, color, or persuasion, religious or political.[284]

By Reconstruction, it was hoped, racial discrimination would now be treated like creedal discrimination—as fundamentally un-American.

These three bases—heredity, geography, and creed—are the only forms of discrimination that seemed to violate the Amendment's guarantee of equal citizenship. To my knowledge, no other form of inequality was mentioned by any participant in the adoption of the Amendment, whether supporter or opponent.

Various scholars have suggested that sex and marital-status discrimination should be included along with race. The principal basis for this analogy is a comment that New York's Robert Hale made in challenging Bingham's initial "equal protection" power. Hale noted that sex and many forms of classifications were no more and no less "unequal" than racial classifications, and thus Congress would have the power to rewrite the entire law of marriage.

But Hale was referring not to equal citizenship, encompassed by the "privileges and immunities of citizens," but to the "extremely vague, loose, and indefinite" language as to "equal protection"[285] found in the February draft. As we saw, when that language was modified by "*of the laws*" in April, the new version satisfied Hale and other Republicans. The context suggests the reason: the qualifier left to the states the authority to make or modify laws defining protection, with the forbidden denial limited to a refusal to enforce such laws.

For the most part, there was a deafening silence as to countless other forms of discrimination, including sex, age, wealth, and so on. One congressman drew a sharp contrast between creedal and racial discrimination and those other classifications. William Lawrence declared that "mere race or color, *as among citizens*, never can" be a licit basis for discrimination. In contrast, "distinctions created by nature of sex, age, insanity, &c, are recognized as modifying conditions and privileges."[286]

Why did Lawrence expressly (and his colleagues tacitly) dismiss any concern with such forms of discrimination? Some scholars have attributed this opinion to blindness as to the injustice of sex and various other "class" distinctions.[287] Like his contemporaries, it seems, Lawrence was woefully ignorant of women's claims to equal rights.

To the contrary, the injustice of sex discrimination was, then, a matter of prominent public discussion. As we noted, the reform of marital coverture was a hot topic. Indeed, while making the Amendment, legislators were pursuing sex equality in various other areas. Some of the same midwestern legislatures that ratified the Amendment also voted for sex equality in the state's universities[288] and proposed state constitutional amendments eliminating "male" as a prerequisite for voting.[289] But at the same time, there is no evidence that anyone claimed that the Amendment compelled such reforms.

Many other proposals of this sort were advanced at this time. In the House of Representatives, for instance, one congressman proposed a measure to ban sex discrimination in federal employment. He seemed to think that his colleagues would agree with his egalitarian opinions. He remarked,

> This is a dictate of common honesty, of reason, and of justice; in fact, instinct, without reason, would feel and understand the justice of this. . . . The question whether men or women should be employed should depend, not on sex, but on qualifications, merits, and claims to Government consideration.[290]

This egalitarian congressman, incidentally, was Ohio's William Lawrence.

Recall that our inquiry is to identify those unequal burdens that represent burdens of alienage. The officials that adopted the Fourteenth Amendment seemed to think that, although sex inequality in some respects was unjust, only hereditary, geographic, and creedal burdens violated the Amendment.

What distinguished these three forms of discrimination from others? Once again, we find an answer to our question "rolling around our feet."[291] These three categories—blood, soil, and creed—are precisely the same that our Republic has always used to distinguish members from nonmembers—and for good cause: These discriminations arise from the nature of the *citizenry*, as a community of households (blood), sharing a common territory (soil), and governed by a common constitution (creed).

But as to ordinary civil rights, any fiscal or regulatory burden is an injustice. Whatever is necessary in defining members from nonmembers becomes, among members, an injustice. A duty at the border of the citizenry becomes a crime among the citizenry. By imposing burdens on undoubted citizens, on the basis of their parentage, place of birth or residence, or creed—the lawmaker effectively calls into question the validity of their citizenship. Even the slightest burden, even a one-penny tax, is an intolerable badge of alienage, and thus an abridgment of the immunities of citizenship.

At the same time, as to political rights, these same distinctions may also be necessary and proper. What's necessary at the border of the citizenry may also be appropriate in distributing political power. From the beginning, our Republic has nakedly discriminated on the basis of creed in assigning political authority. We require all legislators and officers, federal and state, to take an oath to "support this Constitution."[292] And at the Founding (controversially), some states even required some officials to profess a religious creed. During Reconstruction, officials and even voters were subject to new creedal oaths, many of them approved by Congress. While most required mere loyalty to the Union,[293] in at least two states (Arkansas and Alabama), prospective voters had to endorse not only the Union, but also the civil and political equality of all, regardless of race, color, or previous condition of servitude.[294]

As to soil, political inequality is commonplace. From the beginning, we have routinely distributed political rights based on place of residence. Residence in a particular state remains a requirement to represent "the people" thereof, whether as a voter or legislator, whether at the ballot box or in Congress.[295]

Indirect Abridgments of Immunities—and Segregation

In sum, the privileges and immunities of citizens of the United States consist in those affirmative rights and exemptions from certain unequal burdens which privileges and immunities belong, of right, to the citizens of all free government and have been enjoyed throughout the Union of the several states since 1776. These privileges include the right to participate in the territory, markets, intermarriage, tribunals, public discussion, and armed defense of the commonwealth, as such. Conversely, these immunities are exemptions from any fiscal or regulatory burdens imposed on the basis of the citizen's heredity, place of birth or residence, or creed, whether political or religious.

This answer, of course, gives rise to countless other subordinate interpretive questions that are beyond the scope of this study. Still, I provide a brief comment on one perennial issue.

Do these immunities entail the citizen's equal right, regardless of race, creed, and so forth, to certain nonprotective benefits, like public employment, healthcare, and education?

At first glance, the answer must be no. The Equal Protection Clause prohibits the denial of one benefit only—the protection of the laws. The *immunities* of citizenship represent exemptions from burdens and not entitlements to benefits.

Conversely, perhaps one could speak of the *privileges* of public education. But as Earl Maltz has argued, these benefits were created by state law,[296] and indeed had not been enjoyed throughout the Union since 1776, so they could not qualify as fundamental "privileges" of American citizenship that every state must provide to the citizenry.

Still, insofar as governmental benefits are derived from taxes and other takings, any discrimination in the distribution of these revenues would seem to represent an *indirect burden* on the taxpayers. So, for instance, any creedal, geographic, or racial discrimination in the distribution of benefits would thus indirectly but emphatically abridge one of the "immunities of citizens of the United States." As Douglas Smith has elaborated, this same consideration may invalidate all racial preferences: "If the term 'immunity' could be so construed, then to the extent that a race-conscious admissions program imposed unequal burdens on various classes of citizens, it would be unconstitutional."[297]

This inference seems quite persuasive. Any racial, geographic, and creedal discrimination in the distribution of benefits would seem to indirectly abridge the immunities of citizens of the United States. Any laws imposing such indirect *munia* violate the Clause.

Still, various prevalent discriminatory practices would seem to preclude such an interpretation of the Amendment. Then, as now, geographic discrimination was ubiquitous in the distribution of such benefits as education. Then, but less so now, racial discrimination was common (but not ubiquitous) in the distribution of educational benefits, chiefly in the form of racially segregated schools. And this discrimination was legal in northern states like New York, Pennsylvania, and Ohio—the very places that the Amendment's authors said would be unaffected by it.[298]

These questions are difficult to answer. Our inquiry is hampered by both the silence of the Amendment's framers and the obscurity generated by our own heated controversies. Still, the framers probably would have said something like the following.

As to geographic discrimination, the distinction arises by necessity, by the nature of the good provided. If, as was then believed, the household had the primary responsibility for providing food, health, and education to its members, then the political community could only supplement, not supplant, the household. As an auxiliary to the household, these benefits should be financed and distributed on a local basis, close to the household. A state could not, for instance, justly distribute schooling (an extension of the home) on a geography-blind basis. Some attention to the location of the household was necessary.

As to racial discrimination, the nature of the benefit did not require any such separation. Common citizenship required common schools. Indeed, any racially defined burden, requiring an American child to travel further from her home to receive schooling, was adverse to the very nature of the benefit by burdening that household.

Accordingly, while the Amendment was pending, a minority of Americans, chiefly northern African Americans, contended that equal citizenship precluded racially segregated schools. In Fall 1866, conventions of "colored citizens" in Indiana and Illinois insisted on their equal right to the common schools in closest proximity to their homes.[299]

The Illinois Convention of Colored Men made a persuasive constitutional case of obvious relevance to the pending Amendment. By Article IV's Privileges and

Immunities Clause, they were "entitled to equal rights before the law," and thus an immunity against "all discriminations on account of color or race." On this race-blind basis, "all the people" must have "the benefit in common of the free schools."[300]

The Convention rejected the state's current policy, by which colored citizens had separate schools funded by separate taxation. The Convention found the policy still unequal in two respects: (1) colored citizens would not enjoy, in common with others, the land grants once made from the common national property—in which colored citizens had an interest as much as whites; and (2) their children would have additional travel burdens, as they could not enjoy "the well organized and ably conducted schools in the districts *where they reside*."[301]

Nonetheless, most white citizens, in most states, were simply unwilling to accept the interracial household and by extension, the interracial school. Despite supporting an amendment to establish our common citizenship, many were reluctant to accept common schools.

At the same time, the education of the citizenry was an immediate moral and constitutional necessity. And this necessity, I believe, made lawful the immediate establishment of schools, even if still segregated.

Indiana's Governor Morton seemed to understand that this contingent necessity made racial segregation permissible. In his January 1867 address to the Indiana legislature, he recommended both the ratification of the Amendment and the speedy establishment of separate schools "for colored children,"—a reform, he said, was required by the spirit of the Civil Rights Act, the spirit and letter of the state's constitution, and more generally "justice, humanity, and sound policy."[302]

Still, he took pains to provide a justification for this racial separation. He gestured toward a particular contingent necessity: "I would not recommend that white and colored children be placed together in the same schools, believing, as I do, in the *present state of public opinion*, that to do so would create dissatisfaction and conflict, and impair the usefulness of the schools."[303] The people of Indiana were then simply too racist for common schools.

I think it probable that the prevailing opinion among the northern leaders whose support was essential to both winning the Civil War and the passing of the Reconstruction Amendments was as follows:

(1) that human personhood, and therefore freedom, as secured by the Thirteenth Amendment, is prior to citizenship secured by the Fourteenth;
(2) that as to citizenship, the enjoyment of the privileges thereof is more important than an immunity against any indirect racial tax or other such burden;
(3) that education is necessary to maintain and enjoy both this human freedom and these privileges of citizenship, especially participation in the commonwealth's markets and public discussions;
(4) that the brute facts of widespread poverty and ignorance preclude reliance exclusively on privately funded education; and
(5) that at least two other brute facts effectively make racial integration impossible:

(a) the stubborn prejudices of the whites throughout the Union, and
(b) the fresh memories of the unspeakable evils of both slavery and the war to end slavery, especially in the South.

Therefore, the states then had the compelling moral and constitutional duty, under the Thirteenth and Fourteenth Amendments, to secure to all Americans, especially the freedmen, the rights of freedom and citizenship, by the *immediate* establishment of general taxpayer-funded education. The duty was so compelling that the states must acquiesce to present necessity—*only while the necessity prevailed*—of a real but relatively minor violation of the Fourteenth Amendment: an indirect abridgment of the immunity against racial burdens.

Consider, in this regard, these remarks by Chief Justice Chase in 1867:

> Chief Justice Chase was present to-night in Richmond at the dedication of the Normal High School building for colored persons. He delivered an address, and said, by the Grace of God that the fetters had been struck from the limbs of millions of slaves, and they had become free. Having become freedmen, they had now become citizens with all of the *responsibilities and privileges of citizens*; being citizens, *it was necessary that they should be educated to accomplish this end*. The teachers at first came from the north, then sects were formed to further the object, and he was glad to know that the great society of which he had the honor to be President had been instrumental in erecting the building which was being dedicated and which he hoped would accomplish much good. The work of educating the freedmen was just begun, but by organized efforts much would be enforced.
>
> The day was *not far distant* when the States of the South would have a system of free schools in which all might be educated—schools in which there would be *no discrimination*.[304]

Chase, perhaps, thus suggested something like the following:

> Education and segregation today.
>
> Education and segregation tomorrow.
>
> Education and desegregation, some day soon—with all deliberate speed.

Notes

1 Quoted in Joseph B. James, The Framing of the Fourteenth Amendment 30 (1956). *See also* Howard Jay Graham, Everyman's Constitution; Historical Essays on the Fourteenth Amendment, the "Conspiracy Theory," and American Constitutionalism 302 (1968) (identifying Lot Morrill, not Justin Morrill, as the author).

2 *See generally, supra* ch. 2.

3 Ilan Wurman, The Second Founding: An Introduction to the Fourteenth Amendment 137 (2020) (contending that to "abridge" civil rights means to "give civil rights based on arbitrary distinctions"); John Harrison, *Reconstructing the Privileges or Immunities Clause*, 101 Yale L.J. 1385, 1457 (1992) (concluding that the forbidden abridgement extended to restrict a right according to any "arbitrary or irrational" criterion); Christopher Green, Equal Citizenship, Civil Rights and the Constitution The Original Sense of the Privileges or Immunities 43 (2015) (contending that "abridgement . . . was a standard way to express inequality"); William Baude et al., *General Law and the Fourteenth Amendment*, 76 Stan. L. Rev. 1185, 1238–9 (2024) (identifying as legal abridgment any "arbitrary or partial legislation" because it is not at the service of the "public good"). *See* discussion *supra* ch. 3.

4 *See, e.g.*, Ind. Const. art. VII, § 20 (1851); N.Y. Const. art. VI, § 24 (1846); S.C. Const. art. V, § 3 (1868).

5 Pa. Const., Dec. of Rights, § II (1776).

6 *Id.*, Frame of Government, § 10.

7 *See, e.g.*, N.Y. Const. art. VII, § 8 (1821); Ohio Const. art. I, § 11 (1851); Fla. Const. art. I, § 10 (1868); La. Const. art. I, § 5 (1868); *see also* S.C. Const. art. I, §§ 5–6 (1868) & Neb. Const. art. I, §§ 3–4 (1867) (guaranteeing against abridgment both the *person's* right to the freedoms of speech and press and the *people*'s right to assembly).

8 Cong. Globe, 39th Cong. 1st sess. 3039 (June 8).

9 *Scott v. Sandford*, 60 U.S. 393, 417 (1857) (emphasis added).

10 *Hennen v. Hennen*, 12 La. 190, 195 (1838) (emphasis added).

11 Jud Campbell, *The Emergence of Neutrality*, 131 Yale L.J. 861, 887 (2022).

12 *Cincinnati Gazette Co. v. Timberlake*, 10 Ohio St. 548, 555 (1860) (quoting *People v. Crosswell*, 3 Johns. Cas. 337, 393–4, (N.Y. Sup. Ct. 1804) (op. of Kent, J., citing, in turn, argument by Alexander Hamilton).

13 *Cincinnati Gazette*, 10 Ohio St. at 555 (disavowing any intent, by enforcing anti-defamation laws, "to disposition to *abridge* or restrain the liberty of the press, *as thus defined*").

14 *See, e.g.*, William A. Mirola, Redeeming Time: Protestantism and Chicago's Eight-Hour Movement, 1866–1912, at 54 (2014),

15 In Illinois, "while the ratification of the Fourteenth Amendment was pending before the legislature, regulation of monopolistic railroad corporations was discussed with no connection between the two apparently recognized." Joseph B. James, Ratification of the Fourteenth Amendment 172 (1984).

16 Roscoe Conkling, Congress and the President: The Political Problems of 1866, at 25 (1866) (reprinting "Speech of Hon. Roscoe Conkling, Delivered at Mechanics' Hall, Utica, September 13, 1866").

17 *See* Harlan M. Blake, *Employee Agreements Not to Compete*, 73 Harv. L. Rev. 625, 644 (1960) (noting cases, decided roughly contemporaneously with the Amendment, defining the limited enforceability of such contracts).

18 2 James Kent, Commentaries on American Law 137 (George M. Comstock ed. 11th ed. 1867) ("The disability of the wife to contract so as to bind herself arises not from want of discretion, but because she has entered into an indissoluble connection, by which she is placed under the power and protection of her husband").

19 *See, e.g.*, Reverdy Johnson, A Further Consideration of the Dangerous Condition of the Country 15 (1867) (explaining that the Amendment secures every right "incident to citizenship," and to all citizens, "irrespective of age, residence, sex or color").
20 *Speech of Gen. John A. Logan, at Cairo, June 28, 1866*, Chicago Tribune, July 2, 1866, at 1, https://chroniclingamerica.loc.gov/lccn/sn82014064/1866-07-02/ed-1/seq-1/.
21 *Id.*
22 *See* of Ark. Const., art. XII, § 6; Fla. Const., art. V, § 25 (1868); La. Const. art. 123 (1868); S.C. Const. art. XIV, § 8 (1868).
23 Tapping Reeve, The Law of Baron and Femme, at iii. (3d ed. 1862) (quoted in Michael Grossberg, Governing the Hearth: Law and the Family in Nineteenth Century America 27 (2004)).
24 59 U.S. 591 (1856).
25 *Id.* at 593.
26 *See supra* ch. 5.
27 Mo. Const. art. II, § 9 (1865).
28 *Hawkins v. Filkins*, 24 Ark. 286, 320 (1867) (emphasis added).
29 *Id.* at 325.
30 *Cummings v. Missouri*, 71 U.S. 277, 320 (1867) (emphasis added).
31 *Id.* at 322.
32 *Pierce v. Carskadon*, 83 U.S. 234 (1873).
33 *Ex parte Garland*, 71 U.S. 333, 393 (1867) (Miller, J., dissenting) (emphasis added). *Garland*, concerning a federal expurgative oath, was the companion case to *Cummings*, and Miller's dissent in *Garland* was applicable to both cases. *Id.* at 392.
34 *A Candid Confession*, The Wheeling Daily Register, June 20, 1866, at 2, https://chroniclingamerica.loc.gov/lccn/sn84026847/1866-06-20/ed-1/seq-2/.
35 *Id.*
36 *Constitutional Amendment*, The Weekly Caucasian, June 20, 1866, at 2, https://chroniclingamerica.loc.gov/lccn/sn85033995/1866-06-20/ed-1/seq-2/. *See also More Constitution*, The Wheeling Daily Register, July 24, 1868, at 1, https://chroniclingamerica.loc.gov/lccn/sn84026847/1868-07-24/ed-1/seq-1/ ("The second portion of this Amendment declaring that no State shall abridge the privileges or immunities of citizens of the United States, upsets all test oaths, for suitors, lawyers, teachers, and so on. Nevertheless these oaths remain upon the statute books of West Virginia and will continue to be enforced, although abrogated by a Constitutional provision which their authors have approved").
37 *The Test Oath*, The Wheeling Daily Register, June 5, 1866, at 2, https://chroniclingamerica.loc.gov/lccn/sn84026847/1866-06-05/ed-1/seq-2/ (reporting commentary by Reverdy Johnson and other officials correctly predicting the Court's decision and suggesting reasons for a delayed release of the opinion).
38 *Blair v. Ridgely*, 41 Mo. 63, 171–5 (1867) (accepting *Cummings* as a precedent as to the loss of the right to teach but not as to the right to vote); *Murphy & Glover Test Oath Cases*, 41 Mo. 339 (1867). See also Harold Melvin Hyman, Era of the Oath 116 (noting West Virginia's acquiescence)
39 *See, e.g.*, *Ex parte Quarrier*, 4 W. Va. 210 (1870) (noting the recent repeal of the 1866 requirement).
40 *Ex parte Hunter*, 2 W. Va. 122, 144 (1867) (emphasis added).

41 *Ex Parte Garland*, 71 U.S. 333, 384 (1867) (Miller, J., dissenting) ("The right to practise law in the courts as a profession is a privilege granted by the law under such limitations or conditions in each state or government as the lawmaking power may prescribe").

42 Thomas C. Fletcher, First Biennial Message, Jan. 4, 1867, *in* 4 The Messages and Proclamations of the Governors of the State of Missouri 83 (1924) (recommending the repeal of "the ninth section of the second article").

43 *Id.*

44 *Id.* at 81–2 (emphasis added).

45 *Davis v. Pierse*, 7 Minn. 13, 16 (1862).

46 *Id.* at 19, 21–2 (1862) (discussed in Hyman, *supra* note 38, at 116).

47 Calvin Massey, *Privileges or Immunities*, Heritage Guide to the Constitution 501, 501 (2d ed. David F. Forte & Matthew Spaulding, eds. (2014)).

48 John Harrison, *Reconstructing the Privileges or Immunities Clause*, 101 Yale L.J. 1385, 1457–8 (1992) (concluding that the forbidden abridgment extended to restrict a right according to any "arbitrary or irrational" criterion, such that the measure "requires caste-blindness with respect to privileges and immunities of citizens"); Ilan Wurman, The Second Founding: An Introduction to the Fourteenth Amendment 133, 137 (2020) (concluding that the Amendment requires that "one citizen be given the same rights as any other in similar conditions and that any condition must be rational and nonarbitrary"); Green, *supra* note 3, at 43 (contending that "abridgement . . . was a standard way to express inequality"). Two scholars have suggested that the prohibited discrimination is limited to two categories. Philip Hamburger suggests that the Amendment was limited to interstate discrimination. Philip A. Hamburger, *Privileges or Immunities*, 105 Nw. U. L. Rev. 61, 114, 116 (2011) (saying that the Clause provides "[f]urther protection . . . against interstate discrimination"). Raoul Berger wrote that the prohibition extended only to interracial discrimination. Raoul Berger, Government by Judiciary: The Transformation of the Fourteenth Amendment 17–18 (2d ed. 1997).

49 *See, e.g.*, Kurt T. Lash, The Fourteenth Amendment and the Privileges and Immunities of American Citizenship (2014); Richard L. Aynes, *Refined Incorporation and the Fourteenth Amendment*, 33 U. Rich. L. Rev. 289, 299 (1999) ("These threads of history, the evil that prompted the Amendment, the plain meaning of the words of the constitutional Amendment, the legislative history of the Amendment, and the interpretation of the Amendment by constitutional law treatise authors, all converge to support the general conclusion that after the adoption of the Fourteenth Amendment a citizen should be able to enforce the Bill of Rights against the states").

50 *See, e.g.*, Randy E. Barnett & Evan D. Bernick, The Original Meaning of the Fourteenth Amendment: Its Letter and Spirit 22–3, 101 (2021) (mentioning certain civil rights that "specified and protected natural rights"); William Baude et al., *supra* note 3, at 1196–7, 1223 (contending that the Privileges or Immunities Clause protects "civil rights," understood as specifications of "retained natural rights").

51 *See* Articles of Confederation, art. IV (enumerating the rights of "free ingress and regress to and from any other state [and] all the privileges of trade and commerce, subject to the same duties, impositions and restrictions as the inhabitants thereof respectively"); *Campbell v. Morris*, 3 H. & McH. 535, 554 (Md. 1797) (listing "the

peculiar advantage of acquiring and holding real as well as personal property," the protection of such property "by the laws of the state, in the same manner as the property of the citizens of the state is protected" and the exemption from "any taxes or burdens which the property of the citizens is not subject to"); *Corfield v. Coryell*, 6 F. Cas. 546, 552 (C.C.E.D Pa. 1823) (affirming that the privileges and immunities include the "right of a citizen of one state to pass through, or to reside in any other state, for purposes of trade, agriculture, professional pursuits, or otherwise; to claim the benefit of the writ of habeas corpus; to institute and maintain actions of any kind in the courts of the state; to take, hold and dispose of property, either real or personal; and an exemption from higher taxes or impositions than are paid by the other citizens of the state"); *Abbot v. Bayley*, 23 Mass. 89, 92 (1827) (mentioning the "right to sue and be sued as citizens" and "to take and hold real estate"); *Dred Scott v. Sandford*, 60 U.S. 393, 417, 423–4 (1857) (indicating that the privileges and immunities of blacks, if citizens, would include the right to convey real estate and the right to travel wherever one pleases subject only to criminal liabilities for misconduct "for which a white man would be punished").

52 Cong. Globe, 39th Cong., 1st sess. 1115 (Mar. 1).

53 Cong. Globe, 39th Cong., 1st sess. 1757 (Apr. 4, 1866).

54 *Id.*

55 *Id.* at 504 (stating that the proposal "gives the rights of citizenship to all persons without distinction of color"); see also Douglas G. Smith, *A Lockean Analysis of Section One of the Fourteenth Amendment*, 25 Harv. J.L. & Pub. Pol'y 1095, 1111 (noting similar remarks by Representatives William Lawrence (OH) and Martin Thayer (PA) and citing Cong. Globe, 39th Cong., 1st sess. 1152, 1832, 1836).

56 *The Plan of the Reconstruction Committee*, Cleveland Daily Leader, May 1, 1866, at 1, https://chroniclingamerica.loc.gov/lccn/sn85042437/1866-05-01/ed-1/seq-1/.

57 *Letter from Robert Dale Owen*, New-York Tribune, May 19, 1866, at 7, https://chroniclingamerica.loc.gov/lccn/sn83030214/1866-05-19/ed-1/seq-7/.

58 The Wheeling Daily Register, May 1, 1866, at 1, https://chroniclingamerica.loc.gov/lccn/sn84026847/1866-05-01/ed-1/seq-1/ (reprinting report from the *New York World* that the Amendment was attributed to Conkling, who was assisted by Forney).

59 *Reconstruction Report*, The Potter Journal, May 1, 1866, at 2, https://chroniclingamerica.loc.gov/lccn/sn86081096/1866-05-01/ed-1/seq-2/ (printing a letter dated Sunday, April 29, the day after the Committee settled on a proposal).

60 Cong. Globe, 39th Cong., 1st sess. 2459 (May 8).

61 *Id.* at 2462, 2465, 2498, 2502, 2511 (remarks of supporters Garfield, Thayter, Broomall, Raymond, and Eliot); *id.* at 2461, 2467, 2506, 2538 (remarks of opponents Finck, Boyer, Eldridge, and Rogers).

62 *Great Speech of Senator Trumbull*, Chicago Tribune, Aug. 2, 1866, at 4, https://chroniclingamerica.loc.gov/lccn/sn82014064/1866-08-02/ed-1/seq-4/.

63 Speech of Hon. George H. Williams, of Oregon: At Wieting Hall, Syracuse, New York, October 24, 1866, at 5 (1866).

64 Howard Jay Graham, Everyman's Constitution: Historical Essays on the Fourteenth Amendment the 291, n. 73 (2013) ("Virtually every speech in the debates on the amendment—Republican and Democrat alike—said or agreed that the amendment was designed to embody or incorporate the Civil Rights Act."). For discussion in the

states, *see, e.g.*, *Speech of John Sherman at Mozart Hall* (Sept. 28, 1866), in Speeches of the Campaign of 1866, in the States of Ohio, Indiana, and Kentucky 39 (1866) [hereinafter "Campaign Speeches"] ("The first section was an embodiment of the Civil Rights Bill"); *Speech of Hon. Luke P. Poland*, Green-Mountain Freeman, Nov. 7, 1866, at 2, https://chroniclingamerica.loc.gov/lccn/sn84023209/1866-11-07/ed-1/seq-2/ ("The Civil Rights Bill . . . embodies the same principles as are embraced in [Section 1]").

65 Cong. Globe, 39th Cong., 1st sess. 2511 (May 9). But see speech of Poland, *id.* at 2961 (suggesting that the Due Process-Equal Protection Clause and the Civil Rights Act aimed to prohibit the same kind of "partial State legislation").

66 *Speech of Hon. James M. Scovel on the Constitutional Amendment*, The Evening Telegraph, Sept. 11, 1866, at 1, https://chroniclingamerica.loc.gov/lccn/sn83025925/1866-09-11/ed-1/seq-1/.

67 *Speech of Hon. Schuyler Colfax, at Indianapolis, August 7,* in Campaign Speeches, *supra* note 64, at 14.

68 *See supra* chapter 4. *See also Report of the Reconstruction Committee at Last,* The New York Herald, April 30, 1866, at 4, https://chroniclingamerica.loc.gov/lccn/sn83030313/1866-04-30/ed-1/seq-4/ (paraphrasing the first section, that "no State shall make or enforce any law abridging the equal privileges or immunities of citizens of the United States, or denying to any person equal protection under the laws" and commenting that "in regard to the equal privileges and immunities[,] we had supposed the Civil Rights bill was intended to meet the case").

69 *See supra* chapter 4. *Washington Topics and Gossip*, Cleveland Daily Leader, Apr. 18, 1866, at 1, https://chroniclingamerica.loc.gov/lccn/sn85042437/1866-04-18/ed-1/seq-1/.

70 Akhil Reed Amar, The Bill of Rights: Creation and Reconstruction 165 (2008) ("Various critical words of the next phrase—'*make*,' '*any*,' '*law*,' and '*abridge*,'—call to mind the precisely parallel language in parallel sequence of the First Amendment").

71 Michael Zuckert, *On the Fourteenth Amendment: A Textual Analysis*, 48 Perspectives on Pol. Sci. 246, 248 (2019), DOI: 10.1080/10457097.2019.1630208.

72 Amar, *supra* note 70, at 197. *See also* Charles R. Pence, *The Construction of the Fourteenth Amendment*, 25 Am. L. Rev. 536, 537 (1891) ("It would seem therefore too clear for argument that the privileges and immunities of a citizen of the United States are such as are secured to one as a citizen of the United States by its constitution and laws").

73 "These rights are to be determined by a reference to the letter and spirit of our national constitution, and also to the general custom of other nations." William H. Williams, *Arrest of Non-residents for Debt—the Constitutionality of the Law*, 2 Western L.J. 265, 266 (1845).

74 *See* David R. Upham, *The Meanings of the "Privileges and Immunities of Citizens" on the Eve of the Civil War*, 91 Notre Dame L. Rev. 1117, 1152–4, 1157–8 (2016).

75 Cong. Globe, 39th Cong., 1st sess. 1263 (1866).

76 *Id.* at 2542 (May 10).

77 Cong. Globe, 39th Cong., 1st sess. 2765 (May 23).

78 *Governor Dennison's Speech*, *in* Campaign Speeches, *supra* note 64, at 44 (stating that because before the War, citizens could not "go to any of the Southern States and there express [their] opinions freely upon the great questions that were dividing

the American people" therefore "we say now that we will have inserted in the Constitution of the United States, in the form of the proposed amendment, a clause securing to every citizen a right to go where he pleases within the limits of the United States, and then and there to assert his high and noble rights and dignity as an American citizen"); Letter of "Moscow" to Moses Bledsoe, The Tri-Weekly Standard, Oct. 6, 1866, at 2, https://chroniclingamerica.loc.gov/lccn/sn85042146/1866-10-06/ed-1/seq-2/ (enumerating the privileges not to be abridged as follows: "to bear arms, to speak his sentiments freely, to assemble and petition for a redress of grievances, to give testimony, to sue and be sued and to hold property, and to make wills; and no man can deprive him of life, liberty or property without due process of law"). See also David T. Hardy, *Original Popular Understanding of the Fourteenth Amendment as Reflected in the Print Media of 1866–1868*, 30 Whittier L. Rev. 704–6 (2009) (noting that securing to the freedmen the rights of citizenship, including the right to bear arms, was a motive for the *Amendment);* *cf.* Oration of Hon. Rufus Waples, Belmont Chronicle, Aug. 22, 1867, at 1, https://chroniclingamerica.loc.gov/lccn/sn85026241/1867-08-22/ed-1/seq-1/ ("Certainly the right of citizens to meet together to counsel on political affairs is beyond question").

79 *Gov. Jacob Cox's Message to the Legislature*, Ohio Executive Documents 281 (1867), *reprinted in* 2 Reconstruction Amendments: The Essential Documents 335 [hereinafter "Reconstruction Amendments"] (Kurt T. Lash ed. 2021).

80 *Eloquent Speech of Hon. John A. Bingham*, The Wyandot Pioneer, Aug. 23, 1866, at 1, https://chroniclingamerica.loc.gov/lccn/sn87076863/1866-08-23/ed-1/seq-1/.

81 *See* Cong. Globe, 38th Cong. 1st sess. 1202 (Mar. 19, 1864) (Henry Wilson) (charging slavery with nullifying the Privileges and Immunities Clause, which secured the "freedom of religious opinion," and asking rhetorically, as a particularly obnoxious disregard of the "freedom of discussion. . . . On what road of this Republic cursed by slavery have men been free to declare their approval of the divine doctrines of the Declaration of Independence?").

82 *Corfield v. Coryell*, 6 F. Cas. 546, 551–2 (C.C.E.D. Pa. 1823).

83 VA Const., Dec. of Rights, art. I (1776).

84 *See, e.g.*, Barnett and Bernick, *supra* note 50, at 197 (claiming that Washington said that *these* "natural rights were privileges and immunities of citizenship").

85 *See also Douglass v. Stephens*, 1 Del. Ch. 465, 470–1 (1821) (Ridgely, Ch., dissenting) (relying on Blackstone and stating that the "privileges and immunities of citizens," as secured by Article IV, were certain "subordinate rights of the citizen, which serve to protect and maintain inviolate those great and primary rights," that belong to "all men by nature," *viz.*, the "rights of enjoying and defending life and liberty, of acquiring and protecting reputation and property—and, in general, of attaining objects suitable to their condition, without injury to another"). Douglass was cited prominently by counsel in *Corfield. Corfield v. Coryell*, 6 F. Cas. 546, 549 (C.C.E.D. Pa. 1823) (argument of counsel).

86 *Corfield*, 6 F. Cas. at 552.

87 *See, e.g.*, Louise Weinberg, *The McReynolds Mystery Solved*, 89 Denv. U.L. Rev. 133, 136, n. 24 (2011).

88 Cong. Globe, 39th Cong. 1st sess. 2765 (May 23).

89 *Speech of Judge Lawrence at Piqua* (Aug. 15), Bellefontaine Republican, Sept. 21, 1866, at 1.

90 *Tennessee, Governor William Brownlow's Proclamation*, June 19, 1866, *in* Reconstruction Amendments, *supra* note 79, at 243.

91 *Governor's Message* (May 17, 1878), NEB. S. JOUR. 49, 58 (1st–3d sessions, 1867).

92 *See, e.g.*, Charles Fairman, *Does the Fourteenth Amendment Incorporate the Bill of Rights? The Original Understanding*, 2 Stan. L. Rev. 1, 12, 56 (1949).

93 *See generally*, Richard L. Aynes, *On Misreading John Bingham and the Fourteenth Amendment*, 103 Yale L.J. 57 (1993).

94 Green, *supra* note 3, at 117 (resolving the incorporations basic-rights view as an "application of an equality rule to state-to-state disparities").

95 One newspaper editor, however, did make this connection. *The Constitutional Amendment*, Dodgeville Chronicle, Oct. 25, 1866, at 1, https://chroniclingamerica.loc.gov/lccn/sn85033019/1866-10-25/ed-1/seq-1/ ("If a state shall declare that one portion of its citizens may make contracts, but another shall not; that one portion may own land, and another shall not; that one portion, but not another, may carry arms; that one portion may enjoy free speech, but not another, this is an abridgment of that freedom which belongs to all citizens of the United States, and should not be allowed").

96 Akhil Reed Amar, *The Bill of Rights and the Fourteenth Amendment*, 101 Yale L.J. 1193, 1245 (1992) (claiming that "the best reading of the Civil Rights Act suggests that it, too, was understood to incorporate the citizen rights and freedoms of the Bill of Rights").

97 Ilan Wurman, *Reversing Incorporation*, 99 Notre Dame L. Rev. 265, 322 (2023) (finding Amar's account "implausible").

98 Kurt T. Lash, *Enforcing the Rights of Due Process: The Original Relationship between the Fourteenth Amendment and the 1866 Civil Rights Act*, 106 Geo. L.J. 1389 (2018); Kurt Lash, *The State Citizenship Clause*, 25 U. Pa. J. Const. L. 1097 (2024).

99 *See* Sister Mary Jerome Lauer, The Civil Rights Bill of 1866, at 91 (M.A. Thesis, Marquette Univ. 1943), https://www.marquette.edu/library/theses/already_uploaded_to_IR/lauer_m_1943.pdf (providing a nice comparison of Section 1 with the Civil Rights Act).

100 See *supra* text accompanying notes 63–8 (indicating that most commentators who drew the connection cited all of Section 1 and not some part thereof).

101 Barnett and Bernick, *supra* note 50, at 200–1 (indicating that the rights identified as privileges or immunities of citizens (e.g., enumerated in the Civil Rights Act or the Bill of Rights) "can be accurately described as either the means of specifying and protecting natural rights or ensuring impartial treatment of citizens"); Baude, *supra* note 3, at 1223 ("The general-law approach provides the simplest account of how these categories were united in a single phrase").

102 Howard Jay Graham, Everyman's Constitution: Historical Essays on the Fourteenth Amendment, the "Conspiracy Theory," and American Constitutionalism 315 n.80 (1968) ("Senator Howard's own paraphrase seems to indicate selective rather than full or automatic incorporation"); George C. Thomas, *The Fourteenth Amendment and The Bill of Rights: Newspapers and the Fourteenth Amendment: What Did the American Public Know About Section 1?*, 18 J. Contemp. Legal Issues 323, 331 (2009) (noting Donald Dripps' conclusion that Howard's omissions place "him in the selective incorporation camp").

103 Jay S. Bybee, *Taking Liberties With the First Amendment: Congress, Section 5, and the Religious Freedom Restoration Act*, 48 Vand. L. Rev. 1539, 1588 n.230 (1995).

104 *See, e.g.*, Bryan H. Wildenthal, *Nationalizing the Bill of Rights: Revisiting the Original Understanding of the Fourteenth Amendment in 1866–1867*, 68 Ohio St. L.J. 1509, 1607 n.305 (2007) (noting the "fairly extensive—though avowedly non-exhaustive—recitation of Bill of Rights guarantees"); Evan Bernick, *Fourteenth Amendment Confrontation*, 51 Hofstra L. Rev. 1, 43 (2022) (calling Howard's list "explicitly partial and illustrative").

105 Andrew Hyman, *A Comment in Response to Dale Carpenter Regarding Equal Protection*, The Originalism Blog, Nov. 23, 2014, https://originalismblog.typepad.com/the-originalism-blog/2014/11/a-comment-in-response-to-dale-carpenter-regarding-equal-protectionandrew-hyman.html.

106 *Privilege*, Online Etymology Dictionary, https://www.etymonline.com/search?q=privilege; *Immunity*, Online Etymology Dictionary, https://www.etymonline.com/search?q=immunity.

107 10 Op. Att'y Gen. 382, 407 (1862).

108 *Gov. Jacob Cox's Message to the Legislature*, Ohio Executive Documents 281 (1867), *in* Reconstruction Amendments, *supra* note 79, at 305.

109 "And, here, it is pertinent to remark that the affirmative liberties all comprehend 'immunities,' or negative liberties, for their protection. So, the word 'immunities,' it would seem, could have been used alone, in the 14th amendment, to cover all the rights to which the first eight amendments appertain." 2 William Winslow Crosskey, Politics and the Constitution in the History of the United States 1093 (1953).

110 Cong. Globe, 39th Cong. 1st sess. 2944 (June 4) ("I have prepared some remarks with reference to these amendments generally"); The Evening Telegraph, June 5, 1866, at 5, https://chroniclingamerica.loc.gov/lccn/sn83025925/1866-06-05/ed-1/seq-5/ (reporting that Poland "took the floor to deliver a written speech").

111 Cong. Globe, 39th Cong. 1st sess. 2961 (June 5).

112 Chester J. Antieau, *Paul's Perverted Privileges or The True Meaning of the Privileges and Immunities Clause of Article Four*, 9 Wm. & Mary L. Rev. 1, 34 (1967), (declaring the evidence "irrefutable" that the "Congress responsible for proposing the privileges and immunities clause of the Fourteenth Amendment expected thereby to provide better protection for the rights safeguarded by the Fourth Article"); David S. Bogen, Privileges and Immunities: A Reference Guide to the United States Constitution 51 (2003); James E. Bond, No Easy Walk to Freedom: Reconstruction and the Ratification of the Fourteenth Amendment 256–7 (1997); James E. Bond, *The Original Understanding of the Fourteenth Amendment in Illinois, Ohio, and Pennsylvania*, 18 Akron L. Rev. 435, 450 (1985).

113 *Supra* ch. 2.

114 *Supra* ch. 2; see also Upham, *supra* note 74, at 1151–9.

115 Cong. Globe, 39th Cong. 1st sess. 2765 (emphasis added).

116 Chin-Yung Yen, Rights of Citizens and Persons Under the Fourteenth Amendment 31 (Ph.D. Dissertation, Columbia Univ. 1905).

117 The notes are on file with the author and are also available here: https://tifis.org/sources/Howard.pdf. (hereinafter "Howard's Notes").

118 *Id.*

119 *Accord*, Hardy, *supra* note 78, at 714 (2009) (concluding that Howard treated the "Bill of Rights" as "supplementing" the "largely economic liberties listed in Corfield").

120 *Congressional Reports*, National Republican, May 24, 1866, at 3, https://chroniclingamerica.loc.gov/lccn/sn86053571/1866-05-24/ed-1/seq-3/ (skipping both Washington's discussion of *Corfield* and the Bill of Rights and indicating that the Fourteenth Amendment protects the same "privileges and immunities" as Article IV); Daily Age, May 24, 1866, at 1 (including Howard's mention of *Corfield* but omitting the first eight amendments).

121 Cong. Globe, 40th Cong., 3d sess. 1003 (Feb. 8, 1869) (discussed in Green, *supra* note 3, at 56).

122 Cong. Globe, 39th Cong. 1st sess. at 2961 (June 5).

123 Report at xiii–xiv.

124 Lewis L. Gould, Grand Old Party: A History of the Republicans 14 (2012).

125 Abraham Lincoln, Letter to Salmon P. Chase, June 20, 1859, *in* 3 Collected Works 386 (Roy P. Basler ed. 1953).

126 *See, e.g., Campbell v. Morris*, 3 Harr. & McH. 535 (Md. 1797); *Lemmon v. People*, 20 N.Y. 562 (1860).

127 *Kincaid v. Francis*, 3 Tenn. (1 Cooke) 48, 53 (1812) (affirming it "most probable that this clause in the Constitution was intended to compel the general government to extend the same privileges and immunities to the citizens of every State"); *Douglass v. Stephens*, 1 Del. Ch. 465, 476–7 (1821) ("The privileges and immunities to be secured to all citizens of the United States are such only as belong to the citizens of the several States; which includes the whole United States, and must be understood to mean, such privileges as should be common, or the same in every State; and this seems to limit the operation of the clause in the Constitution to federal rules; and to be designed to restrict the powers of Congress as to legislation, so that no privilege or immunity should be granted by it to one citizen of the United States, but such as might be common to all."); *see also Crandall v. State*, 10 Conn. 339, 343 (1834) (noting, but rejecting, the claim that "this section was made to direct, exclusively, the action of the general government, and therefore, can never be applied to state laws").

128 *Barron v. Mayor & City Council of Baltimore*, 32 U.S. 243, 247 (1833) (concluding that because the "Constitution was ordained and established by the people of the United States for themselves, for their own government, and not for the government of the individual States," and because the "powers they conferred on this government were to be exercised by itself," therefore "the limitations on power, if expressed in general terms, are naturally, and we think necessarily, applicable to the government created by the instrument."); *Prigg v. Pennsylvania*, 41 U.S. 615 (concluding that because the clause "is found in the National Constitution," the "natural inference certainly is that the National Government is clothed with the appropriate authority and functions to enforce it").

129 Cong. Globe, 39th Cong. 1st sess. 1291–3 (Feb. 28).

130 *Id.* at 2765 (May 23).

131 *Paul v. Virginia*, 75 U.S. 168, 180 (1869).

132 *Female Suffrage, Report of the Committee on the Judiciary of the House of Representatives* Jan. 30, 1871, *reprinted in* A Hand-Book for Politics 108, 109 (Edward McPherson ed. 1872) (emphasis added).

133 Richard L. Aynes, *Ohio and the Drafting and Ratification of the Fourteenth Amendment, in* 1 History of Ohio Law 370, 382 (Michael Les Benedict & John F. Winkler eds. 2004).

134 See, most prominently, *Dred Scott v. Sandford*, 60 U.S. 393, 422 (1857) (explaining that "so far as mere rights of person are concerned, the provision in question is confined to citizens of a State who are temporarily in another State without taking up their residence there"; *but see Abbot v. Bayley*, 23 Mass. 89, 92 (1827) (affirming that the Clause protected citizens "only in cases of removal from one state to another").

135 See Cong. Globe, 39th Cong., 1st sess. app. at 293 (July 25, 1866) (Shellabarger) (commenting although no state had the right to take away the "fundamental privileges" from "any citizen of the United States" neither "from its own citizens, nor from those coming in from another State," his proposed bill to enforce the Privileges and Immunities Clause was limited to the incoming citizens, in order to "conform this bill to [the prevailing] view of this constitutional provision").

136 Cong. Globe, 39th Cong. 1st sess. 1118 (Mar. 1, 1866) (discussed in Hermine Herta Meyer, The History and the Meaning of the Fourteenth Amendment 64 (1977)).

137 *The Union in Indiana: Large Meeting at New Albany: Another Great Speech by Gov. Morton*, The Evansville Journal, July 21, 1866, at 2, https://newspapers.library.in.gov/?a=d&d=EJ18660721.1.2&e=-------en-20--1--txt-txIN-------; *see also* Reconstruction Amendments, *supra* note 79, at 251.

138 See, most prominently, *Lemmon v. People*, 20 N.Y. 562 (1860) (cited with approval in *Paul v. Virginia*, 75 U.S. 168, 180 & n.7 (1869) (holding that the Privileges and Immunities Clause places "the citizens of each State upon the same footing with citizens of other States").

139 Upham, *supra* note 74, at 113.

140 *The True Union Policy*, Worcester Daily Spy, May 1, 1866, at 2, https://chroniclingamerica.loc.gov/lccn/sn83021205/1866-05-01/ed-1/seq-2/.

141 The Cecil Whig, May 26, 1866, at 2, https://chroniclingamerica.loc.gov/lccn/sn83016348/1866-05-26/ed-1/seq-2/.

142 *Governor Dennison's Speech at Carthage, Ohio* (Oct. 6, 1866) in Campaign Speeches, *supra* note 64, at 44.

143 *American Citizenship*, Chicago Tribune, Oct. 10, 1866, at 2, https://chroniclingamerica.loc.gov/lccn/sn82014064/1866-10-10/ed-1/seq-2/.

144 The Cecil Whig, May 26, 1866, at 2, https://chroniclingamerica.loc.gov/lccn/sn83016348/1866-05-26/ed-1/seq-2/.

145 Burlington Weekly Free Press, May 11, 1866, at 1, https://chroniclingamerica.loc.gov/lccn/sn86072143/1866-05-11/ed-1/seq-1/.

146 *The Fourteenth Amendment*, Chicago Tribune, July 16, 1868, at 2, https://chroniclingamerica.loc.gov/lccn/sn82014064/1868-07-16/ed-1/seq-2/ (declaring that Section 1 would secure the "legal equality of all citizens of the United States" by a "common citizenship" to belong to a citizen "wherever he may be" and no longer a hodge-podge of "citizenships, each varying and to be varied according to the whims and passions of a majority in each State").

147 Cong. Globe, 39th Cong. 1st sess. 2459 (May 8).

148 Cong. Globe, 39th Cong. 1st sess. 2766 (May 23).

149 Cong. Globe, 39th Cong. 1st sess. 1294 (Mar. 9) (relying on *Prigg* to claim that Congress also had power to enforce against the states the Due Process Clause); *id.* at 2512, (May 9) (relying on *Prigg* to contend for power to enforce the Privileges and Immunities Clause).

150 *See, e.g., Ex Parte Bushnell*, 9 Ohio St. 77, 245 (1859) (Sutliff, J., dissenting) ("If, then, congress has power to legislate respecting the duty of the states to surrender fugitives, it has the power to legislate to enforce the duty from each state, whether slave or free, to extend all the privileges and immunities of citizens to the citizens of every other state [or to] legislate for the enforcement of the provision that no person shall 'be deprived of life, liberty, or property without due process of law.' But it is absurd to claim for congress the power to legislate to enforce the duties of the states, in the absence of any such power delegated under the constitution"). On the significance of the *Bushnell* case, see Aynes, *supra* note 93.

151 *Reconstruction*, The Cecil Whig, May 26, 1866, at 2, https://chroniclingamerica.loc.gov/lccn/sn83016348/1866-05-26/ed-1/seq-2/.

152 In its February 1 resolution, the Senate called for an amendment "to declare with greater certainty the power of Congress to enforce and determine, by appropriate legislation, all the guarantees contained in that instrument." As Richard Aynes has observed, "[t]he Senate likely chose the words 'greater certainty' to embrace both those who, like Wilson, thought the enforcement power existed even though it had not been used effectively; and those who, like Bingham, believed no enforcement power existed in the Constitution." Aynes, *supra* note 93, at 80.

153 *Campbell v. Morris*, 3 Harr. & McH. 535, 554 (Md. 1797).

154 Articles of Confederation, art. IV (1781) (listing "free ingress and regress to and from any other state [and] all the privileges of trade and commerce," but "subject to the same duties, impositions and restrictions as the inhabitants thereof respectively").

155 *Campbell*, 3 Harr. & McH. at 554 (mentioning first two privileges, "the peculiar advantage of acquiring and holding real as well as personal property, and that such property shall be protected and secured by the laws of the State, in the same manner as the property of the citizens of the State is protected" and then an immunity, "such property shall not be liable to any taxes, or burdens which the property of the citizens is not subject to").

156 *Corfield v. Coryell*, 6 F. Cas. 546, 551–2 (C.C.E.D. Pa. 1823) (listing various rights "to" do certain things—to travel, reside, institute claims, acquire property, and *then* "an exemption from higher taxes or impositions than are paid by the other citizens of the state" as "some of the particular privileges and immunities of citizens").

157 Meyer, *supra* note 136, at 92 (noting that in both bills, "the term 'immunities' was defined by the provision that all persons without regard to race and color, 'shall be subject to like punishment, pains, penalties, and to none other'").

158 An Act to amend an act entitled "An act to establish a Bureau for the relief of Freedmen and Refugees," and for other purposes (S. No. 60), §§ 7–8, *reprinted in* Edward McPherson, A Political Manual for 1866, at 72, 74 (1866).

159 From George Washington to the Hebrew Congregation in Newport, Rhode Island, August 18, 1790, National Archives, Founders Online, https://founders.archives.gov/documents/Washington/05-06-02-0135.

160 Cong. Globe, 39th Cong. 1st sess. 1117 (Mar. 1) (highlighted in Meyer *supra* note 136, at 92).

161 *Id.* at 157–8.

162 Journal of the Joint Committee of Fifteen on Reconstruction 55–6 (Benjamin Kendrick ed. 1914).

163 Cong. Globe, 39th Cong. 1st sess. 429.
164 *See supra* chapter 2.
165 Cong. Globe, 39th Cong. 1st sess. 1089 (Feb. 28) (emphasis added).
166 Bingham's understanding of this distinction was reflected, again, in his initial redraft of his proposition. As we saw, in apparent imitation of the language of Article I, section 10, Bingham wrote, "No State shall *pass* or enforce any *law* which shall *impair* or deny any of the privileges or immunities of citizens of the United States." *Washington Topics and Gossip*, Cleveland Daily Leader, Apr. 18, 1866, at 1, https://chroniclingamerica.loc.gov/lccn/sn85042437/1866-04-18/ed-1/seq-1/ (emphasis added). To "impair," from Article I, probably encompassed the sense of "burden" (as to an immunity) but not "withhold" (as to a privilege), so he had to amend the text to say, "impair or deny."
167 Cong. Globe, 39th Cong. 1st sess. 1095 (Feb. 28).
168 *Supra* ch. 3.
169 Aynes, *supra* note 93, at 103 n.299 (contending that "of the citizens of the United States" as defining both the "class of rights" and the "class of beneficiaries"); Amar, *supra* note 70, at 170 (contending that privileges and immunities "are paradigmatically rights of and for American citizens").
170 Amar, *supra* note 96, at 1226 n.153.
171 *Conner v. Elliott*, 59 U.S. 591, 593 (1855).
172 *Corfield v. Coryell*, 6 F. Cas. 546, 551 (C.C.E.D. Pa. 1823).
173 *Id.* at 552.
174 Cong. Globe, 39th Cong. 1st sess. 1088 (Feb. 28) (Woodbridge); *id.* at 2465 (May 8) (Thayer).
175 *Id.* at app. 219.
176 Cong. Globe, 39th Cong. 1st sess. 2765.
177 Reconstruction Amendments, *supra* note 79, at 244.
178 Reconstruction Amendments, *supra* note 79, at 362; Message of the Governor to the General Assembly, Jan. 7, 1867, Ill. House Journal, 25th Gen. Ass. 12, 40 (1867).
179 *The Union in Indiana: Large Meeting at New Albany: Another Great Speech by Gov. Morton*, The Evansville Journal, July 21, 1866, at 2, https://newspapers.library.in.gov/?a=d&d=EJ18660721.1.2&e=-------en-20--1--txt-txIN-------; *see also* Reconstruction Amendments, *supra* note 79, at 251 (emphasis added).
180 Johnson, *supra* note 19, at 15.
181 The Legislative Record: Containing the Debates and Proceedings of the Pennsylvania Legislature, for the Session of 1867, app. at vi (George Bergnor, ed. 1867) [hereinafter "Pennsylvania Legislative Debates"] (summarizing Sections 1 and 2 as securing "the privileges of citizenship, and the immunities of impartial suffrage before the law"); *Resolutions of Union League of Philadelphia*, The Evening Telegraph, Aug. 23, 1866, at 6, https://chroniclingamerica.loc.gov/lccn/sn83025925/1866-08-23/ed-1/seq-6/ (endorsing Section 1 for securing both "the rights of citizenship to all persons born or naturalized in the United States" [the Privileges or Immunities Clause] and "equal protection to all in the possession and enjoyment of life, liberty, and property" [the Due Process-Equal Protection Clause]); *Speech of Thomas J. Durant of New Orleans*, Bradford Reporter, Sept. 13, 1866, at 1 (stating that "a citizen of the United States [is entitled] to the enjoyment of all his civil rights and privileges as such"); Speech of Granville Moody, *Pittsburgh Convention*,

The Wyandot Pioneer, Oct. 4, 1866, at 1, https://chroniclingamerica.loc.gov/lccn/sn87076863/1866-10-04/ed-1/seq-1/ (indicating that the Amendment protected the "immunities of citizenship"); "Madison," *The National Question: Constitutional Amendments—National Citizenship*, N.Y, TIMES, Nov. 10, 1866, *in* Reconstruction Amendments, *supra* note 79, at 298 (noting that the Amendment will secure to the citizen the "rights of citizenship as a member of the Union" (citing *Dred Scott*) or stated otherwise, the "rights and privileges of a citizen of the United States" that are summed up in [Corfield]"); *Rescinding the Fourteenth Amendment*, Delaware Gazette, Jan. 24, 1868, at 1, https://chroniclingamerica.loc.gov/lccn/sn83035595/1868-01-24/ed-1/seq-1/ (reprinting editorial of the *Cincinnati Commercial* and referring to "the privileges and immunities that attach to, and are inseparable from citizenship").

182 Cong. Globe, 39th Cong. 1st sess. 1757 (Apr. 4).

183 *Id.* at 1833 (Apr. 7).

184 *Speech of Gen. John A. Logan, at Cairo,* June 28, 1866, Chicago Tribune, July 2, 1866, at 1, https://chroniclingamerica.loc.gov/lccn/sn82014064/1866-07-02/ed-1/seq-1/.

185 Conkling, *supra* note 16, at 25 (1866).

186 As I have explained elsewhere, among other problems, the reading seems inconsistent with the original meaning of the Thirteenth Amendment's first section, the terms of which were first incorporated into the Northwest Ordinance and subsequently in western state constitutions, had *never* been relied on to challenge racial inequality as to civil rights. David R. Upham, *The Understanding of "Neither slavery nor involuntary servitude shall exist" Before the Thirteenth Amendment*, 15 Geo. J.L. & Pub. Pol'y 137 (2017).

187 Lawrence B. Solum, *The Fourteenth Amendment and the Bill of Rights: Incorporation and Originalist Theory*, 18 J. Contemp. Legal Issues 409, 425 (2009).

188 This objection appeared in Andrew Johnson's veto of the Civil Rights Bill. Free blacks, he said, need not "be declared citizens in order that they may be secured in the enjoyment of the civil rights" listed in the Act, for those "rights are, by Federal as well as State laws, secured to all domiciled aliens and foreigners." Cong. Globe, 39th Cong. 1st sess. 1858 (Apr. 9). *Cf. Dred Scott v. Sandford*, 60 U.S. 393, 583–4 (1857) (Curtis, J., dissenting) (contending that "that citizenship, under the Constitution of the United States, is not dependent on the possession of any particular political or even of all civil rights, and any attempt so to define it must lead to error," and that the states have the discretion to "attach a particular privilege or immunity to mere naked citizenship").

189 1 William Blackstone, Commentaries on the Laws of England 360 (1766).

190 Aristotle, The Politics, bk I, at 4 (Carnes Lord, trans., 2d ed. 2013).

191 *See, e.g.*, Fla. Const., art I, § 22 (1868); ALA. CONST. art. I, § 28 (1867).

192 Ga. Const., art. I, § 9 (1868) (emphasis added).

193 Ark. Const., art. I, § 2 (1868) (emphasis added).

194 Quoted in Joseph B. James, The Framing of the Fourteenth Amendment 30 (1956). (Morrill to Sumner, undated [probably Oct. or Nov., 1865], Sumner MSS [Harvard]). Howard Jay Graham remarked that the letter has been sometimes misattributed to Justin Morrill, congressman from Vermont and a member of the Joint Committee on Reconstruction. Howard Jay Graham, Everyman's Constitution; Historical Essays on the Fourteenth Amendment, the "Conspiracy Theory," and American Constitutionalism 302 n. 23 (1968). *See supra* note 1.

195 *Corfield v. Coryell*, 6 F. Cas. 546, 551 (C.C.E.D. Pa. 1823).
196 Howard's Notes, https://tifis.org/sources/Howard.pdf, at 3.
197 Aristotle, Nicomachean Ethics, bk. I, ch. 7, at 14 (Robert C. Bartlett & Susan D. Collins trans. 2011).
198 *The Bill of Rights*, National Archives, https://www.archives.gov/founding-docs/bill-of-rights.
199 *See, e.g.*, *Bank of United States v. Deveaux*, 9 U.S. 61, 85 (1809) (holding the Bank Bill of 1791 expressly gives the corporation what is perhaps "incident to a corporation," *namely*, the "capacity to make contracts and to acquire property . . . [and] to sue and be sued . . . in courts of record, or any other place whatsoever," and that "[t]his power, if not incident to a corporation, is conferred by every incorporating act"); *Commonwealth v. Smith*, 92 Mass. 448, 455 (1865) (explaining that a corporation normally "has the capacity to sue and be sued, the right to make contracts" and the "general power to dispose of and alienate its property").
200 On December 21, 1865, just after the full ratification of the Thirteenth Amendment, Wilson submitted a bill (S. 55) "to maintain and enforce the freedom of the inhabitants of the United States," which was then referred to Trumbull's Judiciary Committee. S. Journal at 59. The bill provided, in part, that "All inhabitants of any State or Territory of the United States, without distinction of color or race, shall be entitled to make and enforce contracts, to sue, be parties, and give evidence in all courts and causes, to lease, purchase, hold, sell, and convey real and personal property, and to have full and equal benefit of all laws and proceedings for the security of person and estate." The text of the bill is found here: https://www.congress.gov/bill/39th-congress/senate-bill/55/text. *See* John P. Frank and Robert F. Munro, *The Original Understanding of "Equal Protection of the Laws,"* 1972 Wash. U. L. Q. 421, 439 & n.48 (1972) (discussing this bill). After the Christmas break, that committee produced the drafts of the eventual Second Freedmen's and Civil Rights Bills, with similar language.
201 17 U.S. 316, 411 (1819) (holding that the "power of creating a corporation" is "incidental to those powers which are expressly given [as] a direct mode of executing them").
202 Siegfried Wiessner, Die Function der Staatsangehörigkeit [The Function of Nationality] 396–7 (1989).
203 *Dred Scott v. Sandford*, 60 U.S. 393, 417 (1857); Cong. Globe, 39th Cong. 1st sess. 2765 (Howard quoting *Corfield*'s mention of the right to travel and reside); *id.* at 1263 (Broomall's list, including "the right of transit, the right of domicil"); *The Union in Indiana: Large Meeting at New Albany: Another Great Speech by Gov. Morton*, The Evansville Journal, July 21, 1866, at 2, https://newspapers.library.in.gov/?a=d&d=EJ18660721.1.2&e=-------en-20--1--txt-txIN-------; *see also* Reconstruction Amendments, *supra* note 79, at 251. The right, of course, included a right of interstate and intrastate travel. *Speech of John Sherman at Mozart Hall* (Sept. 28, 1866), *in* Campaign Speeches, *supra* note 64, at 39 (mentioning the "right to go from county to county, and from State to State").
204 Blackstone, *supra* note 189, at 360 (identifying the right to acquire real property as a privilege of subjecthood); *Dred Scott*, 60 U.S. at 424–5 (indicating that the "right to hold and convey property" is one of "the rights and privileges of citizenship"); *Campbell v. Morris*, 3 Harr. & McH. 535, 554 (Md. 1797) (enumerating, first, "the

peculiar advantage of acquiring and holding real as well as personal property"); *Abbot v. Bayley*, 23 Mass. 89, 92 (1827) (including the right to "take and hold real estate"); Civil Rights Act; Cong. Globe, 39th Cong. 1st sess. 2765 (Howard quoting *Corfield*'s mention of the right "to take, hold and dispose of property, either real or personal," *Corfield v. Coryell*, 6 F. Cas. 546, 552 (C.C.E.D. Pa. 1823)); Cong. Globe, 39th Cong. 1st sess. app. at 217 (Howe's list of "the plainest and most necessary rights of citizenship," including the "right to hold land when they had bought it and paid for it would have been denied them; the right to collect their wages by the processes of the law when they had earned their wages"). Many other sources could be provided.

205 Cong. Globe, 39th Cong. 1st sess. 3035 (June 6) (Senator Henderson, noting that the "members of the people" have the right "to acquire property . . . to enter the professions, to acquire wealth").

206 David R. Upham, *Interracial Marriage and the Original Understanding of the Privileges or Immunities Clause*, 42 Hastings Const. L. Q. 213, 222–7 (2015).

207 *Id.* at 227–31.

208 James Schouler, A Treatise on the Law of the Domestic Relations; Embracing Husband and Wife, Parent and Child, Guardian and Ward, Infancy, and Master and Servant (1870).

209 Upham, *supra* note 206, at 258.

210 *Id.* at 259–73.

211 *See, e.g., Washington v. Eaton*, 29 F. Cas. 345, 348 (C.C.D. D.C. 1833) (noting that "in a qui tam action, the plaintiff always sues for the king, or sovereign, and himself; and not for another *subject* or *citizen*") (emphasis added); *Robison v. Beall*, 26 Ga. 17, 103 (1858) (Lumpkin, J., dissenting) (observing that a statute had conferred a "common right, to *any citizen* of the State, to institute this qui tam action, or prosecution") (emphasis added).

212 *Coe v. Schultz*, 2 Abb. Pr. (n.s.) 193, 195, (N.Y. Sup. Ct. December 1, 1866) (endorsing "the common law principle that any *subject* or *citizen* has the right of his own motion, summarily to abate a public nuisance") (emphasis added).

213 Ariz. Const. art. II § 35 (2006) (stipulating that an unlawfully present "alien shall not be awarded punitive damages in any action in any court in this state").

214 Tenn. Const. art. XI, § 17 (1796) ("Suits may be brought against the State in such manner and in such courts as the Legislature may by law direct: *Provided* The right of bringing suit be limited to the citizens of this State").

215 *Lemmon v. People*, 20 N.Y. 562, 564 (1860).

216 *Id.* at 599–644. For contemporary accounts, *see, e.g., Law Intelligence: Decision in the Lemmon Slave Case*, N.Y. Times, Apr. 16, 1860, https://www.nytimes.com/1860/04/16/archives/law-intelligence-decision-in-the-lemmon-slave-case.html.

217 *Corfield v. Coryell*, 6 F. Cas. 546, 551–2 (C.C.E.D. Pa. 1823) (emphasis added); *accord Davis v. Pierse*, 7 Minn. 13, 16 (1862).

218 Cong. Globe, 39th Cong. 1st sess. 2765 (Howard's remarks); *id.* app. at 217 (Howe's mention of "the right to appear in the courts as suitors for any wrong done them or any right denied them"): *id.* at 1263 (Broomall mentioning the right "to sue"); *Speech of Hon. Schuyler Colfax, at Indianapolis, August 7, in* Campaign Speeches, *supra* note 64, at 14 (mentioning the right "to sue"); *Speech of John Sherman at Mozart Hall* (Sept. 28, 1866), *in id.* at 39 (mentioning the right "to sue").

219 *People v. Hall*, 4 Cal. 399, 403–4 (1854) (emphasis added).

220 Fla. Const. art XVI, § 2 (1865).

221 *At Erie—Gen. Geary's Speech*, The Ebensburg Alleghanian, Sept. 20, 1866, at 1, https://chroniclingamerica.loc.gov/lccn/sn85054846/1866-09-20/ed-1/seq-1/. ("right to sue and be sued, to testify in courts").

222 Cong. Globe, 39th Cong. 1st sess. app. at 237.

223 *"In the Last Ditch,"* The Evening Telegraph, Sept. 27, 1866, at 4, https://chroniclingamerica.loc.gov/lccn/sn83025925/1866-09-27/ed-1/seq-4/ (insisting that the "civil rights" protected by Section 1 included the right "to sue" but also "to act as a witness in a criminal case").

224 *Abbot v. Bayley*, 23 Mass. 89, 92 (1827) (indicating that Article IV secures the "right to sue and be sued as citizens"); *Speech of Gen. John A. Logan, at Cairo, June 28, 1866*, Chicago Tribune, July 2, 1866, at 1, https://chroniclingamerica.loc.gov/lccn/sn82014064/1866-07-02/ed-1/seq-1/ (claiming that the "rights of citizenship" include the "right to sue and be sued"); *At Erie—Gen. Geary's Speech*, The Ebensburg Alleghanian, Sept. 20, 1866, at 1, https://chroniclingamerica.loc.gov/lccn/sn85054846/1866-09-20/ed-1/seq-1/ (stating that the civil rights, guaranteed to the citizen by the Amendment, include the "right to sue and be sued, to testify in courts, and buy and sell real estate"); *Barnes v. Browning*, Indiana Circuit Court (Lafayette, Ind.) (Apr. 13 1866), *reprinted in*, *Judge Test's Decision on the Case Under the Civil Rights Bill*, The Richmond Palladium (Richmond, Ind.), Apr. 26, 1866, at 1, http://chroniclingamerica.loc.gov/lccn/sn86058250/1866-04-26/ed-1/seq-1 (holding that "like all other citizens" the black citizen "is entitled to sue in our courts, and liable to be sued"); *but see Speech of Hon. Schuyler Colfax, at Indianapolis, August 7, in* Campaign Speeches, *supra* note 64, at 14 (conspicuously omitting the right to "be sued").

225 Cong. Globe, 39th Cong. 1st sess. 2765 (Howard's remarks).

226 Northwest Ordinance § 14, arts. 1–2 (U.S. 1787), https://www.archives.gov/milestone-documents/northwest-ordinance.

227 Cong. Globe, 39th Cong. 1st sess. 2765 (Howard's remarks).

228 John Mercer Langston, A Speech on "Equality Before the Law" 19 (1866).

229 Proceedings of the Illinois State Convention of Colored Men, Assembled at Galesburg (Oct. 1866), at 9–10 (1867); *An Address to the People of the State of Illinois*, Chicago Tribune, Oct. 18, 1866, at 1, https://chroniclingamerica.loc.gov/lccn/sn82014064/1866-10-18/ed-1/seq-1/.

230 On "unusual" as contrary to *usus*, *see* John F. Stinneford, *The Original Meaning of Unusual: The Eighth Amendment as a Bar to Cruel Innovation*, 102 Nw. U. L. Rev. 1739 (2008).

231 Cong. Globe, 39th Cong. 1st sess. 2765 (Howard's remarks); *id.* at 2542 (Bingham's remarks).

232 See Upham, *supra* note 74, at 1152–4, 1157–8.

233 *See* 2 James Wilson, Works 443 (1804) (emphasis added).

234 Cong. Globe, 39th Cong. 1st sess. 2765 (Howard's remarks, mentioning "the freedom of speech and of the press," and "the right of the people peaceably to assemble and petition the government for a redress of grievances, a right appertaining to each and all the people"); *Gov. Jacob Cox's Message to the Legislature*, Ohio Executive Documents 281 (1867), *in* Reconstruction Amendments,

supra note 79, at 305; "Madison," *The National Question: Constitutional Amendments—National Citizenship*, N.Y, Times, Nov. 10, 1866, *in* Reconstruction Amendments, *supra* note 79, at 298 (mentioning, among the "rights of the citizen" to be protected by the Amendment, "the right to speak and write his sentiments, regardless of localities; to keep and bears arms in his own defense"); *see generally, supra* note 78.

235 Robert Leider, The Individual Right To Bear Arms For Common Defense (2024), available at SSRN: https://ssrn.com/abstract=4918009 or http://dx.doi.org/10.2139/ssrn.4918009.

236 *Bryan v. Walton*, 14 Ga. 185, 202 (1853).

237 *Dred Scott v. Sandford*, 60 U.S. 393, 417 (1857).

238 Cong. Globe, 39th Cong. 1st sess. 2765.

239 "Madison," *The National Question: Constitutional Amendments—National Citizenship*, N.Y. Times, Nov. 10, 1866, *in* Reconstruction Amendments, *supra* note 79, at 298 (mentioning, among the "rights of the citizen" to be protected by the Amendment, "to keep and bears arms in his own defense"); *To Moses A. Bledsoe, Candidate for the Senate*, The Tri-Weekly Standard, Oct. 6, 1866, at 2, (mentioning, *inter alia*, "the privilege to bear arms, to speak his sentiments freely, to assemble and petition for a redress of grievances"). For a few other sources, *see, e.g.*, Hardy, *supra* note 78 at 704–6.

240 *See generally*, Stephen P. Halbrook, Freedmen, the Fourteenth Amendment, and the Right to Bear Arms, 1866–1876 (1998); Saul Cornell, *The Right to Regulate Arms in the Era of the Fourteenth Amendment: The Emergence of Good Cause Permit Schemes in Post-Civil War Am*erica, 55 U.C. Davis L. Rev. Online 65 (2021).

241 Cong. Globe, 39th Cong., 1st sess. 2765 (May 23).

242 *See, e.g.*, Tex. Const. art. I, § 4 (1869) (declaring that all "men have a natural and indefeasible right to worship God according to the dictates of their own consciences" and that no "man shall be compelled to attend, erect, or support any place of worship, or to maintain any ministry, against his consent."); Va. Const. art. V, § 14 (1870) ("No man shall be compelled to frequent or support any religious worship, place, or ministry whatsoever, nor shall any man be forced, restrained, molested, or burdened in his body or goods, or otherwise suffer on account of his religious opinions or belief").

243 *See also John A. Bingham*, Chicago Tribune, Dec. 12, 1868, at 2, https://chroniclingamerica.loc.gov/lccn/sn82014064/1868-12-12/ed-1/seq-2/ (identifying one of the "immunities" of citizens of the United States as "freedom from . . . unlawful seizures").

244 Mass. Const. art. I, § XIV (1780).

245 David Gray, *Dangerous Dicta*, 72 Wash & Lee L. Rev. 1181, 1191 (2015) (noting this change, but attributing it a communitarian motivation rather than the Framers' uneasy concession to bondage).

246 Mich. Const. art. VI § 25 (1850); S.C. Const. art I, § 22 (1868).

247 *See, e.g.*, The New York Herald, May 24, 1866, at 1, https://chroniclingamerica.loc.gov/lccn/sn83030313/1866-05-24/ed-1/seq-1/; New-York Tribune, May 24, 1866, at 1, https://chroniclingamerica.loc.gov/lccn/sn83030214/1866-05-24/ed-1/seq-1/.

248 As David T. Hardy speculates, either the Associated Press reporter missed the subsequent enumeration, or paraphrased it with "etc.," or Howard exercised his right

to correct the transcript before printing in the Globe. Hardy, *supra* note 78, at 715 n. 118.

249 Fairman, *supra* note 92, at 115–16.

250 Judiciary Act of 1789, 1 Stat. 73 (1789) ("And the trial of issues in fact in the Supreme Court, in all actions at law against citizens of the United States, shall be by jury").

251 The Federalist No. 83, at 503 (Hamilton) (Clinton Rossiter ed., 1961).

252 Fairman, *supra* note 92, at 122, 128 (discussing congressional acceptance of the constitutions of Nebraska and Georgia, upon admission and readmission, respectively).

253 *See supra* ch. 4.

254 Magna Carta, ch. 20, Online Library of Liberty, https://oll.libertyfund.org/pages/1215-magna-carta.

255 *Timbs v. Indiana*, 586 U.S. 146, 149–50 (2019) (holding that the "Excessive Fines Clause is . . . incorporated by the Due Process Clause of the Fourteenth Amendment"); *id.* at 157–70 (Thomas, J., concurring) (contending that freedom from excessive fines is a privilege or immunity of citizenship).

256 Cong. Globe, 39th Cong. 1st sess. 1089 (Feb. 28).

257 *Corfield v. Coryell*, 6 F. Cas. 546, 551–2 (C.C.E.D. Pa. 1823).

258 *Dred Scott v. Sandford*, 60 U.S. 393, 417 (1857) (affirming that if citizens, free black persons would be able to travel to other states, "to go where they pleased at every hour of the day or night without molestation, unless they committed some violation of law for which a white man would be punished").

259 Cong. Globe, 39th Cong. 1st sess. app. at 219. Howe included this remark within a general discussion of the Privileges or Immunities Clause. Christopher Wolfe thus seems mistaken in attributing the comment to the Equal Protection Clause. Christopher Wolfe, The Rise of Modern Judicial Review: From Constitutional Interpretation to Judge-Made Law 140 (1986).

260 Cong. Globe, 39th Cong. 1st sess. 2765.

261 *State ex rel. Garnes v. McCann*, 21 Ohio St. 198, 209–11 (1871) (noting no apparent challenge under the Citizenship and Equal Protection Clauses, and stating that the Privileges or Immunities Clause was "the clause relied on" by the Plaintiff); *People ex rel. Dietz v. Easton*, 10 Abb. Pr. 159, 164–6, (N.Y. Sup. Ct. 1872) (citing *McCann's* discussion of the Privileges or Immunities Clause for the same purpose); *State ex rel. Stoutmeyer v. Duffy*, 7 Nev. 342, 345–6 (1872) (Garber, J., dissenting) (indicating that the majority had tacitly rejected the relator's main claim that segregated schools abridged the privileges of U.S. citizenship). *See also Burns v. State*, 48 Ala. 195, 198 (1872) (striking down the state's bar to interracial marriage on the grounds that the Civil Rights Act secures "the right to make and enforce contracts, amongst which is that of marriage with any citizen capable of entering into that relation," and stating that Section 1 has the same effect, for it prohibits the state from discriminating against African Americans "for any of the causes, or any of the grounds, which previously characterized their want of *citizenship*") (emphasis added); *In re Hobbs*, 12 F. Cas. 262, 263–4 (C.C.N.D. Ga. 1871) (upholding a state's interracial-marriage law as not violative of the Privileges or Immunities Clause); *Lonas v. State*, 50 Tenn. 287, 306–7 (1871) (same); *but see State v. Gibson*, 36 Ind. 389, 392–3 (1871) (noting that [t]he learned attorney for the appellee has not informed us, in his brief, which

one of the clauses of [Section 1] has had the effect to abrogate our laws prohibiting [such] intermarriage" and summarily rejecting the challenge under either such provision); *cf. People v. Washington*, 36 Cal. 658, 671–2 (1869) (suggesting, by italicization, that the Equal Protection Clause incorporated the requirement of the Civil Rights Act whereby the black defendant was equally entitled to the same procedural protections as the white defendant).

262 Journal of the Joint Committee of Fifteen on Reconstruction 83 (Benjamin Kendrick ed. 1914).

263 Reconstruction Amendments, *supra* note 79, at 362

264 *At Erie—Gen. Geary's Speech*, The Ebensburg Alleghanian, Sept. 20, 1866, at 1, https://chroniclingamerica.loc.gov/lccn/sn85054846/1866-09-20/ed-1/seq-1/. *See also, e.g., Speech of Major Gen. Robert C. Schenck*, in Campaign Speeches, *supra* note 64, at 12, 13 (insisting that the Amendment would "prevent unequal legislation" and thus remove from the black citizen the "weight of inequality, in regard to the right of suing and being sued, making contracts, marrying, and educating himself").

265 *See, e.g.*, 9 Brevier Legislative Reports, 1867, at 79 (reporting a remark in the Indiana House that the Privileges or Immunities Clause would "repeal all our State laws making distinctions because of race and color").

266 See chapter 2, *supra*.

267 Cong. Globe, 39th Cong., 1st sess. 2765 (May 23) (noting that the Amendment will prohibit the states from "subjecting one caste of persons to a code not applicable to another"); Pennsylvania Legislative Debates, *supra* note 181, at vii, xxii, xli (stating that the Amendment will make "all castes and colors equal before [the law]," and "destroy all legal caste within our borders" or "every distinction founded upon a difference in the caste, nationality, race or color").

268 Noah Webster, An American Dictionary of the English Language 203 (rev'd ed. 1869). A secondary meaning referred to an "order or class in society." *Id.* In the second sense, the word could refer to any stable grouping. *Compare, e.g., State v. Caesar*, 31 N.C. 391, 409 (1849) (Nash, J., concurring) (noting that in contrast with the statutory racial distinctions, "the common law . . . knows no difference of caste") *with Cost v. Genette*, 1 Port. 212, 214 (Ala. 1834) (referring to the "profession of the law" as a "caste").

269 *American Citizenship*, Chicago Tribune, Oct. 10, 1866, at 2, https://chroniclingamerica.loc.gov/lccn/sn82014064/1866-10-10/ed-1/seq-2/.

270 *Tennessee, Governor William Brownlow's Proclamation*, June 19, 1866, *in* Reconstruction Amendments, *supra* note 79, at 243.

271 *Speech of General Ben. Butler, at Toledo, Ohio,* Oct. 2, 1866, *in* Campaign Speeches, *supra* note 64, at 41 (stating that under Section 1, "every citizen of the United States should have equal rights with every other citizen of the United States, in every State"); *Information for the People: The Proposed Amendment to the Constitution*, The Evening Telegraph, Sept. 26, 1866, at 4 (explaining that under Section 1, "South Carolina must treat Pennsylvanians with the same respect that she treats her own citizens").

272 *John A. Bingham*, Chicago Tribune, Dec. 12, 1868, at 2, https://chroniclingamerica.loc.gov/lccn/sn82014064/1868-12-12/ed-1/seq-2/.

273 *Reconstruction: Judge Kelley's Southern Campaign*, The Evening Telegraph, May 8, 1867, at 1, https://chroniclingamerica.loc.gov/lccn/sn83025925/1867-05-08/ed-1/seq-1/.

274 Cong. Globe, 39th Cong. 1st sess. 252 (Jan. 16) (noting Roscoe Conkling's proposal to establish in the southern states, "human rights to all persons . . . regardless of race, creed, or color"); White Cloud Kansas Chief, Feb. 8, 1866, at 2 (reprinting the Chicago Tribune's declaration that our "National watchword," must be "*equal and exact justice to all*, irrespective of religion, race or color") (emphasis in original).

275 Cong. Globe, 39th Cong. 1st sess. 1833 (Apr. 7) (contending that all men "in their civil rights [are] equal before the law," and this right of equality is not exclusive to "any class or creed, or race or color"); *id.* at 1835 (finding in the Privileges and Immunities Clause the right to the "equal enjoyment" of these civil rights).

276 *The Campaign in Wisconsin: Speech of Senator T.O. Howe, at Madison, Wisconsin, Aug. 10,* Chicago Tribune, Aug. 14, 1866, at 2, https://chroniclingamerica.loc.gov/lccn/sn82014064/1866-08-14/ed-1/seq-2/.

277 *Wisconsin: Proceedings of the State Legislature*, Chicago Tribune, Feb. 12, 1867, at 2, https://chroniclingamerica.loc.gov/lccn/sn82014064/1867-02-12/ed-1/seq-2/; Pennsylvania Legislative Debates, *supra* note 181, app. at xxii (Rep. Taylor).

278 *The Day We Celebrate*, Chicago Tribune, July 4, 1866, at 2, https://chroniclingamerica.loc.gov/lccn/sn82014064/1866-07-04/ed-1/seq-2/.

279 Thomas Jefferson, *The First Inaugural Address 4 March 1801*, Online Library of Liberty, https://oll.libertyfund.org/pages/1801-jefferson-1st-inaugural-address.

280 Cong. Globe, 34th Cong. 3d sess. app. at 1. I thank Christopher Green for bringing this remark to my attention.

281 Cong. Globe, 39th Cong. 1st sess. 157–8 (Jan. 9).

282 *The Constitutional Amendment Discussed By Its Author*, *in* Campaign Speeches, *supra* note 64, at 19 (1866); *see also* Weekly Perrysburg Journal, Sept. 7, 1866, at 1, https://chroniclingamerica.loc.gov/lccn/sn85026193/1866-09-07/ed-1/seq-1/ (reprinting the speech under the title, "Constitutional Amendment: Exposition of its Meaning, and Reasons for Its Adoption"); *see also* Reconstruction Amendments, *supra* note 79, at 264.

283 *See e.g.*, *Impartial Suffrage*, The Weekly Ottumwa Courier, June 11, 1868, at 2, https://chroniclingamerica.loc.gov/lccn/sn84027352/1868-06-11/ed-1/seq-2/ (misquoting Jefferson as having endorsed "Equal and exact justice to all men, of whatever race, creed or condition").

284 An Act To Protect All Citizens in Their Civil and Legal Rights, 18 Stat. 335 (1875) (emphasis added).

285 Cong. Globe, 39th Cong. 1st sess. 1064 (Feb. 27).

286 *Id.* at 1835 (Apr. 7).

287 Steven G. Calabresi & Julia T. Rickert, *Originalism and Sex Discrimination*, 90 Tex. L. Rev. 1, 52–4 (2011) (referring to Lawrence's distinctions as "baseless," "mistaken," and "odd and rather shocking" and categorizing them among other statements that reflect general "misinformation," and "utter ignorance of women's plight").

288 1 Merle Curti & Vernon Carstensen, The University of Wisconsin: A History, 1848–1925, at 119 (1949) (mentioning the legislature's directive of 1866); Dorothy Deach, *Student Opinion Concerning the Admission of Women to the University of Michigan 1867–1872*, *in* Studies in the History of American Education 71, 71 (Charles Eggertsen, ed. 1947) (discussing the state legislature's directive and its eventual implementation).

289 Edward McPherson, A Political Manual for 1867, at 132 (1867) (noting the proposed amendments to the Kansas and Wisconsin constitutions).

290 Cong. Globe, 41st Cong., 2d sess. at 4331 (June 10, 1870).
291 Plato, The Republic 65 (Allan Bloom trans. 1968).
292 Art. VI.
293 *See, e.g.*, Act of Mar. 23, 1867, ch. VI, § 1, 15 STAT 2 (requiring voters to promise to "faithfully support the Constitution and obey the laws of the United States" and to "encourage others so to do").
294 *See* Ala. Const. art. VII, § 4 (1868) & Ark. Const. art. VIII, § 5 (1868) (both requiring voters to "accept the civil and political equality of all men; and agree not to attempt to deprive any person or persons, on account of race, color, or previous condition, of any political or civil right, privilege, or immunity, enjoyed by any other class of men"). *Cf. Carrington v. Rash*, 380 U.S. 89, 94 (1965) (noting that to exclude from voting "a sector of the population because of the way they may vote is constitutionally impermissible").
295 *See* U.S. Const. art I, §§ 2–3.
296 Earl Maltz, *The Speech of Jacob Howard, the Prevalent Rights Theory, and the Decision in Brown v. Board of Education*, The Originalism Blog, Oct. 16, 2019, https://originalismblog.typepad.com/the-originalism-blog/2019/10/the-speech-of-jacob-howard-the-prevalent-rights-theory-and-the-decision-in-brown-v-board-of-educatio.html.
297 *See* Douglas G. Smith, *Originalism and the Affirmative Action Decisions*, 55 Case W. Res. 1, 32 (2004) (nicely elaborating this point, and citing various scholars in support).
298 *See supra* ch. 3.
299 *See, e.g.*, *The Negro in Indiana*, Rutland Weekly Herald, Nov. 15, 1866, at 8 (noting a state's convention demand that "their children share in the advantages of the schools").
300 Proceedings of the Illinois State Convention of Colored Men, Assembled at Galesburg (Oct. 1866), at 9–10 (1867).
301 *Id.* (emphasis added).
302 Journal of the Indiana State Senate, Gen. Assembly, 45th Sess., at 37–8 (1867).
303 *Id.* at 38.
304 The Wheeling Daily Register, Nov. 18, 1867, at 4, https://chroniclingamerica.loc.gov/lccn/sn84026847/1867-11-18/ed-1/seq-4/ (emphasis added).

Conclusion

A Multiracial Republic, If We Can Keep It

I will buy with you, sell with you, talk with you, walk with you, and so following, but I will not eat with you, drink with you, nor pray with you.

—William Shakespeare, Merchant of Venice, act I, sc. 3

In April 1873, in the *Slaughter-House Cases*, the Supreme Court offered its first interpretation of the Fourteenth Amendment. A Louisiana statute had granted a private corporation the exclusive right to maintain a slaughterhouse in New Orleans. Various butchers challenged the law as unconstitutional. They claimed, *inter alia*, that by this regulation, the state had violated the Amendment by (1) depriving them of property without due process of law, (2) denying to them, by an unequal law, the equal protection of the laws, and (3) abridging their rights as citizens of the United States.

The Court, divided five votes to four, rejected each of these challenges. In an opinion written by Republican Samuel Miller, the majority reached its decision based on a series of legal conclusions. To wit,

1. That the Fourteenth Amendment, along with the Thirteenth and Fifteenth, had "one pervading purpose . . . without which none of them would have been even suggested": *viz.*, to secure to the freedmen their rights of "life, liberty, and property."[1]
2. That as to "due process of law," judicial precedent precludes any finding that the regulation at issue was a "deprivation" of the butchers' property.[2]
3. That the guarantee of "equal protection of the laws," which the Court identified as synonymous with "equal protection of the *law*," does indeed prohibit certain unequal laws, but only discriminatory laws involving "gross injustice and hardship" to African Americans—and *perhaps*, in some other cases of "State oppression" by unequal laws.[3]
4. That as to "the privileges and immunities of citizens of the United States,"
    (a) these may be understood in light of the preceding Citizenship Clause, which establishes a "comprehensive definition" of citizenship;[4]
    (b) this Citizenship Clause "clearly" establishes two citizenships: a citizenship of the states, and another of the United States;[5]
    (c) "the privileges and immunities of citizens *of the several States*," as guaranteed by Article IV, consist in rights granted or established by state authority;[6] and

(d) therefore, by analogy, "the privileges [and] immunities of citizens *of the United States*," as guaranteed by the Amendment, consist in the rights granted or established by federal authority or that otherwise "owe their existence to the Federal government, its national character, its Constitution, or its laws."[7]

Within a few years of the decision, these legal conclusions received the general acceptance of the bench and bar. For the most part, these holdings still prevail today.

But in this volume, I have concluded that there was an original official consensus:

1. That the Fourteenth Amendment's original motive was to secure to the freedmen not only the human rights of person and property, but also the fundamental civil rights of citizenship, and to provide that same security to white unionists and white northerners.
2. That the Due Process Clause, by its clear terms, concerns only state deprivations, and not mere regulations, and thus the butchers' claim was not only unprecedented but wholly inconsistent with the plain text of the Amendment.
3. That the Equal Protection Clause, by prohibiting only denials of equal enforcement of "the laws," in no way bans unequal or unjust substantive laws.
4. That as to the Privileges or Immunities Clause,

   (a) the Citizenship Clause could provide no general principle for interpreting the Privileges or Immunities Clause, for the former Clause was a merely partial declaration of citizenship, while the latter Clause protects *all* citizens;
   (b) the Citizenship Clause does not recognize or establish two distinct citizenships, but only a single citizenship of the Union, with a merely contingent and derivative citizenship in a state;
   (c) Article IV, as understood by those drafting the Privileges or Immunities Clause, recognizes certain "privileges and immunities of citizens" as fundamental, and not state-granted, for they have been enjoyed by citizens, as a matter of right, in all the states of our Union since 1776; and
   (d) the "privileges and immunities of citizens of the United States" are precisely these same fundamental civil rights of citizenship.

The *Slaughter-House* decision, then, provides powerful evidence against my conclusions, in two ways. First, the fact that there was such a sharp division in the Court, with Republicans on both sides, suggests the absence of any original official consensus. Second, the fact that the Court's majority, and then the whole legal profession, accepted conclusions so at odds with my own, strongly indicates that even if there was some original consensus, it was not the consensus I set forth here.

To rehabilitate my claims, then, I would have to show evidence of some great rupture. There must have been, between 1868 and 1873, some discernible break, whereby the original consensus was lost or abandoned by American jurists.

The challenge is daunting and cannot be met within this volume. Still, for present purposes, I will here sketch a tentative answer that provides at least some *prima facie* evidence and explanation of this rupture.

First, we should note that evidence of the rupture appears on the very face of the *Slaughter-House* opinions. The Court's members turned their backs on the original understanding. Neither the majority nor the dissenters considered the formal Report of the Joint Committee on Reconstruction, the principal introductory speeches of Representatives Stevens or Senator Howard, or the multiple formal transmittal statements of the state executives. All this history was readily available to the Court.

Second, the majority disregarded even the constitutional text. Justice Miller misquoted Article IV, § 2, so that it read, "The citizens of each State shall be entitled to all *the* privileges and immunities of citizens *of* the several States,"[8] thus adding "the" before "privileges" and replacing "in" with "of" before "the several States."[9] The effect was to rewrite Article IV so as to be tightly parallel with the Amendment, which protects "*the* privileges [and] immunities of citizens *of* the United States." Whether intentional or not, the misquotation plainly bolstered Miller's claim of two distinct citizenships, featuring parallel and closely analogous "privileges and immunities."

Third, contemporaries noticed the rupture. In their dissents, Justice Bradley pointed out this misquotation,[10] and Justice Swayne insisted that the majority's "history" had disregarded the well-known original intent.[11] And a few months after the decision, a learned commentator, citing Senator Trumbull's remarks in Congress, *Corfield v. Coryell*, and Senator Poland's principal speech, demonstrated that Justice Miller's opinion was irreconcilable with the original understanding: The Amendment's Privileges or Immunities Clause was designed to further guarantee the same fundamental privileges and immunities of citizenship already secured by Article IV.[12]

Most telling was the reaction of Matthew Carpenter. As a winning co-counsel in that case, and losing attorney in the contemporaneous *Bradwell v. Illinois*, he had made the same argument that I have made here: The "privileges and immunities of citizens of the United States" are the same "privileges and immunities," protected by Article IV, and as elaborated in *Corfield*, and include the right to travel, to acquire real as well as personal property, and more generally, to participate in the markets and professions.[13]

Soon after the decision in those cases, Carpenter was invited to a reception, a victory party of sorts, at the home of Louisiana's black Lieutenant Governor, Cesar Antoine. The men were joined by other leading African Americans in the state. Carpenter had some disconcerting news for his hosts. Although the Court had reached the right result in upholding the state's law, the Court had disregarded the original understanding of the Privileges or Immunities Clause:

> The recent decision of the U.S. Supreme Court in your Slaughter-house case has very much narrowed *what was always understood* to be the scope and effect of the fourteenth amendment, and virtually decides that only those privileges and immunities which pertain to a citizen of the United States as such, and as contra-distinguished to the privileges which belong to a citizen of a State, are covered by the amendment, and given over to the keeping of the general government.[14]

So the rupture happened and was known. But its cause seems obscure. How was it that, within just a few years of the Fourteenth Amendment's adoption, the whole legal profession could set aside and even nullify the Privileges or Immunities Clause, as originally understood?

One cannot, I think, hastily attribute to a whole generation of lawyers either extreme forgetfulness or extreme dishonesty. Instead, I think there's a more complex answer. I'll sketch my hypothesis here.

When the Amendment was adopted, the American people were beset with three powerful subrational passions that greatly impaired their ability to fairly read and accept their own Constitution. Americans, after the Civil War, proved too commercial, too egalitarian, and too racist for their own Constitution. And the judiciary participated in the same failure, or at least sought to accommodate it.

The first of these subrational factors was the passion for commerce. Americans have long been a restless, commercial people, and at the close of the Civil War, America's commercial interests had an acute case of hubris and fear.

The hubris came with victory. Not only had America's commercial elite shed their fair share of blood, sweat, and tears in the cause of Union and Liberty, but it was precisely their commercial way of life that had been vindicated. Free Labor was the noble means as well as the noble end of the Great Triumph. The fear arose from startling new challenges to traditional economic freedom—employment regulations, price controls, and outright socialism—fears aggravated by the terrifying Paris Commune of 1871.

This hubris and this fear understandably moved certain elites to seek from the courts constitutional protection against populist regulations that seemed novel, arbitrary, and unjust, and at the very least contrary to the spirit of liberty vindicated in Reconstruction. However, this new protection required novel legal arguments that sacrificed constitutional truth in the interest of economic liberty.

A second passion was the love of equality. As a democratic people, Americans are, as Tocqueville observed, passionately fond of equality. And the spirit of the Reconstruction Amendments involved not just liberty but also equality.

The Fourteenth Amendment was profoundly dissatisfying to the devotees of equality, many of them quite wealthy and influential. They sought something more comprehensive, to secure equal political as well as civil rights. Many egalitarians had opposed the Amendment precisely because it had failed to secure equal voting rights for African Americans. And many also objected to the disregard of women's equal right to the suffrage.

Impatient with the indifference, if not hostility, to political equality, the activists turned to activism. Instead of waiting for what would be our Fifteenth and Nineteenth Amendments, the activists decided just to read these rights into the Privileges or Immunities Clause. By 1870, the Fifteenth Amendment formally established racial political equality, but sex equality remained outstanding. So activists continued their efforts in Congress and the courts.

These commercial and egalitarian passions, whether marked by fear, hubris, or impatience, provided the Fourteenth Amendment with many flatterers. But a third passion—American racism—provided the Amendment with its chief foe. And it was this adversary, I think, that was most responsible for the Amendment's misconstruction.

Now, as proven by the 1866 elections, a solid majority of northern whites were strongly in favor of not only emancipation, but also the freedmen's rights to the basic rights of travel, commerce, and so on. And to this extent, many southern whites could acquiesce.

But white Americans, for the most part, were stubbornly unwilling to accept African Americans as full fellow citizens for purposes of (1) the household (interracial marriage and schooling), and (2) shared political authority.

To adapt the language of Shylock in the Merchant of Venice, the average white American said to the black American, "I will buy with you, sell with you, talk with you, walk with you, and so following, but I will not eat with you, drink with you, nor pray with you."[15] And with Shylock, the white American could add, "I will even go to court with you, but I certainly will not intermarry with you, share grandchildren with you, or share political power with you."

But the Fourteenth and Fifteenth Amendments plainly guaranteed full and equal citizenship—which necessarily required the invalidation of all laws imposing any racial burdens (direct or indirect) on Americans' rights as fellow citizens. As fellow citizens, there could be no legal racial barriers to intermarriage, common schools, and common political rights.

For Republicans, American racism posed an acute political problem. In large states like Ohio and New York, where Republicans enjoyed a substantial but not-insurmountable majority, racial apartheid seemed intractable. And any Republican judicial efforts to invalidate segregation threatened to sweep in statewide and national Democratic majorities hostile to the very notion of a multiracial republic. Republicans, and the cause of civil rights, could not afford to lose these voters and these states.

The problem was not unlike that faced by Governor Thomas Fletcher in Missouri a few years prior. The very citizens whose support was needed to secure civil and political rights were stubbornly in favor of local laws that plainly abridged one or more of the fundamental rights of citizenship.

The solution, both for Fletcher in 1867 and for Republicans nationally circa 1872–1873, was disingenuity: to redefine the Privileges or Immunities Clause, so it secured, not these fundamental rights, but only rights created by federal authority. Such redefinition avoided any embarrassing challenges to laws that abridged either the privilege of free discussion (by the imposition of expurgative test oaths on speech) or the immunity against all racially discriminatory burdens (by laws impeding marriage and common schools across racial lines).

At the same time, Republicans could not abandon constitutional civil rights altogether. They needed to find some new constitutional basis for securing African Americans' basic rights to the territory, markets, and tribunals. The solution, for Justice Miller et al., was to repurpose "equal protection of the laws," so that it meant "equal protection of the law," or more precisely "protection by [racially] equal laws." This provision, quite conveniently, spoke of the equal personhood that white Americans would accept, without mentioning the citizenship that made apartheid so anomalous.

As affirmed in the first sentence of our Declaration of Independence, an "equal and separate" station may be consistent with equal personhood, but not common citizenship.[16]

I cannot here prove that such was the motive of either Fletcher in 1867, or the northern Republican jurists of 1873. But the circumstantial evidence points in this direction. Republican leaders plainly had the motive, means, and opportunity.

Moreover, the disingenuous interpretation first appeared precisely in meeting constitutional challenges to racial apartheid. The first such instance occurred in the fall of 1871, in a case challenging Tennessee's ban on interracial marriage. The state's attorney general drew a sharp distinction between the rights of citizens of the United States and the "rights of citizens of States":

> The rights of citizens of the United States, are not the rights of citizens of States, but those political and civil rights, guaranteed by the Constitution of the United States. These are of the most restricted character . . .
>
> Marriage is in no sense a privilege which the citizen has, as a citizen of the United States. They have never attempted to regulate marriage in a State, and they have no right to. It is not claimed or held of the United States, but of the State.[17]

The privileges of U.S. citizenship are, then, those guaranteed by the federal Constitution, or otherwise "claimed" or "held" by federal authority. Interracial marriage is not included.

But if the Privileges or Immunities Clause secures only such constitutionally enumerated rights, what part of the Fourteenth Amendment prohibits the states from discriminating against African Americans?

> What is it that prohibits distinction of race, &c.? The 14th amendment prohibits the denial of *equal protection of the law*.[18]

There, in embryonic form, was the method to be adopted in *Slaughter-House*: both the nullification of the Privileges or Immunities Clause (only federal rights), the misquotation of the Equal Protection Clause (the replacement of "laws" with "law"), and the repurposing of that Clause to now secure equal laws as to race and to an indefinite number of other categories (under that cryptic "&c").

The Tennessee Supreme Court tacitly rejected Heiskell's novelty but upheld the law. The court acknowledged that the Amendment's "privileges and immunities" were the same as those of Article IV, as interpreted in *Corfield*, but concluded that the "right of intermarriage" was not one of them.[19]

But it was in Ohio—the virtual birthplace of the Privileges or Immunities Clause—where a court first endorsed the redefinition of that provision. Here again, racial apartheid was the issue. In upholding segregated schools, the state's highest court, dominated by Republicans, contended that there were "strong reasons for believing that it includes only such privileges or immunities as are derived from, or recognized by, the constitution of the United States."[20] A few months later, a New York judge in another segregation case relied on this Ohio opinion and likewise said that by the best reading of the Amendment, these privileges and immunities are those rights that "arise under the Constitution of the United States, and not those which arise under State laws."[21] The right of education did not "arise under" the Constitution, so it fell outside the scope of the Clause.

By spring 1873, when the Court decided *Slaughter-House*, Justice Miller probably had three main goals. First, he sought to resist the relentless demands of the commercial and egalitarian activists that would destroy states' rights. Second, he hoped, by a strategic retreat, to partly accommodate American apartheid, all while preserving the main purpose of the Amendment—civil equality between black and white—even without a full common citizenship. Finally, he sought to present this settlement via a superficially plausible reading of Section 1.

The school-segregation decisions already provided him with a template. Via a superficially plausible reading—a pretextual textualism, if you will—he could nullify the Privileges or Immunities Clause, so it was no longer available, either for misuse by unruly commercial and egalitarian passions, or for embarrassing challenges to American apartheid. Further, by transferring racial equality to the Equal Protection Clause, he could largely safeguard racial equality without threatening racial apartheid. Equal, but separate, would be enough.

Justice Miller and his colleagues engaged in a strategy that, in an appropriately veiled way, sacrificed constitutional truth in the interest of justice. It was a smart and understandable decision. It was a noble lie.

* * *

Assuming my hypothesis is correct, we might well ask whether the noble lie proved ignoble—even a disaster for our Republic.

The opinion permanently harmed the integrity of the whole American bench and bar. We have never recovered. We have long been governed by a jurisprudence that has no grounding in the text of the Fourteenth Amendment and no other generally accepted basis.

Moreover, this sacrifice of truth has worked injustice, first and foremost to the very group that Justice Miller hoped to serve: African Americans. Carpenter saw the writing on the wall. To the dismay of his black hosts, Carpenter accurately predicted that the Court's anti-originalist decision in *Slaughter-House* laid the groundwork for the future nullification of the Enforcement Acts and other federal civil rights laws.[22] Equal but separate became not just a temporary concession but a permanent norm. And separate and unequal (sometimes *violently* unequal) became the reality.

Moreover, this strategic retreat did injustice to all Americans. The Court arrogated to itself, under "equal protection," an immense power to strike down any law it deemed grossly unreasonable or unfair. And despite Justice Miller's wishes, this potential power would soon be supplemented by similar usurpation under "substantive due process."

Of course, the commercial and egalitarian activists did not go away. The Court's novel "doctrines" provided ample opportunity to solicit the judiciary's aid in striking down state laws, especially under the Warren and Burger Courts. Judicial usurpation eroded government by the people.

Conversely, the Supreme Court would complement its usurpation with abdication. The Court abandoned the traditional principles of actual "due process of law," in favor of procedural novelties. By the twentieth century, law was a "progressive science," so "the methods by which justice is administered are subject to constant fluctuation."[23] But to ensure fairness, overseeing all this lively innovation, would be the self-appointed referees—the courts. The judiciary abandoned the restraining *ratio* of tradition in favor of rule by the fair-minded judge.

American kritocracy worked both ways. The Supreme Court could christen, as eminently reasonable, certain nakedly unconstitutional laws, as in *Plessy v. Ferguson* and *Buck v. Bell*. Conversely, the Court could strike down some (arguably) unreasonable but plainly constitutional regulations, as in *Lochner v. New York* and *Adkins v. Children's Hospital*.

The kritocracy was supposed to be moderate, urbane, reasonable. Still, whether intolerant or permissive, moderate or immoderate, reasonable or unreasonable, it has been all activism—whether by usurpation or abdication.

Further, the abandonment of the original understanding was harmful not only to truth and justice, but also to peace. In "an exceedingly frank and free discussion," as a reporter noted, Carpenter advised black Louisianans to forget about federal protection. After *Slaughter-House*, he rightly predicted, the Enforcement Acts would be struck down, and the federal laws would no longer be a reliable shield. Instead, as "citizens of the United States," southern lacks should rely chiefly on an appeal to arms: "if any white man invades your house or assaults your person, you have the right of self-defense," for after all, "you know how to load a gun, you know how to fire it, and the sacred right of self-defense, the highest of all rights, a right which is above all constitutions, is possessed by you as well."[24]

In other words, an eminent citizen, U.S. Senator, and leading member of the Supreme Court's bar told his fellow citizens, "Forget constitutional self-government. Why don't you learn to shoot white people?"

Above all, the sacrifice of constitutional truth has degraded our great American enterprise. As Hamilton observed in the first number of the *Federalist Papers*, it was the peculiar right and duty of the American people,

> by their conduct and example, to decide the important question, whether societies of men are really capable or not of establishing good government from reflection and choice, or whether they are forever destined to depend for their political constitutions on accident and force.[25]

Our Republic, then, was supposed to exemplify government by popular reason: "it is the reason, alone, of the public, that ought to control and regulate the government." As to popular passions, they "ought to be controlled and regulated by the government."[26]

But from the *Slaughter-House* decision, the American judiciary has deliberately misconstrued the outcome of the American people's deliberations—the Fourteenth Amendment—largely to accommodate the people's commercial, egalitarian, and racist passions. The federal courts thus indulged the people's passions, disobeyed the people's deliberate reason, and established, *sua sponte*, government by judiciary.

To that extent, the Supreme Court's well-intentioned but ignoble lie has left us with a judicial despotism, so often attended by accident and force, including interracial violence. The result has been a tremendous defeat for the cause of peace, truth, justice, and the American way.

Notes

1 *Slaughter-House Cases*, 83 U.S. 26, 70–1 (1873). See also *id.* at 71 (defining the purpose as "the freedom of the slave race, the security and firm establishment of that freedom, and the protection of the newly made freeman and citizen from the oppressions of those who had formerly exercised unlimited dominion over him").
2 *Id.* at 81.
3 *Id.*
4 *Id.* at 73–4.
5 *Id.* at 73.
6 *Id.* at 77 (emphasis added).
7 *Id.* at 79.
8 *Id.* at 75 (emphasis added).
9 *See* Richard L. Aynes, *Constricting the Law of Freedom: Justice Miller, The Fourteenth Amendment, and the Slaughter-House Cases—Freedom: Constitutional Law*, 70 Chi. Kent L. Rev. 627, 646 (1994).
10 *Slaughter-House*, 83 U.S. at 117 (Bradley, J., dissenting).
11 *Id.* at 129 (Swayne, J., dissenting).
12 *Louisiana and the Supreme Court*, The Republic 257, 261–5 (July 1873).
13 *Slaughter-House Cases*, 21 L. Ed. 394, 399, 402 (1873) (argument of Durant, Carpenter, et al. for the defendants in error) (citing *Corfield* for an explanation of "privileges and immunities of citizens" and contending that there "is no reason for giving any more extensive signification to this phrase as used in the Amendment than was given to it as used in the original Constitution"); *Bradwell v. State*, 21 L. Ed. 442, 443–4 (1873) (argument of Carpenter for the plaintiff in error, citing the "opinion of Mr. Justice Washington, in a celebrated case" in discussing the meaning of "privileges and immunities of citizens" and adding these privileges include the right "to buy, hold, and sell land" and pursuing various "avocations," including the "profession of law").
14 *Senator Carpenter: Plain Talk with the Colored People*, New Orleans Republican, May 21, 1873, at 1, https://chroniclingamerica.loc.gov/lccn/sn83016555/1873-05-21/ed-1/seq-1/ (emphasis added).
15 William Shakespeare, Merchant of Venice, act I, sc. 3. I am grateful to my colleague Daniel Burns for showing me the relevance of this remark.
16 Declaration of Independence, para. 1 (U.S. 1776).
17 *Lonas v. State*, 50 Tenn. 287, 292–4 (1871) (argument of counsel).
18 *Id.* at 297 (emphasis in original).
19 *Id.* at 307–8.

20 *State ex rel. Garnes v. McCann*, 21 Ohio St. 198, 209–10 (1872).
21 *People ex rel. Dietz v. Easton*, 10 Abb. Pr. 159, 164 (N.Y. Sup. Ct. 1872).
22 *Id.*
23 *Holden v. Hardy*, 169 U.S. 366, 385–7 (1898).
24 *Id.*
25 Federalist No. 1, at 33 (Clinton Rossiter ed. 1961).
26 *Id.*, No. 49, at 317.

Bibliography

Books and Articles

Amar, Akhil Reed. "Attainder and Amendment 2." *Michigan Law Review* 95 (1996): 203–60.

Amar, Akhil Reed. *The Bill of Rights: Creation and Reconstruction*. New Haven, CT: Yale University Press, 1998.

Amar, Akhil Reed. "The Bill of Rights and the Fourteenth Amendment." *Yale Law Journal* 101 (1992): 1193–284.

Amar, Akhil Reed. "Double Jeopardy Law Made Simple." *Yale Law Journal* 106 (1997): 1807–48.

Ambrose, Graham. "Gunmaking at the Founding." *Stanford Law Review* 77 (2025): 235–80.

Ames, Herman Vandenburg. *The Proposed Amendments to the Constitution of the United States During the First Century of Its History*. Washington, DC: Government Printing Office, 1897.

Antieau, Chester J. "Paul's Perverted Privileges or The True Meaning of the Privileges and Immunities Clause of Article Four." *William & Mary Law Review* 9 (1967): 1–38.

Aristotle. *Nicomachean Ethics*. Translated by Robert C. Bartlett and Susan D. Collins. Chicago, IL: University of Chicago Press, 2011.

Aristotle. *Politics*. Translated by Carnes Lord. 2nd ed. Chicago, IL: University of Chicago Press, 2003.

Avins, Alfred. "Equal Protection against Unnecessary Police Violence and the Original Understanding of the Fourteenth Amendment: A Comment." *Buffalo Law Review* 19 (1970): 599–600.

Aynes, Richard L. "Constricting the Law of Freedom: Justice Miller, the Fourteenth Amendment, and the *Slaughter—House Cases*." *Chicago—Kent Law Review* 70 (1994): 627–46.

Aynes, Richard L. "Enforcing the Bill of Rights Against the States: The History and the Future." *Journal of Contemporary Legal Issues* 18 (2009): 77–110.

Aynes, Richard L. "Ohio and the Drafting and Ratification of the Fourteenth Amendment." In *History of Ohio Law*, edited by Michael Les Benedict and John F. Winkler, 1:370–82. Athens: Ohio University Press, 2004.

Aynes, Richard L. "On Misreading John Bingham and the Fourteenth Amendment." *Yale Law Journal* 103 (1993): 57–104.

Aynes, Richard L. "Refined Incorporation and the Fourteenth Amendment." *University of Richmond Law Review* 33 (1999): 289–322.

Aynes, Richard L. "Unintended Consequences of the Fourteenth Amendment and What They Tell Us About Its Interpretation." *Akron Law Review* 39 (2006): 289–320.

Balkin, Jack M. *Living Originalism*. Cambridge, MA: Belknap Press of Harvard University Press, 2011.

Balkin, Jack M. "The Reconstruction Power." *New York University Law Review* 85 (2010): 1801–69.
Barber, Edward W. "Men and Events in Washington During and After the Civil War." *Collections and Researches Made by the Michigan Pioneer and Historical Society* 30 (1906): 212–26.
Barnes, William H. *History of the Thirty-Ninth Congress of the United States*. New York: Harper & Brothers, 1868.
Barnett, Randy E., and Evan D. Bernick. "No Arbitrary Power: An Originalist Theory of the Due Process of Law." *William & Mary Law Review* 60 (2019): 1599–683.
Barnett, Randy E., and Evan D. Bernick. *The Original Meaning of the Fourteenth Amendment: Its Letter and Spirit*. Cambridge, MA: Harvard University Press, 2021.
Baude, William, Jud Campbell, and Stephen E. Sachs. "General Law and the Fourteenth Amendment." *Stanford Law Review* 76 (2024): 1185–240.
Beauregard, Erving E. "John A. Bingham and the Fourteenth Amendment." *The Historian* 50 (1987): 67–84.
Berger, Raoul. *Government by Judiciary: The Transformation of the Fourteenth Amendment*. 2nd ed. Indianapolis: Liberty Fund, 1997.
Bernick, Evan. "Fourteenth Amendment Confrontation." *Hofstra Law Review* 51 (2022): 1–50.
Bernstein, C'Zar. "Fetal Personhood and the Original Meanings of 'Person' in the Constitution." *Texas Review of Law & Politics* 26 (2022): 485–544.
Blaine, James G. *Twenty Years of Congress: From Lincoln to Garfield*. Norwich, CT: The Henry Hill Publishing Co., 1886.
Blake, Harlan M. "Employee Agreements Not to Compete." *Harvard Law Review* 73 (1960): 625–84.
Blakely, William Addison, ed. *American State Papers Bearing on Sunday Legislation*. Washington, DC: Religious Liberty Association, 1911.
Bodoh, Andrew T. "Liberty Is Not Loco-motion: *Obergefell* and the Originalists' Due Process Fallacy." *Campbell Law Review* 40 (2018): 321–60.
Bogen, David S. *Privileges and Immunities: A Reference Guide to the United States Constitution*. Westport, CT: Greenwood Press, 2003.
Bond, James E. *No Easy Walk to Freedom: Reconstruction and the Ratification of the Fourteenth Amendment*. Westport, CT: Praeger, 1997.
Bond, James E. "The Original Understanding of the Fourteenth Amendment in Illinois, Ohio, and Pennsylvania." *Akron Law Review* 18 (1985): 435–68.
Bork, Robert H. *The Tempting of America: The Political Seduction of the Law*. New York: Free Press, 1989.
Boutwell, George S. *Reminiscences of Sixty Years in Public Affairs*. New York: McClure, Phillips & Co., 1902.
Bradley, Gerard V. "Moral Truth and Constitutional Conservatism." *Louisiana Law Review* 81 (2021): 1317–60.
Brandwein, Pamela. *Rethinking the Judicial Settlement of Reconstruction*. New York: Cambridge University Press, 2011.
Braver, Joshua. "Court-Packing: An American Tradition?" *Boston College Law Review* 61 (2020): 2747–90.
Burkhart, Jeremy D. "William Lawrence: Perspectives of a Reconstruction Republican on the 14th Amendment." University of Akron Constitutional Law Center, 39th Congress

Project, 2010. https://ideaexchange.uakron.edu/cgi/viewcontent.cgi?article=1008&context=conlawakron39th.

Burrell, Thomas H. "*Dobbs v. Jackson Women's Health Organization*: Revisiting the Fourteenth Amendment, Due Process of Law, and American Citizenship." *Ohio Northern University Law Review* 49 (2023): 259–312.

Bybee, Jay S. "Taking Liberties With the First Amendment: Congress, Section 5, and the Religious Freedom Restoration Act." *Vanderbilt Law Review* 48 (1995): 1539–98.

Calabresi, Steven G., and Hannah M. Begley. "Originalism and Same-Sex Marriage." *University of Miami Law Review* 70 (2016): 648–82.

Calabresi, Steven G., and Julia T. Rickert. "Originalism and Sex Discrimination." *Texas Law Review* 90 (2011): 1–54.

Campbell, Jud. "The Emergence of Neutrality." *Yale Law Journal* 131 (2022): 861–946.

Canavan, Francis. "A New Fourteenth Amendment." *Human Life Review* 12 (1986): 30–40.

Carey, George W. *In Defense of the Constitution*. Revised ed. Indianapolis: Liberty Fund, 1995.

Carle, Susan D. "Liquidation and the Fourteenth Amendment." *Florida Law Review* 76 (2024): 103–42.

Chapman, Nathan S., and Michael W. McConnell. "Due Process as Separation of Powers." *Yale Law Journal* 121 (2012): 1672–750.

Chin, Gabriel J. "Reconstruction, Felon Disenfranchisement, and the Right to Vote: Did the Fifteenth Amendment Repeal Section 2 of the Fourteenth Amendment?" *Georgetown Law Journal* 92 (2004): 259–66.

Clark, John G. "Historians and the Joint Committee on Reconstruction." *The Historian* 23 (1961): 348–59.

Colby, Thomas B. "The Federal Marriage Amendment and the False Promise of Originalism." *Columbia Law Review* 108 (2008): 593–636.

Cornell, Saul. "The Right to Regulate Arms in the Era of the Fourteenth Amendment: The Emergence of Good Cause Permit Schemes in Post–Civil War America." *UC Davis Law Review Online* 55 (2021): 1–50.

Corwin, Edward S. "The Doctrine of Due Process of Law before the Civil War." *Harvard Law Review* 24 (1911): 366–85.

Crema, Max, and Lawrence B. Solum. "The Original Meaning of 'Due Process of Law' in the Fifth Amendment." *Virginia Law Review* 108 (2022): 447–526.

Crosskey, William W. *Politics and the Constitution in the History of the United States*. Chicago, IL: University of Chicago Press, 1953.

Curti, Merle, and Vernon Carstensen. *The University of Wisconsin: A History, 1848–1925*. Madison: University of Wisconsin Press, 1949.

Curtis, George Ticknor. *Constitutional History of the United States from Their Declaration of Independence to the Close of Their Civil War*. New York: Harper & Brothers, 1897.

Curtis, Michael Kent. "The Fourteenth Amendment: Recalling What the Court Forgot." *Drake Law Review* 56 (2008): 911–92.

Curtis, Michael Kent. *No State Shall Abridge: The Fourteenth Amendment and the Bill of Rights*. Durham, NC: Duke University Press, 1986.

Dalzell, James M. *John Gray, of Mount Vernon: The Last Soldier of the Revolution*. Washington, DC: Gibson Brothers, Printers, 1868.

Deach, Dorothy. "Student Opinion Concerning the Admission of Women to the University of Michigan 1867–1872." In *Studies in the History of American Education*, edited by Charles Eggertsen, 71–85. Ann Arbor: University of Michigan Press, 1947.

Deforrest, Mark. "Taming a Dragon: Legislative History in Legal Analysis." *Dayton Law Review* 39 (2013): 37–71.
Dolin, Gregory. "Resolving the Original Sin of Bolling v. Sharpe." *Seton Hall Law Review* 44 (2014): 749–836.
Donahue, Charles, Jr. "Magna Carta in the Fourteenth Century: From Law to Symbol? Reflections on the 'Six Statutes.'" *William & Mary Bill of Rights Journal* 25 (2016): 591–620.
Dripps, Donald A. *About Guilt and Innocence: The Origins, Development, and Future of Constitutional Criminal Procedure*. Westport, CT: Praeger, 2003.
Dripps, Donald A. "The Variola Variation." *Constitutional Commentary* 16 (1999): 511–16.
Du Bois, W. E. Burghardt. "A History of the Negro Vote." *The Crisis* 40 (1933): 128–30.
Du Bois, W. E. Burghardt. *Black Reconstruction in America, 1860–1880*. New York: Harcourt, Brace, and Company, 1935.
Dunning, William Archibald. *Essays on the Civil War and Reconstruction*. New York: The Macmillan Co., 1904.
Eastman, John C. "Born in the U.S.A.? Rethinking Birthright Citizenship in the Wake of 9/11." *University of Richmond Law Review* 42 (2008): 955–1000.
Epstein, Richard A. "Of Citizens and Persons: Reconstructing the Privileges or Immunities Clause of the Fourteenth Amendment." *New York University Journal of Law & Liberty* 1 (2005): 334–40.
Fairfax, Robert A., Jr. "Interrogating the Nonincorporation of the Grand Jury Clause." *Cardozo Law Review* 43 (2022): 855–900.
Fairman, Charles. "Does the Fourteenth Amendment Incorporate the Bill of Rights? The Original Understanding." *Stanford Law Review* 2 (1949): 1–56.
Fessenden, Francis. *Life and Public Services of William Pitt Fessenden*. Boston: Houghton, Mifflin and Company, 1907.
Finnis, John. "Abortion Is Unconstitutional." *First Things* 310 (2021): 29–34.
Finnis, John. "The Priority of Persons Revisited." *American Journal of Jurisprudence* 58 (2013): 45–62.
Fish, Peter. "Secrecy and The Supreme Court: Judicial Indiscretion and Reconstruction Politics." *William & Mary Law Review* 8 (1967): 225–33.
Flack, Horace. *The Adoption of the Fourteenth Amendment*. Baltimore: Johns Hopkins Press, 1908.
Flint, H. M., ed. *Life of Stephen A. Douglas, to Which Are Added His Speeches and Reports*. Philadelphia: J. E. Potter, 1863.
Foner, Eric. *Reconstruction: America's Unfinished Revolution, 1863–1877*. New York: Harper & Row, 1988.
Foner, Eric. *The Second Founding: How Civil War and Reconstruction Remade the Constitution*. New York: W. W. Norton & Company, 2019.
Fox, James W., Jr. "Citizenship, Poverty, and Federalism: 1787–1882." *University of Pittsburgh Law Review* 60 (1999): 421–76.
Fox, James W., Jr. "Publics, Meanings & the Privileges of Citizenship." *Constitutional Commentary* 30 (2015): 531–76.
Franck, Matthew J. "What Happened to the Due Process Clause in the Dred Scott Case? The Continuing Confusion over 'Substance versus 'Process.'" *American Political Thought* 4 (2015): 120–48.
Frank, John P., and Robert F. Munro. "The Original Understanding of 'Equal Protection of the Laws.'" *Washington University Law Quarterly* 1972 (1972): 421–39.

Franklin, Frank George. *The Legislative History of Naturalization in the United States.* Chicago, IL: University of Chicago Press, 1906.

Gans, David H. "The 14th Amendment Was Meant to Be a Protection Against State Violence." *The Atlantic*, July 19, 2020.

Garfield, James A. *The Works of James A. Garfield.* Edited by Burke A. Hinsdale. Boston: James R. Osgood and Company, 1882.

Gedicks, Frederick Mark. "An Originalist Defense of Substantive Due Process: Magna Carta, Higher-Law Constitutionalism, and the Fifth Amendment." *Emory Law Journal* 58 (2009): 583–640.

Gorod, Brianne J., and Brian R. Frazelle. "*Timbs v. Indiana*: Revival of a Critical Safeguard?" *Cato Supreme Court Review* 2018–2019 (2019): 147–78.

Gould, Lewis L. *Grand Old Party: A History of the Republicans.* New York: Random House, 2012.

Graber, Mark. "Constructing Constitutional Politics: Thaddeus Stevens, John Bingham, and the Forgotten Fourteenth Amendment." University of Maryland Legal Studies Research Paper No. 2014–37, August 19, 2014. SSRN:https://ssrn.com/abstract =2483355.

Graham, Howard Jay. *Everyman's Constitution: Historical Essays on the Fourteenth Amendment, the "Conspiracy Theory," and American Constitutionalism.* Madison: State Historical Society of Wisconsin, 1968.

Graham, Howard Jay. "The Framing of the Fourteenth Amendment, by Joseph B. James." *Indiana Law Journal* 32 (1957): 285–93.

Gray, David. "Dangerous Dicta." *Washington and Lee Law Review* 72 (2015): 1181–96.

Greeley, Horace. *The American Conflict: A History of the Great Rebellion in the United States of America.* Hartford, CT: O.D. Case & Co., 1865.

Green, Christopher R. *Equal Citizenship, Civil Rights, and the Constitution: The Original Sense of the Privileges or Immunities Clause.* New York: Routledge, 2015.

Green, Christopher R. "Incorporation, Total Incorporation, and Nothing But Incorporation?" *William & Mary Bill of Rights Journal* 24 (2015): 93–135.

Green, Christopher R. "Our Bipartisan Due Process Clause." *George Mason Law Review* 26 (2019): 1147–200.

Green, Christopher R. "The Original Sense of the (Equal) Protection Clause: Pre-Enactment History." *George Mason University Civil Rights Law Journal* 19 (2008): 1–46.

Green, Christopher R. "Twelve Problems with Substantive Due Process." *George Mason Journal of Law & Public Policy* 16 (2018): 397–448.

Gressman, Eugene. "The Unhappy History of Civil Rights Legislation." *Michigan Law Review* 50 (1952): 1323–58.

Grossberg, Michael. *Governing the Hearth: Law and the Family in Nineteenth-Century America.* Chapel Hill: University of North Carolina Press, 2004.

Guelzo, Allen C. *Reconstruction: A Concise History.* New York: Oxford University Press, 2018.

Guminski, Arnold T. "The Rights, Privileges, and Immunities of the American People: A Disjunctive Theory of Selective Incorporation of the Bill of Rights." *Whittier Law Review* 7 (1985): 765–98.

Guthrie, William D. *Lectures on the Fourteenth Article of Amendment to the Constitution of the United States.* Boston: Little, Brown, and Company, 1898.

Halbrook, Stephen P. *Freedmen, the Fourteenth Amendment, and the Right to Bear Arms, 1866–1876.* Westport, CT: Greenwood Press, 1998.

Hamburger, Philip A. "Privileges or Immunities." *Northwestern University Law Review* 105 (2011): 61–147.
Han, William T. "Beyond Presidential Eligibility: The Natural Born Citizen Clause As a Source of Birthright Citizenship." *Drake Law Review* 58 (2010): 457–512.
Hardy, David T. "Original Popular Understanding of the Fourteenth Amendment as Reflected in the Print Media of 1866–1868." *Whittier Law Review* 30 (2009): 704–48.
Harrison, John. "Reconstructing the Privileges or Immunities Clause." *Yale Law Journal* 101 (1992): 1385–474.
Hendrick, Frank. *The Power to Regulate Corporations and Commerce*. New York: G.P. Putnam's Sons, 1906.
Hinman, Mary Karlynn. "The Lost Clause: An Analysis of the Privileges and Immunities of Citizens of the United States." Ph.D. diss., Harvard University, 1967.
Hurd, John C. *The Theory of Our National Existence: As Shown by the Action of the Government of the United States Since 1861*. Boston: Little, Brown, and Company, 1881.
Hyman, Andrew T. "A Comment in Response to Dale Carpenter Regarding Equal Protection." *The Originalism Blog*, November 23, 2014. https://originalismblog.typepad.com/the-originalism-blog/2014/11/a-comment-in-response-to-dale-carpenter-regarding-equal-protectionandrew-hyman.html.
Hyman, Andrew T. "The Little Word 'Due.'" *Akron Law Review* 38 (2005): 1–34.
Hyman, Andrew T. "The Substantive Role of Congress Under the Equal Protection Clause." *Southern University Law Review* 42 (2014): 79–105.
Hyman, Harold M. *A More Perfect Union: The Impact of the Civil War and Reconstruction on the Constitution*. New York: Alfred A. Knopf, 1973.
Hyman, Harold M. *Era of the Oath: Northern Loyalty Tests During the Civil War and Reconstruction*. Philadelphia: University of Pennsylvania Press, 1972.
Ing, Matthew. "Birthright Citizenship, Illegal Aliens, and the Original Meaning of the Citizenship Clause." *Akron Law Review* 45 (2012): 719–68.
James, Joseph B. *The Framing of the Fourteenth Amendment*. Urbana: University of Illinois Press, 1956.
James, Joseph B. *The Ratification of the Fourteenth Amendment*. Macon: Mercer University Press, 1984.
Jordan, Larry L. "Historical Bar: Four Questions About the First Woman to Clerk at the United States Supreme Court." *Alaska Bar Rag* 36 (2012): 4.
Kaczorowski, Robert J. "Congress's Power to Enforce Fourteenth Amendment Rights: Lessons from Federal Remedies the Framers Enacted." *Harvard Journal on Legislation* 42 (2005): 187–272.
Kaczorowski, Robert J. *The Nationalization of Civil Rights: Constitutional Theory and Practice in a Racist Society, 1866–1883*. New York: Fordham University Press, 1987.
Kaczorowski, Robert J. "Revolutionary Constitutionalism in the Era of the Civil War and Reconstruction." *New York University Law Review* 61 (1986): 863–940.
Kelly, Alfred H. "The Fourteenth Amendment Reconsidered, The Segregation Question." *Michigan Law Review* 54 (1956): 1049–86.
Kennedy, Anthony M. "William Rehnquist and Sandra Day O'Connor: An Expression of Appreciation." *Stanford Law Review* 58 (2006): 1663–72.
Kettner, James H. *The Development of American Citizenship, 1608–1870*. Chapel Hill: University of North Carolina Press, 1978.

Kozlowski, Mark. *The Myth of the Imperial Judiciary: Why the Right Is Wrong About the Courts*. New York: Oxford University Press, 2003.

Kull, Andrew. *The Color-Blind Constitution*. Cambridge, MA: Harvard University Press, 1992.

LaRue, Lewis H. "Liberty, Equality, Privileges, Immunities: Lost Knowledge." Washington and Lee University Public Law and Legal Theory Research Paper Series, Working Paper No. 00–4, 2000. SSRN: https://papers.ssrn.com/abstract=247655.

Lash, Kurt T. "An Incomplete Introduction to the Fourteenth Amendment." *Law & Liberty*, January 20, 2021. https://lawliberty.org/an-incomplete-introduction-to-the-fourteenth-amendment/.

Lash, Kurt T. "Enforcing the Rights of Due Process: The Original Relationship between the Fourteenth Amendment and the 1866 Civil Rights Act." *Georgetown Law Journal* 106 (2018): 1389–468.

Lash, Kurt T. *The Fourteenth Amendment and the Privileges and Immunities of American Citizenship*. New York: Cambridge University Press, 2014.

Lash, Kurt T. "The Lost Jurisprudence of the Ninth Amendment." *Texas Law Review* 83 (2005): 597–716.

Lash, Kurt T. "The State Citizenship Clause." *University of Pennsylvania Journal of Constitutional Law* 25 (2023): 1097–149.

Lauer, Sister Mary Jerome. *The Civil Rights Bill of 1866*. M.A. thesis, Marquette University, 1943.

LeBuffe, Francis Peter. *Outlines of Pure Jurisprudence*. New York: Fordham University Press, 1924.

Leider, Robert. "The Individual Right To Bear Arms For Common Defense." SSRN, 2024. https://ssrn.com/abstract=4918009.

Leyland, Herbert Thompson. *The Concept of Due Process of Law in 1866 and Its Influence on the Fourteenth Amendment*. M.A. thesis, University of Wisconsin, 1922.

Lomen, Lucile. "Privileges and Immunities Under the Fourteenth Amendment." *Washington Law Review & State Bar Journal* 18 (1943): 120–35.

Lugosi, Charles I. "Conforming to the Rule of Law: When Person and Human Being Finally Mean the Same Thing in Fourteenth Amendment Jurisprudence." *Georgetown Journal of Law & Public Policy* 4 (2006): 361–406.

Lund, Nelson. "Two Faces of Judicial Restraint (Or Are There More?) in *McDonald v. City of Chicago*." *Florida Law Review* 63 (2011): 487–550.

Maggs, Gregory. "A Critical Guide to Using the Legislative History of the Fourteenth Amendment to Determine the Amendment's Original Meaning." *Connecticut Law Review* 49 (2017): 1069–109.

Magliocca, Gerard N. "Indians and Invaders: The Citizenship Clause and Illegal Aliens." *University of Pennsylvania Journal of Constitutional Law* 10 (2008): 499–541.

Maltz, Earl M. *Civil Rights, the Constitution, and Congress, 1863–1869*. Lawrence: University Press of Kansas, 1990.

Maltz, Earl M. "The Concept of Equal Protection of the Laws—A Historical Inquiry." *San Diego Law Review* 22 (1985): 499–540.

Maltz, Earl M. "The Entire Fourteenth Amendment." SSRN, September 7, 2023. https://papers.ssrn.com/sol3/papers.cfm?abstract_id=4566468.

Maltz, Earl M. "Moving beyond Race: The Joint Committee on Reconstruction and the Drafting of the Fourteenth Amendment." *Hastings Constitutional Law Quarterly* 42 (2015): 287–314.

Maltz, Earl. "The Speech of Jacob Howard, the Prevalent Rights Theory, and the Decision in Brown v. Board of Education." *The Originalism Blog*, October 16, 2019. https://originalismblog.typepad.com/the-originalism-blog/2019/10/the-speech-of-jacob-howard-the-prevalent-rights-theory-and-the-decision-in-brown-v-board-of-education.html.
Maverick, Augustine. *Henry J. Raymond and the New York Press, for Thirty Years: Progress of American Journalism from 1840 to 1870*. Hartford, CT: A.S. Hale & Co., 1870.
Massey, Calvin. "Privileges or Immunities." In *Heritage Guide to the Constitution*, edited by David F. Forte and Matthew Spaulding, 501–6. 2nd ed. Washington, DC: Regnery Publishing, 2014.
Mensel, Robert E. "Jurisdiction in Nineteenth Century International Law and Its Meaning in the Citizenship Clause of the Fourteenth Amendment." *Saint Louis University Public Law Review* 31 (2012): 330–405.
Meyer, Hermine Herta. *The History and Meaning of the Fourteenth Amendment: Judicial Erosion of the Constitution Through the Misuse of the Fourteenth Amendment*. New York: Vantage Press, 1977.
Mirola, William A. *Redeeming Time: Protestantism and Chicago's Eight-Hour Movement, 1866–1912*. Urbana: University of Illinois Press, 2014.
Mitchell, Jonathan P. "Textualism and the Fourteenth Amendment." *Stanford Law Review* 69 (2017): 1237–322.
Moreno, Paul D. *How the Court Became Supreme: The Origins of American Juristocracy*. New York: Encounter Books, 2022.
Nelson, William E. *The Fourteenth Amendment: From Political Principle to Judicial Doctrine*. Rev. ed. Cambridge, MA: Harvard University Press, 1998.
Oberholtzer, Ellis Paxson. *History of the United States Since the Civil War*. New York: The Macmillan Company, 1917.
Office of Legal Policy, Department of Justice. *Wrong Turns on the Road to Judicial Activism: The Ninth Amendment and the Privileges or Immunities Clause*. Washington, DC: U.S. Department of Justice, 1987.
Paulsen, Michael Stokes. "Does the Constitution Prescribe Rules for Its Own Interpretation?" *Northwestern University Law Review* 103 (2009): 857–922.
Pence, Charles R. "The Construction of the Fourteenth Amendment." *American Law Review* 25 (1891): 536–40.
Peterson, Merrill D. *The Great Triumvirate: Webster, Clay, and Calhoun*. New York: Oxford University Press, 1987.
Plato. *The Republic*. Translated by Allan Bloom. New York: Basic Books, 1968.
Pollvogt, Susannah W. "Beyond Suspect Classifications." *University of Pennsylvania Journal of Constitutional Law* 16 (2014): 739–75.
Pomerance, Benjamin. "Justice Denied: The Peculiar History of Rejected United States Supreme Court Nominees." *Albany Law Review* 80 (2017): 627–61.
Porter, David Dixon. *Incidents and Anecdotes of the Civil War*. New York: D. Appleton & Co., 1885.
Ramsey, Michael D. "Originalism and Birthright Citizenship." *Georgetown Law Journal* 109 (2020): 405–528.
Ramsey, Michael D. "The Original Meaning of 'Natural Born.'" *University of Pennsylvania Journal of Constitutional Law* 20 (2017): 199–224.

Rappaport, Mike. "Original Methods Originalism Part I: The Basic Idea and the Different Versions." *Law & Liberty*, May 26, 2017. https://lawliberty.org/original-methods-originalism-part-i-the-basic-idea-and-the-different-versions/.
Rosenthal, Lawrence, and Joyce Lee Malcolm. "Colloquy Debate: McDonald v. Chicago: Which Standard of Scrutiny Should Apply to Gun Control Laws?" *Northwestern University Law Review* 105 (2011): 460–77.
Salter, William. *The Life of James W. Grimes*. New York: D. Appleton and Company, 1876.
Samar, Vincent J. "The Analytic Aposteriori and a New Understanding of Substantive Due Process that Is Exhibited in the Lives of Those Seeking to Marry Someone of the Same Sex." *Saint Louis University Public Law Review* 30 (2011): 377–411.
Sanders, Anthony B. *Baby Ninth Amendments: How Americans Embraced Unenumerated Rights and Why It Matters*. Lawrence: University Press of Kansas, 2023.
Scott, Joshua A. "The Right Thing for the Wrong Reasons? The Incorporation of the Second Amendment in *McDonald v. Chicago*." *Ave Maria Law Review* 9 (2011): 335–79.
Siegan, Bernard H. *The Supreme Court's Constitution: An Inquiry into Judicial Review and Its Impact on Society*. New Brunswick, NJ: Transaction Books, 1987.
Slap, Andrew L. *The Doom of Reconstruction: The Liberal Republicans in the Civil War Era*. New York: Fordham University Press, 2006.
Smith, Douglas G. "A Lockean Analysis of Section One of the Fourteenth Amendment." *Harvard Journal of Law & Public Policy* 25 (2002): 1095–170.
Smith, Douglas G. "Originalism and the Affirmative Action Decisions." *Case Western Reserve Law Review* 55 (2004): 1–45.
Smith, Willard H. "Schuyler Colfax and Reconstruction Policy." *Indiana Magazine of History* 39 (1943): 383–404.
Solum, Lawrence B. "The Fourteenth Amendment and the Bill Of Rights: Incorporation and Originalist Theory." *Journal of Contemporary Legal Issues* 18 (2009): 409–32.
Stahr, Walter. *Salmon P. Chase: Lincoln's Vital Rival*. New York: St. Martin's Press, 2021.
Steiner, Bernard C. *Life of Reverdy Johnson*. Baltimore: The Norman, Remington Co., 1914.
Stevens, Richard G. *Reason and History in Judicial Judgment: Felix Frankfurter and Due Process*. Rev. ed. Lanham, MD: Lexington Books, 2017.
Stinneford, John F. "The Original Meaning of Unusual: The Eighth Amendment as a Bar to Cruel Innovation." *Northwestern University Law Review* 102 (2008): 1739–815.
Sunstein, Cass R. "Originalism for Liberals: Book Review of The Bill of Rights by Akhil Reed Amar & For the People by Akhil Reed Amar and Alan Hirsch." *The New Republic*, September 28, 1998. https://home.uchicago.edu/~csunstei/originalism.html.
Swayne, Wager. *The Ordinance of 1787 and the War of 1861: An Address Delivered Before the New York Commandery of the Military Order of the Loyal Legion*. New York: G.P. Putnam's Sons, 1892.
TenBroek, Jacobus. *The Antislavery Origins of the Fourteenth Amendment*. Berkeley: University of California Press, 1951.
Thomas, George C. "The Fourteenth Amendment and The Bill Of Rights: Newspapers and the Fourteenth Amendment: What Did the American Public Know About Section 1?" *Journal of Contemporary Legal Issues* 18 (2009): 323–60.
Thomas, George C. "When Constitutional Worlds Collide: Resurrecting the Framers' Bill of Rights and Criminal Procedure." *Michigan Law Review* 100 (2001): 145–232.
Thorpe, Francis Newton. *The Constitutional History of the United States*. Chicago: Callaghan and Company, 1901.

Tsesis, Alexander. "The Thirteenth Amendment's Revolutionary Aims." In *The Promises of Liberty: The History and Contemporary Relevance of the Thirteenth Amendment*, edited by Alexander Tsesis, 1–25. New York: Columbia University Press, 2010.
Upham, David R. "The 'Black and Tan Conventions,' Diverse Originalism, and the Fourteenth Amendment." *Mississippi Law Journal* 94 (2025): 1403–24.
Upham, David R. "Interracial Marriage and the Original Understanding of the Privileges or Immunities Clause." *Hastings Constitutional Law Quarterly* 42 (2015): 213–86.
Upham, David R. "The Meanings of the 'Privileges and Immunities of Citizens' on the Eve of the Civil War." *Notre Dame Law Review* 91 (2016): 1117–66.
Upham, David R. "Prenatal Personhood, State Duties, and Congress's Abortion Power Under the Fourteenth Amendment." *Catholic University Law Review* 74 (2025): 427–48.
Upham, David R. "The Understanding of 'Neither Slavery Nor Involuntary Servitude Shall Exist' Before the Thirteenth Amendment." *Georgetown Journal of Law & Public Policy* 15 (2017): 137–71.
Walton, Hanes, Jr., et al. *The African American Electorate: A Statistical History*. Washington, DC: CQ Press, 2012.
Warren, Charles. "The New Liberty Under the Fourteenth Amendment." *Harvard Law Review* 39 (1926): 431–5.
Weinberg, Louise. "The McReynolds Mystery Solved." *Denver University Law Review* 89 (2011): 133–60.
Wiessner, Siegfried. *Die Function Der Staatsangehörigkeit*. Berlin: Duncker & Humblot, 1989.
Wildenthal, Bryan H. "The Lost Compromise: Reassessing the Early Understanding in Court and Congress on Incorporation of the Bill of Rights in the Fourteenth Amendment." *Ohio State Law Journal* 61 (2000): 1051–149.
Wildenthal, Bryan H. "Nationalizing the Bill of Rights: Revisiting the Original Understanding of the Fourteenth Amendment in 1866–67." *Ohio State Law Journal* 68 (2007): 1509–97.
Williams, Ryan C. "The One and Only Substantive Due Process Clause." *Yale Law Journal* 120 (2010): 408–514.
Williams, Ryan C. "Originalism and the Other Desegregation Decision." *Virginia Law Review* 99 (2013): 493–580.
Wolfe, Christopher J. "An Artificial Being: John Marshall and Corporate Personhood." *Harvard Journal of Law and Public Policy* 40 (2017): 201–79.
Wolfe, Christopher J. *The Rise of Modern Judicial Review*. Lanham, MD: Rowman & Littlefield, 1986.
Wolfe, Christopher J. *The Rise of Modern Judicial Review: From Constitutional Interpretation to Judge-Made Law*. Rev. ed. Lanham, MD: Rowman & Littlefield, 1994.
Wurman, Ilan. "Reversing Incorporation." *Notre Dame Law Review* 99 (2023): 265–311.
Wurman, Ilan. *The Second Founding: An Introduction to the Fourteenth Amendment*. New York: Cambridge University Press, 2020.
Yen, Chin-Yung. *Rights of Citizens and Persons Under the Fourteenth Amendment*. Ph.D. diss., Columbia University, 1905.
Zuckert, Michael. "On the Fourteenth Amendment: A Textual Analysis." *Perspectives on Political Science* 48 (2019): 246–51.

Cases

Abbot v. Bayley, 23 Mass. 89 (1827).
Adamson v. California, 332 U.S. 46 (1947).
Adkins v. Children's Hospital, 261 U.S. 525 (1923).
Ainslie v. Martin, 9 Mass. 454 (1813).
Alexander v. Baltimore, 5 Gill 383 (Md. 1847).
Am. Legion v. Am. Humanist Ass'n, 588 U.S. 19 (2019).
American Insurance Company v. Canter, 26 U.S. 511 (1828).
Ames v. Port Huron Log Driving & Booming Co., 11 Mich. 139 (1863).
Anderson v. Baker, 23 Md. 531 (1865).
Baker v. Kelley, 11 Minn. 480 (1866).
Baker v. Wise, 57 Va. 139 (1861).
Bank of Columbia v. Okely, 17 U.S. 122 (1819).
Bank of United States v. Deveaux, 9 U.S. 61 (1809).
Bank One Chicago, NA v. Midwest Bank & Trust Co., 516 U.S. 264 (1996).
Bankhead v. Brown, 25 Iowa 540 (1868).
Barber v. Bryant, 193 F. Supp. 3d 677 (S.D. Miss. 2016).
Barker v. People, 3 Cow. 686 (N.Y. 1824).
Barnes v. Browning, Indiana Circuit Court (Lafayette, Ind.) (Apr. 13, 1866), reprinted in *The Richmond Palladium* (Richmond, Ind.), Apr. 26, 1866, at 1, http://chroniclingamerica.loc.gov/lccn/sn86058250/1866-04-26/ed-1/seq-1.
Barron v. Mayor & City Council of Baltimore, 32 U.S. 243 (1833).
Bartholomew v. People, 104 Ill. 601 (1882).
Beauharnais v. Illinois, 343 U.S. 250 (1952).
Beaupre v. Hoerr, 13 Minn. 366 (1868).
Bennet v. Bennet, 13 N.J. Eq. 114 (1860).
Bertholf v. O'Reilly, 74 N.Y. 509 (1878).
Blair v. Ridgely, 41 Mo. 63 (1867).
Bowlin v. Commonwealth, 65 Ky. 5 (1867).
Bradwell v. Illinois, 83 U.S. 130 (1873).
Briscoe v. President & Dirs. of Bank of Ky., 36 U.S. 257 (1837).
Brown v. Board of Education of Topeka, 347 U.S. 483 (1954).
Brown v. Hummel, 6 Pa. 86 (1847).
Bruch v. Carter, 32 N.J.L. 554 (1867).
Bryan v. Walton, 14 Ga. 185 (1853).
Buck v. Bell, 274 U.S. 200 (1927).
Bullock v. Geomble, 45 Ill. 218 (1867).
Burns v. State, 48 Ala. 195 (1872).
Butterworth v. Dempsey, 229 F. Supp. 754 (D. Conn. 1964).
Campbell v. Morris, 3 H. & McH. 535 (Md. 1797).
Carrington v. Rash, 380 U.S. 89 (1965).
Caruthers v. Andrews, 42 Tenn. 378 (1865).
Catherine H. Barber Mem. Shelter, Inc. v. Town of N. Wilkesboro Bd. of Adjustment, 576 F. Supp. 3d 318 (W.D.N.C. 2021).
Chaloner v. Sherman, 242 U.S. 455 (1917).
Chase v. Hathaway, 14 Mass. 222 (1817).

Chi. & Alton R.R. Co. v. People, 67 Ill. 11 (1873).
Chicago, Burlington & Quincy Railroad Co. v. Chicago, 166 U.S. 226 (1897).
Cincinnati Gazette Co. v. Timberlake, 10 Ohio St. 548 (1860).
Citizens for Const. Integrity v. Census Bureau, 115 F.4th 618 (D.C. Cir. 2024).
City of Boerne v. Flores, 521 U.S. 507 (1997).
Coe v. Schultz, 2 Abb. Pr. (n.s.) 193 (N.Y. Sup. Ct. 1866).
Coffin v. United States, 156 U.S. 432 (1895).
Cohen v. Wright, 22 Cal. 293 (1863).
Commonwealth v. Byrne, 61 Va. 165 (1871).
Commonwealth v. Smith, 92 Mass. 448 (1865).
Comm'r v. Acker, 361 U.S. 87 (1959).
Connecticut Gen. Life Ins. Co. v. Johnson, 303 U.S. 77 (1938).
Conner v. Elliott, 59 U.S. 591 (1855).
Cooper v. Schultz, 32 How. Pr. 107 (N.Y. Comm. Pleas 1866).
Corbin v. Marsh, 63 Ky. 193 (1865).
Corfield v. Coryell, 6 F. Cas. 546 (C.C.E.D. Pa. 1823).
Cost v. Genette, 1 Port. 212 (Ala. 1834).
Coster v. Tide Water Co., 18 N.J. Eq. 54 (1866).
Crandall v. State, 10 Conn. 339 (1834).
Crow v. State, 14 Mo. 237 (1851).
Cummings v. Missouri, 71 U.S. 277 (1867).
Dalton v. State, 6 Blackf. 357 (Ind. 1843).
Darrington v. Bank of Alabama, 54 U.S. 12 (1852).
Davidson v. N.Y.C., 27 How. Pr. 342 (N.Y. Sup. Ct. 1864).
Davis v. Pierse, 7 Minn. 13 (1862).
Den ex dem. Trustees of University v. Foy, 5 N.C. 58 (1805).
Dias v. The Revenge, 7 F. Cas. 637 (C.C.D. Pa. 1814).
District of Columbia v. Heller, 554 U.S. 570 (2008).
Dobbs v. Jackson Women's Health Org., 597 U.S. 215 (2022).
Dorman v. State, 34 Ala. 216 (1859).
Douglass Admin. v. Stevens, 2 Del. Cas. 489 (1819).
Douglass v. Stephens, 1 Del. Ch. 465 (1821).
Dred Scott v. Sandford, 60 U.S. 393 (1857).
East Kingston v. Towle, 48 N.H. 57 (1868).
Elk v. Wilkins, 112 U.S. 94 (1884).
Ex parte Bushnell, 9 Ohio St. 77 (1859).
Ex parte Garland, 71 U.S. 333 (1867).
Ex parte Grace, 12 Iowa 208 (1861).
Ex parte Hunter, 2 W. Va. 122 (1867).
Ex parte Milligan, 71 U.S. 2 (1866).
Ex parte Quarrier, 4 W. Va. 210 (1870).
Ex parte Wilson, 114 U.S. 417 (1885).
Fleming v. Page, 50 U.S. 603 (1850).
Fletcher v. Peck, 10 U.S. 87 (1810).
Gassies v. Ballon, 31 U.S. 761 (1832).
Gibbons v. Ogden, 22 U.S. 1 (1824).
Gibson v. Mason, 5 Nev. 283 (1869).

Goepp v. Bethlehem, 28 Pa. 249 (1857).
Goldberg v. Kelly, 397 U.S. 254 (1971).
Graham v. Richardson, 403 U.S. 365 (1971).
Green v. Shumway, 39 N.Y. 418 (1868).
Greene v. Briggs, 10 F. Cas. 1135 (C.C.D.R.I. 1852).
Griswold v. Connecticut, 381 U.S. 479 (1965).
Groves v. Slaughter, 40 U.S. 449 (1841).
Hall v. Hancock, 32 Mass. 255 (1834).
Harper v. Virginia Bd. of Elections, 383 U.S. 663 (1966).
Hawkins v. Filkins, 24 Ark. 286 (1867).
Heirn v. Bridault, 37 Miss. 209 (1859).
Hennen v. Hennen, 12 La. 190 (1838).
Hepburn v. Griswold, 75 U.S. 603 (1870).
Hoke v. Henderson, 15 N.C. 1 (1833).
Holden v. Hardy, 169 U.S. 366 (1898).
Howell v. Buffalo, 37 N.Y. 267 (1867).
Huber v. Reily, 53 Pa. 112 (1866).
Hurtado v. California, 110 U.S. 516 (1884).
In re Bergen, 3 F. Cas. 261 (C.C.N.C. 1870).
In re Dorsey, 7 Port. 293 (Ala. 1838).
In re Hobbs, 12 F. Cas. 262 (C.C.N.D. Ga. 1871).
In re Janes, 30 How. Pr. 446 (N.Y. Sup. Ct. 1866).
In re Petition of Goodenough, 19 Wis. 274 (1865).
In re Spenser, 22 F. Cas. 921 (C.C.D. Or. 1878).
In re the Oath to be taken by Attorneys & Counsellors, 35 Ga. 286 (1866).
Inglis v. Trustees of Sailor's Snug Harbor, 28 U.S. 99 (1830).
Insurance Co. v. New Orleans, 13 F. Cas. 67 (C.C.D. La. 1870).
Jackson v. White, 20 Johns. 313 (N.Y. 1822).
Jones v. Helms, 452 U.S. 412 (1981).
Jones v. Robbins, 74 Mass. 329 (1857).
Jones' Heirs v. Perry, 18 Tenn. 59 (1836).
Jordan v. Hyatt, 3 Barb. 275 (N.Y. Sup. Ct. 1848).
Kennedy v. Bremerton Sch. Dist., 597 U.S. 507 (2022).
Kincaid v. Francis, 3 Tenn. 48 (1812).
Kneedler v. Lane, 3 Grant 523 (Pa. 1864).
Lander v. State, 12 Tex. 462 (1854).
Lawrence v. Texas, 539 U.S. 558 (2003).
Lawson v. Scott, 9 Tenn. 92 (1825).
Lee v. Back, 30 Ind. 148 (1868).
Legal Tender Cases, 79 U.S. 457 (1871).
Lehman v. McBride, 15 Ohio St. 573 (1863).
Lemmon v. People, 20 N.Y. 562 (1860).
Lincoln v. Smith, 27 Vt. 328 (1856).
Lindsay v. Commissioners, 2 S.C.L. (2 Bay) 38 (Ct. App. 1796).
Littlejohn v. Sch. Bd. of Leon Cnty., 132 F.4th 1232 (11th Cir. 2025).
Live-Stock Dealers' & Butchers' Ass'n v. Crescent City Live-Stock Landing & Slaughter-House Co., 15 F. Cas. 649 (D.C.D. La. 1870).

Lochner v. New York, 198 U.S. 45 (1905).
Lonas v. State, 50 Tenn. 287 (1871).
Loughborough v. Blake, 18 U.S. 317 (1820).
Lynch v. Clarke, 1 Sand. Ch. 583 (N.Y. 1844).
Lyndon v. Danville, 28 Vt. 809 (1856).
Marbury v. Madison, 5 U.S. 137 (1803).
Marguerite v. Chouteau, 3 Mo. 540 (1834).
Marshall v. Baltimore & Ohio R.R., 57 U.S. 314 (1854).
Martin v. Snowden, 59 Va. 100 (1868).
Mason v. Rollins, 16 F. Cas. 1061 (C.C.N.D. Ill. 1869).
McCleskey v. Kemp, 481 U.S. 279 (1987).
McCulloch v. Maryland, 17 U.S. 316 (1819).
McDonald v. City of Chicago, 561 U.S. 742 (2010).
Meyer v. Nebraska, 262 U.S. 390 (1923).
Mississippi v. Johnson, 71 U.S. 475 (1867).
Munn v. Illinois, 94 U.S. 113 (1876).
Murphy & Glover Test Oath Cases, 41 Mo. 339 (1867).
Murray v. M'Carty, 16 Va. 393 (1811).
Murray's Lessee v. Hoboken Land & Improvement Co., 59 U.S. 272 (1856).
Musgrove v. Kornegay, 52 N.C. 71 (1859).
Neil v. Farmer, 9 Ga. 555 (1851).
Nesbitt v. Trumbo, 39 Ill. 110 (1866).
New York State Rifle & Pistol Association, Inc. v. Bruen, 597 U.S. 1 (2022).
Nordyke v. King, 563 F.3d 439 (9th Cir. 2009).
Oklahoma v. Castro-Huerta, 597 U.S. 629 (2022).
Opinion of the Supreme Judicial Court, 44 Me. 507 (1857).
Oregon v. Mitchell, 400 U.S. 112 (1970).
Osborn v. Nicholson, 18 F. Cas. 846 (C.C.E.D. Ark. 1870).
Palko v. Connecticut, 302 U.S. 319 (1937).
Parsons v. Russell, 11 Mich. 113 (1863).
Patterson v. McLean Credit Union, 491 U.S. 164 (1989).
Paul v. Virginia, 75 U.S. 168 (1869).
Payne v. Baldwin, 11 Miss. 661 (1844).
Pennsylvania, D. & M. Steam Navigation Co. v. Dandridge, 8 G. & J. 248 (Md. 1836).
People ex rel. Brooks, 35 Barb. 85 (N.Y. Sup. Ct. 1861).
People ex rel. Dietz v. Easton, 10 Abb. Pr. 159 (N.Y. Sup. Ct. 1872).
People ex rel. Matthews v. Toynbee, 12 How. Pr. 238 (N.Y. 1856).
People ex rel. Nickerson v. ____, 19 Wend. 16 (N.Y. Sup. Ct. 1837).
People ex rel. O'Connell v. Turner, 55 Ill. 280 (1870).
People v. Abbott, 19 Wend. 192 (N.Y. 1838).
People v. Crosswell, 3 Johns. Cas. 337 (N.Y. Sup. Ct. 1804).
People v. Goodwin, 18 Johns. 187 (N.Y. 1820).
People v. Hall, 4 Cal. 399 (1854).
People v. Washington, 36 Cal. 658 (1869).
Pierce v. Carskadon, 83 U.S. 234 (1873).
Pierce v. Underwood, 487 U.S. 552 (1988).
Planned Parenthood of Southeastern Pa. v. Casey, 505 U.S. 833 (1992).

Planters' Bank of Mississippi v. Sharp, 47 U.S. 301 (1848).
Plessy v. Ferguson, 163 U.S. 537 (1896).
Plyler v. Doe, 457 U.S. 202 (1982).
Poe v. Ullman, 367 U.S. 497 (1961).
Poindexter v. Louisiana Financial Assistance Com., 275 F. Supp. 833 (E.D. La. 1967).
Powers v. Inferior Court of Dougherty County, 23 Ga. 65 (1857).
Prigg v. Pennsylvania, 41 U.S. 539 (1842).
Ramsay v. Ramsay, 20 Wis. 507 (1866).
Reed v. Wright, 2 G. Greene 15 (Iowa 1849).
Reidell v. Morse, 36 Mass. 358 (1837).
Renthorp v. Bourg, 4 Mart. (O.S.) 97 (La. 1816).
Reynolds v. Sims, 377 U.S. 533 (1964).
Rison v. Farr, 24 Ark. 161 (1865).
Robison v. Beall, 26 Ga. 17 (1858).
Rockwell v. Nearing, 35 N.Y. 302 (1866).
Roe v. Wade, 410 U.S. 113 (1973).
Rogers v. Soggs, 22 Cal. 444 (1863).
Roosevelt v. Godard, 52 Barb. 533 (N.Y. Gen. Term 1868).
San Mateo County v. Southern Pacific R. Co., 116 U.S. 138 (1885).
Sears v. Cottrell, 5 Mich. 251 (1858).
Sharpless v. Mayor & Citizens of Philadelphia, 21 Pa. 147 (1853).
Slaughter-House Cases, 83 U.S. 36 (1873).
St. Amour v. Rivard, 2 Mich. 294 (1852).
Standeford v. Wingate, 63 Ky. 440 (1866).
Starr v. Hamilton, 22 F. Cas. 1107 (C.C. D. Ore. 1867).
State ex rel. Burlington & M. R. R. Co. v. County of Wapello, 13 Iowa 388 (1862).
State ex rel. Garnes v. McCann, 21 Ohio St. 198 (1871).
State ex rel. Pittman v. Adams, 44 Mo. 570 (1869).
State ex rel. Stoutmeyer v. Duffy, 7 Nev. 342 (1872).
State v. Allmond, 7 Del. 612 (1856).
State v. Caesar, 31 N.C. 391 (1849).
State v. Cummings, 36 Mo. 263 (1865).
State v. Gibson, 36 Ind. 389 (1871).
State v. Heyward, 37 S.C.L. (3 Rich.) 389 (1832).
State v. Millain, 3 Nev. 409 (1867).
State v. Simmon, 2 Spears 761 (S.C. 1844).
Strauder v. West Virginia, 100 U.S. 303 (1880).
Striplin v. Ware, 36 Ala. 87 (1860).
Stuart v. Laird, 5 U.S. 299 (1803).
Students for Fair Admissions, Inc. v. President & Fellows of Harv. Coll., 600 U.S. 181 (2023).
Swift v. Duffield, 5 Serg. & Rawle 38 (Pa. 1819).
Talcott v. Pine Grove, 23 F. Cas. 652 (C.C. Mich. 1872).
Taylor v. Porter & Ford, 4 Hill 140 (N.Y. Sup. Ct. 1843).
Timbs v. Indiana, 586 U.S. 146 (2019).
Toledo, W. & W. R. Co. v. Harmon, 47 Ill. 298 (1868).
Town of Greece v. Galloway, 572 U.S. 565 (2014).
Trimble v. Gordon, 430 U.S. 762 (1977).

Trs. of Dartmouth Coll. v. Woodward, 17 U.S. 518 (1819).
Tuttle v. Wilson, 24 Ill. 553 (1861).
Twining v. New Jersey, 211 U.S. 78 (1908).
United States ex rel. Wheeler v. Williamson, 28 F. Cas. 686 (E.D. Pa. 1855).
United States v. Cruikshank, 92 U.S. 542 (1876).
United States v. Gillies, 25 F. Cas. 1321 (C.C.D. Pa. 1815).
United States v. Hudson, 11 U.S. 32 (1812).
United States v. Rhodes, 27 F. Cas. 785 (C.C.D. Ky. 1867).
United States v. Wilson, 28 F. Cas. 699 (C.C.E.D. Pa. 1830).
United States v. Wong Kim Ark, 169 U.S. 649 (1898).
Van Deusen v. Newcomer, 40 Mich. 90 (1879).
Wammack v. Holloway, 2 Ala. 31 (1841).
Washington v. Eaton, 29 F. Cas. 345 (C.C.D. D.C. 1833).
Weaver v. Lapsley, 43 Ala. 224 (1869).
Westberry v. Gilman Paper Co., 507 F.2d 206 (5th Cir. 1975).
Westervelt v. Gregg, 12 N.Y. 202 (1854).
Winner v. Fitzgerald, 19 Wis. 393 (1865).
Wynehamer v. People, 13 N.Y. 378 (1856).
Yick Wo v. Hopkins, 118 U.S. 356 (1886).
Young v. Hawaii, 896 F.3d 1044 (9th Cir. 2018).

Other Primary Sources

Bingham, John A. *One Country, One Constitution, and One People: Speech of Hon. John A. Bingham, of Ohio, in the House of Representatives, February 28, 1866, In Support of the Proposed Amendment to Enforce the Bill of Rights*. Washington, DC: 1866.
Blackstone, William. *Commentaries on the Laws of England*. Oxford: Clarendon Press, 1766.
Bouvier, John. *A Law Dictionary, Adapted to the Constitution and Laws of the United States of America. Philadelphia*: T. & J. W. Johnson, 1868.
Chase, Salmon P. *The Salmon P. Chase Papers*. Edited by John Niven. Kent, OH: Kent State University Press, 1998.
Colored Conventions Project. https://coloredconventions.org/.
Conkling, Roscoe. *Congress and the President: The Political Problems of 1866*. Utica, NY: Roberts, Printers, 1866.
Congressional Globe. Washington, DC: Blair & Rives, 1834–1873.
"Declaration of Sentiments." In *Woman's Rights Conventions: Seneca Falls & Rochester, 1848*. New York: Arno Press, 1969.
Documentary History of Reconstruction: Political, Military, Social, Religious, Educational & Industrial. Edited by Walter L. Fleming. Cleveland: Arthur H. Clark, 1906.
Documentary History of the Constitution of the United States of America. Washington, DC: Department of State, 1894.
House Journal. Washington, DC: Government Printing Office, 1789–.
Howard, Jacob. "Reconstruction Committee Report." Unpublished manuscript, 1866. Accessed at https://www.tifis.org/sources/Howard.pdf.

Johnson, Reverdy. *A Further Consideration of the Dangerous Condition of the Country: The Causes Which Have Led to It, and the Duty of the People*. Baltimore: Sun Job Printing, 1867.
Journals of the Continental Congress, 1774–1789. Washington, DC: Government Printing Office, 1904–1937.
Kent, James. *Commentaries on American Law*. 2nd ed. New York: Halsted, 1832.
Kent, James. *Commentaries on American Law*. 11th ed. Edited by George M. Comstock. Boston: Little, Brown, and Company, 1867.
Langston, John Mercer. *A Speech on "Equality Before the Law."* St. Louis, MO: Democrat Book and Job Printing House, 1866.
Lash, Kurt T., ed. *The Reconstruction Amendments: The Essential Documents*. Chicago, IL: University of Chicago Press, 2021.
Lemmon Slave Case, Report of the. New York: New York Court of Appeals, 1861.
Library of Congress. *Chronicling America*. https://chroniclingamerica.loc.gov/.
Lincoln, Abraham. *Collected Works*. Edited by Roy P. Basler. New Brunswick, NJ: Rutgers University Press, 1953.
"Louisiana and the Supreme Court." *The Republic* 1 (July 1873): 257–65.
McPherson, Edward. *A Hand-Book for Politics*. Washington, DC: Philip & Solomons, 1872.
McPherson, Edward. *A Political Manual for 1866*. Washington, DC: Philip & Solomons, 1866.
McPherson, Edward. *A Political Manual for 1867*. Washington, DC: Philip & Solomons, 1867.
McPherson, Edward. *The Political History of the United States of America During the Period of Reconstruction (From April 15, 1865 to July 15, 1870)*. Washington, DC: Philip & Solomons, 1871.
National Archives. Founders Online. https://founders.archives.gov/documents/Washington/05-04-02-0087.
Online Etymology Dictionary. https://www.etymonline.com/.
Online Library of Law and Liberty. https://www.libertylawsite.org/.
Opinions of the Principal Officers of the Executive Departments, and Other Papers Relating to Expatriation, Naturalization, and Change of Allegiance. Washington, DC: Government Printing Office, 1873.
Owen, Robert Dale. "Political Results from the Varioloid." *Atlantic Monthly* 35 (June 1875): 664–6.
Pickering, Danby. *The Statutes at Large from 1225 to 1867*. Cambridge: Joseph Bentham, 1869.
Proceedings of the First Three Republican National Conventions. Minneapolis: Charles W. Johnson, 1893.
Proceedings of the Illinois State Convention of Colored Men, Assembled at Galesburg, October 1866. Chicago: Church, Goodman and Donnelley, 1867.
Ramsay, William. *An Elementary Manual of Roman Antiquities*. London: John W. Parker, 1859.
Rawle, William. *A View of the Constitution of the United States of America*. Philadelphia: H. C. Carey & I. Lea, 1825.
Reeve, Tapping. *The Law of Baron and Femme*. 3rd ed. Albany, NY: William Gould, 1862.

Report of the Joint Committee on Reconstruction. H.R. Rep. No. 30, 39th Cong., 1st Sess. Washington, DC: Government Printing Office, 1866.
Rossiter, Clinton, ed. *The Federalist Papers*. New York: New American Library, 1961.
Schouler, James. *A Treatise on the Law of the Domestic Relations; Embracing Husband and Wife, Parent and Child, Guardian and Ward, Infancy, and Master and Servant*. Boston: Little, Brown, and Company, 1870.
Sedgwick, Theodore. *A Treatise on the Rules Which Govern the Interpretation and Application of Statutory and Constitutional Law*. New York: John S. Voorhies, 1857.
Senate Journal. Washington, DC: Government Printing Office, 1789–.
Speeches of the Campaign of 1866 in the States of Ohio, Indiana, and Kentucky. Cincinnati: Cincinnati Commercial, 1866.
Statutes at Large of the United States. Washington, DC: Government Printing Office, 1789–.
Story, Joseph. *Commentaries on the Conflict of Laws*. Boston: Hilliard, Gray, and Company, 1834.
Story, Joseph. *Commentaries on the Constitution of the United States*. Boston: Hilliard, Gray, and Company, 1833.
Story, Joseph. *Commentaries on the Constitution of the United States*. 2nd ed. Edited by William W. Story. Boston: Little, Brown, and Company, 1851.
Swindler, William F., ed. *Sources and Documents of the U.S. Constitutions: National Documents 1492–1800*. Dobbs Ferry, NY: Oceana Publications, 1982.
Teaching American History. https://teachingamericanhistory.org/.
Tucker, St. George. *Blackstone's Commentaries*. Philadelphia: William Young Birch and Abraham Small, 1803.
United States Attorney General. 10 Op. Att'y Gen. 382 (1862).
Webster, Noah. *An American Dictionary of the English Language*. Rev. ed. Philadelphia: J.P. Lippincott, 1869.
Wharton, John. *The Law Lexicon, or Dictionary of Jurisprudence*. London: Stevens and Sons, 1867.
Williams, George H. *Speech of Hon. George H. Williams, of Oregon: At Wieting Hall, Syracuse, New York, October 24, 1866*. Syracuse, NY, 1866.
Wilson, James. *Works*. Philadelphia: Lorenzo Press, 1804.

Index

About the Author

David R. Upham, Ph.D., J.D., is Associate Professor of Law at St. Thomas University College of Law, and Senior Fellow in Politics and Law at the University of Dallas.

www.ingramcontent.com/pod-product-compliance
Ingram Content Group UK Ltd.
Pitfield, Milton Keynes, MK11 3LW, UK
UKHW020220290926
15470UKWH00001B/302

9 781666 943856